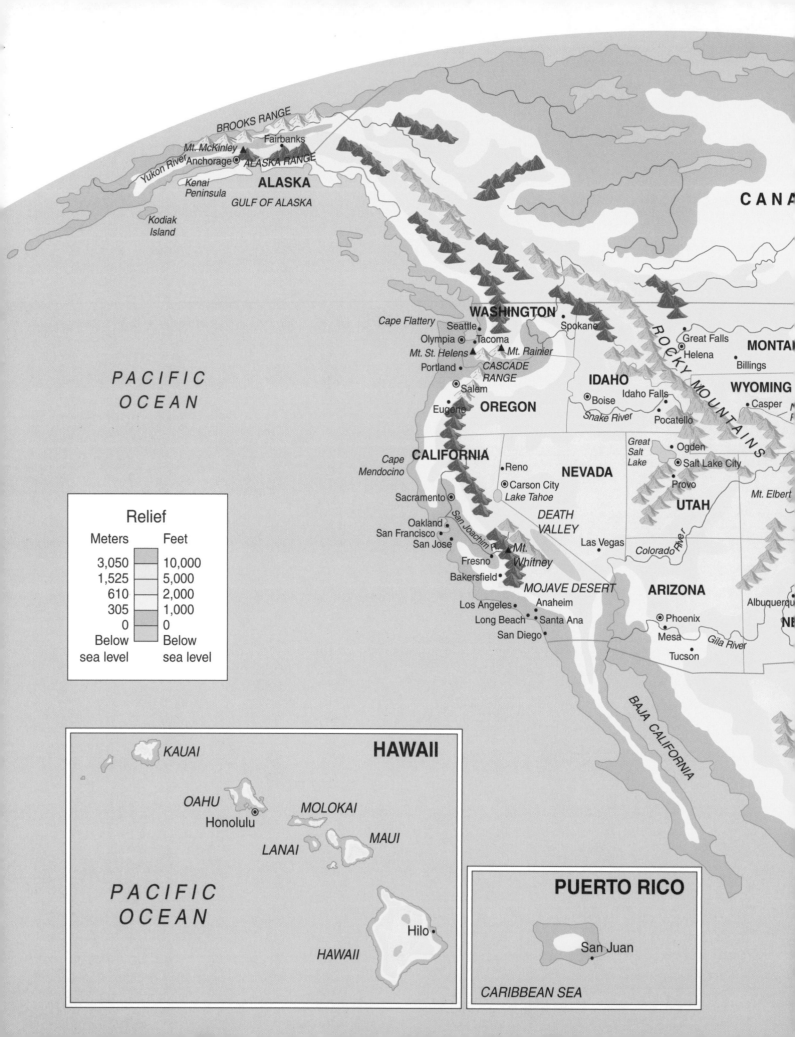

PACIFIC
OCEAN

BROOKS RANGE
Mt. McKinley ▲
Fairbanks •
Yukon River
Anchorage ◉
ALASKA RANGE
Kenai
Peninsula
ALASKA
GULF OF ALASKA
Kodiak
Island

CANA

WASHINGTON
Cape Flattery
Seattle •
Spokane •
Olympia ◉
Tacoma •
Mt. St. Helens ▲
▲ Mt. Rainier
Portland •
CASCADE
RANGE
Salem ◉
OREGON
Eugene •

Great Falls •
Helena ◉
MONTA
Billings •

IDAHO
Boise ◉
Idaho Falls •
Snake River
Pocatello •

WYOMING
Casper •

Cape
Mendocino
CALIFORNIA
Reno •
NEVADA
Great
Salt
Lake
Ogden •
◉ Salt Lake City
Provo •
Sacramento ◉
Carson City ◉
Lake Tahoe
DEATH
VALLEY
UTAH
Mt. Elbert ▲

Oakland •
San Francisco •
San Jose •
San Joachim R.
▲ Mt.
Whitney
Fresno •
Las Vegas •
Colorado River
Bakersfield •
MOJAVE DESERT
ARIZONA
Albuquerqu

Los Angeles •
Anaheim •
Long Beach •
Santa Ana •
San Diego •
Phoenix ◉
Mesa •
Gila River
Tucson •
N

BAJA
CALIFORNIA

Relief

Meters		Feet
3,050		10,000
1,525		5,000
610		2,000
305		1,000
0		0
Below sea level		Below sea level

KAUAI
HAWAII
OAHU
Honolulu ◉
MOLOKAI
LANAI
MAUI

PACIFIC
OCEAN

Hilo •
HAWAII

PUERTO RICO

San Juan •

CARIBBEAN SEA

Why Do You Need This New Edition?

6 good reasons why you should buy this new edition of *THE AFRICAN-AMERICAN ODYSSEY!*

1. In the fifth edition of *The African-American Odyssey*, we have greatly expanded coverage of science and technology and how it impacted African-American history and has in turn been shaped by African Americans. In the early chapters there are new sections on technology in West African civilization and in the ships that carried Africans across the Atlantic Ocean to slavery in America. Another section describes technology in British America's plantation life.

2. A new feature, *Roots of Culture*, examines cultural contributions of African Americans. The feature spotlights the ancient Timbuktu manuscripts, the poetry of Frances Ellen Watkins Harper, the *Freedom's Journal* newspaper, the photography of James van der Zee, the work of Katherine Dunham, and the Freedom Singers of the Civil Rights era.

3. For the twentieth and twenty-first century chapters, there are new sections on W.E.B. Du Bois's Talented Tenth and the *Souls of Black Folk*, on black inventors, and black social scientists, and expanded discussion of radio during the 1930s, including African-American disc jockeys, jazz programs, and *Destination Freedom*.

4. There are new sections on Claudette Colvin, Shirley Chisholm's political career, and the impact of the 2009 recession on employed black women.

5. There are new profiles of Dorothy Height, Mark Dean, Michael Jackson, and Michelle Obama.

6. Chapters 23 and 24 have been reorganized, with the text now ending with updated coverage of the election of 2008 and the first year of the presidency of Barack Obama.

——— FIFTH EDITION ———

The African-American Odyssey

VOLUME I

DARLENE CLARK HINE
Northwestern University

WILLIAM C. HINE
South Carolina State University

STANLEY HARROLD
South Carolina State University

Prentice Hall

Boston   Columbus   Indianapolis   New York   San Francisco   Upper Saddle River
Amsterdam   Cape Town   Dubai   London   Madrid   Milan   Munich   Paris   Montréal   Toronto
Delhi   Mexico City   São Paulo   Sydney   Hong Kong   Seoul   Singapore   Taipei   Tokyo

Editorial Director: Craig Campanella
Publisher: Charlyce Jones Owen
Editorial Assistant: Maureen Diana
Supplements Editor: Emsal Hasan
Senior Manufacturing and Operations Manager
   for Arts & Sciences: Nick Sklitsis
Operations Specialist: Christina Amato
Director of Marketing: Brandy Dawson
Senior Marketing Manager: Maureen E. Prado Roberts
Senior Managing Editor: Ann Marie McCarthy
Senior Project Manager: Denise Forlow
Director of Media and Assessment: Brian Hyland

Media Project Manager: Tina Rudowski
Digital Media Editor: Andrea Messineo
Senior Art Director: Maria Lange
Cover Design: DePinho Design
AV Project Manager: Mirella Signoretto
Full-Service Production, Interior Design, and Composition:
   Mary Tindle/S4Carlisle Publishing Services
Manager, Visual Research: Beth Brenzel
Printer/Binder: Courier Kendallville
Cover Printer: Lehigh-Phoenix Color/Hagerstown
Text Font: New Baskerville, 10/12

Credits and acknowledgments for materials borrowed from other sources and reproduced, with permission, in this textbook, appear on pages **C-1** to **C-2**.

Cover image: Claflin University woodworking shop, 1899 Library of Congress.

Library of Congress Cataloging-in-Publication Data
Hine, Darlene Clark.
  The African-American odyssey / Darlene Clark Hine, William C. Hine,
Stanley Harrold. — 5th ed.
    p. cm.
  Includes bibliographical references and index.
  ISBN-13: 978-0-205-72881-7 (combined volume : alk. paper)
  ISBN-10: 0-205-72881-2 (combined volume : alk. paper)
  ISBN-13: 978-0-205-72886-2 (v. 1 : alk. paper)
  ISBN-10: 0-205-72886-3 (v. 1 : alk. paper)
  ISBN-13: 978-0-205-73593-8 (v. 2 : alk. paper)
  ISBN-10: 0-205-73593-2 (v. 2 : alk. paper)
  [etc.]
  1. African Americans. 2. African Americans—History. I. Hine, William C. II. Harrold, Stanley. III. Title.
  E185.H533 2011
  973'.0496073—dc22
                                          2010023184

10 9 8 7 6 5 4 3

Prentice Hall
is an imprint of

www.pearsonhighered.com

Combined Volume
ISBN 10: 0-205-72881-2
ISBN 13: 978-0-205-72881-7

Examination Copy
ISBN 10: 0-205-72883-9
ISBN 13: 978-0-205-72883-1

Volume 1
ISBN 10: 0-205-72886-3
ISBN 13: 978-0-205-72886-2

Volume 2
ISBN 10: 0-205-73593-2
ISBN 13: 978-0-205-73593-8

To Carter G. Woodson & Benjamin Quarles

DARLENE CLARK HINE

Darlene Clark Hine is Board of Trustees Professor of African-American Studies and Professor of History at Northwestern University. She is a fellow of the American Academy of Arts and Sciences, past President of the Organization of American Historians and of the Southern Historical Association. Hine received her BA at Roosevelt University in Chicago, and her MA and Ph.D. from Kent State University, Kent, Ohio. Hine has taught at South Carolina State University, Purdue University, and at Michigan State University, where she was the John A. Hannah Distinguished Professor of History. She was a fellow at the Center for Advanced Study in the Behavioral Sciences at Stanford University and at the Radcliffe Institute for Advanced Studies at Harvard University. She is the author and/or coeditor of twenty books, most recently *Black Europe and the African Diaspora* (Urbana: University of Illinois Press, 2010) co-edited with Trica Danielle Keaton and Stephen Small; *Beyond Bondage: Free Women of Color in the Americas* (Urbana: University of Illinois Press, 2005) co-edited with Barry Gaspar, *The Harvard Guide to African-American History* (Cambridge: Harvard University Press, 2000) coedited with Evelyn Brooks Higginbotham and Leon Litwack. She coedited a two-volume set with Earnestine Jenkins, *A Question of Manhood: A Reader in U.S. Black Men's History and Masculinity* (Bloomington: Indiana University Press, 1999, 2001); and with Jacqueline McLeod, *Crossing Boundaries: Comparative History of Black People in Diaspora* (Bloomington: Indiana University Press, 2000pk). With Kathleen Thompson she wrote *A Shining Thread of Hope: The History of Black Women in America* (New York: Broadway Books, 1998), and edited with Barry Gaspar *More Than Chattel: Black Women and Slavery in the Americas* (Bloomington: Indiana University Press, 1996). She won the Dartmouth Medal of the American Library Association for the reference volumes coedited with Elsa Barkley Brown and Rosalyn Terborg-Penn, *Black Women in America: An Historical Encyclopedia* (New York: Carlson Publishing, 1993). She is the author of *Black Women in White: Racial Conflict and Cooperation in the Nursing Profession, 1890–1950* (Bloomington: Indiana University Press, 1989). She continues to work on the forthcoming book project *The Black Professional Class: Physicians, Nurses, Lawyers, and the Origins of the Civil Rights Movement, 1890–1955*.

WILLIAM C. HINE

William C. Hine received his undergraduate education at Bowling Green State University, his master's degree at the University of Wyoming, and his Ph.D. at Kent State University. He is a Professor of History at South Carolina State University. He has had articles published in several journals, including *Agricultural History, Labor History,* and the *Journal of Southern History*. He is currently writing a history of South Carolina State University.

STANLEY HARROLD

Stanley Harrold, Professor of History at South Carolina State University, received his bachelor's degree from Allegheny College and his master's and Ph.D. degrees from Kent State University. He is coeditor of *Southern Dissent*, a book series published by the University Press of Florida. In 1991–1992 and 1996–1997 he had National Endowment for the Humanities Fellowships. In 2005 he received an NEH Faculty Research Award. His books include: *Gamaliel Bailey and Antislavery Union* (Kent, Ohio: Kent State University Press, 1986), *The Abolitionists and the South* (Lexington: University Press of Kentucky, 1995), *Antislavery Violence: Sectional, Racial, and Cultural Conflict in Antebellum America* (coedited with John R. McKivigan; Knoxville: University of Tennessee Press, 1999), *American Abolitionists* (Harlow, U.K.: Longman, 2001), *Subversives: Antislavery Community in Washington, D.C., 1828–1865* (Baton Rouge: Louisiana State Univeristy Press, 2003), *The Rise of Aggressive Abolitionism: Addresses to the Slaves* (Lexington: University Press of Kentucky, 2004), *Civil War and Reconstruction: A Documentary Reader* (Oxford, U.K.: Blackwell, 2007) and *Border War: Fighting over Slavery before the Civil War* (Chapel Hill: University of North Carolina Press, 2010). He has published articles in *Civil War History, Journal of Southern History, Radical History Review,* and *Journal of the Early Republic*.

Brief Contents

Contents

3

Black People in Colonial North America, 1526–1763 58

4

Rising Expectations: African Americans and the Struggle for Independence, 1763–1783 86

5

African Americans in the New Nation, 1783–1820 110

8

Opposition to Slavery, 1730–1833   194

ROOTS OF CULTURE

9

Let Your Motto Be Resistance, 1833–1850   216

VISUALIZING THE PAST

10

"And Black People Were at the Heart of It", 1846–1861   240

PART III

THE CIVIL WAR, EMANCIPATION, AND BLACK RECONSTRUCTION: THE SECOND AMERICAN REVOLUTION 266

11

Liberation: African Americans and the Civil War, 1861–1865 268

12

The Meaning of Freedom: The Promise of Reconstruction, 1865–1868 298

13

The Meaning of Freedom: The Failure of Reconstruction, 1868–1877   324

PART IV

SEARCHING FOR SAFE SPACES   348

14

White Supremacy Triumphant: African Americans in the Late Nineteenth Century, 1877–1895   350

VISUALIZING THE PAST
◄ GOING BACK TO AFRICA 378

15

African Americans Challenge White Supremacy, 1877–1918 380

PART V

THE GREAT DEPRESSION AND WORLD WAR II 476

18

Black Protest, the Great Depression, and the New Deal, 1929–1940 478

19

Meanings of Freedom: Culture and Society in the 1930s, 1940s, and 1950s, 1930–1950 508

ROOTS OF CULTURE

22

Black Nationalism, Black Power, Black Arts, 1965–1980 606

VISUALIZING THE PAST

23

African Americans at the Millennium, 1980–2010   642

24

The Triumph of Black Politics: 1980 to the Present, 1980–2010   670

Epilogue:
"A Nation within a Nation"   698

Maps

FIGURES

TABLES

Figures and Tables

"One ever feels his two-ness,—an American, a Negro; two souls, two thoughts, two unreconciled strivings; two warring ideals in one dark body." So wrote W. E. B. Du Bois in 1897. African-American history, Du Bois maintained, was the history of this double-consciousness. Black people have always been part of the American nation that they helped to build. But they have also been a nation unto themselves, with their own experiences, culture, and aspirations. African-American history cannot be understood except in the broader context of American history. American history cannot be understood without African-American history.

Since Du Bois's time our understanding of both African-American and American history has been complicated and enriched by a growing appreciation of the role of class and gender in shaping human societies. We are also increasingly aware of the complexity of racial experiences in American history. Even in times of great racial polarity some white people have empathized with black people and some black people have identified with white interests.

It is in light of these insights that *The African-American Odyssey* tells the story of African Americans. That story begins in Africa, where the people who were to become African Americans began their long, turbulent, and difficult journey, a journey marked by sustained suffering as well as perseverance, bravery, and achievement. It includes the rich culture—at once splendidly distinctive yet tightly intertwined with a broader American culture—that African Americans have nurtured throughout their history. And it includes the many-faceted quest for freedom in which African Americans have sought to counter white oppression and racism with the egalitarian spirit of the Declaration of Independence that American society professes to embody. Nurtured by black historian Carter G. Woodson during the early decades of the twentieth century, African-American history has blossomed as a field of study since the 1950s. Books and articles have appeared on almost every facet of black life. Yet this survey is the first comprehensive college textbook of the African-American experience. It draws on recent research to present black history in a clear and direct manner, within a broad social, cultural, and political framework. It also provides thorough coverage of African-American women as active builders of black culture. *The African-American Odyssey* balances accounts of the actions of African-American leaders with investigations of the lives of the ordinary men and women in black communities. This community focus helps make this a history of a people rather than an account of a few extraordinary individuals. Yet the book does not neglect important political and religious leaders, entrepreneurs, and entertainers. And it gives extensive coverage to African-American art, literature, and music. African-American history started in Africa, and this narrative begins with an account of life on that continent to the sixteenth century and the beginning of the forced migration of millions of Africans to the Americas. Succeeding chapters present the struggle of black people to maintain their humanity during the slave trade and as slaves in North America during the long colonial period.

The coming of the American Revolution during the 1770s initiated a pattern of black struggle for racial justice in which periods of optimism alternated with times of repression. Several chapters analyze the building of black community institutions, the antislavery movement, the efforts of black people to make the Civil War a war for emancipation, their struggle for equal rights as citizens during Reconstruction, and the strong opposition these efforts faced. There is also substantial coverage of African-American military service, from the War for Independence through American wars of the nineteenth and twentieth centuries.

During the late nineteenth century and much of the twentieth century, racial segregation and racially motivated violence that relegated African Americans to second-class citizenship provoked despair, but also inspired resistance and commitment to change. Chapters on the late nineteenth and early twentieth centuries cover the great migration from the cotton fields of the South to the North and West, black nationalism, and the Harlem Renaissance. Chapters on the 1930s and 1940s—the beginning of a period of revolutionary change for African Americans—tell of the economic devastation and political turmoil caused by the Great Depression, the growing influence of black culture in America, the racial tensions caused by black participation in World War II, and the dawning of the civil rights movement. The final chapters tell the story of African Americans during the second half of the twentieth century and beginning of the twenty-first century. They portray the successes of the civil rights movement at its peak during the 1950s and 1960s and the efforts of African Americans to build on those successes during the more conservative 1970s and 1980s. Finally, there are discussions of black life at the turn of the twenty-first century, the election of the first African American President of the United States, Barack Obama, and of the continuing impact of African Americans on life in the United States. In all, *The African-American Odyssey* tells a compelling story of survival, struggle, and triumph over adversity. It will leave students with an appreciation of the central place of black people and black culture in this country and a better understanding of both African-American and American history.

WHAT'S NEW IN THE FIFTH EDITION

- In the fifth edition of *The African-American Odyssey*, we have greatly expanded coverage of science and technology. We have added information concerning how these related aspects of life have impacted African-American history and have in turn been shaped by African Americans.

- In the early chapters there are new sections on technology in West African civilization and in the ships that carried Africans across the Atlantic Ocean to slavery in America. Another section describes technology in British America's plantation life.

- There is more emphasis on the contribution of black scientist Benjamin Banneker to intellectual developments during the Revolutionary Era.

- In the chapters that deal with the nineteenth century, the relationship between technology, cotton production, and slavery receives extended coverage, as does the impact of technology on the underground railroad.

- There is additional coverage of black miners' use of technology during the California gold rush, of slaves who toiled at the Tredegar Ironworks during the Civil War, and of the tools and machinery employed by black families to cultivate and gin cotton during the decades following the war.

- A discussion of the black contribution to the 1893 World's Columbian Exposition in Chicago indicates the growing importance of science and technology as the nineteenth century ended.

- For the twentieth and twenty-first century chapters, there are new sections on W.E.B. Du Bois's Talented Tenth and the *Souls of Black Folk,* on black inventors, and black social scientists.

- There is expanded discussion of radio during the 1930s, including African-American disc jockeys, jazz programs, and *Destination Freedom.*

- There is new coverage of the Tuskegee Airman, especially in regard to aviation technology.

- In Chapter 23 there is a new profile of Mark Dean and his contribution to information technology.

- Chapters 23 and 24 have been reorganized, There are new sections on the arrest of Claudette Colvin, on Shirley Chisholm's political career, and on the impact of the 2009 recession on employed black women.

- There are new Voices Boxes and new profiles of Michael Jackson, Mark Dean, Dorothy Height, and Michelle Obama.

- Finally there is updated coverage of the election of 2008.

ACKNOWLEDGMENTS

In preparing *The African-American Odyssey* we have benefited from the work of many scholars and the help of colleagues, librarians, friends, and family.

Special thanks are due to the following scholars for their substantial contributions to the development of this textbook: Hilary Mac Austin, *Chicago, Illinois*; Brian W. Dippie, *University of Victoria*; Thomas Doughton, *Holy Cross College*; W. Marvin Dulaney, *University of Texas, Arlington*; Sherry DuPree, *Rosewood Heritage Foundation*; Peter Banner-Haley, *Colgate University*; Robert L. Harris Jr., *Cornell University*; Wanda Hendricks, *University of South Carolina*; Rickey Hill, *Mississippi Valley State University*; William B. Hixson, *Michigan State University*; Barbara Williams Jenkins, *South Carolina State University*; Earnestine Jenkins, *University of Memphis*; Hannibal Johnson, *Tulsa, Oklahoma*; Wilma King, *University of Missouri, Columbia*; Karen Kossie-Chernyshev, *Texas Southern University*; Frank C. Martin, *South Carolina State University*; Jacqueline McLeod, *Metropolitan State University, Denver, Colorado*; Freddie Parker, *North Carolina Central University*; Christopher R. Reed, *Roosevelt University*; Linda Reed, *University of Houston*; Marshanda Smith, *Northwestern University*; Mark Stegmaier, *Cameron University*; Robert Stewart, *Trinity School, New York*; Matthew Whitaker, *Arizona State University*; Barbara Woods, *South Carolina State University*; Andrew Workman, *Mills College*; Deborah Wright, *Avery Research Center, College of Charleston*.

We are grateful to the reviewers who devoted valuable time to reading and commenting on *The African-American Odyssey*. Their insightful suggestions greatly improved the quality of the text: Carol Anderson, *University of Missouri, Columbia*; Abel A. Bartley, *Clemson University*; Jennifer L. Baszile, *Yale University*; James M. Beeby, *West Virginia Wesleyan College*; Richard A. Buckelew, *Bethune-Cookman College*; Claude A. Clegg, *Indiana University*; Gregory Conerly, *Cleveland State University*; Delia Cook, *University of Missouri at Kansas City*; Caroline Cox, *University of the Pacific*; Mary Ellen Curtin, *Southwest Texas State University*; Henry Vance Davis, *Ramapo College of NJ*; Roy F. Finkenbine, *Wayne State University*; Abiodun Goke-Pariola, *Georgia Southern University*; Robert Gregg, *Richard Stockton College of NJ*; Keith Griffler, *University of Cincinnati*; John H. Haley, *University of North Carolina at Wilmington*; Robert V. Hanes, *Western Kentucky University*; Julia Robinson, *University of North Carolina at Charlotte*; Ebeneazer Hunter, *De Anza College*; Eric R. Jackson, *Northern Kentucky University*; Wali Rashash Kharif, *Tennessee Technological University*; Joseph Kinner, *Gallaudet University*; Eric Love, *University of Colorado-Boulder*; John F. Marszalek, *Mississippi State University*; Kenneth Mason, *Santa Monica College*; Andrew T. Miller, *Union College*; Diane Batts Morrow, *University of Georgia*; Walter Rucker, *University of Nebraska, Lincoln*; Manisha Sinha, *University of Massachusetts, Amherst*; John David Smith, *North Carolina State University at Raleigh*; Marshall Stevenson, *Ohio State University*; Betty Joe Wallace, *Austin Peay State University*; Matthew C. Whitaker, *Arizona State University*; Harry Williams, *Carleton College*; Vernon J. Williams, Jr., *Indiana University*; Andrew Workman, *Mills College*.

We wish to thank the following reviewers for their insightful comments in preparation for this Fifth Edition: Leslie Alexander, *The Ohio State University*; Richard A. Buckelew, *Bethune Cookman College*; Dr. Jessie Gaston, *California State University, Sacramento*; John W. King, *Temple University*; Lester C. Lamon, *Indiana University, South Bend*; Ruddy Pearson, *American College*; Josh Sides, *California State University, Northridge*; Leslie Wilson, *Montclair State University*; and Marilyn L. Yancy, *Virginia Union University*.

Many librarians provided valuable help tracking down important material. They include Aimee Berry, Ruth Hodges, Doris Johnson, Minnie Johnson, Barbara Keitt, Mary L. Smalls, Ashley Till and Adrienne C.Webber, all of Miller F. Whittaker Library, South Carolina State University; the staff of the interlibrary loan department, Cooper Library, University of South Carolina; and Allan Stokes of the South Caroliniana Library at the University of South Carolina. Marshanda Smith, Research Associate, Northwestern University, provided important documents, other research material, and expert technical and administrative skills.

Seleta Simpson Byrd of South Carolina State University and Linda Werbish of Michigan State University provided valuable administrative assistance.

Each of us also enjoyed the support of family members, particularly Barbara A. Clark, Robbie D. Clark, and Alma J. McIntosh, Emily Harrold, Judy Harrold, Carol A. Hine, Peter J. Hine, and Thomas D. Hine.

Finally, we gratefully acknowledge the essential help of the superb editorial and production team at Prentice Hall: Charlyce Jones Owen, Publisher, whose vision got this project started and whose unwavering support saw it through to completion; Maureen Diana, Editorial Assistant; Rochelle Diogenes, Editor-in-Chief of Development; and Gerald Lombardi, Development Editor, who provided valuable organizational, substantive, and stylistic insights; Maria Lange, Creative Design Director; Anne DeMarinis, who created the book's handsome design; Ann Marie McCarthy, Senior Managing Editor; Denise Forlow, Production Editor and Mary Tindle/S4Carlisle Publishing Services, who saw it efficiently through production; Christine Amato, Operations Manager; Maureen Prado Roberts, Senior Marketing Manager; Emsal Hasan, Supplements Editor; and Alison Lorber, Media Editor.

D.C.H.

W.C.H.

S.H.

FOR INSTRUCTORS	FOR STUDENTS
myhistorylab	**myhistorylab**
www.myhistorylab.com Save Time. Improve Results. MyHistoryLab provides a wealth of resources geared to meet the diverse teaching and learning needs of today's instructors and students.	**www.myhistorylab.com Save Time. Improve Results.** MyHistoryLab's many accessible tools will encourage you to read your text and help you improve your grade in your course.
Instructor's Resource Center www.pearsonhighered .com/irc The Instructor's Resource Center is a Web site where instructors can download the online supplements for *The African-American Odyssey*. Contact your local Pearson representative for an access code or request access online.	**www.coursemart.com** CourseSmart eTextbooks offer the same content as the printed text in a convenient online format—with highlighting, online search, and printing capabilities. You **save 60% over the list price** of the traditional book.
Instructor's Manual with Tests www.pearsonhighered .com/irc Available for download from the Instructor's Resource Center, the Instructor's Manual provides summaries, outlines, learning objectives, lecture and discussion topics, and audio/visual resources for each chapter. The Test Item File includes multiple choice, essay, identification and short-answer, chronology, and map questions.	*African-American Biographies* This collection provides brief biographical sketches of the many African American figures represented in the text. Students can use this as a reference to learn more about the people who have helped to shape both American and African-American history. **Volume 1 ISBN-10: 0-13-193785-5; ISBN-13: 978-0-13-193785-7; Volume 2 ISBN-10: 0-13-193794-4; ISBN-13: 978-0-13-193794-9**
MyTest www.pearsonmytest.com This test generator Web site contains over 1,200 multiple-choice and essay questions. Questions can be edited, and tests can be printed in several different formats.	*A Short Guide to Writing About History, 7/e* Written by Richard Marius, late of Harvard University, and Melvin E. Page, Eastern Tennessee State University, this engaging and practical text explores the writing and researching processes, identifies different modes of historical writing, including argument, and concludes with guidelines for improving style. **ISBN-10: 0-20-567370-8; ISBN-13: 978-0-20-567370-4**
PowerPoint Presentations www.pearsonhighered .com/irc Available online for download from the Instructor's Resource Center, the PowerPoint Presentations include all of the images, maps, and figures from the text and text slides summarizing the content in each chapter.	**Penguin Valuepacks www.pearsonhighered .com/penguin** A variety of Penguin-Putnam texts are available at discounted prices when bundled with *The African-American Odyssey, 5/e*. Texts include works by Frederick Douglass, Martin Luther King, W.E.B. Du Bois and many others.
Transparency Acetates Over 100 transparency acetates are available for use in the classroom and include the maps, figures and charts from the text. **ISBN-10: 0-13-194733-8; ISBN-13: 978-0-13-194733-7**	*Longman American History Atlas* This full-color historical atlas designed especially for college students is a valuable reference tool and visual guide to American history. This atlas includes maps covering the scope of American history. **ISBN-10: 0-32-100486-8; ISBN-13: 978-0-32-100486-4**
Retrieving the American Past Reader Program www.pearsoncustom.com, keyword search/rtap Available through the Pearson Custom Library, the *Retrieving the American Past* (RTAP) program lets you create a textbook or reader that meets your needs and the needs of your course. RTAP gives you the freedom and flexibility to add chapters from several best-selling Pearson textbooks, in addition to *The African-American Odyssey, 5/e* and/or 100 topical reading units written by the History Department of Ohio State University, all under one cover. Choose the content you want to teach in depth, in the sequence you want, at the price you want your students to pay.	

Supplementary Instructional Material

FOR INSTRUCTORS AND STUDENTS

Save TIME. Improve Results. MyHistoryLab is a dynamic website that provides a wealth of re-sources geared to meet the diverse teaching and learning needs of today's instructors and students. MyHistoryLab's many accessible tools will encourage students to read their text and help them improve their grade in their course.

- **Pearson eText**—An e-book version of *The African-American Odyssey, 5/e* is included in MyHistoryLab. Just like the printed text, students can highlight and add their own notes as they read the book online.

- **Gradebook**—Students can follow their own progress and instructors can monitor the work of the entire class. Automated grading of quizzes and assignments helps both instructors and students save time and monitor their results throughout the course.

- **History Bookshelf**—Students may read, download, or print 100 of the most commonly assigned history works like Homer's *The Iliad* or Machiavelli's *The Prince*.

- **Audio Files**—Full audio of the entire text is included to suit the varied learning styles of today's students.

- **MySearchLab**—This website provides students access to a number of reliable sources for online research, as well as clear guidance on the research and writing process.

NEW IN-TEXT REFERENCES TO MYHISTORYLAB RESOURCES

Read/View/See/Watch/Hear/Study and Review Icons integrated in the text connect resources on MyHistoryLab to specific topics within the chapters. The icons are not exhaustive; many more resources are available than those highlighted in the book, but the icons draw attention to some of the most high-interest resources available on MyHistoryLab.

Read the Document Primary and secondary source documents on compelling topics, such as *Brown v. Board of Education of Topeka, Kansas* and George Engel's "Address by a Haymarket Anarchist," enhance topics discussed in each chapter.

See the Map Atlas and interactive maps present both a broad overview and a detailed examination of historical developments.

Watch the Video Video lectures highlight topics ranging from Columbus to Lincoln to President Obama, engaging students on both historical and contemporary topics. Also included are archival videos, such as footage of Ellis Island immigrants in 1903 and the Kennedy-Nixon debate.

Hear the Audio For each chapter there audio files of the text, speeches, readings, and other audio material, such as *Battle Hymn of the Republic* and *The Star Spangled Banner,* that will enrich students' experience of social and cultural history.

Study and Review MyHistoryLab provides a wealth of practice quizzes, tests, flashcards, and other study resources, all available to students online.

ABOUT
The African-American Odyssey

The many special features and pedagogical tools integrated within *The African-American Odyssey* are designed to make the text accessible to students. They include a variety of tools to reinforce the narrative and help students grasp key issues.

SPECIAL FEATURES: TIMELINES

PART-OPENING TIMELINES thematically organize events in African-American history and provide a reference to the many noteworthy individuals discussed in the chapters.

BRIEF CHRONOLOGIES are included throughout the chapters to provide students with a snapshot of the temporal relationship among significant events.

END-OF-CHAPTER TIMELINES establish a chronological context for events in African-American history by relating them to events in American history and in the rest of the world.

1775

AFRICAN AMERICANS AND THE WAR FOR INDEPENDENCE

APRIL 18, 1775	Black Minutemen participate in Battle of Lexington and Concord.
MAY 10, 1775	The Second Continental Congress convenes in Philadelphia.
JUNE 15, 1775	Congress appoints George Washington commander in chief of the new Continental Army.
JUNE 17, 1775	Black men fight with the Patriots at Bunker Hill.
JULY 9, 1775	George Washington bans African-American enlistment in the Continental Army.
NOVEMBER 7, 1775	Lord Dunmore, the royal governor of Virginia, offers freedom to slaves who will fight for the British.
DECEMBER 30, 1775	Washington allows black reenlistments in the Continental Army.

PRIMARY SOURCE DOCUMENTS AND BIOGRAPHIES

VOICES

MARIA W. STEWART ON THE CONDITION OF BLACK WORKERS

Maria W. Stewart (1803–1879) was the first black female public speaker in the United States. She was strong willed and spoke without qualification what she believed to be the truth. At times she angered both black and white people. In the following speech, which she delivered in Boston in September 1831, Stewart criticized the treatment accorded to black workers—especially black female workers—in the North.

Tell us no more of southern slavery; for with few exceptions, although I may be very erroneous in my opinion, yet I consider our condition but little better than that. . . . After all, methinks there are no chains so galling as those that bind the soul, and exclude it from the vast field of useful and scientific knowledge. . . .

I have asked several [white] individuals of my sex, who transact business for themselves, if providing our girls were to give them the most satisfactory references, they would not be willing to grant them an equal opportunity with others? Their reply has been—for their own part, they had no objection; but as it was not the custom, were they to take them into their employ, they would be in danger of losing the public patronage.

And such is the powerful force of prejudice. Let our girls possess whatever amiable qualities of soul they may; let their characters be fair and spotless as innocence itself; let their natural taste and ingenuity be what they may; it is impossible for scarce an individual of them to rise above the condition of servants. . . .

I observed a piece . . . respecting us, asserting that we were lazy and idle. I confute them on that point. Take us generally as a people, we are neither lazy nor idle; and considering how little we have to excite or stimulate us, I am almost astonished that there are so many industrious and ambitious ones to be found. . . .

Again it was asserted that we were "a ragged set, crying for liberty." I reply to it, the whites have so long and so loudly proclaimed the theme of equal rights and privileges, that our souls have caught the flame also, ragged as we are. As far as our merit deserves, we feel a common desire to rise above the condition of servants and drudges. I have learnt, by bitter experience, that the continual hard labor deadens the energies of the soul, and benumbs the faculties of the mind; the ideas become confined, the mind barren, and, like the scorching sands of Arabia, produces nothing; or like the uncultivated soil, brings forth thorns and thistles. . . .

Most of our color have dragged out a miserable existence of servitude from the cradle to the grave. . . . Do you [women] ask, why

INVENTORS

In some cases, members of the black elite owed their success to technological innovations. Some black inventors had been born in slavery; others had not. Some participated in black community life; others did not.

In 1834 Henry Blair of Maryland became the first African American to patent an invention—a horse-drawn mechanized corn seed planter. In 1836 he patented a similar cotton seed planter. Henry Boyd was much better known than Blair. Boyd, born in Kentucky in 1802, apprenticed as a cabinetmaker, purchased his freedom in 1826, and moved to Cincinnati. In 1835, as that city's leading bed manufacturer, he patented the "Boyd Bedstead." Versions of this "corded four poster" sold from between $8.00 and $125.00 (about $264 and $550 today). In 1844 Boyd produced more than 1,000 of them.

Lewis Temple was another prominent black inventor of the period. Born free in Richmond, Virginia, Temple moved to New Bedford, Massachusetts. In 1845, at this whaling port, Temple, a blacksmith, devised the toggle harpoon. Set with a wooden pin, the barbed toggle secured a whale to a harpooner's line on impact. Although Temple did not patent this invention, he made a good living manufacturing it before his death in 1854. At the same time Temple devised his harpoon, Joseph Hawkins of West Windsor, New Jersey, patented "a gridiron used to broil meat," which preserved juices as the meat cooked.

One of the best-known stories of early nineteenth-century black inventions, however, has been called into question. James Forten's biographer finds no

are you wretched and miserable? I reply, look at many of the most worthy and most interesting of us doomed to spend our lives in gentlemen's kitchens. Look at our young men, smart, active, and energetic, with souls full with ambitious fire; if they look forward, alas! What are their prospects? They can be nothing but the humblest laborers, on account of their dark complexions; hence many of them lose their ambition, and become worthless. . . .

▶ *Is Stewart correct in assuming that conditions for black northerners were little better than those for slaves?*
▶ *According to Stewart, what was the impact of northern white prejudice on black workers?*

Source: Maria W. Stewart, "Lecture Delivered at the Franklin Hall, Boston, September 21, 1831," as quoted in Roy Finkenbine, *Sources of the African-American Past: Primary Sources in American History* (New York: Longman, 1997), 36–52.

VOICES boxes provide students with first-person perspectives on key events in African-American history. Brief introductions and study questions help students analyze these primary source documents and relate them to the text.

PROFILES boxes provide biographical sketches that highlight the contributions and personalities of both prominent individuals and ordinary people, illuminating common experiences among African Americans at various times and places.

PROFILE: Solomon Northup

Solomon Northup's aspirations as a musician led in 1841 to his kidnapping and sale into slavery. For 12 years, he labored in the cotton and sugar regions of Louisiana, interacted with slaves and masters, and experienced firsthand what it was like to be caught up in a brutal labor system.

Northup was born free at Minerva, New York, in about 1808. His parents were prosperous farmers, and he became a farmer too, although he also worked occasionally as a violinist. He lived in Saratoga Springs, New York, with his wife and three children until March 1841, when two white men suggested that he become a musician in their circus, which was performing in Washington, D.C.

Enticed by the prospect of good wages and a chance to perform, Northup left with the two men without informing his wife or anyone else. Within two days of arriving in Washington, he was drugged, robbed of his money and free papers, chained, and sold to slave traders. After experiencing a terrible beating with a wooden paddle and a rope, Northup was shipped to New Orleans and sold to William Ford, who owned a cotton plantation and sawmill in Louisiana's Red River region.

As Ford's slave, Northup worked at the mill "piling lumber and chopping logs." Northup liked Ford and regarded him to be a "model master" who treated his slaves well and read scripture to them each Sunday. But when Ford became insolvent and sold his slaves, Northup had to deal with a series of brutal masters. They employed him as a carpenter, as a field hand on cotton and sugar plantations, and finally as a slave driver.

At one point when he was cutting lumber and building cabins, Northup was surprised to have several "large and stout" black women join in the forestry work. Later he observed women performing other demanding physical labor. "There are lumberwomen

as well as lumbermen in the forests of the South," he reported. "In fact . . . they perform their share of all the labor required by the planters. They plough, dray, drive team, clear wild lands, work on the highway and so forth."

Subsequently, Northup spent ten years as a slave of Edwin Epps, a cotton planter, who when drunk enjoyed forcing his slaves to dance. Northup noted that Epps's slaves received a meager diet of corn and bacon. They slept in crude, crowded cabins on planks of wood. During harvest season, "it was rarely that a day passed by without one or more whippings" as slaves failed to pick their quota. During a three-year period, Epps hired Northup out to "sugar plantations during the season of cane-cutting and sugar making" for $1.00 per day.

Northup had become Epps's slave driver by 1852, when he set in motion the events that led to his rescue. Deeply disturbed by being forced to whip other slaves, Northup conspired with a Canadian carpenter to smuggle a letter to two white business-men in Saratoga Springs. The letter led the governor of New York to send Henry B. Northup—a member of the family that had owned Solomon Northup's father—to Louisiana to present evidence that Solomon Northup was a free man. By January 1853, he had been reunited with his family in New York. In July of that year he published *Twelve Years a Slave*, which sold over 30,000 copies and earned him enough money to purchase a home for his family in Glens Falls, New York, where he died in 1863.

SPECIAL TOPIC FEATURES

VISUALIZING THE PAST   These two-page features analyze important aspects of African-American history through photographs. A brief narrative introduction provides a careful examination of the historical implications of each topic. The six features follow related chapters.

ROOTS OF CULTURE   NEW to this edition, this feature examines cultural contributions of African Americans. The six *Roots of Culture* features spotlight the ancient Timbuktu manuscripts, the poetry of Frances Ellen Watkins Harper, the *Freedom's Journal* newspaper, slave rebellions, the photography of James van der Zee, the work of Katherine Dunham, and the Freedom Singers of the Civil Rights era and appear at the end of related chapters.

STUDY AIDS

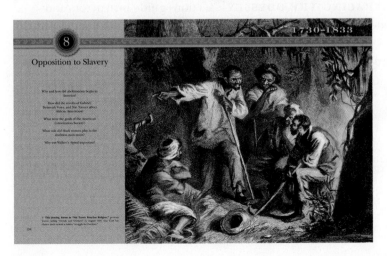

CHAPTER OPENERS   Each chapter opens with a provocative image that gives students a visual introduction to the chapter content and **chapter opening questions** that provide an inquiry-based approach that encourages students to think about the material they are about to read.

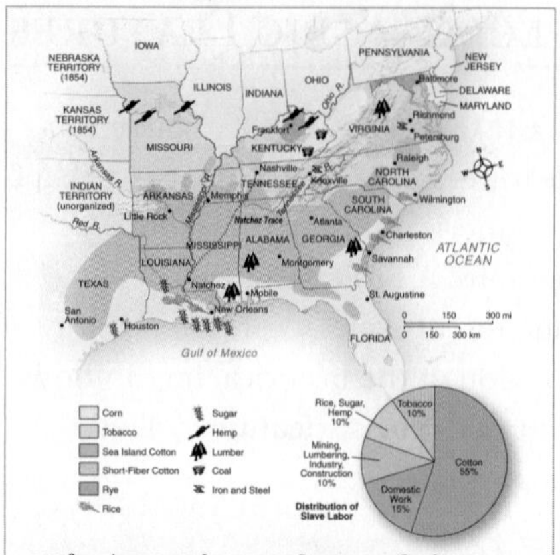

MAP 6–3 AGRICULTURE, INDUSTRY, AND SLAVERY IN THE OLD SOUTH, 1850

The experience of the African American in slavery varied according to their occupation and the region of the South in which they lived.

▶ *To what degree did climate affect the type of crop slaves produced?*

See the Map *Explore this map at* **www.myhistorylab.com**

MAPS The text includes an abundance of maps that help students visualize the geographical context of events and grasp significant trends. **Map questions** challenge students to review their understanding of the maps in context.

GLOSSARIES Key terms are first bold-faced in the chapters and included in an alphabetical **Glossary of Key Terms and Concepts** at the end of the text.

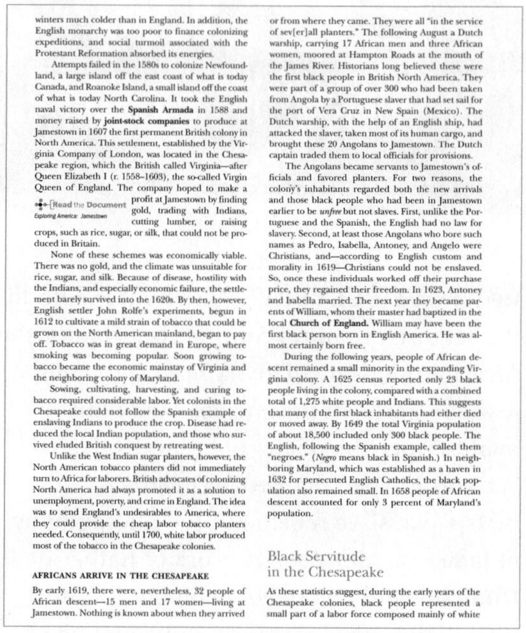

winters much colder than in England. In addition, the English monarchy was too poor to finance colonizing expeditions, and social turmoil associated with the Protestant Reformation absorbed its energies.

Attempts failed in the 1580s to colonize Newfoundland, a large island off the east coast of what is today Canada, and Roanoke Island, a small island off the coast of what is today North Carolina. It took the English naval victory over the **Spanish Armada** in 1588 and money raised by **joint-stock companies** to produce at Jamestown in 1607 the first permanent British colony in North America. This settlement, established by the Virginia Company of London, was located in the Chesapeake region, which the British called Virginia—after Queen Elizabeth I (r. 1558–1603), the so-called Virgin Queen of England. The company hoped to make a profit at Jamestown by finding gold, trading with Indians, cutting lumber, or raising crops, such as rice, sugar, or silk, that could not be produced in Britain.

Read the Document *Exploring America: Jamestown*

None of these schemes was economically viable. There was no gold, and the climate was unsuitable for rice, sugar, and silk. Because of disease, hostility with the Indians, and especially economic failure, the settlement barely survived into the 1620s. By then, however, English settler John Rolfe's experiments, begun in 1612 to cultivate a mild strain of tobacco that could be grown on the North American mainland, began to pay off. Tobacco was in great demand in Europe, where smoking was becoming popular. Soon growing tobacco became the economic mainstay of Virginia and the neighboring colony of Maryland.

Sowing, cultivating, harvesting, and curing tobacco required considerable labor. Yet colonists in the Chesapeake could not follow the Spanish example of enslaving Indians to produce the crop. Disease had reduced the local Indian population, and those who survived eluded British conquest by retreating west.

Unlike the West Indian sugar planters, however, the North American tobacco planters did not immediately turn to Africa for laborers. British advocates of colonizing North America had always promoted it as a solution to unemployment, poverty, and crime in England. The idea was to send England's undesirables to America, where they could provide the cheap labor tobacco planters needed. Consequently, until 1700, white labor produced most of the tobacco in the Chesapeake colonies.

AFRICANS ARRIVE IN THE CHESAPEAKE

By early 1619, there were, nevertheless, 32 people of African descent—15 men and 17 women—living at Jamestown. Nothing is known about when they arrived or from where they came. They were all "in the service of sev[er]all planters." The following August a Dutch warship, carrying 17 African men and three African women, moored at Hampton Roads at the mouth of the James River. Historians long believed these were the first black people in British North America. They were part of a group of over 300 who had been taken from Angola by a Portuguese slaver that had set sail for the port of Vera Cruz in New Spain (Mexico). The Dutch warship, with the help of an English ship, had attacked the slaver, taken most of its human cargo, and brought these 20 Angolans to Jamestown. The Dutch captain traded them to local officials for provisions.

The Angolans became servants to Jamestown's officials and favored planters. For two reasons, the colony's inhabitants regarded both the new arrivals and those black people who had been in Jamestown earlier to be *unfree* but not slaves. First, unlike the Portuguese and the Spanish, the English had no law for slavery. Second, at least those Angolans who bore such names as Pedro, Isabella, Antoney, and Angelo were Christians, and—according to English custom and morality in 1619—Christians could not be enslaved. So, once these individuals worked off their purchase price, they regained their freedom. In 1623, Antoney and Isabella married. The next year they became parents of William, whom their master had baptized in the local **Church of England.** William may have been the first black person born in English America. He was almost certainly born free.

During the following years, people of African descent remained a small minority in the expanding Virginia colony. A 1625 census reported only 23 black people living in the colony, compared with a combined total of 1,275 white people and Indians. This suggests that many of the first black inhabitants had either died or moved away. By 1649 the total Virginia population of about 18,500 included only 300 black people. The English, following the Spanish example, called them "negroes." (*Negro* means black in Spanish.) In neighboring Maryland, which was established as a haven in 1632 for persecuted English Catholics, the black population also remained small. In 1658 people of African descent accounted for only 3 percent of Maryland's population.

Black Servitude in the Chesapeake

As these statistics suggest, during the early years of the Chesapeake colonies, black people represented a small part of a labor force composed mainly of white

END OF CHAPTER RESOURCES

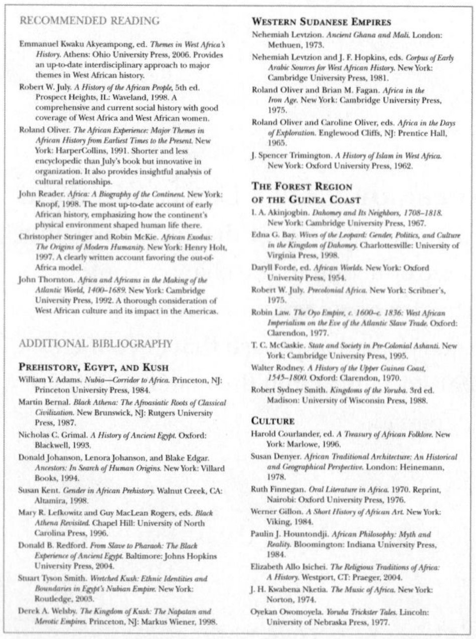

RECOMMENDED READING

Emmanuel Kwaku Akyeampong, ed. *Themes in West Africa's History.* Athens: Ohio University Press, 2006. Provides an up-to-date interdisciplinary approach to major themes in West African history.

Robert W. July. *A History of the African People,* 5th ed. Prospect Heights, IL: Waveland, 1998. A comprehensive and current social history with good coverage of West Africa and West African women.

Roland Oliver. *The African Experience: Major Themes in African History from Earliest Times to the Present.* New York: HarperCollins, 1991. Shorter and less encyclopedic than July's book but innovative in organization. It also provides insightful analysis of cultural relationships.

John Reader. *Africa: A Biography of the Continent.* New York: Knopf, 1998. The most up-to-date account of early African history, emphasizing how the continent's physical environment shaped human life there.

Christopher Stringer and Robin McKie. *African Exodus: The Origins of Modern Humanity.* New York: Henry Holt, 1997. A clearly written account favoring the out-of-Africa model.

John Thornton. *Africa and Africans in the Making of the Atlantic World, 1400–1689.* New York: Cambridge University Press, 1992. A thorough consideration of West African culture and its impact in the Americas.

ADDITIONAL BIBLIOGRAPHY

PREHISTORY, EGYPT, AND KUSH

William Y. Adams. *Nubia—Corridor to Africa.* Princeton, NJ: Princeton University Press, 1984.

Martin Bernal. *Black Athena: The Afroasiatic Roots of Classical Civilization.* New Brunswick, NJ: Rutgers University Press, 1987.

Nicholas C. Grimal. *A History of Ancient Egypt.* Oxford: Blackwell, 1993.

Donald Johanson, Lenora Johanson, and Blake Edgar. *Ancestors: In Search of Human Origins.* New York: Villard Books, 1994.

Susan Kent. *Gender in African Prehistory.* Walnut Creek, CA: Altamira, 1998.

Mary R. Lefkowitz and Guy MacLean Rogers, eds. *Black Athena Revisited.* Chapel Hill: University of North Carolina Press, 1996.

Donald B. Redford. *From Slave to Pharaoh: The Black Experience of Ancient Egypt.* Baltimore: Johns Hopkins University Press, 2004.

Stuart Tyson Smith. *Wretched Kush: Ethnic Identities and Boundaries in Egypt's Nubian Empire.* New York: Routledge, 2003.

Derek A. Welsby. *The Kingdom of Kush: The Napatan and Meroitic Empires.* Princeton, NJ: Markus Wiener, 1998.

WESTERN SUDANESE EMPIRES

Nehemiah Levtzion. *Ancient Ghana and Mali.* London: Methuen, 1973.

Nehemiah Levtzion and J. F. Hopkins, eds. *Corpus of Early Arabic Sources for West African History.* New York: Cambridge University Press, 1981.

Roland Oliver and Brian M. Fagan. *Africa in the Iron Age.* New York: Cambridge University Press, 1975.

Roland Oliver and Caroline Oliver, eds. *Africa in the Days of Exploration.* Englewood Cliffs, NJ: Prentice Hall, 1965.

J. Spencer Trimington. *A History of Islam in West Africa.* New York: Oxford University Press, 1962.

THE FOREST REGION OF THE GUINEA COAST

I. A. Akinjogbin. *Dahomey and Its Neighbors, 1708–1818.* New York: Cambridge University Press, 1967.

Edna G. Bay. *Wives of the Leopard: Gender, Politics, and Culture in the Kingdom of Dahomey.* Charlottesville: University of Virginia Press, 1998.

Daryll Forde, ed. *African Worlds.* New York: Oxford University Press, 1954.

Robert W. July. *Precolonial Africa.* New York: Scribner's, 1975.

Robin Law. *The Oyo Empire, c. 1600–c. 1836: West African Imperialism on the Eve of the Atlantic Slave Trade.* Oxford: Clarendon, 1977.

T. C. McCaskie. *State and Society in Pre-Colonial Ashanti.* New York: Cambridge University Press, 1995.

Walter Rodney. *A History of the Upper Guinea Coast, 1545–1800.* Oxford: Clarendon, 1970.

Robert Sydney Smith. *Kingdoms of the Yoruba.* 3rd ed. Madison: University of Wisconsin Press, 1988.

CULTURE

Harold Courlander, ed. *A Treasury of African Folklore.* New York: Marlowe, 1996.

Susan Denyer. *African Traditional Architecture: An Historical and Geographical Perspective.* London: Heinemann, 1978.

Ruth Finnegan. *Oral Literature in Africa.* 1970. Reprint, Nairobi: Oxford University Press, 1976.

Werner Gillon. *A Short History of African Art.* New York: Viking, 1984.

Paulin J. Hountondji. *African Philosophy: Myth and Reality.* Bloomington: Indiana University Press, 1984.

Elizabeth Allo Isichei. *The Religious Traditions of Africa: A History.* Westport, CT: Praeger, 2004.

J. H. Kwabena Nketia. *The Music of Africa.* New York: Norton, 1974.

Oyekan Owomoyela. *Yoruba Trickster Tales.* Lincoln: University of Nebraska Press, 1977.

RECOMMENDED READING and **ADDITIONAL BIBLIOGRAPHY** lists direct students to more information about the subject of each chapter.

RETRACING THE ODYSSEY sections guide instructors and students to educational sites that explore the diverse dimensions of African-American history.

REVIEW QUESTIONS help students to synthesis and review the content they have read within the chapter.

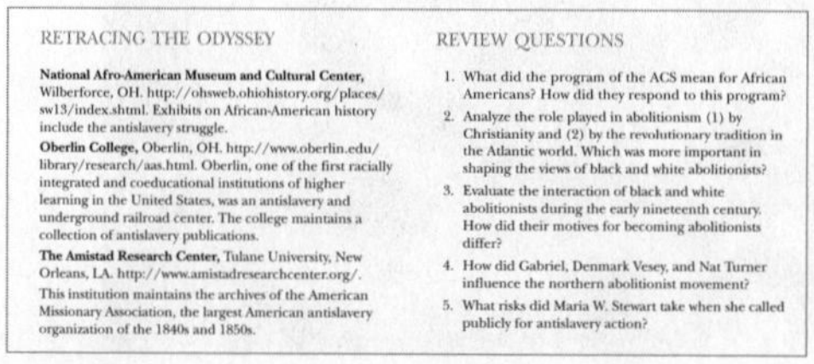

RETRACING THE ODYSSEY

National Afro-American Museum and Cultural Center, Wilberforce, OH. http://ohsweb.ohiohistory.org/places/sw13/index.shtml. Exhibits on African-American history include the antislavery struggle.

Oberlin College, Oberlin, OH. http://www.oberlin.edu/library/research/aas.html. Oberlin, one of the first racially integrated and coeducational institutions of higher learning in the United States, was an antislavery and underground railroad center. The college maintains a collection of antislavery publications.

The Amistad Research Center, Tulane University, New Orleans, LA. http://www.amistadresearchcenter.org/. This institution maintains the archives of the American Missionary Association, the largest American antislavery organization of the 1840s and 1850s.

REVIEW QUESTIONS

1. What did the program of the ACS mean for African Americans? How did they respond to this program?
2. Analyze the role played in abolitionism (1) by Christianity and (2) by the revolutionary tradition in the Atlantic world. Which was more important in shaping the views of black and white abolitionists?
3. Evaluate the interaction of black and white abolitionists during the early nineteenth century. How did their motives for becoming abolitionists differ?
4. How did Gabriel, Denmark Vesey, and Nat Turner influence the northern abolitionist movement?
5. What risks did Maria W. Stewart take when she called publicly for antislavery action?

WWW.MYHISTORYLAB.COM

Myhistorylab is an online resource that offers students and instructors numerous study aids, review materials, and activities to make the study of African-American history an enjoyable learning experience. The wealth of resources on the MyHistorylab site include chapter assessment, documents, images, videos, audio, a History Bookshelf, as well as tools for effective learning and writing.

NEW! myhistorylab ICONS

References to relevant primary source documents, audio files, visual sources, interactive maps and activities available on the MyHistoryLab Web site have been added throughout each chapter. These references are identified by icons that connect the MyHistorylab sources to the specific content within the text. Students should look these icons as they read the chapter and explore the additional content online at www.myhistorylab.com.

◀◉┤**Read** the **Document** Primary source documents, the History Bookshelf, and learning activities.

◀◉┤**See** the **Map** Interactive and Atlas maps.

((◉┤**Hear** the **Audio** Audio files of *The African-American Odyssey* textbook and audio clips of readings, music, and speeches.

◀◉┤**Watch** the **Video** Video lectures and archival footage.

government. Between 1791 and 1796, he used his astronomical observations and mathematical calculations to publish an almanac predicting the positions in the earth's night sky of the sun, moon, and constellations.

Like Wheatley, Banneker thoroughly assimilated white culture and well understood the fundamental issues of human equality raised by the American Revolution. In 1791 he sent Thomas Jefferson, who was then U.S. secretary state, a copy of his almanac to refute Jefferson's claim in *Notes on the State of Virginia* that black people were inherently inferior intellectually to white people. Noting Jefferson's commitment to the biblical statement that God had created "us all of one flesh" and Jefferson's words in the Declaration of Independence, Banneker called the great man to account concerning slavery.

◀◉┤Read the Document
Benjamin Banneker–Letter to Thomas Jefferson (1791)

Referring to the Declaration, Banneker wrote, "You were then impressed with proper ideas of the great valuation of liberty, and the free possession of those blessings, to which you were entitled by nature; but, Sir, how pitiable is it to reflect, that altho you were so fully convinced of the benevolence of the Father of Mankind, and of his equal and impartial distribution of these rights and privileges . . . that you should at the Same time counteract his mercies, in detaining by fraud and violence so numerous a part of my brethren, under groaning captivity and cruel oppression."

African Americans in the War for Independence

In the words of historian Benjamin Quarles, "The Negro's role in the Revolution can best be understood by realizing that his major loyalty was not to a place nor to a people, but to a principle." When it came to fighting between Patriots on one side and the British and their Loyalist American allies on the other, African Americans joined the side that offered freedom. In the South, where the British held out the promise of freedom in exchange for military service, black men eagerly fought on the British side as **Loyalists**. In the North, where white Patriots were more consistently committed to human liberty than in the South, black men just as eagerly fought on the Patriot side (see Map 4–2). In contrast, American Indians, hoping to counter white expansion westward, almost always fought on the British side.

◀◉┤Watch the Video
The American Revolution as Different Americans Saw It

The war began in earnest in August 1776 when the British landed a large army at Brooklyn, New York, and drove Washington's **Continental Army** across New Jersey into Pennsylvania. The military and diplomatic turning point in the war came the following year at Saratoga, New York, when a poorly executed British strategy to take control of the Hudson River resulted in British general John Burgoyne's surrender of his entire army to Patriot forces. This victory led France and other European powers to enter the war against Britain. Significant fighting ended in October 1781 when Washington and the French forced Lord Cornwallis to surrender another British army at Yorktown, Virginia.

When Washington had organized the Continental Army in July 1775, he forbade the enlistment of new black troops and the reenlistment of black men who had served at Lexington and Concord, Bunker Hill, and other early battles. Shortly thereafter, all 13 states followed Washington's example. Several reasons account for Washington's decision and its ratification

The title page of the 1795 edition of Benjamin Banneker's *Pennsylvania, Delaware, Maryland, and Virginia Almanac.* Banneker was widely known during the late eighteenth century as a mathematician and astronomer.

NEW myhistorylab CONNECTIONS

At the end of each chapter, the references in the chapter are listed again along with additional resources that relate directly to the content students will have read in the chapter.

myhistorylab Connections

www.myhistorylab.com
Review what you've learned in this chapter and explore the many documents, images, research tools, and activities for this chapter to learn more about African-American history.

✓◉┤**Study** and **Review**

READ ◀◉┤Read the Document	LISTEN ((◉┤Hear the Audio	RESEARCH mysearchlab	EXPLORE ◀◉┤Watch the Video
• Herodotus on Carthaginian Trade and on the City of Meroë	Hear the audio files for Chapter 1.	Consider these questions in a short research paper.	• Africa as an Urban Not Rural Place
• A Tenth-Century Arab Description of the East African Coast	• *Ghana: Ewe-Atingbekor from Roots of Black Music in America*	*What were the key features of West African society and culture? What place did slavery have in that society?*	• West African States
• Ghana and Its People in the Mid-Eleventh Century			• States, Societies, and Cities in Medieval West Africa
• Muslim Reform in Songhai			◀◉┤See the Map
• Job Hortop and the British Enter the Slave Trade (1567)			• Africa: Climatic Regions and Early Sites
• Leo Africanus' Description of West Africa (1500)			

I

BECOMING
AFRICAN AMERICAN

King Mbunza

	to 1500	**1500–1700**

RELIGION

The Library Company
of Philadelphia

300s CE Axum adopts Christianity

750s Islam begins to take root in West Africa

1300s–1500s Timbuktu flourishes as a center of Islamic learning

1324 Mansa Musa's pilgrimage to Mecca

c. 1500 Portuguese convert Kongo kings to Christianity

CULTURE

1600s African versions of English and French—Gullah, Geechee, and Creole—begin to develop

1600s–1700s African-American folk culture appears among the slaves

POLITICS & GOVERNMENT

c. 3150–30 BCE Independence of Ancient Egypt

1st century CE Fall of Kush

8th century CE Decline of Axumite Empire in Ethiopia

c. 750–1076 Empire of Ghana

1230–1468 Empire of Mali

1400s–1700s Expansion of Benin

1468–1571 Empire of Songhai

1500s Rise of Akan states

1607 Jamestown founded

1696 South Carolina Slave Code enacted

SOCIETY & ECONOMY

10th century Islamic slave trade across the Sahara and Central Africa begins

1472 First Portuguese slave traders in Benin

1481 First "slave factory" in Elmira on the Guinea coast

1502 First mention of African slaves in the Americas

1518 Spanish *Asiento* begins

c. 1520 Sugar plantations begin in Brazil

1619 First African slaves arrive in Jamestown

1620s Chesapeake tobacco plantations increase the demand for slaves

1624 First black child reported born in British North America

1660s Chattel slavery emerges in the southern colonies

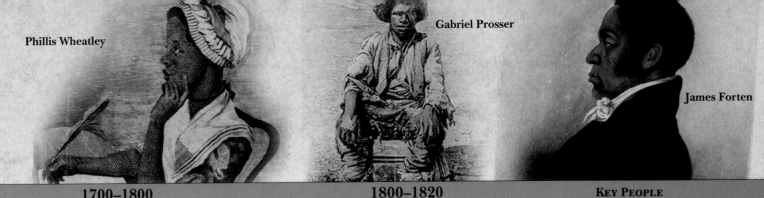

Phillis Wheatley

Gabriel Prosser

James Forten

1700–1800	1800–1820	KEY PEOPLE

1700–1800

c. 1738 First Great Awakening: George Whitefield preaches to African Americans

1780 Lemuel Haynes becomes first ordained black Congregationalist minister

1794 Mother Bethel Church founded in Philadelphia

St. Thomas's Episcopal Church established under Absalom Jones

1740s Lucy Terry Prince publishes poetry

1760 Jupiter Hammon publishes a book of poetry

1773 Phillis Wheatley's *Poems on Various Subjects*

1775 Prince Hall founds first African-American Masonic Lodge

1780 First African-American mutual aid society founded in Newport, Rhode Island

1787 Free African Society founded in Philadelphia

1791–1795 Benjamin Banneker's *Almanac* published

1793 Philadelphia's Female Benevolent Society of St. Thomas founded

1773 Massachusetts African Americans petition the legislature for freedom

1775 Black militiamen fight at Lexington and Concord

1776 Declaration of Independence

1777 Vermont prohibits slavery

1782 Virginia allows manumission

1783 Massachusetts allows male black taxpayers to vote

1787 Congress bans slavery in the Northwest Territory

1789 U.S. Constitution includes the Three-Fifths clause

1793 Congress passes First Fugitive Slave Act

1712 New York City slave rebellion

1739 Stono slave revolt in South Carolina

1776–1783 100,000 slaves flee southern plantations

1781–1783 20,000 black Loyalists depart with British troops

1793 Eli Whitney invents the cotton gin

1800–1820

1808 Abyssinian Baptist Church organized in New York City

1811 African Presbyterian Church established in Philadelphia under Samuel E. Cornish

1816 African Methodist Episcopal Church established

1818 Mother Bethel Church establishes the Augustine School

1807 Britain abolishes the Atlantic slave trade

1808 U.S. abolishes the Atlantic slave trade

1820 Missouri Compromise

First settlement of Liberia by African Americans

William Ranney, "The Battle of Cowpens." Oil on canvas. Photo by Sam Holland. Courtesy South Carolina State House.

1800 Gabriel's rebellion in Charleston

1811 Deslondes's rebellion in Louisiana

KEY PEOPLE

King Piankhy of Kush (r. c. 750 BCE)

Sundiata of Mali (c. 1235 CE)

Emperor Mansa Musa of Mali (r. 1312–1337)

King Sunni Ali of Songhai (r. 1464–1492)

King Askia Muhammed Toure of Songhai (r. 1492–1528)

King Nzinga Mbemba (Affonso I) of Kongo (r. 1506–1543)

Ayuba Suleiman Diallo of Bondu (c. 1701–1773)

Jupiter Hammon (1711–c. 1806)

Crispus Attucks (1723–1770)

Benjamin Banneker (1731–1806)

Prince Hall (1735–1807)

Elizabeth Freeman (1744–1811)

Absalom Jones (1746–1818)

Olaudah Equiano (c. 1745–1797)

James Forten (1746–1818)

Peter Salem (1750–1816)

Phillis Wheatley (c. 1753–1784)

Richard Allen (1760–1831)

Paul Cuffe (1759–1817)

Daniel Coker (1780–1846)

Gabriel (d. 1800)

Charles Deslondes (d. 1811)

Africa

What are the geographical
characteristics of Africa?

Where and how did humans originate?

Why are ancient African civilizations
important?

Why is West Africa significant for
African-American history?

How did the legacies of West African
society and culture influence the way
African Americans lived?

▶ **The craftsmen of the Kingdom of Benin** gained wide renown
for the bronze reliefs they produced.

These [West African] nations think themselves the foremost men in the world, and nothing will persuade them to the contrary. They imagine that Africa is not only the greatest part of the world but also the happiest and most agreeable.

Father Cavazzi, 1687

◀ **West Africans** were making iron tools long before Europeans arrived in Africa.

The ancestral homeland of most black Americans is West Africa. Other regions—Angola and East Africa—were caught up in the great Atlantic slave trade that carried Africans to the New World from the sixteenth to the nineteenth centuries. But West Africa was the center of the trade in human beings. Knowing the history of West Africa therefore is important for understanding the people who became the first African Americans.

That history is best understood within the larger context of the history and geography of the whole African continent. This chapter begins with a survey of

((•— Hear the Audio
Hear the audio files for Chapter 1 at www.myhistorylab.com

the larger context. It emphasizes the aspects of the broader African experience that shaped life in West Africa before the arrival of Europeans in that region. It then explores West Africa's unique heritage and the facets of its culture that have influenced the lives of African Americans from the Diaspora—the original forced dispersal of Africans from their homeland—to the present.

A Huge and Diverse Land

Africa, the second largest continent in the world (only Asia is larger), is bounded by the Mediterranean Sea to the north, the Atlantic Ocean to the west, and the Indian Ocean and the Red Sea to the east. A narrow strip of land in its northeast corner connects it to the Arabian Peninsula and beyond that to Asia and Europe.

From north to south, Africa is divided into a succession of climatic zones (see Map 1–1). Except for a fertile strip along the Mediterranean coast and the agriculturally rich Nile River valley, most of the northern third of the continent consists of the Sahara Desert. For thousands of years, the Sahara limited contact between the rest of Africa—known as sub-Saharan Africa—and the Mediterranean coast, Europe, and Asia. South of the Sahara is a semidesert region known as the Sahel, and south of the Sahel is a huge grassland, or savanna, stretching from Ethiopia west to the Atlantic Ocean. Arab adventurers named this savanna *Bilad es Sudan*, meaning "land of the black people," and the term *Sudan* designates this entire region rather than simply the modern East African nation of Sudan. Much of the habitable part of West Africa falls within the savanna. The rest lies within the northern part of a **rain forest** that extends east from the Atlantic coast over most of the central part of the continent. Another region of savanna borders the rain forest to the south, followed by another desert—the Kalahari—and another coastal strip at the continent's southern extremity.

The Birthplace of Humanity

Paleoanthropologists—scientists who study the evolution and prehistory of humans—have concluded that the origins of humanity lie in the savanna regions of Africa. All people today, in other words, are very likely

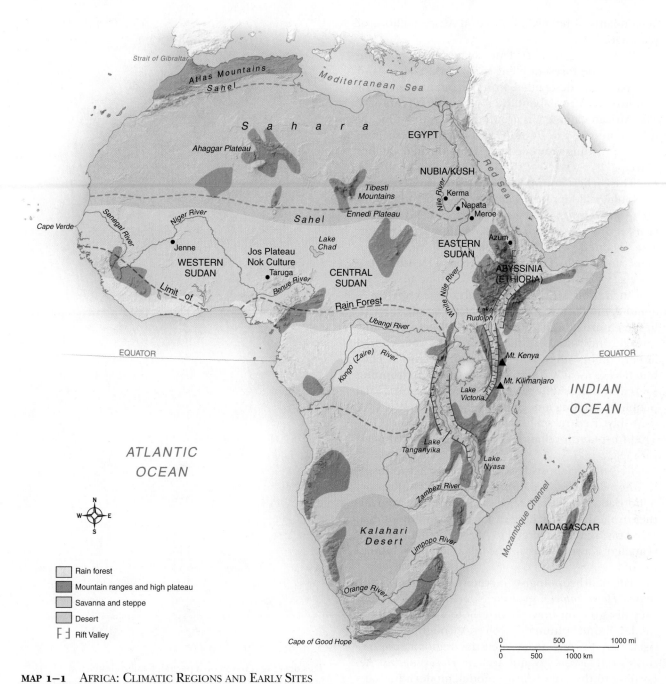

MAP 1–1   AFRICA: CLIMATIC REGIONS AND EARLY SITES

Africa is a large continent with several climatic zones. It is also the home of several early civilizations.

▶ *What impact did the variety of climatic zones have on the development of civilization in Africa?*

⊙ See the Map   *Explore this map at* **www.myhistorylab.com**

descendants of beings who lived in Africa millions of years ago.

Fossil and genetic evidence suggests that both humans and the forest-dwelling great apes (gorillas and chimpanzees) descended from a common ancestor who lived in Africa about five to ten million years ago. The African climate was growing drier at that time, as it has continued to do into the present. Forests gave way to spreading savannas dotted with isolated patches of trees.

The earliest known *hominids* (the term designates the biological family to which humans belong) were the *Ardipithecines*, who emerged about 4.5 million years ago. These creatures walked upright but otherwise retained primitive characteristics and did not make stone tools. They were succeeded by Australopithecus, who probably did not make stone tools. The first such tools are associated with the emergence—about 2.4 million years ago—of *Homo habilis*, the earliest creature designated as within the *homo* (human) lineage. Individuals of the *Homo habilis* species had larger brains than the australopithecines. They butchered meat with stone cutting and chopping tools and built shelters with stone foundations. Like people in **hunting and gathering societies** today, they probably lived in small bands in which women foraged for plant food and men hunted and scavenged for meat.

Recently scientists have found *Homo habilis* fossils in the Caucasus region of southeastern Europe. A more advanced human, *Homo erectus*, spread even farther from Africa, reaching eastern Asia and Indonesia. *Homo erectus*, who emerged in Africa about 1.6 million years ago, is associated with the first evidence of human use of fire.

Paleoanthropologists agree that modern humans, *Homo sapiens*, evolved from *Homo erectus*, but they disagree on how. According to a multiregional model, modern humans evolved throughout Africa, Asia, and Europe from ancestral regional populations of *Homo erectus* and archaic *Homo sapiens*. According to the out-of-Africa model, modern humans emerged in Africa some 200,000 years ago and began migrating to the rest of the world about 100,000 years ago, eventually replacing all other existing hominid populations. Both of these models are consistent with recent genetic evidence, and both indicate that all living peoples are closely related. The "Eve" hypothesis, which supports the out-of-Africa model, suggests that all modern humans are descended from a single African woman. The multiregional model maintains that a continuous exchange of genetic material allowed archaic human populations in Africa, Asia, and Europe to evolve simultaneously into modern humans.

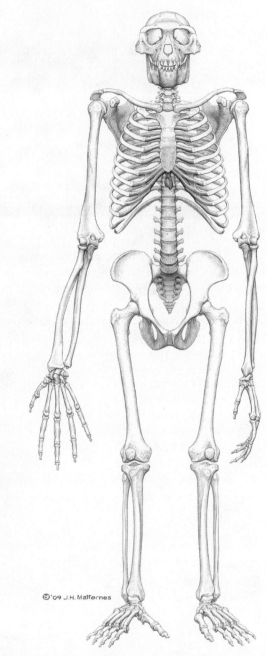

This drawing is based on a partial, fossilized skeleton discovered at Afar, Ethiopia, in 1994. The anthropologists who found the remains concluded in 2009 that the bones are those of a female Ardipithecus ramidus (nicknamed "Ardi") who lived 4.5 million years ago. Ardi shows that hominids diverged from apes much earlier than previously believed and fortifies existing evidence that human origins lay in Africa.

Ancient Civilizations and Old Arguments

The earliest civilization in Africa and one of the two earliest civilizations in world history is that of ancient Egypt (see Map 1–1), which emerged in the Nile River valley in the fourth millennium BCE. Mesopotamian civilization, the other of the two, emerged in the valleys of the Tigris and Euphrates rivers in southwest Asia with the rise of the city-states of Sumer. In both regions, civilization appeared at the end of a long process in which hunting and gathering gave way to agriculture. The settled village life that resulted from this transformation permitted society to become increasingly **hierarchical** and specialized. Similar processes gave rise to civilization in the Indus valley in India around 2300 BCE, in China—with the founding of the Shang dynasty—around 1500 BCE, and in Mexico and Andean South America during the first millennium BCE.

The race of the ancient Egyptians and the nature and extent of their influence on later Western civilizations have long been a source of controversy that reflects more about the racial politics of recent history than it reveals about the Egyptians themselves. It is not clear whether they were an offshoot of their Mesopotamian contemporaries, whether they were representatives of a group of peoples whose origins were in both Africa and southwest Asia, or whether the ancestors of both the Egyptians and Mesopotamians were black Africans. What is clear is that the ancient Egyptians exhibited a mixture of racial features and spoke a language related to the languages spoken by others in the fertile regions of North Africa and southwest Asia.

In this context the argument over the racial identity of the Egyptians is unlikely to be resolved, for they did not regard themselves in a way related to modern racial terminology. The argument began in the nineteenth century when African Americans and white liberals sought to refute claims by racist pseudoscientists that people of African descent were inherently inferior to whites. Unaware of the achievements of West African civilization, those who believed in human equality used evidence that the Egyptians were black to counter assertions that African Americans were incapable of civilization.

Recently there has been a more scholarly debate between Afrocentricists and traditionalists. Afrocentricists regard ancient Egypt as an essentially black civilization closely linked to other indigenous African civilizations to its south. They maintain not only that the Egyptians influenced later African civilizations but also that they had a decisive impact on the Mediterranean Sea region, including ancient Greece and Rome. Therefore, in regard to philosophy and science, black Egyptians were the originators of Western civilization. Traditionalists respond that modern racial categories have no relevance to the world of the ancient Egyptians. The ancient Greeks, they argue, developed the empirical method of inquiry and notions of individual freedom that characterize Western civilization. What is not under debate, however, is Egypt's contribution to the spread of civilization throughout the Mediterranean region. No one doubts that in religion, commerce, and art, Egypt strongly influenced Greece and subsequent Western civilizations.

EGYPTIAN CIVILIZATION

Egypt was, as the Greek historian Herodotus observed 2,500 years ago, the "gift of the Nile." A gentle annual flooding regularly irrigates the banks of this great river, leaving behind deposits of fertile soil. The Nile allowed Egyptians to cultivate wheat and barley and herd goats, sheep, pigs, and cattle in an otherwise

Only the head remains of what was once a statue of Egyptian queen Hatshepsut, who lived from 1508 to 1458 BCE and ruled for 22 years. Hatshepsut was noted for encouraging trade.

desolate region. The Nile also provided the Egyptians with a transportation and communications artery, while their desert surroundings protected them from foreign invasion. Egypt became a unified kingdom around 3150 BCE. A succession of 31 dynasties ruled the kingdom before the Roman Empire conquered it in 30 BCE. Between 1550–1100 BCE, Egypt expanded beyond the Nile valley, creating an empire over the coastal regions of southwest Asia as well as over Libya and Nubia in Africa. It was during this period that Egypt's kings began using the title *pharaoh*, which means "great house." After 1100 BCE, Egypt fell prey to a series of outside invaders. With the invasion of Alexander the Great's Macedonian army in 331 BCE, Egypt's ancient culture began a long decline under the pressure of Greek ideas and institutions (see Map 1–2).

Before then, Egypt had resisted change for thousands of years. Kings presided over a hierarchical society. Beneath them were classes of warriors, priests, merchants, artisans, and peasants. Scribes, who were masters of Egypt's complex **hieroglyphic** writing, staffed a large bureaucracy. Egyptian society was also **patrilineal** and **patriarchal.** Royal incest was customary. Each king often chose a sister to be his queen. Kings maintained numerous concubines. Other men could also take additional wives if the first wife failed to produce children. Egyptian women nonetheless held a high status compared with women in much of the rest of the ancient world. They owned property independently of their husbands, oversaw household slaves, controlled the education of their children, held public office, served as priests, and operated businesses. There were several female rulers, one of whom, Hatshepsut, reigned for 20 years (1478–1458 BCE).

A complex polytheistic religion shaped Egyptian life. Although there were innumerable gods, two of the more important were the sun god Re (or Ra), who represented the immortality of the Egyptian state, and Osiris, the god of the Nile, who embodied each person's immortality. Personal immortality and the immortality of the state merged in the person of the king, as expressed in Egypt's elaborate royal tombs. The most dramatic examples of those tombs, the Great Pyramids at Giza near the modern city of Cairo, were built more than 4,500 years ago to protect the bodies of three Egyptian kings so that their souls might enter the life to come. The pyramids also symbolized the power of the Egyptian state and have endured as embodiments of the grandeur of Egyptian civilization.

KUSH, MEROË, AND AXUM

To the south of Egypt in the upper Nile valley, in what is today the nation of Sudan, lay the ancient region known as Nubia. As early as the fourth millennium BCE,

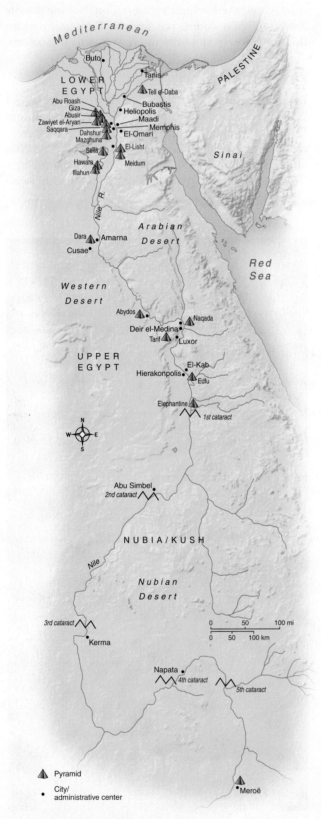

MAP 1–2   ANCIENT EGYPT AND NUBIA

▶ *What does this map indicate about the relationship between ancient Egypt and Nubia/Kush?*

the black people who lived there interacted with the Egyptians. Archaeological evidence suggests that grain production and the concept of monarchy may have arisen in Nubia and then spread north to Egypt. But Egypt's population was always much larger than that of Nubia, and during the second millennium BCE, Egypt used its military power to make Nubia an Egyptian colony and control Nubian copper and gold mines. Egyptians also imported ivory, ebony, leopard pelts, and slaves from Nubia and required the sons of Nubian nobles to live in Egypt as hostages.

Egyptian religion, art, hieroglyphics, and political structure influenced Nubia. Then, with Egypt's decline during the first millennium BCE, the Nubians established an independent kingdom known as Kush, which had its capital at Kerma on the Nile River. During the eighth century BCE, the Kushites took control of upper (meaning southern because the Nile flows from south to north) Egypt, and in about 750 BCE, the Kushite king Piankhy added lower Egypt to his realm. Piankhy became pharaoh and founded Egypt's twenty-fifth dynasty, which ruled until the Assyrians, who invaded Egypt from southwest Asia, drove the Kushites out in 663 BCE.

Kush itself remained independent for another thousand years. Its kings continued for centuries to call themselves pharaohs and had themselves buried in pyramid tombs covered with Egyptian hieroglyphics. They and the Kushite nobility practiced the Egyptian religion and spoke the Egyptian language. In 540 BCE a resurgent Egyptian army destroyed Kerma, and the Kushites moved their capital southward to Meroë. The new capital traded with East Africa, with regions to the west across Sudan, and with the Mediterranean world by way of the Nile River. The development of a smelting technology capable of exploiting local deposits of iron transformed the city into Africa's first industrial center.

Read the Document
Herodotus on Carthaginian Trade and on the City of Meroë

Kush's wealth attracted powerful enemies, and in 23 BCE a Roman army invaded. But it was the decline of Rome and its Mediterranean economy that hurt Kush the most. As the Roman Empire grew weaker and poorer, its trade with Kush declined, and Kush, too,

The ruined pyramids of Meroë on the banks of the upper Nile River are not as old as those at Giza in Egypt, and they differ from them stylistically. But they nonetheless attest to the cultural connections between Meroë and Egypt.

weakened. During the early fourth century CE, it fell to the neighboring Noba people, who in turn fell to the kingdom of Axum, whose warriors destroyed Meroë.

Located in what is today Ethiopia, Axum emerged as a nation during the first century BCE as **Semitic** people from the Arabian Peninsula settled among a local black population. By the time it absorbed Kush during the fourth century CE, Axum had become the first Christian state in sub-Saharan Africa. By the eighth century, shifting trade patterns, environmental depletion,

This giant stele at Axum demonstrates the spread of Egyptian architecture into what is today Ethiopia. Probably erected during the first century CE, before Axum converted to Christianity, this is the last of its kind still standing.

and Islamic invaders combined to reduce Axum's power. It nevertheless retained its unique culture and its independence.

West Africa

For centuries, legend has held that the last kings of Kush retreated across the savanna to West Africa, bringing with them artistic motifs, the knowledge of iron making, and the concepts of divine kingship and centralized government. No archaeological evidence supports this belief. By the fifth century BCE in what is today Libya, Garamantian **Berbers**—the indigenous people of northwestern Africa—independently introduced pyramids, Egyptian gods, and ancestor worship to the western Sahara region. But a distinctive West African civilization had independent roots. Ironworking arose earlier in West Africa than it did at Meroë. The immediate birthright of most African Americans, then, is to be found not in the ancient civilizations of the Nile valley—although those civilizations are part of the heritage of all Africans—but thousands of miles away among the civilizations that emerged in West Africa during the first millennium BCE.

Like Africa as a whole, West Africa is physically, ethnically, and culturally diverse. Much of West Africa south of the Sahara Desert falls within the **savanna** that spans the continent from east to west. West and south of the savanna, however, are extensive forests. They cover Senegambia (modern Senegal and Gambia), the southwest coast of West Africa, and the lands located along the coast of the Gulf of Guinea. These two environments—savanna and forest—were home to a variety of cultures and languages. Patterns of settlement in the region ranged from isolated homesteads and hamlets to villages, towns, and cities.

West Africans began cultivating crops and tending domesticated animals between 1000 BCE and 200 CE. Those who lived on the savanna usually adopted settled village life well before those who lived in the forests. The early farmers produced grains—millet, rice, and sorghum—while tending cattle and goats. By 500 BCE, beginning with the Nok people of the forest region, some West Africans were producing iron tools and weapons.

From early times, the peoples of West Africa traded among themselves and with the peoples who lived across the Sahara Desert in North Africa. This extensive trade became an essential part of the region's economy and formed the basis for the three great western Sudanese empires that successively dominated the region, from before 800 CE until the beginnings of the modern era.

ANCIENT GHANA

The first known kingdom in western Sudan was Ghana (see Map 1–3). Founded by the Soninke people in the area north of the modern republic of Ghana, the kingdom's origins are unclear. It may have arisen as early as the fourth century CE or as late as the eighth century when Arab merchants began to praise its wealth. Its name comes from the Soninke word for king, which Arab traders mistakenly applied to the entire kingdom.

Because they possessed superior iron weapons, the Soninke were able to dominate their neighbors and forge an empire through constant warfare. Ghana's boundaries reached into the Sahara Desert to its north and into modern Senegal to its south. But the empire's real power lay in commerce.

Ghana's kings were known in Europe and southwest Asia as the richest of monarchs, and it was trade that produced their wealth. The key to this trade was the camel, introduced into Africa from Asia during the first century CE. The camel's ability to endure long journeys on small amounts of water dramatically increased trade across the Sahara between western Sudan and the coastal regions of North Africa.

Ghana traded in several commodities. From North Africa came silk, cotton, glass beads, horses, mirrors, dates, and especially salt—a scarce necessity in the torridly hot western Sudan. In return, Ghana exported pepper, slaves, and especially gold. The slaves were usually war captives, and the gold came from mines in the Wangara region to the southwest of Ghana. The Soninke did not mine the gold themselves. Instead, the kings of Ghana grew rich by taxing it as it passed through their lands.

Before the fifth century CE, Roman merchants and Berbers were West Africa's chief partners in the trans-Sahara trade. As Roman power declined and Islam spread across North Africa during the seventh and eighth centuries, Arabs replaced the Romans. Arab merchants settled in Saleh, the Muslim part of Kumbi Saleh, Ghana's capital, which by the twelfth century had become an impressive city. There were stone houses and tombs and as many as 20,000 people. Visitors remarked the splendor of Kumbi Saleh's royal

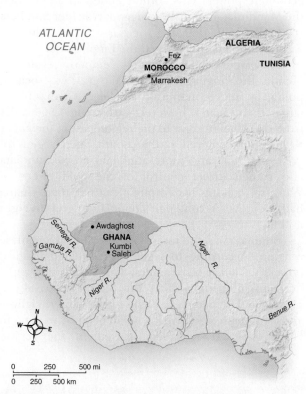

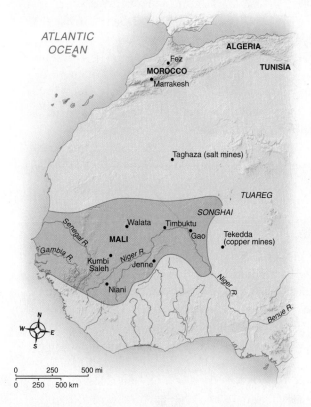

MAP 1–3   THE EMPIRES OF GHANA AND MALI

The western Sudanese empires of Ghana and Mali helped shape West African culture. Ghana existed from as early as the fourth century CE to 1076. Mali dominated western Sudan from 1230 to 1468.

▶ *What does this map suggest concerning the historical relationship between ancient Ghana and Mali?*

VOICES

AL BAKRI DESCRIBES KUMBI SALEH AND GHANA'S ROYAL COURT

Nothing remains of the documents compiled by Ghana's Islamic bureaucracy. As a result, accounts of the civilization are all based on the testimony of Arab or Berber visitors. In this passage, written in the eleventh century, Arab geographer Al Bakri describes the great wealth and power of the king of Ghana and suggests there were tensions between Islam and the indigenous religion of the Soninke.

The city of Ghana [Kumbi Saleh] consists of two towns lying in a plain. One of these towns is inhabited by Muslims. It is large and possesses twelve mosques. . . . There are imams and muezzins, and assistants as well as jurists and learned men. Around the town are wells of sweet water from which they drink and near which they grow vegetables. The town in which the king lives is six miles from the Muslim one, and bears the name Al Ghaba [the forest]. The land between the two towns is covered with houses. The houses of the inhabitants are of stone and acacia wood. The king has a palace and a number of dome-shaped dwellings, the whole surrounded by an enclosure like the defensive wall of a city. In the town where the king lives, and not far from the hall where he holds his court of justice, is a mosque where pray the Muslims who come on diplomatic missions. Around the king's town are domed buildings, woods, and copses where live the sorcerers of these people, the men in charge of the religious cult. . . .

Of the people who follow the king's religion, only he and his heir presumptive, who is the son of his sister, may wear sewn clothes. All the other people wear clothes of cotton, silk, or brocade, according to their means. All men shave their beards and women shave their heads. The king adorns himself like a woman, wearing necklaces and bracelets, and when he sits before the people he puts on a high cap decorated with gold and wrapped in a turban of fine cotton. The court of appeal [for grievances against officials] is held in a domed pavilion around which stand ten horses with gold embroidered trappings. Behind the king stand ten pages holding shields and swords decorated with gold, and on his right are the sons of the subordinate kings of his country, all wearing splendid garments and their hair mixed with gold. . . . When the people professing the same religion as the king approach him, they fall on their knees and sprinkle their heads with dust, for this is their way of showing him their respect. As for the Muslims, they greet him only by clapping their hands.

court. Saleh had several mosques, and some Soninke converted to Islam, although it is unclear whether the royal family joined them. Muslims dominated the royal bureaucracy and introduced Arabic writing to the region.

Commercial and religious rivalries led to Ghana's decline during the twelfth century. The Almoravids, who were Islamic Berbers from what is today Morocco, had been Ghana's principal competitors for control of the trans-Sahara trade. In 992 Ghana's army captured Awdaghost, the Almoravid trade center northwest of Kumbi Saleh. Driven as much by religious fervor as by economic interest, the Almoravids retaliated in 1076 by conquering Ghana. The Soninke regained their independence in 1087, but a little over a century later the Sosso, a previously tributary people, destroyed Kumbi Saleh.

Read the Document
Ghana and Its People in the Mid-Eleventh Century

THE EMPIRE OF MALI, 1230–1468

Following the defeat of Ghana by the Almoravids, western Sudanese peoples competed for political and economic power. This contest ended in 1235 when the Mandinka, under their legendary leader Sundiata (c. 1210–1260), defeated the Sosso at the Battle of Kirina. Sundiata then forged the Empire of Mali.

Mali, which means "where the emperor resides" in Mende, the language of the Mandinka, was socially, politically, and economically similar to Ghana. It was larger than Ghana, however—stretching 1,500 miles from the Atlantic coast to the region east of the Niger River—and centered farther south, in a region of greater rainfall and more abundant crops. Sundiata also gained direct control of the gold mines of Wangara, making his empire wealthier than Ghana had been. As a result, Mali's population grew to eight million.

Sundiata was also important for western Sudanese religion. According to legend, he wielded magical powers to defeat his enemies. This suggests he practiced an indigenous faith. But Sundiata was also a Muslim and helped make Mali—at least superficially—an Islamic state. West Africans had been converting to Islam since Arab traders arrived in the region

▶ *What does this passage indicate about life in ancient Ghana?*
▶ *According to Al Bakri, in what ways do customs in Kumbi Saleh differ from customs in Arab lands?*

Source: Roland Oliver and Caroline Oliver, *Africa in the Days of Exploration* (Upper Saddle River, NJ: Prentice Hall, 1965), 9–10. Reprinted with permission.

centuries before, although many converts, like Sundiata, continued to practice indigenous religions. By his time, most merchants and bureaucrats were Muslims, and the empire's rulers gained stature among Arab states by converting to Islam.

To administer their vast empire at a time when communication was slow, Mali's rulers relied on personal and family ties with local chiefs. Commerce, bureaucracy, and scholarship also helped hold the empire together. Mali's most important city was Timbuktu, which had been established during the eleventh century beside the Niger River near the southern edge of the Sahara.

By the thirteenth century, Timbuktu had become a major hub for trade in gold, slaves, and salt. It attracted merchants from throughout the Mediterranean world and became a center of Islamic learning. The city had several mosques, 150 Islamic schools, a law school, and many book dealers. It supported a cosmopolitan community and impressed visitors with its absence of religious and ethnic intolerance. Even though Mali enslaved war captives and traded slaves, an Arab traveler noted in 1352–1353, "the Negroes possess some admirable qualities. They are seldom unjust, and have a greater abhorrence of injustice than any other people."

Mali reached its peak during the reign of Mansa Musa (r. 1312–1337). One of the wealthiest rulers the world has known, Musa made himself and Mali famous when in 1324 he undertook a pilgrimage across Africa to the Islamic holy city of Mecca in Arabia. With an entourage of 60,000, a train of one hundred elephants, and a propensity for distributing huge amounts of gold to those who greeted him along the way, Musa amazed the Islamic world. After his death, however, Mali declined. In 1468, one of its formerly subject peoples, the Songhai, captured Timbuktu, and their leader, Sunni Ali, founded a new West African empire.

THE EMPIRE OF SONGHAI, 1464–1591

Like the Mandinka and Soninke before them, the Songhai were great traders and warriors. The Songhai had seceded from Mali in 1375, and under Sunni Ali (r. 1464–1492), they built the last and largest of the

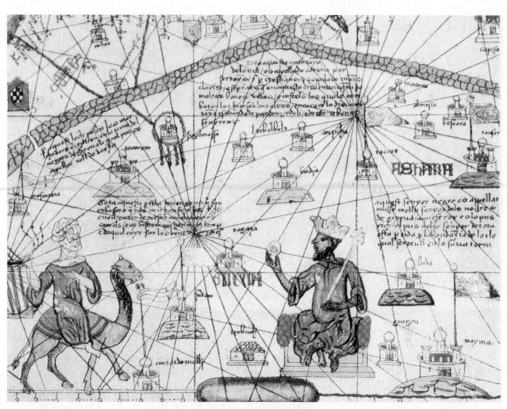

Mansa Musa, who ruled the West African Empire of Mali from 1312 to 1337, is portrayed at the bottom center of this portion of the fourteenth-century Catalan Atlas. Musa's crown, scepter, throne, and the huge gold nugget he displays symbolize his power and wealth.

western Sudanese empires (see Map 1–4). Sunni Ali required conquered peoples to pay tribute but otherwise let them run their own affairs. Nominally a Muslim, he—like Sundiata—was reputedly a great magician who derived power from the traditional spirits.

When Sunni Ali died by drowning, Askia Muhammad Toure led a successful revolt against Ali's son and made himself king of Songhai. The new king (r. 1492–1528) extended the empire north into the Sahara, west into Mali, and east to include the trading cities of Hausaland. He centralized the administration of the empire, replacing local chiefs with members of his family, substituting taxation for tribute, and establishing a bureaucracy to regulate trade.

A devout Muslim, Muhammad Toure used his power to spread the influence of Islam within the empire. During a pilgrimage to Mecca in 1497, he established diplomatic relations with Morocco and Egypt and recruited Muslim scholars to serve at the Sankore Mosque at Timbuktu. The mosque became a center for the study of theology, law, mathematics, and medicine. Despite these efforts, by the end of Muhammad Toure's reign—the aging ruler, senile and blind, was

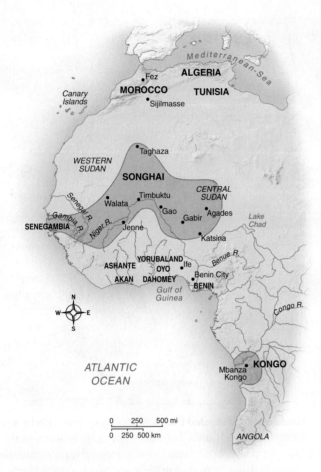

MAP 1–4 WEST AND CENTRAL AFRICA, C. 1500
This map shows the Empire of Songhai (1464–1591), the Kongo kingdom (c. 1400–1700), and the major kingdoms of the West African forest region.

▶ *How did the western Sudanese empires' geographical location make them susceptible to slave trading?*

deposed by family members—Islamic culture remained weak in West Africa outside urban areas.

●●◐ Read the **Document**
Muslim Reform in Songhai

Peasants, who made up 95 percent of the population, spoke a variety of languages, continued to practice indigenous religions, and remained loyal to their local chiefs.

Songhai reached its peak of influence under Askia Daud (r. 1549–1582). However, the political balance of power in West Africa was changing rapidly, and, lacking new leaders as resourceful as Sunni Ali or Muhammad Toure, Songhai failed to adapt. Since the 1430s, adventurers from the European country of Portugal had been establishing trading centers along the Guinea Coast, seeking gold and diverting it from the trans-Sahara trade. Their success threatened the

Arab rulers of North Africa, Songhai's traditional partners in the trans-Sahara trade. In 1591 the king of Morocco, hoping to regain access to West African gold, sent an army of 4,000—mostly Spanish mercenaries armed with muskets and cannons—across the Sahara to attack Gao, Songhai's capital. Only 1,000 of the soldiers survived the grueling march to confront Songhai's elite cavalry at Tondibi on the approach to Gao. But the Songhai forces were armed only with bows and lances that were no match for firearms, and the mercenaries routed them. Its army destroyed, the Songhai empire fell apart. The center of Islamic scholarship in West Africa shifted east from Timbuktu to Hausaland. The Moroccans soon left the region, and West Africa was without a government powerful enough to intervene when the Portuguese, other Europeans, and the African kingdoms of the Guinea Coast became more interested in trading for human beings than for gold.

THE WEST AFRICAN FOREST REGION

The area called the forest region of West Africa, which includes stretches of savanna, extends 2,000 miles along the Atlantic coast from Senegambia in the northwest to the former kingdom of Benin (modern Cameroon) in the east. Among the early settlers of the forest region were the Nok, who, in what is today southern Nigeria, created around 500 BCE a culture noted for its ironworking technology and its terracotta sculptures. But significant migration into the forests began only after 1000 CE, as the western Sudanese climate became increasingly dry.

Because people migrated south from Sudan in small groups over an extended period, the process brought about considerable cultural diversification. A variety of languages, economies, political systems, and traditions came into existence. Some ancient customs survived, such as dividing types of agricultural labor by gender and living in villages composed of extended families. Nevertheless, the forest region became a patchwork of diverse ethnic groups with related but various ways of life.

Colonizing a region covered with thick vegetation was hard work. In some portions of the forest, agriculture did not supplant hunting and gathering until the fifteenth and sixteenth centuries. In more open parts of the region, however, small kingdoms emerged centuries earlier. Benin City, for example, dates to the thirteenth century and Ife in Nigeria to the eleventh. Although none of these kingdoms ever grew as large as the empires of western Sudan, some were powerful. The kings claimed semidivine status, but the nobility and urban elites limited their power. Kings sought to extend their power by conquering and assimilating

The Nok people of what is today Nigeria produced terra-cotta sculptures like this one during the first millennium BCE. They also pioneered, between 500 and 450 BCE, iron smelting in West Africa.

neighboring peoples. Secrecy and elaborate ritual marked royal courts, which were also centers of patronage for art and religion.

The peoples of the forest region are of particular importance for African-American history because of the role they played in the Atlantic slave trade as both slave traders and victims. Space limitations permit only a survey of the most important of these peoples, beginning with those of Senegambia in the northwest.

The inhabitants of Senegambia shared a common history and spoke closely related languages, but they were not politically united. Parts of the region had been incorporated within the empires of Ghana and Mali and had been exposed to Islamic influences. Senegambian society was strictly hierarchical, with royalty at the top and slaves at the bottom. Most people were farmers, growing rice, millet, sorghum, plantains, beans, and bananas. They supplemented their diet with fish, oysters, rabbits, and monkeys.

Southeast of Senegambia, the Akan states emerged during the sixteenth century as the gold trade provided local rulers with the wealth they needed to clear forests and initiate agricultural economies. The rulers traded gold from mines they controlled for slaves, who did the difficult work of cutting trees and burning refuse. Then settlers received open fields from the rulers in return for a portion of their produce and services. When Europeans arrived, they traded guns for gold, and the guns allowed the

The great mosque at the West African city of Jenne was first built during the fourteenth century CE. It demonstrates the importance of Islam in the region's trading centers.   Roderick J. McIntosh, Rice University

Akan states to expand. During the late seventeenth century, one of them, the Ashantee, created a well-organized and densely populated kingdom, comparable in size to the modern country of Ghana. By the eighteenth century, this kingdom dominated the central portion of the forest region and used its army to capture slaves for sale to European traders.

To the east of the Akan states (in modern Benin and western Nigeria) lived the people of the Yoruba culture. They gained ascendancy in the area as early as 1000 CE by trading kola nuts and cloth to the peoples of the western Sudan. The artisans of the Yoruba city of Ife gained renown for their fine bronze, brass, and terra-cotta sculptures. Ife was also notable for the prominent role women played in commerce.

This carved wooden ceremonial offering bowl is typical of a Yoruba art form that has persisted for centuries. It reflects religious practices as well as traditional hairstyle and dress.

During the seventeenth century, the Oyo people, employing a well-trained cavalry, imposed political unity on part of the Yoruba region. They, like the Ashantee, became extensively involved in the Atlantic slave trade.

West of the Oyo were the Fon people, who formed the Kingdom of Dahomey, which rivaled Oyo as a center for the slave trade. The king of Dahomey was an absolute monarch who, to ensure the loyalty of potential rivals, took thousands of wives for himself from leading Fon families.

At the eastern end of the forest region was the Kingdom of Benin, which controlled much of what is today southern Nigeria. The people of this kingdom shared a common heritage with the Yoruba, who played a role in its formation during the thirteenth century. Throughout Benin's history, the Obas (kings), who claimed divine status, struggled for power with the kingdom's hereditary nobility.

After a reform of its army during the fifteenth century, Benin expanded to the Niger River in the east, to the Gulf of Guinea to the south, and into Yoruba country to the west. The kingdom peaked during the late sixteenth century. European visitors noted the size and sophistication of its capital, Benin City. There skilled artisans produced the fine bronze sculptures for which the region is still known. The city's wealthy class dined on beef, mutton, chicken, and yams. Its streets, unlike those of European cities of the time, were free of beggars.

Benin remained little influenced by Islam or Christianity, but like other coastal kingdoms, it joined in the Atlantic slave trade. Beginning in the late fifteenth century, the Oba allowed Europeans to trade for gold, pepper, ivory, and slaves. Initially, the Oba forbade the sale of his subjects, but his large army—the first in the forest region to have European firearms—captured others for the trade as it conquered neighboring regions. By the seventeenth century, Benin's prosperity depended on the slave trade. As the kingdom declined during the eighteenth century, it began to sell its own people to European slave traders.

To Benin's east was Igboland, a densely populated but politically weak region along the Niger River. The Igbo people lived in one of the stateless societies common in West Africa. In these societies, families rather than central authorities ruled. Village elders provided local government, and life centered on family homesteads. Igboland had long exported fieldworkers and skilled artisans to Benin and other kingdoms. When Europeans arrived, they expanded this trade, which brought many Igbos to the Americas (see Map 1–5).

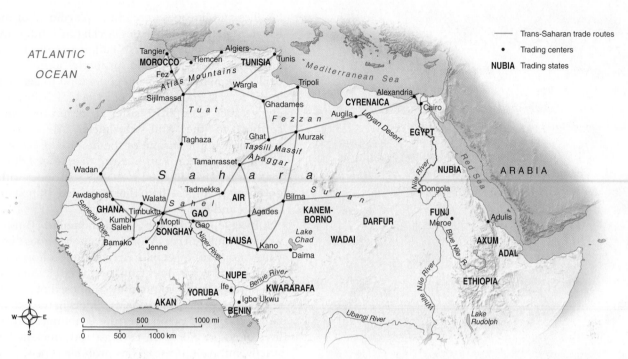

MAP 1–5 TRANS-SAHARAN TRADE ROUTES
Ancient trade routes connected sub-Saharan West Africa to the Mediterranean coast. Among the commodities carried southward were silk, cotton, horses, and salt. Among those carried northward were gold, ivory, pepper, and slaves.

▶ *What was the significance of the trans-Sahara trade in West African history?*

Kongo and Angola

Although the forebears of most African Americans originated in West Africa, a large minority came from Central Africa. In particular, they came from the area around the Congo River and its tributaries and from the region to the south that the Portuguese called Angola. The people of these regions had much in common with those of the Guinea Coast. They divided labor by gender, lived in villages of extended families, and gave semidivine status to their kings. Like the people of West Africa, they were ensnared in the Atlantic slave trade as it grew to immense proportions after 1500.

During the fourteenth and fifteenth centuries, much of the Congo River system, with its fertile valleys and abundant fish, came under the control of the Kingdom of Kongo. This kingdom's wealth also derived from access to salt and iron and trade with the interior of the continent. Nzinga Knuwu, who was *Mani Kongo* (the Kongolese term for king) when Portuguese expeditions arrived in the late fifteenth century, surpassed other African rulers in welcoming the intruders. His son Nzinga Mbemba tried to convert the kingdom to Christianity and remodel it along European lines. The resulting unrest, combined with Portuguese greed and the effects of the slave trade, undermined royal authority and ultimately led to the breakup of the kingdom and the disruption of the entire Kongo-Angola region.

West African Society and Culture

West Africa's great ethnic and cultural diversity makes it hazardous to generalize about the social and cultural background of the first African Americans. The dearth of written records from the region south of Sudan compounds the difficulties. But working with a variety of sources, including oral histories, traditions, and archaeological studies, historians have pieced together a broad understanding of the way the people of West Africa lived at the beginning of the Atlantic slave trade.

Watch the **Video**
States, Societies, and Cities in Medieval West Africa

FAMILIES AND VILLAGES

By the early sixteenth century, most West Africans were farmers. They usually lived in hamlets or villages of extended families and clans called **lineages.** Generally,

VOICES

A DUTCH VISITOR DESCRIBES BENIN CITY

Benin City was one of the few towns of the Guinea Coast that were open to European travelers before the nineteenth century. As this account by a Dutch visitor in 1602 suggests, many of them compared it favorably to the cities of Europe.

The town seemeth to be very great; when you enter into it, you go into a great broad street, not paved, which seems to be seven or eight times broader than the Warmoes street in Amsterdam; which goeth right out and never crooks. . . . It is thought that street is a mile long [this is a Dutch mile, equal to about four English miles] besides the suburbs. At the gate where I entered on horseback, I saw a very high bulwark, very thick of earth, with a very deep broad ditch. . . . Without this gate there is a great suburb. When you are in the great street aforesaid, you see many great streets on the sides thereof, which also go right forth. . . . The houses in this street stand in good order, one close and even with the other, as the houses in Holland stand. . . . Their rooms within are four-square, over them having a roof that is not close[d] in the middle, at which place the rain, wind, and light come in, and therein they lie and eat their meat; they have other places besides, as kitchens and other rooms. . . .

The King's Court is very great, within it having many great four-square plains, which round about them have galleries, wherein there is always watch kept. I was so far within the Court that I passed over four such great plains, and wherever I looked, still I saw gates upon gates to go into other places. . . . I went as far as any Netherlander was, which was to the stable where his best horses stood, always passing a great long way. It seems that the King has many soldiers; he has also many gentlemen, who when they come to the court ride upon horses. . . . There are also many men slaves seen in the town, that carry water, yams, and palm-wine, which they say is for the King; and many carry grass, which is for their horses; and all of this is carried into the court.

▶ *According to the Dutch visitor, how does Benin City compare to Amsterdam?*

▶ *What seems to impress the Dutch visitor most about Benin City?*

Source: *A Short History of Africa* by Roland Oliver and J. D. Fage (Penguin Books 1962, Sixth Edition 1988). Copyright Roland Oliver and J. D. Fage, 1962, 1966, 1970, 1972, 1975, 1988. Reprinted with permission.

families and lineages were either patrilineal or **matrilineal.** In patrilineal societies, social rank and property passed in the male line from fathers to sons. In matrilineal societies, rank and property, although controlled by men, passed from generation to generation in the female line. A village chief in a matrilineal society was succeeded by his sister's son, not his own. According to the Arab chronicler Al Bakri, the succession to the throne of the empire of Ghana followed this pattern. But, like the people of Igboland, many West Africans lived in stateless societies with no government other than that provided by extended families and lineages.

In extended families, **nuclear families** (husband, wife, and children) or in some cases **polygynous families** (husband, wives, and children) acted as economic units. Nuclear and polygynous families existed in the context of a broader family community composed of grandparents, aunts, uncles, and cousins. Elders in the extended family had great power over the economic and social lives of its members. In contrast with ancient Egypt, strictly enforced incest taboos prohibited people from marrying within their extended family.

Villages tended to be larger on the savanna than in the forest. A nuclear or polygynous family unit might have several houses. In nuclear households, the husband occupied the larger house and his wife the smaller. In polygynous households, the husband had the largest house, and his wives lived in smaller ones.

Villagers' few possessions included cots, rugs, stools, and wooden storage chests. Their tools and weapons included bows, spears, iron axes, hoes, and scythes. Households used grinding stones, baskets, and ceramic vessels to prepare and store food. Villagers in both the savanna and forest regions produced cotton for clothing, but their food crops were distinct. West Africans in the savanna cultivated millet, rice, and sorghum as their dietary staples; kept goats and cattle for milk and cheese; and supplemented their diets with peas, okra, watermelons, and nuts. Yams, rather than grains, were the dietary staple in the forest region. Other important forest region crops included bananas and coco yams, both derived from Indonesia.

Farming in West Africa was not easy. Drought was common on the savanna. In the forest, diseases carried by the tsetse fly sickened draft animals, and agricultural plots (because they had to be cleared by hand) averaged just two or three acres per family. Although private landownership prevailed, West Africans generally worked land communally, dividing tasks by gender. Among the Akan of the Guinea Coast, for example, men cleared the land of trees and underbrush, and women tended the fields, planting, weeding, and

one lineage occupied each village, although some large lineages peopled several villages. Each extended family descended from a common ancestor, and each lineage claimed descent from a mythical personage. Depending on the ethnic group involved, extended

PROFILE: Nzinga Mbemba (Affonso I) of Kongo

Nzinga Mbemba, baptized Dom Affonso, ruled as the Mani Kongo (r. c. 1506–1543 CE). His life illustrates the complex and tragic relationships between the African coastal kingdoms and Europeans in search of power, cultural hegemony, and wealth.

Mbemba was a son of Nzinga Knuwu, who, as Mani Kongo, established diplomatic ties with Portugal. Portuguese vessels had first reached Kongo in 1482, and in 1491 the Portuguese king sent a formal mission to Mbanza Kongo (the City of Kongo). Amid considerable ceremony, Knuwu converted to Christianity because conversion gave him access to Portuguese musketeers he needed to put down a rebellion. Mbemba served as his father's general in the ensuing successful campaign.

By 1495, internal politics and Knuwu's inability to accept Christian monogamy had led him to renounce his baptism and banish Christians—both Portuguese and Kongolese—from Mbanza Kongo. Mbemba, who was a sincere Christian, became their champion in opposition to a traditionalist faction headed by his half brother Mpanza. Following Knuwu's death in 1506, the two princes fought over the succession. Mbemba's victory led to his coronation as Affonso and the execution of Mpanza.

By then Mbemba had learned to speak, read, and write Portuguese. He gained at least outward respect from the Portuguese monarchy as a ruler and Christian missionary. Soon hundreds of Portuguese advisers, priests, artisans, teachers, and settlers lived in Mbanza Kongo and its environs. In 1516 a Portuguese priest described Mbemba as "not . . . a man but an angel sent by the Lord to this kingdom to convert it. . . . Better than we, he knows the Prophets and the Gospel of Our Lord Jesus Christ." Mbemba destroyed images and shrines associated with Kongo's traditional religion, replaced them with crucifixes and images of saints, built Christian churches in Mbanza Kongo, and had some of his opponents burned.

While seeking the spiritual salvation of his nation, Mbemba hoped also to modernize it on a European model. He dressed in Portuguese clothing, had his sons and other young men educated in Portugal, and began schools for the children of Kongo's nobility. He corresponded with Portuguese kings, and his son Dom Henrique, who became a Christian bishop, represented Kongo at the Vatican, where he addressed the pope in Latin in 1513.

Mbemba put too much faith in his Portuguese patrons and too little in the traditions of his people. By 1508, Portuguese priests traded in slaves and lived with Kongolese mistresses. This disturbed Mbemba not because he opposed slavery but because the priests undermined his authority. He was supposed to have a monopoly over the slave trade, and he did not want his own people subjected to it.

Mbemba's complaints led to a formal agreement with Portugal in 1512 called the *Regimento*, which only made matters worse. It placed restrictions on the priests and pledged continued Portuguese military assistance. But it also recognized Portuguese merchants' right to trade for copper, ivory, and slaves, and it exempted the Portuguese from punishment under local law. Soon the slave trade and related corruption increased, as did unrest among Mbemba's increasingly unhappy subjects. In 1526, Mbemba created a commission to ensure that only war captives could be enslaved. When this strategy failed, he begged the Portuguese king, "In these kingdoms there should not be any trade in slaves or market for slaves."

In response, Portugal made alliances with Kongo's neighbors and withdrew much of its support from Mbemba, who died surrounded by scheming merchants, corruption, and dissension. In 1568—a quarter century after his death—Kongo became a client state of Portugal, and the slave trade expanded.

▶ **Affonso I** gives an audience to foreign ambassadors at his royal court.

harvesting. Women also cared for children, prepared meals, and manufactured household pottery.

WOMEN

In general, men dominated women in West Africa. As previously noted, men often had two or more wives, and, to a degree, custom held women to be the property of men. But West African women also enjoyed an amount of freedom that impressed Arabs and Europeans. In ancient Ghana, women sometimes served as government officials. Later, in the forest region, they sometimes inherited property and owned land—or at least controlled its income. Women—including enslaved women—in the royal court of Dahomey held high government posts. Ashantee noblewomen could own property, although they themselves could be considered inheritable property. The Ashantee queen held her own court to administer women's affairs.

Women retained far more sexual freedom in West Africa than was the case in Europe or southwest Asia. Ibn Battuta, a Muslim Berber who visited Mali during the fourteenth century, was shocked to discover that in this Islamic country "women show no bashfulness before men and do not veil themselves, though they are assiduous in attending prayer." Battuta was even more dumbfounded to learn that West African women could have male friends and companions other than their husbands or relatives.

Sexual freedom in West Africa was, however, more apparent than real. Throughout the region **secret societies** instilled in men and women ethical standards of behavior. The most important secret societies were the women's *Sande* and the men's *Poro*. They initiated boys and girls into adulthood and provided sex education. They also established standards for personal conduct by emphasizing female virtue and male honor. Other secret societies influenced politics, trade, medical practice, recreation, and social gatherings.

CLASS AND SLAVERY

Although many West Africans lived in stateless societies, most of them lived in hierarchically organized states headed by monarchs who claimed divine or semidivine status. Most of these monarchs' power was far from absolute, but they commanded armies, taxed commerce, and accumulated wealth. Beneath the royalty were classes of landed nobles, warriors, bureaucrats, and peasants. Lower classes included blacksmiths, butchers, weavers, woodcarvers, and tanners.

Slavery had been part of this hierarchical social structure since ancient times. Although common throughout West Africa, slavery was less so in the forest region than on the savanna. It took many forms and was not necessarily a permanent condition. Like people in other parts of the world, West Africans held war captives—including men, women, and children—to be without rights and suitable for enslavement. In Islamic regions, masters had obligations to their slaves similar to those of a guardian for a ward and were responsible for their slaves' religious well-being. In non-Islamic regions, the children of slaves acquired legal protections, such as the right not to be sold away from the land they occupied.

Slaves who served either in the royal courts of a West African kingdom or in a kingdom's armies often exercised power over free people and could acquire property. Also, the slaves of peasant farmers often had standards of living similar to those of their masters. Slaves who worked under overseers in gangs on large estates were far less fortunate. However, the children and grandchildren of these enslaved agricultural workers gained employment and privileges similar to those of free people. Slaves retained a low social status, but in many respects slavery in West African societies functioned as a means of **assimilation.**

RELIGION

There were two religious traditions in fifteenth-century West Africa: Islamic and indigenous. Islam, which Arab traders introduced into West Africa, took root first in the Sudanese empires and remained more prevalent in the cosmopolitan savanna. Even there it was stronger in cities than in rural areas because it was the religion of merchants and bureaucrats. Islam fostered literacy in Arabic, the spread of Islamic learning, and the construction of mosques. Islam is resolutely monotheistic, asserting that Allah is the only God. It recognizes its founder, Muhammad, as well as Abraham, Moses, and Jesus, as prophets but regards none of them as divine.

West Africa's indigenous religions remained strongest in the forest region. They were **polytheistic** and **animistic,** recognizing many divinities and spirits. Beneath an all-powerful but remote creator god, lesser gods represented the forces of nature or were associated with particular mountains, rivers, trees, and rocks. Indigenous West African religion, in other words, saw the force of God in all things.

In part because practitioners of West African indigenous religions perceived the creator god to be unapproachable, they invoked the spirits of their ancestors and turned to magicians and oracles for divine assistance. Like the Chinese, they believed the spirits of their ancestors could influence their lives. Therefore, ceremonies to sustain ancestral spirits and their power over the earth became central to traditional West African religions. These rituals were part of everyday life, making organized churches and professional clergy rare. Instead, family members with an

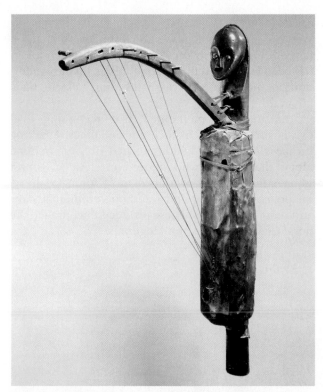

This six-string wooden harp is a rare example of the type of instrument West African musicians and storytellers used to accompany themselves.

inclination to do so assumed religious duties. These individuals encouraged their relatives to participate in ceremonies that involved music, dancing, and animal sacrifice in honor of deceased ancestors. Funerals were especially important because they symbolized the linkage between the living and the dead.

ART AND MUSIC

As in other parts of the world, religious belief and practice influenced West African art. West Africans, seeking to preserve the images of their ancestors, excelled in woodcarving and sculpture in **terra-cotta,** bronze, and brass. Throughout the region, artists produced wooden masks representing in highly stylized manners ancestral spirits and gods. Wooden and terra-cotta figurines, sometimes referred to as **"fetishes,"** were also common. West Africans used them in funerals, in rituals related to ancestral spirits, in medical practice, and in coming-of-age ceremonies. In contrast to masks and fetishes, the great bronze sculptures of Benin had political functions. They were realistic in portraying their subjects, which consisted of kings, warriors, and nobles rather than gods and spirits.

West African music also served religion. Folk musicians employed such instruments as drums, xylophones, bells, flutes, and mbanzas (predecessor to the banjo) to produce a highly rhythmic accompaniment to the dancing associated with religious rituals. A **call-and-response** style of singing also played a vital role in ritual. Vocal music, produced in a full-throated but often raspy style, had polyphonic textures and sophisticated rhythms.

((•—[Hear the Audio
Ghana: Ewe-Atsiagbekor from Roots of Black Music in America

LITERATURE: ORAL HISTORIES, POETRY, AND TALES

West African literature was part of an oral tradition that passed from generation to generation. At its most formal, trained poets and musicians who served kings and nobles created it. But it was also a folk art that expressed the views of the common people.

At a king's court there could be several poet-musicians who had high status and specialized in poems glorifying rulers and their ancestors by linking fact and fiction. Drums and horns often accompanied recitations of these poems. Court poets also used their trained memories to recall historical events and precise genealogies. The self-employed poets, called *griots,* who traveled from place to place were socially inferior to court poets but functioned in a similar manner. Both court poets and griots were men. Women were more involved in folk literature. They joined men in creating and performing work songs. They led in creating and singing dirges, lullabies, and satirical verses. Often these forms of literature used a call-and-response style.

Just as significant for African-American history were the West African prose tales. Like similar stories in other parts of Africa, these tales took two forms: those with human characters and those with animal characters who represented humans. The tales centered on human characters dealt with such subjects as creation, the origins of death, worldly success, and romantic love. They frequently involved magical objects and potions.

The animal tales aimed to entertain and to teach lessons. They focused on small creatures, often referred to as "trickster characters," who were pitted against larger beasts. Among the heroes were the hare, the spider, and the mouse. Plots centered on the ability of these weak animals to outsmart larger and meaner antagonists, such as the snake, leopard, and hyena. These animal characters had human emotions and goals. They were presented in human settings, although they retained animal characteristics.

In West Africa, these tales represented the ability of common people to counteract the power of kings and nobles. When the tales reached America, they became allegories for the struggle between enslaved African Americans and their powerful white masters.

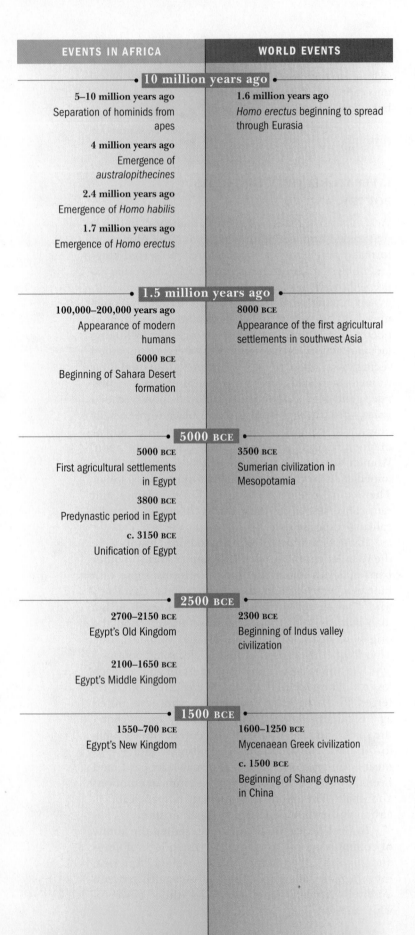

EVENTS IN AFRICA	WORLD EVENTS
• 10 million years ago •	
5–10 million years ago Separation of hominids from apes	**1.6 million years ago** *Homo erectus* beginning to spread through Eurasia
4 million years ago Emergence of *australopithecines*	
2.4 million years ago Emergence of *Homo habilis*	
1.7 million years ago Emergence of *Homo erectus*	
• 1.5 million years ago •	
100,000–200,000 years ago Appearance of modern humans	**8000 BCE** Appearance of the first agricultural settlements in southwest Asia
6000 BCE Beginning of Sahara Desert formation	
• 5000 BCE •	
5000 BCE First agricultural settlements in Egypt	**3500 BCE** Sumerian civilization in Mesopotamia
3800 BCE Predynastic period in Egypt	
c. 3150 BCE Unification of Egypt	
• 2500 BCE •	
2700–2150 BCE Egypt's Old Kingdom	**2300 BCE** Beginning of Indus valley civilization
2100–1650 BCE Egypt's Middle Kingdom	
• 1500 BCE •	
1550–700 BCE Egypt's New Kingdom	**1600–1250 BCE** Mycenaean Greek civilization
	c. 1500 BCE Beginning of Shang dynasty in China

TECHNOLOGY

West African technology was also distinctive and important. Although much knowledge about this technology has been lost, iron refining and forging, textile production, architecture, and rice cultivation helped shape life in the region.

As previously mentioned, iron technology had existed in West Africa since ancient times. Smelting furnaces employing bellows turned ore into refined metal. Blacksmiths, who enjoyed an elevated, almost supernatural status, produced tools for agriculture, weapons for hunting and war, and ceremonial staffs and religious amulets. These products encouraged the development of cities and kingdoms.

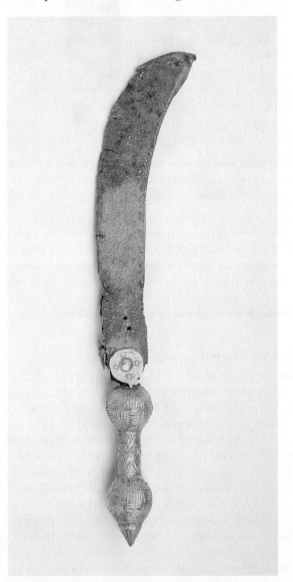

This is an Ashantee sword from West Africa. It is sheathed in a ray-skin cover and has a gold handle. Although this sword dates to early modern times, it is likely that Ashantee craftsmen constructed similar swords much earlier.

Architecture embodied Islamic and indigenous elements, with the former predominant on the savanna and the latter in the forest region. Building materials consisted of stone, mud, and wood. Builders in dry regions relied on stone and mud to build walls and relied on thatch supported by wooden beams for roofs. In some parts of the savanna, mud plaster covered stone walls. In other parts, walls consisted entirely of mud brick or packed earth. Public buildings reached large proportions, and some mosques served 3,000 worshippers. Massive stone or mud walls surrounded cities and towns.

Hand looms for household production existed throughout Africa for thousands of years, and cloth made from pounding bark persisted in the forest region into modern times. But trade and Islamic influences led to commercial textile production. By the ninth century CE, large looms, some equipped with pedals, produced narrow strips of wool or cotton. Men, rather than women, made cloth and tailored it into embroidered Islamic robes, shawls, hats, and blankets, which Muslim merchants traded over wide areas.

Of particular importance for African-American history, West Africans living along rivers in coastal regions had produced rice since approximately 1000 BCE. Portuguese who arrived during the fifteenth century CE reported large diked rice fields. Deliberate flooding of these fields, transplanting sprouts, and intensive cultivation were practices that reemerged in the colonial South Carolina low country.

CONCLUSION

In recent years, paleoanthropologists, archaeologists, and historians have revealed much about Africa's history and prehistory, but much remains to be learned concerning the past of this vast and diverse continent. The evolution of humans, the role of ancient Egypt in world history, and Egypt's relationship to Nubia and Kush are topics that continue to attract wide interest.

Although all of Africa contributed to their background, the history of African Americans begins in West Africa, the region from which the ancestors of most of them were unwillingly wrested. Historians have discovered, as subsequent chapters will show, that West Africans taken to America and their descendants in America preserved much more of their ancestral way of life than scholars once believed possible. West African family organization, work habits, language structures and some words, religious beliefs, legends and stories, pottery styles, art, and music all reached America. These African legacies, although often sharply modified, influenced the way African Americans and other Americans lived in their new land and continue to shape American life.

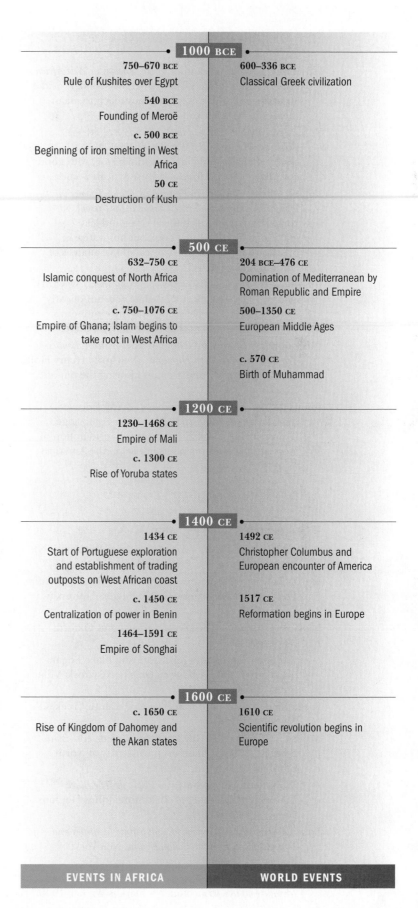

1000 BCE

750–670 BCE
Rule of Kushites over Egypt

540 BCE
Founding of Meroë

c. 500 BCE
Beginning of iron smelting in West Africa

50 CE
Destruction of Kush

600–336 BCE
Classical Greek civilization

500 CE

632–750 CE
Islamic conquest of North Africa

c. 750–1076 CE
Empire of Ghana; Islam begins to take root in West Africa

204 BCE–476 CE
Domination of Mediterranean by Roman Republic and Empire

500–1350 CE
European Middle Ages

c. 570 CE
Birth of Muhammad

1200 CE

1230–1468 CE
Empire of Mali

c. 1300 CE
Rise of Yoruba states

1400 CE

1434 CE
Start of Portuguese exploration and establishment of trading outposts on West African coast

c. 1450 CE
Centralization of power in Benin

1464–1591 CE
Empire of Songhai

1492 CE
Christopher Columbus and European encounter of America

1517 CE
Reformation begins in Europe

1600 CE

c. 1650 CE
Rise of Kingdom of Dahomey and the Akan states

1610 CE
Scientific revolution begins in Europe

EVENTS IN AFRICA   **WORLD EVENTS**

RECOMMENDED READING

Emmanuel Kwaku Akyeampong, ed. *Themes in West Africa's History*. Athens: Ohio University Press, 2006. Provides an up-to-date interdisciplinary approach to major themes in West African history.

Robert W. July. *A History of the African People*, 5th ed. Prospect Heights, IL: Waveland, 1998. A comprehensive and current social history with good coverage of West Africa and West African women.

Roland Oliver. *The African Experience: Major Themes in African History from Earliest Times to the Present*. New York: HarperCollins, 1991. Shorter and less encyclopedic than July's book but innovative in organization. It also provides insightful analysis of cultural relationships.

John Reader. *Africa: A Biography of the Continent*. New York: Knopf, 1998. The most up-to-date account of early African history, emphasizing how the continent's physical environment shaped human life there.

Christopher Stringer and Robin McKie. *African Exodus: The Origins of Modern Humanity*. New York: Henry Holt, 1997. A clearly written account favoring the out-of-Africa model.

John Thornton. *Africa and Africans in the Making of the Atlantic World, 1400–1689*. New York: Cambridge University Press, 1992. A thorough consideration of West African culture and its impact in the Americas.

ADDITIONAL BIBLIOGRAPHY

PREHISTORY, EGYPT, AND KUSH

William Y. Adams. *Nubia—Corridor to Africa*. Princeton, NJ: Princeton University Press, 1984.

Martin Bernal. *Black Athena: The Afroasiatic Roots of Classical Civilization*. New Brunswick, NJ: Rutgers University Press, 1987.

Nicholas C. Grimal. *A History of Ancient Egypt*. Oxford: Blackwell, 1993.

Donald Johanson, Lenora Johanson, and Blake Edgar. *Ancestors: In Search of Human Origins*. New York: Villard Books, 1994.

Susan Kent. *Gender in African Prehistory*. Walnut Creek, CA: Altamira, 1998.

Mary R. Lefkowitz and Guy MacLean Rogers, eds. *Black Athena Revisited*. Chapel Hill: University of North Carolina Press, 1996.

Donald B. Redford. *From Slave to Pharaoh: The Black Experience of Ancient Egypt*. Baltimore: Johns Hopkins University Press, 2004.

Stuart Tyson Smith. *Wretched Kush: Ethnic Identities and Boundaries in Egypt's Nubian Empire*. New York: Routledge, 2003.

Derek A. Welsby. *The Kingdom of Kush: The Napatan and Meroitic Empires*. Princeton, NJ: Markus Wiener, 1998.

WESTERN SUDANESE EMPIRES

Nehemiah Levtzion. *Ancient Ghana and Mali*. London: Methuen, 1973.

Nehemiah Levtzion and J. F. Hopkins, eds. *Corpus of Early Arabic Sources for West African History*. New York: Cambridge University Press, 1981.

Roland Oliver and Brian M. Fagan. *Africa in the Iron Age*. New York: Cambridge University Press, 1975.

Roland Oliver and Caroline Oliver, eds. *Africa in the Days of Exploration*. Englewood Cliffs, NJ: Prentice Hall, 1965.

J. Spencer Trimington. *A History of Islam in West Africa*. New York: Oxford University Press, 1962.

THE FOREST REGION OF THE GUINEA COAST

I. A. Akinjogbin. *Dahomey and Its Neighbors, 1708–1818*. New York: Cambridge University Press, 1967.

Edna G. Bay. *Wives of the Leopard: Gender, Politics, and Culture in the Kingdom of Dahomey*. Charlottesville: University of Virginia Press, 1998.

Daryll Forde, ed. *African Worlds*. New York: Oxford University Press, 1954.

Robert W. July. *Precolonial Africa*. New York: Scribner's, 1975.

Robin Law. *The Oyo Empire, c. 1600–c. 1836: West African Imperialism on the Eve of the Atlantic Slave Trade*. Oxford: Clarendon, 1977.

T. C. McCaskie. *State and Society in Pre-Colonial Ashanti*. New York: Cambridge University Press, 1995.

Walter Rodney. *A History of the Upper Guinea Coast, 1545–1800*. Oxford: Clarendon, 1970.

Robert Sydney Smith. *Kingdoms of the Yoruba*. 3rd ed. Madison: University of Wisconsin Press, 1988.

CULTURE

Harold Courlander, ed. *A Treasury of African Folklore*. New York: Marlowe, 1996.

Susan Denyer. *African Traditional Architecture: An Historical and Geographical Perspective*. London: Heinemann, 1978.

Ruth Finnegan. *Oral Literature in Africa*. 1970. Reprint, Nairobi: Oxford University Press, 1976.

Werner Gillon. *A Short History of African Art*. New York: Viking, 1984.

Paulin J. Hountondji. *African Philosophy: Myth and Reality*. Bloomington: Indiana University Press, 1984.

Elizabeth Allo Isichei. *The Religious Traditions of Africa: A History*. Westport, CT: Praeger, 2004.

J. H. Kwabena Nketia. *The Music of Africa*. New York: Norton, 1974.

Oyekan Owomoyela. *Yoruba Trickster Tales*. Lincoln: University of Nebraska Press, 1977.

RETRACING THE ODYSSEY

National Museum of African Art, Smithsonian Institution, Washington, D.C. http://africa.si.edu/index2.html. The museum exhibits visual art from African regions south of the Sahara Desert. It includes art from ancient Benin and ancient Kerma in Nubia. There is also an exhibit of African musical instruments.

African Collection, National History Museum of Los Angeles County, Los Angeles, CA. http://www.nhm.org/africa/home.html. This collection includes about 5,000 objects representing African cultures.

African Gallery, University of Pennsylvania Museum of Archaeology and Anthropology, Philadelphia, PA. http://www.museum.upenn.edu/new/exhibits/galleries/africa.shtml. The gallery includes a collection of Benin bronzes.

Chattanooga African American Museum, Chattanooga, TN. http://caamhistory.org/. The museum includes an exhibit dealing with African culture and history.

REVIEW QUESTIONS

1. What was the role of Africa in the evolution of modern humanity?

2. Discuss the controversy concerning the racial identity of the ancient Egyptians. What is the significance of this controversy for the history of African Americans?

3. Compare and contrast the western Sudanese empires with the forest civilizations of the Guinea Coast.

4. Discuss the role of religion in West Africa. What was the African religious heritage of black Americans?

5. Describe West African society on the eve of the expansion of the Atlantic slave trade. What were the society's strengths and weaknesses?

PEARSON myhistorylab Connections

www.myhistorylab.com
Review what you've learned in this chapter and explore the many documents, images, research tools, and activities for this chapter to learn more about African-American history.

✔● Study and Review

READ
●●●● Read the Document

- Herodotus on Carthaginian Trade and on the City of Meroë

- A Tenth-Century Arab Description of the East African Coast

- Ghana and Its People in the Mid-Eleventh Century

- Muslim Reform in Songhai

- Job Hortop and the British Enter the Slave Trade (1567)

- Leo Africanus' Description of West Africa (1500)

LISTEN
((●● Hear the Audio

Hear the audio files for Chapter 1.

- *Ghana: Ewe-Atsiagbekor from Roots of Black Music in America*

RESEARCH
mysearchlab

Consider these questions in a short research paper.

What were the key features of West African society and culture? What place did slavery have in that society?

EXPLORE
(●● Watch the Video

- Africa as an Urban Not Rural Place

- West African States

- States, Societies, and Cities in Medieval West Africa

(●● See the Map

- Africa: Climatic Regions and Early Sites

THE ANCIENT MANUSCRIPTS OF TIMBUKTU

Timbuktu, ancient Mali's most important city, was an important center for a thriving trade in gold, salt, and slaves. It was also a city of spectacular intellectual and cultural achievements. Its many mosques and schools helped support a book trade that was famous throughout the region. The city took pride in its intellectual accomplishments. Many of the ancient manuscripts that exist today were carefully preserved as family treasures by the residents of the area over many generations. The manuscripts provide compelling evidence of the skill and sophistication of Mali's scientists, physicians, philosophers, and theologians. They also demonstrate the fact that Africa has a rich legacy of written culture, aspects of which crossed the Atlantic with the enslaved Africans who were transported to the Americas.

Islam was a powerful force in West Africa, but its practitioners were largely concentrated in cities like Timbuktu. What might explain this fact?

Many of Timbuktu's ancient texts are still housed in the libraries of private families in Mali.

This text was written to train scholars in the field of astronomy. On this page, the text and diagram describe and demonstrate the rotation of the heavens.

Islamic mystics played an important part in Timbuktu's religious life. This diagram explains the life of the mystics, which revolved around the teaching of their master.

2

Middle Passage

How did the arrival of the Europeans
affect Africa?

How did the slave trade in Africa differ
from the Atlantic slave trade?

What was the "Middle Passage"?

What happened to Africans after
they crossed the Atlantic?

How were slaves treated
in the Americas?

Why did the Atlantic slave trade end?

▶ **After Great Britain** banned the Atlantic slave trade in 1807,
British warships enforced the ban. The people portrayed in this
early nineteenth-century woodcut were rescued from a slave ship
by the H.M.S. *Undine*.

They felt the sea-wind tying them into one nation of eyes and shadows and groans, in the one pain that is inconsolable, the loss of one's shore. They had wept, not for their wives only, their fading children, but for strange, ordinary things. This one, who was a hunter wept for a sapling lance whose absent heft sang in his palm's hollow. One, a fisherman, for an ocher river encircling his calves; one a weaver, for the straw fisherpot he had meant to repair, wilting in water. They cried for the little thing after the big thing. They cried for a broken gourd.

Derek Walcott, *Omeros*

◀ This modern print portrays small boats transporting West African captives to European slavers during the 1700s.

((•── Hear the Audio
Here the audio files for Chapter 2 at www.myhistorylab.com

These words of a modern black West Indian poet express the sorrow and loss the Atlantic slave trade inflicted on the enslaved Africans it tore from their homelands. This huge enterprise, which lasted for more than three centuries, brought millions of Africans 3,000 miles across the Atlantic Ocean to the Americas. It was the largest forced migration in history. By the eighteenth century, the voyage across the ocean in European ships called "slavers" had become known as the **"Middle Passage."** British sailors coined this innocuous phrase to describe the middle leg of a triangular journey first from England to Africa, then from Africa to the Americas, and finally from the Americas back to England. Yet today Middle Passage denotes an unbelievable descent into an earthly hell of cruelty and suffering. It was from the Middle Passage that the first African Americans emerged.

This chapter describes the Atlantic slave trade and the Middle Passage. It explores their origins both in European colonization in the Americas and in the slave trade that had existed in Africa itself for centuries. It focuses on the experience of the enslaved people whom the trade brought to America. For those who survived, the grueling journey was a prelude to servitude on huge agricultural factories called plantations. Many who became African Americans first experienced plantation life in the West Indies—the Caribbean islands—where they were prepared for lives as slaves in the Americas through a process called "seasoning."

The European Age of Exploration and Colonization

The origins of the Atlantic slave trade and its long duration were products of Western Europe's expansion of power that began during the fifteenth century and continued into the twentieth century. For a variety of economic, technological, and demographic reasons, Portugal, Spain, the Netherlands, France, England, and other nations sought to explore, conquer, and colonize in Africa, Asia, and the Americas. Their efforts had important consequences for these areas.

Portugal took the lead during the early 1400s when its ships reached Africa's western coast. Portuguese captains hoped to find Christian allies there against the Muslims of North Africa and spread Christianity. But they were more interested in trade with African kingdoms, as were the Spanish, Dutch, English, and French who followed them.

Even more attractive than Africa to the Portuguese and their European successors as sources of trade and wealth were India, China, Japan, and the East Indies (modern Indonesia and Malaysia). In 1487 the Portuguese explorer Bartolomeu Dias discovered the Cape of Good Hope at the southern tip of Africa and thereby established that it was possible to sail around Africa to reach India and regions to its east. Ten years later Vasco da Gama initiated this route on behalf of Portuguese commerce. A similar desire to reach these eastern regions motivated the Spanish monarchy to finance Christopher Columbus's westward voyages that began in 1492.

Columbus, who believed the earth to be much smaller than it is, hoped to reach Japan or India by sailing west, thereby opening a direct trade route between Spain and these eastern countries. Columbus's mistake led to his accidental landfall in the Americas. In turn, that encounter led to the European conquest, settlement, and exploitation of North and South America and the Caribbean islands, where Columbus first landed. Columbus and those who followed him quickly enslaved indigenous Americans (American Indians) as laborers in fields and mines. Almost as quickly, many indigenous peoples either died of European diseases and overwork or escaped beyond the reach of European power. Consequently, European colonizers needed additional laborers. This demand for a workforce in the Americas caused the Atlantic slave trade.

Watch the Video
What Is Columbus's Legacy?

West African artists recorded the appearance of Europeans who came to trade in gold, ivory, and human beings. This Benin bronze relief sculpture, dating to the late sixteenth or early seventeenth century, portrays two Portuguese men.

The Slave Trade in Africa

Slave labor was not peculiar to the European colonies in the Americas. Slavery and slave trading had existed in all cultures for thousands of years. As Chapter 1 indicates, slave labor was common in West Africa, although it was usually less oppressive than it became in the Americas.

When Portuguese voyagers first arrived at Senegambia, Benin, and Kongo, they found a thriving commerce in slaves. These kingdoms represented the southern extremity of an extensive trade conducted by Islamic nations that involved the capture and sale of Europeans and North African Berbers as well as black people from south of the Sahara Desert. Although Arabs nurtured antiblack prejudice, race was not the major factor in this Islamic slave trade. Arab merchants and West African kings, for example, imported white slaves from Europe.

In West Africa, Sudanese horsemen conducted the Islamic slave trade. The horsemen invaded the forest region to capture people who could not effectively resist—often they belonged to stateless societies. The trade dealt mainly in women and children who as slaves were destined for lives as concubines and domestic servants in North Africa and southwest Asia. This pattern contrasted with that of the later Atlantic slave trade, which primarily sought young men for agricultural labor in the Americas. The West African men who constituted a minority of those subjected to the trans-Sahara slave trade were more likely to become soldiers than fieldworkers in such North African states as Morocco and Egypt.

The demand for slaves in Muslim countries remained high from the tenth through the fifteenth centuries because many slaves died from disease or were freed and assimilated into Arab society. The trans-Sahara slave trade therefore rivaled the extensive trade in gold across the Sahara and helped make such West African cities as Timbuktu, Walata, Jenne, and Gao wealthy. According to historian Roland Oliver, the Atlantic slave trade did not reach the proportions of the trans-Sahara slave trade until 1600 (see Figure 2–1).

The Origins of the Atlantic Slave Trade

When Portuguese ships first arrived off the **Guinea Coast,** their captains traded chiefly for gold, ivory, and pepper, but they also wanted slaves. As early as 1441, Antam Goncalvez of Portugal enslaved a Berber and

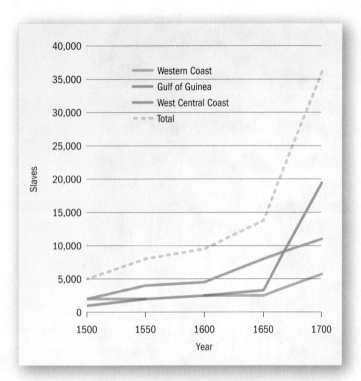

FIGURE 2–1 ESTIMATED ANNUAL EXPORTS OF SLAVES FROM WESTERN AFRICA TO THE AMERICAS, 1500–1700

Source: John Thornton, *Africa and Africans in the Making of the Atlantic World, 1400–1680* (New York: Cambridge University Press, 1992), 118.

Although the overwhelming majority of Africans who were caught up in the Atlantic slave trade went to the Americas, a few reached Europe. This sixteenth-century drawing by German artist Albrecht Dürer depicts Katharina, a servant of a Portuguese official who lived in Antwerp.   Albrecht Dürer (1471–1528). "Portrait of the Moorish Woman Katharina." Drawing. Uffizi Florence, Italy. Photograph © Foto Marburg/Art Resource, NY

his West African servant and took them home as gifts for a Portuguese prince. During the following decades, Portuguese raiders captured hundreds of Africans to work as domestic servants in Portugal and Spain.

But usually the Portuguese and the other European and white Americans who succeeded them did not capture and enslave people themselves. They instead purchased slaves from African traders. This arrangement began formally in 1472 when the Portuguese merchant Ruy do Siqueira gained permission from the Oba (king) of Benin to trade for slaves, as well as for gold and ivory, within the borders of the Oba's kingdom. Siqueira and other Portuguese found that a commercial infrastructure already existed in West Africa that could distribute European trade goods and procure slaves. The rulers of Benin, Dahomey, and other African kingdoms restricted the Europeans to a few points on the coast, and the kingdoms raided the interior to supply the Europeans with slaves.

Interethnic rivalries in West Africa led to the warfare that produced these slaves during the sixteenth century. Although Africans were initially reluctant to sell members of their own ethnic group to Europeans,

they did not at first consider it wrong to sell members of their own race to foreigners. In fact, neither Africans nor Europeans had yet developed a concept of racial solidarity. However, by the eighteenth century, at least the victims of the trade believed that such solidarity *should* exist. Ottobah Cugoano, who had been captured and sold during that century, wrote, "I must own to the shame of my countrymen that I was first kidnapped and betrayed by [those of] my own complexion."

Until the early sixteenth century, Portuguese seafarers conducted the Atlantic slave trade on a tiny scale to satisfy a limited market for domestic servants in Portugal and Spain. Other European countries had no demand for slaves because their workforces were already too large. But the impact of Columbus's voyages drastically changed the slave trade. The Spanish and Portuguese—followed by the Dutch, English,

MAP 2–1   THE ATLANTIC AND ISLAMIC SLAVE TRADES
Not until 1600 did the Atlantic slave trade reach the proportions of the Islamic slave trade. The map shows the principal sources of slaves, primary routes, and major destinations.

▶ *According to this map, which region in the Americas imported the most slaves?*

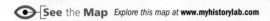 **See the Map** Explore this map at **www.myhistorylab.com**

and French—established colonies in the Caribbean, Mexico, Central America, and South America. Because disease and overwork caused the number of American Indians in these regions rapidly to decline, Europeans relied on the Atlantic slave trade to replace them as a source of slave labor (see Map 2–1). As early as 1502, African slaves lived on the island of Hispaniola—modern Haiti and the Dominican Republic (see Map 2–2). During the sixteenth century, gold and silver mines in Spanish Mexico and Peru and especially sugar plantations in Portuguese Brazil produced an enormous demand for labor. Consequently, the Atlantic slave trade grew to huge and tragic proportions to meet that demand (see Table 2–1).

MAP 2–2 SLAVE COLONIES OF THE SEVENTEENTH AND EIGHTEENTH CENTURIES

This map indicates regions in North America, the West Indies, and South America that had, during the seventeenth and eighteenth centuries, significant populations of enslaved people of African descent.

▶ *What European powers controlled the regions of North America and the Caribbean islands shown in this map?*

TABLE 2–1 ESTIMATED SLAVE IMPORTS BY DESTINATION, 1451–1870

Destination	Total Slave Imports
British North America	500,000
Spanish America	2,500,000
British Caribbean	2,000,000
French Caribbean	1,600,000
Dutch Caribbean	500,000
Danish Caribbean	28,000
Brazil	4,000,000
Old World	200,000

Source: Hugh Thomas, *The Slave Trade: The Story of the Atlantic Slave Trade, 1440–1870* (New York: Simon & Schuster, 1997), 804. Reprinted with permission.

Growth of the Atlantic Slave Trade

Because Europe provided an insatiable market for sugar, cultivation of this crop in the Americas became extremely profitable. Sugar plantations employing slave labor spread from Portuguese-ruled Brazil to the Caribbean islands. Later the cultivation of coffee in Brazil and of tobacco, rice, and **indigo** in British North America added to the demand for African slaves. By 1510 Spain had joined Portugal in the enlarged Atlantic slave trade, and a new, harsher form of slavery had appeared in the Americas. Unlike slavery in Africa, Asia, and Europe, slavery in the Americas was based on race, as only Africans and American Indians were enslaved. Most of the slaves were men or boys who were employed as agricultural laborers rather than soldiers or domestic servants. They became **chattel**—meaning personal property—of their masters and lost their customary rights as human beings. Men and boys predominated in part because Europeans believed they were stronger laborers than women and girls.

Watch the Video
From Trianglar Trade to an Atlantic System: Rethinking the Links That Created the Atlantic World

Another factor was that West Africans preferred to have women do agricultural work and therefore tended to withhold them from the Atlantic trade.

Portugal and Spain dominated the Atlantic slave trade during the sixteenth century. They shipped about 2,000 Africans per year to their American colonies, with the most by far going to Brazil. From the beginning of the trade until its nineteenth-century abolition, about 6,500,000 of the approximately 11,328,000 Africans taken to the Americas went to Brazil and Spain's colonies. Both the Portuguese and the Spanish monarchies granted monopolies over the trade to private companies. In Spain this monopoly became known in 1518 as the *Asiento* (meaning "contract"). The profits from the slave trade were so great that by 1550 the Dutch, French, and English were becoming involved. During the early seventeenth century, the Dutch drove the Portuguese from the West African coast and became the principal European slave-trading nation. For the rest of that century, most Africans came to the Americas in Dutch ships—including a group of 20 in 1619 who until recently were considered to have been the first of their race to reach British North America.

The Dutch also shifted the center of sugar production to the West Indies. England and France followed, with the former taking control of Barbados and Jamaica and the latter taking Saint Domingue (Haiti), Guadeloupe, and Martinique. With the development of tobacco as a **cash crop** in Virginia and Maryland during the 1620s and with the continued expansion of sugar production in the West Indies, the demand for African

The Portuguese established the city of Luanda in 1575. This eighteenth-century print portrays the city when it was at its height as a center for the shipment of enslaved Africans to Brazil.   The Granger Collection, New York

slaves grew. The result was that England and France competed with the Dutch to control the Atlantic slave trade. After a series of wars, England emerged supreme. It had driven the Dutch out of the trade by 1674. Victories over France and Spain led in 1713 to English control of the *Asiento*, which allowed English traders the exclusive right to supply slaves to all of Spain's American colonies. After 1713, English ships dominated the slave trade, carrying about 20,000 slaves per year from Africa to the Americas. At the peak of the trade during the 1790s, they transported 50,000 per year.

The profits from the Atlantic slave trade, together with those from the sugar and tobacco produced in the Americas by slave labor, were invested in England and helped fund the **Industrial Revolution** during the eighteenth century. In turn, Africa became a market for cheap English manufactured goods (see Map 2–3). Eventually, two triangular trade systems developed. In one, traders carried English goods to West Africa and exchanged the goods for slaves. Then the traders carried the slaves to the West Indies and exchanged them for sugar, which they took back to England on the third leg of the triangle. In the other triangular trade, white Americans from Britain's New England colonies carried rum to West Africa to trade for slaves. From Africa they took the slaves to the West Indies to exchange for sugar or molasses—sugar syrup—which they then took home to distill into rum.

Read the Document
England Asserts Her Dominion through Legislation in 1660

The African-American Ordeal from Capture to Destination

Recent scholarship indicates that the availability of large numbers of slaves in West Africa resulted from the warfare that accompanied the formation of states in

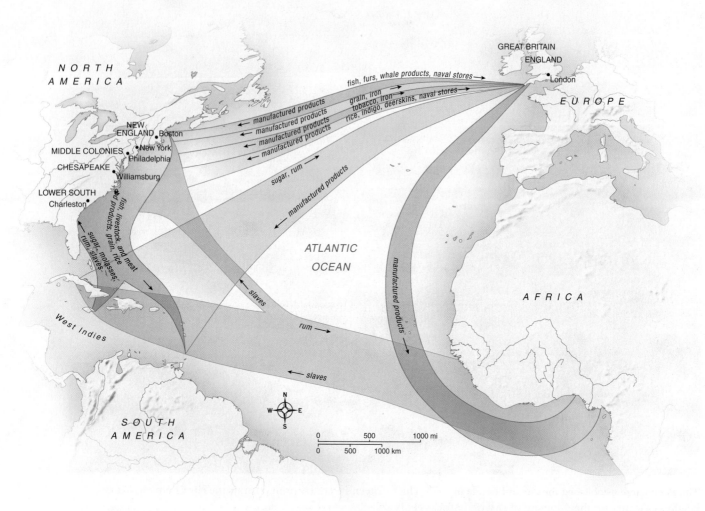

MAP 2–3   ATLANTIC TRADE AMONG THE AMERICAS, GREAT BRITAIN, AND WEST AFRICA DURING THE SEVENTEENTH
AND EIGHTEENTH CENTURIES

Often referred to as a triangular trade, this map shows the complexity of early modern Atlantic commerce, of which the slave
trade was a major part.

▶ *What does this map suggest about the economy of the Atlantic world between 1600 and 1800?*

that region. Captives suitable for enslavement were a
by-product of these wars. Senegambia and nearby
Sierra Leone, then Oyo, Dahomey, and Benin, became,
in turn, centers of the trade. Meanwhile, on the west coast
of Central Africa, slaves became available as a result of the
conflict between the expanding Kingdom of Kongo
and its neighbors. The European traders provided the
aggressors with firearms but did not instigate the wars.
Instead, they used the wars to enrich themselves.

Sometimes African armies enslaved the inhabitants
of conquered towns and villages. At other times, raid-
ing parties captured isolated families or kidnapped

individuals. As warfare spread to the interior, captives
had to march for hundreds of miles to the coast where
European traders awaited them. The raiders tied the
captives together with rope or secured them with
wooden yokes about their necks. It was a shocking experience, and many captives died from hunger, exhaustion, and exposure during the journey. Others killed
themselves rather than submit to their fate, and the
captors killed those who resisted.

Once the captives reached the coast, those destined for the Atlantic trade went to fortified structures
called **factories.** Portuguese traders constructed the

In this late eighteenth-century drawing, African slave traders conduct a group of bound captives from the interior of Africa toward European trading posts.

first factory at Elmina on the Guinea Coast in 1481—the Dutch captured it in 1637. Such factories contained the headquarters of the traders, warehouses for their trade goods and supplies, and dungeons or outdoor holding pens for the captives. In these pens, slave traders divided families and—as much as possible—ethnic groups to prevent rebellion. The traders stripped captives naked and inspected them for disease and physical defects. Those considered fit for purchase were branded like cattle with a hot iron bearing the symbol of a trading company.

In a rare account of such proceedings from a captive's point of view, Olaudah Equiano described during the 1780s how horrifying such treatment could be. The white slave traders, with their "horrible looks, red faces, and long hair," appeared to be savages who acted with a "brutal cruelty" that went beyond anything their victims had previously experienced. Many of the captives feared the Europeans were cannibals who would take them to their country for food. According to historian Gary Nash, such fears were the product of deliberate European brutalization of the

captives, part of an attempt to destroy the Africans' self-respect and self-identity.

THE CROSSING

After being held in a factory for weeks or months, captives faced the frightening prospect of leaving their native land for a voyage across an ocean that many of them had never before seen. Sailors rowed them out in large canoes to slave ships offshore. One English trader recalled that during the 1690s "the negroes were so wilful and loth to leave their own country, that they often leap'd out of the canoos, boat and ship, into the sea, and kept under water till they were drowned."

Once at sea, the slave ships followed the route Columbus had established during his voyages to the Americas: from the Canary Islands off West Africa to the Windward Islands in the Caribbean. Because ships taking this route enjoyed prevailing winds and westward currents, the passage normally lasted between two and three months. But the time required for the crossing varied widely. The larger ships were able to reach the Caribbean in 40 days, but some voyages could take up to six months.

Both human and natural causes accounted for such delays. During the three centuries that the Atlantic slave trade endured, Western European nations often fought each other, and slave ships became prized targets. As early as the 1580s, English "sea dogs," such as John Hawkins and Sir Francis Drake, attacked Spanish ships to steal their human cargoes. Outright piracy peaked between 1650 and 1725 when demand for slaves in the West Indies increased. There were also such potentially disastrous natural forces as doldrums—long windless spells at sea—and hurricanes, which could destroy ships, crews, and cargoes.

THE SLAVERS AND THEIR TECHNOLOGY

Slave ships (called **slavers**) varied in size but grew larger over the centuries. A ship's tonnage determined how many slaves it could carry, with the formula being two slaves per ton. A ship of 200 tons might therefore carry 400 slaves. But captains often ignored the formula. Some kept their human cargo light, calculating that smaller loads lowered mortality and made revolt less likely. But most captains were "tight packers" who squeezed human beings together hoping that large numbers would offset increased deaths. The 120-ton *Henrietta Marie*, a British ship that sailed from London on its final voyage in 1699, should have been fully loaded with 240 slaves. Yet it carried 350 from West Africa when it set out for Barbados and Jamaica. Another ship designed to carry 450 slaves usually carried 600.

The slavers' cargo space was generally only five feet high. Ships' carpenters halved this vertical space by building shelves, so slaves might be packed above and below on planks that measured only 5.5 feet long and 1.3 feet wide. Consequently, slaves had only about 20 to 25 inches of headroom. To add to the discomfort, the crews chained male slaves together in pairs to help prevent rebellion and lodged them away from women and children.

The most frequently reproduced illustration of a slaver's capacity for human cargo comes from the *Brookes*, which sailed from Liverpool, England, during the 1780s. At 300 tons, the *Brookes* was an exceptionally large ship for its time, and the diagrams show how tightly packed were the slaves it transported. Although those who wished to abolish the Atlantic slave trade created the diagrams, their bias does not make the diagrams less accurate. In fact, as historian James Walvin points out, the precise, unemotional renderings of the *Brookes*'s geometrically conceived design scarcely indicate the physical suffering it caused. The renderings do not show the constant shifting, crushing, and chafing

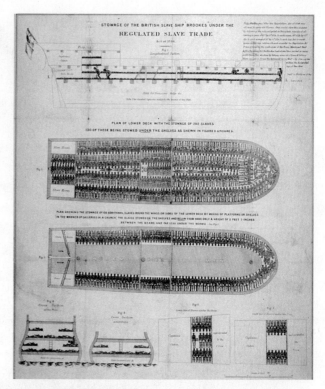

Plan of the British slave ship *Brookes,* 1788. This plan, which may undercount the human cargo the *Brookes* carried, shows how tightly Africans were packed aboard slave ships.

among the human cargo caused by the movement of the ship at sea. Also, during storms the crew often neglected to feed the slaves, empty the tubs used for excrement, take slaves on deck for exercise, tend to the sick, or remove the dead.

Mortality rates were high because the crowded, unsanitary conditions encouraged seaboard epidemics. Between 1715 and 1775, slave deaths on French ships averaged 15 percent. The highest recorded mortality rate was 34 percent. By the nineteenth century, the death rate had declined to 5 percent. Overall, one-third of the Africans subjected to the trade perished between their capture and their embarkation on a slave ship. Another third died during the Middle Passage or during "seasoning" on a Caribbean island. It would have been slight consolation to the enslaved to learn that, because of the seaboard epidemics, the death rate among slaver crews was proportionally higher than their own.

As historian Marcus Rediker notes, by the eighteenth century Europeans regarded slavers as "useful machines." The large three-masted, full-rigged vessels, with their "cast-iron cannon . . . harnessed unparalleled mobility, speed, and destructive power." They were not only well armed to protect against those who might attempt to steal their human cargo but also built to be durable and stable, although they rarely lasted more than ten years. By 1750 shipbuilders in Liverpool built slavers to order. The ships combined varieties of wood to produce strength, flexibility, and resistance to tropical ship worms that could bore into hulls. By 1800 they used copper sheathing to provide better protection below water. They used lattice doors, portholes, and funnels to ventilate slave quarters, which became healthier as time passed. They also maintained a special "hardware of bondage," including iron manacles, shackles, collars, branding implements, and thumbscrews.

A SLAVE'S STORY

In his book *The Interesting Narrative of the Life of Olaudah Equiano or Gustavus Vassa, the African*, published in 1789, former slave Olaudah Equiano provides a vivid account of a West African's capture, sale to traders, and voyage to America in 1755. Although recent evidence suggests Equiano *may* have been born in South Carolina rather than West Africa, scholars respect the accuracy of his account. He tells the story of a young Igbo, the dominant ethnic group in what is today southern Nigeria. African slave raiders capture him when he is ten years old and force him to march along with other captives to the Niger River or one of its tributaries, where they trade him to other Africans. His new captors take him to the coast and sell him to European slave traders whose ships sail to the West Indies.

Read the **Document**
A Slave Tells of His Capture in Africa in 1798

The boy's experience at the coastal slave factory convinces him he has entered a hell, peopled by evil spirits. The stench caused by forcing many people to live in close confinement makes him nauseated and emotionally agitated. His African and European captors try to calm him with liquor. But because he is not accustomed to alcohol, he becomes disoriented and more convinced of his impending doom. When the sailors lodge him with others below deck on the ship, he is so sick that he loses his appetite and hopes to die. Instead, because he refuses to eat, the sailors take him on deck and whip him. Later the boy witnesses the flogging of a white crewman. The man dies, and the sailors throw his body into the sea just as they disposed of dead Africans.

During the time the ship is in port awaiting a full cargo of slaves, the boy spends much time on deck. After putting to sea, however, he usually remains below deck with the other slaves where "each had scarcely room to turn himself." There, the smells of unwashed bodies and of the toilet tubs, "into which the children often fell and were almost suffocated," create a loathsome atmosphere. The darkness, the chafing of chains on flesh, and the shrieks and groans of the sick and disoriented provide "a scene of horror almost inconceivable."

When slaves are allowed to get fresh air and exercise on deck, the crew strings up nets to prevent them from jumping overboard. Even so, two Africans who are chained together evade the nets and jump into the ocean, preferring drowning to staying on board. The boy shares their desperation. As the ship goes beyond sight of land, he and the other captives believe they lose "even the least glimpse of hope of [re]gaining the shore" and returning to their country. Equiano, in his first-person narrative, insisted that "many more" would have jumped overboard "if they had not been prevented by the ship's crew."

Read the **Document**
An African Captive Tells the Story of Crossing the Atlantic in a Slave Ship in 1789

Attempts to keep the slaves entertained and in good humor seldom succeeded. Crews sometimes forced the slaves to dance and sing, but their songs, as slave-ship surgeon Alexander Falconbridge testified, were "melancholy lamentations, of their exile from their native country." Depression among the Africans led to a catatonia that contemporary observers called melancholy or extreme nostalgia. Falconbridge noted that the slaves had "a strong attachment to their native country" and a "just sense of the value of liberty."

Although the traders, seeking to lessen the possibility of shipboard conspiracy and rebellion, separated individuals who spoke the same language, the boy described by Equiano manages to find adults who speak Igbo. They explain to him the purpose of the voyage, which he learns is to go to the white people's country to labor for them rather than to be eaten by them. He does not realize that work on a West Indian island could be a death sentence.

A CAPTAIN'S STORY

John Newton, a white captain of a slave ship, who was born in London in 1725, provides another perspective on the Middle Passage. In 1745 Newton, as an **indentured servant,** joined the crew of a slaver bound for Sierra Leone. Indentured servants lost their freedom for a specified number of years either because they sold it or because they were being punished for debt or crime. In 1748, on the return voyage to England, Newton survived a fierce Atlantic storm and, thanking God, became an evangelical Christian. Like most people of his era, Newton saw no contradiction between his newfound faith and his participation in the enslavement and ill treatment of men, women, and children. When he became a slaver captain in 1750, he read Bible passages to his crew twice each Sunday and

PROFILE: Olaudah Equiano

For many years historians have regarded Olaudah Equiano's autobiography, *The Interesting Narrative of the Life of Olaudah Equiano or Gustavus Vassa, the African. Written by Himself* (1789), as one of the few authentic descriptions of the trade from an African point of view. Recently, however, Equiano's African birth, if not his general accuracy, has been questioned. Vincent Carretta, author of *Equiano the African: Biography of a Self-Made Man* (2005), discovered two documents—a 1759 baptismal record and a 1777 ship muster roll—indicating that Equiano was born in South Carolina in about 1747 rather than—as Equiano claimed—in Nigeria in 1745. It appears that Equiano had not used an African name for himself before he published his autobiography. But, as several scholars have noted, an African in the Atlantic world during the eighteenth century had good reason to hide his true identity and claim to have been born in America. Even Carretta does not flatly assert that Equiano lied about his African birth. Carretta, in fact, validates Equiano's autobiography by treating Equiano's description of his capture, experience on the Middle Passage, and enslavement "as if it were true."

Although the controversy over Equiano's birthplace may never be resolved, it is certain that he was a young slave in Virginia when a visiting British sea captain named Michael Henry Pascal purchased him in 1754. Pascal commanded a merchant ship and employed Equiano as his personal servant. Pascal also gave him the name Gustavus Vassa (after the king of Sweden), which Equiano used for the rest of his life. Pascal and Equiano traveled extensively and served together in North America during the French and Indian War of 1754–1763. As a result, both of them were with General James Wolfe in 1759 at Quebec, Canada, where the British won the decisive battle of the war. Equiano also lived in England, where he received the schooling that allowed him to work as "a shipping clerk and amateur navigator on the ship of his . . . [third] master, the Quaker Robert King of Philadelphia, trading chiefly between [North] America and the West Indies."

In 1766 growing antislavery sentiment among Quakers led King to allow Equiano to purchase his freedom for 40 pounds sterling. This was more money than most eighteenth-century British laborers earned in a year. Thereafter, Equiano toured the Mediterranean, sailed to the Arctic and Central America, converted to Calvinism, and became a leader in the British movement against the slave trade. In 1787 he helped organize a colony for emancipated British slaves at Sierra Leone in West Africa. Just before embarking for that country, however, dissention and confusion in the enterprise cost him his position as Commissary for Stores for the Black Poor. His autobiography, which he wrote shortly thereafter, proved to be a greater contribution to the anti–slave trade cause. The book also became a major source of income for Equiano.

In April 1792 he married an Englishwoman, Susanna Cullen, with whom he had two daughters. Their marriage notice recognized him "as the champion and advocate for procuring the suppression of the slave trade." When Equiano died on March 31, 1797, he was, according to Carretta, "probably the wealthiest and most famous person of African descent in the Atlantic world."

Equiano is significant for his account of the Atlantic slave trade and his service in the British struggle against that trade. His extraordinary life reveals how baseless the assumption was among Europeans and persons of European descent that black people were naturally suited for slavery.

◀ *Portrait of a Negro Man, Olaudah Equiano, 1780s* (previously attributed to Joshua Reynolds) by English School (eighteenth century). EX 17082 Portrait of a Negro Man, Olaudah Equiano, 1780s, (previously attributed to Joshua Reynolds) by English School (18th century) Royal Albert Memorial Museum, Exeter, Devon, UK/Bridgeman Art Library.

This mezzotint, engraved by J. R. Smith in 1793, follows a 1788 painting by English artist George Moreland. The title of the painting is "The Slave Trade." In what would have been an unusual event, Morland shows two English sea captains abducting Africans. The picture reflects moral opposition to the trade.

forbade swearing. But he treated his human cargoes as harshly as any other slaver captain.

Newton was 25 when he became captain of the *Duke of Argyle,* an old 140-ton vessel that he converted into a slaver after it sailed from Liverpool on August 11, 1750. Near the Cape Verde Islands, off the coast of Senegambia, carpenters began making the alterations required for packing Africans below deck. Newton also put the ship's guns and ammunition in order to protect against pirates or African resistance. On October 23 the *Duke of Argyle* reached Frenchman's Bay, Sierra Leone, where Newton observed other ships from England, France, and New England anchored offshore. Two days later, Newton purchased two men and a woman from traders at the port, but he had to sail to several other ports to accumulate a full cargo. Leaving West Africa for the open sea on May 23, 1751, the ship delivered its slaves to Antigua in the West Indies on July 3.

Poor health forced Newton to retire from the slave trade in 1754. Ten years later he became an Anglican priest, and from 1779 until his death in 1807 Newton served as rector of St. Mary Woolnoth Church in London. By the late 1770s, he had repented his involvement in the slave trade and had become one of its leading opponents. Together with William Cowper—a renowned poet—Newton published the *Olney Hymns* in 1779. Among the selections included in this volume was "Amazing Grace," which Newton wrote as a reflection on divine forgiveness for his sins. For several reasons, Newton and other religious Britons had begun to perceive an evil in the slave trade that, despite their piety, they had failed to see earlier.

PROVISIONS FOR THE MIDDLE PASSAGE

Slave ships left Liverpool and other European ports provisioned with food supplies for their crews. These included beans, cheese, beef, flour, and grog, a mixture of rum and water. When the ships reached the Guinea Coast in West Africa, their captains purchased pepper, palm oil, lemons, limes, yams, plantains, and coconuts. Because slaves were not accustomed to European foods, the ships needed these staples of the African diet. Meat and fish were rare luxuries on board, and crews did not share them with slaves. In the voyage Equiano describes, crew members at one point caught far more fish than they could eat but threw what was left overboard instead of giving it to the Africans who were exercising on deck. The captives "begged and prayed for some . . . but in vain." The sailors whipped those Africans who filched a few fish for themselves.

The crew usually fed the slaves twice per day in shifts. Cooks prepared vegetable pulps, porridge, and stews for the crew to distribute in buckets as the slaves assembled on deck during good weather or below deck during storms. At the beginning of the voyage, each slave received a wooden spoon for dipping into the buckets, which about ten individuals shared. But in the confined confusion below deck, slaves often lost their spoons. They then had to eat from the buckets with their unwashed hands, which spread disease.

Although slaver captains realized it was in their interest to feed their human cargoes well, they often skimped on supplies to save money and make room for more slaves. Therefore, the food on a slave ship was often insufficient to prevent malnutrition and weakened immune systems among people already traumatized by separation from their families and homelands. As a result, many Africans died during the Middle Passage from diseases amid the horrid conditions that were normal aboard the slave ships. Others died from depression: they refused to eat despite the crew's efforts to force food down their throats.

SANITATION, DISEASE, AND DEATH

Diseases such as malaria, yellow fever, measles, smallpox, hookworm, scurvy, and dysentery constantly threatened African cargoes and European crews during the Middle Passage. Death rates were astronomical on board the slave ships before 1750. Mortality dropped after that date because ships became faster and ships' surgeons knew more about hygiene and diet. There were also early forms of vaccinations against smallpox, which may have been the worst killer of slaves on ships. But, even after 1750, poor sanitation led to many deaths. It is important to remember that before the early twentieth century, no civilization had developed a germ theory of disease. Physicians blamed human illnesses on poisonous atmospheres and imbalances among bodily fluids.

Usually slavers provided only three or four toilet tubs below deck for enslaved Africans to use during the Middle Passage. They had to struggle among themselves to get to the tubs, and children had a particularly difficult time. Those too ill to reach the tubs excreted where they lay, and diseases such as dysentery, which

are spread by human waste, thrived. Dysentery, known by contemporaries as "the bloody flux," vied with smallpox to kill the most slaves aboard ships. Alexander Falconbridge reported that during one dysentery epidemic, "the deck, that is, the floor of [the slaves'] rooms, was so covered with blood and mucus which had proceeded from them in consequence of the flux, that it resembled a slaughter-house. It is not in the power of human imagination, to picture to itself a situation more dreadful or disgusting."

John Newton's stark, unimpassioned records of slave deaths aboard the *Duke of Argyle* indicate even more about how the Atlantic slave trade devalued human life. Newton recorded deaths at sea only by number. He wrote in his journal, "Bury'd a man slave No. 84 . . . bury'd a woman slave, No. 47." Yet Newton probably was more conscientious than other slaver captains in seeking to avoid disease. During his 1750 voyage, he noted only eleven deaths. These included ten slaves—five men, one woman, three boys, and one girl—and one crewman. Compared with the usual high mortality rates, this was an achievement.

What role ships' surgeons—general practitioners in modern terminology—played in preventing or inadvertently encouraging deaths aboard slave ships is difficult to determine. Some of them were outright frauds. Even the best were limited by the primitive medical knowledge that existed between the fifteenth and nineteenth centuries. Captains rewarded the surgeons with "head money" for the number of healthy slaves who arrived in the Americas, but the surgeons could also be blamed for deaths at sea that reduced the value of the human cargo.

Many surgeons recognized that African remedies were more likely than European medications to alleviate the slaves' illnesses. The surgeons collected herbs and foods along the Guinea Coast. They learned African nursing techniques, which they found more effective in treating onboard diseases than European procedures. What the surgeons did not understand and regarded as superstition was the holistic nature of African medicine. African healers maintained that body, mind, and spirit were interconnected elements of the totality of a person's well-being.

The enslaved Africans were often just as dumbfounded by the beliefs and actions of their captors. They thought they had entered a world of bad spirits when they boarded a slaver, and they attempted to counteract the spirits with rituals from their homeland. John Newton noted that during one voyage he feared slaves had tried to poison the ship's drinking water. He was relieved to discover that they were only

> **Read the Document**
> *A Slave Ship Surgeon Writes about the Slave Trade in 1788*

VOICES

The Journal of a Dutch Slaver

The following account of slave trading on the West African coast is from a journal kept on the Dutch slaver St. Jan *between March and November 1659. Although written from a European point of view, it describes the conditions Africans faced on such ships.*

We weighed anchor, by the order of the Hon'ble Director, Johan Valckenborch, and the Hon'ble Director, Jasper van Heussen to proceed on our voyage to Rio Reael [on the Guinea Coast] to trade for slaves for the hon'ble company.

March 8. Saturday. Arrived with our ship before Ardra, to take on board the surgeon's mate and a supply of tamarinds for refreshment for the slaves; sailed again next day on our voyage to Rio Reael.

17. Arrived at Rio Reael in front of a village called Bany, where we found the company's yacht, named the *Vrede*, which was sent out to assist us to trade for slaves.

In April. Nothing was done except to trade for slaves.

May 6. One of our seamen died. . . .

22. Again weighed anchor and ran out of Rio Reael accompanied by the yacht *Vrede;* purchased there two hundred and nineteen head of slaves, men, women, boys and girls, and set our course for the high land of Ambosius, for the purpose of procuring food there for the slaves, as nothing was to be had at Rio Reael.

June 29. Sunday. Again resolved to proceed on our voyage, as there also but little food was to be had for the slaves in consequence of the great rains which fell every day, and because many of the slaves were suffering from the bloody flux in consequence of the bad provisions we were supplied with at El Mina. . . .

July 27. Our surgeon, named Martyn de Lanoy, died of the bloody flux.

Aug. 11. Again resolved to pursue our voyage towards the island of Annebo, in order to purchase there some refreshments for the slaves. . . .

Aug. 15. Arrived at the island Annebo, where we purchased for the slaves one hundred half tierces of beans, twelve hogs, five thousand coconuts, five thousand sweet oranges, besides some other stores.

Sept. 21. The skipper called the ships officers aft, and resolved to run for the island of Tobago and to procure water there; otherwise we should have perished for want of water, as many of our water casks had leaked dry.

24. Friday. Arrived at the island of Tobago and hauled water there, also purchased some bread, as our hands had had no ration for three weeks.

Nov. 1. Lost our ship on the Reef of Rocus [north of Caracas], and all hands immediately took to the boat, as there was no prospect of saving the slaves, for we must abandon the ship in consequence of the heavy surf.

4. Arrived with the boat at the island of Curaco; the Hon'ble Governor Beck ordered two sloops to take the slaves off the wreck, one of which sloops with eighty four slaves on board, was captured by a privateer [pirate vessel].

▶ *What dangers did the slaves and crew on board the* St. Jan *face?*

▶ *What is the attitude of the author of the journal toward slaves?*

Source: Elizabeth Donnan, ed., *Documents Illustrative of the History of the Slave Trade to America*, 4 vols. (Washington, DC: Carnegie Institute, 1930–35), 1: 141–45. Reprinted with permission.

putting what he called "charms" in the water supply. Such fetishes, representing the power of spirits, were important in West African religions. What the slaves hoped to accomplish is not clear. But Newton, as a Christian, held their beliefs in contempt. "If it please God [that] they make no worse attempts than to charm us to death, they will not harm us," he wrote.

RESISTANCE AND REVOLT AT SEA

Although Newton ridiculed African religion, he was relieved that the slaves were not planning to poison the crew or mutiny. Because many enslaved Africans refused to accept their fate, slaver captains had to be vigilant. Uprisings were common, and Newton himself put down a potentially serious one aboard the *Duke of Argyle*. Twenty men had broken their chains below deck but were apprehended before they could assault the crew.

Most such rebellions took place while a ship prepared to set sail, the African coast was in sight, and the slaves could still hope to return home. But some revolts occurred on the open sea, where it was unlikely the Africans, even if their revolt succeeded, could return to their homes or regain their freedom. Both sorts of revolt indicate that not even capture, forced march to the coast, imprisonment, branding, and sale could break the spirit of many captives. These Africans preferred to face death rather than accept bondage.

John Atkins, an English slaver surgeon who made many voyages between Africa and the Americas during the 1720s, noted that although the threat of revolt diminished on the high seas, it never disappeared:

> When we are slaved and out at sea, it is commonly imagined that the *Negroes*['] Ignorance of Navigation, will always be a Safeguard [against revolt]; yet, as many of them think themselves bought to eat, and more, that Death will send them into their own Country, there has not been wanting Examples of rising and killing a Ship's Company, distant from Land, though not so often as on the Coast: But once or twice is enough to shew, a Master's Care and Diligence should never be over till the Delivery of them.

Later in the eighteenth century, a historian used the prevalence of revolt to justify the harsh treatment of Africans on slave ships. Edward Long wrote that "the many acts of violence they [the slaves] have committed by murdering whole crews and destroying ships when they had it left in their power to do so, have made this rigour wholly chargeable on their own bloody and malicious disposition, which calls for the same confinement as if they were wolves or wild boars."

Failed slave mutineers could expect harsh punishment, although profit margins influenced sentences. Atkins chronicled how the captain of the *Robert*, which sailed from Bristol, England, punished the ringleaders, who were worth more, less harshly than their followers who were not as valuable. Atkins related that

> Captain Harding, weighing the Stoutness and Worth of the two [ringleaders], did, as in other Countries they do by Rogues of Dignity, whip and scarify them only; while three others, Abettors, but not Actors, nor of Strength for it, he sentenced to cruel Deaths; making them first eat the Heart and Liver of one of them killed. The Woman [who had helped in the revolt] he hoisted up by the Thumbs, whipp'd and slashed her with Knives, before the other Slaves, till she died.

Other slaves resisted their captors by drowning or starving themselves. Thomas Phillips, captain of the slaver *Hannibal* during the 1690s, commented, "We had about 12 negroes did wilfully drown themselves and others starved themselves to death; for 'tis their belief that when they die they return home to their own country and friends again." As previously indicated, captains used nets to prevent deliberate drowning. To deal with self-imposed starvation, they used hot coals or a metal device called a *speculum oris* to force individuals to open their mouths for feeding.

CRUELTY

The Atlantic slave trade required more capital than any other maritime commerce during the seventeenth and eighteenth centuries. The investments for the ships, the exceptionally large crews they employed, the navigational equipment, the armaments, the purchase of slaves in Africa, and the supplies of food and water needed to feed hundreds of passengers were phenomenal. The aim was to carry as many Africans in healthy condition to the Americas as possible in order to make the large profits that justified such expenditures. Yet, as we have indicated, conditions aboard the vessels were abysmal.

Scholars have debated how much deliberate cruelty the enslaved Africans suffered from ships' crews. The West Indian historian Eric Williams asserts that the horrors of the Middle Passage have been exaggerated. Many writers, Williams contends, are led astray by the writings of those who, during the late eighteenth and early nineteenth centuries, sought to abolish the slave trade. In his view—and that of other historians—the difficulties of the Middle Passage were similar to those of European indentured servants who suffered high mortality rates on the voyage to America.

From this perspective the primary cause of death at sea on all ships carrying passengers across the Atlantic to the Americas was epidemic disease, against which medical practitioners had few tools before the twentieth century. Contributing factors included inadequate means of preserving food from spoilage and failure to prevent freshwater from becoming contaminated during the long ocean crossing. According to Williams, overcrowding by slavers was only a secondary cause for the high mortality rates.

Such observations help place conditions aboard the slave ships in a broader perspective. Cruelty and suffering are, to some degree, historically relative in that practices acceptable in the past are now considered inhumane. Yet cruelty aboard slavers must also be placed in a cultural context. Cultures distinguish between what constitutes acceptable behavior to their own people on the one hand and to strangers on the other. For Europeans, Africans were cultural strangers, and what became normal in the Atlantic slave trade was in fact exceptionally cruel compared to how Europeans treated each other. Slaves below deck received only one-half the space allocated on board to European soldiers, free emigrants, indentured servants, and convicts. Europeans regarded slavery itself as a condition suitable only for non-Christians. And as strangers, Africans were subject to brutalization by European crew members who often cared little about the physical and emotional damage they inflicted.

PROFILE: Ayuba Suleiman Diallo of Bondu

Ayuba Suleiman Diallo, known to Europeans as Job ben Solomon, was one of the many West Africans caught up in the Atlantic slave trade. But his experience was far from typical. Because he had family connections, was literate in Arabic, and used his aristocratic personality to gain favor among Europeans, Diallo was able to escape enslavement and return to his native land. His story reveals much about the bonds of wealth and class in the Atlantic world during the early eighteenth century.

Diallo was born in about 1701 at the village of Marsa located in the eastern Senegambian region of Bondu. His father, the imam of the local mosque and village head, taught him Arabic and the Koran when he was a child and prepared him to become a merchant. That Samba Geladio Jegi, the future king of the nearby kingdom of Futa Toro, was a fellow student suggests the standing of Diallo's family. Diallo, following Muslim and West African custom, had two wives. He married the first of them when he was fifteen and she was eleven, the second when he was 28.

In February 1730, Diallo was on his way to the Gambia River to sell two slaves to an English trader when he was himself captured by Mandingo warriors and sold as well. Although the English slaver captain was willing to ransom Diallo, his ship sailed before Diallo's father could send the money. As a result, Diallo was shipped with other Africans to Annapolis, Maryland, and delivered to Vachell Denton, factor for William Hunt, a London merchant. Shortly thereafter, Diallo was sold to a Mr. Tolsey, who operated a tobacco plantation on Maryland's eastern shore.

Although Diallo was "about five feet ten inches high . . . and naturally of a good constitution," his "religious abstinence" and the difficulties he had experienced during the Middle Passage unsuited him for fieldwork. Therefore, Tolsey assigned him to tending cattle. In June 1731, however, after a young white boy repeatedly interrupted his prayers, Diallo

escaped to Dover, Delaware, where he was apprehended and jailed. There, Thomas Bluett, who published in 1734 an account of Diallo's adventures, discovered that Diallo was literate in Arabic, pious in his religious devotions, and—according to Bluett's stereotypical notions—"no common slave." Bluett provided this information to Tolsey, who on Diallo's return allowed him a quiet place to pray and permitted him to write a letter in Arabic to his father.

The letter reached James Oglethorpe, the director of England's slave-trading Royal African Company, who arranged to purchase Diallo from Tolsey and in March 1733 transport him by ship to England. Accompanied by Bluett, Diallo learned during the long voyage to speak, read, and write English. In London, Bluett contacted several well-to-do gentlemen who raised 60 pounds to secure Diallo's freedom and, with the aid of the Royal African Company, return him to Senegambia. Before he left England in July 1734, Diallo had an audience with King George II, met with the entire royal family, dined with members of the nobility, and received expensive gifts.

Diallo's wives and children greeted him on his return to his village, but much had changed during his absence. Futa Toro had conquered Bondu, and as a result Diallo's family had suffered economically. In addition, the slave trade in Senegambia had intensified and Morocco had begun to interfere militarily in the region. Grateful to his English friends, Diallo used his influence in these difficult circumstances to help the Royal African Company hold its share of the trade in slaves and gold until the company disbanded in 1752. Able to differentiate between his fortunes and those of others, he retained commercial ties to the British until his death in 1773.

▶ **"The Fortunate Slave,"** an illustration of African slavery in the early eighteenth century by Douglas Grant (1968). From "Some Memoirs of the Life of Job," by Thomas Bluett, 1734. The New York Public Library/Art Resource, NY

VOICES

DYSENTERY (OR THE BLOODY FLUX)

Alexander Falconbridge (d. 1792) served as ship's surgeon on four British slavers between 1780 and 1787. In 1788 he became an opponent of the trade and published An Account of the Slave Trade on the Coast of Africa. *Here he describes in gruesome detail conditions in slave quarters during a dysentery epidemic that he mistakenly attributes to stale air and heat.*

Some wet and blowing weather having occasioned the portholes to be shut, and the grating to be covered, fluxes and fevers among the Negroes ensued. While they were in this situation, my profession requiring it, I frequently went down among them, till at length their apartments became so extremely hot, as to be only sufferable for a very short time. . . . It is not in the power of the human imagination, to picture to itself a situation more dreadful or disgusting. Numbers of the slaves having fainted, they were carried upon deck, where several of them died, and the rest were, with great difficulty, restored. It had nearly proved fatal to me also. The climate was too warm to admit the wearing of any clothing but a shirt, and that I had pulled off before I went down; notwithstanding which, by only continuing among them for about a quarter of an hour, I was so overcome with the heat, stench, and foul air, that I had nearly fainted; and it was not without assistance, that I could get upon deck. The consequence was, that I soon after fell sick of the same disorder, from which I did not recover for several months. . . .

The place allotted for the sick Negroes is under the half deck, where they lie on the bare planks. By this means, those who are emaciated, frequently have their skin, and even their flesh, entirely rubbed off, by the motion of the ship, from the prominent parts of the shoulders, elbows, and hips, so as to render the bones in those parts quite bare. And some of them, by constantly lying in the blood and mucus, that had flowed from those afflicted with the flux, and which . . . is generally so violent as to prevent their being kept clean, have their flesh much sooner rubbed off, than those who have only to contend with the mere friction of the ship. The excruciating pain which the poor sufferers feel from being obliged to continue in such a dreadful situation, frequently for several weeks, in case they happen to live so long, is not to be conceived or described. Few, indeed, are ever able to withstand the fatal effects of it. The utmost skill of the surgeon is here ineffectual. . . .

The surgeon, upon going between decks, in the morning, to examine the situation of the slaves, frequently finds several dead; and among the men, sometimes a dead and living Negroe fastened by their irons together. When this is the case, they are brought upon the deck, and being laid on the grating, the living Negroe is disengaged, and the dead one thrown overboard. . . .

AFRICAN WOMEN ON SLAVE SHIPS

For similar reasons, African women did not enjoy the same protection against unwanted sexual attention from European men that European women received. Consequently, sailors during long voyages attempted to sate their sexual appetites with enslaved women. African women caught in the Atlantic slave trade were worth half the price of African men in Caribbean markets, and as a result, captains took fewer of them on board their vessels. Perhaps because the women were less valuable commodities, crew members felt they had license to abuse them sexually. The separate below-deck compartments for women on slave ships also made them easier targets than they otherwise might have been.

Historian Barbara Bush speculates that the horrid experience of the Middle Passage may have influenced black women's attitudes toward sexuality and procreation. This, in turn, may help explain why slave populations in the Caribbean and Latin America failed to reproduce themselves: exhaustion, terror, and disgust can depress sex drives.

Landing and Sale in the West Indies

As a slaver neared the West Indies, the crew prepared its human cargo for landing and sale. They allowed the slaves to shave, wash with freshwater, and exercise. Those bound for the larger Caribbean islands or for the British colonies of southern North America often received some weeks of rest in the easternmost islands of the West Indies. **((•─Hear the Audio** *I Just Come from the Fountain* French slave traders typically rested their slave passengers on **Martinique.** The English preferred **Barbados.** Sale to white plantation owners followed. Then began a period of what the planters called "seasoning," up to two years of acculturating slaves and breaking them in to plantation routines.

The process of landing and sale that ended the Middle Passage was often as protracted as the events that

▶ *Could slave traders have avoided the suffering described in this passage?*
▶ *What impact would such suffering have had on those who survived it?*

Source: Alexander Falconbridge, *An Account of the Slave Trade on the Coast of Africa* (London: privately printed, 1788), in John H. Bracey Jr. and Manisha Sinha, *African American Mosaic: A Documentary History from the Slave Trade to the Twenty-first Century* (Upper Saddle River, NJ: Prentice Hall, 2004), 1: 24.

began it in Africa. After anchoring at one of the Lesser Antilles Islands—Barbados, St. Kitts, or Antigua—English slaver captains haggled with the agents of local planters over numbers and prices. They then determined whether to sell all their slaves at their first port of call, sell some of them, sail to another island, or sail to such North American ports as Charleston, Williamsport, or Baltimore. If the market looked good in the first port, the captain might still take a week or more to sell his cargo. The captain of the *James*, who landed at Barbados in 1676, just as the cultivation of cane sugar there was becoming extremely profitable, sold most of his slaves in three days. "May Thursday 25th . . . sold 163 slaves. May Friday 26th. We sold 70 slaves. May Saturday 27th. Sold 110 slaves," he recorded in his journal.

Often, captains and crew had to do more to prepare slaves for sale than allow them to clean themselves and exercise. The ravages of cruelty, confinement, and disease could not be easily remedied. According to legend, young African men and women arrived in the Americas with gray hair, and captains used dye to hide such indications of age before the slaves went to market. Slaves were also required to oil their bodies to conceal blemishes, rashes, and bruises. Ships' surgeons used hemp to plug the anuses of those suffering from dysentery to block the bloody discharge the disease caused.

The humiliation continued as the slaves went to market. Once again they suffered close physical inspection from potential buyers, which—according to Equiano—caused "much dread and trembling among us" and "bitter cries." Unless a single purchaser agreed to buy an entire cargo of slaves, auctions took place either on deck or in sale yards on shore. However, some captains employed "the scramble." In these barbaric spectacles, the captain established standard prices for men, women, and children; herded the Africans together in a corral; and then allowed buyers to rush pell-mell among them to grab and rope together the slaves they desired.

Seasoning

Seasoning followed sale. On Barbados, Jamaica, and other Caribbean islands, planters divided slaves into three categories: **Creoles** (slaves born in the Americas), old Africans (those who had lived in the Americas

This nineteenth-century engraving suggests the humiliation Africans endured as they were subjected to physical inspections before being sold.

for some time), and new Africans (those who had just survived the Middle Passage). Creole slaves were worth three times the value of unseasoned new Africans, whom planters and Creole slaves called "salt-water Negroes" or "Guinea-birds." Seasoning began the process of making new Africans more like Creoles.

In the West Indies, this process involved not only an apprenticeship in the work routines of the sugar plantations on the islands. It also prepared many slaves for resale to North American planters, who preferred "seasoned" slaves to "unbroken" ones who came directly from Africa. In fact, most of the Africans who ended up in the British colonies of North America before 1720 had gone first to the West Indies. By that date, the demand for slave labor in the islands had become so great that they could spare fewer slaves for resale to the North American market. Thereafter, as a result, slave imports into the tobacco-, rice-, and later cotton-growing regions of the American South came directly from Africa and had to be seasoned by their American masters. But many slaves still came to North America from the Caribbean, to which they had been brought from Africa or where they had been born.

In either case, seasoning was a disciplinary process intended to modify the behavior and attitude of slaves and make them effective laborers. As part of this

Slaves in this nineteenth-century painting are preparing a field for cultivation on the island of Antigua, a British possession in the West Indies. As had been the case in earlier centuries, the men and women work in gangs under the direction of a white overseer who carries a whip.

process, the slaves' new masters gave them new names: Christian names, generic African names, or names from classical Greece and Rome (such as Jupiter, Achilles, or Plato).

The seasoning process also involved learning European languages. Masters in the Spanish Caribbean were especially thorough teachers. Consequently, although Spanish-speaking African slaves and their descendants retained African words, they could be easily understood by any Spanish-speaking person. In the French and English Caribbean islands and in parts of North America, however, slave society produced Creole dialects that in grammar, vocabulary, and intonation had distinctive African linguistic features. These Africanized versions of French and English, including the Gullah dialect

still prevalent on South Carolina's sea islands and the Creole most Haitians speak today, were difficult to understand for those who spoke more standardized dialects.

During seasoning, masters or overseers broke slaves into plantation work by assigning them to one of several work gangs. The strongest men joined the first or "great gang," which did the heavy fieldwork of planting and harvesting. The second gang, including women and older men, did lighter fieldwork, such as weeding. The third gang, composed of children, worked shorter hours and performed such tasks as bringing food and water to the field gangs. Other slaves became domestic servants. New Africans served apprenticeships with old Africans from their same ethnic group or with Creoles.

Some planters looked for cargoes of young people, anticipating that they might be more easily **acculturated** than older Africans. One West Indian master in 1792 recorded his hopes for a group of children: "From the late Guinea sales, I have purchased altogether twenty boys and girls, from ten to thirteen years old." He emphasized that "it is the practice, on bringing them to the estate, to distribute them in the huts of Creole blacks, under their direction and care, who are to feed them, train them to work, and teach them their new language."

Planters had to rely on old Africans and Creoles to train new recruits because white people were a minority in the Caribbean. Later, a similar demographic pattern developed in parts of the cotton-producing American South. In both regions, therefore, African custom shaped the cooperative labor of slaves in gangs. But the use of old Africans and Creoles as instructors and the appropriation of African styles of labor should not suggest leniency. Although the plantation overseers, who ran day-to-day operations, could be white, of mixed race, or black, they invariably imposed strict discipline. Drivers, who directed the work gangs, were almost always black. But they carried whips and frequently punished those who worked too slowly or showed disrespect. Planters assigned recalcitrant new Africans to the strictest overseers and drivers.

Planters housed slaves undergoing seasoning with the old Africans and Creoles who were instructing them. The instructors regarded such additions to their households as economic opportunities because the new Africans provided extra labor on the small plots of land that West Indian planters often allocated to slaves. Slaves could sell surplus root vegetables, peas, and fruit from their gardens and save to purchase freedom for themselves or others. Additional workers helped produce larger surpluses to sell at local markets, thereby reducing the time required to accumulate a purchase price.

New Africans also benefited from this arrangement. They learned how to build houses in their new land and how to cultivate vegetables to supplement the food the planter provided. Even though many Africans brought building skills and agricultural knowledge with them to the Americas, old Africans and Creoles helped teach them how to adapt their skills and knowledge to a new climate, topography, building materials, and social organization.

The End of the Journey: Masters and Slaves in the Americas

By what criteria did planters assess the successful seasoning of new Africans? The first criterion was survival. Already weakened and traumatized by the Middle Passage, many Africans did not survive seasoning. Historian James Walvin estimates that one-third died during their first three years in the West Indies. African men died at a greater rate than African women, perhaps because they did the more arduous fieldwork.

A second criterion was that the Africans had to adapt to new foods and a new climate. The foods included salted codfish traded to the West Indies by New England merchants, Indian corn (maize), and varieties of squash not available in West Africa. The Caribbean islands, like West Africa, were tropical, but North America was much cooler. Even within the West Indies, an African was unlikely to find a climate exactly like the one he or she had left behind.

A third criterion was learning a new language. Planters did not require slaves to speak the local language, which could be English, French, Spanish, Danish, or Dutch, fluently. But slaves had to speak a creole dialect well enough to obey commands. A final criterion was psychological. When new Africans ceased to be suicidal, planters assumed they had accepted their status and their separation from their homeland.

It would have suited the planters if their slaves had met all these criteria. Yet that would have required the Africans to have been thoroughly desocialized by the Middle Passage, and they were not. As traumatic as that

Group of Negros, as imported to be sold for Slaves.

This print, published in 1793, portrays a group of Africans who arrived during the 1720s in Suriname, in northern South America. Although the artist creates an almost festive scene, a slave trader is driving them with a stick.

voyage was—for all the shock of capture, separation from loved ones, and efforts to dehumanize them—most Africans who entered plantation society in the Americas had not been stripped of their memories or their culture. When their ties to their villages and families were broken, they created bonds with shipmates that simulated blood relationships. Such bonds became the basis of new extended families. So similar were these new synthetic families to those that had existed in West Africa that slaves considered sexual relations among shipmates and former shipmates incestuous.

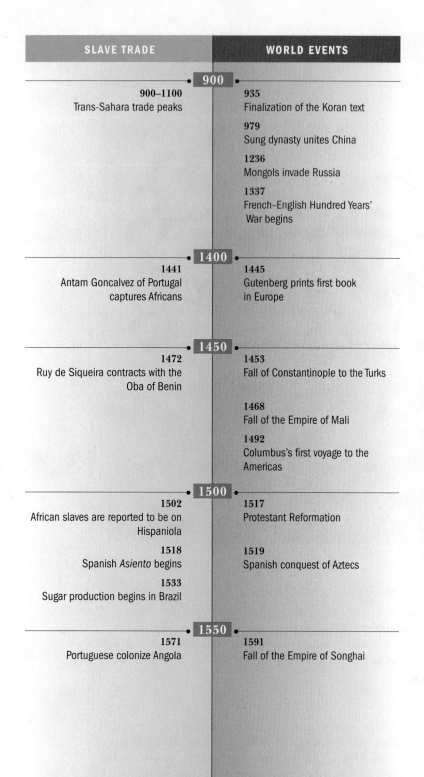

SLAVE TRADE	WORLD EVENTS
900	
900–1100 Trans-Sahara trade peaks	**935** Finalization of the Koran text
	979 Sung dynasty unites China
	1236 Mongols invade Russia
	1337 French–English Hundred Years' War begins
1400	
1441 Antam Goncalvez of Portugal captures Africans	**1445** Gutenberg prints first book in Europe
1450	
1472 Ruy de Siqueira contracts with the Oba of Benin	**1453** Fall of Constantinople to the Turks
	1468 Fall of the Empire of Mali
	1492 Columbus's first voyage to the Americas
1500	
1502 African slaves are reported to be on Hispaniola	**1517** Protestant Reformation
1518 Spanish *Asiento* begins	**1519** Spanish conquest of Aztecs
1533 Sugar production begins in Brazil	
1550	
1571 Portuguese colonize Angola	**1591** Fall of the Empire of Songhai

As this suggests, African slaves did not lose all their culture during the Middle Passage and seasoning in the Americas. Their value system never totally replicated that of the plantation. Despite their ordeal, the Africans who survived the Atlantic slave trade and slavery in the Americas were resilient. Seasoning did modify their behavior. Yet the claim that it obliterated African Americans' cultural roots is incorrect. Anthropologist Melville Herskovits in 1941 raised questions about this issue that still shape debate about the African-American experience.

Herskovits asked, "What discussions of world view might not have taken place in the long hours when [Creole] teacher and [new African] pupil were together, reversing their roles when matters only dimly sensed by the American-born slave were explained [by his pupil] in terms of African conventions he had never analyzed?" How many African beliefs and methods of coping with life and the supernatural were retained and transmitted by such private discussions? How much did African cultural elements, such as dance, song, folklore, moral values, and etiquette, offset the impulse to accept European values?

The Ending of the Atlantic Slave Trade

The cruelties associated with the Atlantic slave trade contributed to its abolition in the early nineteenth century. During the late 1700s, English abolitionists led by Thomas Clarkson, William Wilberforce, and Granville Sharp began a religiously oriented moral crusade against slavery and the slave trade. Because the English had dominated the Atlantic trade since 1713, Britain's growing antipathy became crucial to the trade's destruction. But it is debatable whether moral outrage alone prompted this humanitarian effort. By the late 1700s, England's industrializing economy was less dependent on the slave trade and the entire plantation system than it had been previously. To maintain its prosperity, England needed raw materials and markets for its manufactured goods. Slowly but surely its ruling classes realized it was more profitable to invest in industry and other forms of trade and to leave Africans in Africa.

So morals and economic self-interest combined when Britain abolished the Atlantic slave trade in 1807 and tried to enforce that abolition on other nations through a naval patrol off the African coast. The following year, the U.S. Congress joined in outlawing the Atlantic trade. Although American, Brazilian, and Spanish slavers defied these prohibitions for years, the forced migration from Africa to the Americas dropped to a tiny percentage of what it had been at its peak. Ironically, the coastal kingdoms of Guinea and western Central Africa fought most fiercely to keep the trade going because their economies had become dependent on it. This persistence gave the English, French, Belgians, and Portuguese an excuse to establish colonial empires in Africa during the nineteenth century in the name of suppressing the slave trade.

CONCLUSION

Over more than three centuries, the Atlantic slave trade brought more than eleven million Africans to the Americas. Several million died in transit. Of those who survived, most came between 1701 and 1810, when more Africans than Europeans reached the New World. Most Africans went to the sugar plantations of the Caribbean and Brazil. Only 500,000 went to the British colonies of North America, either directly or after seasoning in the West Indies. From them have come the nearly 40 million African Americans alive today.

This chapter has described the great forced migration across the Atlantic that brought Africans into slavery in the Americas. We still have much to learn about the origins of the trade, its relationship to the earlier trans-Sahara trade, and its involvement with state formation in West and western Central Africa. Historians continue to debate how cruel the trade was, the ability of transplanted Africans to preserve their cultural heritage, and why Britain abolished the trade in the early nineteenth century.

We are fortunate that a few Africans who experienced the Middle Passage recorded their testimony. Otherwise, we would find its horror even more difficult to comprehend. Even more important, however, is that so many survived the horrible experience of the Atlantic slave trade and carried on. Their struggle testifies to the human spirit that is at the center of the African-American experience.

RECOMMENDED READING

Barbara Bush. *Slave Women in Caribbean Society, 1650–1838.* Bloomington: Indiana University Press, 1990. Contains an insightful discussion of African women, their introduction to slavery in the Americas, and their experience on sugar plantations.

Basil Davidson. *The African Slave Trade: Revised and Expanded Edition.* Boston: Little, Brown, 1980. Originally published in 1961, this book has been superseded in some respects by more recent studies. But it places the trade in both African and European contexts.

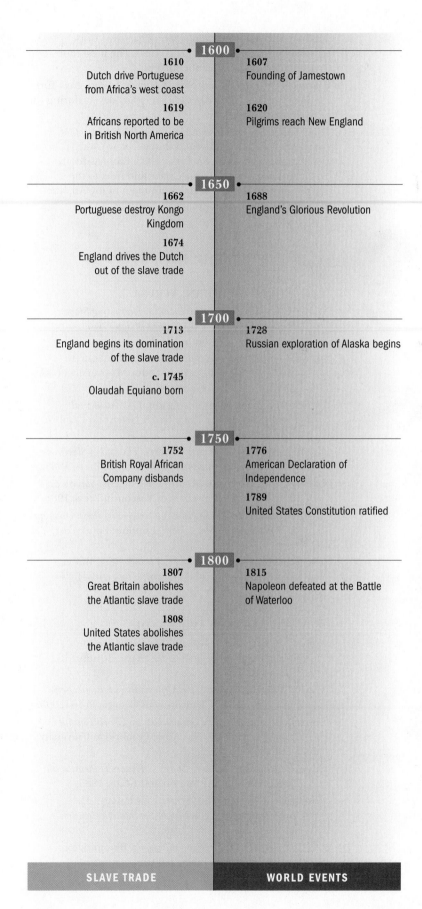

1600

1610
Dutch drive Portuguese from Africa's west coast

1619
Africans reported to be in British North America

1607
Founding of Jamestown

1620
Pilgrims reach New England

1650

1662
Portuguese destroy Kongo Kingdom

1674
England drives the Dutch out of the slave trade

1688
England's Glorious Revolution

1700

1713
England begins its domination of the slave trade

c. 1745
Olaudah Equiano born

1728
Russian exploration of Alaska begins

1750

1752
British Royal African Company disbands

1776
American Declaration of Independence

1789
United States Constitution ratified

1800

1807
Great Britain abolishes the Atlantic slave trade

1808
United States abolishes the Atlantic slave trade

1815
Napoleon defeated at the Battle of Waterloo

SLAVE TRADE   **WORLD EVENTS**

Herbert S. Klein. *The Atlantic Slave Trade*. New York: Cambridge University Press, 1999. The most thorough and current study of the subject.

Marcus Rediker. *The Slave Ship: A Human History*. New York: Viking, 2007. Describes life on board slavers during the eighteenth century.

John Thornton. *Africa and Africans in the Making of the Atlantic World, 1400–1800*, 2nd ed. New York: Cambridge University Press, 1998. Emphasizes the contributions of Africans, slave and free, to the economic and cultural development of the Atlantic world during the slave trade centuries.

ADDITIONAL BIBLIOGRAPHY

THE SLAVE TRADE IN AFRICA

Walter Hawthorne. *Planting Rice and Harvesting Slaves: Transformations along the Guinea-Bissau Coast, 1400–1900*. Portsmouth, NH: Heinemann, 2003.

Bernard Lewis. *Race and Slavery in the Middle East: An Historical Enquiry*. New York: Oxford University Press, 1990.

Patrick Manning. *Slavery and African Life: Occidental, Oriental, and African Slave Trades*. New York: Cambridge University Press, 1990.

Suzanne Miers and Richard Roberts. *The End of Slavery in Africa*. Madison: University of Wisconsin Press, 1988.

Claire C. Robertson and Martin A. Klein, eds. *Slavery in Africa*. Madison: University of Wisconsin Press, 1983.

Elizabeth Savage, ed. *The Human Commodity: Perspectives on the Trans-Saharan Slave Trade*. London: Frank Cass, 1992.

John K. Thornton. *The Kingdom of Kongo: Civil War and Transition, 1641–1718*. Madison: University of Wisconsin Press, 1983.

THE ATLANTIC SLAVE TRADE

Anne C. Bailey. *African Voices of the Atlantic Slave Trade: Beyond the Silence and the Shame*. Boston: Beacon, 2005.

Vincent Carretta. *Equiano the African: Biography of a Self-Made Man*. Athens: University of Georgia Press, 2005.

Emma Christopher. *Slave Ship Sailors and Their Captive Cargoes, 1730–1807*. New York: Cambridge University Press, 2006.

Edward Reynolds. *Stand the Storm: A History of the Atlantic Slave Trade*. London: Allison and Busby, 1985.

Rosemarie Robotham, ed. *Spirits of the Passage: The Transatlantic Slave Trade in the Seventeenth Century*. New York: Simon & Schuster, 1997.

Lief Svalesen. *The Slave Ship Fredensborg*. Bloomington: Indiana University Press, 2000.

Hugh Thomas. *The Slave Trade: The Story of the Atlantic Slave Trade, 1440–1870*. New York: Simon & Schuster, 1997.

Vincent Bakpetu Thompson. *The Making of the African Diaspora in the Americas, 1441–1900*. New York: Longman, 1987.

James Walvin. *Making the Black Atlantic: Britain and the African Diaspora*. New York: Cassell, 2000.

THE WEST INDIES

Edward Brathwaite. *The Development of Creole Society in Jamaica, 1770–1820*. New York: Oxford University Press, 1971.

William Claypole and John Robottom. *Caribbean Story: Foundations*. Kingston: Longman, 1980.

Melville J. Herskovits. *The Myth of the Negro Past*. Boston: Beacon, 1941.

Clarence J. Munford. *The Black Ordeal of Slavery and Slave Trading in the French West Indies, 1625–1715*. Lewiston, NY: Mellen, 1991.

Keith Albert Sandiford. *The Cultural Politics of Sugar: Caribbean Slavery and Narratives of Colonialism*. New York: Cambridge University Press, 2000.

RETRACING THE ODYSSEY

The Henrietta Marie. http://www.historical-museum.org/exhibits/hm/henmarie.htm. This is a slave ship placed on traveling display by the Museum of Southern Florida in Miami. The *Henrietta Marie* sank in 1701 after delivering slaves to Jamaica.

Chattanooga African American Museum, Chattanooga, TN. http://www.caamhistory.org/. The museum includes an exhibit dealing with the Atlantic slave trade.

REVIEW QUESTIONS

1. How did the Atlantic slave trade reflect the times during which it existed?

2. Think about Olaudah Equiano's experience as a young boy captured by traders and brought to a slave ship. What new and strange things did he encounter? How did he explain these things to himself? What kept him from descending into despair?

3. How could John Newton reconcile his Christian faith with his career as a slave-ship captain?

4. What human and natural variables could prolong the Middle Passage across the Atlantic? How could delay make the voyage more dangerous for slaves and crew?

5. How could Africans resist the dehumanizing forces of the Middle Passage and seasoning and use their African cultures to build black cultures in the New World?

PEARSON myhistorylab Connections

www.myhistorylab.com

Review what you've learned in this chapter and explore the many documents, images, research tools, and activities for this chapter to learn more about African-American history.

✓● Study and Review

READ

●●●● Read the Document

- Christopher Columbus, from The Journal of Christopher Columbus (1492)

- England Asserts Her Dominion through Legislation in 1660

- A Slave Tells of His Capture in Africa in 1798

- An African Captive Tells the Story of Crossing the Atlantic in a Slave Ship in 1789

- A Slave Ship Surgeon Writes about the Slave Trade in 1788

- Congress Prohibits Importation of Slaves (1807)

LISTEN

((●● Hear the Audio

Hear the audio files for Chapter 2.

- *I Just Come from the Fountain* by Michael LaRue

RESEARCH

mysearchlab

Consider these questions in a short research paper.

Why was the history of slavery repressed for so long? Why has interest in the subject grown in the past quarter of a century?

EXPLORE

◉● Watch the Video

- What Is Columbus's Legacy?

- From Trianglar Trade to an Atlantic System: Rethinking the Links That Created the Atlantic World

- Atlantic Connections: Sugar, Smallpox, and Slavery

◉● See the Map

- The Atlantic and Islamic Slave Trades

●●●● Read the Document

- Exploring America: Racism in American History

The Voyage to Slavery

The voyage to the slavery began with captured Africans shackled together at the neck, forced to march to factories where they were held in dungeons or outdoor holding pens. Many captives died from hunger, exhaustion, and exposure. Others killed themselves rather than submit to their fate or were killed if they resisted. Families and ethnic groups were divided. Once considered fit for purchase, captives were branded like cattle with a hot iron bearing the symbol of a trading company. Those sent to the Atlantic slave trade continued the journey in the cargo space of slave ships that were only five feet high. Packed above and below ship planks that measured only 5.5 feet long and 16 inches wide, slaves had very little headroom. Male slaves were chained together in pairs. Many captains carried more slaves than a ship was built to handle, squeezing human beings together to offset high death rates by carrying more slaves. During storms the crew often neglected to feed the slaves, empty the tubs used for excrement, take slaves on deck for exercise, tend to the sick, or remove the dead.

◀ **These diagrams show how slaves were crowded** below deck on slave ships with little or no room between them.

◀ **Fort San Sebstian in Ghana** where slaves were imprisoned while awaiting transport.

Slaves were housed in prison-type pens once they arrived in America until they could be sold at market. This photo shows the interior view of one such pen in Alexandria, Virginia, used in the 1800s.

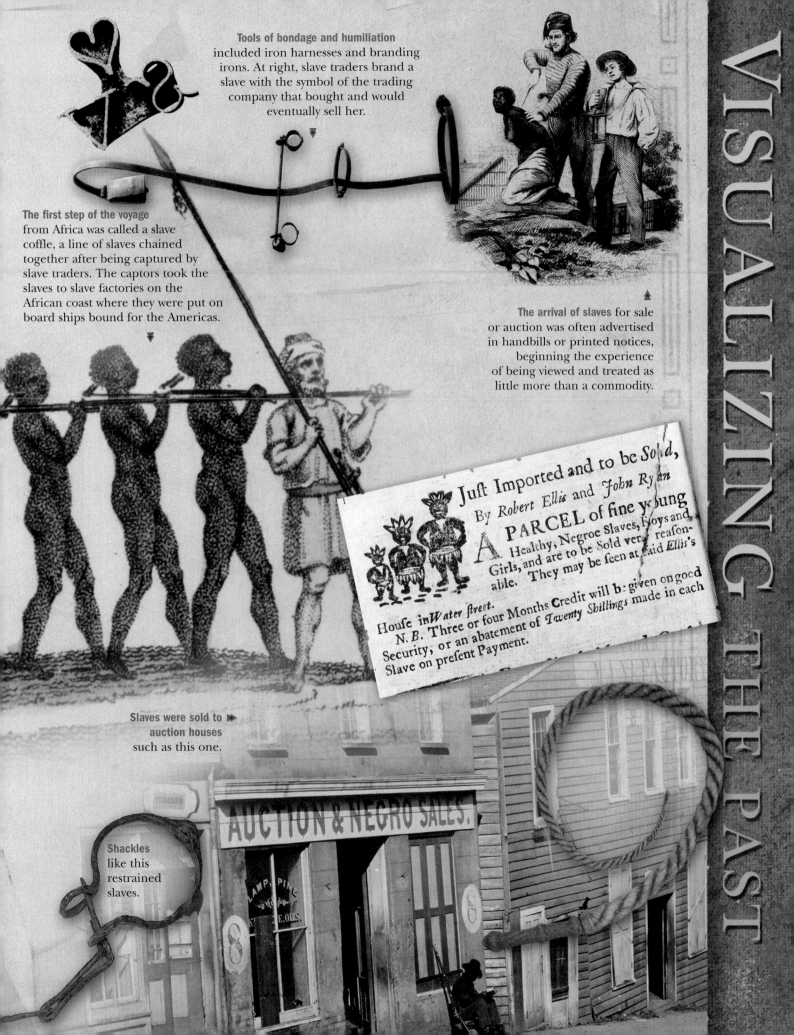

Tools of bondage and humiliation included iron harnesses and branding irons. At right, slave traders brand a slave with the symbol of the trading company that bought and would eventually sell her.

The first step of the voyage from Africa was called a slave coffle, a line of slaves chained together after being captured by slave traders. The captors took the slaves to slave factories on the African coast where they were put on board ships bound for the Americas.

The arrival of slaves for sale or auction was often advertised in handbills or printed notices, beginning the experience of being viewed and treated as little more than a commodity.

Just Imported and to be Sold, By *Robert Ellis* and *John Ryan* A PARCEL of fine young Healthy, Negroe Slaves, Boys and Girls, and are to be Sold very reasonable. They may be seen at said *Ellis's* House in *Water street*. N.B. Three or four Months Credit will be given on good Security, or an abatement of *Twenty Shillings* made in each Slave on present Payment.

Slaves were sold to ▶▶ auction houses such as this one.

AUCTION & NEGRO SALES.

Shackles like this restrained slaves.

Black People in Colonial North America

Who were the peoples of colonial
North America?

How did black servitude develop
in the Chesapeake?

What were the characteristics
of plantation slavery from 1700 to 1750?

How did the experience of African
Americans under French and Spanish
rule in North America compare to that
in the British colonies?

How did slavery affect black women
in colonial America?

How did African Americans
resist slavery?

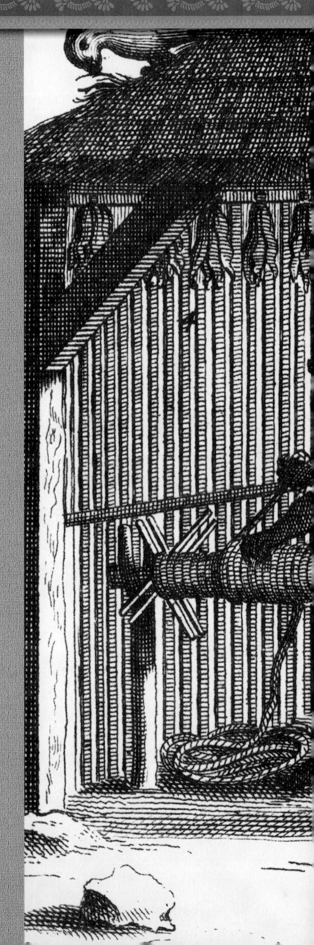

▶ **This eighteenth-century woodcut** shows enslaved black men, women,
and children engaged in the steps involved in the curing of tobacco.
Courtesy of the Library of Congress

Whereas, the plantations and estates of this Province [of South Carolina] cannot be well and sufficiently managed and brought into use, without the labor and service of negroes and other slaves; and forasmuch as the said negroes and other slaves brought unto the People of the Province for that purpose, are of barbarous, wild, savage natures, and such as renders them wholly unqualified to be governed by the laws, customs, and practices of this Province; . . . it is absolutely necessary, that such other constitutions, laws and orders, should in this Province be made and enacted, for the good regulating and ordering of them, as may restrain the disorderly rapines and inhumanity, to which they are naturally prone and induced; and may also tend to the safety and security of the people of this Province and their estates.

From the introduction to the original South Carolina Slave Code of 1696

◀ **The slavery codes** regulated slaves and asserted the rights of slave owners.

((•— **Hear** the **Audio**
Hear the audio files for Chapter 3
at **www.myhistorylab.com**

African Americans lived in North America for nearly three centuries before the United States gained independence from Great Britain in 1783. During that long time period, most of them were slaves in British, French, and Spanish colonies. As a result, they left scant written testimony about their lives. Their history, therefore, must be learned through archaeology and the writings of the white settlers who enslaved and oppressed them.

The passage that begins this chapter is an excellent example of what we can learn about African-American history by reading between the lines in the official publications of the colonial governments. As historian Winthrop D. Jordan points out, the founders of South Carolina in 1696 borrowed much of this section of the colony's law code from the British colony of Barbados in the Caribbean.

The code indicates that the British Carolinians believed they needed the labor of enslaved Africans for their colony to prosper. It also shows that the colonial British feared Africans and their African-American descendants. This ambivalence among white Americans concerning African Americans shaped life in colonial South Carolina and in other British colonies in North America. The same ambivalence persisted in the minds of white southerners into the twentieth century. The dichotomy of white economic dependence on black people and fear of black revolt was a central fact of American history and provided a rationale for racial oppression.

The opening passage also reveals the willingness of British and other European settlers in North America to brand Africans and their American descendants as "barbarous, wild, [and] savage." Although real cultural differences underlay such negative perceptions, white people used them to justify oppressing black people. Unlike white people, black people by the 1640s could be enslaved for life. Black people did not enjoy the same legal protection as white people and were punished more harshly.

This chapter describes the history of African-American life in colonial North America from the early sixteenth century to the end of the **French and Indian War** in 1763. It briefly covers the black experience in Spanish Florida, in New Spain's borderlands in the Southwest, and in French Louisiana but concentrates on the British colonies that stretched along the eastern coast of the continent. During the seventeenth century, the plantation system that became a central part of black life in

America for nearly two centuries took shape in the Chesapeake tobacco country and in the low country of South Carolina and Georgia. Unfree labor, which in the Chesapeake had originally involved both white and black people, solidified into a system of slavery based on race. Although the plantation system did not develop in Britain's northern colonies, race-based slavery existed in them as well. African Americans responded to these conditions by interacting with other groups, preserving parts of their African culture, seeking strength through religion, and resisting and rebelling against enslavement.

The Peoples of North America

In the North American colonies during the seventeenth and eighteenth centuries, African immigrants gave birth to a new African-American people. Born in North America and forever separated from their ancestral homeland, they preserved a surprisingly large core of their African cultural heritage. Meanwhile, a new natural environment and contacts with people of American Indian and European descent helped African Americans shape a way of life within the circumstances that slavery forced on them. To understand the early history of African Americans, we must first briefly discuss the other peoples of colonial North America.

AMERICAN INDIANS

Historians and anthropologists group the original inhabitants of North America together as American Indians. (The terms *Amerinds* and *Native Americans* are also used, with the latter term including Inuits [Eskimos].) But when the British began to colonize the Atlantic coastal portion of this huge region during the early seventeenth century, the indigenous peoples who lived there had no such all-inclusive name. They spoke many different languages, lived in diverse environments, and considered themselves distinct from one another. Like other Indian peoples of the Western Hemisphere, they descended from Asians who, at least 12,000 years ago, had migrated eastward by coastal waterways and across a land bridge connecting Siberia and Alaska. Europeans called them Indians as a result of Christopher Columbus's mistaken assumption in 1492 that he had landed on islands near the "Indies," by which he meant near Southeast Asia.

In Mexico, Central America, and Peru, American Indian peoples developed complex, densely populated civilizations with hereditary monarchies, formal religions, armies, and social classes. Cultural developments in Mexico and the northward spread of the cultivation of maize (corn) influenced the indigenous peoples of what is today the United States. In the Southwest, the Anasazi and later Pueblo peoples developed farming communities. Beginning around 900 CE, they produced pottery, studied astronomy, built large adobe towns, and struggled against a drying climate. Farther east in what is known as the Woodlands region, the Adena culture flourished in the Ohio River valley as early as 1000 BCE and attained the social organization required to construct large burial mounds. Between the tenth and fourteenth centuries CE, what is known as the Mississippian culture established a civilization, marked by extensive trade routes, division of labor, and urban centers. The largest such center was Cahokia—located near modern St. Louis, Missouri—which at its peak had a population of about 30,000.

Climatic change and warfare destroyed the Mississippian culture during the fourteenth century, and only remnants of it existed when Europeans and Africans arrived in North America. By that time, a diverse variety of American Indian cultures existed in what is today the eastern portion of the United States. People resided in towns and villages, supplementing their agricultural economies with fishing and hunting. They held land communally, generally allowed women a voice in ruling councils, and—although warlike—regarded battle as an opportunity for young men to prove their bravery rather than as a means of conquest. Gravely weakened by diseases that settlers unwittingly brought from Europe, the woodlands Indians of North America's coastal regions were ineffective in resisting British settlers during the seventeenth century. Particularly in the Southeast, the British developed an extensive trade in Indian slaves.

Because American Indians were experts at living harmoniously with the natural resources of North America, they influenced the way people of African and European descent came to live there as well. Indian crops, such as corn, pumpkins, beans, and squash, became staples of the newcomers' diets. On the continent's southeastern coast, British cultivation of tobacco, another Indian crop, secured the economic survival of the Chesapeake colonies of Virginia and Maryland and led directly to the enslavement of Africans in them. The Indian canoe became a means of river transportation for black and white people, and Indian moccasins became common footwear for everyone.

The relationships between black people and American Indians during colonial times were complex. Although Indian nations often provided refuge to escaping black slaves, Indians sometimes became slaveholders and on occasion helped crush black revolts. Some black men assisted in the Indian slave trade

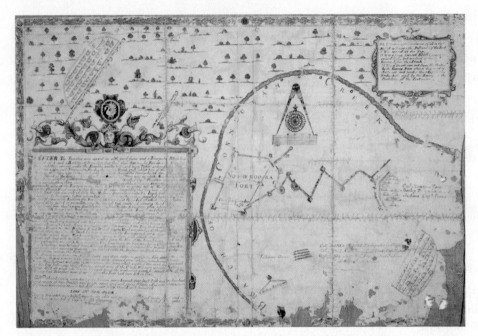

Escaping slaves in the Carolinas during the early eighteenth century sometimes found shelter with the Tuscaroras and other Indian tribes. This map, drawn during a colonial expedition against the Tuscaroras in 1713, shows a Tuscarora fort that escaped slaves probably helped design and build.

and sometimes helped defend European colonists against Indian attacks. Nevertheless, people of African and Indian descent frequently found themselves in similarly oppressive circumstances in Britain's American colonies. Although white officials attempted to keep them apart, social and sexual contacts between the two groups were frequent. Some interracial black-Indian settlements—and a few black-Indian-white settlements— have persisted to the present.

THE SPANISH EMPIRE

Following Christopher Columbus's voyage in 1492, the Spanish rapidly built a colonial empire in the Americas. Mining of gold and silver, as well as the production of sugar, tobacco, and leather goods, provided a firm economic foundation. But few Spaniards came to the Western Hemisphere. Consequently, Spain's colonial economy rested first on the forced labor of the Indian population and then increasingly on enslaved Africans when the Indian population declined from disease and overwork. Overseers in the mines and fields often brutally worked Africans and Indians to death. But because the Spanish were few, some of the African and Indians who survived were able to gain freedom and become tradesmen, small landholders, and militiamen. Often they were of mixed race and identified with their former masters rather than with the oppressed people beneath

them in society. African, Indian, and Spanish customs intermingled in what became a multicultural colonial society. Its center was in the West Indian islands of Cuba and Santo Domingo, Mexico, and northern South America. On its northern periphery were lands that are now part of the United States: Florida, Texas, Arizona, New Mexico, and California.

Africans came early to these borderlands. In 1526 Luis Vasquez de Ayllon brought one hundred African slaves with him from Hispaniola (modern Haiti and the Dominican Republic) in an attempt to establish a Spanish colony near what is now Georgetown, South Carolina. A decade later, slaves who were either African or of African descent accompanied Hernando de Soto on a Spanish expedition from Florida to the Mississippi River. In 1565 Africans helped construct the Spanish settlement of St. Augustine in Florida, which is now the oldest city in the continental United States. In 1528 a Spanish expedition that departed Cuba to search for gold in western Florida and the Gulf Coast included a slave of African descent named Esteban. Following a shipwreck, Esteban reached the coast of Texas. After a brief captivity among the local Indians, he and other survivors made their way south to Mexico City.

THE BRITISH AND JAMESTOWN

While the powerful Spanish empire colonized warm, populous, and wealthy regions of the Americas, the relatively less powerful British acquired lands that were cooler, less populous, and deficient in easily acquired wealth. The British, like the Africans and the American Indians, were not a single nation. The British Isles— consisting principally of Britain and Ireland and located off the northwest coast of Europe—were the homeland of the English, Welsh, Scots, and Irish. By the seventeenth century, the English dominated the other ethnic groups. But at that time, the Kingdom of England was, compared to Spain, a poor country notable mainly for producing wool.

England's claim to the east coast of North America rested on the voyage of John Cabot, who sailed in 1497, just five years after Columbus's first westward voyage. But, unlike the Spanish who rapidly created an empire in the Americas, the English were slow to establish themselves in the region Cabot had reached. This was partly due to the harsher North American climate, with winters much colder than in England. In addition, the English monarchy was too poor to finance colonizing expeditions, and social turmoil associated with the Protestant Reformation absorbed its energies.

Attempts failed in the 1580s to colonize Newfoundland, a large island off the east coast of what is today Canada, and Roanoke Island, a small island off the coast of what is today North Carolina. It took the English naval victory over the **Spanish Armada** in 1588 and money raised by **joint-stock companies** to produce at Jamestown in 1607 the first permanent British colony in North America. This settlement, established by the Virginia Company of London, was located in the Chesapeake region, which the British called Virginia—after Queen Elizabeth I (r. 1558–1603), the so-called Virgin Queen of England. The company hoped to make a profit at Jamestown by finding gold, trading with Indians, cutting lumber, or raising crops, such as rice, sugar, or silk, that could not be produced in Britain.

Read the Document
Exploring America: Jamestown

None of these schemes was economically viable. There was no gold, and the climate was unsuitable for rice, sugar, and silk. Because of disease, hostility with the Indians, and especially economic failure, the settlement barely survived into the 1620s. By then, however, English settler John Rolfe's experiments, begun in 1612 to cultivate a mild strain of tobacco that could be grown on the North American mainland, began to pay off. Tobacco was in great demand in Europe, where smoking was becoming popular. Soon growing tobacco became the economic mainstay of Virginia and the neighboring colony of Maryland.

Sowing, cultivating, harvesting, and curing tobacco required considerable labor. Yet colonists in the Chesapeake could not follow the Spanish example of enslaving Indians to produce the crop. Disease had reduced the local Indian population, and those who survived eluded British conquest by retreating west.

Unlike the West Indian sugar planters, however, the North American tobacco planters did not immediately turn to Africa for laborers. British advocates of colonizing North America had always promoted it as a solution to unemployment, poverty, and crime in England. The idea was to send England's undesirables to America, where they could provide the cheap labor tobacco planters needed. Consequently, until 1700, white labor produced most of the tobacco in the Chesapeake colonies.

AFRICANS ARRIVE IN THE CHESAPEAKE

By early 1619, there were, nevertheless, 32 people of African descent—15 men and 17 women—living at Jamestown. Nothing is known about when they arrived or from where they came. They were all "in the service of sev[er]all planters." The following August a Dutch warship, carrying 17 African men and three African women, moored at Hampton Roads at the mouth of the James River. Historians long believed these were the first black people in British North America. They were part of a group of over 300 who had been taken from Angola by a Portuguese slaver that had set sail for the port of Vera Cruz in New Spain (Mexico). The Dutch warship, with the help of an English ship, had attacked the slaver, taken most of its human cargo, and brought these 20 Angolans to Jamestown. The Dutch captain traded them to local officials for provisions.

The Angolans became servants to Jamestown's officials and favored planters. For two reasons, the colony's inhabitants regarded both the new arrivals and those black people who had been in Jamestown earlier to be *unfree* but not slaves. First, unlike the Portuguese and the Spanish, the English had no law for slavery. Second, at least those Angolans who bore such names as Pedro, Isabella, Antoney, and Angelo were Christians, and—according to English custom and morality in 1619—Christians could not be enslaved. So, once these individuals worked off their purchase price, they regained their freedom. In 1623, Antoney and Isabella married. The next year they became parents of William, whom their master had baptized in the local **Church of England.** William may have been the first black person born in English America. He was almost certainly born free.

During the following years, people of African descent remained a small minority in the expanding Virginia colony. A 1625 census reported only 23 black people living in the colony, compared with a combined total of 1,275 white people and Indians. This suggests that many of the first black inhabitants had either died or moved away. By 1649 the total Virginia population of about 18,500 included only 300 black people. The English, following the Spanish example, called them "negroes." (*Negro* means black in Spanish.) In neighboring Maryland, which was established as a haven in 1632 for persecuted English Catholics, the black population also remained small. In 1658 people of African descent accounted for only 3 percent of Maryland's population.

Black Servitude in the Chesapeake

As these statistics suggest, during the early years of the Chesapeake colonies, black people represented a small part of a labor force composed mainly of white people. From the 1620s to the 1670s, black and white people worked in the tobacco fields together, lived together, and slept together (and also did these things with American Indians). They were all unfree indentured servants.

Indentured servitude had existed in Europe for centuries. In England, parents indentured—or, in other words, apprenticed—their children to "masters," who then controlled their lives and had the right to their labor for a set number of years. In return, the masters supported the children and taught them a trade or profession. Unrestrained by modern notions of human equality and democracy, masters could exercise brutal authority over those bound to them.

As the demand for labor to produce tobacco in the Chesapeake expanded, indentured servitude came to include adults who sold their freedom for two to seven years in return for the cost of their voyage to North America. Instead of training in a profession, the servants could improve their economic standing by remaining as free persons in America after completing their period of servitude.

When Africans first arrived in Virginia and Maryland, they entered into similar contracts, agreeing to work for their masters until the proceeds of their labor recouped the cost of their purchase. Indentured servitude could be harsh in the tobacco colonies because masters sought to get as much labor as they could from their servants before the indenture ended. Most indentured servants died from overwork or disease before regaining their freedom. But those who survived, black people as well as white people, could expect eventually to leave their masters and seek their fortunes as free persons.

The foremost example in early Virginia of a black man who emerged from servitude to become a tobacco planter himself is Anthony Johnson. (See the Profile.) But Johnson was not the only person of African descent who became a free property owner during the first half of the seventeenth century. Here and there, black men seemed to enjoy a status similar to their white counterparts. Free black men in the Chesapeake participated fully in the commercial and legal life of the colonies. They owned land, farmed, lent money, sued in the courts, served as jurors and minor officials, and at times voted.

This suggests that before the 1670s the English in the Chesapeake did not draw a strict line between white freedom and black slavery. Yet, since the early 1600s, the ruling elite had treated black servants differently than white servants. Over the decades, the region's British population gradually came to assume that persons of African descent were inalterably alien. This sentiment did not become universal among the white poor during the colonial period. But it was a foundation for what historian Winthrop D. Jordan calls the "unthinking decision" among the British in the Chesapeake to establish **chattel slavery.** In this form of slavery, Africans and people of African descent became their master's private property on a level with livestock.

RACE AND THE ORIGINS OF BLACK SLAVERY

Between 1640 and 1700, the British tobacco-producing colonies stretching from Delaware to northern Carolina underwent a social and demographic revolution. An economy once based primarily on the labor of white indentured servants became an economy based on the labor of black slaves. In Virginia, for example, the slave population in 1671 was less than 5 percent of the colony's total non-Indian population. White indentured servants outnumbered black slaves by three to one. By 1700, however, slaves constituted at least 20 percent of Virginia's population. Probably most agricultural laborers were slaves.

Although historians debate how this extraordinary change occurred, several interrelated factors brought it about. Some of these factors are easily understood. Others are more complicated and profound because they involve basic assumptions about the American nation.

Several economic and demographic developments led to the mass enslavement of people of African descent in the tobacco colonies. First, during the second quarter of the seventeenth century, Britain's Caribbean sugar colonies set a precedent for enslaving Africans. Second, fewer poor white people came to the tobacco colonies as they found better opportunities for themselves in other regions of British North America. Third, as Britain gained increased control over the Atlantic slave trade, African slaves became less costly.

These changing circumstances provide the context for the beginnings of black slavery as a major phenomenon in British North America. Yet race and class were crucial in shaping the *character* of slavery in the British mainland colonies. From the first arrival of Africans in the Chesapeake, those English who exercised authority made decisions that qualified the apparent social mobility the Africans enjoyed. The English had historically distinguished between how they treated each other and how they treated those who were physically and culturally different from them. Such discrimination had been the basis of English colonial policies toward the Irish—whom England had been trying to conquer for centuries—and the American Indians. Because the English considered Africans even more different from themselves than either the Irish or the Indians, they assumed from the beginning that Africans were generally inferior.

Therefore, although black and white servants residing in the Chesapeake during the early seventeenth century had much in common, their masters made distinctions between them based on race. The few women of African descent who arrived in the Chesapeake during those years worked in the tobacco fields with the male servants, while most white women performed domestic duties. Also, unlike white servants, black servants usually did not have surnames, and early census reports listed them separately from white people. By the 1640s, black people could not bear arms, and local Anglican priests (although not those in England) maintained that persons of African descent could not become Christians. Although sexual contacts among blacks, whites, and Indians were common, colonial authorities soon discouraged them. In 1662 Virginia's **House of Burgesses** (the colony's legislature) declared that "any christian [white person]" who committed "Fornication with a negro man or woman, he or shee soe offending" would pay double the fine set for committing the same offense with a white person.

These distinctions suggest that the status of black servants had never been the same as that of white servants. But only starting in the 1640s do records indicate a predilection toward making black people slaves rather

●•●─┤**Read** the **Document**
Maryland Addresses the Status of Slaves in 1644

than servants. During that decade, courts in Virginia and Maryland began to reflect an assumption that it was permissible for persons of African descent to serve their master for life rather than a set term. By then black men, women, and children often sold for higher prices than their white counterparts on the explicit provision that black people would serve "for their Life tyme," or "for ever."

THE EMERGENCE OF CHATTEL SLAVERY

Legal documents and statute books reveal that, during the 1660s, other aspects of chattel slavery emerged in the Chesapeake colonies. Bills of sale began to stipulate that the children of black female servants would also be servants for life. In 1662 the House of Burgesses decreed that a child's condition—free or unfree—followed that of the mother. This ran counter to English common law, which assumed that a child's status derived from the father. The change permitted masters to exploit their black female servants sexually without having to acknowledge the children who might result from such contacts. Just as significant, by the mid-1660s statutes in the Chesapeake colonies assumed servitude to be the natural condition of black people.

With these laws, slavery in British North America emerged in the form that it retained until the American Civil War: a racially defined system of perpetual involuntary servitude that compelled almost all black people to work as agricultural laborers. **Slave codes** enacted between 1660 and 1710 further defined American slavery as a system that sought as much to control persons of African descent as to exploit their labor. Slaves could not testify against white people in court, own property, leave their master's estate without a pass, congregate in groups larger than three or four, enter into contracts, or marry, nor, of course, could they bear arms. Profession of Christianity no longer protected a black person from enslavement, nor was conversion a cause for **manumission.** In 1669 the House of Burgesses exempted from felony charges masters who killed a slave while administering punishment.

By 1700, just as the slave system began to expand in the southern colonies, enslaved Africans and African Americans had been reduced legally to the status of domestic animals except that, unlike

●•●─┤**Read** the **Document**
Virginia Law on Indentured Servitude (1705)

animals (or masters who abused slaves), the law held slaves to be strictly accountable for their transgressions.

BACON'S REBELLION
AND AMERICAN SLAVERY

The series of events that led to the enslavement of black people in the Chesapeake tobacco colonies preceded their emergence as the great majority of laborers in those colonies. The dwindling supply of white indentured servants, the growing availability of Africans, and preexisting white racial biases affected this transformation. But the key event in bringing it about was the rebellion led by Nathaniel Bacon in 1676.

Bacon was an English aristocrat who had recently migrated to Virginia. The immediate cause of his rebellion was a disagreement between him and the colony's royal governor William Berkeley over Indian policy. Bacon's followers were mainly white indentured servants and former indentured servants who resented the control the tobacco-planting elite exercised over the colony's resources and govern-

●•●─┤**Read** the **Document**
Declaration against the Proceedings of Nathaniel Bacon (1676)

ment. That Bacon also appealed to black slaves to join his rebellion indicates that poor white and black people still had a chance to unite against the **master class.**

Before such a class-based, biracial alliance could be realized, Bacon died of dysentery, and his rebellion collapsed. But the uprising convinced the colony's elite that continuing to rely on white agricultural laborers, who could become free and get guns, was dangerous. By switching from indentured white servants to an enslaved black labor force that would never become free or control firearms, the planters hoped to avoid class conflict among white people. Increasingly thereafter, white Americans perceived that both their freedom from class conflict and their prosperity rested on denying freedom to black Americans.

Plantation Slavery, 1700–1750

The reliance of Chesapeake planters on slavery to meet their labor needs was the result of racial prejudice, the declining availability of white indentured servants, the increasing availability of Africans, and fear of white class conflict. When, following the shift from indentured white to enslaved black labor, the demand for tobacco in Europe increased sharply, the newly dominant slave labor system expanded rapidly.

TOBACCO COLONIES

Between 1700 and 1770, some 80,000 Africans arrived in the tobacco colonies, and even more African Americans were born into slavery there (see Figure 3–1). Tobacco planting spread from Virginia and Maryland to

PROFILE: Anthony Johnson

Little is known of the individual Africans and African Americans who lived in North America during the seventeenth and eighteenth centuries. A lack of contemporary accounts prevents us from truly understanding their personalities. In rare instances, however, black people emerge from bits and pieces of information preserved in court records. This is the case for Anthony Johnson and his family. Their accomplishments cast light on African-American life in the seventeenth-century Chesapeake.

Anthony Johnson arrived at Jamestown in 1621 from England, but his original home may have been Angola. He was fortunate the following year to escape death in an Indian attack on Jamestown. He was one of four out of 56 inhabitants on the Bennett plantation, where he labored, to survive. He was also lucky to wed "Mary a Negro Woman," who in 1625 was the only woman residing at Bennett's.

In 1635 Johnson's master, Nathaniel Littleton, released him from further service. Johnson, like other free men of this time and place, then scrambled to acquire wealth in the form of land, livestock, and human beings. He received his own 250-acre plantation in 1651 under the "headright system," by which the colonial government encouraged population growth by awarding 50 acres of land for every new servant a settler brought to Virginia.

This meant that Johnson had become the master of five servants, some of them white. His estate was on a neck of land between two creeks that flowed into the Pungoteague River in Northampton County. A few years later his relatives, John and Richard Johnson, also acquired land in this area. John brought eleven servants to the colony and received 550 acres, and Richard brought two and received one hundred acres.

The Johnson estates existed among white-owned properties in the same area. Like their white neighbors, the Johnsons were not part of the planting elite. But they owned their own land, farmed, and had social, economic, and legal relations with other colonists. Anthony Johnson in particular engaged in litigation that tells us much about black life in early Virginia.

In 1654, his lawsuit against his black servant John Casor and a white neighbor set a precedent in favor of black slavery but also revealed Johnson's legal rights. Casor claimed that Johnson "had kept him his serv[an]t seven years longer than hee should or ought." Johnson, whom court records described as an "old Negro," responded that he was entitled to "ye Negro [Casor] for his life." Johnson momentarily relented when he realized that if he persisted in his suit, Casor could win damages against him. Shortly thereafter, however, Johnson brought suit against his white neighbor Robert Parker, whom Johnson charged had detained Casor "under pretense [that] the s[ai]d John Casor is a freeman." This time the court ruled in Johnson's favor. It returned Casor to him and required Parker to pay court costs.

During the 1660s, the extended Johnson family moved to Somerset, Maryland, where its members had acquired additional land. They were still prospering as planters during the early eighteenth century. Some family members moved on to New Jersey and others to Delaware, where some of them intermarried with the Nanticoke Indians. Historian John H. Russell exaggerated when he claimed in 1913 that black people in the seventeenth century had roughly the same opportunities as free white servants. But industrious and lucky black people at that time could achieve a social and economic standing that became nearly impossible for their descendants.

Delaware and North Carolina and from the coastal plain to the foothills of the Appalachian Mountains. In the process, American slavery began to assume the form it kept for the next 165 years.

By 1750, 144,872 slaves lived in Virginia and Maryland, accounting for 61 percent of all the slaves in British North America. Another 40,000 slaves lived in the rice-producing regions of South Carolina and Georgia, accounting for 17 percent. Unlike in the sugar colonies of the Caribbean, where white people were a tiny minority, they constituted a majority in the tobacco colonies and a large minority in the rice colonies. Also, most white southerners did not own slaves. Nevertheless, the economic development of the region depended on enslaved black laborers.

The conditions under which those laborers lived varied. Most slaveholders farmed small tracts of land and owned fewer than five slaves. These masters and their slaves worked together and developed close personal relationships. Other masters owned thousands of acres of land and rarely saw most of their slaves. During the early eighteenth century, the great planters divided their slaves among several small holdings. They did this to avoid concentrating potentially rebellious Africans in one area. As the proportion of newly arrived Africans in the slave population declined later in the century, larger concentrations of slaves became more common.

Before the mid-eighteenth century, nearly all slaves—both men and women—worked in the fields. On the smaller farms, they worked with their master. On larger estates, they worked for an overseer, who was usually white. Like other agricultural workers, enslaved African Americans normally worked from sunup to sundown with breaks for food and rest. Even during colonial times, they usually had Sunday off.

From the beginnings of slavery in North America, masters tried to make slaves work harder and faster while slaves sought to conserve their energy, take breaks, and socialize with each other. African men

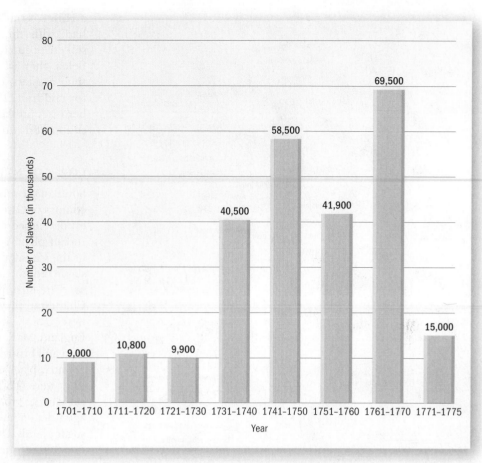

FIGURE 3–1 AFRICANS BROUGHT AS SLAVES TO BRITISH NORTH AMERICA, 1701–1775
The rise in the number of captive Africans shipped to British North America during the early eighteenth century reflects the increasing dependence of British planters on African slave labor. The declines in slave imports during the periods 1751 to 1760 and 1771 to 1775 resulted from disruptions to commerce associated with the French and Indian War (or Seven Years' War) and the struggle between the colonies and Great Britain that preceded the American War for Independence.   Source: From *The American Colonies: From Settlement of Independence*, by R. C. Simmons (© R. C. Simmons, 1976) is reproduced by permission of PFD (www.pfd.co.uk) on behalf of R. C. Simmons.

1619–1662

FROM SERVITUDE TO SLAVERY

1619	Thirty-two Africans reported to be living at Jamestown; 20 more arrive.
1621	Anthony Johnson arrives at Jamestown.
1624	First documented birth of a black child occurs at Jamestown.
1640	A black man is sentenced to servitude for life.
1651	Anthony Johnson receives estate of 250 acres.
1661	House of Burgesses (the Virginia colonial legislature) recognizes that black servants would retain that status throughout their life.
1662	House of Burgesses affirms that a child's status—slave or free—follows the status of her or his mother.

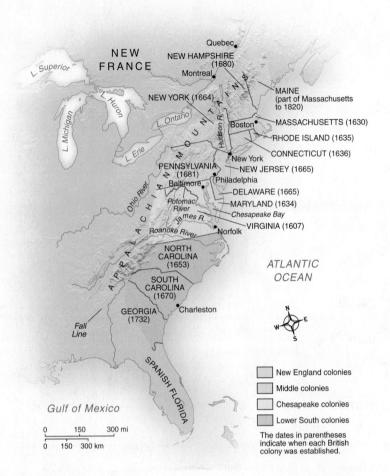

MAP 3–1   REGIONS OF COLONIAL NORTH AMERICA, 1683–1763
The British colonies on the North American mainland were divided into four regions. They were bordered on the south by Spanish Florida and to the west by regions claimed by France.

▶ *How did African Americans in the British colonies benefit from the close proximity of regions controlled by France and Spain?*

👁️‍🗨️ See the **Map** *European Claims in America, c. 1750*

regarded field labor as women's work and tried to avoid it. But, especially if they had incentives, enslaved Africans could be efficient workers. One incentive to which both slaves and masters looked forward was the annual harvest festival. These festivals were held in both Africa and Europe and became common throughout the British colonies early in the eighteenth century.

After 1750 some black men began to hold such skilled occupations on plantations as carpenter, smith, carter, cooper, miller, potter, sawyer, tanner, shoemaker, and weaver. By 1768 one South Carolina planter noted that "in established Plantations, the Planter has Tradesmen of all kinds in his Gang of Slaves, and 'tis a Rule with them, never to pay Money for what can be made upon their Estates, not a Lock,

a Hinge, or a Nail if they can avoid it." Black women had, with the exception of weaving, less access to skilled occupations. When they did not work in the fields, they were domestic servants in the homes of their masters, cooking, washing, cleaning, and caring for children. These duties could be extremely taxing because, unlike fieldwork, they did not end when the sun went down.

LOW-COUNTRY SLAVERY

South of the tobacco colonies, on the coastal plain or low country of Carolina and Georgia, a distinctive slave society developed (see Map 3–1). The influence of the West Indian plantation system was much stronger here than in the Chesapeake, and rice, not tobacco, became the staple crop.

The first British settlers who arrived in 1670 at Charleston (in what would later become South Carolina) were mainly immigrants from Barbados rather than England. Many of them had been slaveholders on that island and brought slaves with them. Therefore, in the low country, black people were never indentured servants. They were chattel from the start. The region's subtropical climate discouraged white settlement and encouraged dependence on black labor the way it did in the sugar islands. During the early years of settlement, nearly one-third of the immigrants were African, most of them male. By the early eighteenth century, more Africans had arrived than white people. White Carolinians also enslaved more American Indians than other British colonists did, and during the early 1700s, Indians accounted for approximately one-quarter of the colony's slave population. Carolina also became the center of an Indian slave trade. Although official colonial policy sought to keep Africans and Indians apart, black slaves sometimes helped acquire and transport Indian slaves. Carolina exported Indian slaves to the West Indies and to other mainland British colonies.

By 1740 the Carolina low country had 40,000 slaves, who constituted 90 percent of the population in the region around Charleston. In all, 94,000 Africans arrived at Charleston between 1706 and 1776, which made it North America's leading port of entry for Africans during the eighteenth century. A Swiss immigrant commented in 1737 that the region "looks more like a negro country than like a country settled by white people."

During its first three decades, Carolina supplied Barbados with beef and lumber. Because West Africans from the Gambia River region were skilled herders, white settlers sought them out as slaves. Starting around 1700, however, the low-country planters concentrated on growing rice. Rice had been grown in West Africa for thousands of years, and many of the enslaved Africans who reached Carolina had the skill required to cultivate it in America. Economies of scale, in which an industry becomes more efficient as it grows larger, were more important in the production of rice than tobacco. Although tobacco could be profitably produced on small farms, rice required large acreages. Therefore, large plantations on a scale similar to those on the sugar islands of the West Indies became the rule in the low country.

In 1732 King George II of England chartered the colony of Georgia to serve as a buffer between South Carolina and Spanish Florida. James Oglethorpe, who received the royal charter, wanted to establish a refuge for England's poor, who were expected to become virtuous through their own labor. Consequently, in 1734 he and the colony's other trustees banned slavery in Georgia. But economic difficulties, combined with land hunger among white South Carolinians, soon led to the ban's repeal. During the 1750s, rice cultivation and slavery spread into Georgia's coastal plain. By 1773 Georgia had as many black people—15,000—as white people.

●▪—Read the Document
James Oglethorpe to the Trustees (1733)

As on Barbados, absentee plantation owners became the rule in South Carolina and Georgia. In these colonies planters preferred to live in Charleston or Savannah where sea breezes provided relief from the heat. Meanwhile, enslaved Africans on low-country plantations suffered a high mortality rate from diseases, overwork, and poor treatment, just as did their counterparts on Barbados and other sugar islands. Therefore, unlike the slave population in the Chesapeake colonies, the slave population in the low country did not grow by natural reproduction. Instead, until shortly before the American Revolution, it grew through continued arrivals from Africa.

Low-country slave society developed striking paradoxes in race relations. As the region's black population grew, white people became fearful of revolt, and by 1698 Carolina had the strictest slave code in North America. In 1721, Charleston organized a "Negro watch" to enforce a curfew on its black population, and watchmen could shoot recalcitrant Africans and African Americans on sight. Yet, as the passage that begins this chapter indicates, black people in Carolina faced the quandary of being both feared and needed by white people. Even as persons of European descent grew fearful of black revolt, the colony in 1704 authorized the arming of enslaved black men when needed for defense against Indian and Spanish raids.

Of equal significance was the appearance in Carolina and to some extent in Georgia of distinct classes among people of color. Like the low-country society

VOICES

A DESCRIPTION OF AN EIGHTEENTH-CENTURY VIRGINIA PLANTATION

The following eyewitness account of a large Virginia plantation in Fairfax County indicates the sorts of skilled labor slaves performed by the mid-eighteenth century. George Mason, one of Virginia's leading statesmen during the Revolutionary War era, owned this plantation, which he named Gunston Hall in 1758. The account is by one of Mason's sons.

My father had among his slaves carpenters, coopers, sawyers, blacksmiths, tanners, curriers, shoemakers, spinners, weavers and knitters, and even a distiller. His woods furnished timber and plank for the carpenters and coopers, and charcoal for the blacksmith, his cattle killed for his own consumption and for sale supplied skins for tanners, curriers, and shoemakers, and his sheep gave wool and his fields produced cotton and flax for the weavers and spinners, and his orchards fruit for the distiller. His carpenters and sawyers built and kept in repair all the dwelling-houses, barns, stables, ploughs, harrows, gates, &c., on the plantations and the outhouses at the home house. His coopers made the hogsheads the tobacco was prized in and the tight casks to hold the cider and other liquors. The tanners and curriers with the proper vats &c., tanned and dressed the skins as well for upper as for lower leather to the full amount of the consumption of the estate, and shoemakers made them into shoes for the negroes. . . . The blacksmith did all the iron work required by the establishment, as making and repairing ploughs, harrows, teeth chains, bolts, &c., &c. The spinners, weavers and knitters made all the coarse cloths and stockings used by the negroes, and nearly all worn by the children of it. The distiller made every fall a good deal of apple, peach and persimmon brandy. . . . Moreover, all the beeves and hogs for consumption or sale were driven up and slaughtered there at the proper seasons, and whatever was to be preserved was salted and packed away for after distribution.

▶ What does this passage indicate about plantation life in mid-eighteenth-century Virginia?

▶ How does the description of black people presented here compare to the passage from the South Carolina statute book that begins this chapter?

Source: Edmond S. Morgan, *Virginians at Home: Family Life in the Eighteenth Century* (Williamsburg, VA: Colonial Williamsburg, 1952), 53–54. Reprinted with permission.

itself, such classes were more similar to those in the Caribbean sugar islands than to the mainland colonies to the north. A Creole population that had absorbed European values lived alongside white people in Charleston and Savannah. Members of this Creole population were frequently mixed-race relatives of their masters and enjoyed social and economic privileges denied to slaves who labored on the nearby rice plantations. Yet this urban mixed-race class was under constant white supervision.

In contrast, slaves who lived in the country retained considerable autonomy in their daily routines. The intense cultivation required to produce rice encouraged the evolution of a "task system" of labor on the low-country plantations. Rather than working in gangs as in the tobacco colonies, slaves on rice plantations had daily tasks. When they completed these tasks, they could work on plots of land assigned to them or do what they pleased without white supervision. Because black people were the great majority in the low-country plantations, they also preserved more of their African heritage than did black people who lived in the region's cities or in the more northerly British mainland colonies.

PLANTATION TECHNOLOGY

During the American colonial era, most people of African descent living on southern plantations employed technologies associated with raising and processing crops for distant markets. A minority gained technical skills associated with a variety of trades.

In tobacco-growing regions, the harvest began a process of preparing leaves for market. Slaves hung plants in "tobacco houses," whose open construction kept out sunlight and rain while allowing breezes to circulate and dry the leaves. After six weeks, slaves removed the leaves and packaged them in wooden barrels for shipment. On low-country rice plantations, slaves built, operated, and maintained irrigation systems. They threshed, winnowed, and pounded rice to remove the husks. At first they performed these labor-intensive operations by hand. By the mid-eighteenth century, however, masters introduced "winnowing fans and pounding mills" powered by draft animals. Also, during the eighteenth century, low-country slave artisans built the vats, pumps, and structures required for turning indigo plants into a blue dye that was popular in Europe. As the indigo fermented in vats—releasing noxious fumes—slaves pumped in water, stirred and beat the plants into pulp, drained away blue liquid, solidified it with lime, dried it, and cut it into blocks.

Enslaved carpenters used a variety of hand tools to construct the buildings required for all these processes. They also built other plantation buildings. Slave sawyers operated water-powered mills to cut lumber. Other slaves made barrels. They cut and prepared oak staves—a process that took three years—trimmed the staves, soaked them, and bound them with iron hoops. Plantation blacksmiths used charcoal-burning hearths and billows to form the hoops from iron ingots and—using tongs and hammers—pounded the hoops into shape on anvils. They used a similar process to fashion nails, axe and hammer heads, hooks, horse shoes, hinges, and locks.

Like carpentry, tanning was essential. But, like indigo production, it was a laborious, smelly, and extended operation. Slaves cooked deer and cow hides in lime to remove fur and then washed off the lime with a mixture of animal dung, salt, and water. They used *tannin*, a chemical found in tree bark, to cure the hides. After drying, softening, stretching, and trimming, slave craftsmen used the leather to make shoes, boots, garments, and other articles.

Slave Life in Early America

Little evidence survives of the individual lives of enslaved black people in colonial North America. This is because they, along with American Indians and most white people of that era, were poor and illiterate and kept no records. Yet recent studies provide a glimpse of their material culture.

Eighteenth-century housing for slaves was minimal and often temporary. In the Chesapeake, small log cabins predominated. They had dirt floors, brick fireplaces, wooden chimneys, and few, if any, windows. African styles of architecture were more common in coastal South Carolina and Georgia. In these regions, slaves built the walls of their houses with tabby—a mixture of lime, oyster shells, and sand—or, occasionally, mud. In either case, the houses had thatched roofs. Early in the eighteenth century, when single African men made up the mass of the slave population, these structures were used as dormitories. Later they housed generations of black families.

The amount of furniture and cooking utensils the cabins contained varied from place to place and according to how long the cabins were occupied. In some cabins, the only furniture consisted of wooden boxes for both storage and seating and planks for beds. But a 1697 inventory of items contained in a slave cabin in Virginia includes chairs, a bed, a large iron kettle, a brass kettle, an iron pot, a frying pan, and a "beer barrel." Enslaved black people, like contemporary Indians and white people, used hollowed-out gourds for cups and carted water in wooden buckets for drinking, cooking, and washing. As the eighteenth century progressed, slave housing on large plantations became more substantial, and slaves acquired tables, linens, chamber pots, and oil lamps. Yet primitive, poorly furnished log cabins persisted in many regions even after the abolition of slavery in 1865.

At first, slave dress was minimal during summer. Men wore breechcloths; women wore skirts, leaving their upper bodies bare; and children went naked until puberty. Later men wore shirts, trousers, and hats while working in the fields. Women wore shifts (loose, simple dresses) and covered their heads with handkerchiefs. In winter, masters provided heavier cotton and woolen clothing and cheap leather shoes. In the early years, much of the clothing, or at least the cloth used to make it, came from England. Later, as the account of George Mason's Gunston Hall plantation indicates, homespun fabric made by slaves replaced English cloth. From the seventeenth century onward, slave women brightened clothing with dyes made from bark, decorated clothing with ornaments, and created African-style head wraps, hats, and hairstyles. In this manner, African Americans retained a sense of personal style compatible with West African culture.

Food consisted of corn, yams, salt pork, and occasionally salt beef and salt fish. Slaves also caught fish and raised chickens and rabbits. When, during the eighteenth century, farmers in the Chesapeake began planting wheat, slaves baked biscuits. In the South Carolina low country, rice became an important part of African-American diets, but even there corn was the staple. During colonial times, slaves occasionally supplemented this limited diet with vegetables that they raised in their own gardens, such as cabbage, cauliflower, black-eyed peas, turnips, collard greens, and rutabagas.

Miscegenation and Creolization

When Africans first arrived in the Chesapeake during the early seventeenth century, they interacted culturally and physically with white indentured servants and with American Indians. This mixing of peoples changed all three groups. Interracial sexual contacts—miscegenation—produced people of mixed race. Meanwhile, cultural exchanges became an essential part of the process of creolization that led African

SLAVES' QUARTERS IN THE CELLAR OF THE OLD KNICKERBOCKER MANSION.

This 1876 drawing romanticizes the home life of slaves. The Knickerbocker Mansion is located in Schaghticoke, New York, and dates to 1770.

parents to produce African-American children. When, as often happened, miscegenation and creolization occurred together, the change was both physical and cultural. However, the dominant British minority in North America during the colonial period defined persons of mixed race as black. Although enslaved mulattoes—those of mixed African and European ancestry—enjoyed some advantages over slaves who had a purely African ancestry, mulattoes as a group did not receive enhanced legal status.

Miscegenation between blacks and whites and blacks and Indians was extensive throughout British North America during the seventeenth and eighteenth centuries. But it was less extensive and accepted than it was in the European sugar colonies in the Caribbean, in Latin America, or in French Canada, where many French men married Indian women. British North America was exceptional because many more white women migrated there than to Canada, Latin America, or the Caribbean. Therefore, white men were far less likely to take black or Indian wives and concubines. Sexual relations between Africans and Indians were also more limited than they were elsewhere because the coastal Indian population had drastically declined before large numbers of Africans arrived.

Yet miscegenation between black people and the remaining Indians was extensive, and there were striking examples of black-white marriage in seventeenth-century Virginia. In 1656 in Northumberland County, a mulatto woman named Elizabeth Kay successfully sued for her freedom and immediately thereafter married her white lawyer. In Norfolk County in 1671, Francis Skiper had to pay a tax on his wife Anne because she was black. In Westmoreland County in 1691, Hester Tate, a white indentured servant, and her husband James Tate, a black slave, had four children. One was apprenticed to her master and the other three to his.

Colonial assemblies banned such interracial marriages mainly to keep white women from bearing mulatto children. The assemblies feared that having free white mothers might allow persons of mixed race to sue and gain their freedom, thereby creating a legally recognized mixed-race class. Such a class, wealthy white people feared, would blur the distinction between the dominant and subordinate races and weaken white supremacy. The assemblies did far less to prevent white male masters from sexually exploiting their black female slaves—although they considered such exploitation immoral—because the children of such liaisons would be slaves.

The Origins of African-American Culture

Creolization and miscegenation transformed the descendants of the Africans who arrived in North America into African Americans. Historians long believed that in this process the Creoles lost their African heritage. But since Melville J. Herskovits published *The Myth of the Negro Past* in 1941, scholars have found many African legacies not only in African-American culture but in American culture in general.

The second generation of people of African descent in North America did lose their parents' native languages and their ethnic identity as Igbos, Angolans, or Senegambians. But they retained a generalized West African heritage and passed it on to their descendants. Among the major elements of that heritage were family structure and notions of kinship, religious concepts and practices, African words and modes of expression, musical style and instruments, cooking methods and foods, folk literature, and folk arts.

The preservation of the West African extended family was the basis of African-American culture. Because most Africans imported into the British colonies during the late seventeenth and early eighteenth centuries were males, most black men of that era could not have wives and children. It was not until the Atlantic slave trade declined briefly during the 1750s that sex ratios became more balanced and African-American family life began to flourish. Without that family life, black people could not have maintained as much of Africa as they did.

Even during the Middle Passage, enslaved Africans created "fictive kin relationships" for mutual support, and in dire circumstances,

This eighteenth-century painting of slaves on a South Carolina plantation provides graphic proof of the continuities between West African culture and the emerging culture of African Americans. The religious dance, the drum and banjo, and elements of the participants' clothing are all West African in origin.

Abby Aldrich, Rockefeller Folk Art Museum, Colonial Williamsburg Foundation, VA.

African Americans continued to improvise family structures. By the mid-eighteenth century, however, extended black families based on biological relationships dominated. Black people retained knowledge of their kinship ties to second and third cousins over several generations and wide stretches of territory. These extended families had roots in Africa but were also a result of—and a reaction to—slavery. West African **incest taboos** encouraged slaves to pick mates who lived on plantations other than their own. The sale of slaves away from their immediate families also tended to extend families over wide areas. Once established, such far-flung kinship relationships helped others, who were forced to leave home, to adapt to new conditions under a new master. Kinfolk also sheltered escapees.

Extended families also influenced African-American naming practices, which in turn reinforced family ties. Africans named male children after close relatives. This custom survived in America because boys were more likely to be separated from their parents by being sold than girls were. Having one's father's name or grandfather's name preserved one's family identity. Also, early in the eighteenth century, when more African Americans began to use surnames, they clung to the name of their original master. This reflected a West African predisposition to link a family name with a certain location. Like taking a parent's name, it helped maintain family relationships despite repeated scatterings.

The result was that African Americans preserved given and family names over many generations. Black men continued to bear such African names as Cudjo, Quash, Cuffee, and Sambo, and black women such names as Quasheba and Juba. Even when masters imposed demeaning classical names, such as Caesar, Pompey, Venus, and Juno, black Americans passed them on from generation to generation.

Bible names did not become common among African Americans until the mid-eighteenth century. This was because before that time masters often refused to allow slaves to be converted to Christianity. As a result, African religions—both indigenous and Islamic—persisted in parts of America well into the nineteenth century. The indigenous religions in particular maintained a premodern perception of the unity of the natural and the supernatural, the secular and the sacred, and the living and the dead. Black Americans continued to perform an African circle dance known as the "ring shout" at funerals, and they decorated graves with shells and pottery in the West African manner. They looked to recently arrived Africans for religious guidance, held bodies of water to be sacred, remained in daily contact with their ancestors through **spirit possession,** and practiced **divination** and magic. When they became ill, they turned to "herb doctors" and "root workers." Even when many African Americans began to convert to Christianity during the mid-eighteenth century, West African religious thought and practice shaped their lives.

THE GREAT AWAKENING

The major turning point in African-American religion came in conjunction with the religious revival known as the Great Awakening. This extensive social movement of the mid- to late-eighteenth century grew out of growing dissatisfaction among white Americans with a deterministic and increasingly formalistic style of Protestantism that seemed to deny most people a chance for salvation. During the early 1730s in western Massachusetts, a Congregationalist minister named Jonathan Edwards began an emotional and participatory ministry aimed at bringing more people into the church. Later that decade, George Whitefield, an Englishman who with John Wesley founded the Methodist Church, carried a similarly evangelical style of Christianity to the mainland colonies. In his sermons, Whitefield appealed to emotions, offered salvation to all who believed in Christ, and—although he did not advocate emancipation—preached to black people as well as white people.

Some people of African descent had converted to Christianity before Whitefield's arrival in North America. But two factors had prevented widespread black conversion. First, most masters feared that converted slaves would interpret their new religious status as a step toward freedom and equality. A South Carolina minister lamented in 1713 that "the Masters of Slaves are generally of Opinion that a Slave grows worse by being a Christian; and therefore instead of instructing them in the principles of Christianity . . . malign and traduce those that attempt it." Second, many slaves remained devoted to their ancestral religions and were not attracted to Christianity.

With the Great Awakening, however, a process of general conversion began. African Americans did indeed link the spiritual equality preached by evangelical ministers with a hope for earthly equality. They tied salvation for the soul with liberation for the body. They recognized that the preaching style Whitefield and other evangelicals adopted had much in common with West African "spirit possession." As in West African religion, eighteenth-century revivalism in North America emphasized personal rebirth, singing, movement, and emotion. The practice of total body immersion during baptism in rivers, ponds, and lakes that gave the Baptist church its name paralleled West African water rites.

Read the Document

Exploring America: The Great Awakening

Because it drew African Americans into an evangelical movement that helped shape American society, the Great Awakening increased mutual black-white acculturation. Revivalists appealed to the poor of all races and emphasized spiritual equality. Evangelical Anglican, Baptist, Methodist, and Presbyterian churches welcomed black people. Members of these biracial churches addressed each other as *brother* and *sister*. Black members took communion with white members and served as church officers. The same church discipline applied to both races. By the late eighteenth century, a few black men gained ordination as priests and ministers and—often while still enslaved—preached to white congregations. They thereby influenced white people's perception of how services should be conducted.

Black worshipers also influenced white preachers and white religion. In 1756, a white minister in Virginia noted that African Americans spent nights in his kitchen. He recorded in his diary that "sometimes, when I have awakened about two or three a-clock in the morning, a torrent of sacred harmony poured into my chamber, and carried my mind away to Heaven."

Other factors, however, favored the development of a distinct African-American church. From the start, white churches seated black people apart from white people, belying claims to spiritual equality. Black members took communion *after* white members. Masters also tried to use religion to instill in their chattels such self-serving Christian virtues as meekness, humility, and obedience. Consequently, when they could, African Americans established their own churches. Dancing, shouting, clapping, and singing became especially characteristic of their religious meetings. Black spirituals probably date from the eighteenth century, and like African-American Christianity itself, they blended West African and European elements.

African Americans also retained the West African assumption that the souls of the dead returned to their homeland and rejoined their ancestors. Reflecting this family-oriented view of death, African-American funerals were often loud and joyous occasions with dancing, laughing, and drinking. Perhaps most important, the emerging black church reinforced black people's collective identity and helped them persevere in slavery.

LANGUAGE, MUSIC, AND FOLK LITERATURE

Although African Americans did not retain their ancestral languages, those languages contributed to the **pidgins** and creolized languages that became **Black English** by the nineteenth century. It was in the low country, with its large and isolated black populations, that African-English creoles lasted the longest. The

Gullah and Geechee dialects of the sea islands of South Carolina and Georgia, which combine African words and grammatical elements with a basically English structure, are still spoken today. In other regions, where black people were less numerous, the creole languages were less enduring. Nevertheless, they contributed many words to American—particularly southern—English. Among them are *yam, banjo* (from mbanza), *tote, goober* (peanut), *buckra* (white man), *cooter* (tortoise), *gumbo* (okra), *nanse* (spider), *samba* (dance), *tabby* (a form of concrete), and *voodoo*.

Music was another essential part of West African life, and it remained so among African Americans, who preserved an antiphonal, call-and-response style of singing with an emphasis on improvisation, complex rhythms, and a strong beat. They sang while working and during religious ceremonies. Early on, masters banned drums and horns because of their potential for long-distance communication among slaves. But

This photograph depicts two versions of the African *mbanza*. They feature leather stretched across a gourd, a wooden neck, and strings made of animal gut. In America, such instruments became known as banjos.

the African banjo survived in America, and African Americans quickly adopted the violin and guitar. At night, in their cabins or around communal fires, slaves accompanied these instruments with bones and spoons. Music may have been the most important aspect of African culture in the lives of American slaves. Eventually, African-American music influenced all forms of American popular music.

West African folk literature also survived in North America. African tales, proverbs, and riddles—with accretions from American Indian and European stories—entertained, instructed, and united African Americans. Just as the black people on the sea islands of South Carolina and Georgia were most able to retain elements of African language, so did their folk literature remain closest to its African counterpart. Africans used tales of how weak animals like rabbits outsmarted stronger animals like hyenas and lions to symbolize the power of the common people over unjust rulers. African Americans used similar tales to portray the ability of slaves to outsmart and ridicule their masters.

THE AFRICAN-AMERICAN IMPACT ON COLONIAL CULTURE

African Americans also influenced the development of white culture. As early as the seventeenth century, black musicians performed English ballads for white audiences in a distinctively African-American style. Meanwhile, in the northern and Chesapeake colonies, people of African descent helped determine how all Americans celebrated. By the eighteenth century, slaves in these regions organized black election or coronation festivals that lasted for several days. Sometimes called *Pinkster* and ultimately derived from Dutch-American pre-Easter celebrations, these festivities included parades, athletics, food, music, dancing, and mock coronations of kings and governors. Although dominated by African Americans, they attracted white observers and a few white participants.

The African-American imprint on southern diction and phraseology is especially clear. Because black women often raised their master's children, generations of white children acquired African-American speech patterns and intonations. Black people also influenced white notions about portents, spirits, and folk remedies. Seventeenth- and eighteenth-century English lore about such things was not that different from West African lore, and white Americans consulted black conjurers and "herb doctors." Black cooks in early America influenced both white southern and African-American eating habits. Preferences for barbecued pork, fried chicken, black-eyed peas, okra, and collard and mustard greens owed much to West African culinary traditions.

VOICES

A POEM BY JUPITER HAMMON

Jupiter Hammon (1711–1806?) was a favored slave living in Long Island, New York, when on Christmas Day 1760 he composed "An Evening Thought: Salvation by Christ, with Penitential Cries," an excerpt of which appears here. A Calvinist preacher and America's first published black poet, Hammon was deeply influenced by the Great Awakening's emphasis on repentance and Christ's spiritual sovereignty.

Salvation comes by Jesus Christ alone,
    The only Son of God;
Redemption now to every one,
    That love his holy Word.
Dear Jesus we would fly to Thee,
    And leave off every Sin,
Thy tender Mercy well agree;
    Salvation from our King.
Salvation comes from God we know,
    The true and only One;
It's well agreed and certain true,
    He gave his only Son.
Lord hear our penitential Cry:
    Salvation from above
It is the Lord that doth supply,
    With his Redeeming Love.
Dear Jesus let the Nations cry,
    And all the People say,
Salvation comes from Christ on high,
    Haste on Tribunal Day.
We cry as Sinners to the Lord,
    Salvation to obtain;
It is firmly fixt his holy Word,
    Ye shall not cry in vain.

▶ *What elements in Hammond's poem might have appealed to African Americans of his time?*

▶ *Does Hammond suggest a relationship between Christ and social justice?*

Source: Dorothy Porter, ed., *Early Negro Writing, 1760–1837* (1971; reprint, Baltimore: Black Classic Press, 1995).

African Americans also used West African culture and skills to shape the way work was done in the American South during and after colonial times. Africans accustomed to collective agricultural labor imposed the **"gang system"** on most American plantations. Masters learned that their slaves worked harder

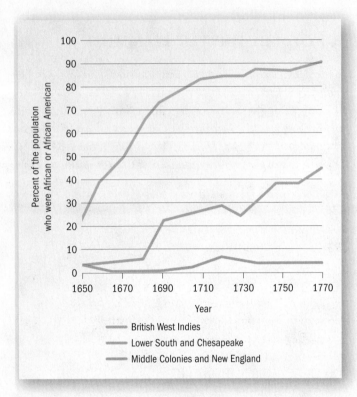

FIGURE 3–2 AFRICANS AS A PERCENTAGE OF THE TOTAL POPULATION OF THE BRITISH AMERICAN COLONIES 1650–1770

Time on the Cross: The Economics of Negro Slavery by Robert W. Fogel and Stanley L. Engerman.

Copyright © 1974. Reprinted by permission of W. W. Norton & Company, Inc.

and longer in groups. Their work songs were also an African legacy, as was the slow, deliberate pace of their labor. By the mid-eighteenth century, masters often employed slaves as builders. As a result, African styles and decorative techniques influenced southern colonial architecture. Black builders introduced African-style high-peaked roofs, front porches, wood carvings, and elaborate ironwork.

Slavery in the Northern Colonies

The British mainland colonies north of the Chesapeake had histories, cultures, demographics, and economies that differed considerably from those of the southern colonies. Organized religion played a much more important role in the foundation of most of the northern colonies than it did in those of the South (except for Maryland). In New England, where the Pilgrims settled in 1620 and the Puritans in 1630, religious utopianism shaped colonial life. The same was true in the West Jersey portion of New Jersey, where members of the English pietist Society of Friends (Quakers) settled during

the 1670s, and in Pennsylvania, which William Penn founded in 1682 as a Quaker colony. Quakers, like other pietists, emphasized nonviolence and a divine spirit within all humans. These beliefs disposed some Quakers to become early opponents of slavery.

Even more important than religion in shaping life in northern British North America were a cooler climate, sufficient numbers of white laborers, lack of a staple crop, and a diversified economy. All these circumstances made black slavery in the colonial North less extensive than and different from, its southern counterparts.

By the end of the colonial period during the 1770s, only 50,000 African Americans lived in the northern colonies in comparison to 400,000 in the southern colonies. In the North, black people were 4.5 percent of the total population, compared with 40 percent in the South. But, as in the South, the northern black population varied in size from place to place. By 1770 enslaved African Americans constituted 10 percent of the population of Rhode Island, New Jersey, New York, and Pennsylvania (see Figure 3–2).

New York City had a particularly large black population—20 percent of its total by 1750. This dated to 1626 when the city bore the name New Amsterdam and served as the main port of New Netherlands, a Dutch colony stretching along the Hudson River. By 1638, free and enslaved Africans constituted a large part of the city's small but cosmopolitan population. They spoke a variety of European languages and converted to a variety of Christian churches. The English conquered New Netherlands in 1664, but as late as the 1810s, many African Americans in and about New York City still spoke Dutch.

Like all Americans during the colonial era, most northern slaves were agricultural laborers. But, in contrast to those in the South, slaves in the North typically lived in their master's house. They worked with their master, his family, and one or two other slaves on a small farm. In northern cities, which were often home ports for slave traders, enslaved people of African descent worked as artisans, shopkeepers, messengers, domestic servants, and general laborers.

Consequently, most northern African Americans led lives that differed from their counterparts in the South. Mainly because New England had so few slaves, but also because of Puritan religious principles, slavery there was least oppressive. White people had no reason to suspect that the small and dispersed black population posed a threat of rebellion. The local slave codes were milder than in the South and, except for the ban on miscegenation, not rigidly enforced. New England slaves could legally own, transfer, and inherit property. From the early seventeenth century onward, Puritans converted the Africans and African Americans who came

London Coffee House.

This eighteenth-century drawing of Philadelphia's London Coffee House suggests the routine nature of slave auctions in early America. The main focus is on architecture. The sale of human beings is merely incidental. John F. Watson, "Annals of Philadelphia," being a collection of memoirs, anecdotes, and incidents of Philadelphia. The London Coffee House. The Library Company of Philadelphia.

among them to Christianity, recognizing their spiritual equality before God.

In the middle colonies of New York, New Jersey, and Pennsylvania, where black populations were larger and hence perceived by white people to be more threatening, the slave codes were stricter and penalties harsher. But even in these colonies, the curfews imposed on Africans and African Americans and restrictions on their ability to gather together were less well enforced than they were farther south.

These conditions encouraged rapid assimilation. Because of their small numbers, frequent isolation from others of African descent, and close association with their masters, northern slaves usually had fewer opportunities to preserve an African heritage. However, there was an increase in African customs among black northerners between 1740 and 1770. Before that time, most northern slaves had been born or "seasoned" in the South or the West Indies. Then, during the mid-eighteenth century, direct imports of African slaves into the North temporarily increased. With them came knowledge of African life. But overall,

the less harsh and more peripheral nature of slavery in this region limited the retention of African perspectives, just as it allowed the slaves more freedom than most of their southern counterparts enjoyed.

Slavery in Spanish Florida and French Louisiana

Just as slavery in Britain's northern colonies differed from slavery in its southern colonies, slavery in Spanish Florida and French Louisiana—areas that later became parts of the United States—had distinctive characteristics. People of African descent, brought to Florida and Louisiana during the sixteenth, seventeenth, and eighteenth centuries, had different experiences from those who arrived in the British colonies. They and their descendants learned to speak Spanish or French rather than English, and they became Roman Catholics rather than Protestants. The routes to freedom were also more plentiful in the Spanish and French colonies than they were in Britain's plantation colonies.

The Spanish monarchy regarded the settlement it established at St. Augustine in 1565 as primarily a military outpost, and plantation agriculture was not significant in Florida under Spanish rule. Therefore, the number of slaves in Florida remained small, and black men were needed more as soldiers than as fieldworkers. As militiamen, they gained power that eluded slaves in most of the British colonies, and as members of the Catholic Church, they acquired social status. By 1746 St. Augustine had a total population of 1,500, including about 400 black people. When the British took control of Florida in 1763, these local people of African descent retreated along with the city's white inhabitants to Cuba. It was with the British takeover that plantation slavery began to grow in Florida.

When the French in 1699 established their Louisiana colony in the lower Mississippi River valley, their objective, like that of the Spanish in Florida, was primarily military. In 1720 few black people (either slave or free) lived in the colony. During the following decade, Louisiana imported about 6,000 slaves, most of whom were male and from Senegambia. Although they faced harsh conditions and many died, by 1731 black people outnumbered white people in the colony. Some of the Africans worked on plantations growing tobacco and indigo. But most lived in the port city of New Orleans, where many became skilled artisans, lived away from their masters, became Roman Catholics, and gained freedom. Unfortunately, early in its history, New Orleans also became a place where it was socially acceptable for white men to exploit black women sexually. This custom eventually created a sizable mixed-race population with elaborate social gradations based on the amount of white ancestry a person had and the lightness of his or her skin. Unlike the case in Florida, Louisiana's distinctive black and mixed-race population did not leave when the colony became part of the United States in 1803.

African Americans in New Spain's Northern Borderlands

What is today the southwestern portion of the United States was from the sixteenth century until 1821 the northernmost part of New Spain. Centered on Mexico, this Spanish colony reached into Texas, California, New Mexico, Colorado, and Arizona. The first people of African descent who entered this huge region were members of Spanish exploratory expeditions. As we mentioned earlier, the best known of them is Esteban, an enslaved Moor (the Spanish term for a dark-skinned Muslim) who survived a shipwreck on the Texas coast in 1529 and joined Spanish explorer Alvar Núñez Cabeza

de Vaca in an arduous seven-year trek from Texas to Mexico City. Esteban, a skilled interpreter, later explored regions in what are today New Mexico and Arizona. Black men also accompanied Francisco Vásquez de Coronado's 1540–1542 search across the Southwest for the mythical Seven Cities of Cibola as well as Spanish expeditions along the upper regions of the Rio Grande in 1593 and 1598. During the seventeenth century, black soldiers participated in the Spanish conquest of Pueblo Indians. Some black or mulatto women also joined in Spanish military expeditions. The best known of them was Isabel de Olvena, who traveled with an expedition through New Mexico in 1600.

During the colonial era, however, New Spain's North American borderlands had far fewer black people than there were in the British colonies. In part this was because the total non-Indian population in the borderlands was extremely small. As late as 1792, only around 3,000 colonists lived in Texas, including about 450 described as black or mulatto. There were even fewer colonists in New Mexico and California, where people of mixed African, Indian, and Spanish descent were common. Black men in the borderlands gained employment as sailors, soldiers, tradesmen, cattle herders, and day laborers. Some of them were slaves, but others had limited freedom. In contrast to the British colonies, in New Spain's borderlands most slaves were Indians. They worked as domestics and as agricultural laborers or were marched south to Mexico, where they labored in gold and silver mines.

Also in contrast to the British mainland colonies, where no formal aristocracy existed but where white insistence on racial separation gradually grew in strength,

This detail of a mural located in the Arizona capitol building shows, on its extreme right, the former slave Esteban, who wears a blue turban. During the early 1500s, shipwrecked Esteban traveled through Texas to Mexico. Later he joined Spanish expeditions that explored what are now New Mexico and Arizona.

both hereditary rank and racial fluidity existed in New Spain's borderlands. In theory, throughout the Spanish empire in the Americas, "racial purity" determined social status, with Spaniards of "pure blood" at the top and Africans and Indians at the bottom. In Texas free black people and Indians suffered legal disabilities. They paid special taxes and could not own guns or travel freely. But almost all of the Spaniards who moved north from Mexico were themselves of mixed race, and people of African and Indian descent could more easily acquire status than they could in the British colonies. In the borderlands black men held responsible positions at Roman Catholic missions. A few acquired large landholdings called *ranchos*.

In this painting African Americans await sale to slave traders, who stand at the doorway on the left.

Black Women in Colonial America

The lives of black women in early North America varied according to the colony in which they lived. The differences between Britain's New England colonies and its southern colonies are particularly clear. In New England, where religion and demographics made the boundary between slavery and freedom permeable, black women distinguished themselves in a variety of ways. The thoroughly acculturated Lucy Terry Prince of Deerfield, Massachusetts, published poetry during the 1740s and gained her freedom in 1756. Other black women succeeded as bakers and weavers. But in the South, where most black women of the time lived, they had few opportunities for work beyond the tobacco and rice fields and domestic labor in the homes of their masters.

Hear the Audio
Bars Fight, poem by Lucy Terry; read by Arna Bontemps

During the late seventeenth and the eighteenth centuries, approximately 90 percent of southern black women worked in the fields, as was customary for women in West Africa. White women also did fieldwork, but masters considered black women to be tougher than white women and therefore able to do more hard physical labor. Black women also mothered their children and cooked for their families, a chore that involved lugging firewood and water and tending fires as well as preparing meals. Like other women of their time, colonial black women suffered from inadequate medical attention while giving birth. But because black women worked until the moment they delivered, they were more likely than white women to experience complications in giving birth and to bear low-weight babies.

As the eighteenth century passed, more black women became house servants. Yet most jobs as maids, cooks, and body servants went to the young, the old, or the infirm. Black women also wet-nursed their master's children. None of this was easy work. Those who did it were under constant white supervision and were particularly subject to the sexual exploitation that characterized chattel slavery.

European captains and crews molested and raped black women during the Middle Passage. Masters and overseers similarly used their power to force themselves on female slaves. The results were evident in the large mixed-race populations in the colonies and in the psychological damage it inflicted on African-American women and their mates. In particular, the sexual abuse of black women by white men disrupted the emerging black families in North America because black men usually could not protect their wives from it.

Although black women were more expensive than white indentured servants—because, unlike the children of white indentured servants, their children would become their master's property—slave traders and slaveholders never valued black women as highly as they did black men. Until 1660 the British mainland colonies imported twice as many African men as women. Thereafter, the ratio dropped to three African men for every two women, and by the mid-eighteenth century, natural population growth among African Americans had corrected the sexual imbalance.

Black Resistance and Rebellion

That masters regularly used their authority to abuse black women sexually and thereby humiliate black men dramatizes the oppressiveness of a slave system based on race and physical force. Masters often rewarded black women who became their mistresses, just as masters and overseers used incentives to get more labor from field hands. But slaves who did not comply in either case faced a beating. Slavery in America was always a system that relied ultimately on physical force to deny freedom to African Americans. From its start, black men and women responded by resisting their masters as well as they could.

Such resistance ranged from sullen goldbricking (shirking assigned work) to sabotage, escape, and rebellion. Before the late eighteenth century, however, resistance and rebellion were not part of a coherent antislavery effort. Before the spread of ideas about natural human rights and universal liberty associated with the American and French revolutions, slave resistance and revolt did not aim to destroy slavery as a social system. Africans and African Americans resisted, escaped, and rebelled but not as part of an effort to free all slaves. Instead, they resisted to force masters to make concessions within the framework of slavery and escaped and rebelled to relieve themselves, their friends, and their families from intolerable disgrace and suffering.

African men and women newly arrived in North America openly defied their masters. They frequently refused to work and often could not be persuaded by punishment to change their behavior. "You would really be surpris'd at their Perseverance," one frustrated master commented. "They often die before they can be conquered." Africans tended to escape in groups of individuals who shared a common homeland and language. When they succeeded, they usually became "outliers," living nearby and stealing from their master's estate. Less frequently, they headed west, where they found some safety among white frontiersmen, Indians, or interracial banditti. In 1672 Virginia's colonial government began paying bounties to anyone who killed outliers, and six decades later, the governor of South Carolina offered similar rewards. In some instances, escaped slaves, known as *maroons*—a term derived from the Spanish word *cimarron*, meaning wild—established their own settlements in inaccessible regions.

Read the Document
Runaway Notices from the South Carolina Gazette (1732 and 1737)

The most durable of such maroon communities in North America existed in the Spanish colony of Florida. In 1693 the Spanish king officially made this colony a refuge for slaves escaping from the British colonies, although he did not free slaves who were already there. Many such escapees joined the Seminole Indian nation and thereby gained protection between 1763 and 1783, when the British ruled Florida, and after 1821 when the United States took control. It was in part to destroy this refuge for former slaves that the United States fought the Seminole War from 1835 to 1842. Other maroon settlements existed in the South Carolina and Georgia backcountry and the **Great Dismal Swamp** of southern Virginia.

As slaves became acculturated, forms of slave resistance changed. To avoid punishment, African Americans replaced open defiance with more subtle day-to-day obstructionism. They malingered, broke tools, mistreated domestic animals, destroyed crops, poisoned their masters, and stole. Not every slave who acted this way, of course, was consciously resisting enslavement, but masters assumed that they were. In 1770, Benjamin Franklin, who owned slaves, complained to a European friend, "Perhaps you may imagine the Negroes to be mild-tempered, tractable Kind of People. Some of them indeed are so. But the Majority are of plotting Disposition, dark, sullen, malicious, revengeful and cruel in the highest Degree." Acculturation also brought different escape patterns. Increasingly, the more assimilated slaves predominated among escapees. Most of them were young men who left on their own and relied on their knowledge of American society to pass as free. Although some continued to head for maroon settlements, most sought safety among relatives, in towns, or in the North Carolina piedmont, where there were few slaves.

Rebellions were far rarer in colonial North America than resistance or escape. More and larger rebellions broke out during the early eighteenth century in Jamaica and Brazil. This discrepancy resulted mainly from demographics: in the sugar-producing colonies, black people outnumbered white people by six or eight to one, but in British North America black people were a majority only in the low country. The larger the proportion of slaves in a population, the more likely they were to rebel. Also, by the mid-eighteenth century, most male slaves in the British mainland colonies were Creoles with families, who had more to lose from a failed rebellion than did the single African men who made up the bulk of the slave population farther south.

Nevertheless, there were waves of rebellion in British North America from 1710 to 1722 and 1730 to 1741. Men born in Africa took the lead in these revolts, and the two most notable ones occurred in New York City in 1712 and near Charleston, South Carolina, in 1739. In New York, 27 Africans, taking revenge for "hard usage," set fire to an outbuilding. When white men arrived to put out the blaze, the rebels attacked them with muskets, hatchets, and swords. They killed nine of the white men and wounded six. Shortly thereafter, local militia units captured the rebels. Six of the rebels killed themselves; the other 21 were executed— some brutally. In 1741 another revolt conspiracy in New York led to another mass execution. Authorities put to death 30 black people and four white people convicted of helping them.

Even more frightening for most white people was the rebellion that began at Stono Bridge within 20 miles of Charleston in September 1739. Under the leadership of a man named Jemmy or Tommy, 20 slaves who had recently arrived from Angola broke into a "wearehouse, & then plundered it of guns & ammunition." They killed the warehousemen, left their severed heads on the building's steps, and fled toward Florida. Other slaves joined the Angolans until their numbers reached one hundred. They sacked plantations and killed approximately 30 more white people. But when they stopped to celebrate their victories and beat drums to attract other slaves, planters on horseback aided by

•••—Read the Document
The Slaves Revolt in South Carolina in 1739

Indians routed them, killing 44 and dispersing the rest. Many of the rebels, including their leader, remained at large for up to three years, as did the spirit of insurrection. In 1740 Charleston authorities arrested 150 slaves and hanged ten daily to quell that spirit.

In South Carolina and other southern colonies, white people never entirely lost their fear of slave revolt. Whenever slaves rebelled or were rumored to rebel, the fear became intense. As the quotation that begins this chapter indicates, the unwillingness of many Africans and African Americans to submit to enslavement pushed white southerners into a siege mentality that became a determining factor in American history.

CONCLUSION

Studying the history of black people in early America is both painful and exhilarating. It is painful to learn of their enslavement, the emergence of racism in its modern form, and the loss of so much of the African heritage. But it is exhilarating to learn how much of that heritage Africans and African Americans preserved, how they resisted their oppressors and forged strong family bonds, and how an emerging African-American culture began to influence all aspects of American society.

The varieties of black life during the colonial period also help us understand the complexity of African-American society later in American history. Although they had much in common, black people in the Chesapeake, in the low country, in Britain's northern colonies, in Spanish Florida, in French Louisiana, and in New Spain's borderlands had different experiences, different relationships with white people and Indians, and different prospects. Those who lived in the fledgling colonial towns and cities differed from those who were agricultural laborers. The lives of those who worked on small farms were different from the lives of those who served on large plantations.

Finally, African-American history during the colonial era raises fundamental issues about contingency and determinism in human events. Did economic necessity, racism, and class interest make the development of chattel slavery in the Chesapeake inevitable? Or, had things gone otherwise (e.g., if Bacon's Rebellion had not occurred or had turned out differently), might African Americans in that region have retained more rights and access to freedom? What would have been the impact of that freedom on the colonies to the north and south of the Chesapeake?

RECOMMENDED READING

Ira Berlin. *Many Thousands Gone: The First Two Centuries of Slavery in North America*. Cambridge, MA: Belknap Press, 1998. Berlin presents an impressive synthesis of black life in slavery during the seventeenth and eighteenth centuries that emphasizes the ability of black people to shape their lives in conflict with the will of masters.

Winthrop D. Jordan. *White over Black: American Attitudes toward the Negro, 1550–1812*. Chapel Hill: University of North Carolina Press, 1968. This classic study provides a probing and detailed analysis of the cultural and psychological forces that led white people to enslave black people in early America.

Philip D. Morgan. *Slave Counterpoint: Black Culture in the Eighteenth-Century Chesapeake and Lowcountry*. Chapel Hill: University of North Carolina Press, 1998. Comparative history at its best, this book illuminates the lives of black people in important parts of British North America.

Oscar Reiss. *Blacks in Colonial America*. Jefferson, NC: McFarland, 1997. Although short on synthesis and eccentric in interpretation, this book is packed with information about black life in early America.

Betty Wood. *Slavery in Colonial America 1619–1776*. Lanham, MD: Roman & Littlefield, 2005. This is a brief history that emphasizes life among the slaves.

Peter H. Wood. *Black Majority: Negroes in Colonial South Carolina from 1670 through the Stono Rebellion*. New York: Norton, 1974. This is the best account available of

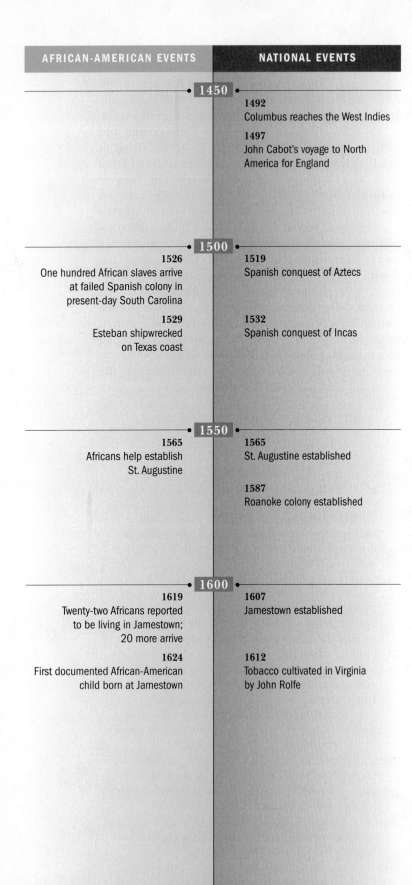

AFRICAN-AMERICAN EVENTS	NATIONAL EVENTS
	1450
	1492 Columbus reaches the West Indies
	1497 John Cabot's voyage to North America for England
	1500
1526 One hundred African slaves arrive at failed Spanish colony in present-day South Carolina	**1519** Spanish conquest of Aztecs
1529 Esteban shipwrecked on Texas coast	**1532** Spanish conquest of Incas
	1550
1565 Africans help establish St. Augustine	**1565** St. Augustine established
	1587 Roanoke colony established
	1600
1619 Twenty-two Africans reported to be living in Jamestown; 20 more arrive	**1607** Jamestown established
1624 First documented African-American child born at Jamestown	**1612** Tobacco cultivated in Virginia by John Rolfe

slavery and the origins of African-American culture in the colonial low country.

Donald R. Wright. *African Americans in the Colonial Era: From African Origins through the American Revolution.* 2nd ed. Arlington Heights, IL: Harlan Davidson, 2000. Wright provides a brief but well-informed survey of black history during the colonial period.

ADDITIONAL BIBLIOGRAPHY

COLONIAL SOCIETY

Wesley Frank Craven. *The Southern Colonies in the Seventeenth Century, 1607–1689.* Baton Rouge: Louisiana State University Press, 1949.

Jack P. Greene. *Pursuits of Happiness: The Social Development of Early Modern British Colonies and the Formation of American Culture.* Chapel Hill: University of North Carolina Press, 1988.

John J. McCusker and Russell R. Menard. *The Economy of British America, 1607–1789.* Chapel Hill: University of North Carolina Press, 1985.

Gary B. Nash. *Red, White, and Black: The Peoples of Early America.* 3rd ed. Englewood Cliffs, NJ: Prentice Hall, 1992.

ORIGINS OF SLAVERY AND RACISM IN THE WESTERN HEMISPHERE

Robin Blackburn. *The Making of New World Slavery: From the Baroque to the Modern 1492–1800.* New York: Verso, 1997.

David Brion Davis. *Inhuman Bondage: The Rise and Fall of Slavery in the New World.* New York: Oxford University Press, 2006.

Seymour Drescher. *From Slavery to Freedom: Comparative Studies of the Rise and Fall of Atlantic Slavery.* New York: New York University Press, 1999.

David Eltis. *The Rise of African Slavery in the Americas.* New York: Cambridge University Press, 2000.

Frank Tannenbaum. *Slave and Citizen: The Negro in the Americas.* New York: Knopf, 1946.

Betty Wood. *The Origins of American Slavery: Freedom and Bondage in the English Colonies.* New York: Hill and Wang, 1997.

THE CHESAPEAKE

Barbara A. Faggins. *Africans and Indians: An Afrocentric Analysis of Contacts between Africans and Indians in Colonial Virginia.* New York: Routledge, 2001.

Allan Kulikoff. *Tobacco and Slaves: The Development of Southern Cultures in the Chesapeake, 1680–1800.* Chapel Hill: University of North Carolina Press, 1986.

Gloria L. Main. *Tobacco Colony: Life in Early Maryland, 1650–1720.* Princeton, NJ: Princeton University Press, 1982.

Edmund S. Morgan. *American Slavery, American Freedom: The Ordeal of Colonial Virginia.* New York: Norton, 1975.

Isaac Rhys. *The Transformation of Virginia, 1740–1790.* New York: Norton, 1982.

Mechal Sobel. *The World They Made Together: Black and White Values in Eighteenth-Century Virginia.* Princeton, NJ: Princeton University Press, 1987.

THE CAROLINA AND GEORGIA LOW COUNTRY

Judith Ann Carney. *Black Rice: The African Origins of Rice Cultivation in the Americas.* Cambridge, MA: Harvard University Press, 2001.

Alan Gallay. *The Indian Slave Trade: The Rise of the English Empire in the American South, 1670–1717.* New Haven, CT: Yale University Press, 2002.

Julia Floyd Smith. *Slavery and Rice Culture in Low Country Georgia, 1750–1860.* Knoxville: University of Tennessee Press, 1985.

Betty Wood. *Slavery in Colonial Georgia, 1730–1775.* Athens: University of Georgia Press, 1984.

Jeffrey R. Yount. *Domesticating Slavery: The Master Class in Georgia and South Carolina, 1670-1837.* Chapel Hill: University of North Carolina Press, 1999.

THE NORTHERN COLONIES

Lorenzo J. Greene. *The Negro in Colonial New England, 1620–1776.* 1942. Reprint, New York: Atheneum, 1968.

Leslie M. Harris. *In the Shadow of Slavery: African Americans in New York City, 1626–1863.* Chicago: University of Chicago Press, 2003.

Graham R. Hodges. *Root and Branch: African Americans in New York and East Jersey, 1613–1863.* Chapel Hill: University of North Carolina Press, 1999.

Edgar J. McManus. *Black Bondage in the North.* Syracuse, NY: Syracuse University Press, 1973.

William D. Piersen. *Black Yankees: The Development of an Afro-American Subculture in Eighteenth-Century New England.* Amherst: University of Massachusetts Press, 1988.

SPANISH BORDERLANDS AND LOUISIANA

Lynn Robinson Bailey. *Indian Slave Trade and the Southwest: A Study of Slave-Taking and the Traffic in Indian Captives.* Los Angeles: Westernlore, 1966.

Gwendolyn Midlo Hall. *Africans in Colonial Louisiana: The Development of Afro-Creole Culture in the Eighteenth Century.* Baton Rouge: Louisiana State University Press, 1992.

Thomas N. Ingersoll. *Mammon and Manon in Early New Orleans: The First Slave Society in the Deep South, 1718–1819.* Knoxville: University of Tennessee Press, 1999.

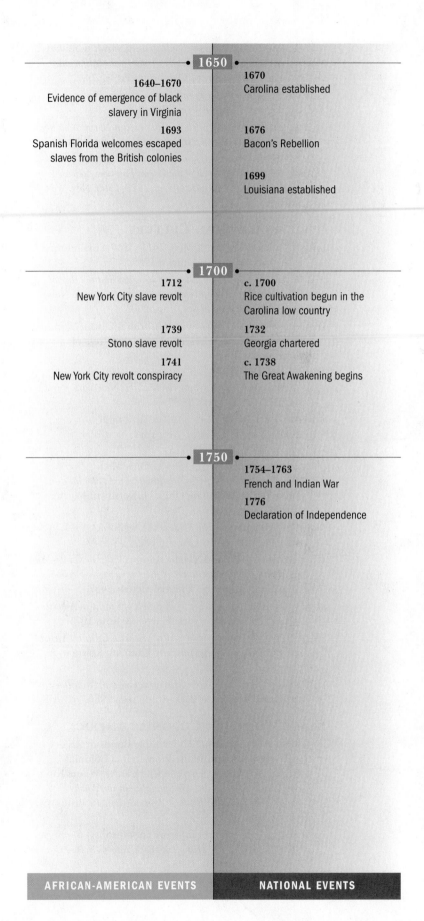

1650

1640–1670
Evidence of emergence of black slavery in Virginia

1693
Spanish Florida welcomes escaped slaves from the British colonies

1670
Carolina established

1676
Bacon's Rebellion

1699
Louisiana established

1700

1712
New York City slave revolt

1739
Stono slave revolt

1741
New York City revolt conspiracy

c. 1700
Rice cultivation begun in the Carolina low country

1732
Georgia chartered

c. 1738
The Great Awakening begins

1750

1754–1763
French and Indian War

1776
Declaration of Independence

AFRICAN-AMERICAN EVENTS   NATIONAL EVENTS

John L. Kessell. *Spain in the Southwest: A Narrative History of Colonial New Mexico, Arizona, Texas, and California.* Norman: University of Oklahoma Press, 2002.

Jane Landers. *Black Society in Spanish Florida.* Urbana: University of Illinois Press, 1999.

Michael M. Swann. *Migrants in the Mexican North: Mobility, Economy, and Society in a Colonial World.* Boulder, CO: Westview, 1989.

Quintard Taylor. *In Search of the Racial Frontier: African Americans in the American West, 1528–1990.* New York: Norton, 1998.

AFRICAN-AMERICAN CULTURE

John B. Boles. *Black Southerners, 1619–1869.* Lexington: University Press of Kentucky, 1983.

Joanne Brooks. *American Lazarus: Religion and the Rise of African American and Native American Literature.* New York: Oxford University Press, 2003.

Dickson D. Bruce. *The Origins of African American Literature, 1680–1865.* Charlottesville: University Press of Virginia, 2001.

Margaret W. Creel. *A Peculiar People: Slave Religion and Community Culture among the Gullahs.* New York: New York University Press, 1988.

Sylvaine A. Diouf. *Servants of Allah: African Muslims Enslaved in the Americas.* New York: New York University Press, 1998.

Michael Gomez. *Exchanging Our Country Marks: The Transformation of African Identities in the Colonial and Antebellum South.* Chapel Hill: University of North Carolina Press, 1998.

Melville J. Herskovits. *The Myth of the Negro Past.* 1941. Reprint, Boston: Beacon, 1990.

Linda Marinda Heywood. *Central Africans, Atlantic Creoles, and the Making of the Foundation of the Americas 1585–1660.* New York: Cambridge University Press, 2007.

Henry Mitchell. *Black Belief: Folk Beliefs of Blacks in America and West Africa.* New York: Harper & Row, 1975.

Sheila S. Walker, ed. *African Roots/American Culture: Africa and the Creation of the Americas.* Lanham: Rowman & Littlefield, 2001.

Joel Williamson. *New People: Miscegenation and Mulattoes in the United States.* New York: Free Press, 1980.

BLACK WOMEN IN COLONIAL AMERICA

Joan Rezner Gunderson. "The Double Bonds of Race and Sex: Black and White Women in a Colonial Virginia Parish." In Darlene Clark Hine, Wilma King, and Linda Reed, eds., *We Specialize in the Wholly Impossible: A Reader in Black Women's History.* Brooklyn, NY: Carlson, 1995.

Darlene Clark Hine and Kathleen Thompson. *A Shining Thread of Hope: The History of Black Women in America.* New York: Broadway, 1998.

Jane Kamensky. *The Colonial Mosaic: American Women, 1600–1760: Rising Expectations from the Colonial Period to the American Revolution.* New York: Oxford University Press, 1995.

Jenny Sharpe. *Ghosts of Slavery: A Literary Archaeology of Black Women's Lives.* Minneapolis: University of Minnesota Press, 2003.

RESISTANCE AND REVOLT

Herbert Aptheker. *American Negro Slave Revolts.* 1943. Reprint, New York: International Publishers, 1974.

Thomas J. Davis. *A Rumor of Revolt: The "Great Negro Plot" in Colonial New York.* New York: Free Press, 1985.

Merton L. Dillon. *Slavery Attacked: Southern Slaves and Their Allies, 1619–1865.* Baton Rouge: Louisiana State University Press, 1990.

Eugene D. Genovese. *From Rebellion to Revolution: Afro-American Slave Revolts in the Making of the Modern World.* Baton Rouge: Louisiana State University Press, 1979.

Gerald W. Mullin. *Flight and Rebellion: Slave Resistance in Eighteenth-Century Virginia.* New York: Oxford University Press, 1972.

Michael Mullin. *Africa in America: Slave Acculturation and Resistance in the American South and the British Caribbean, 1736–1831.* Urbana: University of Illinois Press, 1992.

John K. Thornton. *Africa and Africans in the Making of the Atlantic World, 1400–1800.* New York: Cambridge University Press, 1992.

RETRACING THE ODYSSEY

African Americans at Jamestown, Colonial National Historical Park, Jamestown and Yorktown, Virginia. http://www.nps.gov/jame/historyculture/african-americans-at-jamestown.htm. This program covers the period from 1619, the date of the first reports concerning black inhabitants at Jamestown, to 1705 when Virginia formally adopted a slave code.

Colonial Williamsburg, Williamsburg, Virginia. http://www.history.org/. The "Enslaving Virginia Tour" allows visitors to "explore [the] conditions that led to slavery's development in the Jamestown/Virginia colony."

Charles H. Wright Museum of African American History, Detroit, Michigan. http://www.maah-detroit.org/. The "Of the People: The African American Experience" exhibit includes material dealing with the memory of Africa and the "survival of the spirit."

REVIEW QUESTIONS

1. Based on your reading of this chapter, do you believe racial prejudice among British settlers in the Chesapeake led them to enslave Africans? Or did the unfree condition of the first Africans to arrive at Jamestown lead to racial prejudice among the settlers?

2. Why did vestiges of African culture survive in British North America? Did these vestiges help or hinder African Americans in dealing with enslavement?

3. Compare and contrast eighteenth-century slavery as it existed in the Chesapeake, in the low country of South Carolina and Georgia, and in the northern colonies.

4. What were the strengths and weaknesses of the black family in the eighteenth century?

5. How did enslaved Africans and African Americans preserve a sense of their own humanity?

myhistorylab Connections

www.myhistorylab.com
Review what you've learned in this chapter and explore the many documents, images, research tools, and activities for this chapter to learn more about African-American history.

✓● Study and Review

READ
●●●─Read the Document

- Maryland Addresses the Status of Slaves in 1664
- Virginia Law on Indentured Servitude (1705)
- The Selling of Joseph (1700)
- A Virginian Describes the Difference between Servants and Slaves in 1722
- Runaway Notices from the *South Carolina Gazette* (1732 and 1737)
- The Slaves Revolt in South Carolina in 1739
- Lucy Terry Prince, "Bars Fight" (1746)
- James Oglethorpe to the Trustees (1733)
- James Oglethorpe, The Stono Rebellion (1739)
- Declaration against the Proceedings of Nathaniel Bacon (1676)

LISTEN
((●─Hear the Audio

Hear the audio files for Chapter 3.

- *Bars Fight,* poem by Lucy Terry; read by Arna Bontemps

RESEARCH
mysearchlab

Consider this question in a short research paper.

How did the evolving economy of the British colonies come to depend on a race-based system of slavery?

EXPLORE
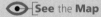See the Map

- Regions of Colonial North America, 1683–1763
- The Colonies to 1740

●●●─Read the Document

- Exploring America: Jamestown
- Exploring America: The Great Awakening

4

Rising Expectations:
African Americans and the Struggle for Independence

What was the crisis in the British Empire?

What did the Declaration of Independence mean to African Americans?

How did African Americans contribute to the Enlightenment?

What roles did African Americans play in the War for Independence?

How did the American Revolution weaken slavery?

▶ **African Americans fought on both sides** in the American War for Independence. In this nineteenth-century painting, a black Patriot aims his pistol at a British officer during the Battle of Cowpens, fought in South Carolina in 1781. William Ranney, "The Battle of Cowpens." Oil on Canvas. Photo by Sam Holland. Courtesy of South Carolina State House.

To the Honorable Legislature of the State of Massachusetts Bay, January 13, 1777:

The petition of a great number of blacks detained in a state of slavery in the bowels of a free & Christian country humbly sheweth that your petitioners apprehend we have in common with all other men a natural and unalienable right to that freedom which the Great Parent of the Universe hath bestowed equally on all mankind, and which they have never forfeited by any compact or agreement whatever.

Lancaster Hill, et al.

◀ **Because of southern opposition,** the Declaration of Independence was edited to exclude criticism of the slave trade. Instead, the Declaration accused the British of inciting slaves to revolt against their masters.

As the preceding quotation indicates, African Americans of the 1770s understood the revolutionary thought of their time. When a large minority of America's white population demanded independence from Britain on the basis of a natural human right to freedom, many black Americans asserted their right to be

((•— **Hear** the **Audio**
Hear the audio files for Chapter 4
at **www.myhistorylab.com** liberated from slavery. It took a momentous change in outlook from that of earlier ages for either group to perceive freedom as a right. Just as momentous was the dawning awareness among white people of the contradiction between claiming freedom for themselves and denying it to others.

The Great Awakening had nurtured humanitarian opposition to slavery. But secular thought, rooted in the European Enlightenment, shaped a revolutionary ethos in America. According to the precepts of the Enlightenment, all humans had natural, God-given rights that could not be taken from them without their consent. In 1777, the African-American petitioners in Massachusetts alluded to these precepts.

If the Enlightenment shaped the revolutionary discourse of the late eighteenth century, it was the French and Indian War, fought between 1754 and 1763, that made the American struggle for independence possible. The outcome of that war, which pitted the British, Americans, and their American Indian allies against the French and their Indian allies, created a volatile situation in the thirteen British colonies. That situation, in turn, produced the American War for Independence and efforts by many enslaved African Americans to gain their freedom.

In this chapter we explore the African-American quest for liberty during the 20 years between 1763, when the French and Indian War ended, and 1783, when Britain recognized the independence of the United States. During this period, African Americans exercised an intellectual and political leadership that had far-ranging implications. A few black writers and scientists emerged, black soldiers fought in battle, black artisans proliferated, and—particularly in the North—black activists publicly argued against enslavement. Most important, many African Americans used the War for Independence to gain their freedom. Some were Patriots fighting for American independence. Others were Loyalists fighting for the British. Still others simply used the dislocations war caused to escape their masters.

The Crisis of the British Empire

The great struggle for empire between Great Britain and France created the circumstances within which an independence movement and rising black hopes for freedom developed in America. Starting in 1689, the British and French fought a series of wars in Europe, India, North America, Africa, and the Caribbean. This great conflict climaxed during the French and Indian

War that began in North America in 1754, spread to Europe in 1756 (where it was called the Seven Years' War), and from there extended to other parts of the world.

The war sprang from competing British and French efforts to control the Ohio River valley and its lucrative **fur trade.** In 1754 and 1755, the French and their Indian allies defeated Virginian and British troops in this region and then attacked the western frontier of the British colonies. Not until 1758 did Britain undertake the vigorous and expensive military effort that by 1763 had forced France to withdraw from North America. Britain took Canada from France and Florida from France's ally Spain. In compensation, Spain received New Orleans and the huge French province of Louisiana in central North America (see Map 4–1).

These changes had momentous consequences. Deprived of their ability to play off Britain against France and Spain, the American Indian nations east of the Mississippi River had great difficulty resisting white encroachment. Although the Florida swamps remained a refuge for escaping slaves, fugitives lost their Spanish protectors. Americans no longer had to face French and Spanish threats on their frontiers. The bonds between Britain and the thirteen colonies rapidly weakened.

These last two consequences were closely linked. The colonial assemblies had not always supported the war effort against the French. American merchants had traded with the enemy. Therefore, after the war ended, British officials decided that Americans should be taxed to pay their share of the costs of empire and that their

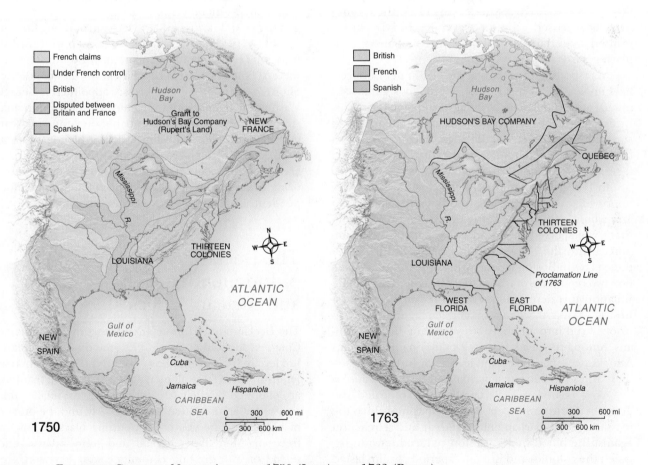

MAP 4–1   EUROPEAN CLAIMS IN NORTH AMERICA, 1750 (LEFT) AND 1763 (RIGHT)

These maps illustrate the dramatic change in the political geography of North America that resulted from the British victory in the French and Indian War (1754–1763). It eliminated France as a North American power. France surrendered Canada and the Ohio River valley to Britain. Spain ceded Florida to Britain and, as compensation, received Louisiana from France.

▶ *What was the significance for African Americans of these political changes and, in particular, of Great Britain's acquisition of Florida?*

commerce should be more closely regulated. In England it seemed entirely reasonable that the government should proceed in this manner. But white Americans had become accustomed to governing themselves, trading with whom they pleased, and paying only local taxes. They were well aware that with the French and Spanish gone, they no longer needed British protection. Therefore, many resisted when the British Parliament asserted its power to tax and govern them.

During the 1760s Parliament repeatedly passed laws that many Americans considered oppressive. The Proclamation Line of 1763 aimed to placate Britain's Indian allies by forbidding American settlement west of the crest of the Appalachian Mountains. The Sugar Act of 1764 levied **import duties** designed, for the first time in colonial history, to raise revenue for Britain rather than simply to regulate American trade. In 1765 the Stamp Act, also passed to raise revenue, heavily taxed printed materials, such as deeds, newspapers, and playing cards.

Read the Document

Exploring America: The Stamp Act

In response, Americans at the Stamp Act Congress held in New York City in October 1765 took a first step toward united resistance. By agreeing not to import British goods, the congress forced Parliament in 1766 to repeal the Stamp Act. But the Sugar Act and Proclamation Line remained in force, and Parliament remained determined to exercise greater control in America.

In 1767 Parliament forced the New York assembly to provide quarters for British troops and enacted the Townshend Acts (named after the British finance minister), which taxed glass, lead, paint, paper, and tea imported into the colonies from Britain. Resistance to these taxes in Boston led the British government to station two regiments of troops there in 1768. The volatile situation this deployment created led in 1770 to the Boston Massacre, when a small detachment of British troops fired into an angry crowd, killing five Bostonians. Among the dead was a black sailor named Crispus Attucks, who had taken the lead in accosting the soldiers and soon became a martyr to the Patriot cause.

As it turned out, Parliament had repealed the Townshend duties, except the one on tea, before the massacre. This parliamentary retreat and a reaction against the bloodshed in Boston reduced tension between the colonies and Britain. A period of calm lasted until May 1773, when Parliament passed the Tea Act.

The Tea Act gave the British East India Company a monopoly over all tea sold in the American colonies. A huge but debt-ridden entity, the East India Company governed India for the British Empire and had exclusive rights to import tea from China to Britain. At the time, Americans drank a great deal of tea, and Parliament hoped the tea monopoly would save the company from bankruptcy. But American merchants assumed the act was the first step in a plot to bankrupt them. Because it had huge tea reserves, the East India Company could sell its tea much more cheaply than colonial merchants could. Other Americans believed the Tea Act was a trick to get them to pay the tax on tea by lowering its price. They feared that once Americans paid the tax on tea, British leaders would use it as a precedent to raise additional taxes.

To prevent this, Boston's radical **Sons of Liberty** in December 1773 dumped a shipload of tea into the harbor. In response, Britain in early 1774 sent more troops to Boston and punished the city economically, sparking resistance throughout the colonies that eventually led to American independence. **Patriot** leaders organized the Continental Congress, which met in Philadelphia in September 1774 and demanded the repeal of all "oppressive" legislation. By November, Massachusetts Minutemen—members of an irregular militia—had begun to stockpile arms in the villages surrounding Boston.

In April 1775 Minutemen clashed with British troops at Lexington and Concord near Boston. This was the first battle in what became a war for independence. Shortly thereafter, Congress appointed George Washington commander in chief of the Continental Army. Before he took command, however, the American and British forces at Boston fought a bloody battle at Bunker Hill. After a year during which other armed clashes occurred and the British rejected a compromise, Congress in July 1776 declared the colonies to be independent states, and the war became a revolution.

The Declaration of Independence and African Americans

The Declaration of Independence that the Continental Congress adopted on July 4, 1776, was drafted by a slaveholder in a slaveholding country. When Thomas Jefferson wrote "that all men are created equal; that they are endowed by their Creator with certain unalienable rights; that among these are life, liberty, and the pursuit of happiness," he was not supporting black claims for freedom. Men like Jefferson and John Adams, who served on the drafting committee with Jefferson, frequently distinguished between the rights of white men of British descent and a lack of rights for people of color. In 1765 Adams had written that God had "never intended the American colonists 'for Negroes . . . and therefore never intended us for slaves.'" So convinced were Jefferson and his colleagues that black people could not claim the same rights as white people that they felt no need to qualify their words proclaiming universal liberty.

PROFILE: Crispus Attucks

Crispus Attucks was a fugitive slave who escaped in 1750 from his Framingham, Massachusetts, master. Attucks's father was black, his mother Indian. His master described him as "a mulatto fellow, about 27 years old, named Crispus, 6 feet 2 inches height, short, curl'd hair, his knees nearer together than common." During his 20 years as a fugitive, Attucks worked as a sailor, with Boston as his home port.

Attucks shared the anti-British sentiment that developed after the French and Indian War. This is not surprising since the tightening restrictions Parliament placed on American trade affected his livelihood as a seaman. In Boston, British soldiers were the most obvious target of such resentment. Bostonians had insulted and thrown rocks at them for some time before Attucks joined a motley crowd that, armed with clubs and sticks, accosted a small detachment of troops on the chilly evening of March 5, 1770. Attucks was not the only African American in the mob. One pro-British witness described those who gathered as "saucy boys, Negroes and mulattoes, Irish Teagues and outlandish Jack Tars [sailors]."

Although eyewitness accounts differ, Attucks probably took the lead in confronting Captain Thomas Preston and the nine soldiers under his command. A black witness maintained that Attucks, "a stout man with a long cordwood stick," hit a soldier, which led the troops to fire on the mob. John Adams, who defended the soldiers in court, credited this account, and Attucks was almost certainly the first to die when the soldiers, with their backs to a wall, fired.

Samuel Adams, John's cousin, and other Patriots in Boston declared the 47-year-old Attucks the first martyr to British oppression. They carried his coffin, along with those of three of the other four men who were killed, to Faneuil Hall—called the "Cradle of Liberty" because of its association with revolutionary rhetoric. There Attucks lay in state for three days with the other victims of what Americans immediately called the Boston Massacre. From this hall 10,000 mourners accompanied four hearses to Boston's Middle Burying Ground. The inscription on the monument raised to commemorate the martyrs reads as follows:

Long as in freedom's cause the wise contend,
Dear to your country shall your fame extend;
While to the world the lettered stone shall tell
Where Caldwell, Attucks, Gray, and Maverick fell.

Bostonians celebrated the anniversary of the massacre annually until the 1840s. They revived the practice in 1858 to protest the Supreme Court's decision in *Dred Scott v. Sanford* that African Americans were not citizens of the United States. At about the same time, African Americans in Cincinnati formed the "Attucks Guards" to resist enforcement of the Fugitive Slave Law. After the Civil War, black abolitionist William C. Nell linked the service of black men in defense of the Union to Attucks's sacrifice "in defense of this nation's freedom."

Attucks has remained a symbol of African-American patriotism. In 1967, at the height of the Vietnam War, the Newark, New Jersey, Board of Education, at the expressed desire of the city's large black community, made March 5 an annual holiday in honor of Attucks. This was the first holiday to recognize an African American.

▶ **The death of Crispus Attucks** in the Boston Massacre.

The draft declaration that Jefferson, Adams, and Benjamin Franklin submitted to Congress for approval did denounce the Atlantic slave trade as a "cruel war against human nature itself, violating its most sacred rights of life and liberty in the persons of a distant [African] people." But Congress deleted this passage because delegates from the Deep South objected to it. The final version of the Declaration referred to slavery only to accuse the British of arousing African Americans to revolt against their masters.

Yet, although Jefferson and the other delegates did not mean to encourage African Americans to hope the American War for Independence could become a war against slavery, that is what African Americans believed it could be. Black people heard Patriot speakers make unqualified claims for human equality and natural rights. They read accounts of such speeches and listened as white people discussed them. In response, African Americans began to assert that such principles logically applied as much to them as to the white population. They forced white people to confront the contradiction between the new nation's professed ideals and its reality. Most white people did not deny that black people were human beings. White citizens therefore had to choose between accepting the literal meaning of the Declaration, which meant changing American society, or rejecting the revolutionary ideology that supported their claims for independence.

THE IMPACT OF THE ENLIGHTENMENT

At the center of that ideology was the European Enlightenment. The roots of this intellectual movement, also known as the Age of Reason, lay in Renaissance secularism and humanism dating back to the fifteenth century. But it was Isaac Newton's *Principia Mathematica*, published in England in 1687, that shaped a new way of perceiving human beings and their universe.

Newton used mathematics to portray an orderly, balanced universe that ran according to natural laws that humans could discover through reason. Newton's insights supported the rationalized means of production and commerce associated with the Industrial Revolution that began in England during the early eighteenth century. An emerging market economy required the same sort of rational use of resources that Newton discovered in the universe. But what made the Enlightenment of particular relevance to the **Age of Revolution** was John Locke's application of Newton's ideas to politics.

In his essay "Concerning Human Understanding," published in 1690, Locke maintained that human society—like the physical universe—ran according to natural laws. He contended that at the base of human laws were natural rights all people shared. Human

beings, according to Locke, created governments to protect their natural individual rights to life, liberty, and private property. If a government failed to perform this basic duty and became oppressive, he insisted, the people had the right to overthrow it. Although conceived nearly a century before the 1777 Massachusetts petition with which this chapter begins, Locke's ideas underlie this appeal on behalf of black liberty. Locke also maintained that the human mind at birth was a *tabula rasa* (i.e., knowledge and wisdom were not inherited but were acquired through experience). Locke saw no contradiction between these principles and human slavery. However, during the eighteenth century, that contradiction became increasingly clear.

Most Americans became acquainted with Locke's ideas through pamphlets that a radical English political minority produced during the early eighteenth century. This literature portrayed the British government of the day as a conspiracy aimed at depriving British subjects of their natural rights, reducing them to slaves, and establishing tyranny. After the French and Indian War, Americans, both black and white, interpreted British policies and actions from this same perspective.

The influence of such pamphlets is clear between 1763 and 1776 when white Patriot leaders charged that the British government sought to enslave them by depriving them of their rights as Englishmen. When they made these charges, they had difficulty denying that they themselves deprived African Americans of their natural rights. George Washington, for example, declared in 1774 that "the crisis is arrived when we must assert our rights, or submit to every imposition, that can be heaped upon us, till custom and use shall make us tame and abject, as the blacks we rule over with such arbitrary sway."

AFRICAN AMERICANS IN THE REVOLUTIONARY DEBATE

During the 1760s and 1770s, when powerful slaveholders such as George Washington talked of liberty, natural rights, and hatred of enslavement, African Americans listened. Most of them had been born in America, they had absorbed English culture, they were united as a people, and they knew their way in colonial society. Those who lived in or near towns and cities had access to public meetings and newspapers. They were aware of the disputes with Great Britain and the contradictions between demanding liberty for oneself and denying it to others. They understood that the ferment of the 1760s had shaken traditional assumptions about government, and many of them hoped for more changes.

The greatest source of optimism for African Americans was the expectation that white Patriot leaders would realize that their revolutionary principles were incompatible with slavery. Those in England who believed that white Americans must submit to British authority pointed out the contradiction. Samuel Johnson, London's most famous writer, asked, "How is it that we hear the loudest yelps for liberty among the drivers of negroes?" But white Americans made similar comments. As early as 1763, James Otis of Massachusetts warned that "those who every day barter away other mens['] liberty, will soon care little for their own." Thomas Paine, whose pamphlet *Common Sense* rallied Americans to endorse independence in 1776, asked them to contemplate "with what consistency, or decency they complain so loudly of attempts to enslave them, while they hold so many hundred thousands in slavery; and annually enslave many thousands more."

Such principled misgivings among white people about slavery helped improve the situation for black people in the North and upper South during the war. But African Americans acting on their own behalf played a key role. In January 1766 slaves marched through Charleston, South Carolina, shouting "Liberty!" In the South Carolina and Georgia low country and in the Chesapeake, slaves escaped in massive numbers throughout the revolutionary era.

The drawing portrays a black youngster joining in a Boston demonstration against the Stamp Act of 1765.

This drawing depicts James Armistead (1760-1831) who, as an enslaved young man, served as a Patriot spy during the War for Independence. Under the command of the Marquis de Lafayette, whose name Armistead later added to his own, he infiltrated British camps in Virginia. He provided information that helped George Washington force the British surrender at Yorktown in 1781.

VOICES

BOSTON'S SLAVES LINK THEIR FREEDOM TO AMERICAN LIBERTY

In April 1773 a committee of slaves from Boston submitted this petition to the delegate to the Massachusetts General Court from the town of Thompson. The petition, which overflows with sarcasm, demonstrates African-American familiarity with the principles of the Enlightenment and the irony of white Americans' contention that Britain aimed to enslave them. Its authors are of two minds about their society. They see both the potential for black freedom and the entrenched prejudice of white Americans. Note that the authors propose to go to Africa if they gain their freedom.

Boston, April 20th, 1773

Sir, The efforts made by the legislative of this province in their last sessions to free themselves from slavery, gave us, who are in that deplorable state, a high degree of satisfaction. We expect great things from men who have made such a noble stand against the designs of their *fellow-men* to enslave them. We cannot but wish and hope Sir, that you will have the same grand object, we mean civil and religious liberty, in view in your next session. The divine spirit of *freedom*, seems to fire every humane breast on this continent, except such as are bribed to assist in executing the execrable plan.

We are very sensible that it would be highly detrimental to our present masters, if we were allowed to demand all that of *right* belongs to us for past services; this we disclaim. Even the *Spaniards*, who have not those sublime ideas of freedom that English men have, are conscious that they have no right to all the services of their fellow-men, we mean the *Africans*, whom they have purchased with their money; therefore they allow them one day in a week to work for themselves, to enable them to earn money to purchase the residue of their time. . . . We do not pretend to dictate to you Sir, or to the Honorable Assembly, of which you are a member. We acknowledge our obligations to you for what you have already done, but as the people of this province seem to be actuated by the principles of equity and justice, we cannot but expect your house will again take our deplorable case into serious consideration, and give us that ample relief which, *as men*, we have a natural right to.

But since the wise and righteous governor of the universe, has permitted our fellow men to make us slaves, we bow in submission to him, and determine to behave in such a manner as that we can have reason to expect the divine approbation of, and assistance in, our peaceable and lawful attempts to gain our freedom.

We are willing to submit to such regulations and laws, as may be made relative to us, until we leave the province, which we determine to do as soon as we can, from our joynt labours procure money to transport ourselves to some part of the Coast of *Africa*, where we propose settlement. We are very desirous that you should have instructions relative to us, from your town, therefore we pray you to communicate this letter to them, and ask this favor for us.

In behalf of our fellow slaves in this province, and by order of their Committee.

Peter Bestes,
Sambo Freeman,
Felix Holbrook,
Chester Joie.
For the Representative of the town of Thompson.

Rumors of slave uprisings spread throughout the southern colonies. However, it was in New England—the heartland of anti-British radicalism—that African Americans formally made their case for freedom. As early as 1701, a Massachusetts slave won his liberty in court, and there were eleven similar suits before 1750. As the revolutionary era began, such cases multiplied. In addition, although slaves during the seventeenth and early eighteenth centuries had based their **freedom suits** on contractual technicalities, during the revolutionary period, they increasingly sued on the basis of principles of universal liberty. They did not always win their cases—John Adams, a future president, was the lawyer who defeated one such case in Boston in 1768—but they set precedents.

African Americans in Massachusetts, New Hampshire, and Connecticut also petitioned their colonial or state legislatures for gradual emancipation. These petitions, worded like the one at the start of this chapter, indicate that the black men who signed them were familiar with revolutionary rhetoric. African Americans learned this rhetoric as they joined white radicals to confront British authority.

> ●◀━ Read the Document
> *Slave Petition to the Governor of Massachusetts (1774)*

▶ *What is the object of this petition?*
▶ *What Enlightenment principles does the petition invoke?*
▶ *What is the significance of the slaves' vow to go to Africa if freed?*

Source: Gary B. Nash, *Race and Revolution* (Madison, WI: Madison House, 1990), 173–74.

In 1765 black men in Boston demonstrated against the Stamp Act. They rioted against British troops there in 1768 and joined Crispus Attucks in 1770. Black Minutemen stood with their white comrades at Lexington and Concord. In 1773 black petitioners from Boston told a delegate to the colonial assembly, "We expect great things from men who have made such a noble stand against the designs of their *fellow-men* to enslave them. . . . The divine spirit of *freedom*, seems to fire every human breast."

Black Enlightenment

Besides influencing radical political discourse during the revolutionary era, the Enlightenment also shaped the careers of America's first black intellectuals. Because it emphasized human reason, the Enlightenment led to the establishment of colleges, academies, and libraries in Europe and America. These institutions usually served a tiny elite, but newspapers and pamphlets made science and literature available to the masses. The eighteenth century was also an era in which amateurs could make serious contributions to human knowledge. Some of these amateurs, such as Thomas Jefferson and Benjamin Franklin, were rich and well educated. They made discoveries in botany and electricity while pursuing political careers. What is striking is that some African Americans, whose advantages were far more limited, also became scientists and authors.

Because they had easier access to evangelical Protestantism than to secular learning, most African Americans who gained intellectual distinction during the late eighteenth century owed more to the Great Awakening than to the Enlightenment. The best known of these is Jupiter Hammon, a Long Island slave who published religious poetry in the 1760s. There were also Josiah Bishop and Lemuel Haynes, black ministers to white church congregations in Virginia and New England. But Phillis Wheatley and Benjamin Banneker, who were directly influenced by the Enlightenment, became the most famous black intellectuals of their time.

PHILLIS WHEATLEY AND POETRY

Wheatley came to Boston from Africa—possibly near the Gambia River—in 1761 aboard a slaver. She was seven or eight years old, small, frail, and nearly naked.

◆●◆─Read the Document
Phillis Wheatley, Poems on Various Subjects, Religious and Moral (1772)

John Wheatley, a wealthy merchant, purchased her as a servant for his wife. Although Phillis spoke no English when her ship docked, she was soon reading and writing in that language and studying Latin. She pored over the Bible and became a fervent Christian. She also read the fashionable poetry of British author Alexander Pope and became a poet herself by the age of thirteen.

For the rest of her short life, Wheatley wrote poems to celebrate important events. Like Pope's, Wheatley's poetry reflected the values of the Enlightenment. She aimed to blend thought, image, sound, and rhythm to provide a perfectly balanced composition. In 1773 the Wheatleys sent her to London where her first book of poems—the first book ever by an African-American woman and the second by any American woman—was published under the title *Poems on Various Subjects, Religious and Moral*. The Wheatleys freed Phillis after her return to Boston, although she continued to live in their house until both of them died. In 1778 she married John Peters, a black grocer, and was soon mired in illness and poverty. Two of her children died in infancy, and she died in December 1784 giving birth to her third child, who died with her.

Wheatley was an advocate and symbol of the adoption of white culture by black people. Before her marriage, she lived almost exclusively among white people and absorbed their values. For example, although she lamented the

((•●─Hear the Audio
On Being Brought from Africa to America, poem by Phillis Wheatley; read by Jean Brannon

sorrow her capture had caused her parents, she was grateful to have been brought to America:

> 'Twas mercy brought me from my Pagan land,
> Taught my benighted soul to understand
> That there's a God, that there's a Saviour too:
> Once I redemption neither sought nor knew.

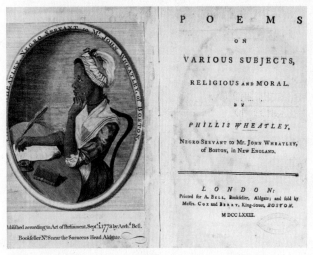

A frontispiece portrait of Phillis Wheatley precedes the title page of her first book of poetry, which was published in 1773. The portrait suggests Wheatley's small physique and studious manner.

VOICES

PHILLIS WHEATLEY ON LIBERTY AND NATURAL RIGHTS

Phillis Wheatley wrote the following letter to Samson Occom, an American-Indian minister, in 1774, after her return from England and as tensions between Britain and its American colonies intensified. In it, she links divine order, natural rights, and an inner desire for personal liberty. She expresses optimism that Christianity and the emergence of order in Africa will lead to the end of the Atlantic slave trade. And she hopes that God will ultimately overcome the avarice of American slaveholders ("our modern Egyptians") and let them see the contradiction between their words and deeds.

February 11, 1774

Rev'd and honor'd Sir, I have this Day received your obliging kind Epistle, and am greatly satisfied with your Reasons respecting the Negroes, and think highly reasonable what you offer in Vindication of their natural Rights. Those that invade them cannot be insensible that the divine Light is chasing away the thick Darkness which broods over the Land of Africa; and the Chaos which has reign'd so long, is converting into beautiful Order, and reveals more and more clearly, the glorious Dispensation of civil and religious Liberty, which are so inseparably united, that there is little or no Enjoyment of one without the other. Otherwise, perhaps, the Israelites had been less solicitous for their Freedom from Egyptian Slavery; I don't say they would have been contented without it. By no Means, for in every human Breast, God has implanted a Principle, which we call Love of Freedom; it is impatient of Oppression, and pants for Deliverance. And by the leave of our modern Egyptians, I will assert that the same principle lives in us. God grant Deliverance in his own Way and Time, and get him honor upon all those whose Avarice impels them to countenance and help forward the Calamities of their fellow Creatures. This I desire not for their Hurt, but to convince them of the strange Absurdity of their Conduct whose Words and Actions are so diametrically opposite. How well the cry for Liberty, and the reverse Disposition for the exercise of oppressive Power over others agree, I humbly think it does not require the Penetration of a Philosopher to determine.

Phillis Wheatley

▶ *How does this letter reflect principles associated with the Enlightenment?*
▶ *What insights does this letter provide into Wheatley's views on slavery and its abolition?*

Source: Roy Finkenbine, ed., *Sources of the African-American Past: Primary Sources in American History* (New York: Longman, 1997), 22–23.

But Wheatley did not simply copy her masters' views. Although the Wheatleys were loyal to Britain, she became a fervent Patriot. She attended Boston's Old North Church, a hotbed of anti-British sentiment, and wrote poems supporting the Patriot cause. In early 1776, for example, she lavishly praised George Washington, "fam'd for thy valour, for thy virtues more," and received effusive thanks from the general.

Wheatley also became an advocate and symbol of John Locke's ideas concerning the influence of environment on human beings. White leaders of the Revolution and intellectuals debated whether black people were inherently inferior in intellect to white people or whether this perceived black inferiority was the result of enslavement. Some slaveholders, such as Thomas Jefferson—who held racist assumptions about innate black inferiority—dismissed Wheatley's work as "below the dignity of criticism." But those who favored an environmental perspective considered Wheatley an example of what people of African descent could achieve if freed from oppression. She made her own views clear:

> Some view our sable race with scornful eye,
> "Their colour is a diabolic dye."
> Remember, Christians, *Negroes*, black as *Cain*,
> May be refin'd, and join th' angelic train.

BENJAMIN BANNEKER AND SCIENCE

In the breadth of his achievement, Benjamin Banneker is even more representative of the Enlightenment than Phillis Wheatley. Like hers, his life epitomizes a flexibility concerning race that the revolutionary era briefly promised to expand.

Banneker was born free in Maryland in 1731 and died in 1806. The son of a mixed-race mother and an African father, he inherited a farm near Baltimore from his white grandmother. As a child, Banneker attended a racially integrated school. Later his farm gave him a steady income and the leisure to study literature and science.

With access to the library of his white neighbor George Ellicott, Banneker "mastered Latin and Greek and had a good working knowledge of German and French." By the 1770s he had a reputation as a man "of uncommonly soft and gentlemanly manners and of pleasing colloquial powers." Like Jefferson, Franklin, and others of his time, Banneker was fascinated with mechanics and in 1770 constructed a clock. He also wrote a treatise on bees. However, he gained international fame as a mathematician and astronomer. Because of his knowledge in these disciplines, he became a member of the survey commission for Washington, D.C. This made him the first black civilian employee of the U.S.

government. Between 1791 and 1796, he used his astronomical observations and mathematical calculations to publish an almanac predicting the positions in the earth's night sky of the sun, moon, and constellations.

Like Wheatley, Banneker thoroughly assimilated white culture and well understood the fundamental issues of human equality raised by the American Revolution. In 1791 he sent Thomas Jefferson, who was then U.S. secretary state, a copy of his almanac to refute Jefferson's claim in *Notes on the State of Virginia* that black people were inherently inferior intellectually to white people. Noting Jefferson's commitment to the biblical statement that God had created "us all of one flesh" and Jefferson's words in the Declaration of Independence, Banneker called the great man to account concerning slavery.

Read the **Document**
Benjamin Banneker–Letter to Thomas Jefferson (1791)

Referring to the Declaration, Banneker wrote, "You were then impressed with proper ideas of the great valuation of liberty, and the free possession of those blessings, to which you were entitled by nature; but, Sir, how pitiable is it to reflect, that altho you were so fully convinced of the benevolence of the Father of Mankind, and of his equal and impartial distribution of these rights and privileges . . . that you should at the Same time counteract his mercies, in detaining by fraud and violence so numerous a part of my brethren, under groaning captivity and cruel oppression."

African Americans in the War for Independence

In the words of historian Benjamin Quarles, "The Negro's role in the Revolution can best be understood by realizing that his major loyalty was not to a place nor to a people, but to a principle." When it came to fighting between Patriots on one side and the British and their Loyalist American allies on the other, African Americans joined the side that offered freedom. In the South, where the British held out the promise of freedom in exchange for military service, black men eagerly fought on the British side as **Loyalists.** In the North, where white Patriots were more consistently committed to human liberty than in the South, black men just as eagerly fought on the Patriot side (see Map 4–2). In contrast, American Indians, hoping to counter white expansion westward, almost always fought on the British side.

Watch the **Video**
The American Revolution as Different Americans Saw It

The war began in earnest in August 1776 when the British landed a large army at Brooklyn, New York, and drove Washington's **Continental Army** across New Jersey into Pennsylvania. The military and diplomatic turning point in the war came the following year at Saratoga, New York, when a poorly executed British strategy to take control of the Hudson River resulted in British general John Burgoyne's surrender of his entire army to Patriot forces. This victory led France and other European powers to enter the war against Britain. Significant fighting ended in October 1781 when Washington and the French forced Lord Cornwallis to surrender another British army at Yorktown, Virginia.

When Washington had organized the Continental Army in July 1775, he forbade the enlistment of new black troops and the reenlistment of black men who had served at Lexington and Concord, Bunker Hill, and other early battles. Shortly thereafter, all thirteen states followed Washington's example. Several reasons account for Washington's decision and its ratification

The title page of the 1795 edition of Benjamin Banneker's *Pennsylvania, Delaware, Maryland, and Virginia Almanac.* Banneker was widely known during the late eighteenth century as a mathematician and astronomer.

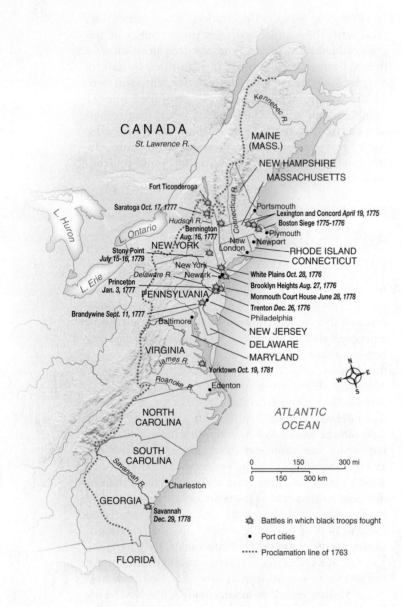

MAP 4–2 MAJOR BATTLES OF THE AMERICAN WAR FOR INDEPENDENCE, INDICATING THOSE IN WHICH BLACK TROOPS PARTICIPATED

Black troops fought on both sides during the American War for Independence and participated in most of the major battles.

Adapted from *The Atlas of African-American History and Politics*, 1/e, by A. Smallwood and J. Elliot, © 1998, The McGraw-Hill Companies. Reproduced with permission of The McGraw-Hill Companies.

▶ *Why is it significant that most of these battles were in the North?*

👁 See the Map *The American Revolution*

by the **Continental Congress.** Although several black men had served during the French and Indian War, the colonies had traditionally excluded African Americans from militia service. Like others before them, Patriot leaders feared that if they enlisted African-American soldiers, it would encourage slaves

to leave their masters without permission. White people—especially in the South—also feared that armed black men would endanger the social order. Paradoxically, white people simultaneously believed black men were too cowardly to be effective soldiers. Although apparently contradictory, these last two beliefs persisted into the twentieth century.

BLACK LOYALISTS

Because so many Patriot leaders resisted employing black troops, by mid-1775 the British had taken the initiative in recruiting African Americans. During the spring of that year, from Maryland southward, rumors circulated that the British would instigate slave revolt. In North Carolina, for example, the white populace believed that British agents promised to reward black individuals who murdered their masters. However, no such uprisings occurred.

Instead, many slaves escaped and sought British protection as Loyalists. Thomas Jefferson later claimed that 30,000 slaves escaped in Virginia alone. The British employed most black men who escaped to their lines as laborers and foragers. During the siege at Yorktown in 1781, the British used the bodies of black laborers who had died of smallpox in a primitive form of biological warfare to try to infect the Patriot army. Even so, many black refugees fought for British or Loyalist units.

Black Loyalists were most numerous in the low country of South Carolina and Georgia. At the end of the war in 1783, approximately 20,000 African Americans left with the British forces as they evacuated Savannah and Charleston. A few who remained became known as "the plunderers of Georgia." They carried out guerrilla warfare there until 1786.

The most famous British appeal to African Americans to fight for the empire in return for freedom came in Virginia. On November 7, 1775, Lord Dunmore, the last royal governor of the Old Dominion, issued a proclamation offering to liberate slaves who joined "His Majesty's Troops . . . for the more speedily reducing this Colony to a proper sense of their duty to His Majesty's crown and dignity."

Among those who responded to Dunmore's offer was Ralph Henry, a 26-year-old slave of Patrick Henry. Perhaps Ralph Henry recalled his famous master's "Give me liberty or give me death" speech. Another who joined Dunmore's troops was James Reid, who later became a leader of Britain's colony for former slaves in Sierra Leone in West Africa. Reid's 16-year-old wife came with him, and they both served with the Royal Artillery. In 1780 at least 20 of Thomas Jefferson's slaves joined Cornwallis's army when it invaded Virginia.

1775

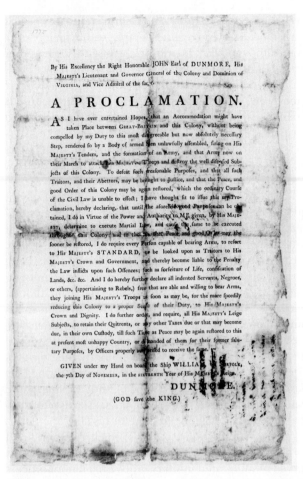

This is a broadside version of Lord Dunmore's November 7, 1775, proclamation calling on black men in Virginia to fight on the British side in the American War for Independence in return for their freedom.

AFRICAN AMERICANS AND THE WAR FOR INDEPENDENCE

APRIL 18, 1775	Black Minutemen participate in Battle of Lexington and Concord.
MAY 10, 1775	The Second Continental Congress convenes in Philadelphia.
JUNE 15, 1775	Congress appoints George Washington commander in chief of the new Continental Army.
JUNE 17, 1775	Black men fight with the Patriots at Bunker Hill.
JULY 9, 1775	George Washington bans African-American enlistment in the Continental Army.
NOVEMBER 7, 1775	Lord Dunmore, the royal governor of Virginia, offers freedom to slaves who will fight for the British.
DECEMBER 30, 1775	Washington allows black reenlistments in the Continental Army.

Dunmore recruited black soldiers out of desperation, then became the strongest advocate—on either the British or the American side—of their fighting ability. When he issued his appeal, Dunmore had only 300 British troops and had been driven from Williamsburg, Virginia's colonial capital. Mainly because Dunmore had to seek refuge on British warships, only about 800 African Americans managed to reach his forces. Defeat by the Patriots at the Battle of Great Bridge in December 1775 curtailed his efforts.

But Dunmore's proclamation and the black response to it struck a tremendous psychological blow against his enemies. Of Dunmore's 600 troops at Great Bridge, half were African Americans whose uniforms bore the motto "Liberty to Slaves." As more and more Virginia slaves escaped, masters blamed Dunmore. Throughout the war, other British and Loyalist commanders followed his example, recruiting thousands of black men who worked and sometimes fought in

exchange for their freedom. More African Americans became active Loyalists than Patriots during the war.

Five hundred of Dunmore's black troops died of typhus or smallpox. When he had to abandon Virginia, the remainder sailed with his fleet to New York City (which had become British headquarters in America). One of them, the notorious Colonel Tye, conducted guerrilla raids in Monmouth County, New Jersey, for years. Until he was killed in 1780, Tye and his interracial band of about 25 Loyalists plundered villages, spiked cannons to make them incapable of firing, and kidnapped Patriot officers. When the war ended, many black Loyalists, like those in Charleston and Savannah, joined white Loyalists in leaving the United States. Some of them went first to Acadia (now Nova Scotia) and then on to Sierra Leone. Others went to the British West Indies, where some faced reenslavement.

BLACK PATRIOTS

Washington's July 1775 policy to the contrary, black men fought on the Patriot side from the beginning of the Revolutionary War to its conclusion. Before Washington's arrival in Massachusetts, there were black Minutemen at Lexington and Concord, and some of the same men distinguished themselves at Bunker Hill. Among them were Peter Salem, Caesar Dickerson, Pomp Fisk, Prince Hall, Cuff Hayes, Barzillai Lew, Salem Poor, Caesar Weatherbee, and Cuff Whittemore. Lew was a veteran of the French and Indian War. Hall became a prominent black leader. Poor, who wintered with Washington's army at Valley

For many years historians presumed that Peter Salem is the black soldier portrayed in this detail from John Trumbull's contemporary oil painting *The Battle of Bunker Hill.* Instead the soldier is Asaba Grosvenor, a slave who accompanied his master in the fighting.

Forge in Pennsylvania in 1777–1778, received a commendation for bravery at Bunker Hill.

Dunmore's use of African-American soldiers prompted Washington to reconsider his ban on black enlistment. "If that man, Dunmore," he wrote in late 1775, "is not crushed before the Spring he will become the most dangerous man in America. His strength will increase like a snowball running down hill. Success will depend on which side can arm the Negro faster." After receiving encouragement from black veterans, Washington, on December 30, 1775, allowed African-American reenlistment in the Continental Army. Congress, fearful of alienating slaveholders, initially would not allow him to go further. By the end of 1776, however, troop shortages forced Congress and the state governments to recruit black soldiers in earnest for the Continental Army and state militias.

Even then, South Carolina and Georgia refused to permit black men to serve in regiments raised within their boundaries, although black men from these states joined other Patriot units.

The Patriot recruitment policy changed most quickly in New England. In early 1777 Massachusetts opened its militia to black men, and Rhode Island formed a black regiment. Connecticut enabled masters to free their slaves to serve as substitutes for the masters or their sons in the militia or Continental Army. New York and New Jersey adopted similar statutes.

Also in 1777, when Congress set state enlistment quotas for the Continental Army, state recruitment officers began to fill those quotas with black men so that white men might serve closer to home in the militia. Meanwhile, the southern states of Delaware, Maryland, Virginia, and North Carolina reluctantly began enlisting free black men. Of these states, only Maryland allowed slaves to serve in return for freedom, but the others sometimes allowed slaves to enlist as substitutes for their masters, which usually led to freedom. Black men asserted that if they were to fight in a war for liberty, their own liberty had to be ensured. When one master informed his slave that both of them would be fighting for liberty, the slave replied "that it would be a great satisfaction to know that he was indeed going to fight for his liberty."

Except for Rhode Island's black regiment and some companies in Massachusetts, black Patriots served in integrated military units. Enrollment officers often did not specify a man's race when he enlisted, so it is difficult to know precisely how many black men were involved. The figure usually given is 5,000 black soldiers out of a total Patriot force of 300,000. A few black men, such as Salem Poor, became junior officers. Others were drummers and fifers, sailors on privateers (merchant vessels armed and authorized by a government to raid enemy shipping) commissioned by the Continental Congress, and informants and spies. Like others who gathered intelligence behind enemy lines, African Americans who informed and spied risked being hanged if they were captured.

Black men fought on the Patriot side in nearly every major battle of the war (see Map 4–2). Prince Whipple and Oliver Cromwell crossed the Delaware River with Washington on Christmas night 1776 to surprise Hessian mercenaries (German troops hired to fight on the British side) at Trenton, New Jersey. Others fought at Monmouth, Saratoga, Savannah, Princeton, and Yorktown. In 1777 a Hessian officer reported, "No [Patriot] regiment is to be seen in which there are not Negroes in abundance, and among them are able bodied, strong and brave fellows."

Black women also supported the Patriot cause. Like white women, black women, such as James Reid's

The Patriots of African Descent Monument was erected at Valley Forge National Historical Park in 1933. Cal Massey designed the monument, and Phil Sumpter executed the relief sculpture portraying three black Revolutionary War soldiers who served among George Washington's troops.

wife, sometimes accompanied their soldier husbands into army camps, if not into battle. A few black women also demonstrated their sympathy for the Patriots in defiance of British authority. When the British occupied Philadelphia in 1777, they put Patriot prisoners of war in the city jail. The following year, a local Patriot correspondent reported that a free black woman, "having received two hard dollars for washing, and hearing of the distress of our prisoners in the goal, went to market and bought some neck beef and two heads, with some green[s], and made a pot of as good broth as she could; but having no more money to buy bread, she got credit of a baker for six loaves of bread, all of which she carried to our unfortunate prisoners."

The Revolution and Emancipation

The willingness of African Americans to risk their lives in the Patriot cause encouraged northern legislatures to emancipate slaves within their borders. By the late 1770s, most of these legislatures were debating abolition. Petitions and lawsuits initiated by black people in Massachusetts, Connecticut, New Hampshire, and elsewhere encouraged such consideration. But it took an emerging market economy, the Great Awakening, and the Enlightenment to establish the cultural context in which people who believed deeply in the sanctity of private property could consider such a momentous change. Economic, religious, and intellectual change had convinced many white Americans that slavery should be abolished.

Enlightenment rationalism was a powerful antislavery force. In the light of reason, slavery appeared to be inefficient, barbaric, and oppressive. But rationalism alone could not convince white Americans that black people should be released from slavery. White people also had to believe general emancipation was in their self-interest and their Christian duty.

In the North, where all these forces operated and the economic stake in slave labor was relatively small, emancipation made steady progress. In the Chesapeake, where some of these forces operated, emancipationist sentiment grew, and many masters manumitted their slaves, but there was no serious threat to the slave system. In the low country of South Carolina and Georgia, where economic interests and white solidarity against large black populations outweighed intellectual and religious considerations, white commitment to black bondage remained absolute.

The movement among white people to abolish slavery began within the Society of Friends. This religious group, whose members were known as Quakers, had always emphasized conscience, human brotherhood, and nonviolence. Moreover, many leading Quaker families engaged in international business ventures that required workers who were educated, efficient, and moral. This predisposed such Quakers against a system that forced workers to be uneducated, recalcitrant, and often ignorant of Christian religion. Although members of the Society of Friends had owned and traded slaves for generations, growing numbers of Quakers concluded that slaveholding was sinful.

During the 1730s Benjamin Lay, a former slaveholder who had moved from Barbados to the Quaker-dominated colony of Pennsylvania, began to exhort his fellow Friends to disassociate themselves from owning and buying slaves. A decade later John Woolman, from southern New Jersey, urged northeastern and Chesapeake Quakers to emancipate their slaves. With assistance from British Quakers, Woolman and Anthony Benezet, a Philadelphia teacher, convinced the society's 1758 annual meeting to condemn slavery and the slave trade.

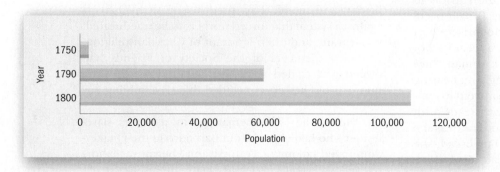

WHEREAS the NEGROES in the counties of Briſtol and Worceſter, the 24th of March laſt, petitioned the Committees of Correſpondence for the county of Worceſter (then convened in Worceſter) to aſſiſt them in obtaining their freedom. THEREFORE, In County Convention, June 14th, 1775. RESOLVED, That we abhor the enſlaving of any of the human race, and particularly of the NEGROES in this country. And that whenever there ſhall be a door opened, or opportunity preſent, for any thing to be done toward the emancipating the NEGROES; we will uſe our influence and endeavour that ſuch a thing may be effected, Atteſt. WILLIAM HENSHAW, Clerk.

The Patriot newspaper *Massachusetts Spy* published this antislavery resolution on June 21, 1775. It indicates the initiative taken by black abolitionists and the sympathetic response of white Patriots.

When the conflict with Britain made human rights a political as well as a religious issue, Woolman and Benezet carried their abolitionist message beyond the Society of Friends. They thereby merged their sectarian crusade with the rationalist efforts of such northern white revolutionary leaders as former slaveholder Benjamin Franklin of Philadelphia and John Jay and Alexander Hamilton—who continued to own slaves—of New York. Under Quaker leadership, antislavery societies organized in the North and the Chesapeake. The societies joined African Americans in petitioning northern legislatures and, in one instance, the Continental Congress to act against slavery or the slave trade.

▶▶▶ **Read** the **Document**

An Early Abolitionist Speaks Out against Slavery in 1757

FIGURE 4–1 THE FREE BLACK POPULATION OF THE BRITISH NORTH AMERICAN COLONIES IN 1750 AND OF THE UNITED STATES IN 1790 AND 1800

The impact of revolutionary ideology and a changing economy led to a great increase in the free black population during the 1780s and 1790s.

Source: *A Century of Population Growth in the United States. 1790–1900* (1909), 80. Data for 1750 estimated.

THE REVOLUTIONARY IMPACT

In calling for emancipation, the antislavery societies emphasized black service in the war against British rule and the religious and economic progress of northern African Americans. They also contended that emancipation would prevent black rebellions. As a result, by 1784 all the northern states except New Jersey and New York had undertaken either immediate or gradual abolition of slavery. Delaware, Maryland, and Virginia made manumission easier. Even the Deep South saw efforts to mitigate the most brutal excesses that slavery encouraged among masters. Many observers believed the Revolution had profoundly improved the prospects for African Americans.

In fact, the War for Independence dealt a heavy, although not mortal, blow to slavery (see Figure 4–1). While northern states prepared to abolish involuntary servitude, an estimated 100,000 slaves escaped from their masters in the South. In South Carolina alone, approximately 25,000 escaped—about 30 percent of the state's black population. Twenty thousand black people left with the British at the end of the war (see Map 4–3). Meanwhile, numerous escapees found their way to southern cities or to the North, where they joined an expanding free black class.

In the Chesapeake, as well as in the North, individual slaves gained freedom either in return for service in the war or because their masters had embraced Enlightenment principles. Philip Graham of Maryland, for example, freed his slaves, commenting that holding one's "fellow men in bondage and slavery is repugnant to the gold law of God and the unalienable right of mankind as well as to every principle of the late glorious revolution which has taken place in America." The Virginia legislature ordered masters to free slaves who had fought for American independence.

Those Chesapeake slaves who did not become free also made gains during the Revolution because the war hastened the decline of tobacco raising. As planters switched to wheat and corn, they required fewer year-round, full-time workers. This encouraged them to free their excess labor force or to negotiate contracts that let slaves serve for a term of years rather than for life. Another alternative was for masters to allow slaves—primarily males—to practice skilled trades instead of doing fieldwork. Such slaves

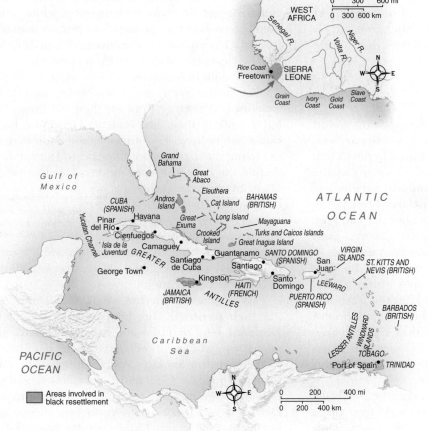

MAP 4–3   THE RESETTLEMENT OF BLACK LOYALISTS AFTER THE AMERICAN WAR FOR INDEPENDENCE

Like their white Loyalist counterparts, many black Loyalists left with the British following the Patriot victory. Most of those who settled in Nova Scotia soon moved on to Great Britain or the British free black colony of Sierra Leone. Some black migrants to the British Caribbean were reenslaved. Adapted from *The Atlas of African-American History and Politics*, 1/e, by A. Smallwood and J. Elliot, © 1998, The McGraw-Hill Companies. Reproduced with permission of The McGraw-Hill Companies.

▶ *What does the arrival of some black Loyalists in Sierra Leone indicate about Great Britain's changing attitudes toward slavery?*

often "**hired their own time**" in return for giving their masters a large percentage of their wages.

Even those slaves who remained agricultural workers had more time to garden, hunt, and fish to supply themselves and their families with food and income. They gained more freedom to visit relatives who lived on other plantations, attend religious meetings, and interact with white people. Masters tended to refrain from the barbaric punishments used in the past, to improve slave housing, and to allow slaves more access to religion.

In South Carolina and Georgia, greater autonomy for slaves during the revolutionary era took a different form. The war increased absenteeism among masters and reduced contacts between the black and white populations. The black majorities in these regions grew larger, more isolated, and more African in culture as South Carolina and Georgia imported more slaves from Africa. The constant arrival of Africans helped the region's African-American population retain a distinctive culture and the Gullah dialect. The increase in master absenteeism also permitted the task system of labor to expand. As historian Peter Kolchin notes, although African Americans in the North and the Chesapeake lived near white people and interacted with them, "in the coastal region of the lower South, most blacks lived in a world of their own, largely isolated from whites, and developed their own culture and way of life."

THE REVOLUTIONARY PROMISE

Even though the northern states were moving toward general emancipation during the revolutionary era, most newly free African Americans lived in the Chesapeake. They gained their freedom by serving in the war or escaping or because of economic and ideological change. As a result, a substantial free black population emerged in the Chesapeake after the war. Free African Americans had, of course, always lived there—Anthony Johnson is a prominent example—but before the Revolution they were few. In 1782 Virginia had only 1,800 free people within a total black population of 220,582. By 1790 the state had 12,766 free people within a total black population of 306,193. By 1810 it was 30,570 within 423,088. Free black populations also grew in Delaware and Maryland, where—unlike Virginia—the number of slaves began a long decline.

But in South Carolina and Georgia, the free black class remained tiny. Most low-country free black people were the children of white slave owners. They tended to be less independent of their former masters than their Chesapeake counterparts and lighter complexioned because their freedom was often a result of a family relationship to their masters.

In the North and the Chesapeake, free African Americans frequently moved to cities. Boston, New York, Philadelphia, Baltimore, Richmond, and Norfolk gained substantial free black populations after the Revolution. Black women predominated in this migration because they could more easily find jobs as domestics in the cities than in rural areas. Cities also offered free black people opportunities for community development that did not exist in thinly settled farm country. Although African Americans often used their new mobility to reunite families disrupted by slavery, relocating to a city could disrupt families that had survived enslavement. It took about a generation for stable, urban, two-parent households to emerge.

Newly freed black people also faced economic difficulty, and their occupational status often declined. Frequently they emerged from slavery without the economic resources needed to become independent farmers, shopkeepers, or tradespeople. In the North such economic restraints sometimes forced them to remain with their former masters long after formal emancipation. To make matters worse, white artisans used legal and extralegal means to protect themselves from black competition. Therefore, African Americans who had learned trades as slaves had difficulty employing their skills in freedom.

Yet, in the North and Chesapeake, most African Americans refused to work for their old masters and left the site of their enslavement. Those who had escaped had to leave. For others, leaving indicated a desire to put the stigma of servitude behind and embrace, despite the risks, the opportunities freedom offered. Many former masters did not understand this desire and criticized their former chattels for not staying on as hired hands. One white Virginian complained, "I cannot help thinking it is too generally the case with all those of colour to be ungrateful."

Read the **Document**
A Free African American Petitions the Government for Emancipation of All Slaves (1777)

Many African Americans took new names to signify their freedom. They adopted surnames such as *Freedom, Liberty,* or *Justice* and dropped classical given names such as *Pompey* and *Caesar.* Some paid homage to their African ancestry and complexion by taking surnames such as *Africa* and *Guinea, Brown,* and *Coal.* Others, however, expressed their aspirations in a racially stratified society by replacing African given names like *Cuffee* and *Quash* with Anglicized biblical names and the surnames of famous white people.

CONCLUSION

In the Peace of Paris signed in September 1783, Britain recognized the independence of the United States, acquiesced in American control of the territory between the Appalachian Mountains and the Mississippi River, and returned Florida to Spain (see Map 4–4). Both sides promised to return confiscated property—including slaves—to their owners, but neither side complied. As the United States gained recognition of its independence, African Americans could claim they had helped secure it. As soldiers in the Continental Army or in Patriot state militias, many black men fought and died for the revolutionary cause. Others supported the British. African Americans, like white Americans, had been divided over the War for Independence. Yet both those black men and women who chose the Patriot side and those who became Loyalists had freedom as their goal.

This chapter has sought to place the African-American experience during the struggle for independence in the broad context of revolutionary ideology derived from the Enlightenment. Black men and women, such as Benjamin Banneker and Phillis

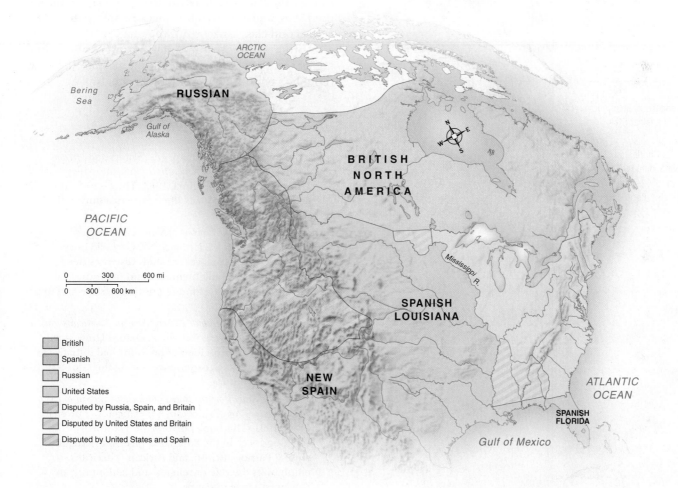

MAP 4–4 NORTH AMERICA, 1783

This map shows the political geography of North America following British recognition of the independence of the United States in 1783.

▶ *Why was this division of territory important for African Americans?*

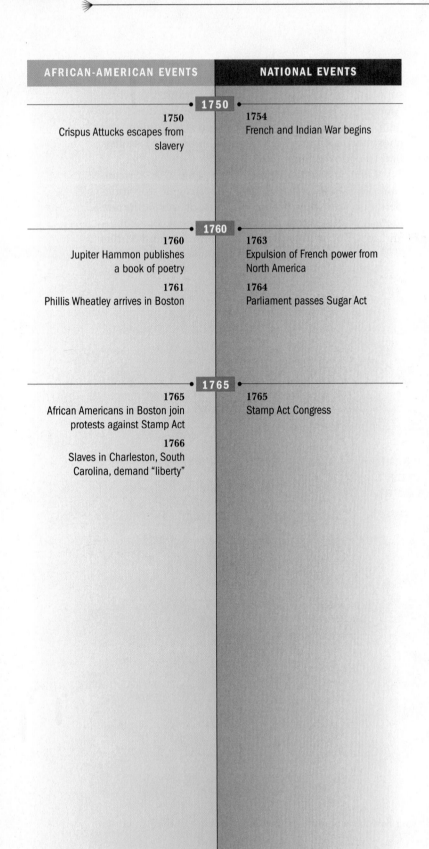

AFRICAN-AMERICAN EVENTS	NATIONAL EVENTS
1750 Crispus Attucks escapes from slavery	**1754** French and Indian War begins
1760 Jupiter Hammon publishes a book of poetry	**1763** Expulsion of French power from North America
1761 Phillis Wheatley arrives in Boston	**1764** Parliament passes Sugar Act
1765 African Americans in Boston join protests against Stamp Act	**1765** Stamp Act Congress
1766 Slaves in Charleston, South Carolina, demand "liberty"	

Wheatley, exemplified the intellectually liberating impact of eighteenth-century rationalism and recognized its application to black freedom.

During the war, and with the assistance of white opponents of slavery, African Americans combined arguments for natural rights with action to gain freedom. The American Revolution seemed about to fulfill its promise of freedom to a minority of African Americans, and they were ready to embrace the opportunities it offered. By the war's end in 1783, slavery was dying in the North and seemed to be on the wane in the Chesapeake. The first steps toward forming free black communities had been taken. Black leaders and intellectuals had emerged. Although most of their brothers and sisters remained in slavery, although the slave system began to expand again during the 1790s, and although free black people achieved *at best* second-class citizenship, they had made undeniable progress. Yet African Americans were also learning how difficult freedom could be despite the new republic's embrace of revolutionary ideals.

RECOMMENDED READING

Ira Berlin and Ronald Hoffman, eds. *Slavery and Freedom in the Age of the American Revolution.* Charlottesville: University Press of Virginia, 1983. The essays in this collection focus on black life in America during the revolutionary era.

David Brion Davis. *The Problem of Slavery in the Age of Revolution, 1770–1823.* Ithaca, NY: Cornell University Press, 1975. This magisterial study discusses the influence of the Enlightenment and the Industrial Revolution on slavery and opposition to slavery in the Atlantic world.

Douglas R. Egerton. *Death or Liberty: African Americans and Revolutionary America.* New York: Oxford University Press, 2009. Egerton focuses on individual initiative as central to the black experience during the late eighteenth century.

Sylvia R. Frey. *Water from the Rock: Black Resistance in a Revolutionary Age.* Princeton, NJ: Princeton University Press, 1991. This book portrays the War for Independence in the South as a three-way struggle among Patriots, British, and African Americans. It emphasizes the role of religion and community in black resistance to slavery.

Benjamin Quarles. *The Negro in the American Revolution.* 1961. Reprint, New York: Norton, 1973. This classic study remains the most comprehensive account of black participation in the War for Independence. It also demonstrates the impact of the war on black life.

Ellen Gibson Wilson. *The Loyal Blacks.* New York: G. P. Putnam's Sons, 1976. This book discusses why many

African Americans chose the British side in the War for Independence. It also focuses on the fate of those loyal blacks who departed Nova Scotia in Canada for Sierra Leone.

ADDITIONAL BIBLIOGRAPHY

THE CRISIS OF THE BRITISH EMPIRE

Stephen Conway. *The British Isles and the War of American Independence.* New York: Oxford University Press, 2000.

Edward Countryman. *The American Revolution.* Revised ed. New York: Hill and Wang, 2003.

Douglas E. Leach. *Roots of Conflict: British Armed Forces and Colonial Americans, 1677–1763.* Chapel Hill: University of North Carolina Press, 1986.

Pauline Maier. *From Resistance to Revolution: Colonial Radicals and the Development of American Opposition to Britain, 1765–1776.* New York: Knopf, 1972.

Peter David Garner Thomas. *Revolution in America: Britain and the Colonies, 1765–1776.* Cardiff, UK: University of Wales, 1992.

THE IMPACT OF THE ENLIGHTENMENT

Bernard Bailyn. *The Ideological Origins of the American Revolution.* Cambridge, MA: Harvard University Press, 1967.

Henry Steele Commager. *The Empire of Reason: How Europe Imagined and America Realized the Enlightenment.* Garden City, NY: Anchor, 1977.

Paul Finkelman. *Slavery and the Founders: Race and Liberty in the Age of Jefferson.* London: M. E. Sharpe, 1996.

J. G. A. Pocock. *The Machiavellian Moment: Florentine Political Thought and the Atlantic Republican Tradition.* Princeton, NJ: Princeton University Press, 1975.

Frank Shuffelton, ed. *The American Enlightenment.* Rochester, NY: University of Rochester Press, 1993.

AFRICAN AMERICANS AND THE AMERICAN REVOLUTION

Lerone Bennett Jr. *Before the Mayflower: A History of Black America,* 6th ed. Chicago: Johnson, 1987, Chapter 3.

Ira Berlin. "The Revolution in Black Life," in Alfred F. Young, ed., *The American Revolution: Explorations in the History of American Radicalism.* DeKalb: Northern Illinois University Press, 1976, 349–82.

Merton L. Dillon. *Slavery Attacked: Southern Slaves and Their Allies, 1619–1865.* Baton Rouge: Louisiana State University Press, 1990, Chapter 2.

Woody Holton. *Forced Founders: Indians, Debtors, Slaves, and the Making of the American Revolution in Virginia.* Chapel Hill: University of North Carolina Press, 1999.

Sidney Kaplan and Emma Nogrady Kaplan. *The Black Presence in the Era of the American Revolution.* Amherst: University of Massachusetts Press, 1989.

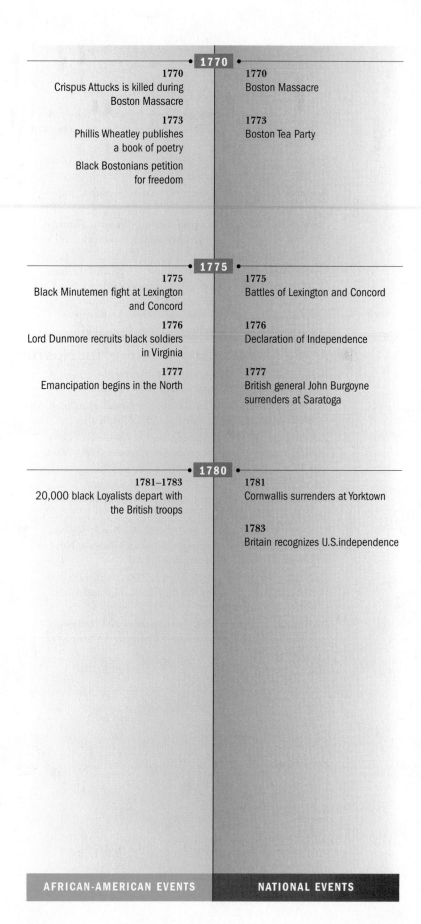

1770

1770
Crispus Attucks is killed during Boston Massacre

1770
Boston Massacre

1773
Phillis Wheatley publishes a book of poetry

Black Bostonians petition for freedom

1773
Boston Tea Party

1775

1775
Black Minutemen fight at Lexington and Concord

1775
Battles of Lexington and Concord

1776
Lord Dunmore recruits black soldiers in Virginia

1776
Declaration of Independence

1777
Emancipation begins in the North

1777
British general John Burgoyne surrenders at Saratoga

1780

1781–1783
20,000 black Loyalists depart with the British troops

1781
Cornwallis surrenders at Yorktown

1783
Britain recognizes U.S. independence

AFRICAN-AMERICAN EVENTS   **NATIONAL EVENTS**

Peter Kolchin. *American Slavery, 1619–1877*. New York: Hill and Wang, 1993, Chapter 3.

Duncan McLeod. *Slavery, Race, and the American Revolution*. New York: Cambridge University Press, 1974.

Gary B. Nash. *Forging Freedom: The Formation of Philadelphia's Black Community, 1720–1840*. Cambridge, MA: Harvard University Press, 1988.

John W. Pulis. *Moving On: Black Loyalists in the Afro-Atlantic World*. New York: Garland, 1999.

Simon Schama. *Rough Crossings: Britain, the Slaves, and the American Revolution*. New York: Ecco, 2006.

David Waldstreicher. *Runaway America: Benjamin Franklin, Slavery, and the American Revolution*. New York: Hill and Wang, 2004.

Peter H. Wood. "'The Dream Deferred': Black Freedom Struggles on the Eve of White Independence," in Gary Y. Okihiro, ed., *In Resistance: Studies in African, Caribbean, and Afro-American History*. Amherst: University of Massachusetts Press, 1986, 166–87.

ANTISLAVERY AND EMANCIPATION IN THE NORTH

Robin Blackburn. *The Overthrow of Colonial Slavery, 1776–1848*. New York: Verso, 1988, Chapter 3.

Merton L. Dillon. *The Abolitionists: The Growth of a Dissenting Minority*. New York: Norton, 1974, Chapter 1.

Joanne Pope Melish. *Disowning Slavery: Gradual Emancipation and "Race" in New England, 1780–1860*. Ithaca, NY: Cornell University Press, 1998.

Gary B. Nash. *The Forgotten Fifth: African Americans in the Age of Revolution*. Cambridge, MA: Harvard University Press, 2006.

Gary B. Nash and Jean R. Soderlund. *Freedom by Degrees: Emancipation in Pennsylvania and Its Aftermath*. New York: Oxford University Press, 1991.

James Brewer Stewart. *Holy Warriors: The Abolitionists and American Slavery*. Rev. ed. New York: Hill and Wang, 1997, Chapter 1.

Arthur Zilversmit. *The First Emancipation: The Abolition of Slavery in the North*. Chicago: University of Chicago Press, 1967.

BIOGRAPHY

Silvio A. Bedini. *The Life of Benjamin Banneker: The First African-American Man of Science*. Baltimore: Maryland Historical Society, 1999.

Henry Louis Gates Jr. *The Trials of Phillis Wheatley*. New York: Basic Civitas Books, 2003.

William Henry Robinson. *Phillis Wheatley and Her Writings*. New York: Garland, 1984.

RETRACING THE ODYSSEY

Colonial Williamsburg, Williamsburg, Virginia. http://www.history.org/visit/planYourVisit/revCity/. This is the largest historical restoration site in America. It emphasizes the period on the "eve of the American Revolution." Take the "Other Half Tour," which deals with "the lives and livelihoods of eighteenth-century African Americans."

Crispus Attucks' Grave, Granary Burial Ground, Boston, Massachusetts. http://www.thefreedomtrail.org/visitor/granary.html. Attucks is buried with the other victims of the Boston Massacre.

REVIEW QUESTIONS

1. How did the Enlightenment affect African Americans during the revolutionary era?
2. What was the relationship between the American Revolution and black freedom?
3. What was the role of African Americans in the War for Independence? How did their choices in this conflict affect how the war was fought?
4. How did the American Revolution encourage assimilation among African Americans? How did it discourage assimilation?
5. Why did a substantial class of free African Americans emerge from the revolutionary era?

myhistorylab Connections

www.myhistorylab.com
Review what you've learned in this chapter and explore the many documents, images,
research tools, and activities for this chapter to learn more about African-American history.

✓● Study and Review

READ
●●●● Read the Document

- Slave Petition to the Governor of Massachusetts (1774)

- Phillis Wheatley, *Poems on Various Subjects, Religious and Moral* (1772)

- An American Patriot Tries to Stir Up the Soldiers of the American Revolution (1776)

- Benjamin Banneker—Letter to Thomas Jefferson (1791)

- An Early Abolitionist Speaks Out against Slavery in 1757

- A Free African American Petitions the Government for Emancipation of All Slaves (1777)

- Report on Impending Ending of Slave Trade (1792)

- Proclamation of Lord Dunmore (November 14, 1775)

LISTEN
((●● Hear the Audio

Hear the audio files for Chapter 4.

- *On Being Brought from Africa to America*, poem by Phillis Wheatley; read by Jean Brannon

RESEARCH
mysearchlab

Consider these questions in a short research paper.

How did African Americans participate in the struggle for independence? What expectations did they have about the new nation they were helping create?

EXPLORE
Watch the Video

- The American Revolution as Different Americans Saw It

◉ See the Map

- European Claims in North America (1750 and 1763)

- Revolutionary War: Northern Theater (1775-1780)

- The American Revolution

●●●● Read the Document

- Exploring America: The Stamp Act

- Exploring America: Geography of the American Revolution

5

African Americans in the New Nation

What forces worked for black freedom after the Revolution?

Why did slavery survive in the new United States?

What were the characteristics of early free black communities?

How did the War of 1812 affect African Americans?

What impact did the Missouri Compromise have on African Americans?

▶ **This recent photograph portrays** one of several buildings used as slave quarters on Boone Hall Plantation, South Carolina. Built during the mid-seventeenth century, the small brick building housed two African-American families into the Civil War years.

Anytime, anytime while I was a slave, if one minute's freedom had been offered to me, and I had been told I must die at the end of that minute, I would have taken it—just to stand one minute on God's earth a free woman—I would.

Elizabeth Freeman

This, my dear brethren, is by no means the greatest thing we have to be concerned about. Getting our liberty in this world is nothing to our having the liberty of the children of God. . . . What is forty, fifty, or sixty years, when compared to eternity?

Jupiter Hammon

Death or Liberty.

Proposed inscription for a flag to be used in Gabriel's planned rebellion of 1800.

◀ **Thousands of** African Americans won their own freedom by escaping to the North before the Civil War.

Hear the Audio
Hear the audio files for Chapter 5 at **www.myhistorylab.com**

Except that they were all born slaves in eighteenth-century America, Elizabeth Freeman, Jupiter Hammon, and Gabriel had little in common. Freeman was an illiterate domestic servant when, in 1781, she sued for her freedom in Massachusetts. Hammon, who lived in Long Island, New York, was a poet and orthodox Calvinist preacher who enjoyed the support of his master and never sought his freedom. Gabriel was a literate, skilled slave who in 1800 masterminded a conspiracy to overthrow slavery in Virginia.

In this chapter, we explore how African Americans as diverse as Freeman, Hammon, and Gabriel helped shape the lives of black people during America's early years as an independent republic. We also examine how between 1783 and 1820 the forces for black liberty vied with the forces of slavery and inequality. The end of the War for Independence created great expectations among African Americans. But by 1820, when the **Missouri Compromise** confirmed the power of slaveholders in national affairs, black people in the North and the South had long known that the struggle for freedom was far from over.

That struggle took place at the state and local as well as the regional and national levels. The forces involved in it were often impersonal. They included the emergence of a market economy based on wage labor in the North and an economy based on the production of cotton by slave labor in the South. In addition, a revolutionary ideology encouraged African Americans to seek freedom, by force if necessary.

Meanwhile, economic self-interest encouraged white northerners to limit black freedom, and fear of race war caused white southerners to strengthen the slave system.

Yet individuals and groups also shaped African-American life in the new nation. As urban, church-centered black communities arose, men and women—both slave and free—influenced culture, politics, economics, and perceptions of race. This was particularly true in the North and the Chesapeake but also to a lesser degree in the Deep South. These were years of considerable progress for African Americans, although they ended with free black people facing deteriorating conditions in the North and with slavery spreading westward across the South.

Forces for Freedom

After the War for Independence ended in 1783, a strong trend in the North and the Chesapeake favored emancipation. It had roots in economic change, evangelical Christianity, and a revolutionary ethos based on the natural rights doctrines of the Enlightenment. African Americans took advantage of these forces to escape from slavery, purchase the freedom of their families and themselves, sue for freedom in court, and petition state legislatures to grant them equal rights.

In the postrevolutionary North, slavery, although widespread, was not economically essential. Farmers could hire hands during the labor-intensive seasons of planting and harvesting more efficiently than they could maintain a year-round slave labor force. Northern slaveholders had wealth and influence, but they lacked the overwhelming authority of their southern counterparts. Moreover, transatlantic immigration brought to the North plenty of white laborers, who worked cheaply and resented slave competition. As the Great Awakening initiated a new religious morality, as natural rights doctrines flourished, and as a market economy based on wage labor emerged, northern slaveholders had difficulty defending perpetual black slavery.

In Chapter 4, we saw that emancipation in the North was a direct result of the War for Independence. But the *process* of doing away with slavery unfolded in these states only after the war. Meanwhile, the national Congress set an important precedent in discouraging the expansion of slavery, and antislavery societies proliferated in the North and upper South.

NORTHERN EMANCIPATION

In comparison to other parts of the Atlantic world, emancipation in the northern portion of the United States began early. Its first stages preceded the revolt that had by 1804 ended slavery in Haiti, the first independent black republic. It preceded by a much greater margin the initiation in 1838 of peaceful, gradual abolition of slavery in the British Empire and the end of slavery in 1848 in the French colonies. Northern emancipation was exceptional in that it was not the result of force or intervention by an imperial power. Although free black communities were emerging throughout the Western Hemisphere, those in the North were distinctive because they included the bulk of the region's black population.

Emancipation in the North did not follow a single pattern. Instead, the New England states of Massachusetts (which included Maine until it became a separate state in 1820), Connecticut, Rhode Island, New Hampshire, and Vermont moved more quickly than did the mid-Atlantic states of Pennsylvania, New York, and New Jersey (see Map 5–1). Slavery collapsed in the New England states because African Americans who lived there refused to remain in servitude and because most white

1777–1804

THE ABOLITION OF SLAVERY IN THE NORTH

1777	Vermont constitutional convention prohibits slavery within what becomes the fourteenth state.
1780	Pennsylvania begins gradually abolishing slavery within its borders.
1783	Massachusetts's Supreme Court abolishes slavery there.
1784	Connecticut and Rhode Island adopt gradual abolition plans.
1785	New Jersey and New York legislatures defeat gradual abolition plans.
1799	The New York legislature provides for gradual abolition.
1804	New Jersey becomes the last northern state to initiate gradual abolition.

New Englanders acquiesced. The struggle against slavery in the middle states was longer and harder because more white people had a vested interest there in maintaining it.

Vermont and Massachusetts (certainly) and New Hampshire (probably) abolished slavery immediately during the 1770s and 1780s. Vermont, where there had never been more than a few slaves, prohibited slavery in the constitution it adopted in 1777. Massachusetts,

This engraving originally appeared in Boston in 1793, with the caption, "Cuffe near him . . . grasps his hand." It suggests the progress African Americans had made in the North but also the contempt in which many white northerners held them. The object of the picture is to ridicule Massachusetts governor John Hancock for participating in a black celebration.   The Library Company of Philadelphia

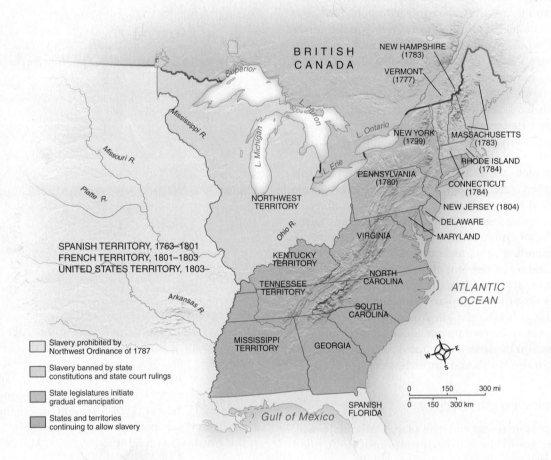

MAP 5–1   EMANCIPATION AND SLAVERY IN THE EARLY REPUBLIC

This map indicates the abolition policies adopted by the states of the Northeast between 1777 and 1804, the antislavery impact of the Northwest Ordinance of 1787, and the extent of slavery in the South during the early republic.

▶ *Why did the states and territories shown in this map adopt different policies toward African Americans?*

in its constitution of 1780, declared "that all men are born free and equal; and that every subject is entitled to liberty." Although this constitution did not specifically ban slavery, within a year Elizabeth Freeman and other slaves in Massachusetts sued under it for their freedom. Freeman, while serving as a waitress at her master's home in Sheffield, Massachusetts, overheard "gentlemen" discussing the "free and equal" clause of the new constitution. Shortly thereafter, she contacted a prominent local white lawyer, Theodore Sedgwick Sr., who agreed to represent her in court.

Meanwhile, another Massachusetts slave, Quok Walker, left his master and began living as a free person. In response, Walker's master sought a court order to force Walker to return to slavery. This case led in

1783 to a Massachusetts Supreme Court ruling that "slavery is . . . as effectively abolished as it can be by the granting of rights and privileges wholly incompatible and repugnant to its existence." Another judge used similar logic to grant Freeman her liberty. These decisions encouraged other Massachusetts slaves to sue for their freedom or to leave their masters because the courts had ruled unconstitutional the master's claim to his human chattel.

As a result, the first U.S. census in 1790 found no slaves in Massachusetts. Even before then, black men in the state had gained the right to vote. In 1780 Paul and John Cuffe, free black brothers who lived in Dartmouth, protested with five other free black men to the state legislature that they were being taxed without representation. The courts finally decided in 1783 that African-American men who paid taxes in Massachusetts could vote there. This was a rare victory. Before the Civil War, only a few New England states permitted black men to vote on the same basis as white men.

New Hampshire's record on emancipation is less clear than that of Vermont and Massachusetts. In 1779 black residents petitioned the New Hampshire legislature for freedom. Evidence also indicates that court rulings based on New Hampshire's 1783 constitution, which was similar to that of Massachusetts, refused to recognize human property. Nevertheless, New Hampshire still had about 150 slaves in 1792. Slavery may have withered away there rather than having been abolished by the courts.

In Connecticut and Rhode Island, the state legislatures, rather than individual African Americans, took the initiative against slavery. In 1784 these states adopted gradual abolition plans, which left adult slaves in bondage but proposed to free their children over a period of years. In Connecticut all children born to enslaved mothers after March 1, 1784, became free at age 25. Rhode Island's plan was less gradual. Beginning that same March 1, it freed the children of enslaved women at birth. By 1790 only 3,763 slaves remained in New England out of a total black population there of 16,882. By 1800 only 1,339 slaves remained in the region, and by 1810 only 418 were left (108 in Rhode Island and 310 in Connecticut).

In New Jersey, New York, and Pennsylvania, the investment in slaves was much greater than in New England. After considerable debate, the Pennsylvania legislature in 1780 voted that the children of enslaved mothers would be free at age 28. Under this scheme, Pennsylvania still had 403 slaves in 1830 (see Table 5–1). But many African Americans in the state gained their freedom much earlier by lawsuits or by simply leaving their masters. Emancipation came even more slowly in New York and New Jersey. In 1785 their legislatures *defeated* proposals for gradual abolition. White revolutionary leaders, such as Alexander Hamilton and John Jay, worked for abolition in New York, and Quakers had long advocated it in New Jersey. But these states had relatively large slave populations, powerful slaveholders, and white workforces fearful of free black competition.

In 1799 the New York legislature finally agreed that male slaves born after July 4 of that year were to be free at age 28 and females at age 25. In 1804 New Jersey adopted a similar law that freed male slaves born after July 4 of that year at age 25 and females at age 21. Under this plan, New Jersey still had 18 slaves in 1860.

THE NORTHWEST ORDINANCE OF 1787

Nearly as significant as the actions of northern states against slavery was Congress's decision to limit slavery's expansion. During the 1780s, Congress drew its authority from a constitution known as the Articles of Confederation. The Articles created a weak central government that lacked power to tax or to regulate commerce. Despite its weaknesses, this government acquired jurisdiction over the region west of the Appalachian Mountains and east of the Mississippi River, eclipsing several states' conflicting land claims.

During the War for Independence, increasing numbers of white Americans had migrated across the Appalachians into this huge region. The migrants— some of whom brought slaves with them—provoked hostilities with American Indian nations. Those who moved into the Old Northwest also faced British opposition, and those who moved into the Old Southwest contested against Spanish forces for control of that area. In response to these circumstances, Congress formulated policies to protect the migrants and provide for their effective government. The new nation's leaders also disparaged the westward expansion of slavery, and Thomas Jefferson sought to deal with both issues. First, he suggested that the western region be divided into separate territories and prepared for statehood. Second, he proposed that after 1800 slavery be banned from the entire region stretching from the Appalachians to the Mississippi River and from Spanish Florida (Spain had regained Florida in 1783) to British Canada.

In 1784 Jefferson's antislavery proposal failed by a single vote to pass Congress. Three years later, Congress adopted the **Northwest Ordinance.** This legislation

TABLE 5–1	SLAVE POPULATIONS IN THE MID-ATLANTIC STATES, 1790–1860							
	1790	**1800**	**1810**	**1820**	**1830**	**1840**	**1850**	**1860**
New York	21,324	20,343	15,017	10,888	75	4		
New Jersey	11,432	12,343	19,851	7,557	2,243	674	236	18
Pennsylvania	3,737	1,706	795	211	403	64		

Source: Philip S. Foner, *History of Black Americans, from Africa to the Emergence of the Cotton Kingdom*, vol. 1 (Westport, CT: Greenwood, 1975), 374.

PROFILE: Elizabeth Freeman

Known as Mum Bett, Elizabeth Freeman showed a strength of character that impressed everyone she met. She was probably born in 1744 in Claverack, New York. As her parents were African slaves, she was also a slave. After the death of her first master in 1758, Freeman and her sister became the property of Colonel John Ashley, a judge, in Sheffield, Massachusetts. She married young, gave birth to her only child—a daughter—and became a widow when her husband was killed fighting on the Patriot side in the War for Independence.

Freeman, who was illiterate, may have first learned of natural rights when in 1773 a group of men met at Ashley's home to draft a protest against British policies in the American colonies. "Mankind . . . have a right to the undisturbed Enjoyment of their lives, their Liberty and Property," the document declared. She took these words to heart, and when she learned while serving as a waitress in 1780 that Massachusetts had adopted a bill of rights asserting that all people were born free and equal, she was ready to apply the doctrine to herself.

In 1781 Freeman received "a severe wound" to her arm when she attempted to protect her sister from Ashley's wife, who "in a fit of passion" was threatening her with a hot kitchen shovel. Outraged at this attack, Freeman left the Ashley home and refused to return. Instead, she engaged the legal assistance of Theodore Sedgwick Sr. in a suit for her freedom on the basis of Massachusetts's new bill of rights. The jury found in Freeman's favor and required Ashley to pay her 30 shillings in damages. It was at this point that Mum Bett changed her name legally to Elizabeth Freeman. Shortly thereafter, the Massachusetts Supreme Court declared slavery unconstitutional throughout the state.

For the remainder of her active life, Freeman worked as a paid domestic servant in the Sedgwick household and moved with the Sedgwicks to Stockbridge in 1785. Because Theodore Sedgwick Sr.'s wife was emotionally unstable, Freeman became a surrogate mother to the Sedgwick children, who later testified to her "superior instincts," abilities as a nurse, efficiency, and bravery.

During the 1830s, Theodore Sedgwick Jr. told British writer Harriet Martineau that in 1786 some participants in Shays's Rebellion entered the Sedgwick home while Theodore Sr. was away. Acting quickly to hide the family's silverware, Freeman confronted the men with a kitchen shovel similar to the one her former mistress had used against her. While advising the men "that they 'dare not strike a woman,'" she threatened to use the shovel against any one of them who disturbed the family possessions, and she managed to usher them out with only minor damage to the Sedgwicks' property.

Freeman earned enough while employed by the Sedgwicks to purchase her own home and retire. When she died, she left a small estate to her daughter, grandchildren, and great grandchildren. She left another legacy to the Sedgwick children. When Theodore Jr. became an abolitionist during the 1830s, he credited Freeman as the source of his conviction that black people were not inferior to white people. Earlier, his brother Charles had the following lines inscribed on Freeman's gravestone: "She never violated a trust, nor failed to perform a duty. In every situation of domestic trial, she was the most efficient helper, and the tenderest friend. Good mother fare well."

◀ **This portrait of Elizabeth Freeman** was painted in watercolor on ivory by Elizabeth Sedgwick in 1811, thirty years after Freeman initiated her famous lawsuit.

applied the essence of Jefferson's plan to the region north of the Ohio River—what historians call the Old Northwest. The ordinance provided for the orderly sale of land, support for public education, territorial government, and the eventual formation of new states. Unlike Jefferson's plan, the ordinance banned slavery immediately. But, because it applied only to the Northwest Territory, the ordinance left the huge region south of the Ohio River open to slavery expansion.

Even in parts of the Old Northwest, some African Americans remained unfree after 1787. The first governor of the territory forced those who had been slaves before the adoption of the ordinance to remain slaves. Then in 1803, when Ohio became a state, the remainder of the Northwest Territory legalized indentured servitude. The result was that in southern parts of what became Illinois and Indiana, a few African Americans remained in bondage well into the nineteenth century.

Yet, by preventing slaveholders from taking slaves legally into areas north of the Ohio River, the ordinance set a precedent for excluding slavery from U.S. territories. Whether Congress had the power to do this became a contentious issue after President Jefferson annexed the huge Louisiana Territory in 1803 (see p. 120). The issue divided northern and southern politicians until the Civil War.

ANTISLAVERY SOCIETIES IN THE NORTH AND THE UPPER SOUTH

While African Americans helped destroy slavery in the northeastern states and Congress blocked its advance into the Old Northwest, a few white people organized to spread antislavery sentiment. In 1775 Quaker abolitionist Anthony Benezet organized the first antislavery society in the world. In 1787 it became the **Pennsylvania Society for Promoting the Abolition of Slavery,** and Benjamin Franklin became its president. Similar societies emerged in Delaware in 1788 and Maryland in 1789. By 1800, there were abolition societies in New Jersey, Connecticut, and Virginia. Organized antislavery sentiment also arose in the new slave states of Kentucky and Tennessee. But such societies never appeared in the Deep South.

●●●⊣Read the Document
John Wesley, "Thoughts upon Slavery" (1774)

From 1794 to 1832, antislavery societies cooperated within the loose framework of the **American Convention for Promoting the Abolition of Slavery and Improving the Condition of the African Race.** Only white people participated in these Quaker-dominated organizations, although members often cooperated with black leaders. As the northern states adopted abolition plans, the societies focused their attention on Delaware, Maryland, and Virginia. They aimed at gradual, compensated emancipation. They encouraged masters to free their slaves, attempted to protect free black people from reenslavement, and frequently advocated sending freed black people out of the country.

Experience with emancipation in the northern states encouraged the emphasis on gradual abolition. So did the reluctance of white abolitionists to challenge the property rights of masters. Abolitionists also feared that immediate emancipation might lead masters to abandon elderly slaves and assumed that African Americans would require long training before they could be free. All of this played into the hands of slaveholders who, like Thomas Jefferson, opposed slavery in the abstract but had no intention of freeing their own slaves.

The antislavery societies of the Upper South tended to be small and short lived. A Wilmington, Delaware, society established in 1788 peaked at 50 members and ceased to exist in 1800. The Maryland society organized in 1781 with six members grew to 250 in 1797 but disbanded in 1798. African Americans and their white friends, nevertheless, hoped that antislavery sentiment was advancing southward.

MANUMISSION AND SELF-PURCHASE

Another hopeful sign for African Americans was that after the Revolution most southern states liberalized their manumission laws. In general, masters could free individual slaves by deed or will. They no longer had to go to court or petition a state legislature to prove that an individual they desired to free had performed a "meritorious service." Virginia led the way in 1782 by repealing its long-standing ban on private manumissions. Delaware followed in 1787, as did Maryland in 1790, Kentucky in 1792, and the slaveholding territory of Missouri in 1804.

As a result, hundreds of slaveholders in the Upper South began freeing slaves. Religious sentiment and natural rights principles motivated many of these masters. Even though most of them opposed general emancipation, they considered the slave system immoral. Yet noble motives were not always most important. Masters often profited from self-purchase agreements they negotiated with their slaves. Slaves raised money by marketing farm produce or hiring themselves out for wages and then paid for their eventual freedom in installments. Masters liked the installments because they provided additional income in addition to what they otherwise received from a slave.

Masters also sometimes manumitted slaves who were no longer profitable investments. A master might

The title of this 1811 painting by German-American artist John Lewis Krimmel is *Pepper-Pot, a Scene in the Philadelphia Market*. Slavery still existed in Pennsylvania when Krimmel recorded this scene. It is likely, however, that the black woman who is selling pepper-pot (a type of stew) was free.

2001-196-1 Krimmel, John Lewis. Pepper Pot, A Scene in the Philadelphia Market.

Philadelphia Museum of Art: Gift of Mr. and Mrs. Edward B. Leisenring, Jr. in honor of

the 125th anniversary of the museum, 2001. Sumpter Priddy III, Inc.

be switching from tobacco to wheat or corn—crops that did not need a year-round workforce. Or a master might manumit older slaves whose best years as workers were behind them. Frequently, however, slaves—usually young men—presented their masters with the choice of either manumitting them after a term of years or having them escape immediately.

Self-purchase often left African Americans in precarious financial condition. Sometimes they used up their savings to buy their freedom. In other instances, they went into debt to their former masters, to white lawyers who acted as their agents, or to other white people who had loaned them money to cover their purchase price. After receiving money from a slave, some masters reneged on their agreement to manumit. Many of the freedom suits that became common in the Upper South during this period resulted from such unethical behavior.

THE EMERGENCE OF A FREE BLACK CLASS IN THE SOUTH

As a result of manumission, self-purchase, and freedom suits, the free black population of the Upper South blossomed. Maryland and Virginia had the largest free black populations. Between 1790 and 1820, the number of free African Americans in Maryland climbed from 8,043 to 39,730 and in Virginia from 12,766 to 36,889. By 1820 the Upper South (Delaware, Maryland, Virginia, District of Columbia, Kentucky, Missouri, North Carolina, and Tennessee) had a free black population of 114,070, compared with a northern free black population of 99,281. However, most of the Upper South's black population remained in slavery while the North's was on the way to general emancipation. In the North, 83.9 percent of African Americans were free in 1820, compared with 10.6 percent of those in the Upper South.

In the Deep South (South Carolina, Georgia, Florida, Louisiana, Alabama, and Mississippi), both the percentage and the absolute numbers of free black people remained much smaller. During the eighteenth century, neither South Carolina nor Georgia restricted the right of masters to manumit their slaves, but far fewer masters in these states exercised this right after the Revolution than was the case in the Chesapeake. Manumission declined in Louisiana following its annexation to the United States in 1804. Generally, masters in the Deep South freed only their illegitimate slave children, other favorites, or those unable to work. Only 20,153 free black people lived in the Deep South in 1820. In North Carolina, a transitional area between the Upper and Deep South, the state legislature made manumission more difficult after 1777. But many masters—especially those who were Quakers—nevertheless freed their slaves or let them live in quasi freedom.

The emergence of a free black class in the South, especially in the Deep South, produced social strata more similar to those in Latin America than was the case in the North. As in the Caribbean, South America, and portions of Mexico, there were dominant white people, free people of color, and slaves. In southern cities, such as Charleston, Savannah, and New Orleans, some free African Americans not only identified economically and culturally with their former masters but also acquired slaves.

Forces for Slavery

The forces for black freedom in the new republic rested on widespread African-American dissatisfaction with slavery, economic change, Christian morality, and revolutionary precepts. Most black northerners had achieved freedom by 1800, three-quarters were free by 1810, and by 1840 only 0.7 percent remained in slavery. Yet for the nation as a whole and for the mass of African Americans, the forces favoring slavery proved to be stronger. Abolition took place in the North, where slavery was weak. In the South, where it was strong, slavery thrived and expanded. Virginia, for example, had 293,427 slaves in 1790, and—despite manumissions and escapes—it had 425,153 in 1820. Even more significant, although Virginia continued to have the largest population of enslaved African Americans in the country, slave populations grew more quickly in North Carolina, South Carolina, and Georgia. Meanwhile, slavery expanded westward. When Tennessee was still a territory in 1790, it had 3,417 slaves. By 1820 the state of Tennessee had 80,107 slaves.

THE U.S. CONSTITUTION

The U.S. Constitution, which went into effect in 1789, became a major force in favor of the continued enslavement of African Americans. During the War for Independence, the Continental Congress had provided a weak central government for the United States, as each of the thirteen states retained control over its own internal affairs. The Articles of Confederation, which served as the American constitution from 1781 to 1789, formalized this system of divided sovereignty.

Watch the Video
Slavery and the Constitution

However, by the mid-1780s, wealthy and powerful men perceived that the Confederation Congress was too weak to protect their interests. Democratic movements in the states threatened property rights. Congress's inability to regulate commerce led to trade disputes among the states, and its inability to tax prevented it from maintaining an army and navy. Congress could not control the western territories, and, most frightening to the wealthy, it could not help states suppress popular uprisings, such as that led by Daniel Shays in western Massachusetts in 1786.

The fears Shays's Rebellion caused led directly to the Constitutional Convention in Philadelphia that in 1787 produced the Constitution under which the United States is still governed. The new constitution gave the central government power to regulate commerce, to tax, and to have its laws enforced in the states. But the convention could not create a more powerful central government without first making important concessions to southern slaveholders.

The delegates to the convention omitted the words *slave* and *slavery* from the Constitution. But they included clauses designed to maintain the enslavement of African Americans in the southern states. These clauses provided for continuing the Atlantic slave trade another 20 years, for national military aid in suppressing slave revolts, and for returning to their masters slaves who escaped to other states. The Constitution also enhanced representation for slaveholders in Congress and in the Electoral College that elected the president and vice president.

Humanitarian opposition to the Atlantic slave trade had mounted during the revolutionary era. Under pressure from black activists—such as Prince Hall of Boston—and Quakers, northern state legislatures during the 1780s forbade their citizens to engage in the slave trade. Rhode Island led the way in 1787. Massachusetts, Connecticut, and Pennsylvania followed in 1788. Economic change in the Upper South also prompted opposition to the trade. Virginia, for example, banned the importation of slaves from abroad nearly a decade before Rhode Island.

Yet convention delegates from South Carolina and Georgia maintained that their states had an acute labor shortage. They threatened that citizens of these states would not tolerate a central government that could stop them from importing slaves—at least not in the near future. Torn between these conflicting perspectives, the convention compromised by including a provision in the Constitution that prohibited Congress from abolishing the slave trade until 1808.

Read the Document
Congress Prohibits Importation of Slaves (1807)

During the 20 years before 1808, when Congress banned the trade, thousands of Africans were brought into the southern states. Between 1804 and 1808, for example, 40,000 entered through Charleston. Overall, more slaves entered the United States between 1787 and 1808 than during any other 20-year period in American history. Such huge numbers helped fuel the westward expansion of the slave system.

Other proslavery clauses of the Constitution aimed to counteract slave rebellion and escape. The Constitution gave Congress power to put down "insurrections" and "domestic violence." It also provided that persons "held to service or labour in one State, escaping into another . . . shall be delivered up on claim of the party to whom such service or labour may be due." This clause was the basis for the **Fugitive Slave Act of 1793,** which allowed masters or their agents to pursue slaves across state lines, capture them, and take them before a magistrate. There, on presentation of satisfactory evidence, masters could regain legal custody of the person they claimed. This act did not stop slaves from escaping from Virginia and Maryland to Pennsylvania. But it did extend the power of masters into the North, force the federal and northern state governments to uphold slavery, create personal tragedies for those who were recaptured, and encourage the kidnapping of free black northerners falsely claimed as escapees.

Finally, the Constitution strengthened the political power of slaveholders through the Three-Fifths Clause. This clause was also a compromise between northern and southern delegates. Southern delegates wanted slaves to be counted toward representation in the national government but not counted for purposes of taxation. Northern delegates wanted just the opposite. The **Three-Fifths Clause** provided that a slave be counted as three-fifths of a free person in determining a state's representation in the House of Representatives and in the Electoral College. Slaves would be counted similarly if and when Congress instituted a per capita tax.

This gave southern slaveholders increased representation on the basis of the number of slaves they owned—slaves who, of course, had no vote or representation. The South gained enormous political advantage from it. If not for the Three-Fifths Clause, for example, northern nonslaveholder John Adams would have been reelected president in 1800 instead of losing the presidency to southern slaveholder Thomas Jefferson. For many years, this clause contributed to the domination of the U.S. government by slaveholding southerners, even though the South's population steadily fell behind the North's. That Congress never instituted a per capita tax made this victory for slaveholders all the more remarkable.

Four other factors, however, were more important than constitutional provisions in fostering the continued enslavement of African Americans in the new republic: increased cultivation of cotton, the Louisiana Purchase, declining revolutionary fervor, and intensified white racism.

COTTON

The most obvious of the four developments was the increase in cotton production. By the late eighteenth century, Britain led the world in textile manufacturing. As mechanization made the spinning of cotton cloth more economical, Britain's demand for raw cotton increased dramatically. The United States led in filling that demand as a result of Eli Whitney's invention of the **cotton gin** in 1793. This simple machine provided an easy and quick way to remove the seeds from the type of cotton most commonly grown in the South.

British demand combined with the cotton gin encouraged cotton production in the United States to rise from 3,000 to 178,000 bales between 1790 and 1810 (each bale of cotton weighed 480 pounds). Cotton became by far the most lucrative U.S. export. Southern cotton production also encouraged the

Harpers Weekly **printed this "conjectural work" in 1869.** Although the clothing warn by the men and women shown reflects styles of a later era, the machine suggests how slaves used the gin Eli Whitney invented in 1793.

development of textile mills in New England, thereby creating a proslavery alliance between the "lords of the lash and the lords of the loom."

Cotton reinvigorated the slave-labor system, which spread rapidly across Georgia and later into Alabama, Mississippi, Louisiana, and eastern Texas. Cotton cultivation also existed in South Carolina, North Carolina, Arkansas, and parts of Virginia and Tennessee. To make matters worse for African Americans, the westward expansion of cotton production encouraged an internal slave trade. Masters in the old tobacco-growing regions of Maryland, Virginia, and other states began to support themselves by selling their slaves to the new cotton-growing regions (see Figure 5–1).

THE LOUISIANA PURCHASE AND AFRICAN AMERICANS IN THE LOWER MISSISSIPPI VALLEY

The Jefferson administration's purchase of Louisiana from France in 1803 accelerated the westward expansion of slavery and the **domestic slave trade.** The purchase nearly doubled the area of the United States. That slavery might extend over this vast region became an issue of great importance to African Americans.

◉ See the Map
The Louisiana Purchase

The purchase also brought under American sovereignty those black people, both free and slave, who lived in the portion of the territory that centered on the city of New Orleans. As Chapter 3 indicates, black life in the New Orleans area had developed a distinctive pattern under French rule from 1699 to 1763, under Spanish rule from 1763 to 1801, and again under French rule from

1801 to 1803. Although people of African descent were a majority of the area's population, they consisted of two distinct groups. First were the free people of color who called themselves Creoles. They were usually craftsmen and shopkeepers, spoke French, belonged to the Roman Catholic Church, and aspired to equal rights with other free inhabitants. Some of them bought and sold slaves. Their numbers had increased under Spanish rule as urban slaves purchased their freedom. This route to freedom became more difficult under American sovereignty, but, as a group, Louisiana's free people of color remained optimistically integrationist in outlook.

It was, nevertheless, the second black group that grew more rapidly. It consisted of slaves, most of whom had come directly from Africa and worked on Louisiana plantations. Spain had encouraged white Americans to settle in the lower Mississippi valley. The Americans, in turn, demanded more strictly enforced slave codes and the expansion of the external slave trade. At first the slaves produced tobacco and indigo, but by the 1790s sugar and cotton had emerged as the crops of the future. As demand for these crops grew, conditions for slaves in Louisiana became increasingly harsh, especially after the region became part of the United States. The slaves' rural location, their predominantly African culture, and, eventually, their Protestant religion cut them off from free people of color. In 1770 the region that later became the state of Louisiana had a slave population of 5,600. By 1810 it had 34,660, and by 1820 the slave population numbered 149,654. This tremendous growth, involving an extremely harsh form of slavery in a huge region, constituted a warning to all opponents of that institution. With the termination of the external slave trade, the notorious slave markets of New Orleans became the dreaded destination of thousands of African Americans "sold south" by their masters in the domestic slave trade.

CONSERVATISM AND RACISM

The waning of revolutionary humanitarianism and the rise of a more intense racism among white people were less tangible forces than cotton production and the Louisiana Purchase, but they were just as important in strengthening slavery. They also made life more difficult for free African Americans.

By the 1790s white Americans had begun a long retreat from the egalitarianism of the revolutionary era. In the North and the Chesapeake, most white people became less willing to challenge the prerogatives of slaveholders and more willing to accept slavery as suitable for African Americans. Most Marylanders and

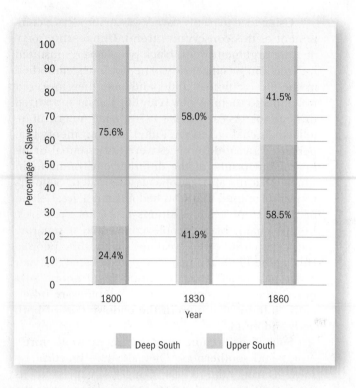

FIGURE 5–1 DISTRIBUTION OF THE SOUTHERN SLAVE POPULATION, 1800–1860

The demand for slaves in the cotton-growing Deep South produced a major shift in the distribution of the slave population.

Virginians came to think of emancipation as best left to the distant future. This outlook strengthened the slaveholders and their nonslaveholding white supporters in the Deep South who had never embraced the humanitarian precepts of the Enlightenment and Great Awakening.

Increasing proslavery sentiment among white Americans stemmed, in part, from revulsion against the radicalism of the French Revolution that had begun in 1789. Reports from France of bloody class and religious warfare, disruption of the social order, and redistribution of property led most Americans to value property rights—including rights to human property—and order above equal rights. In addition, as cotton production spread westward and the value of slaves soared, rationalist and evangelical criticism of human bondage withered. Antislavery sentiment in the Upper South that had flourished among slaveholders, nonslaveholders, Deists, Methodists, and Baptists became increasingly confined to African Americans and Quakers. During the early 1800s, manumissions began a long decline.

Using race to justify slavery was an important component of this conservative trend. Unlike white people, the argument went, black people were unsuited for freedom or citizenship. The doctrines embodied in the Declaration of Independence, therefore, did not apply to them. A new scientific racism supported this outlook. As early as the 1770s, some American intellectuals challenged the Enlightenment theory that perceived racial differences were not essential or inherent but results of the different environments in which Africans and Europeans originated. Scholars instead proposed that God had created a great chain of being from lesser creatures to higher creatures. In this chain, black people constituted a separate species as close to the great apes as to white people. During the 1780s Thomas Jefferson reflected this view when he argued that "scientific observation" supported the conclusion that black people were inherently "inferior to whites in the endowments of both body and mind."

Such views became common among white northerners and southerners. They also had practical results. During the 1790s Congress expressed its determination to exclude African Americans from the benefits of citizenship in "a white man's country." A 1790 law limited the granting of naturalized citizenship to "any alien, being a white person." In 1792 Congress limited enrollment in state militias to "each and every free, able-bodied white male citizen." These laws implied that African Americans had no place in the United States except as slaves. They suggested that the free black class was an anomaly and, in the opinion of most white people, a dangerous anomaly.

The Emergence of Free Black Communities

The competing forces of slavery and racism, on one hand, and freedom and opportunity, on the other, shaped the growth of African-American communities in the early American republic. A distinctive black culture had existed since the early colonial period. But enslavement had limited black community life. The advent of large free black populations in the North and Upper South after the Revolution allowed African Americans to establish autonomous and dynamic communities. They appeared in Philadelphia, Baltimore, Newport (Rhode Island), Richmond, Norfolk (Virginia), New York, and Boston. Although smaller and less autonomous, there were also free black communities in such Deep South cities as Charleston, Savannah, and New Orleans. As free black people in these cities acquired a modicum of wealth and education, they established institutions that have shaped African-American life ever since.

A combination of factors encouraged African Americans to form these distinctive institutions. First, as they emerged from slavery, they realized they would have inferior status in white-dominated organizations or not be allowed to participate in them at all. Second, black people valued the African heritage they had preserved over generations in slavery. They wanted institutions that would perpetuate their heritage.

The earliest black community institutions were mutual aid societies. Patterned on similar white organizations, these societies were like modern insurance companies and benevolent organizations. They provided for their members' medical and burial expenses and helped support widows and children. African Americans in Newport, Rhode Island, organized the first black mutual aid society in 1780. Seven years later, Richard Allen and Absalom Jones established the more famous Free African Society in Philadelphia.

Most early free black societies admitted only men, but similar organizations for women appeared during the 1790s. In 1793 Philadelphia's Female Benevolent Society of St. Thomas took over the welfare functions of the city's Free African Society. Other black women's organizations in Philadelphia during the early republic included the Benevolent Daughters, established in 1796 by Sarah Allen (the wife of the Rev. Richard Allen); the Daughters of Africa, established in 1812; the American Female Bond Benevolent Society, formed in 1817; and the Female Benezet Society, formed in 1818.

These ostensibly secular societies maintained a decidedly Christian moral character. They insisted that their members meet standards of middle-class propriety and, in effect, became self-improvement as well as mutual aid societies. Members had to pledge to refrain from fornication, adultery, drunkenness, and other "disreputable behavior." By the early 1800s, such societies also organized resistance to kidnappers who sought to recapture fugitive slaves or enslave free African Americans.

Because the societies provided real benefits and reflected black middle-class aspirations, they spread to every black urban community. More than one hundred such organizations existed in Philadelphia alone by 1830. Although these societies were more common in the North than in the South, Baltimore had about 30 of them by that same year, and Charleston, South Carolina, had at least two. One of them was the Brown Fellowship, founded in 1790, which admitted only black men with light complexions. The other was open to all free black men in Charleston.

Of particular importance were the black Freemasons because, unlike other free black organizations, the Masons united black men from several northern cities. Combining rationalism with secrecy and obscure ritual, Freemasonry was a major movement among European and American men during the late eighteenth and early nineteenth centuries. Opportunities for male bonding, wearing fancy regalia, and achieving prestige in a supposedly ancient hierarchy attracted both black and white men. As historians James Oliver Horton and Lois E. Horton suggest, black people drew special satisfaction from the European-based order's claims to have originated in ancient Egypt, which black people associated with their own African heritage.

The most famous black Mason of his time was Prince Hall, the Revolutionary War veteran and abolitionist.

This late eighteenth-century portrait of Prince Hall (1735?–1807) dressed as a gentleman places him among Masonic symbols. A former slave, a skilled craftsman and entrepreneur, an abolitionist, and an advocate of black education, Hall is best remembered as the founder of the African Lodge of North America, popularly known as the Prince Hall Masons.

During the 1770s he began in Boston what became known as the **Prince Hall Masons.** Hall's relationship to Masonry epitomizes the free black predicament in America.

In 1775 the local white Masonic lodge in Boston rejected Hall's application for membership because of his black ancestry. Therefore, Hall, who was a Patriot, organized African Lodge No. 1 on the basis of a limited license he secured from a British Masonic lodge associated with the British army that then occupied Boston. The irony of this situation compounded when, after the War for Independence, American Masonry refused to grant the African Lodge a full charter. Hall again had to turn to the British Masons, who approved his application in 1787. Under this British charter, Hall in 1791 organized the African Grand Lodge of North America (later renamed the Prince Hall Grand Lodge) and became its first grand master. Even before this he had begun authorizing black lodges in other cities, including Philadelphia and Providence, Rhode Island.

THE ORIGINS OF INDEPENDENT BLACK CHURCHES

Although black churches emerged at least a decade later than black benevolent associations, the churches quickly became the core of African-American communities. Not only did these churches attend to the spiritual needs of free black people and—in some southern cities—slaves, but their pastors also became the primary African-American leaders. Black church buildings housed schools, social organizations, and antislavery meetings.

During the late eighteenth century, as the egalitarian spirit of the Great Awakening waned among white Baptists, Methodists, and Episcopalians, separate but not independent black churches appeared in the South. The biracial churches the Awakening spawned had never embraced African Americans on an equal basis with white people, and as time passed, white people denied black people significant influence in church governance. White parishioners also subjected African Americans to segregated seating, communion services, Sunday schools, and cemeteries. In response African Americans formed separate black congregations, usually headed by black ministers but subordinate to white church hierarchies. The first such congregations appeared during the 1770s in South Carolina and Georgia.

In contrast to these subordinate churches, a truly independent black church emerged gradually in Philadelphia between the 1780s and the early 1800s. The movement for such a church began within the

VOICES

RICHARD ALLEN ON THE BREAK WITH ST. GEORGE'S CHURCH

It took an emotionally wrenching experience to convince Richard Allen, Absalom Jones, and other black Methodists that they must break their association with St. George's Church. Allen published the following account in 1831 as part of his autobiography, The Life Experiences and Gospel Labors of the Rt. Rev. Richard Allen. *Although many years had passed since the incident, Allen's account retains a strong emotional immediacy.*

A number of us usually attended St. George's church in Fourth street; and when the colored people began to get numerous in attending the church, they moved us from the seats we usually sat on, and placed us around the wall, and on Sabbath morning, we went to the church and the sexton stood at the door, and told us to go in the gallery. He told us to go, and we would see where to sit. We expected to take the seats over the ones we formerly occupied below, not knowing any better. We took those seats. Meeting had begun and they were nearly done singing, and just as we got to the seats, the elder said, "Let us pray." We had not been long upon our knees before I heard considerable scuffling and low talking. I raised my head up and saw one of the trustees, H M, having hold of the Rev. Absalom Jones, pulling him up off his knees, and saying, "You must get up—you must not kneel here." Mr. Jones replied, "Wait until prayer is over." Mr. H M said, "No, you must get up now, or I will call for aid and force you away." Mr. Jones said, "Wait until prayer is over, and I will get up and trouble you no more." With that he [H M] beckoned to one of the other trustees, Mr. L S to come to his assistance. He came, and went to William White to pull him up. By this time prayer was over, and we all went out of the church in a body, and they were no more plagued with us in the church. . . . We then hired a storeroom, and held worship by ourselves. Here we were pursued with threats of being disowned, and read publicly out of meeting if we did continue worship in the place we had hired; but we believed the Lord would be our friend. We got subscription papers out to raise money to build the house of the Lord.

▶ *What sparked the confrontation Allen describes?*
▶ *How did white leaders respond to the withdrawal of the church's black members?*

Source: *The Life Experiences and Gospel Labors of Rt. Rev. Richard Allen*, 1833.

city's white-controlled St. George's Methodist Church. Richard Allen and Absalom Jones, who led the movement, could rely for help on the Free African Society they established in 1787.

◆●━ Read the Document
Preamble of the Free African Society (1787)

Allen in 1780 and Jones in 1783 had purchased their freedom. In 1786 Allen, a fervent Methodist since the 1770s, received permission from St. George's white leadership to use the church in the evenings to preach to black people. Jones joined Allen's congregation. Soon they and other black members of St. George's chafed under policies they considered un-Christian and insulting. But during the 1780s, Allen's and Jones's faith that Methodist egalitarianism would prevail over discrimination undermined their efforts to create a separate black Methodist church.

The break finally came in 1792 when St. George's white leaders grievously insulted the church's black members. An attempt by white trustees to prevent Jones from praying in what the trustees considered the white section of the church led black members to walk out. "We all went out of the church in a body," recalled Allen, "and they were no more plagued with us in the church."

St. George's white leaders fought hard and long to control the expanding and economically valuable black congregation. Yet other white Philadelphians, led by abolitionist Benjamin Rush, applauded the concept of an independent "African church." Rush and other sympathetic white people contributed to the

Raphaelle Peale, the son of famous Philadelphia portraitist Charles Wilson Peale, completed this oil portrait of the Reverend Absalom Jones (1746–1818) in 1810. Reverend Jones is shown in his ecclesiastical robes holding a Bible in his hand.

new church's building fund. When construction began in 1793, Rush and at least one hundred other white people joined with African Americans at a banquet to celebrate the occasion.

However, the black congregation soon split. When the majority determined that the new church would be Episcopalian rather than Methodist, Allen and a few others refused to join. The result was *two* black churches in Philadelphia. St. Thomas's Episcopal Church, with Jones as priest, opened in July 1794 as an African-American congregation within the white-led national Episcopal Church. Then Allen's Mother Bethel congregation became the first truly independent black church. The white leaders of St. George's tried to control Mother Bethel until 1816. That year Mother Bethel became the birthplace of the **African Methodist Episcopal (AME) Church.** Allen became the first bishop of this organization, which quickly spread to other cities in the North and the South.

The more significant among the other AME congregations were Daniel Coker's in Baltimore, the AME Zion in New York, and those in Wilmington, Delaware; Salem, New Jersey; and Attleboro, Pennsylvania. Other independent black churches formed at this time out of similar conflicts with white-led congregations. Among them were the African Baptist Church established in Boston in 1805 and led by Thomas Paul from 1806 to 1808, the Presbyterian Evangelical Society founded in 1811 by John Gloucester, the Abyssinian Baptist Church organized in New York City in 1808 by Paul, and the African Presbyterian Church established in Philadelphia by Samuel E. Cornish in 1822.

THE FIRST BLACK SCHOOLS

Schools for African-American children, slave and free, date to the early 1700s. In both North and South, white clergy, including the Massachusetts Congregationalist Cotton Mather, ran the schools. So did Quakers, early abolition societies, and missionaries acting for the Anglican Society for the Propagation of the Gospel in Foreign Parts. But the first schools established by African Americans to instruct African-American children arose after the Revolution. The new black mutual aid societies and churches created and sustained them.

Schools for black people organized or taught by white people continued to flourish. But black people also founded their own schools because local white authorities regularly refused either to admit black children to public schools or to maintain adequate separate black schools. For example, in 1796, when Prince Hall failed to convince Boston's city council to provide a school for black students, he had the children taught in his home and that of his son Primus. By 1806 Hall's school was meeting in the basement of the new African Meeting House, which housed Thomas Paul's African Baptist Church.

Hall was not the first to take such action. As early as 1790, Charleston's Brown Fellowship operated a school for its members' children. Free black people in Baltimore supported schools during the same decade, and during the early 1800s, similar schools opened in Washington, D.C. Such schools frequently employed white teachers. Not until Philadelphia's Mother Bethel Church established the Augustine School in 1818 did

This drawing portrays Philadelphia's Bethel African Methodist Episcopal Church as it appeared in 1829. It had been built in 1793 under the direction of Richard Allen, the first bishop of the AME denomination, and had been "rebuilt" in 1803. The Library Company of Philadelphia

This lithograph, c. 1887, portrays the New York African Free School, No. 2. The New York Manumission Society established the original school in 1787, at 137 Mulberry Street in New York City. Men who later became prominent black abolitionists, such as Henry Highland Garnet and James McCune Smith, attended the school during the 1820s.

VOICES

ABSALOM JONES PETITIONS CONGRESS ON BEHALF OF FUGITIVES FACING REENSLAVEMENT

Absalom Jones wrote his petition to Congress on behalf of four black men who had been manumitted in North Carolina. Because they were in danger of being reenslaved, they had taken refuge in Philadelphia. The men, under whose names the petition appears in the Annals of Congress, *were Jupiter Nicholson, Jacob Nicholson, Joe Albert, and Thomas Pritchet. Jones provided brief accounts of their troubles. Here we include only the important general principles that Jones invoked. Southern representatives argued that accepting a petition from alleged slaves would set a dangerous precedent, and Congress refused to accept the petition.*

To the President, Senate, and House of Representatives,

The Petition and Representation of the under-named Freemen, respectfully showeth:

That, being of African descent, the late inhabitants and natives of North Carolina, to you only, under God, can we apply with any hope of effect, for redress of our grievances, having been compelled to leave the State wherein we had a right of residence, as freemen liberated under the hand and seal of humane and conscientious masters, the validity of which act of justice in restoring us to our native right of freedom, was confirmed by judgment of the Superior Court of North Carolina . . . yet, not long after this decision, a law of that State was enacted, under which men of cruel disposition, and void of just principle, received countenance and authority in violently seizing, imprisoning, and selling into slavery, such as had been so emancipated; whereby we were reduced to the necessity of separating from some of our nearest and most tender connections, and seeking refuge in such parts of the Union where more regard is paid to the public declaration in favor of liberty and the common right of man, several hundreds, under our circumstances, having, in consequence of the said law, been hunted day and night, like beasts of the forest, by armed men with dogs, and made a prey of as free and lawful plunder . . .

We beseech your impartial attention to our hard condition, not only with respect to our personal sufferings, as freemen, but as a class of that people who, distinguished by color, are therefore with a degrading partiality, considered by many, even of those in eminent stations, as unentitled to that public justice and protection which is the great object of Government. . . .

If, notwithstanding all that has been publicly avowed as essential principles respecting the extent of human right to freedom; notwithstanding we have had that right restored to us,

a school for black children exist that was entirely administered and taught by African Americans.

These schools faced great difficulties. Many black families could not afford the fees, but rather than turn children away, the schools strained their meager resources by taking charity cases. Some black parents also believed education was pointless when African Americans often could not get skilled jobs. White people feared competition from skilled black workers, believed black schools attracted undesirable populations, and—particularly in the South—feared that educated free African Americans would encourage slaves to revolt.

so far as was in the power of those by whom we were held as slaves, we cannot claim the privilege of representation in your councils, yet we trust we may address you as fellow-men, who, under God, the sovereign Ruler of the Universe, are intrusted with the distribution of justice, for the terror of evil-doers, the encouragement of protection of the innocent, not doubting that you are men of liberal minds, susceptible of benevolent feelings and clear conception of rectitude to a catholic extent, who can admit that black people . . . have natural affections, social and domestic attachments and sensibilities; and that, therefore, we may hope for a share in your sympathetic attention while we represent that the unconstitutional bondage in which multitudes of our fellows in complexion are held, is to us a subject sorrowfully affecting; for we cannot conceive their condition (more especially those who have been emancipated and tasted the sweets of liberty, and again reduced to slavery by kidnappers and man-stealers) to be less afflicting or deplorable than the situation of citizens of the United States, captured and enslaved through the unrighteous policy prevalent in Algiers . . . may we not be allowed to consider this stretch of power, morally and politically, a Governmental defect, if not a direct violation of the declared fundamental principles of the Constitution; and finally, is not some remedy for an evil of such magnitude highly worthy of the deep inquiry and unfeigned zeal of the supreme Legislative body of a free and enlightened people?

▶ *On what principles does Jones believe the U.S. government is bound to act?*

▶ *What does Jones's petition indicate concerning the legal status of African Americans?*

Source: *Annals of Congress*, 4 Cong., 2 sess. (January 23, 1797), 2015–18.

Threats of violence against black schools and efforts to suppress them were common. The case of Christopher McPherson exemplifies these dangers. McPherson, a free African American, established a night school for black men at Richmond, Virginia, in 1811 and hired a white teacher. All went well until McPherson advertised the school in a local newspaper. In response, white residents forced the teacher to leave the city, and local authorities had McPherson committed to the state lunatic asylum. Nevertheless, similar schools continued to operate in the North and Upper South, producing a growing class of literate African Americans.

Black Leaders and Choices

By the 1790s an educated black elite existed in the North and the Chesapeake. It provided leadership for African Americans in religion, economic advancement, and racial politics. Experience had driven members of this elite to a contradictory perception of themselves and of America. On the one hand, they were acculturated, patriotic Americans who had achieved some personal well-being and security. On the other hand, they knew that American society had not lived up to its revolutionary principles. They lamented the continued enslavement of the mass of African Americans, and they had misgivings about the future.

Prominent among these leaders were members of the clergy. Two of the most important of them were Richard Allen and Absalom Jones. Besides organizing his church, Allen opened a school in Philadelphia for black children, wrote against slavery and racial prejudice, and made his home a refuge for fugitive slaves. A year before his death in 1831, Allen presided over the first national black convention.

Jones, too, was an early abolitionist. In 1797 his concern for fugitives facing reenslavement led him to become the first African American to petition Congress. His petition anticipated later abolitionists in suggesting that slavery violated the spirit of the U.S. Constitution and that Congress could abolish it.

Other influential black ministers of the late eighteenth and early nineteenth centuries were Jupiter Hammon of Long Island, Daniel Coker of Baltimore, John Chavis of Virginia, and Lemuel Haynes of New England. Hammon, who is quoted at the beginning of this chapter, became a well-known poet. Coker, who was of mixed race, conducted a school, cofounded the AME Church, and advocated black migration to Africa. Chavis also combined preaching and teaching. Born free, he served on the Patriot side in the War for Independence and entered the College of New Jersey (Princeton) in 1792. Thereafter he became a Presbyterian missionary among African Americans in Virginia, Maryland, and North Carolina and gained a wide reputation as a biblical scholar. Haynes was perhaps even better known for his intellectual accomplishments. The son of a white mother and black father, Haynes served with the Minutemen and Continental Army, spoke against slavery, and in 1780 became the first ordained black Congregationalist minister, serving as pastor to white congregations.

Vying with clergy for influence were African-American entrepreneurs. Prince Hall, for example, owned successful leather dressing and catering businesses in Boston, and Peter Williams, principal founder of New York's AME Zion Church, was a prosperous tobacco merchant. Another prominent black businessman was James Forten of Philadelphia, described as "probably the most noteworthy free African-American entrepreneur in the early nineteenth century." Born to free parents in 1766, Forten was a Patriot during the War for Independence, learned the craft of sail making, and became the owner of his own business in 1798. For the rest of his life, he advocated equal rights and abolition.

American patriotism, religious conviction, organizational skill, intellectual inquisitiveness, and antislavery activism delineate the lives of most free black leaders in this era. Yet these leaders often were torn in their perceptions of what was best for African Americans. Hammon and Chavis accommodated slavery and racial oppression. They condemned slavery and lauded human liberty, but they were not activists. They maintained that God would eventually end injustice. As late as 1836, Chavis, who lived in the South, wrote, "Slavery is a national evil no one doubts, but what is to be done? . . . All that can be done, is to make the best of a bad bargain. . . . I am clearly of the opinion that immediate emancipation would be to entail the greatest earthly curse upon my brethren according to the flesh."

Allen, Jones, Hall, and Forten were more optimistic than Hammon and Chavis about the ability of African Americans to mold their destiny in the United States. Although they each expressed misgivings, they believed that, despite setbacks, the egalitarian principles of the American Revolution would prevail if black people insisted on liberty. Forten never despaired that African Americans would be integrated into the larger American society on the basis of their individual talent and enterprise. Although he was often frustrated, Hall pursued for four decades a strategy based on the assumption that white authority would reward black protest and patriotism. In 1786, when Daniel Shays led his revolt of white farmers in western Massachusetts, Hall offered to raise 700 black volunteers to help defeat the

PROFILE: James Forten

James Forten was one of the few black leaders of the early American republic to live well beyond that era. His long career as a determined opponent of slavery linked the time of Prince Hall and Richard Allen to that of the militant abolitionists William Lloyd Garrison and Frederick Douglass (see Chapters 8 and 9). From the 1790s until his death in 1842, Forten used his wealth and organizational talents to build a cohesive black community in Philadelphia. But he also struggled to create a broader American community based on merit rather than on racial privilege.

Forten was born in Philadelphia in 1766. Family tradition held that one of his great grandfathers was an African who had been brought to Delaware in the late 1600s. His paternal grandfather was one of the first Pennsylvania slaves to purchase his freedom.

As a child, Forten learned to read and write at a school run by Quaker abolitionist Anthony Benezet and acquired Benezet's broad humanistic philosophy. In 1781 Forten volunteered to serve as a powder boy with a cannon crew on board the American privateer *Royal Louis*. He proved himself a brave sailor in battle. He was also deeply patriotic. When taken prisoner and offered special treatment by the son of a British officer, Forten declared, "No, NO! I am here a prisoner for the liberties of my country; *I never, NEVER, shall prove a traitor to her interests.*" As a result of his defiance, Forten spent seven months on a rotting prison ship in New York harbor.

After his release Forten walked back to Philadelphia and became an apprentice sail maker. He became foreman in 1786 and bought the business in 1798. By 1807 he employed an interracial workforce of 30 members and by 1832 had acquired a fortune of about $100,000—a large sum at the time.

Throughout the 1780s and most of the 1790s, Forten stood aloof from Philadelphia's developing black community. He did not join the Free African Society or help establish separate black churches. He only emerged as an active black leader in 1797 when he joined Richard Allen and Absalom Jones in establishing the African Masonic Lodge of Pennsylvania, which Prince Hall came to Philadelphia to install. Forten then joined 80 other Philadelphia African Americans to petition Congress to repeal the Fugitive Slave Law of 1793.

By 1817 Forten had become a major opponent of black migration to Africa. Although he had previously endorsed some colonization schemes, he had come to believe such efforts were racist because they assumed that black people were not suited for American citizenship. Rather than commit resources to sending African Americans to other parts of the world, he was determined to improve their standing in the United States. In 1809 he joined Allen and Jones in creating a self-improvement organization, the Society for the Suppression of Vice and Immorality. By 1830 he hoped to use the newly organized Black National Convention movement to train young black men for skilled trades.

Forten also became an important influence on the white abolitionist leader William Lloyd Garrison. Forten welcomed Garrison to his home, introduced him to other black leaders, and helped finance his antislavery newspaper, the *Liberator*. In 1833 Forten joined Garrison, Arthur Tappan, Lewis Tappan, and other white and black abolitionists in organizing the American Antislavery Society, pledged to the peaceful immediate abolition of slavery without colonization of the former slaves and without compensation to slaveholders. Increasingly radical during his remaining years, Forten advocated an end to war, favored equal rights for women, and resisted the enforcement of the Fugitive Slave Law. He also helped establish the American Moral Reform Society. He demonstrated his commitment to women's rights in the way he raised his daughters, Sarah, Margaretta, and Harriet, who carried on his activism.

James Forten, by an unknown artist.

insurgency. Allen and Jones put more emphasis on separate black institutions than did Forten or Hall. Yet they were just as willing to organize, protest, and petition to establish the rights of black people as American citizens.

MIGRATION

African Americans, however, had another alternative: migration from the United States to establish their own society free from white prejudices. In 1787 British philanthropists, including Olaudah Equiano, had established Freetown in Sierra Leone on the West African coast as a refuge for former slaves. As we mentioned in Chapter 4, some African Americans who had been Loyalists during the American Revolution settled there. Other black and white Americans proposed that free black people should settle western North America or in the Caribbean islands. There were great practical obstacles to mass black migration to each of these regions. Migration was expensive, was difficult to organize, and involved long, often fruitless negotiations with foreign governments. But no black leader during the early national period was immune to the appeal of such proposals.

Aware of Freetown, Hall in 1787 petitioned the Massachusetts legislature to support efforts by black Bostonians to establish a colony in Africa. Although he recognized black progress in Massachusetts, Hall maintained that he and others found themselves "in many respects, in very disagreeable and disadvantageous circumstances; most of which must attend us so long as we and our children live in America." By the mid-1810s, a few influential white Americans had also decided that there was no place in the United States for free African Americans. In 1816 they organized the **American Colonization Society.** Under its auspices, Coker in 1820 led the first party of 86 African Americans to the new colony of Liberia on the West African coast.

The major black advocate of migration to Africa during this period, however, was Paul Cuffe, the son of an Ashantee father and Wampanoag Indian mother. He became a prosperous New England sea captain and, by the early 1800s, cooperated with British humanitarians and entrepreneurs to promote migration. He saw African-American colonization in West Africa as a way to end the Atlantic slave trade, spread Christianity, create a refuge for free black people, and make profits. Before his death in 1817, Cuffe had influenced not only Coker but also—at least temporarily—Forten, Allen, and Jones to consider colonization as a viable alternative for African Americans.

SLAVE UPRISINGS

While, after the Revolution, black northerners grew increasingly aware of the limits to their freedom, black southerners faced perpetual slavery. As cotton production expanded westward, as new slave states entered the Union, and as masters in such border slave states as Maryland and Virginia turned away from the revolutionary commitment to gradual emancipation, slaves faced several choices.

Some lowered their expectations and loyally served their masters. Most continued patterns of day-to-day resistance. Many escaped. A few risked their lives to join forceful revolutionary movements to destroy slavery. When just several hundred out of hundreds of thousands of slaves rallied behind Gabriel in 1800 near Richmond or behind Charles Deslondes in 1811 near New Orleans, they frightened white southerners. But they raised hopes for freedom among countless African Americans.

The egalitarian principles of the American and French revolutions influenced Gabriel and Deslondes. Unlike earlier slave rebels, they acted not to revenge personal grievances or to establish maroon communities but to destroy slavery because it denied natural human rights to its victims. The American Declaration of Independence and the legend of Haiti's Toussaint Louverture provided the intellectual foundations for their efforts. Louverture, against great odds, had led the enslaved black people of the French sugar colony of Saint Domingue—modern Haiti—to freedom and independence. This bitter and bloody struggle lasted from 1791 to 1804. Many white planters fled the island with their slaves to take refuge in Cuba, Jamaica, South Carolina, Virginia, and, somewhat later, Louisiana. The Haitian slaves carried the spirit of revolution with them to their new homes.

During the early 1790s, black unrest and rumors of revolt mounted in Virginia. The state militia arrested suspected plotters, who got off with whippings. In this revolutionary atmosphere, Gabriel, the human property of Thomas Prosser Sr., prepared to lead a massive slave insurrection. Gabriel was an acculturated and literate blacksmith well aware of the rationalist and revolutionary currents of his time. He was also a large and powerful man with a violent temper. In 1799 a local court convicted him of "'biting off a considerable part of [the] left Ear' of a white neighbor."

While the ideology of the American Revolution shaped Gabriel's actions, he also perceived that white people were politically divided and distracted by an

Toussaint Louverture (1744–1803) led the black rebellion in the French colony of St. Domingue on the Caribbean island of Hispaniola that led to the creation of the independent black republic of Haiti in 1804. Louverture became an inspiration for black rebels in the United States.

undeclared naval war with France. He enjoyed secret support from a few white people and hoped poor white people would rally to his cause as he and his associates planned to kill those who supported slavery and take control of central Virginia.

But on August 30, 1800—the day set for the uprising—two slaves revealed the plan to white authorities while a tremendous thunderstorm prevented Gabriel's followers from assaulting Richmond. Then Virginia governor—and future U.S. president—James Monroe quickly had suspects arrested. Gabriel, who relied on white allies to get to Norfolk, was among the last captured. In October he and 26 others, convicted of "conspiracy and insurrection," were hanged. By demonstrating that slaves could organize for large-scale rebellion, they left a legacy of fear among slaveholders and hope for liberation among southern African Americans.

The far less famous Louisiana Rebellion took place under similar circumstances. By the early

1800s, refugees from Haiti had settled with their slaves in what was then known as Orleans Territory. As they arrived, rumors of slave insurrection spread across the territory. The rumors became reality on January 8, 1811, when Deslondes, a Haitian native and slave driver on a plantation north of New Orleans, initiated a massive revolt in cooperation with maroons.

Although no record of Deslondes's rhetoric survives and his goals may have been less ideologically coherent than Gabriel's, he organized a force of at least 180 men and women. They marched south along the Mississippi River toward New Orleans, with leaders on horseback and with flags and drums but few guns. The revolutionaries plundered and burned plantations but killed only two white people and one recalcitrant slave. On January 10 a force of about 700 territorial militia, slaveholding vigilantes, and U.S. troops overwhelmed them. The "battle" was a massacre. Well-armed white men slaughtered 66 rebels and captured 30. They tried the captives without benefit of counsel, found 22 (including Deslondes) guilty of rebellion, and shot them. Then they cut off the hands of the executed men and displayed them on pikes to warn other African Americans of the consequences of revolt.

THE WHITE SOUTHERN REACTION

Although Deslondes's uprising was one of the few major slave revolts in American history, Gabriel's conspiracy and events in Haiti left the more significant legacy. For generations, enslaved African Americans regarded Louverture as a black George Washington and recalled Gabriel's revolutionary message. The networks among slaves that Gabriel established survived his death, and, as the domestic slave trade carried black Virginians southwestward, they carried his promise of liberation with them. White southerners responded to these black revolutionary currents by rejecting the egalitarian values of the Enlightenment. Because white southerners feared race war and believed emancipation would encourage African Americans to begin such a war, most of them determined to make black bondage stronger, not weaker.

Beginning with South Carolina in December 1800, southern states outlawed assemblies of slaves, placed curfews on slaves and free black people, and made manumissions more difficult. The old colonial practice of white men on horseback patrolling slave quarters revived. Assuming that revolutionaries like Gabriel received encouragement from northern white abolitionists, white southerners became suspicious of such outsiders as Yankee peddlers, evangelicals, and foreigners. Assuming that local free African Americans were even more involved in slave uprisings, some white southerners advocated forcing them to leave. This brought about an odd alliance between white advocates of expulsion and black advocates of emigration to Africa.

The War of 1812

Many of the themes developed in this chapter—African-American patriotism, opportunities for freedom, migration sentiment, and influences pushing slaves toward revolutionary action—are reflected in the black experience during the U.S. war with Britain that began in 1812 and lasted until early 1815. The roots of this conflict lay in a massive military and economic struggle between Britain and France for mastery over the Atlantic world. The struggle lasted from 1793, during the French Revolution, to the defeat of Napoleon Bonaparte by a British-led coalition in 1815.

British military support for American Indian resistance in the Old Northwest, an American desire to annex Canada, and especially Britain's interference with American ships trading with Europe drew the United States into the war. Although the United States won important victories, it failed to achieve its major objective—the conquest of Canada—and the war ended in a draw. Yet many Americans regarded the war as a second struggle for independence, and, as during the American Revolution, black military service and white fear of slave revolt played important roles (see Map 5-2).

By 1812 prejudice and fear of revolt had nearly nullified positive white memories of black Patriot soldiers during the Revolution. The Militia Act of 1792 eliminated armed black participation in all state militias except that of North Carolina. In 1798 the secretary of the navy ended black service on American warships. Because of the news from Haiti and because of Gabriel's conspiracy, most white southerners joined John Randolph of Virginia in regarding African Americans as "an internal foe." Therefore, when the war with Britain began, the southern states refused to enlist black men for fear they would use their guns to

MAP 5-2   THE WAR OF 1812

As during the War for Independence, African Americans fought on both sides during the War of 1812. Some joined the British army that burned Washington, D.C. Others helped the United States win control of Lake Erie in 1813 and stop the British invasion of Louisiana at the Battle of New Orleans in 1815.

▶ *What was at stake for African Americans in the War of 1812?*

◉ See the Map *Explore this map at www.myhistorylab.com*

aid slave revolts. Meanwhile, a lack of enthusiasm for the war, combined with the absence of a British threat to their part of the country, kept northern states from mobilizing black troops in 1812 and 1813.

Southern fears of slave revolt mounted during the spring of 1813 when the British invaded the Chesapeake. As they had during the Revolution, British generals offered slaves freedom in Canada or the British West Indies in return for help. In response, African Americans joined the British army that burned Washington, D.C., in 1814 and attacked Baltimore.

The threat this British army posed to Philadelphia and New York led to the first active black involvement in

21 "We Have Met the Enemy and They Are Ours"

Perry's Famous Victory on Lake Erie in War of 1812, Erie, Pa.   99824

The Battle of Put-in Bay, fought on Lake Erie in September 1813, was a notable American victory during the War of 1812. This postcard suggests the prevalence of black sailors among American commandant Oliver Hazard Perry's crew.

the war on the American side. The New York state legislature authorized two black regiments, offered freedom to slaves who enlisted, and promised compensation to their masters. Meanwhile, African Americans in Philadelphia and New York City volunteered to help build fortifications. In Philadelphia, James Forten, Richard Allen, and Absalom Jones patriotically raised a "Black Brigade," which never saw action because the British halted when they failed to capture Baltimore.

African-American men did fight, however, at two of the war's most important battles. During the naval engagement at Put-in-Bay on Lake Erie in September 1813, which secured control of the Great Lakes for the United States, one-quarter of Commandant Oliver Hazard Perry's 400 sailors were black. Although Perry had been prejudiced against using these men, he praised their valor. At the Battle of New Orleans—fought in January 1815, about a month after a peace treaty had been negotiated but not ratified—African Americans also fought bravely. Yet white memories of Deslondes's uprising almost prevented them from being allowed to fight on the American side. Many white people feared that the local free black militia, which dated back to the Spanish occupation of Louisiana from 1763 to 1801, would make common cause with slaves and the British

rather than take the American side. In defiance of such fears, General Andrew Jackson included the black militia in his force defending New Orleans and offered them equal pay and benefits. At least 600 free black men fought on the American side at the Battle of New Orleans, and Jackson lived up to his promise of equal treatment. It was a choice, he later informed President James Madison, between having the free African Americans "in our ranks or . . . in the ranks of the enemy."

The Missouri Compromise

After 1815, as the United States emerged from a difficult war, sectional issues between the North and South, which constitutional compromises and the political climate had pushed into the background, revived. The nation's first political parties—the Federalist and the Republican—had failed to confront slavery as a national issue. The northern wing of the modernizing Federalist Party had abolitionist tendencies. But during the 1790s when they controlled the national government, the Federalists did not raise the slavery issue. Then the victory of the state-rights-oriented Republican Party in 1800 fatally weakened the Federalists as a

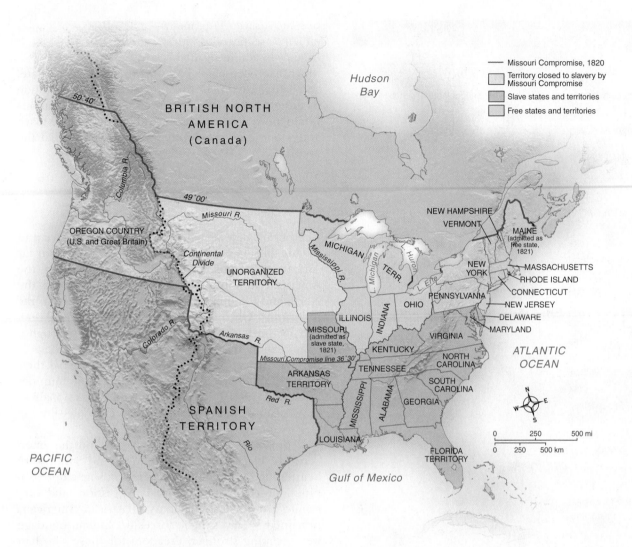

MAP 5-3   THE MISSOURI COMPROMISE OF 1820

Under the Missouri Compromise, Missouri entered the Union as a slave state, Maine entered as a free state, and Congress banned slavery in the huge unorganized portion of the old Louisiana Territory north of the 36° 30′ line of latitude.

▶ *Which section of the United States did the Missouri Compromise favor?*

⊙ See the Map *Explore this map at* www.myhistorylab.com

national organization and brought a series of proslavery administrations to power in Washington.

It took innovations in transportation and production that began during the 1810s, as well as the rapid disappearance of slavery in the northern states, to transform the North into a region consciously at odds with the South's traditional culture and slave-labor economy. The first major expression of intensifying sectional differences over slavery and its expansion came in 1819 when the slaveholding Missouri Territory, which had been carved out of the Louisiana Territory, applied for admission to the Union as a slave state. Northerners expressed deep reservations about the creation of a new slave state. Many of them feared

it would destroy the political balance between the sections and encourage the expansion of slavery elsewhere. The aged Thomas Jefferson called this negative northern reaction a "fire bell in the night." It awakened slaveholders to an era in which the slavery issue could no longer be excluded from national politics.

African Americans also appreciated the significance of the Missouri crisis. Black residents of Washington, D.C., crowded into the U.S. Senate gallery as that body debated the issue. Finally, Henry Clay of Kentucky, the slaveholding Speaker of the House of Representatives, directed an effort that produced in 1820 a compromise that temporarily quieted discord. This Missouri Compromise (see Map 5–3) permitted Missouri to

AFRICAN-AMERICAN EVENTS	NATIONAL EVENTS
• **1775** •	
1775 First antislavery society formed	**1776** Declaration of Independence
1777 Vermont bans slavery	**1777** Battle of Saratoga
• **1780** •	
1780 Pennsylvania begins gradual emancipation	**1781** Articles of Confederation ratified
1781 Elizabeth Freeman begins her legal suit for freedom	**1783** Great Britain recognizes independence of the United States
1782 Virginia repeals its ban on manumission	
1783 Massachusetts bans slavery and black men gain the right to vote there	
1784 Connecticut and Rhode Island begin gradual abolition	
• **1785** •	
1785 New Jersey and New York defeat gradual emancipation	**1786** Shays's Rebellion
1787 Northwest Ordinance bans slavery in the territory north of the Ohio River	**1787** Constitutional Convention
	1789 Constitution ratified; George Washington becomes president
• **1790** •	
1793 Congress passes Fugitive Slave Law	
1794 Mother Bethel Church established in Philadelphia	
New York adopts gradual abolition plan	

become a slave state; maintained a sectional political balance by admitting Maine,

Read the **Document**
Missouri Admitted to Statehood, Slavery at Issue (1820)

which had been part of Massachusetts, as a free state; and banned slavery north of the 36° 30′ line of latitude in the old Louisiana Territory. Yet sectional relations would never be the same, and a new era of black and white antislavery militancy soon confronted the South.

CONCLUSION

The period between the War for Independence and the Missouri Compromise was a time of transition for African Americans. On one hand, the legacy of the American Revolution brought emancipation in the North and a promise of equal opportunity with white Americans. On the other hand, by the 1790s slavery and racism had begun to grow stronger. Through a combination of antiblack prejudice among white people and African Americans' desire to preserve their own cultural traditions, black urban communities arose in the North, Upper South, and, occasionally—in Charleston and Savannah, for example—in the Deep South.

Spreading freedom in the North and the emergence of black communities North and South were heartening developments. There were new opportunities for education, spiritual expression, and economic growth. But the mass of African Americans remained in slavery. The forces for human bondage were growing stronger. Freedom for those who had gained it in the Upper South and North was marginal and precarious.

Gabriel's conspiracy in Virginia and Deslondes's rebellion in Louisiana indicated that revolutionary principles persisted among black southerners. But these rebellions and British recruitment of slaves during the War of 1812 convinced most white southerners that black bondage had to be permanent. Therefore, African Americans looked to the future with mixed emotions. A few determined that the only hope for real freedom lay in migration from the United States.

RECOMMENDED READING

Ira Berlin. *Slaves without Masters: The Free Negro in the Antebellum South.* New York: New Press, 1974. The early chapters of this classic study indicate the special difficulties the first large generation of free black southerners faced.

Douglas R. Egerton. *Gabriel's Rebellion: The Virginia Slave Conspiracies of 1800 and 1802.* Chapel Hill: University of North Carolina Press, 1993. This most recent account of Gabriel's conspiracy emphasizes both the revolutionary context within which he acted and his legacy.

Philip S. Foner. *History of Black Americans, from Africa to the Emergence of the Cotton Kingdom.* Westport, CT: Greenwood, 1975. This is the first volume of a comprehensive three-volume history of African Americans. It is detailed and informative about black life between 1783 and 1820.

Jaees Oliver Horton and Lois E. Horton. *In Hope of Liberty: Culture, Community, and Protest among Northern Free Blacks, 1700–1860.* New York: Oxford University Press, 1997. This is a well-written interpretation of the northern free black community and its origins.

Sidney Kaplan and Emma Nogrady Kaplan. *The Black Presence in the Era of the American Revolution,* Rev. ed. Amherst: University of Massachusetts Press, 1989. This delightfully written book provides informative accounts of black leaders who lived during the early American republic.

Gary B. Nash. *Forging Freedom: The Formation of Philadelphia's Black Community, 1720–1840.* Cambridge, MA: Harvard University Press, 1988. This path breaking study of a black community analyzes the origins of separate black institutions.

Donald R. Wright. *African Americans in the Early Republic, 1789–1831.* Arlington Heights, IL: Harlan Davidson, 1993. This is a brief but comprehensive account that reflects recent interpretations.

ADDITIONAL BIBLIOGRAPHY

EMANCIPATION IN THE NORTH

James D. Essig. *The Bonds of Wickedness: American Evangelicals against Slavery, 1770–1808.* Philadelphia: Temple University Press, 1982.

David N. Gellman. *Emancipating New York: The Politics of Slavery and Freedom, 1777–1827.* Baton Rouge: Louisiana State University Press, 2006.

Joanne Pope Melish. *Disowning Slavery: Gradual Emancipation and "Race" in New England, 1780–1860.* Ithaca, NY: Cornell University Press, 1998.

Gary B. Nash and Jean R. Soderlund. *Freedom by Degrees: Emancipation in Pennsylvania and Its Aftermath.* New York: Oxford University Press, 1991.

Arthur Zilversmit. *The First Emancipation: The Abolition of Slavery in the North.* Chicago: University of Chicago Press, 1967.

PROSLAVERY FORCES

Paul Finkelman. *Slavery and the Founders: Race and Liberty in the Age of Jefferson.* Armonk, NY: M. E. Sharpe, 1996.

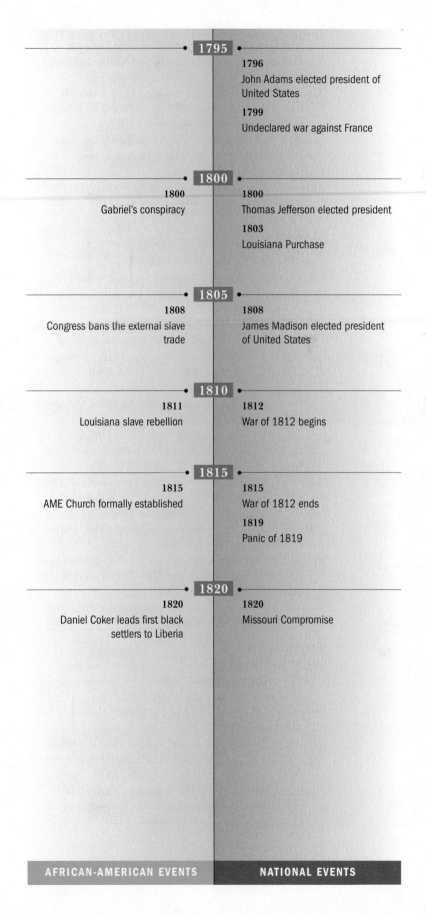

Charles F. Irons. *The Origins of Proslavery Christianity: White and Black Evangelicals in Colonial and Antebellum Virginia.* Chapel Hill: University of North Carolina Press, 2008.

Donald G. Nieman. *Promises to Keep: African Americans and the Constitutional Order, 1776 to the Present.* New York: Oxford University Press, 1991.

Donald L. Robinson. *Slavery in the Structure of American Politics, 1765–1820.* New York: Harcourt Brace Jovanovich, 1971.

Larry E. Tise. *Proslavery: A History of the Defense of Slavery in America, 1701–1840.* Athens: University of Georgia Press, 1987.

FREE BLACK INSTITUTIONS AND MIGRATION MOVEMENTS

Eddie S. Glaude. *Exodus! Religion, Race, and Nation in Early Nineteenth-Century Black America.* Chicago: University of Chicago Press, 2000.

Sheldon H. Harris. *Paul Cuffe: Black America and the African Return.* New York: Simon & Schuster, 1972.

Leon Litwack. *North of Slavery: The Negro in the Free States.* Chicago: University of Chicago Press, 1961.

William A. Muraskin. *Middle-Class Blacks in a White Society: Prince Hall Freemasonry in America.* Berkeley: University of California Press, 1975.

Richard S. Newman. *Freedom's Prophet: Bishop Richard Allen, the AME Church, and the Black Founding Fathers.* New York: New York University Press, 2008.

Lamont D. Thomas. *Paul Cuffe: Black Entrepreneur and Pan-Africanist.* Urbana: University of Illinois Press, 1988.

Heather Andrea Williams. *Self-Taught: African American Education in Slavery and Freedom.* Chapel Hill: University of North Carolina Press, 2005.

Julie Winch. *Philadelphia's Black Elite: Activism, Accommodation, and the Struggle for Autonomy, 1787–1848.* Philadelphia: Temple University Press, 1988.

———. *A Gentleman of Color: The Life of James Forten.* New York: Oxford University Press, 2002.

THE SOUTH

John Hope Franklin. *The Free Negro in North Carolina, 1790–1860.* 1943. Reprint, New York: Russell and Russell, 1969.

Peter Kolchin. *American Slavery, 1619–1877.* New York: Hill and Wang, 1993.

John Chester Miller. *The Wolf by the Ears: Thomas Jefferson and Slavery.* 1977. Reprint, Charlottesville: University Press of Virginia, 1991.

T. Stephen Whitman. *The Price of Freedom: Slavery and Manumission in Baltimore and Early National Maryland.* Lexington: University of Kentucky Press, 1997.

SLAVE REVOLTS, RESISTANCE, AND ESCAPES

Herbert Aptheker. *American Negro Slave Revolts.* 1943. Reprint, New York: International, 1983.

Merton L. Dillon. *Slavery Attacked: Southern Slaves and Their Allies, 1619–1865.* Baton Rouge: Louisiana State University Press, 1990.

Eugene D. Genovese. *From Rebellion to Revolution: Afro-American Slave Revolts in the Making of the Modern World.* Baton Rouge: Louisiana State University Press, 1979.

John R. McKivigan and Stanley Harrold, eds. *Antislavery Violence: Sectional, Racial, and Cultural Conflict in Antebellum America.* Knoxville: University of Tennessee Press, 1999.

Gerald W. Mullin. *Flight and Rebellion: Slave Resistance in Eighteenth-Century Virginia.* New York: Oxford University Press, 1972.

James Sidbury. *Ploughshares into Swords: Race, Rebellion, and Identity in Gabriel's Virginia, 1730–1810.* New York: Cambridge University Press, 1998.

RETRACING THE ODYSSEY

Monticello, Charlottesville, Virginia. http://www.monticello.org/. One hundred and thirty African Americans worked on this plantation during the late eighteenth and early nineteenth centuries.

Amherst History Museum, Amherst, Massachusetts. http://www.amhersthistory.org/. An exhibit on free black people who lived in eighteenth-century Amherst.

Afro-American Historical and Cultural Museum, Philadelphia, Pennsylvania. http://www.aampmuseum.org/. The collection includes an exhibit on black churches, 1740–1977.

REVIEW QUESTIONS

1. Which were stronger in the early American republic, the forces in favor of black freedom or of continued enslavement?

2. How did African Americans achieve emancipation in the North?

3. How was the U.S. Constitution, as it was drafted in 1787, proslavery? How was it antislavery?

4. Why were separate institutions important in shaping the lives of free black people during the late eighteenth and early nineteenth centuries?

5. Why did Gabriel believe he and his followers could abolish slavery in Virginia through an armed uprising?

myhistorylab Connections

www.myhistorylab.com
Review what you've learned in this chapter and explore the many documents, images,
research tools, and activities for this chapter to learn more about African-American history.

✓ Study and Review

READ

Read the Document

- John Wesley, "Thoughts upon Slavery" (1774)

- Preamble of the Free African Society (1787)

- Venture Smith Narrative (1798)

- Congress Prohibits Importation of Slaves (1807)

- Absalom Jones, Sermon on the Abolition of the International Slave Trade (1808)

- Missouri Admitted to Statehood, Slavery at Issue (1820)

- An Architect Describes African-American Music and Instruments in 1818

- The United States Constitution and the Bill of Rights

LISTEN

Hear the Audio

Hear the audio files for Chapter 5.

RESEARCH

mysearchlab

Consider this question in a short research paper.

How did the Missouri Compromise of 1820 shape the lives of African Americans?

EXPLORE

Watch the Video

- Slavery and the Constitution

See the Map

- The Missouri Compromise of 1820

- The Louisiana Purchase

- The War of 1812

Read the Document

- Ratification of the Constitution

PART II

SLAVERY, ABOLITION, AND THE QUEST FOR FREEDOM: THE COMING OF THE CIVIL WAR, 1793–1861

Anthony Burns

	1770–1800	1800–1830
RELIGION	**1775** Philadelphia Quakers organize first antislavery society in America Late 1700s–1830s Second Great Awakening	**1819** Episcopal Diocese of New York excludes black delegates from annual conventions **1820s** Semisecret churches spread among slaves **1829** Oblate Sisters of Providence founded in Baltimore, first African-American order of Roman Catholic nuns
CULTURE	**Early 1800s** Growth of folk tales among slaves	**1820s–1830s** Numerous black literary societies established in northern cities
POLITICS & GOVERNMENT		**1804–1849** Black laws in midwestern states restrict rights of African Americans **1807** New Jersey disfranchises black voters **1818** Connecticut bans new black voters **1820** Missouri Compromise **1821** New York retains property qualification for black voters **1822** Rhode Island disfranchises black voters
SOCIETY & ECONOMY	**1784** Society for the Promotion of the Abolition of Slavery founded	**1800** Gabriel's conspiracy **1812** African schools become part of Boston's public schools **1816** American Colonization Society founded **1822** Denmark Vesey's conspiracy **1827** *Freedom's Journal* begins publication

Harriet Tubman

Frederick Douglas

Sojourner Truth

1830–1850	1850–1870	NOTEWORTHY INDIVIDUALS

1840s Mother Bethel Church in Philadelphia has largest black congregation in the United States

1853 Episcopal Diocese of New York readmits black delegates

1840s–1850s Paintings of Robert Duncanson

1845 *Narrative of the Life of Frederick Douglass* published

1848 Okah Tubee's fictionalized autobiography published

UNCLE TOM'S CABIN

1852 *Uncle Tom's Cabin* published

1853 William W. Brown, first African-American novelist, publishes *Clotel*

Elizabeth Taylor Greenfield makes her singing debut in New York before a white audience

Solomon Northup publishes *Twelve Years as a Slave*

1854 Frances Ellen Watkins Harper publishes *Poems*

1855 William C. Nell publishes *The Colored Patriots of the American Revolution*

1859 Harriet Wilson publishes first novel by an African-American woman

1832 Virginia rejects gradual emancipation

1836–1841 "Gag rule" prohibits Congress from considering petitions regarding slavery

1838 Pennsylvania disfranchises black voters

1846–1848 Mexican War

1846 Wilmot Proviso

1847 Liberia becomes an independent republic

1848 Free Soil party founded

1850 Compromise of 1850 includes stronger Fugitive Slave Act

1851 Indiana bans African Americans from residing in the state

1855–1856 "Bleeding Kansas"

1857 Dred Scott decision

1858 Arkansas reenslaves free blacks who refuse to leave the state

1859 John Brown raids Harpers Ferry

1860 Lincoln elected president

1860–1861 Eleven southern states secede and form the Confederacy

1861 Civil War begins

1831 Nat Turner's revolt

William Lloyd Garrison begins publication of *The Liberator*

1832 First black women's abolitionist organization founded

1833 American Anti-Slavery Society founded

1834 African Free Schools become part of New York's public schools

1835 Abolitionist postal campaign begins

1836 Elijah P. Lovejoy killed by antiabolitionist mob

1839 *Amistad* mutiny

1843 Henry H. Garnet's *Address to the Slaves*

1847 Frederick Douglass begins publication of the *North Star*

Missouri bans education of free blacks

1851 "Battle" of Christiana

1853 Rochester Convention

1854 Ashmun Institute, first black institution of higher education in the United States, founded

1860 U.S. slave population put at 3,953,760

Life in the Cotton Kingdom

Why did slavery expand in the Cotton Kingdom?

What types of labor did slaves perform in the South?

What was the domestic slave trade?

How did African Americans adapt to life under slavery?

How have historians evaluated slavery and slaves?

▶ **Cutting sugarcane** on a plantation in Louisiana.

There may be humane masters, as there certainly are inhumane ones; there may be slaves well-clothed, well-fed, and happy, as there surely are those half-clad, half-starved, and miserable; nevertheless, the institution that tolerates such wrong and inhumanity . . . is a cruel, unjust, and barbarous one.

Solomon Northup, *Twelve Years a Slave: Narrative of Solomon Northup*

CASH!

All persons that have SLAVES to dispose of, will do well by giving me a call, as I will give the **HIGHEST PRICE FOR Men, Women, & CHILDREN.**

Any person that wishes to sell, will call at Hill's tavern, or at Shannon Hill for me, and any information they want will be promptly attended to.

Thomas Griggs.

Charlestown, May 7, 1835.

◄ **A slave buyer** offers cash for men, women, and children in this 1835 advertisement.

Solomon Northup, a free black man, had been kidnapped into slavery during the 1840s. After twelve years in bondage, he finally escaped. In this passage he identifies the central cruelty of slavery. It was not that some masters failed to provide slaves with adequate food, clothing, and shelter while others did. Nor was it that some masters treated their slaves brutally while others did not. The central cruelty of slavery was that it gave masters nearly absolute power over their slaves. The sufferings of African Americans in slavery were not caused by abuses in an otherwise benevolent institution. They were caused by the institution itself.

In this chapter we describe the life of black people in the slave South from the rise of the Cotton Kingdom during the early 1800s to the eve of the Civil War in 1860. As we have indicated in previous chapters, African Americans suffered brutal oppression on southern plantations. But they also developed means of coping with that oppression, resisting it, and escaping. Between 1820 and 1861, slavery in the South was at its peak as a productive system and means of white

((•─ Hear the Audio

Hear the audio files for Chapter 6 at **www.myhistorylab.com**

control over black southerners. We describe the extent of that slave system, how it varied across the South, and how it operated. We investigate the slave communities that African-American men, women, and children built.

The Expansion of Slavery

Eli Whitney's invention of the cotton gin in 1793 made the cultivation of cotton profitable on the North American mainland. It was the key to the rapid and extensive expansion of slavery from the Atlantic coast to Texas. By 1811 cotton growing had spread across South Carolina, Georgia, and parts of North Carolina and Virginia. By 1821 it had crossed Alabama and reached Mississippi, Louisiana, and parts of Tennessee. It then expanded again into Arkansas, Florida, and eastern Texas (see Map 6–1). Enslaved black labor cleared forests and drained swamps to make these lands fit for cultivation.

The expansion of the cotton culture led to the removal of the American Indians—some of them slaveholders—who inhabited this vast region. During the 1830s and 1840s, the U.S. Army forced the Cherokee, Chickasaw, Choctaw, Creek, and most Seminole to leave their ancestral lands for Indian Territory in what is now Oklahoma. Many Indians died during this forced migration, and the Cherokee remember it as "The Trail of Tears." Yet the Cherokees created in Oklahoma an economy dependent on black slave labor. By 1860 there were 7,000 slaves there, 14 percent of the population.

Far fewer slaves lived in the other western territories. Kansas never had more than a few dozen slaves during the 1850s and had none after 1858. In New Mexico in 1850, there were about 40 black slaves and 3,000 American Indian slaves. When Utah Territory legalized slavery in 1852, only about 26 enslaved black people were living there, and by 1860 Utah still had just 29 black people. Although California entered the Union as a state in 1850 under a constitution that banned slavery, two years later more than 300 illegally held slaves worked there as prospectors or servants.

SLAVE POPULATION GROWTH

In contrast to the Far West, during the period of territorial expansion a tremendous increase in the number of African Americans in bondage occurred in the region stretching from the Atlantic coast to Texas. Although the predominantly male slave populations in Latin American countries failed to reproduce

PROFILE: Solomon Northup

Solomon Northup's aspirations as a musician led in 1841 to his kidnapping and sale into slavery. For twelve years, he labored in the cotton and sugar regions of Louisiana, interacted with slaves and masters, and experienced firsthand what it was like to be caught up in a brutal labor system.

Northup was born free at Minerva, New York, in about 1808. His parents were prosperous farmers, and he became a farmer too, although he also worked occasionally as a violinist. He lived in Saratoga Springs, New York, with his wife and three children until March 1841, when two white men suggested that he become a musician in their circus, which was performing in Washington, D.C.

Enticed by the prospect of good wages and a chance to perform, Northup left with the two men without informing his wife or anyone else. Within two days of arriving in Washington, he was drugged, robbed of his money and free papers, chained, and sold to slave traders. After experiencing a terrible beating with a wooden paddle and a rope, Northup was shipped to New Orleans and sold to William Ford, who owned a cotton plantation and sawmill in Louisiana's Red River region.

As Ford's slave, Northup worked at the mill "piling lumber and chopping logs." Northup liked Ford and regarded him to be a "model master" who treated his slaves well and read scripture to them each Sunday. But when Ford became insolvent and sold his slaves, Northup had to deal with a series of brutal masters. They employed him as a carpenter, as a field hand on cotton and sugar plantations, and finally as a slave driver.

At one point when he was cutting lumber and building cabins, Northup was surprised to have several "large and stout" black women join in the forestry work. Later he observed women performing other demanding physical labor. "There are lumberwomen as well as lumbermen in the forests of the South," he reported. "In fact . . . they perform their share of all the labor required by the planters. They plough, dray, drive team, clear wild lands, work on the highway and so forth."

Subsequently, Northup spent ten years as a slave of Edwin Epps, a cotton planter, who when drunk enjoyed forcing his slaves to dance. Northup noted that Epps's slaves received a meager diet of corn and bacon. They slept in crude, crowded cabins on planks of wood. During harvest season, "it was rarely that a day passed by without one or more whippings" as slaves failed to pick their quota. During a three-year period, Epps hired Northup out to "sugar plantations during the season of cane-cutting and sugar making" for $1.00 per day.

Northup had become Epps's slave driver by 1852, when he set in motion the events that led to his rescue. Deeply disturbed by being forced to whip other slaves, Northup conspired with a Canadian carpenter to smuggle a letter to two white business-men in Saratoga Springs. The letter led the governor of New York to send Henry B. Northup—a member of the family that had owned Solomon Northup's father—to Louisiana to present evidence that Solomon Northup was a free man. By January 1853, he had been reunited with his family in New York. In July of that year he published *Twelve Years a Slave*, which sold over 30,000 copies and earned him enough money to purchase a home for his family in Glens Falls, New York, where he died in 1863.

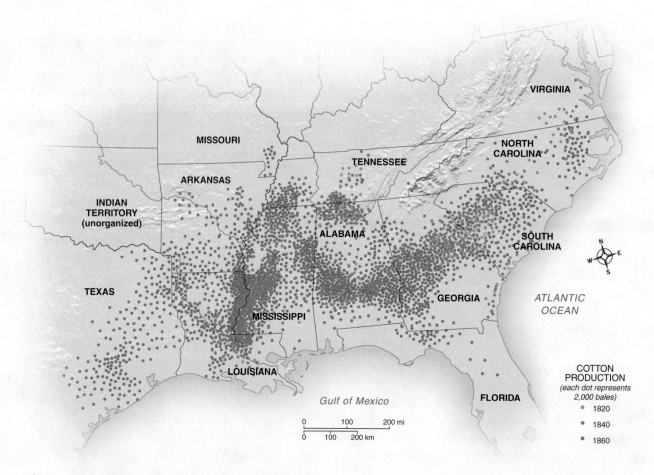

MAP 6–1   COTTON PRODUCTION IN THE SOUTH, 1820–1860

Cotton production expanded westward between 1820 and 1860 into Alabama, Mississippi, Louisiana, Texas, Arkansas, and western Tennessee. Sam Bowers Hilliard, *Atlas of Antebellum Southern Agriculture* (Louisiana State University Press, 1984), 67–71.

▶ *Why did cotton production spread westward?*

themselves and declined drastically before general emancipation, the slave population of the United States grew almost sixfold between 1790 and 1860, from 697,897 to 3,953,760 (see Table 6–1). But slaves were not equally distributed across the region. Western North Carolina, eastern Tennessee, western Virginia, and most of Missouri never had many slaves. Their numbers grew fastest in the newer cotton-producing states, such as Alabama and Mississippi (see Map 6–2).

Virginia had the largest slave population throughout the period. But between 1820 and 1860, that population increased by only 15 percent, from 425,153 to 490,865. During the same 40 years, the slave population of Louisiana increased by 209 percent, from 149,654 to 462,198, and that of Mississippi by 1,231 percent, from 32,814 to 436,631. By 1860 Mississippi

and South Carolina were the only states with more slaves than free inhabitants.

OWNERSHIP OF SLAVES IN THE OLD SOUTH

Slaveholders were as unevenly distributed as slaves and, unlike slaves, were declining in number. In 1830, 1,314,272 white southerners (36 percent of a total white southern population of 3,650,758) owned slaves. In 1860 only 383,673 white southerners (4.7 percent of a total white southern population of 8,097,463) owned slaves. Even counting the immediate families of slaveholders, only 1,900,000 (or less than 25 percent of the South's white population) had a direct interest in slavery in 1860.

Almost half of the South's slaveholders owned fewer than five slaves, only 12 percent owned more than 20 slaves, and just 1 percent owned more than 50 slaves. Yet more than half the slaves belonged to masters who had 20 or more slaves. So, although the typical slaveholder owned few slaves, the typical slave lived on a sizable plantation.

Since the time of Anthony Johnson in the mid-1600s, a few black people had been slaveholders, and this class continued to exist. In 1830, only 2 percent of free African Americans owned slaves. This amounted to 3,775 individuals. Many of them became slaveholders to protect their families from sale and disruption. This was because, as the nineteenth century progressed, southern states made it more difficult for masters to manumit slaves and for slaves to purchase their freedom. The states also threatened to expel former slaves from their territory. In response, black men and women sometimes purchased relatives who were in danger of sale to traders and who—if legally free—might be forced by white authorities to leave a state.

Some African Americans, however, purchased slaves for financial reasons and passed those slaves on to their heirs. Most black people who became masters for financial reasons owned five or fewer slaves. But William Johnson, a wealthy free black barber of Natchez, Louisiana, owned many slaves whom he employed on a plantation he purchased. Some black women, such as Margaret Mitchell Harris of South Carolina and Betsy Somayrac of Natchitoches, Louisiana, also became slaveholders for economic reasons. Harris was a successful rice planter who inherited 21 slaves from her white father. She prospered by carefully managing her resources in land and slaves. By the time she sold out in 1849, she had more than 40 slaves and nearly 1,000 acres that produced 240,000 pounds of rice per year.

Slave Labor in Agriculture

Agricultural laborers constituted 75 percent of the South's slave population. About 55 percent of the slaves cultivated cotton, 10 percent grew tobacco, and 10 percent produced sugar, rice, or hemp. About 15 percent were domestic servants, and the remaining 10 percent worked in trades and industries.

TOBACCO

During the 1800s, tobacco remained important in Virginia, Maryland, Kentucky, and parts of North Carolina and Missouri (see Map 6–3). A difficult crop to produce, tobacco required a long growing season and careful cultivation. In the spring slaves had to transfer seedlings from sterilized seedbeds to

TABLE 6–1 U.S. SLAVE POPULATION, 1820 AND 1860

	1820	1860
United States	1,538,125	3,953,760
North	19,108	64
South	1,519,017	3,953,696
Upper South	965,514	1,530,229
Delaware	4,509	1,798
Kentucky	127,732	225,483
Maryland	107,397	87,189
Missouri	10,222	114,931
North Carolina	205,017	331,059
Tennessee	80,107	275,719
Virginia	425,153	490,865
Washington, D.C.	6,377	3,185
Lower South	553,503	2,423,467
Alabama	41,879	435,080
Arkansas	1,617	111,115
Florida	*	61,745
Georgia	149,654	462,198
Louisiana	69,064	331,726
Mississippi	32,814	436,631
South Carolina	258,475	402,406
Texas	*	182,566

*Florida and Texas were not states in 1820.

Source: *Slaves without Masters: The Free Negro in the Antebellum South*. Copyright © 1974 by Ira Berlin. Reprinted by permission of The New Press. www.thenewpress.com

well-worked and manured soil. Then they had to hoe weeds, pick off insects, and prune lower leaves so the topmost leaves grew to their full extent. Slaves also built scaffolds to cure the tobacco leaves and made the barrels in which the tobacco was shipped to market.

Robert Ellett, a former slave, recalled that when he was just eight years old he worked in Virginia "a-worming tobacco." He "examined tobacco leaves, pull[ed] off the worms, if there were any, and killed them." He claimed that if an overseer discovered that slaves had overlooked worms on the tobacco plants, the slaves were whipped or forced to eat the worms. Nancy Williams, another Virginia slave, recalled that sometimes as a punishment slaves had to inhale burning tobacco until they became nauseated.

RICE

Unlike the cultivation of tobacco, which spread west and south from Maryland and Virginia, rice production remained confined to the low country of South Carolina and Georgia. As they had since colonial times, slaves in these coastal regions worked according

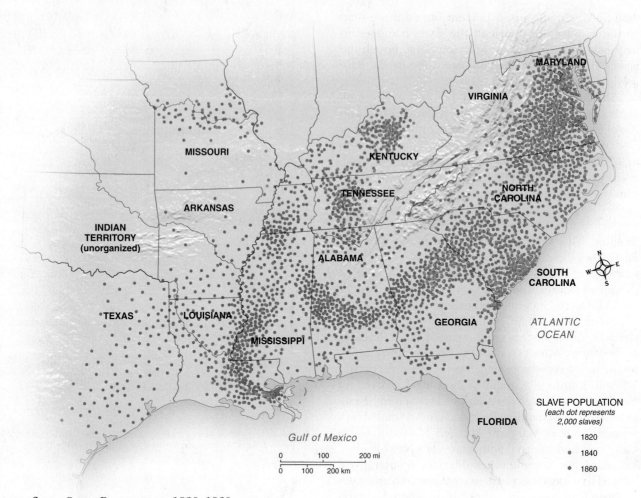

MAP 6–2 SLAVE POPULATION, 1820–1860

Slavery spread southwestward from the Upper South and the eastern seaboard following the spread of cotton cultivation.

Atlas of Antebellum Southern Agriculture, by Sam Bowers Hillard, pp. 67–71, 1984.

▶ *What does this map suggest concerning black life in the South?*

to task systems that allowed them considerable autonomy. Because rice fields needed to be flooded for the seeds to germinate, slaves maintained elaborate systems of dikes and ditches. Influenced by West African methods, they sowed, weeded, and harvested the rice crop.

Rice cultivation was labor intensive, and rice plantations needed large labor forces to grow and harvest the crop and maintain the fields. By 1860 twenty rice plantations had 300 to 500 slaves, and eight others had between 500 and 1,000. The only American plantation employing more than 1,000 slaves was in the rice-producing region. These vast plantations represented sizable capital investments, and masters or overseers carefully monitored slave

productivity. Although slaves enjoyed considerable leeway in how they performed their assigned duties, those who missed a day's work risked forfeiting their weekly allowance "of either bacon, sugar, molasses, or tobacco."

SUGAR

Another important crop that grew in a restricted region was sugar, which slaves cultivated on plantations along the Mississippi River in southern Louisiana. Commercial production of sugarcane did not begin in Louisiana until the 1790s. It required a consistently warm climate, a long growing season, and at least 60 inches of rain per year.

Raising sugarcane and refining sugar also required constant labor. Together with the great profitability of the sugar crop, these demands encouraged masters to work their slaves hard. Slave life on sugar plantations was harsh, and African Americans across the South feared being sent to labor on them. Historian Paul W. Gates details the work of slaves on sugar plantations:

> Fresh land was constantly being cleared, and the wood was used for fuel in the sugarhouses or was sold to steamboats. Levees had to be raised; ditching and draining was never completed. Planting, numerous hoeings, cutting, loading and unloading the cane, putting it through the mill, feeding the boilers, moving the huge hogsheads of sugar and molasses and drawing them to the boat landing, setting aside the seed cane, hauling the bagasse to the fields—all this took much labor.

Slaves did this work in hot and humid conditions, adding to the toll it took on their strength and health. Because cane could not be allowed to stand too long in the fields, harvest time was hectic. As one former slave recalled, "On cane plantations in sugar time, there is no distinction as to the days of the week. They [the slaves] worked on the Sabbath as if it were Monday or Thursday."

COTTON

Although tobacco, rice, and sugar were economically significant, cotton was by far the South's and the country's most important staple crop. By 1860 cotton exports amounted to more than 50 percent of the annual dollar value of all U.S. exports (see Figure 6–1). This was almost ten times the value of its nearest export competitors, wheat and wheat flour.

Cotton as a crop did not require cultivation as intensive as that needed for tobacco, rice, or sugar. But the cotton culture was so extensive that cotton planters as a group employed the most slave labor. By 1860, out of the 2,500,000 slaves employed in agriculture in the United States, 1,815,000 of them produced cotton. Cotton drove the South's economy and its westward expansion. Even in rice-producing South Carolina and sugar-producing Louisiana, cotton was dominant, and cotton plantations employed the bulk of the slave populations.

Although long-staple cotton continued to be grown on the sea islands of South Carolina and Georgia, most American cotton was the hardier short-staple variety that flourished over much of the South. Demand for cotton fiber in the textile mills of Britain and New England stimulated the westward spread of cotton cultivation. Between 1830 and 1860, this

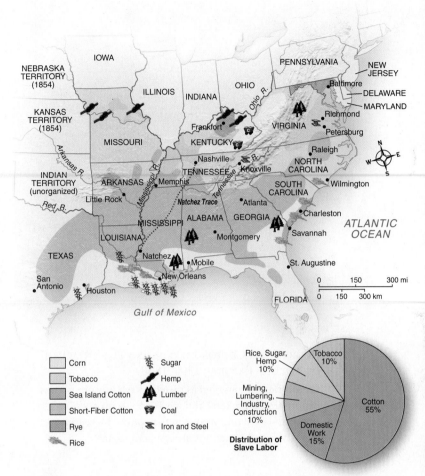

MAP **6–3** AGRICULTURE, INDUSTRY, AND SLAVERY IN THE OLD SOUTH, 1850

The experience of the African American in slavery varied according to their occupation and the region of the South in which they lived.

▶ *To what degree did climate affect the type of crop slaves produced?*

◉ See the Map *Explore this map at* **www.myhistorylab.com**

demand increased by at least 5 percent per year. In response—and with the essential aid of Whitney's cotton gin—American production of cotton rose from 10,000 bales in 1793 to 500,000 annually during the 1820s to 4,491,000 bales in 1860. The new states of Alabama, Louisiana, and Mississippi led this mounting production.

Picturesque scenes of ripening cotton fields are part of the romantic image of the Old South that novels, songs, and movies have perpetuated for so long. Even a former slave could recall that "few sights are more pleasant to the eye than a wide cotton field

((●— **Hear** the **Audio**
Pick a Bale of Cotton

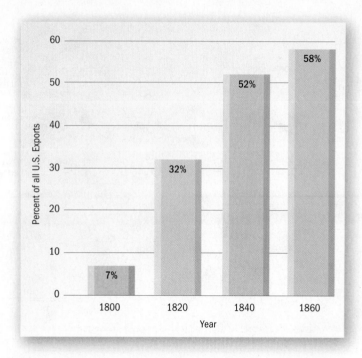

FIGURE 6–1   COTTON EXPORTS AS A PERCENTAGE OF ALL U.S. EXPORTS, 1800–1860
Cotton rapidly emerged as the country's most important export crop after 1800 and was key to its prosperity. Because slave labor produced the cotton, increasing exports strengthened the slave system itself.

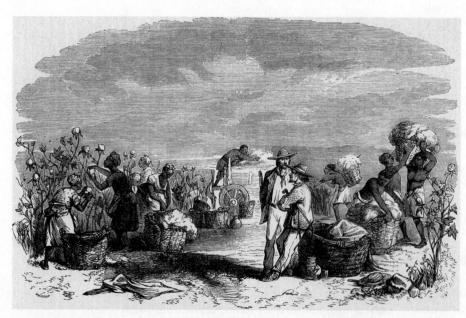

In this engraving, which dates to about 1860, slaves harvest cotton under white supervision on a southern plantation. Note the division of labor with women picking and men packing and carrying.   The Granger Collection, New York

when it is in full bloom. It presents an appearance of purity, like an immaculate expanse of light, new-fallen snow." Yet such scenes mask the backbreaking labor enslaved African Americans performed and the anxiety and fear they experienced.

During the early nineteenth century, potential profits drew white farmers to the rich Black Belt lands of Mississippi and Alabama. Rapid population growth allowed Mississippi to gain statehood in 1817 and Alabama in 1819. By 1860 these states had become the leading cotton producers. They also had the greatest concentration of plantations with one hundred or more slaves. Twenty-four of Mississippi's slaveholders each owned between 308 and 899 slaves.

As huge agricultural units drew in labor, the price of slaves increased. During the 1830s, a prime male field hand sold in the New Orleans slave market for $1,250 (more than 35,000 current dollars). Prices dipped during the hard times of the early 1840s. But, by the 1850s, such slaves cost $1,800 (more than 50,000 current dollars). Young women usually sold for up to $500 less than young men. Elderly slaves, unless they were highly skilled, sold for far less.

The enslaved men and women who worked in the cotton fields rose before dawn when the master or overseer sounded the plantation bell or horn. They ate breakfast and then assembled in work gangs of 20 or 25 under the control of black slave drivers. They plowed and planted in the spring. They weeded with heavy hoes in the summer and harvested in the late fall. During harvest season, adult slaves picked about 200 pounds of cotton per day. Regardless of the season, the work was hard, and white overseers whipped those who seemed to be lagging. Slaves usually got a two-hour break at midday in the summer and an hour to an hour and a half in the winter. Then they returned to the fields until sunset, when they went back to their cabins for dinner and an early bedtime enforced by the master or overseer.

Frederick Law Olmsted, a northern traveler, described a large gang of Mississippi slaves he saw in 1854 marching home early because of rain:

> First came, led by an old driver carrying a whip, forty of the largest and strongest women I ever saw together; they were all in a single uniform dress of a bluish check stuff, the skirts reaching little below the knee; their legs and feet were bare; they carried themselves loftily, each having a hoe over the shoulder, and walking with a

free, powerful swing. Behind them came the [plow hands and their mules], thirty strong, mostly men, but a few of them women. . . . A lean and vigilant white overseer, on a brisk pony, brought up the rear. The men wore small blue Scotch bonnets; many of the women handkerchiefs, turban fashion. . . . They were evidently a picked lot. I thought every one could pass for a "prime" cotton hand.

COTTON AND TECHNOLOGY

Agricultural technology in the Cotton Kingdom was primitive compared to that in the Old Northwest. Free northwestern farmers by the 1840s used a variety of machines, drawn by teams of horses and constructed of wood and iron, to plant, cultivate, and harvest crops. In contrast southern slave workers relied on simple plows and harrows, drawn by a single mule—as well as handheld shovels, rakes, and heavy hoes—to perform similar work. Masters did not trust slaves with expensive machinery. They also preferred to invest in slaves and land rather than labor-saving devices. And the nature of the South's major crop had an essential impact. Because cotton ripened unevenly, nineteenth-century mechanical harvesters could not discern which plants were ready for harvest. Therefore, three times each harvest season, enslaved men, women, and children picked cotton bolls by hand. They had long sacks tied to their waists or hung from their shoulders to hold the bolls.

Nineteenth-century technology nevertheless impacted slaves' lives. Although the South lagged behind the North and Britain in applying steam power to transportation, it surpassed continental Europe and other regions of the world. After 1811 the Mississippi River teamed with steamboats. Railroads helped open the Old Southwest to cotton production, which encouraged the growth of the domestic slave trade and the disruption of black families.

In some instances technology improved plantation conditions. Early in the nineteenth century, cotton gins became much larger and more efficient than the ones Eli Whitney designed during the 1790s. Enslaved men operated gins powered by mules attached to long "sweeps" walking in circles. Once bolls had been cleaned of their seeds, slaves used presses, driven by huge screws turned by either man or mule power, to form bales. Slaves packaged the bales in cloth bagging and took them by wagon to river steamboat landings for shipment to market.

●●●[**Read** the **Document**
Frederick Law Olmsted, from A Journey in the Seabord States (1856)

By the early nineteenth century many slaves in Delaware, Maryland, and Virginia were cultivating wheat rather than tobacco. This 1831 lithograph portrays a demonstration of Cyrus McCormick's automatic reaper. It indicates the adaptability of slave labor to new technology.

The technology available to enslaved women on cotton plantations was less sophisticated. They used heavy cast-iron kettles for cooking food and washing clothes. Washing involved boiling garments in soapy water, beating them with "battling sticks" on "battling blocks," and returning them for another boiling before hanging them out to dry.

OTHER CROPS

Besides cotton, sugar, tobacco, and rice, slaves in the Old South produced other crops, including hemp, corn, wheat, oats, rye, white potatoes, and sweet potatoes. They also raised cattle, hogs, sheep, and horses. The hogs and corn were mainly for consumption on the plantations. But all the hemp and much of the other livestock and wheat were raised for the market. In fact, wheat replaced tobacco as the main cash crop in much of Maryland and Virginia. The transition to wheat encouraged many planters to substitute free labor for slave labor, but slaves continued to grow wheat in the South until the Civil War.

Kentucky was the center of the hemp industry. Before the Civil War, planters used hemp, which is closely related to marijuana, to make rope and bagging for cotton bales. This tied Kentucky economically to the Deep South. But, because hemp required much less labor than rice, sugar, or cotton, Kentucky developed a distinctive slave system. Three slaves could tend 50 acres of hemp, so slave labor forces were much smaller than elsewhere.

Robert Wickliffe, the largest Kentucky slaveholder during the 1840s, owned 200 slaves—a large number but far fewer than his counterparts in the Cotton Belt.

House Servants and Skilled Slaves

About 75 percent of the slave workforce in the nineteenth century consisted of field hands. But because masters wanted to make their plantations as self-sufficient as possible, they also employed slaves as house servants and skilled craftsmen. Slaves who did not have to do field labor were an elite. Those who performed domestic duties, drove carriages, or learned a craft considered themselves privileged. However, they were also suspended between two different worlds.

House slaves worked as cooks, maids, butlers, nurses, and gardeners. Their work was less physically demanding than fieldwork, and they often received better food and clothing. Nevertheless, nineteenth-century kitchen work was grueling, and maids and butlers were on call at all hours. House servants' jobs were also more stressful than field hands' jobs because the servants were under closer white supervision.

In addition, house servants were by necessity cut off from the slave community centered in the slave quarters. Yet, as Olmsted pointed out during the 1850s, house servants rarely sought to become field hands. Conversely, field hands had little desire to be exposed to the constant surveillance house servants had to tolerate. As Olmsted put it,

> Slaves brought up to housework dread to be employed at field-labor; and those accustomed to the comparatively unconstrained life of the Negro-settlement detest the close control and careful movements required of the house-servants. It is a punishment of a lazy field hand to employ him in menial duties at the house . . . and it is equally a punishment to a neglectful house-servant, to banish him to the field-gangs.

Skilled slaves tended to be even more of a slave elite than house servants. As had been true earlier, black men had a decided advantage over black women—apart from those who were seamstresses—in becoming skilled. Slave carpenters, blacksmiths, and millwrights built and maintained plantation houses, slave quarters, and machinery. Because they might need to travel to get tools or spare parts, such skilled slaves gained a more cosmopolitan outlook than field hands or house servants. They got a taste of freedom, which from the masters' point of view was dangerous.

As plantation slavery declined in the Chesapeake, skilled slaves could leave their master's estate to "hire their time." Either they or their masters negotiated labor contracts with employers who needed their expertise. In effect, these slaves worked for money. Although masters often kept all or most of what they earned, some of these skilled slaves merely paid their master a set rate and lived as independent contractors.

Urban and Industrial Slavery

Most skilled slaves who hired their time lived in the South's towns and cities, where they interacted with free black communities. Many of them resided in Baltimore and New Orleans, which were major ports and the Old South's largest cities. But there were others in such smaller southern urban centers as Richmond and Norfolk, Virginia; Atlanta and Augusta, Georgia; Washington, D.C.; Charleston, South Carolina; Louisville, Kentucky; and Memphis, Tennessee.

Slave populations in southern cities were often large, although they tended to decline between 1800 and 1860. In 1840 slaves were a majority of Charleston's population of 29,000. They nearly equaled white residents in Memphis and Augusta, which had total populations of 14,700 and 6,000, respectively. Slaves were almost one-quarter of New Orleans's population of 145,000 (see Map 6–4).

As the young Frederick Douglass found when his master sent him from rural Maryland to Baltimore during the late 1830s, life in a city could be much more complicated for a slave than life on a plantation. When urban slaves were not working for their masters, they could earn money for themselves, and as a result, masters had a harder time controlling their lives. Those who contracted to provide their masters with a certain amount of money per year could live on their own, buying their own food and clothing. "You couldn't pay me," observed one slave woman, "to live at home if I could help myself."

Urban slaves served as domestics, washwomen, waiters, artisans, stevedores, drayers, hack drivers, and general laborers. (Douglass was an apprentice caulker in a shipyard.) In general, they did the urban work that foreign immigrants undertook in northern cities. If urban slaves purchased their freedom, they usually continued in the same work they had done as slaves. Particularly in border cities like Baltimore, Louisville, and Washington, urban slaves increasingly relied on their free black neighbors—and sympathetic white people—to escape north. Urban masters often let slaves purchase their freedom over a term of years to keep them from leaving. In Baltimore, during the early

MAP 6–4   POPULATION PERCENTAGES IN THE SOUTHERN STATES, 1850

The percentages of slaves, free African Americans, and white people varied from state to state. In the Upper South, white populations were substantially larger than black populations. In the Deep South, however, the races were more in balance.

Faragher John Mack; Armitage, Susan H.; Buhle, Mari Jo; Czitrom, Daniel, *Out of Many: A History of the American People, Combined Volume, Media and Research Updated,* 4th © 2005. Printed and Electronically reproduced by permission of Pearson Education, Inc., Upper Saddle River, New Jersey.

▶ *In which two states were there black majorities in 1850, and why?*

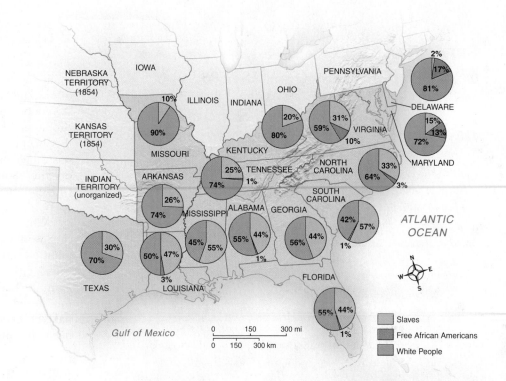

nineteenth century, this "**term slavery**" was gradually replacing slavery for life.

Industrial slavery overlapped with urban slavery, but southern industries that employed slaves were often in rural areas. By 1860 about 5 percent of southern slaves— approximately 200,000 people—worked in industry. Enslaved men, women, and children worked in textile mills in South Carolina and Georgia, sometimes beside white people. In Richmond and Petersburg, Virginia, during the 1850s, about 6,000 slaves, most of whom were men, worked in factories producing chewing tobacco. Richmond's famous Tredegar Iron Works also employed a large slave workforce. So did earlier southern iron-works in Virginia, Maryland, northern Tennessee, and southern Kentucky.

The bulk of the 16,000 people who worked in the South's lumber industry in 1860 were slaves. Under the supervision of black drivers, they felled trees, operated sawmills, and delivered lumber. Slaves also did most of the work in the naval stores industry of North Carolina and Georgia, manufacturing tar, turpentine, and related products. In western Virginia, they labored in the salt works of the Great Kanawha River Valley, producing the salt used to preserve meat—especially the southern mainstay salt pork. During the 1820s many workers in the Maryland Chemical Works in Baltimore, which manufactured industrial chemicals, pigments, and medicines, were slaves. Most southern

Enslaved black women often had the responsibility of raising their masters' young children. The women's duties sometimes forced them to neglect the needs of their own children.

VOICES

FREDERICK DOUGLASS ON THE READINESS OF MASTERS TO USE THE WHIP

This passage from the Narrative of the Life of Frederick Douglass, An American Slave, *published in 1845, suggests the volatile relationship between slaves and masters that could quickly result in violence. As Douglass makes clear, masters and overseers used the whip not just to force slaves to work but also to enforce a distinction between what was proper and even laudable for white men and what was forbidden behavior for slaves.*

It would astonish one, unaccustomed to a slaveholding life, to see with what wonderful ease a slaveholder can find things of which to make occasion to whip a slave. A mere look, word, or motion—a mistake, accident, or want of power—are all matters for which a slave may be whipped at any time. Does a slave look dissatisfied? It is said, he has the devil in him, and it must be whipped out. Does he speak loudly when spoken to by his masters? Then he is getting high-minded, and should be taken down a button-hole lower. Does he forget to pull off his hat at the approach of a white person? Then he is wanting in reverence, and should be whipped for it. Does he ever venture to vindicate his conduct, when censured for it? Then he is guilty of impudence—one of the greatest crimes of which a slave can be guilty. Does he ever venture to suggest a different mode of doing things from that pointed out by his master? He is indeed presumptuous, and getting above himself; and nothing less than a flogging will do for him. Does he, while plowing, break a plough—or, while hoeing, break a hoe? It is owing to his carelessness, and for it a slave must always be whipped.

▶ *Why did masters and overseers whip slaves?*
▶ *Given the behavior by masters that Douglass describes, how were slaves likely to act around white people?*

Source: Roy Finkenbine, ed., *Sources of the African-American Past* (New York: Longman, 1997), 43–44.

industrialists did not purchase slaves. Instead they hired slaves from their masters. The industrial work slaves performed was often dangerous and tiring. But, as historian John B. Boles points out, slaves came to prefer industrial jobs to plantation labor. Like urban slaves, industrial slaves had more opportunities to advance themselves, enjoyed more autonomy, and often received cash incentives. Industrial labor, like urban labor, was a path to freedom for some.

Punishment

Those who used slave labor, whether on plantations, small farms, in urban areas, or industry, frequently offered incentives to induce slaves to perform well. Yet slave labor by definition is forced labor based on the threat of physical punishment. Masters denied that this brutal aspect detracted from what they claimed was the essentially benign and paternalistic character of the South's "peculiar institution." After all, Christian masters found support in the Bible for using corporal punishment to chastise servants.

White southerners also believed that African Americans would not work unless threatened with beatings. Olmsted reported that in Mississippi he had observed a young girl subjected to "the severest corporal punishment" he had ever seen. The white overseer, who had administered the flogging with a rawhide whip "across her naked loins and thighs," told Olmsted that the girl had been shirking her duties. He claimed that "if I hadn't

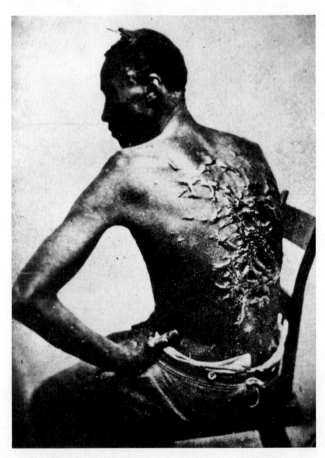

In this 1863 photograph a former Louisiana slave displays the scars that resulted from repeated whippings. Although this degree of scarring is exceptional, few slaves were able to avoid being whipped at least once in their lives.

[punished her so hard] she would have done the same thing again to-morrow, and half the people on the plantation would have followed her example. Oh, you've no idea how lazy these niggers are. . . . They'd never do any work at all if they were not afraid of being whipped."

Fear of the lash drove slaves to work and to cooperate among themselves for mutual protection. Parents and older relatives taught slave children how to avoid punishment and still resist masters and overseers. They worked slowly—but not too slowly—and feigned illness to maintain their strength. They broke tools and injured mules, oxen, and horses to tacitly protest their condition. This pattern of covert resistance and physical punishment caused anxiety for both masters and slaves. Resistance (described in more detail in Chapter 3) often forced masters to reduce work hours and improve conditions. Yet few slaves escaped being whipped at least once during their lives in bondage.

The Domestic Slave Trade

The expansion of the Cotton Kingdom south and west combined with the decline of slavery in the Chesapeake to stimulate the domestic slave trade. As masters in Delaware, Maryland, Virginia, North Carolina, and Kentucky trimmed excess slaves from their workforces—

Read the **Document**
A Slave Tells of His Sale at Auction (1848)

or switched entirely from slave to wage labor—they sold men, women, and children to slave traders. The traders in turn shipped these unfortunate people to the slave markets of New Orleans and other cities for resale. Masters also sold slaves as punishment, and fear of being "sold down river" led many slaves in the Chesapeake to escape. A vicious circle resulted: masters sold slaves south to prevent their escape, and slaves escaped to avoid being sold south.

Some slave songs record the anxiety of those facing separation from loved ones as a result of the domestic trade. One song laments the sale of a man sold away from his wife and family:

William Rino sold Henry Silvers;
Hilo! Hilo!
Sold him to de Gorgy [Georgia] trader;
Hilo! Hilo!
His wife she cried, and children bawled
Hilo! Hilo!
Sold him to de Gorgy trader;
Hilo! Hilo!

. . .

See wives and husbands sold apart,
Their children's screams will break my heart;—

There's a better day coming,
Will you go along with me?
There's a better day a coming,
Go sound the jubilee!

The number of people traded was huge and, considering that many of them were ripped away from their families, tragic. Starting in the 1820s, about 150,000 slaves per decade moved toward the southwest either with their masters or traders. Between 1820 and 1860, an estimated 50 percent of the slaves of the Upper South moved involuntarily into the Southwest.

Traders operated compounds called slave prisons or slave pens in Baltimore; Washington, D.C.; Alexandria and Richmond, Virginia; Lexington, Kentucky; Charleston, South Carolina; and in smaller cities. Most of the victims of the

Read the **Document**
E. S. Abdy, Description of a Washington, D.C., Slave Pen (1835)

trade moved on foot in groups called **coffles,** chained or roped together. From the 1810s onward, northern and European visitors to Washington noted the coffles passing before the U.S. Capitol. There was also a considerable coastal trade in slaves from Chesapeake ports to New Orleans, and by the 1840s some traders were carrying their human cargoes in railroad cars.

The domestic slave trade demonstrated the falseness of slaveholders' claims that slavery was a benign institution. Driven by economic necessity, profit, or a desire to frustrate escape plans, masters in the Upper South irrevocably separated husbands and wives, mothers and children, and brothers and sisters. Traders sometimes tore babies from their mothers' arms. The journey from the Chesapeake to Mississippi, Alabama, or Louisiana could be long and hard, and some slaves died along the way. A few managed to keep in touch with those they had left behind through letters and travelers. But most could not, and after the abolition of slavery in 1865, many African Americans used their new freedom to travel across the South looking for relatives from whom they had been separated long before.

SLAVE FAMILIES

The families that enslaved African Americans sought to preserve had been developing in America since the seventeenth century. However, such families had no legal standing. Most enslaved men and women could choose their own mates, although masters sometimes arranged such things. Masters encouraged pairings among female and

Read the **Document**
Farm Journal Reports on the Care and Feeding of Slaves (1836)

male slaves because they assumed correctly that husbands and fathers would be less rebellious than single men.

Masters also knew that they would benefit if their human chattel reproduced. As Thomas Jefferson put it, "I consider a [slave] woman who brings [gives birth to] a child every two years as more profitable than the best man on the farm. What she produces is an addition to the capital, while his labors disappear in mere consumption."

Families were also the core of the African-American community in slavery. Even though no legal sanctions supported slave marriages and the domestic slave trade could sunder them, many such marriages endured. Before they wed, some couples engaged in courting rituals, while others rejected "such foolishness." Similarly, slave weddings ranged from simply "taking up" and living together to religious ceremonies replete with food and frolics.

PROFILE: William Ellison

The life of William Ellison, who was born a slave in the Fairfield district of South Carolina in 1790 and named *April* by his master, exemplifies several of the themes of this chapter. He was a skilled slave, used what he knew to save enough to purchase his freedom, and subsequently became a slaveholder himself. His story came to light in 1935 when three white children, playing in the crawlspace under his former home, discovered his personal papers.

The son of a slave mother and an unknown white father, Ellison received special treatment from his owner, who apprenticed him at age twelve to a skilled white craftsman named William McCreight. Together with several white apprentices, Ellison learned carpentry, blacksmithing, and how to repair cotton gins. He also learned how to conduct a business. He did so well that in 1816, when he was 26, he purchased his freedom.

Once free, Ellison petitioned a court to change his name from his slave name *April* to *William*, in honor of his mentor—or perhaps his father. With freedom, skills, and a new name, Ellison opened a gin-making and gin-repair shop in Statesburg, South Carolina. Like the Natchez, Mississippi, barber William Johnson, Ellison achieved a respectable reputation among his white clients and neighbors as a churchgoing businessman. On the surface at least, his ties to his slave past diminished as he prospered. Because his income depended on white slaveholders, he did nothing to antagonize them.

As a result, Ellison became one of the wealthiest owners of real and personal property in the South. He owned hundreds of acres of farmland and woodland worth at least $8,250 (about 231,000 current dollars). As early as 1820, he owned two slaves. In 1830 he owned four, and in 1840 he owned 26. By 1860 he owned 63 and was worth in personal property alone $53,000 (about 1,500,000 current dollars).

Ellison assigned tasks to his slaves according to their gender and age. The field hands—mostly women and children—produced 80 bales of cotton each in 1850. They also raised thousands of bushels of corn, sweet potatoes, and other vegetables each year. The gin shop workers—men and adolescent boys—worked as blacksmiths, carpenters, and mechanics.

When South Carolina seceded from the Union in December 1860 and the Civil War began a few months later, Ellison and his family were caught between two contradictory forces. During the war, South Carolina's state government considered free African Americans potential traitors and curtailed their liberty. Meanwhile, the Union moved relentlessly toward immediate, uncompensated emancipation. Ellison, who died on December 5, 1861, did not live to see the emancipation of his slaves in 1865. But his children did. They also saw the destruction of his business when its newly emancipated workers refused to continue to work for the Ellisons as free men and women.

◄ **William Ellison's house** near Columbia, South Carolina.

"Jumping the broom" was often part of these ceremonies, although this custom was not African but European. During the 1930s former slave Tempie Herndon recalled her wedding ceremony conducted by "de nigger preacher dat preached at de plantation church." In particular, she remembered that after the religious ceremony, "Marse George got to have his little fun" by having the newlyweds jump backward over a broomstick. "You got to do dat to see which one gwine be boss of your household," she commented. "If both of dem jump over without touchin' it, dey won't gwine be no bossin', dey just gwine be congenial." In fact, more equality existed between husbands and wives in slave marriages than in those of the masters. Southern white concepts of patriarchy required male dominance. But because black men lacked power, their wives were more like partners than servants.

Slave couples usually lived together in cabins on their master's property. They had little privacy because nineteenth-century slave cabins were rude, small, one-room dwellings that two families might have to share. But couples who shared cabins were generally better off than husbands and wives who were the property of different masters and lived on different plantations. In these cases, children lived with their mother, and their father visited when he could in the evenings. Work patterns that changed with the seasons or with the mood of a master could interfere with such visits. So could the requirement that slaves have passes to leave home.

CHILDREN

Despite these difficulties, slave parents were able to instruct their children in family history, religion, and the skills required to survive in slavery. They sang to their children and told them stories full of folk wisdom. In particular, they impressed on them the importance of extended family relationships. The ability to rely on grandparents, aunts and uncles, cousins, and honorary relatives was a hedge against the family disruption that the domestic slave trade might inflict. In this manner, too, the extended black family provided slaves with the independent resources they needed to avoid complete physical, intellectual, cultural, and moral subjugation to their masters.

During an age when infant mortality rates were much higher than they are today, those rates for black southerners were even higher than they were for white people. There were several reasons for this. Enslaved black women usually had to do field labor up to the time they delivered a child, and their diets lacked necessary nutrients. Consequently, they tended to have babies whose weights at birth were less than normal. Enslaved infants were also more likely than other

This woodcut of a black father being sold away from his family appeared in *The Child's Anti-Slavery Book* in 1860. Family ruptures, like the one shown, were among the more common and tragic aspects to slavery, especially in the upper South, where masters claimed slavery was "mild."

children to be subject to such postpartum maladies as rickets, tetany, tetanus, high fevers, intestinal worms, and influenza. More than 50 percent of slave children died before the age of five.

Slaveholders contributed to high infant mortality rates probably more from ignorance than malevolence. It was, after all, in the master's economic self-interest to have slave mothers produce healthy children. Masters often allowed mothers a month to recuperate after giving birth and several months thereafter off from field-work to nurse their babies. Although this reduced the mother's productivity, the children's labor might make up the loss when they entered the plantation workforce. Unfortunately, many infants needed more than a few months of breast-feeding to survive.

The care of slave children varied with the size of a slaveholder's estate, the region it was in, and the mother's work. House servants could carry their babies with them while they did their work. On small farms, slave women strapped their babies to their backs or left them at the edge of fields, so they could nurse them periodically, although the latter practice risked exposing an infant to ants, flies, or mosquitoes. On larger plantations, mothers could leave a child with an elderly or infirm adult. This encouraged a sense of community and a shared responsibility among the slaves for all black children on a plantation.

VOICES

A SLAVEHOLDER DESCRIBES A NEW PURCHASE

In this letter to her mother, a white Louisiana woman, Tryphena Blanche Holder Fox, describes her husband's purchase of a slave woman and her children. Several things are apparent in the letter— that investing in slaves was expensive, that the white woman's only concern for the slave woman and her children was their economic value, that it was up to the white woman to supervise the new slaves, and that the slave woman showed her displeasure with her situation.

Hygiene [Jesuit Bend, Louisiana]
Sunday, Dec. 27th 1857

Dear Mother,

We are obliged to save every dollar he can "rake & scrape" to pay for a negro woman. . . . She has two likely children . . . and is soon to have another, and he only pays fourteen hundred for the three. She is considered an excellent bargain . . . he would not sell her and the children for less than $2,000. She came & worked two days, so we could see what she was capable of. . . . She was sold by a Frenchman. . . . He has a family of ten & she had all the work to do besides getting her own wood & water from the river. She was not used to do this, and gave them a great deal of trouble. . . . How much trouble she will give me, I don't know, but I think I can get along with her, passable well any how. Of course it increased my cares, for having invested so much in one purchase, it will be to my interest to see that the children are well taken care of & clothed and fed. All of them give more or less trouble. . . .

▶ *What does Tryphena reveal about the management of slaves?*
▶ *What does she indicate about the ability of slaves to force concessions from their masters?*

Source: Tryphena Blanche Holder Fox to Anna Rose Holder, December 27, 1857, Mississippi Department of Archives and History, Jackson, Mississippi.

As children grew older, they spent much time in unsupervised play, often with white children. Boys played marbles and ball games; girls skipped rope and tended to their dolls. A game of hiding and whipping, similar to the more recent cops and robbers, was a childish commentary on a violent system.

Slave childhood was short. Early on, parents and others taught youngsters about the realities of plantation life. As early as age six, children undertook so-called light chores. Work became more taxing as the children grew older, until, between the ages of eight and twelve, they performed adult fieldwork. Sale away from their families, particularly in the Upper South, also accelerated progress to adulthood.

SEXUAL EXPLOITATION

As with forced separations, masters' sexual exploitation of black women disrupted enslaved families. Abuse of black women began during the Middle Passage and continued after the abolition of slavery in the United States in 1865.

Long-term relationships between masters and enslaved women were common in the nineteenth-century South. Such continuing relationships rested not on overt coercion but on masters' implicit power and authority. The relationship between Thomas Jefferson and his slave Sally Hemings is the most infamous of these. DNA and circumstantial evidence indicate that Jefferson and Hemings had a long sexual relationship that produced four children who survived to adulthood. It began in 1787 when Hemings served as caretaker to one of Jefferson's daughters at his household in Paris, where he was U.S. ambassador to France. At that time Jefferson was 44 and Hemings about fourteen. She was pregnant when she returned to Virginia in 1789, although the child probably died in infancy.

There is evidence that Hemings and her children enjoyed special privileges on Jefferson's Monticello plantation. But, by modern standards, her relationship to Jefferson began with statutory rape, and Hemings's unfree status and that of her children limited her ability to resist his sexual advances. Two of Hemings's children, a man named Beverly and a woman named Harriet, were "allowed" to escape in 1821 or 1822. Thereafter, they lived as white people in Washington, D.C. Two others, Madison and Eston, gained freedom as young men under Jefferson's will. Jefferson never freed Sally Hemings. Instead, his daughter permitted her to leave Monticello shortly after his death in 1826. She lived with Madison and Eston in Charlotte, Virginia, until her death in 1835.

Even more common than relationships like that of Jefferson and Hemings were instances in which masters, overseers, and their sons forced slave women to have sex against their will. This routine rape caused great distress. Former slave Harriet Jacobs wrote in her autobiography, "I cannot tell how much I suffered in the presence of these wrongs, nor how I am still pained by the retrospect." One of the more notorius antebellum (pre–Civil War) cases of forced sexual exploitation occurred in Missouri during the 1850s. It involved 60-year-old Robert Newsom and Celia, a fourteen-year-old girl he had purchased in 1850. Newsom repeatedly raped Celia until she killed him in 1855. Celia's attorneys put up a spirited defense at her trial. They argued that an 1845 Missouri law that made it a crime to "take any woman unlawfully against her will and by force, menace or duress, compel her to be defiled" gave Celia a right to defend her virtue. But the white male jury convicted her of murder anyway, and she was executed.

White southerners justified sexual abuse of black women in several ways. They maintained that black women were naturally promiscuous and seduced white men. Some proslavery apologists argued that the sexual exploitation of black women by white men reduced prostitution and promoted purity among white women. These apologists ignored the devastating emotional impact of sexual exploitation on black women. They failed to note that the rape of black women by white men emphasized in the most degrading manner the inability of black men to protect their wives and daughters.

DIET

The slaves' diet hardly raised the moral issues associated with the sexual exploitation of black women by white men. The typical plantation's weekly ration of one peck of cornmeal (about 14 pounds) and three to four pounds of salt pork or bacon was enough to maintain an adult's body weight and, therefore, appeared to be adequate. But even when black men and women added vegetables, eggs, and poultry that they raised or fish and small game that they caught, this diet was (according to modern medical science) deficient in calcium, vitamin C, riboflavin, protein, and iron and other minerals. Because these nutrients are essential to the health of people who perform hard labor in a hot climate, slaves frequently suffered from chronic illnesses. They often complained about being hungry and the poor quality of their food. As one song went,

> We raise de wheat,
> Dey gib us de corn;
> We bake de bread,
> Dey gib us de crust;
> We sif' de meal,
> Dey gib us de huss;
> We peel de meat,
> Dey gib us de skin

Yet masters and white southerners generally consumed the same sort of food that slaves ate, and, in

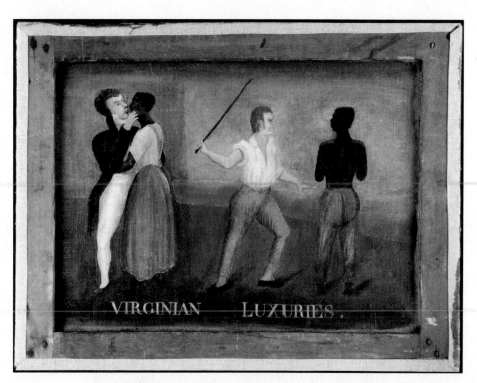

Throughout its existence, slavery in America encouraged white men to exploit black women for sexual purposes and to abuse black men and women physically. *Virginian Luxuries,* painted c. 1810, aimed to expose and ridicule these practices.

comparison to people in other parts of the Atlantic world, enslaved African Americans were not undernourished. Although adult slaves were on average an inch shorter than white northerners, they were three inches taller than new arrivals from Africa, two inches taller than slaves who lived in the West Indies, and one inch taller than British Royal Marines.

African-American cooks, primarily women, developed a distinctive cuisine based on African culinary traditions. They seasoned foods with salt, onions, pepper, and other spices and herbs. They fried meat and fish, served sauce over rice, and flavored vegetables with bits of smoked meat. The availability in the South of such African foods as okra, yams, collard greens, benne seeds, and peanuts strengthened their culinary ties to that continent. Cooking also gave black women the ability to control part of their lives and demonstrate their creativity.

CLOTHING

Enslaved men and women had less control over what they and their children wore than how they cooked. Although skilled slaves often produced the shoes and clothing plantation workers wore, slaves in general rarely had the time or skill to make their own clothes. They went barefoot during the warm months and wore cheap shoes, usually made by local cobblers, in the winter. Slaveholding women, with the help of trained female house servants, sewed the clothes slaves wore.

This clothing was usually made of homespun cotton or wool. Some slaves also received hand-me-downs from masters and overseers. Although the distribution of clothing varied widely over time and space and according to the generosity of masters, slaves usually received clothing allotments twice a year. At the fall distribution, slave men received two outfits for the cold weather along with a jacket and a wool cap. At the spring distribution, they received two cotton outfits. Slave drivers wore garments of finer cloth and greatcoats during the winter. Butlers and carriage drivers wore liveries appropriate to their public duties. Slave women received at each distribution two simple dresses of calico or homespun. In the winter they wore capes or cloaks and covered their heads with kerchiefs or bonnets.

Because masters gave priority to clothing adult workers, small children often went naked during the warm months. Depending on their ages and the season, children received garments called *shirts* if worn by boys and *shifts* if worn by girls. "I ain' neber had no pants 'till de year befo' de [Civil] war. All de li'l boys wo' shu't-tail shu'ts, jes' a slip to de knees," recalled

Black children began doing "light chores" in cotton fields at an early age. These girls are collecting cotton boles that older workers missed.

former Louisiana slave Jacob Branch. This androgynous garb lasted until children reached "about twelve or fourteen," when they began doing adult work.

Although they received standard-issue clothing, black women particularly sought to individualize what they wore. They changed the colors of clothes with dyes they extracted from roots, berries, walnut shells, oak leaves, and indigo. They wove threads of different color into their clothes to make "checkedy" and other patterns. Former slave Morris Sheppard remembered that with his mother "everything was stripedy."

HEALTH

Low birth weight, diet, and clothing all affected the health of slaves. Before the 1830s diseases were endemic among them, and death could come quickly. Much of this ill health resulted from overwork in the South's hot, humid summers, exposure to cold during the winter, and poor hygiene. Slave quarters, for example, rarely had privies; human waste could contaminate drinking water; and food was prepared under unsanitary conditions. Dysentery, typhus, food poisoning, diarrhea, hepatitis, tuberculosis, typhoid fever, salmonella, and intestinal worms were common and often fatal maladies.

The South's warm climate encouraged mosquito-borne diseases like yellow fever and malaria, the growth of bacteria, and the spread of viruses. Interaction between people of African and European descent increased the types of illnesses. Smallpox, measles, and gonorrhea were European diseases. Malaria, hookworm, and yellow fever came from Africa. The sickle-cell blood trait protected people of African descent from malaria but could cause sickle-cell anemia, a painful, debilitating, and fatal disease.

African Americans were also more susceptible to certain other afflictions than were persons of European descent. They suffered from lactose intolerance, which greatly limited the amount of calcium they could absorb from dairy products, and from a limited ability to acquire vitamin D from sunlight in temperate regions. Because many slaves lost calcium through perspiration while working, these characteristics led to a high incidence of debilitating diseases. These included, according to historian Donald R. Wright, "blindness or inflamed and watery eyes; lameness or crooked limbs; loose, missing or rotten teeth; and skin sores. Also, they made African Americans much more apt than whites to suffer from a number of often fatal diseases—tetanus, intestinal worms, diphtheria, whooping cough, pica (or dirt eating), pneumonia, tuberculosis, and dysentery."

However, black southerners constituted the only New World slave population that grew by natural reproduction. Although the death rate among slaves was higher than among white southerners, it was similar to that of Europeans. Slave health also improved after 1830, when their rising economic value persuaded masters to improve slave quarters, provide warmer winter clothing, reduce overwork, and hire physicians to care for bond people. During the 1840s and 1850s, slaves were more likely than white southerners to be cared for by a physician, although there was often little that nineteenth-century doctors could do to combat disease.

Enslaved African Americans also used traditional remedies—derived from Africa and passed down by generations of women—to treat the sick. Wild cherry bark and herbs like pennyroyal or horehound went into teas to treat colds. Slaves used jimsonweed tea to counter rheumatism and chestnut leaf tea to relieve asthma. One former slave recalled that her grandmother dispensed syrup to treat colic and teas to cure fevers and stomachaches. Some of these folk remedies were more effective than those prescribed by white physicians. This was especially true of kaolin, a white clay that black women used to treat dysentery.

The Socialization of Slaves

African Americans had to acquire the skills needed to protect themselves and their loved ones from a brutal slave system. Folktales, often derived from Africa but on occasion from American Indians, helped pass such skills from generation to generation. Parents, other relatives, and elderly slaves generally told such tales to teach survival, mental agility, and self-confidence.

The heroes of the tales are animal tricksters with human personalities. Most famous is Brer Rabbit, who in his weakness and cleverness represents African Americans in slavery. Although the tales portray Brer Rabbit as far from perfect, he uses his wits to overcome threats from strong and vicious antagonists, principally Brer Fox, who represents slaveholders. By hearing these stories and rooting for Brer Rabbit, slave children learned how to conduct themselves in a difficult environment.

They learned to watch what they said to white people, not to talk back, to withhold information about other African Americans, and to dissemble. In particular, they refrained from making antislavery statements and camouflaged their awareness of how masters exploited them. As Henry Bibb, who escaped from slavery, put it, "The only weapon of self defense that I could use successfully was that of deception." Another former slave, Charshee Charlotte Lawrence-McIntyre, summed up the slave strategy in rhyme: "Got one mind for the boss to see; got another for what I know is me."

Masters tended to miss the subtlety of the divided consciousness of their bond people. When slaves refused to do simple tasks correctly, masters saw it as black stupidity rather than resistance. Sometimes outsiders, such as white northern missionary Charles C. Jones, understood more clearly what was going on. In 1842 Jones observed,

> Persons live and die in the midst of Negroes and know comparatively little of their real character. The Negroes form a distinct class in the community, and keep themselves very much to themselves. They are one thing before the whites and another before their own color. Deception towards the former is characteristic of them, whether bond or free. . . . It is habit—long established custom, which descends from generation to generation.

Religion

Along with family and socialization, religion helped African Americans cope with slavery. Some masters denied their slaves access to Christianity, and some slaves ignored the religion. In New Orleans, Baltimore, and a few other locations, there were Roman Catholic slaves, who were usually the human property of Roman Catholic masters. In Maryland during the 1830s, the Jesuits, an order of Roman Catholic priests and brothers, collectively owned approximately 300 slaves. But by the mid-nineteenth century, most American slaves practiced a Protestantism similar but not identical to that of most white southerners.

Biracial Baptist and Methodist congregations persisted in the South longer than they did in northern cities. The southern congregations usually had racially segregated seating, but black and white people joined in communion and church discipline. They shared cemeteries.

Read the **Document**
Charles C. Jones, The Religious Instruction of the Negroes in the United States (1842)

Many masters during the nineteenth century sponsored plantation churches for slaves, and white missionary organizations also supported such churches.

In the plantation churches, white ministers told their black congregations that Christian slaves must obey their earthly masters as they did God. This was not what slaves wanted to hear. Cornelius Garner, a former slave, recalled that "dat ole white preacher jest was telling us slaves to be good to our marsters. We ain't keer'd a bit 'bout dat stuff he was telling us 'cause we wanted to sing, pray, and serve God in our own way." At times slaves walked out on ministers who preached obedience.

Instead of services sponsored by masters, slaves preferred a semisecret black church they conducted

British artist John Antrobus completed this painting in about 1860. It is named *Plantation Burial* and suggests the importance of religion among enslaved African Americans.   John Antrobus, "Negro Burial." Oil painting. The Historic New Orleans Collection. #1960.46

themselves under the leadership of self-called, often illiterate black preachers. They emphasized Moses and deliverance from bondage rather than consistent theology or Christian meekness. Services involved singing, dancing, shouting, moaning, and clapping. According to historian Peter Kolchin, slaves mixed in African "potions, concoctions, charms, and rituals [used] to ward off evil, cure sickness, harm enemies, and produce amorous behavior" with this black Christianity. European settlers in America during the previous century had also melded Christian and non-Christian beliefs and practices. So it is not surprising that white as well as black people continued to seek the help of African-American conjurers.

((•●─[Hear the Audio
Go Down Moses; Come by Hyar
traditional; sung by Bernice Reagon

The Character of Slavery and Slaves

For over a century, historians have debated the character of the Old South's slave system and the people it held in bondage. During the 1910s southern historian Ulrich B. Phillips portrayed slavery as a benign, paternalistic institution in which Christian slaveholders cared for largely content slaves. Slavery, Phillips argued—as had the slaveholders themselves—rescued members of an inferior race from African barbarism and permitted them to rise as far as they possibly could toward civilization. With different emphasis, historian Eugene D. Genovese has, since the 1960s, also placed paternalism at the heart of southern plantation slavery.

•●●─[Read the Document
Southern Novel Depicts Slavery (1832)

Other historians, however, deny paternalism had much to do with a system that rested on force. Since the 1950s they have contended that slaveholders exploited their bond people in a selfish quest for profits. Although some slaveholders were concerned about the welfare of their slaves, this brutal portrait of slavery is persuasive at the dawn of the twenty-first century. Many masters never met their slaves face to face. Most slaves suffered whippings at some point in their lives, and over half the slaves caught up in the domestic slave trade were separated from their families.

Scholars have also compared slavery in the American South with its counterpart in Latin America. Historians note that slaves in Latin American countries influenced by Roman law and the Roman Catholic Church enjoyed more protection from abusive masters than did slaves in the United States, where English law and Protestant Christianity dominated. Routes to freedom, through self-purchase and manumission, were more available in Latin America than in the Old South. There was more interracial marriage and therefore, some historians maintain, less racism in Latin America than in the United States. But other historians have established that protections offered by law and religion to slaves in Latin America were more theoretical than practical. They argue that racism there merely took a different form than it did in the United States. Certainly the mortality rate among Latin American slaves was far greater than among slaves in the American South. This implies that the conditions under which slaves labored in Latin America were even harsher than the grim conditions slaves often faced in the United States.

Another debate has centered on the character of enslaved African Americans. Historians such as Phillips argued that African Americans were genetically predisposed to being slaves and were therefore usually content. In 1959 Stanley M. Elkins changed the debate by arguing that black people were not inherently inferior or submissive but that concentration-camp-like conditions on plantations made them into childlike "Sambos." They were, according to Elkins, as dependent on their masters as inmates in Nazi extermination camps were on their guards.

A scholarly reaction to Elkins's study led to current understandings of the character of African Americans in slavery. Since the 1960s historians have argued that rather than dehumanizing black people, slavery led them to create institutions that allowed them some control over their lives. Slaves built families, churches, and communities. According to these historians, African-American resistance forced masters to accept African work patterns and black autonomy in the slave quarters. Although these historians may idealize the strength of slave communities within a brutal plantation context, they have enriched our understanding of slave life.

CONCLUSION

African-American life in slavery during the time of the Cotton Kingdom is a vast subject. As slavery expanded westward before 1860, it varied from region to region and according to the crops that slaves cultivated. Although cotton became the South's most important product, many African-American slaves continued to produce tobacco, rice, sugar, and hemp. In the Chesapeake, slaves grew wheat. Others tended livestock or worked in cities and industry. Meanwhile, enslaved African Americans continued to build the community institutions that allowed them to maintain their cultural autonomy and persevere within a brutal system.

The story of African Americans in southern slavery is one of labor, perseverance, and resistance. Black labor was responsible for the growth of a southern economy that helped produce prosperity throughout the United States. Black men and women preserved and expanded an African-American cultural heritage that included African, European, and American Indian roots. They resisted determined efforts to dehumanize them. They developed family relationships, communities, churches, and traditions that helped them preserve their character as a people.

RECOMMENDED READING

Ira Berlin. *Generations in Captivity: A History of African-American Slaves.* Cambridge, MA: Harvard University Press, 2003. Portrays slavery in the Cotton Kingdom as the product of a series of negotiations between masters and slaves over the terms of captivity.

Charles B. Dew. *Bonds of Iron: Masters and Slaves at Buffalo Forge.* New York: Norton, 1994. Dew offers an excellent account of one type of industrial slavery in the Old South.

Michael P. Johnson and James L. Roark. *Black Masters: A Free Family of Color in the Old South.* New York: Norton, 1984. This book provides a full account of William Ellison and his slaveholding black family.

Norrece T. Jones Jr. *Born a Child of Freedom, yet a Slave: Mechanisms of Control and Strategies of Resistance in Antebellum South Carolina.* Middleton, CT: Wesleyan University Press, 1990. This book explores how masters controlled slaves and how slaves resisted.

Wilma King. *Stolen Childhood: Slave Youth in Nineteenth-Century America.* Bloomington: Indiana University Press, 1995. This is the most up-to-date account of enslaved black children. It is especially useful concerning the children's work.

Melton A. McLaurin. *Celia, a Slave.* Athens: University of Georgia Press, 1991. This is the most complete study of an enslaved woman's response to sexual exploitation. MacLaurin establishes the social and political contexts for this famous case.

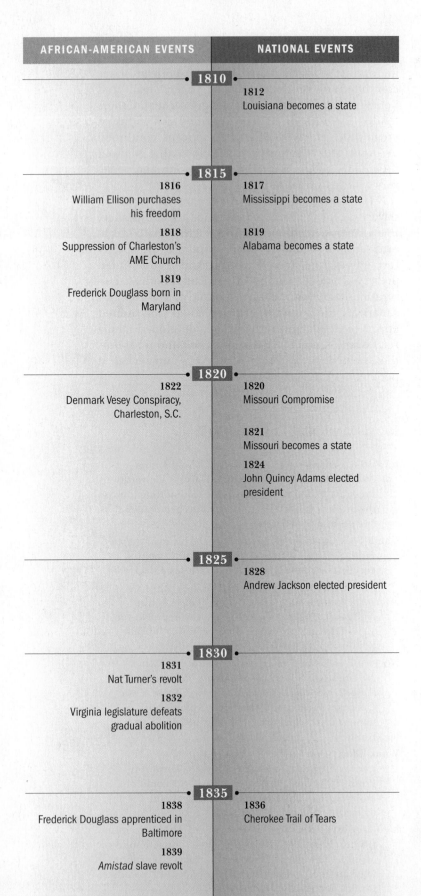

AFRICAN-AMERICAN EVENTS	NATIONAL EVENTS
	1810
	1812 Louisiana becomes a state
	1815
1816 William Ellison purchases his freedom	**1817** Mississippi becomes a state
1818 Suppression of Charleston's AME Church	**1819** Alabama becomes a state
1819 Frederick Douglass born in Maryland	
	1820
1822 Denmark Vesey Conspiracy, Charleston, S.C.	**1820** Missouri Compromise
	1821 Missouri becomes a state
	1824 John Quincy Adams elected president
	1825
	1828 Andrew Jackson elected president
	1830
1831 Nat Turner's revolt	
1832 Virginia legislature defeats gradual abolition	
	1835
1838 Frederick Douglass apprenticed in Baltimore	**1836** Cherokee Trail of Tears
1839 *Amistad* slave revolt	

ADDITIONAL BIBLIOGRAPHY

SLAVERY AND ITS EXPANSION

Stanley M. Elkins. *Slavery: A Problem in American Institutional and Intellectual Life.* 3rd ed. Chicago: University of Chicago Press, 1976.

Eugene D. Genovese. *The Political Economy of Slavery: Studies in the Economy and Society of the Slave South.* 1961. Reprint, New York: Random House, 1967.

Roger G. Kennedy. *Mr. Jefferson's Lost Cause: Land, Farmers, Slavery, and the Louisiana Purchase.* New York: Oxford University Press, 2003.

Larry Koger. *Black Slaveowners: Free Black Slave Masters in South Carolina, 1790–1860.* 1985. Reprint, Columbia: University of South Carolina Press, 1994.

Peter Kolchin. *American Slavery 1619–1877.* New York: Hill and Wang, 1993.

Donald P. McNeilly. *The Old South Frontier: Cotton Plantations and the Formation of Arkansas Society, 1819–1861.* Fayetteville: University of Arkansas Press, 2000.

John H. Moore. *The Emergence of the Cotton Kingdom in the Old Southwest.* Baton Rouge: Louisiana State University Press, 1988.

Larry Eugene Rivers. *Slavery in Florida: Territorial Days to Emancipation.* Gainsville: University Press of Florida, 2000.

Kenneth M. Stampp. *The Peculiar Institution: Slavery in the Antebellum South.* 1956. Reprint, New York: Vintage Books, 1989.

URBAN AND INDUSTRIAL SLAVERY

Ronald L. Lewis. *Coal, Iron, and Slaves: Industrial Slavery in Maryland and Virginia, 1715–1865.* Westport, CT: Greenwood, 1979.

Robert S. Starobin. *Industrial Slavery in the Old South.* New York: Oxford University Press, 1970.

Midori Takagi. *Rearing Wolves to Our Own Destruction: Slavery in Richmond, Virginia, 1782–1865.* Charlottesville: University Press of Virginia, 1999.

Richard C. Wade. *Slavery in the Cities: The South 1820–1860.* 1964. Reprint, New York: Oxford University Press, 1967.

THE DOMESTIC SLAVE TRADE

Steven Deyle. *Carry Me Back: the Domestic Slave Trade in American Life.* New York: Oxford University Press, 2005.

Walter Johnson. *Soul by Soul: Life inside the Antebellum Slave Market.* Cambridge, MA: Harvard University Press, 1999.

Michael Tadman. *Speculators and Slaves: Masters, Traders, and Slaves in the Old South.* 1989. Reprint, Madison: University of Wisconsin Press, 1996.

THE SLAVE COMMUNITY

John W. Blassingame. *The Slave Community: Plantation Life in the Antebellum South.* 2nd ed. New York: Oxford University Press, 1979.

Janet Duitsman Cornelius. *Slave Missions and the Black Church in the Antebellum South.* Columbia: University of South Carolina Press, 1999.

Wilma A. Dunaway. *The African-American Family in Slavery and Emancipation.* New York: Cambridge University Press, 2003.

Eugene D. Genovese. *Roll, Jordan, Roll: The World the Slave Made.* 1974. Reprint, Vintage Books, 1976.

Herbert Gutman. *The Black Family in Slavery and Freedom.* 1976. Reprint, Vintage Books, 1977.

Charles Joyner. *Down by the Riverside: A South Carolina Community.* Urbana: University of Illinois Press, 1984.

Ann Patton Malone. *Sweet Chariot: Slave Family and Household Structure in Nineteenth-Century Louisiana.* Chapel Hill: University of North Carolina Press, 1992.

Leslie Howard Owens. *This Species of Property: Slave Life and Culture in the Old South.* 1976. Reprint, New York: Oxford University Press, 1977.

Todd L. Savitt. *Medicine and Slavery: The Diseases and Health Care of Blacks in Antebellum Virginia.* Urbana: University of Illinois Press, 1978.

Maria Jenkins Schwartz. *Born in Bondage: Growing up Enslaved in the Antebellum South.* Cambridge, MA: Harvard University Press, 2000.

ENSLAVED WOMEN

David Barry Gaspar and Darlene Clark Hine, eds. *More Than Chattel: Black Women and Slavery in the Americas.* Bloomington: Indiana University Press, 1996.

Thavolia Glymph. *Out of the House of Bondage: The Transformation of the Plantation Household.* New York: Cambridge University Press, 2008.

Darlene Clark Hine, Wilma King, and Linda Reed, eds. *"We Specialize in the Wholly Impossible": A Reader in Black Women's History.* Brooklyn, NY: Carlson, 1996.

Joshua D. Rothman. *Notorious in the Neighborhood: Sex and Families across the Color Line in Virginia 1787–1861.* Chapel Hill: University of North Carolina Press, 2003.

Deborah Gray White. *Ar'n't I a Woman? Female Slaves in the Plantation South.* New York: Norton, 1985.

Jean Fagan Yellin. *Harriet Jacobs: A Life.* New York: Basic Civitas, 2003.

SLAVE CULTURE AND RELIGION

John B. Boles, ed. *Masters and Slaves in the House of the Lord: Race and Religion in the American South, 1740–1870.* Lexington: University Press of Kentucky, 1988.

Janet Duitsman Cornelius. *When I Can Read My Title Clear: Literacy, Slavery, and Religion in the Antebellum South.* Columbia: University of South Carolina Press, 1991.

———. *Slave Missions and the Black Church in the Antebellum South.* Columbia: University of South Carolina Press, 1999.

Sharla M. Fett. *Working Cures: Healing, Health, and Power on Southern Slave Plantations.* Chapel Hill: University of North Carolina Press, 2002.

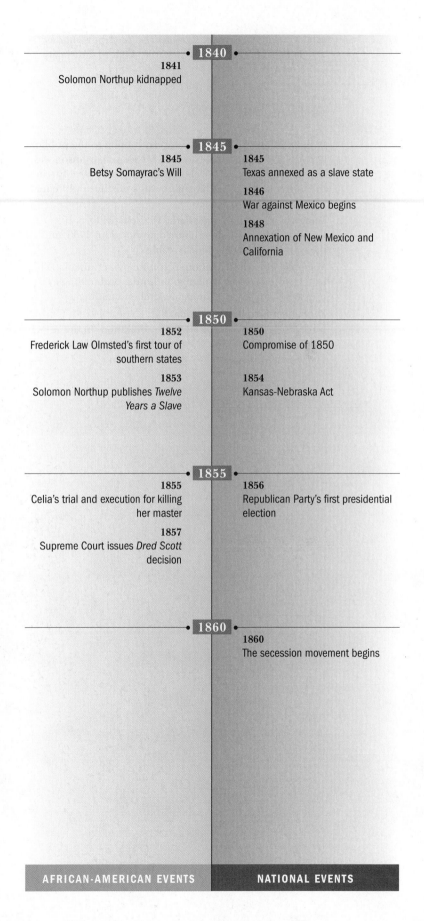

1840

1841
Solomon Northup kidnapped

1845

1845
Betsy Somayrac's Will

1845
Texas annexed as a slave state

1846
War against Mexico begins

1848
Annexation of New Mexico and California

1850

1852
Frederick Law Olmsted's first tour of southern states

1853
Solomon Northup publishes *Twelve Years a Slave*

1850
Compromise of 1850

1854
Kansas-Nebraska Act

1855

1855
Celia's trial and execution for killing her master

1857
Supreme Court issues *Dred Scott* decision

1856
Republican Party's first presidential election

1860

1860
The secession movement begins

AFRICAN-AMERICAN EVENTS   NATIONAL EVENTS

Albert J. Raboteau. *Slave Religion: The "Invisible Institution" in the Antebellum South.* New York: Oxford University Press, 1978.

RETRACING THE ODYSSEY

William Johnson House (not currently open to the public) **and Melrose Plantation,** Natchez, Mississippi. Johnson was one of the rare black slaveholders, and John T. McMurrin, the owner of Melrose Plantation, was a northern white man who became a slaveholder.

Hampton Plantation State Park, McClellanville, South Carolina. The plantation house dates to about 1750, and the outbuildings include slave cabins.

Magnolia Mound Plantation, Baton Rouge, Louisiana. This historic site includes a plantation house, outbuildings, an overseer's house, and a separate kitchen building.

Zephaniah Kingsley Plantation, Fort George Island, Florida. Kingsley's was an interracial family. Buildings on the plantation include the oldest standing plantation house in Florida and thirty-two slave quarters.

REVIEW QUESTIONS

1. How did the domestic slave trade and the exploitation of black women by white males affect slave families?

2. How significant were black slaveholders in the history of slavery?

3. How did urban and industrial slavery differ from plantation slavery in the Old South?

4. What impact did housing, nutrition, and disease have on the lives of slaves between 1820 and 1860?

5. How did black Christianity differ from white Christianity in the Old South? How did black Christianity in the South differ from black Christianity in the North?

PEARSON myhistorylab Connections

www.myhistorylab.com

Review what you've learned in this chapter and explore the many documents, images, research tools, and activities for this chapter to learn more about African-American history.

✓ Study and Review

READ
Read the Document

- State Laws Govern Slavery (1824)

- A Muslim Slave Speaks Out (1831)

- Southern Novel Depicts Slavery (1832)

- E. S. Abdy, *Description of a Washington, D.C., Slave Pen* (1835)

- Charles C. Jones, *The Religious Instruction of the Negroes in the United States* (1842)

- Frederick Douglass, excerpt from *Narrative of the Life* (1845)

- A Slave Tells of His Sale at Auction (1848)

- Georgia Slave Codes (1848)

- Farm Journal Reports on the Care and Feeding of Slaves (1836)

- A Slave Girl Tells of Her Life (1861)

- Frederick Law Olmsted, from *A Journey in the Seabord States* (1856)

LISTEN
Hear the Audio

Hear the audio files for Chapter 6.

- *Pick a Bale of Cotton*

- *Come by Hyar* traditional; sung by Bernice Reagon

- *Go Down Moses*

RESEARCH
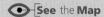

Consider these questions in a short research paper.

How did blacks resist the oppression of the slave system?

What steps did whites take to eliminate resistance?

EXPLORE
See the Map

- Agriculture, Industry, and Slavery in the Old South (1850)

Free Black People in Antebellum America

What were the demographics of black freedom?

How did the policies of the Jacksonian Democrats favor slaveholders?

How was black freedom limited in the North?

What were the characteristics of northern black communities?

What institutions did African Americans rely on most?

How did free African Americans live in the South and the West?

▶ **This lithograph, published in 1818** by antislavery author Jesse Torrey Jun, depicts a free black man still in handcuffs and leg irons after an attempt to kidnap him into slavery. He is relating details of his experience to a sympathetic white man. The sparsely furnished attic room reflects the living conditions of many free African Americans of the time. Courtesy of the Library of Congress

166

O ur vices and our degradation are ever arrayed against us, but our virtues are passed by unnoticed. And what is still more lamentable, our [white] friends, to whom we concede all the principles of humanity and religion, from these very causes seem to have fallen into the current of popular feeling and are imperceptibly floating on the stream—actually living in the practice of prejudice, while they abjure it in theory, and feel it not in their hearts.

Freedom's Journal,
March 16, 1827

◄ **Blacks who escaped** from slavery lived in fear that they might be sought by masters who often posted monetary offers for the return of runaway slaves.

Journalist Samuel Cornish wrote this passage in 1827 when he introduced himself to his readers as the coeditor of the first African-American newspaper. He knew that pervasive white prejudice limited the lives of black people. During the 40 years before the Civil War, such prejudice was nearly as common in the North as in the South. The northern states had, of course, abolished slavery, and free black people in the North enjoyed more rights than they did in the South. But

((•⊢ **Hear the Audio**

Hear the audio files for Chapter 7 at **www.myhistorylab.com**

that made many white northerners more hostile toward African Americans than white southerners generally were.

While southern legislatures considered expelling free black people from their states, northern legislatures—particularly in the Old Northwest—restricted black people's ability to move into their states. White workers, North and South, fearing competition for jobs, sponsored legislation that limited most free African Americans to menial employment. White people also required most black people to live in segregated areas of cities. Yet such ghettoized African-American communities cultivated a dynamic cultural legacy and built enduring institutions.

This chapter picks up the story of free black communities that began in Chapter 5. It provides a portrait of free African Americans between 1820 and the start of the Civil War. Like the revolutionary era, the antebellum period was a time of hope and fear. The numbers of free African Americans steadily increased. But the number of slaves increased much faster.

Demographics of Freedom

In 1820 there were 233,504 free African Americans in the United States. In comparison, there were 1,538,125 slaves and 7,861,931 white people. Of the free African Americans, 99,281 lived in the North, 114,070 in the Upper South, and only 20,153 in the Deep South (see Map 7–1). Free people of color accounted for 2.4 percent of the American population and 3 percent of the southern population. More black women than black men were free in 1820, and—particularly in urban areas—this remained true throughout the period. As the southern states made freedom suits and manumission more difficult, the northern free black population increased more rapidly than the free black populations in either the Upper or the Deep South.

By 1860 the free African-American population had reached 488,070. Of these, 226,152 lived in the North, 224,963 in the Upper South, and 36,955 in the Deep South (see Figures 7–1 and 7–2). A few thousand free black people also lived in the west beyond Missouri, Arkansas, and Texas. Meanwhile, the number of slaves had increased to just under four million, and massive immigration had tripled the white population to 26,957,471. Because the white population grew so quickly, the proportion of free African Americans dropped to just 1.6 percent of the total American

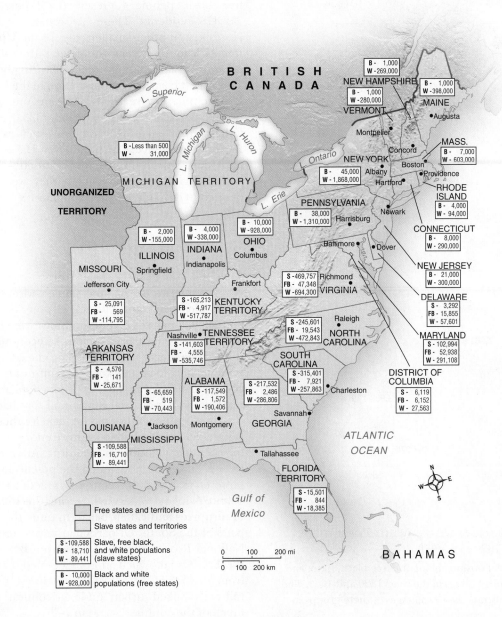

MAP 7–1   THE SLAVE, FREE BLACK, AND WHITE POPULATIONS OF THE UNITED STATES IN 1830

This map does not distinguish the slave from the free black population of the free states, although the process of gradual emancipation in several northeastern states was still under way and some black northerners remained enslaved.   Source: For slave states, Ira Berlin, *Slaves without Masters: The Free Negro in the Antebellum South* (New York: New Press, 1971); for free states, *Historical Statistics of the United States* (Washington: GPO, 1960). Note: Figures for free states are rounded to the nearest thousand.

▶ *Which states had the largest and the smallest free black populations in 1830?*

⊙ See the Map *Explore this map at* **www.myhistorylab.com**

population and to 2.1 percent of the southern population by 1861, when the Civil War began the process of making all black people free.

In 1860, 47.3 percent of the free black population lived in cities, compared with only 32.9 percent of white people. Of the urban African Americans, 62.5 percent lived in cities with populations over 100,000. As a result, free African Americans accounted for a significantly larger percentage of the population of large cities than they did of the total American population. In Baltimore

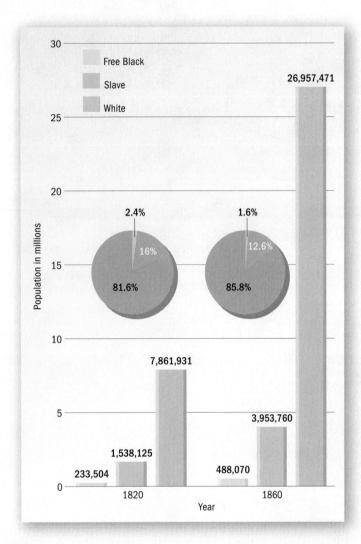

FIGURE 7–1 THE FREE BLACK, SLAVE, AND WHITE POPULATIONS OF THE UNITED STATES IN 1820 AND 1860

The bar graph shows the relationship among the free black, slave, and white populations in the United States in the years 1820 and 1860. The superimposed pie charts illustrate the percentages of these groups in the population in the same years.

free black people represented 12 percent of the 212,418 residents. There, as well as in Richmond, Norfolk, and other smaller cities of the Upper South, free African Americans interacted with enslaved populations to create communities embracing both groups. The largest black urban population in the North was in Philadelphia, where 22,185 African Americans made up 4.2 percent of approximately 533,000 residents. Other important northern cities—such as New York; Boston; Providence; Cincinnati; New Haven, Connecticut; and New Bedford, Massachusetts—had much smaller black populations, but they were still large enough to develop dynamic communities.

The Jacksonian Era

After the War of 1812, free African Americans—like other Americans of the time—witnessed rapid economic, social, and political change. Between 1800 and 1860, a **market revolution** transformed the North into a modern industrial society. An economy based on subsistence farming, goods produced by skilled artisans, and local markets grew into one marked by commercial farming, factory production, and national markets. The Industrial Revolution that had begun in Britain a century earlier set the stage for these changes. But transportation had to improve enormously to allow for such a revolution in America. After 1807, when Robert Fulton demonstrated the practicality of steam-powered river vessels, steamboats speeded travel on the country's inland waterways. During the 1820s a system of turnpikes and canals began to unite the North and parts of the South. Of particular importance were the National Road (extending west from Baltimore) and the Erie Canal, which in 1825 opened a water route from New York City to the Old Northwest. By the 1830s railroads linked urban and agricultural regions in much of the country (see Map 7–2).

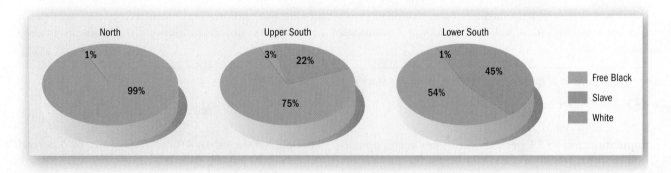

FIGURE 7–2 THE FREE BLACK, SLAVE, AND WHITE POPULATIONS BY REGION, 1860

These pie charts compare the free black, slave, and white populations of the North, Upper South, and Lower South in 1860. Note the near balance of the races in the Lower South.

MAP 7–2   TRANSPORTATION REVOLUTION
This map shows the principal American canals and roads built by 1830 and the principal railroad lines built by 1850.
A growing transportation network cut travel time and shipping costs, which encouraged commerce.

▶ *How did the transportation revolution affect African Americans?*

As faster transportation revolutionized trade, as a factory system began to replace small shops run by artisans, and as cities expanded, northern society profoundly changed. A large urban working class arose. Artisans and small farmers feared for their future. Entrepreneurs began to replace the traditional social elite. The North also became increasingly different from a still largely premodern South. By the 1820s northern states bristled with reform movements designed to deal with the social dislocations the market revolution had caused.

The market revolution also helped create mass political parties as communications improved, populations became more concentrated, and wage workers became more assertive. By 1810 states had begun dropping the property qualifications that had limited citizens' right to vote. One by one, they moved toward universal white manhood suffrage. This trend doomed the openly elitist Federalist Party and disrupted its foe, the Republican Party. As the market revolution picked up during the 1820s, unleashing hopes and fears among Americans, politicians recognized the need for more broadly based political parties.

The 1824 presidential election, in which four candidates ran as Republicans but none received a majority of the popular or electoral vote, marked a turning point. War hero Andrew Jackson of Tennessee led the field, but in early 1825 Congress—exercising its duty to decide such elections—elected Secretary of State John Quincy Adams of Massachusetts. As president, Adams paradoxically represented both the old elitist style of politics and the entrepreneurial spirit of emerging northern capitalism. Adams, along with Henry Clay—Adams's secretary of state—promoted industrialization through a national program of federal aid. But Jackson's supporters claimed that Clay and Adams, by combining their forces in Congress, had cheated the general out of the presidency. Led by Martin Van Buren of New York, they organized a new Democratic Party to counter the Adams-Clay program. By appealing to slaveholders—who believed economic nationalism favored the North over the South—and to "the common man" throughout the country, the Democrats defeated Adams and elected Jackson in 1828.

Jackson was a strong but controversial president. During the **Nullification Crisis** of 1832–1833, he acted as a nationalist in facing down South Carolina's attempt to nullify—to block—the collection of the U.S. tariff (tax) on imports within the state. Otherwise, Jackson, who owned many slaves, promoted states' rights, economic localism, and the territorial expansion of slavery. In opposition

▸▸▸ Read the Document
Senator Sees Slavery as a "Positive Good" (1837)

to Jackson, Henry Clay—a Kentucky slaveholder—and others formed the Whig Party.

A national organization that fought the Democrats for power from 1834 to 1852, the Whig Party mixed traditional and modern politics. It was a mass political party, but many of its leaders questioned the legitimacy of mass parties. It favored a nationalist approach to economic policy, which made it more successful in the North than in the South. It also opposed territorial expansion, worried about the growing number of immigrants, and endorsed the moral values of evangelical Protestantism. In contrast to Democratic politicians who increasingly made racist appeals to antiblack prejudices among white voters, Whigs generally adopted a more conciliatory tone on race. By the late 1830s, a few northern Whigs claimed their party opposed slavery and racial oppression. They were, however, exaggerating. The Whigs often nominated slaveholders for the presidency, and few Whig politicians defended the rights of African Americans.

Limited Freedom in the North

Addressing an interracial audience in Boston in 1846, white abolitionist Joseph C. Lovejoy described the North as a land "partially free." Lovejoy was especially concerned that the Fugitive Slave Law of 1793 extended into the northern states the power of southern masters to enslave African Americans. But white northerners also limited black freedom by enacting **black laws.** They also rarely allowed black men to vote; often advocated segregated housing, schools, and transportation; and limited African Americans' employment opportunities.

The Fugitive Slave Law endangered the freedom of northern black men, women, and children. Those who had escaped from slavery, of course, lived in fear that as long as they stayed in the United States they might be seized and returned to their erstwhile masters. But any black northerner could be kidnapped, taken to a southern state, and enslaved under the aegis of this law. Throughout the antebellum period, vigilance against kidnapping was an important part of northern African-American life.

BLACK LAWS

As indicated in previous chapters, the racially egalitarian impulse of the revolutionary era had by the 1790s begun to wane among white Americans. Meanwhile, the dawning Romantic Age—characterized by a sentimental fascination with uniqueness—encouraged a general belief that each ethnic and racial group had its own inherent spirit that set it apart from others. As white

Americans began to perceive self-reliance, intellectual curiosity, the capacity for self-government, military valor, and an energetic work ethic as inherently "Anglo-Saxon" characteristics, they began to believe other racial groups lacked these virtues. As Samuel Cornish suggested, even those white people who befriended black people considered them outsiders in a "white man's country."

Most white northerners wanted nothing to do with African Americans. They paradoxically dismissed black people as incapable of honest work and feared black competition for jobs. Contact with African Americans, they believed, had degraded white southerners and would also corrupt white northerners if permitted. Therefore, as historian Leon Litwack puts it, "Nearly every northern state considered, and many adopted, measures to prohibit or restrict the further immigration of Negroes."

Read the **Document**
North Carolina Codes (1855)

Such measures were more prevalent in the Old Northwest than in the Northeast. Ohio, Illinois, Indiana, Michigan, Iowa, and Wisconsin all limited or banned black immigration and discriminated against black residents. But in 1821 a bill to keep black people from entering Massachusetts failed to reach a vote in the state legislature on the grounds that it was inconsistent with "love of humanity." In Pennsylvania, which had a much larger influx of southern African Americans than Massachusetts, the legislature defeated attempts to limit their entry.

Between 1804 and 1849, Ohio's "black laws" required that African Americans entering the state produce legal evidence that they were free, register with a county clerk, and post a $500 bond "to pay for their support in case of want." State and local authorities rarely enforced these provisions, and by the time the Ohio **Free Soil Party** brought about their repeal in 1849, about 25,000 African Americans lived in the state. But these rules made black people insecure. In 1829 Cincinnati used them to force between 1,100 and 2,200 black residents to depart. Moreover, other provisions of Ohio's black laws were rigorously enforced, including those that prohibited black testimony against white people, black service on juries, and black enlistment in the state militia.

In 1813 Illinois Territory threatened that African Americans who tried to settle within its borders would be repeatedly whipped until they left. In 1847, long after it had become a state, Illinois mandated that African Americans who sought to become permanent residents could be fined. Those who could not pay the fine could be sold at public auction into indentured servitude. Indiana citizens ratified a state constitution in 1851 that explicitly banned all African Americans from the state, and Michigan, Iowa, and Wisconsin followed Indiana's example. Yet, as in Ohio, these states

Eliza, Nellie, and Margaret Copeland in an 1854 portrait by W. M. Prior. The Copeland family was one of the few African-American families in antebellum America affluent enough to commission such a portrait. Note the girls' fine clothing.   Three Sisters of the Copeland Family, 1854; William Matthew Prior, American (1806–1873). Oil on canvas; 26 7/8 × 36 1/2 in. (68.3 × 92.7 cm). Bequest of Martha C. Karolik for the M. and M. Karolik Collection of American Paintings, 1815–1865, 48.467. Courtesy, Museum of Fine Arts, Boston. Reproduced with permission. © 2004 Museum of Fine Arts, Boston. All Rights Reserved.

rarely enforced such restrictive laws. As long as they did not feel threatened, white people were usually willing to tolerate a few black people (see Table 7–1).

DISFRANCHISEMENT

The disfranchisement of black voters was common throughout the North—except in most of New England—during the antebellum decades. The same white antipathy to African Americans that led to exclusionary legislation supported the movement to deny black men the right to vote (no women could vote anywhere in the United States during most of the

TABLE 7–1   BLACK POPULATION IN THE STATES OF THE OLD NORTHWEST, 1800–1840

	1800	1810	1820	1830	1840
Ohio	337	1,899	4,723	9,574	17,345
Michigan		144	174	293	707
Illinois		781	1,374	2,384	3,929
Indiana	298	630	1,420	3,632	7,168
Iowa					188

Source: James Oliver Horton and Lois E. Horton, *In Hope of Liberty: Culture, Community, and Protest among Northern Free Blacks, 1700–1860* (New York: Oxford University Press, 1997), 104.

nineteenth century). Because northern antiblack sentiment was so strong in the Old Northwest, before the Civil War no black men were ever allowed to vote in Ohio, Indiana, Illinois, Michigan, Wisconsin, and Iowa. But the older northern states had allowed black male suffrage, and efforts to curtail it were by-products of Jacksonian democracy.

During the eighteenth and early nineteenth centuries, the dominant elite in the northeastern states had used property qualifications to prevent poor black and white men from voting. Because black people were generally poorer than white people, these property qualifications gave most white men the right to vote and denied it to most black men. Under such circumstances, white people saw no danger in letting a few relatively well-to-do black men exercise the franchise. It was the egalitarian movement to remove property qualifications that led to the outright disfranchisement of most black voters in the Northeast.

Both advocates and opponents of universal white male suffrage opposed allowing all black men to vote. They alleged that in certain places black men would be elected to office, morally suspect African Americans would corrupt the political process, black people would be encouraged to try to mix socially with white people, and justifiably angry white people would react violently. Therefore, the movement for universal white manhood suffrage transformed a class issue into a racial one. Although some New England states rejected disfranchisement of black voters, this was not the case in those northeastern states with the largest black populations.

New Jersey stopped allowing black men to vote in 1807 and in 1844 adopted a white-only suffrage provision in its state constitution. In 1818 Connecticut determined that, although black men who had voted before that date could continue to vote, no new black voters would be allowed. At the other extreme, Maine, New Hampshire, Vermont, and Massachusetts—none of which had a significant African-American minority—made no effort to deprive black men of the vote. In the middle were Rhode Island, New York, and Pennsylvania, which had protracted struggles over the issue.

In 1822 Rhode Island denied that black men were eligible to vote in its elections, but in 1842 a popular uprising against the state's conservative government extended the franchise to all men, black and white. In New York an 1821 state constitutional convention defeated an attempt to disfranchise all black men. Instead, it raised the property qualification for black voters while eliminating it for white voters. To vote in New York, black men had to have property worth $250 (approximately 7,000 current dollars) and pay taxes, whereas white men simply had to pay taxes or

serve in the state militia. This provision denied the right to vote to nearly all of the 10,000 black men who had previously voted in the state. African Americans nevertheless remained active in New York politics. As supporters of the Liberty Party in 1844, the Whig Party in 1846, and the **Free-Soil Party** in 1848, they fought unsuccessfully to regain equal access to the polls.

A similar protracted struggle in Pennsylvania resulted in a more absolute elimination of black suffrage. From 1780 to 1837, black men who met property qualifications could vote in some of this state's counties but not in others. Then, in 1838, delegates to a convention to draft a new state constitution voted 77 to 45 to enfranchise all white men and disfranchise all black men. Although such African-American leaders as Robert Purvis, Peter Gardner, and Frederick Hinton organized to prevent the new constitution from being adopted, Pennsylvanians ratified it by a vote of 113,971 to 112,759. As late as 1855, black Pennsylvanians, arguing that without the right to vote they faced mounting repression, petitioned Congress to help them gain equal access to the polls. But their efforts failed. Just before the Civil War, 93 percent of northern black people lived in states that either denied or limited black men's right to vote.

SEGREGATION

Exclusionary legislation was confined to the Old Northwest, and not all northern states disfranchised black men. But no black northerner could avoid being victimized by a pervasive determination among white people to segregate society.

Northern hotels, taverns, and resorts turned black people away unless they were the servants of white guests. African Americans either were banned from public lecture halls, art exhibits, and religious revivals or could attend only at certain times. When they were allowed in churches and theaters, they had to sit in segregated sections. Ohio excluded African Americans from state-supported poorhouses and insane asylums. In relatively enlightened Massachusetts, prominent black abolitionist and orator Frederick Douglass was "within the space of a few days . . . turned away from a menagerie on Boston Common, a lyceum [a public lecture hall] and revival meeting in New Bedford, [and] an eating house."

African Americans faced special difficulty trying to use public transportation. They could ride in stagecoaches only if there were no white passengers. As rail travel became more common during the late 1830s, companies set aside special cars for African Americans. In Massachusetts in 1841, a railroad first used the term **Jim Crow,** which derived from a blackface minstrel act, to describe these cars. Later the term came to define other forms of racial segregation as well. In cities, many omnibus and streetcar companies barred African Americans entirely, even though urban black people had little choice but to try to use these means of transportation. Steamboats refused to rent cabins to African Americans. They had to remain on deck at night and during storms. All African Americans, regardless of their wealth or social standing, endured such treatment.

In this atmosphere, black people learned to distrust white people. A correspondent of Frederick Douglass's newspaper, the **North Star,** wrote in 1849 that there seemed "to be a fixed determination on the part of our oppressors in this country to destroy every vestige of self-respect, self-possession, and manly independence left in the colored people." Even when African Americans interacted with white people on an ostensibly equal basis, there were underlying tensions. James Forten's wealthy granddaughter Charlotte Forten, who attended an integrated school in Boston, wrote in her diary, "It is hard to go through life meeting contempt with contempt, hatred with hatred, fearing with too good

reason, to love and trust hardly any one whose skin is white—however lovable, attractive, and congenial."

African Americans moving to northern cities were not surprised to find segregated black neighborhoods. A few wealthy black people lived in white urban neighborhoods, and a few northern cities, such as Cleveland and Detroit, had no patterns of residential segregation. But in most cases, a white belief that black neighbors led to lowered property values produced such patterns. There were "Nigger Hill" in Boston, "Little Africa" in Cincinnati, "Hayti" in Pittsburgh, and Philadelphia's "Southside." Conditions in these ghettoes were often dreadful, but they provided a refuge from constant insult and a place where black institutions could develop.

Because African Americans representing all social and economic classes lived in segregated neighborhoods, the quality of housing in them varied. But, at its worst, such housing was bleak and dangerous. One visitor called the black section of New York City's Five Points "the worst hell of America," and other black urban neighborhoods

This nineteenth-century lithograph depicts a street scene in the notorious Five Points neighborhood of New York City. Amid deteriorating buildings, black people are shown to be victims of poverty, crime, and immorality.

were just as bad. People lived in unheated shacks and shanties, in dirt-floored basements, or in houses without doors and windows. These conditions nurtured disease, infant mortality, alcoholism, and crime. Southern visitors to northern cities blamed the victims, insisting that the plight of many urban black northerners proved that African Americans were better off in slavery.

Black Communities in the Urban North

Northern African Americans lived in both rural and urban areas during the antebellum decades, but it was urban neighborhoods, with their more concentrated black populations, that nurtured black community life (see Table 7–2). African-American urban communities of the antebellum period developed from the free black communities that had emerged from slavery in the North during the late eighteenth century. The communities varied from city to city and from region to region, yet they had much in common and interacted with each other. Resilient families, poverty, class divisions, active church congregations, the continued development of voluntary organizations, and concern for education characterized them. Particularly in the Northeast, urban black communities attracted people of American Indian descent who often married African Americans.

THE BLACK FAMILY

As they became free, northern African Americans left their masters and established their own households. Some left more quickly than others, and in states such as New York and New Jersey, where gradual emancipation extended into the nineteenth century, the process continued into the 1820s. By then the average black family in northern cities had two parents and between two and four children. However, in both the Northeast and Old Northwest, single-parent black families, usually headed by women, became increasingly common during the antebellum period. In Cincinnati black families headed by women increased from 11 percent in 1830 to more than 22 percent in 1850. The difficulty black men had gaining employment may have influenced this trend. It certainly was a function of a high mortality rate among black men, which made many black women widows during their forties.

Both financial need and African-American culture encouraged black northerners to take in boarders and create extended families. By 1850 approximately one-third of black adults in such cities as Boston, Buffalo, Chicago, Detroit, and Cincinnati boarded. Economic considerations determined such arrangements, but friendship and family relationships also played a part. Sometimes entire nuclear families boarded, but most boarders were young, single, and male. As historians James Oliver Horton and Lois E. Horton put it, "The opportunity to rely on friends and family for shelter enhanced the mobility of poor people who were often forced to move to find employment. It provided financial assistance when people were unemployed; it provided social supports for people who faced discrimination; and it saved those who had left home or run away from slavery from social isolation."

THE STRUGGLE FOR EMPLOYMENT

The rising tide of immigration from Europe hurt northern African Americans economically. Before 1820 black craftsmen had been in demand, but, given the choice, white people preferred to employ other white people, and black people suffered. To make matters worse for African Americans, white workers excluded young black men from apprenticeships, refused to work with black people, and used violence to prevent employers from hiring black workers when white workers were unemployed. By the 1830s these practices had driven African Americans from the skilled trades. For the rest of the antebellum period, most northern black men performed menial day labor, although a few worked as coachmen, teamsters, waiters, barbers, carpenters, masons, and plasterers. By the 1850s black men were losing to Irish immigrants unskilled work as longshoremen, drayers, railroad workers, hod carriers, porters, and shoe shiners and positions in such skilled trades as barbering.

TABLE 7–2   FREE BLACK POPULATION OF SELECTED CITIES, 1800–1850

City	1800	1850
Baltimore	2,771	25,442
Boston	1,174	1,999
Charleston	951	3,441
New Orleans	800 (estimated)	9,905
New York	3,499	13,815
Philadelphia	4,210	10,736
Washington	123	8,158

Source: Adapted from "The Free Black in Urban America, 1800–1850: The Shadow of a Dream," by Dr. Leonard P. Curry, p. 250. Copyright © 1981 University of Chicago Press, Chicago, IL. Reprinted by permission of the author.

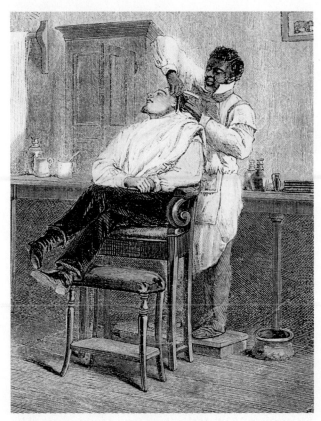

Barbering was one of the skilled trades open to black men during the antebellum years. Several wealthy African Americans began their careers as barbers.

By 1847, 80 percent of employed black men in Philadelphia did unskilled labor. Barbers and shoemakers predominated among those black workers with skills. Only .5 percent held factory jobs. Among employed black women, 80 percent either washed clothes or worked as domestic servants. Three-quarters of the remaining 20 percent were seamstresses. By the 1850s black women, too, were losing work to Irish immigrants. A few became prostitutes. About 5 percent of black men and women were self-employed, selling food or second-hand clothing.

Unskilled black men often could not find work. When they did work, they received low wages. To escape such conditions in Philadelphia and other ports, they became sailors. By 1850 about 50 percent of the crewmen on American merchant and whaling vessels were black. Not only did these sailors have to leave their families for months at a time and endure brutal conditions at sea, but they also risked imprisonment if their ship anchored at southern ports.

THE NORTHERN BLACK ELITE

Despite the poor prospects of most northern African Americans, a northern black elite emerged during the first six decades of the nineteenth century. Membership in this elite could be achieved through talent, wealth, occupation, family connections, complexion, and education. The elite led in the development of black institutions and culture, in the antislavery movement, and in the struggle for racial justice. It was also the bridge between the black community and sympathetic white people.

Although few African Americans achieved financial security during the antebellum decades, black people could become rich. Segregated neighborhoods gave rise to a black professional class of physicians, lawyers, ministers, and undertakers who served an exclusively black clientele. Black merchants could gain wealth selling to black communities. Other relatively well-off African Americans included skilled tradesmen, such as carpenters, barbers, waiters, and coachmen, who generally found employment among white people.

Although less so than in the South, complexion also influenced social standing among African Americans in the North, especially in cities like Cincinnati that were close to the South. White people often preferred to hire people of mixed race, successful black men often chose light-complexioned brides, and African Americans generally accepted white notions of human beauty.

By the 1820s the black elite had become better educated and more socially polished than its less wealthy black neighbors, yet it could never disassociate itself from them. Segregation and discriminatory legislation in the North applied to all African Americans regardless of class and complexion, and all African Americans shared a common culture and history.

Conspicuous among the black elite were entrepreneurs who, against considerable odds, gained wealth and influence in the antebellum North. As we noted in Chapter 5, James Forten was one of the first of them, and several other examples indicate the character of such people. John Remond—who as a child migrated from Curacao, a Dutch-ruled island in the Caribbean, to Salem, Massachusetts—and his wife, Nancy Lenox Remond, became prosperous restaurateurs, caterers, and retailers. Their fortune subsidized the abolitionist careers of their son Charles Lenox Remond and daughter Sarah Parker Remond. Louis Hayden, who escaped from slavery in Kentucky in 1845, had by 1849 become a successful haberdasher and an abolitionist in Boston. Perhaps most successful were Stephen Smith and his partner William Whipper, who had extensive business interests in southeast Pennsylvania. (See *Profile* on page 182.)

VOICES

MARIA W. STEWART ON THE CONDITION OF BLACK WORKERS

Maria W. Stewart (1803–1879) was the first black female public speaker in the United States. She was strong willed and spoke without qualification what she believed to be the truth. At times she angered both black and white people. In the following speech, which she delivered in Boston in September 1831, Stewart criticized the treatment accorded to black workers—especially black female workers—in the North.

Tell us no more of southern slavery; for with few exceptions, although I may be very erroneous in my opinion, yet I consider our condition but little better than that. . . . After all, methinks there are no chains so galling as those that bind the soul, and exclude it from the vast field of useful and scientific knowledge. . . .

I have asked several [white] individuals of my sex, who transact business for themselves, if providing our girls were to give them the most satisfactory references, they would not be willing to grant them an equal opportunity with others? Their reply has been—for their own part, they had no objection; but as it was not the custom, were they to take them into their employ, they would be in danger of losing the public patronage.

And such is the powerful force of prejudice. Let our girls possess whatever amiable qualities of soul they may; let their characters be fair and spotless as innocence itself; let their natural taste and ingenuity be what they may; it is impossible for scarce an individual of them to rise above the condition of servants. . . .

I observed a piece . . . respecting us, asserting that we were lazy and idle. I confute them on that point. Take us generally as a people, we are neither lazy nor idle: and considering how little we have to excite or stimulate us, I am almost astonished that there are so many industrious and ambitious ones to be found. . . .

Again it was asserted that we were "a ragged set, crying for liberty." I reply to it, the whites have so long and so loudly proclaimed the theme of equal rights and privileges, that our souls have caught the flame also, ragged as we are. As far as our merit deserves, we feel a common desire to rise above the condition of servants and drudges. I have learnt, by bitter experience, that the continual hard labor deadens the energies of the soul, and benumbs the faculties of the mind; the ideas become confined, the mind barren, and, like the scorching sands of Arabia, produces nothing: or like the uncultivated soil, brings forth thorns and thistles. . . .

Most of our color have dragged out a miserable existence of servitude from the cradle to the grave. . . . Do you [women] ask, why

INVENTORS

In some cases, members of the black elite owed their success to technological innovations. Some black inventors had been born in slavery; others had not. Some participated in black community life; others did not.

In 1834 Henry Blair of Maryland became the first African American to patent an invention—a horse-drawn mechanized corn seed planter. In 1836 he patented a similar cotton seed planter. Henry Boyd was much better known than Blair. Boyd, born in Kentucky in 1802, apprenticed as a cabinetmaker, purchased his freedom in 1826, and moved to Cincinnati. In 1835, as that city's leading bed manufacturer, he patented the "Boyd Bedstead." Versions of this "corded four poster" sold from between $8.00 and $125.00 (about $264 and $550 today). In 1844 Boyd produced more than 1,000 of them.

Lewis Temple was another prominent black inventor of the period. Born free in Richmond, Virginia, Temple moved to New Bedford, Massachusetts. In 1845, at this whaling port, Temple, a blacksmith, devised the toggle harpoon. Set with a wooden pin, the barbed toggle secured a whale to a harpooner's line on impact. Although Temple did not patent this invention, he made a good living manufacturing it before his death in 1854. At the same time Temple devised his harpoon, Joseph Hawkins of West Windsor, New Jersey, patented "a gridiron used to broil meat," which preserved juices as the meat cooked.

One of the best-known stories of early nineteenth-century black inventions, however, has been called into question. James Forten's biographer finds no

are you wretched and miserable? I reply, look at many of the most worthy and most interesting of us doomed to spend our lives in gentlemen's kitchens. Look at our young men, smart, active, and energetic, with souls filled with ambitious fire; if they look forward, alas! What are their prospects? They can be nothing but the humblest laborers, on account of their dark complexions; hence many of them lose their ambition, and become worthless. . . .

▶ *Is Stewart correct in assuming that conditions for black northerners were little better than those for slaves?*
▶ *According to Stewart, what was the impact of northern white prejudice on black workers?*

Source: Maria W. Stewart, "Lecture Delivered at the Franklin Hall, Boston, September 21, 1831," as quoted in Roy Finkenbine, *Sources of the African-American Past: Primary Sources in American History* (New York: Longman, 1997), 30–32.

evidence to substantiate a contemporary claim that Forten "invented an improvement in the management of sails" that "came into general use."

PROFESSIONALS

The northern black elite also included physicians and lawyers. Among the physicians, some, such as James McCune Smith and John S. Rock, received medical degrees. Smith, the first African American to earn a medical degree, graduated from the University of Glasgow in Scotland in 1837 and practiced in New York City until his death in 1874. Rock, who had been a dentist in Philadelphia, graduated from the American Medical College in 1852 and practiced medicine in Boston until 1860 when he undertook the study of law. In 1865 he became the first African American to argue a case before the U.S. Supreme Court.

Either because they had been forced out of medical school or they chose not to go, other prominent black physicians practiced medicine without having earned a degree. (This was legal in the nineteenth century.) James Still of Medford, New Jersey, had meager formal education but used natural remedies to develop a successful practice among black and white people. The multitalented Martin R. Delany, who had been born free in Charles Town, Virginia, in 1812, practiced medicine in Pittsburgh after having been expelled

from Harvard Medical School at the insistence of two white classmates.

Prominent black attorneys included Macon B. Allen, who gained admission to the Maine bar in 1844, and Robert Morris, who qualified to practice law in Massachusetts in 1847. Both Allen and Morris apprenticed with white attorneys, and Morris had a particularly successful and lucrative practice. Yet white residents thwarted his attempt to purchase a mansion in a Boston suburb.

ARTISTS AND MUSICIANS

Although they rarely achieved great wealth and have not become famous, black artists and musicians were also part of the northern African-American elite. Among the best-known artists were Robert S. Duncanson, Robert Douglass, Patrick Reason, and Edmonia Lewis. Several of them supported the antislavery movement through their artistic work.

John S. Rock, portrayed in an 1860 *Harper's Weekly* illustration, was born free in Salem, New Jersey in 1825. He earned a medical degree in 1852 and practiced law beginning in 1861.

Educated at Oberlin College, Edmonia Lewis (1843–1911?) studied sculpture in Rome and emerged as one of the more prolific American artists of the late nineteenth century.

Douglass, a painter who studied in England before establishing himself in Philadelphia, and Reason, an engraver, created portraits of abolitionists during the 1830s. Reason also etched illustrations of the sufferings of slaves. Duncanson, who was born in Cincinnati and worked in Europe between 1843 and 1854, painted landscapes and portraits. Lewis, the daughter of a black man and a Chippewa woman, enrolled with abolitionist help at Oberlin College in Ohio and studied sculpture in Rome. Her works, which emphasized African-American themes, came into wide demand after the Civil War.

The reputations of black professional musicians of the antebellum period have suffered in comparison with the great tradition of black folk music epitomized by spirituals. But in Philadelphia a circle of black musicians wrote and performed a wide variety of music for orchestra, voice, and solo instruments. Similar circles existed in New Orleans, Boston, Cleveland, New York, Baltimore, and St. Louis. The best-known professional black singer of the period was Elizabeth Taylor Greenfield, who was born a slave in Mississippi and raised by Quakers in Philadelphia. Known as the "Black Swan," Taylor gained renown for her vocal range.

AUTHORS

The antebellum era was a golden age of African-American literature. Driven by suffering in slavery and limited freedom in the North, black authors portrayed an America that had not lived up to its revolutionary ideals. Black autobiography recounted life in bondage and dramatic escapes. Although the antislavery movement promoted the publication of scores of such narratives, the best known is Frederick Douglass's classic *Narrative of the Life of Frederick Douglass, an American Slave*, published in 1845.

African Americans also wrote history, novels, and poetry. In 1855 William C. Nell published *The Colored Patriots of the American Revolution*, which reminded its readers that black men had fought for American freedom. William Wells Brown, who had escaped from slavery in Kentucky, became the first African-American novelist. His *Clotel, or the President's Daughter*, published in 1853, used the affair between Thomas Jefferson and Sally Hemings to explore in fiction the moral ramifications of slaveholders who fathered children with their bondwomen. Another black novelist of the antebellum years was Martin R. Delany. His *Blake, or the Huts of America*, a story of emerging revolutionary consciousness among southern slaves, ran as a serial in the *Weekly Anglo-African* during 1859. Black poets included George M. Horton, a slave living in

Frances Ellen Watkins Harper (1825–1911) was born free in Baltimore. During the 1850s, she published antislavery poetry and traveled across the North as an antislavery speaker.

North Carolina, who in 1829 published *The Hope of Liberty*, and James W. Whitfield of Buffalo, who in 1853 lampooned the song "My Country 'tis of Thee" when he wrote the following:

> America, it is to thee
> Thou boasted land of liberty,—
> Thou land of blood, and crime, and wrong.

African-American women who published fiction during the period included Frances Ellen Watkins Harper and Harriet E. Wilson. Harper was born free in Baltimore in 1825. Associated with the antislavery cause in Pennsylvania and Maine, she published poems that depicted the sufferings of slaves. Her first collection, *Poems on Various Subjects*, appeared in 1854. Wilson published *Our Nig: Or, Sketches from the Life of a Free Black, in a Two-Story White House, North* in 1859. This was the first novel published by a black woman in the United States. In the genre of autobiographical fiction, it compared the lives of black domestic workers in the North with those of southern slaves. Wilson's book, however, received little attention during her lifetime, and until the 1980s critics believed a white author had written it.

At about the same time that Wilson wrote *Our Nig*, Hanna Crafts, who had recently escaped from slavery in North Carolina, wrote *The Bondwoman's Narrative*. Unpublished until 2002, this melodramatic autobiographical novel tells the story of a house slave and her escape to freedom.

African-American Institutions

In the antebellum decades, the black institutions that had appeared during the revolutionary era in urban areas of the North, Upper South, and—to a lesser extent—the Deep South grew in strength, numbers,

and variety. This was the result of growing black populations, the exertions of the African-American elite, and the persistence of racial exclusion and segregation. Black institutions of the time included schools, mutual aid organizations, benevolent and fraternal societies, self-improvement and temperance associations, literary groups, newspapers and journals, and theaters. But, aside from families, the most important black community institution remained the church.

CHURCHES

Black church buildings were community centers. They housed schools and meeting places for other organizations. Antislavery societies often met in churches, and the churches harbored fugitive slaves. All of this went hand in hand with the community leadership black ministers provided. They began schools and various voluntary associations. They

Read the Document
Address to the Free People of Color (1830)

This lithograph depicts the bishops of the African Methodist Episcopal church and suggests both the church's humble origins and its remarkable growth during the antebellum years. Founder Richard Allen is portrayed at the center.

PROFILE: Stephen Smith and William Whipper, Partners in Business and Reform

Black people in antebellum America had great difficulty succeeding in business. In most states, northern and southern, African-American entrepreneurs faced limited educational opportunities, inequality before the law, disfranchisement, and pervasive prejudice. To make their fortunes, they had to compete in a marketplace white people dominated. Yet a few African Americans, aided by skill, determination, and luck, acquired great wealth. Some who did, such as William Ellison of South Carolina (see *Profile* on page 154 in Chapter 6), had little sympathy for the less fortunate. But others used their affluence to improve conditions for other African Americans. Black Pennsylvanians Stephen Smith and William Whipper, who linked their commercial success to reform efforts, illustrate this point.

Both Smith and Whipper were children of black mothers and white fathers. Both of their mothers were domestic servants in white households. Smith was born unfree in Dauphin County, south-central Pennsylvania, in about 1795. Whipper was born free in nearby Lancaster, Pennsylvania, in about 1804. Nothing suggests that either of them had a formal education.

When Smith was five years old, his master apprenticed him to Thomas Boule, who owned a lumber business. During his late teens, Smith became manager of Boule's business. In 1816 he purchased his freedom, married, and began his own lumber company. Shortly thereafter, he began purchasing real estate. Not far away, Whipper grew up and struck out on his own. During the 1820s, he worked as a steam scourer in Philadelphia. In 1834 he opened a grocery store in the same city.

The two men became partners in 1835. They had phenomenal success despite a mob attack that same year on their office. They operated one of the largest lumbering businesses in southeast Pennsylvania and expanded into selling coal. By 1842, when Smith moved to Philadelphia and left Whipper in charge of their Columbia operations, the two men had invested $9,000 (approximately 252,000 current dollars) in a bridge company and had bank deposits totaling $18,000 (about $504,000 today). By 1850, they owned—in addition to their lumber and coal business—22 railroad cars and $27,000 (about $756,000 today) worth of bank stock. They grossed $100,000 (nearly $2,800,000 today) per year. Smith continued to excel in real-estate acquisition, owning at one point 52 brick houses in Philadelphia. He was, perhaps, the richest African American in antebellum America.

The two men were partners in reform as well as business. Both of them began during the 1830s as integrationists who, based on their experience, believed that white society would accept African Americans who worked to uplift themselves. Early on, Whipper made his grocery a center for temperance and antislavery activities. He became a leader at the Black National Conventions, while Smith became an African Methodist Episcopal minister and builder of churches. They were both active in the underground railroad and opened their homes to escaped slaves. Despite their business success, however, during the 1850s they grew more pessimistic about peaceful reform as a way to gain black rights in the United States. Whipper began to promote black migration to Canada. In 1858 Smith hosted a meeting at which white antislavery activist John Brown discussed his plan to incite slave revolt in the South. Clearly, Smith and Whipper as African Americans experienced the double consciousness that W. E. B. Du Bois later so eloquently identified.

◀ **William Whipper**, c. 1835.

spoke against slavery, racial oppression, and what they considered weaknesses among African Americans. However, black ministers never spoke with one voice. Throughout the antebellum decades, many followed Jupiter Hammon in admonishing their congregations that preparing one's soul for heaven was more important than gaining equal rights on earth.

By 1846 the independent African Methodist Episcopal (AME) Church had 296 congregations in the United States and Canada with 17,375 members. In 1848 Frederick Douglass maintained that the AME Mother Bethel Church in Philadelphia was "the largest church in this Union," with 2,000 to 3,000 worshipers each Sunday. The AME Zion Church of New York City was probably the second largest black congregation, with about 2,000 members.

Most black Baptist, Presbyterian, Congregationalist, Episcopal, and Roman Catholic congregations remained affiliated with white denominations, although they were rarely represented in regional and national church councils. For example, the Episcopal Diocese of New York in 1819 excluded black ministers from its annual conventions, maintaining that African Americans "*are* socially degraded, and are not regarded as proper associates for the class of persons who attend our convention." Not until 1853 was white abolitionist William Jay able to convince New York Episcopalians to admit black representatives.

Many northern African Americans continued to attend white churches. To do so, they had to submit to the same second-class status that had driven Richard Allen and Absalom Jones to establish separate black churches in Philadelphia during the 1790s. Throughout the antebellum years, northern white churches required their black members to sit in special sections during services, provided separate Sunday schools for black children, and insisted that black people take communion after white people. Even Quakers, who spearheaded white opposition to slavery in the North and South, often provided separate seating for black people at their meetings.

During the 1830s and 1840s, some black leaders criticized the existence of separate black congregations and denominations. Frederick Douglass called them "negro pews, on a higher and larger scale." Such churches, Douglass and others maintained, were part and parcel of a segregationist spirit that divided America according to complexion. Douglass also denounced what he considered the illiteracy and anti-intellectual bias of most black ministers. Growing numbers of African Americans, nevertheless, regarded such churches as sources of spiritual integrity and legitimate alternatives to second-class status among white Christians.

VOICES

THE CONSTITUTION OF THE PITTSBURGH AFRICAN EDUCATION SOCIETY

Compared with black southerners, black northerners were fortunate to have access to education, and education societies were prominent among black self-improvement organizations. In January 1832 a group headed by John B. Vashon, a local black barber and philanthropist, met at Pittsburgh's African Church to establish such a society and a school. The following extracts from its constitution indicate the group's motives and plans.

Whereas, ignorance in all ages has been found to debase the human mind, and to subject its votaries to the lowest vices, and most abject depravity—and it must be admitted, that ignorance is the sole cause of the present degradation and bondage of the people of color in these United States—that the intellectual capacity of the black man is equal to that of the white, and that he is equally susceptible of improvement, all ancient history makes manifest; and even modern examples put beyond a single doubt.

We, therefore, the people of color, of the city and vicinity of Pittsburgh, and State of Pennsylvania, for the purpose of dispersing the moral gloom that has so long hung around us, have, under Almighty God, associated ourselves together, which association shall be known by the name of the *Pittsburgh African Education Society.* . . .

It shall be the duty of the Board of Managers . . . to purchase such books and periodicals as the Society may deem it expedient, they shall have power to raise money by subscription or otherwise, to purchase ground, and erect thereon a suitable building or buildings for the accommodation and education of youth, and a hall for the use of the Society. . . .

▶ *Why would this group claim that black ignorance was the "sole cause" of black degradation and enslavement?*

▶ *Why was the Pittsburgh African Education Society necessary?*

Source: Dorothy Porten, ed., *Early Negro Writing, 1760–1837* (1971; reprint, Baltimore: Black Classics, 1995), 120–22.

SCHOOLS

Education, like religion, was racially segregated in the North between 1820 and 1860. Tax-supported compulsory public education for children in the United States began in Massachusetts in 1827 and spread throughout the Northeast and Old Northwest during the 1830s. Some public schools, such as those in Cleveland, Ohio, during the 1850s, were racially integrated. But usually, as soon as 20 or more African-American children appeared in a school district, white parents demanded that black children attend separate schools. White people claimed that black children lacked mental capacity and lowered the quality of education. White people also feared that opening schools to black children would encourage more black people to live in the school district.

How to educate African-American children who were not allowed to attend school with white children became a persistent issue in the North. Until 1848 Ohio and the other states of the Old Northwest simply excluded black children from public schools and refused to allocate tax revenues to support separate facilities. The northeastern states were more willing to undertake such expenditures. But across the North, white people were reluctant to use tax dollars to fund education for African Americans. As a result, appropriations for black public schools lagged far behind those for public schools white children attended.

This tendency extended to cities where African-American leaders and white abolitionists had created private schools for black children. In 1812 the African School, established by Prince Hall in 1798, became part of Boston's public school system. As a result, like newly created black public schools in the city, it began to suffer from inadequate funding and a limited curriculum. The African Free Schools, opened in New York City in 1787 by the New York Society for Promoting the Manumission of Slaves, had a similar fate. In 1834, when these schools became part of New York's public school system, funding and attendance declined. By the 1850s public support for the city's black schools had become negligible.

Woefully inadequate public funding resulted in poor education or none at all for most black children across the North. The few black schools were dilapidated and overcrowded. White teachers who taught in them received lower pay than those who taught in white schools, and black teachers received even less, so teaching was generally poor. Black parents, however, were often unaware that their children received an inadequate education. Even black and white abolitionists tended to expect less from black students than from white students.

Some black leaders defended segregated schools as better for black children than integrated ones. They probably feared that the real choice was between separate black schools or none at all. But, by the 1830s, most northern African Americans favored racially integrated public education, and during the 1840s Frederick Douglass became a leading advocate for such a policy. Douglass, other black leaders, and their white abolitionist allies made the most progress in Massachusetts, where by 1845 all public schools, except for those in Boston, had been integrated. After a ten-year struggle, the Massachusetts legislature finally ended segregated schools in that city too. This victory encouraged the opponents of segregated public schools across the North. By 1860 integration had advanced among the region's smaller school districts. But, except for those in Boston, urban schools remained segregated on the eve of the Civil War.

In fact, the black elite had more success gaining admission to northern colleges during the antebellum period than most African-American children had in gaining an adequate primary education. Some colleges served African Americans exclusively. Ashmum Institute in Oxford, Pennsylvania, was founded in 1854 to prepare black missionaries who would go to Africa. Ashmum, later renamed Lincoln University, was the first black institution of higher learning in the United States. Another exclusively black college was Wilberforce University, founded by the AME Church in 1855 near Columbus, Ohio. Earlier some northern colleges had begun to admit a few black students. They included Bowdoin in Maine, Dartmouth in New Hampshire, Harvard and Mount Pleasant in Massachusetts, Oneida Institute in New York, and Western Reserve in Ohio. Because of its association with the antislavery movement, Oberlin College in Ohio became the most famous biracial institution of higher learning during the era. By 1860 many northern colleges, law schools, medical schools, and seminaries admitted black applicants, although not on an equal basis with white applicants.

VOLUNTARY ASSOCIATIONS

The African-American mutual aid, benevolent, self-improvement, and fraternal organizations that originated during the late eighteenth century proliferated during the antebellum decades. So did black literary and temperance associations.

Mutual aid societies became especially attractive to black women. In 1830 black women in Philadelphia had 27 such organizations, compared with 16 for black men. By 1855 Philadelphia had 108 black mutual aid societies, enrolling 9,762 members, with a combined annual income of $29,600 (approximately 812,000 current dollars). Among black benevolent societies, African Dorcas Associations were especially prevalent. Started in 1828 in New York City by black women, these societies distributed used clothing to the poor, especially poor schoolchildren. During the early 1830s, black women also began New York City's Association for the Benefit of Colored Orphans, which operated an orphanage that by 1851 had helped 524 children. Other black benevolent organizations in New York maintained the Colored Seaman's Home and a home for the elderly.

Meanwhile, the Prince Hall Masons created new lodges in the cities of the Northeast and the Chesapeake. Beginning during the 1840s, Black Odd Fellows lodges also became common. But more prevalent were self-improvement, library, literary, and temperance organizations. These manifested the reform spirit that swept the North and the Upper South during the antebellum decades. Closely linked to evangelical Protestantism, reformers maintained that the moral regeneration of individuals was essential to perfecting society. African Americans shared this belief and formed myriad organizations to put it into practice.

Among the more prestigious of the societies for black men were the Phoenix Literary Society, established in New York City in 1833 and the Philadelphia Library Company of Colored Persons, founded in 1833. There were also Pittsburgh's Theban Literary Society, founded in 1831, and Boston's Adelphi Union for the Promotion of Literature and Science, established in 1836. Black women had the Female Literary Society of Philadelphia, founded in 1831, and New York City's Ladies Literary Society, founded in 1834. The Ladies Literary Society of Buffalo emerged in the mid-1830s, and Boston's Afric-American Female Intelligence Society began in 1832.

Black temperance societies were even more widespread than literary and benevolent organizations, although they also tended to be more short lived. Like their white counterparts, black temperance advocates were middle-class activists who sought to stop those lower on the social ladder from abusing alcoholic beverages. The temperance societies organized lecture series and handed out literature that portrayed the negative physical, economic, and moral consequences of liquor. Whether such societies were effective is debatable, but they helped unite black communities.

Free African Americans in the Upper South

Life for free black people in the South during the antebellum period differed from that in the North. The free black experience in the Upper South also differed from what it was in the Deep South. In general, free African Americans in the North, despite the limits on their liberty, had opportunities their southern counterparts did not enjoy. Each of the southern regions, nevertheless, offered some advantages to free black residents.

The free black people of the Upper South had much in common with their northern counterparts. In particular, African Americans in the Chesapeake cities of Baltimore, Washington, Richmond, and Norfolk had ties to black northerners, ranging from family and church affiliations to business connections and membership in fraternal organizations. But significant differences that resulted from the South's agricultural economy and slavery set free people of color in the Upper South apart. Although nearly half the free black population in the North lived in cities, only one-third did so in the Upper South, hampering the development of black communities there.

A more important difference was the impact of slavery on the lives of free African Americans in the Upper South. Unlike black northerners, free black people in the Upper South lived alongside slaves. Many had family ties to slaves and were more directly involved than black northerners in the slaves' suffering. They did so in several capacities, including efforts to prevent the sale south of relatives and friends, reimbursing masters for manumissions, and funding for freedom suits. They also earned a reputation among white southerners as inveterate harborers of escaped slaves. Southern white politicians and journalists used the close connection between free black southerners and slaves to justify limiting the freedom of the former group.

Free black people of the Upper South were also more at risk of *being* enslaved than were black northerners. Except for Louisiana, with its French and Spanish heritage, all southern states assumed African Americans were slaves unless they could prove otherwise. Free black people had to carry **free papers** and renew them periodically. They could be enslaved if their papers were lost or stolen, and sheriffs routinely arrested them on the grounds that they might be fugitive slaves. Even when those arrested proved they were free, they were sometimes sold as slaves to pay the cost of imprisoning them. Free African Americans who got into debt in the South risked being sold into slavery to pay off their creditors.

As the antebellum period progressed, the distinction between free and enslaved African Americans narrowed in the Upper South. Although a few northern states allowed black men to vote, no southern state did after 1835 when North Carolina followed Tennessee—the only other southern state to allow black suffrage—in revoking the right to vote among property-owning black men. Free black people of the Upper South also had more difficulty traveling, owning firearms, congregating in groups, and being out after dark than did black northerners. Although residential segregation was less pronounced in southern cities than in the North, African Americans of the Upper South faced a more thorough exclusion from hotels, taverns, trains and coaches, parks, theaters, and hospitals.

Free black people in the Upper South experienced various degrees of hardship in earning a living, although, during the nineteenth century, their employment expanded as slavery declined in Maryland and northern Virginia. Free persons of color in rural areas were generally tenant farmers. Some had to sign labor contracts that reduced them to semislavery. But others owned land, and a few owned slaves. Rural free African Americans also worked as miners, lumberjacks, and teamsters. In Upper South urban areas, most free black men were unskilled day laborers, waiters,

1828–1834

EARLY BLACK LITERARY SOCIETIES

1828	Reading Room Society (Philadelphia)
1829	New York African Clarkson Society
1830	New York Philomathean Society
1831	Female Literary Society (Philadelphia), Theban Literary Society (Pittsburgh)
1832	Afric-American Female Intelligence Society (Boston), Tyro and Literary Association (Newark, NJ)
1833	Library Company of Colored Persons (Philadelphia), Phoenix Literacy Society (New York)
1834	Minerva Literary Association (Philadelphia), Ladies Literary Society (New York), New York Garrison Literary Association, Literary and Religious Institution (Hartford, CT), Washington Conventional Society (Washington, DC)

whitewashers, and stevedores. Free black women worked as laundresses and domestic servants. As in the North, the most successful African Americans were barbers, butchers, tailors, caterers, merchants, and those teamsters and hack drivers who owned their own horses and vehicles. Before 1850 free black people in the Upper South had less competition from European immigrants for jobs than was the case in northern cities. Therefore, although the Upper South had fewer factories than the North, more free black men worked in them. This changed during the 1850s when Irish and German immigrants competed against free black people in the Upper South just as they did in the North for all types of employment. As in the North, immigrants often used violence to drive African Americans out of skilled trades.

These circumstances made it more difficult for free black people in the Upper South to maintain community institutions. In addition, the measures white authorities adopted to prevent slave revolt limited free black autonomy, and such measures became pervasive after the revolt Nat Turner led in southern Virginia in 1831. Many black churches and schools had to close or curtail their activities. The Baltimore Conference of the AME Church, which had been expanding during the 1820s, declined during the early 1830s. Some states required that black churches have white ministers, and some black ministers left for the North. Yet free black southerners persevered. During the late 1830s, new black churches organized in Louisville and Lexington, Kentucky, and in St. Louis, Missouri. Between 1836 and 1856, the Baltimore AME Conference rebounded and more than doubled its membership. By 1860 Baltimore had 15 black churches. Louisville had nine, and Nashville, St. Louis, and Norfolk had four each. Most of these churches ministered to both enslaved and free members.

Black schools and voluntary associations also survived white efforts to suppress them, although the schools faced great challenges. Racially integrated schools and public funding for segregated black schools were out of the question in the South. Most black children received no formal education. Black churches, a few white churches, and a scattering of black and white individuals maintained what educational facilities the Upper South had for black children. The schools met—often sporadically—in churches or private homes and generally lacked books, chalkboards, and desks. Particularly noteworthy were the efforts of the Oblate Sisters of Providence, who constituted the first black Roman Catholic religious order in the United States, and John F. Cook, who for 20 years conducted a black school in Washington, D.C.

Mother Mary Elizabeth Clovis Lange, O.S.P. (c. 1784–1882), was born in Haiti. She organized the Oblate Sisters of Providence in Baltimore in 1828. This Roman Catholic order helped black refugees from Haiti and operated a school for the refugees' children.

Elizabeth Clovis Lange, who was of Haitian descent, established the Oblate Sisters of Providence, an order of Roman Catholic nuns, in Baltimore in 1829 to provide a free education to the children of French-speaking black refugees from the Haitian Revolution. The sisters taught English, math, composition, and religion. Cook, who was an AME and Presbyterian minister, taught similar subjects at his Union Seminary from 1834 until his death in 1854. Both the sisters and Cook confronted persecution and inadequate funding. Cook had to flee Washington temporarily in 1835 to avoid being killed. Nevertheless, he passed his school on to his son, who kept it going through the Civil War. Meanwhile, the Oblate Sisters had become influential in the black community. They built a chapel in Baltimore in 1836 that became the first black Catholic church in the United States.

Black voluntary associations, particularly in urban areas of the Upper South, fared better than black schools. By 1838 Baltimore had at least 40 such organizations, including chapters of the Prince Hall Masons, Black Odd Fellows, literary societies, and temperance groups. In Norfolk, the Masons enrolled slaves as well as freemen. As in the North, black women organized their own voluntary associations. Washington's Colored Female Roman Catholic Beneficial Society, for example, provided death benefits for its members. Black benevolent organizations in the Upper South also sought to apprentice orphans to black tradesmen; sponsored fairs, picnics, and parades; and provided protection against kidnappers.

Free African Americans in the Deep South

More than half the South's free black population lived in Maryland, Delaware, and Virginia. To the west and south of these states, the number of free people of color in each state declined sharply. The smaller free black populations in Kentucky, Tennessee, Missouri, and North Carolina had much in common with that in the Chesapeake states. But free African Americans who lived in the Deep South were different from their counterparts in other southern regions.

Neither the natural rights ideology of the revolutionary era nor changing economic circumstances led to many manumissions in the Deep South. Free black people there were not only far fewer than in either the Upper South or the North but also "largely the product of illicit sexual relations between black slave women and white men." Slaveholder fathers either manumitted their mixed-race children or let them buy their freedom. However, some free black people of the Deep South traced their ancestry to free mixed-race refugees from Haiti, who sought during the 1790s to avoid that island nation's bloody revolutionary struggle by fleeing to Charleston, Savannah, and New Orleans.

A three-caste system similar to that in Latin America developed in the antebellum Deep South. It included white people, free black people, and slaves. Most free African Americans in the region identified more closely with their former masters than with slaves. To ensure the loyalty of such free people of color, powerful white people provided them with employment, loans, protection, and such special privileges as the ability to vote and to testify against white people. Some states and municipalities formalized this relationship by requiring free African Americans to have white guardians—often their blood relatives. Some people of mixed descent crossed the racial boundary and passed as white.

The relationship between free African Americans of the Deep South and their former masters was also evident in religion. An AME church existed in Charleston until 1818, when the city authorities suppressed it, fearing it would become a center of sedition. African Baptist churches existed in Savannah during the 1850s. In 1842 New Orleans's Sisters of the Holy Family became the second Roman Catholic religious order for black women in the United States. But free black people in the region were more likely than those farther north to remain in white churches largely because they identified with the white elite.

In the Deep South, free African Americans—over half of whom lived in cities—were more concentrated in urban areas than were their counterparts in the North and Upper South. Although Deep South cities restricted their employment opportunities, free black people in Charleston, Savannah, Mobile, and New Orleans maintained stronger positions in the skilled trades than free black people in the Upper South or the North. By 1860 in Charleston, three-quarters of the free black men worked in skilled trades. Free African Americans made up only 15 percent of Charleston's male population. Yet they constituted 25 percent of its carpenters, 40 percent of its tailors, and 75 percent of its millwrights. In New Orleans, free black men predominated as carpenters, masons, bricklayers, barbers, tailors, cigar makers, and shoemakers. In both cities, free African Americans compared favorably to white people in their ratio of skilled to unskilled workers. The close ties between free black people and the upper-class white people who did business with them explain much of this success.

Despite these ties, free black communities comparable to those in the Upper South and North arose in the cities of the Deep South. Although they usually lacked separate black churches as community centers, free African Americans in the region created other institutions. In Charleston the Brown Fellowship Society survived throughout the antebellum period. Charleston also had a chapter of the Prince Hall Masons, and free black men and women in the city maintained other fraternal and benevolent associations. In addition to similar sorts of organizations, the free black elite in New Orleans published literary journals and supported an opera house. During the 1850s, Savannah—where black churches did exist—had at least three black volunteer fire companies, a porters' association, and several benevolent societies.

Because black churches were rare, wealthy African Americans and fraternal organizations organized private schools for black children in the cities of the Deep South. In Charleston the Brown Fellowship Society organized an academy. New Orleans had several schools, most of which were conducted in French—the first or second language for many free black people in the city. Some of the wealthier free black families in these cities sent their children to Europe for education, and the literacy rate among free black people in both Charleston and New Orleans was markedly high for the antebellum period.

In all, free people of color in the Deep South differed substantially from those in the Upper South and the North. Their ties to the white slaveholding class gave them tangible advantages. However, they were not without sympathy for those who remained in slavery, and white authorities were never certain of their loyalty to the slave regime. In particular, white people feared contact between free African Americans in the ports of the Deep South and black northerners—especially black sailors. As a new round of slave unrest began in the South and a more militant northern antislavery movement got under way during the 1820s, free black people in the Deep South faced difficult circumstances.

Free African Americans in the Far West

Free black communities in the North, Upper South, and Deep South each had unique features, and all of them had existed for decades by the antebellum period. In the huge region stretching from the Great Plains to the Pacific coast, which had become part of the United States by the late 1840s, free black people were rare. Black communities there were just emerging in a few isolated localities. As historian Quintard Taylor notes, the 4,000 "nominally free" African Americans who lived in California in 1860 constituted "75 percent of the free black population of the West." In the major slaveholding state of Texas, census figures indicate that a tiny free black population decreased from 397 in 1850 to 355 in 1860. The prevalence of discriminatory "black laws" in the region's states and territories partially explains the small number of free black westerners. Like similar laws in the states of the Old Northwest, these laws either banned free African Americans entirely or restricted the activities of those who were allowed to settle. Nevertheless, a few black families sought economic opportunities in the West. During the 1840s they joined white Americans in settling Oregon. The California gold rush of 1849 had by 1852 attracted about 2,000 African Americans, most of whom were men, among hundreds of thousands of white Americans.

Painted in 1858 by Thomas Waterman Wood, *Market Woman* portrays a young woman carrying produce she has purchased. There is no indication of her status as either free or enslaved. The portrait provides an example of how black women dressed in antebellum America.

Usually black Californians lived and worked in multicultural communities that also included people of Chinese, Jamaican, Latin American, and white American descent. But in a few localities, African Americans predominated. Some black Californians were prosperous gold prospectors. Others worked as steamship stewards, cooks, barbers, laundresses, mechanics, saloonkeepers, whitewashers, porters, and domestics. By the early 1850s, there were black communities centered on churches in San Francisco, Sacramento, and Los Angeles. In 1851 Bernard Fletcher established an AME church in Sacramento, and the following year, John Jamison Moore established an AME Zion church in San Francisco. As in the East, these black communities organized benevolent and self-help societies. Although most African Americans who went west were men, black women sometimes accompanied their husbands and families. Those who were better off raised funds for AME churches and voluntary associations. Others worked as cooks, laundresses, and prostitutes. (For more on free African Americans in California, see Chapter 10.)

CONCLUSION

During the antebellum period, free African-American communities that had emerged during the revolutionary era grew and fostered black institutions. Particularly in the urban North, life in these segregated communities foreshadowed the pattern of black life from the end of the Civil War into the twentieth century. Although the black elite could gain education, professional expertise, and wealth despite white prejudices, most northern people of color were poor. Extended families, churches, segregation, political marginality, and limited educational opportunities still influence African-American life today.

Life for free black people in the Upper South and Deep South was even more difficult. Presumed to be slaves if they could not prove otherwise, black people confronted more danger of enslavement and restrictive legislation than in the North. But energetic black communities existed in the Upper South throughout the antebellum period. In the Deep South, the small free black population was better off economically than were free black people in other regions, but it depended on white slaveholders, who were unreliable allies as sectional controversy mounted. The antislavery movement, secession, and the Civil War would have a more profound impact on the free black communities in the South than in the North. Although it is not wise to generalize about free black people in the trans-Mississippi West, their presence on the Pacific coast in particular demonstrates their involvement in the westward expansion that characterized the United States during the antebellum years. Their West Coast communities indicate the adaptability of black institutions to new circumstances.

RECOMMENDED READING

Ira Berlin. *Slaves without Masters: The Free Negro in the Antebellum South.* New York: New Press, 1971. This classic study is still the most comprehensive treatment of free African Americans in the antebellum South.

W. Jeffrey Bolster. *Black Jacks: African American Seamen in the Age of Sail.* Cambridge, MA: Harvard University Press, 1997. *Black Jacks* explores the lives of black seamen between 1740 and 1865.

Leonard Curry. *The Free Black in Urban America, 1800–1850: The Shadow of the Dream.* Chicago: University of Chicago Press, 1981. Curry provides a comprehensive

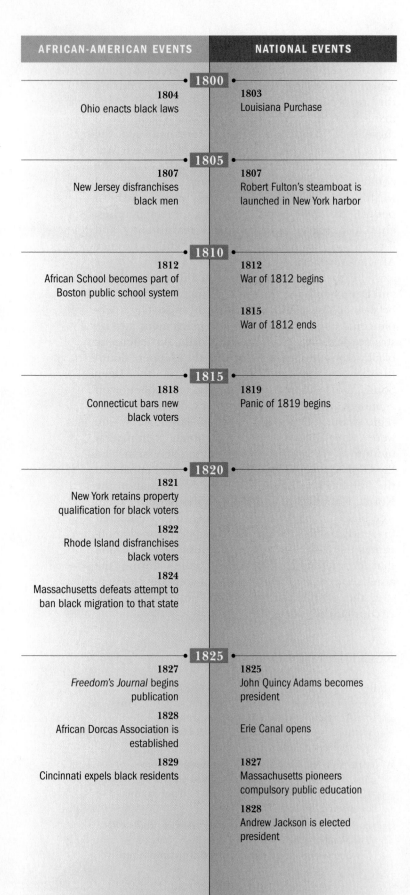

AFRICAN-AMERICAN EVENTS

1800

1804
Ohio enacts black laws

1805

1807
New Jersey disfranchises
black men

1810

1812
African School becomes part of
Boston public school system

1815

1818
Connecticut bars new
black voters

1820

1821
New York retains property
qualification for black voters

1822
Rhode Island disfranchises
black voters

1824
Massachusetts defeats attempt to
ban black migration to that state

1825

1827
Freedom's Journal begins
publication

1828
African Dorcas Association is
established

1829
Cincinnati expels black residents

NATIONAL EVENTS

1803
Louisiana Purchase

1807
Robert Fulton's steamboat is
launched in New York harbor

1812
War of 1812 begins

1815
War of 1812 ends

1819
Panic of 1819 begins

1825
John Quincy Adams becomes
president

Erie Canal opens

1827
Massachusetts pioneers
compulsory public education

1828
Andrew Jackson is elected
president

account of urban African-American life in the antebellum period.

Philip S. Foner. *History of Black America: From the Emergence of the Cotton Kingdom to the Eve of the Compromise of 1850*. Westport, CT: Greenwood Press, 1983. This second volume of Foner's three-volume series presents a wealth of information about African-American life between 1820 and 1861, especially about the northern black community.

James Oliver Horton and Lois E. Horton. *In Hope of Liberty: Culture, Community, and Protest among Northern Free Blacks, 1700–1860*. New York: Oxford University Press, 1997. The authors focus on how the northern black community responded to difficult circumstances, especially during the antebellum decades.

Leon F. Litwack. *North of Slavery: The Negro in the Free States, 1790–1860*. Chicago: University of Chicago Press, 1961. This book emphasizes how northern white people treated African Americans. It is an essential guide to the status of African Americans in the antebellum North.

Quintard Taylor. *In Search of the Racial Frontier: African Americans in the American West, 1528–1990*. New York: Norton, 1998. This is the first book-length study of black westerners.

ADDITIONAL BIBLIOGRAPHY

COMMUNITY STUDIES

Tommy L. Bogger. *Free Blacks in Norfolk, Virginia, 1790–1860: The Darker Side of Freedom*. Charlottesville: University Press of Virginia, 1997.

Letitia Woods Brown. *Free Negroes in the District of Columbia, 1790–1846*. New York: Oxford University Press, 1972.

Melvin Patrick Ely. *Israel on the Appomattox: A Southern Experiment in Black Freedom from the 1790s through the Civil War*. New York: Knopf, 2004.

Leslie M. Harris. *In the Shadow of Slavery: African Americans in New York City, 1626–1863*. Chicago: University of Chicago Press, 2003.

James Oliver Horton. *Free People of Color: Inside the African-American Community*. Washington, DC: Smithsonian Institution Press, 1993.

James Oliver Horton and Lois E. Horton. *Black Bostonians: Family Life and Community Struggle in the Antebellum North*. New York: Holmes and Meier, 1979.

Gary B. Nash. *Forging Freedom: The Formation of Philadelphia's Black Community, 1720–1840*. Cambridge, MA: Harvard University Press, 1988.

Christopher Phillips. *Freedom's Port: The African-American Community of Baltimore, 1790–1860*. Urbana: University of Illinois Press, 1997.

Bernard E. Powers Jr. *Black Charlestonians: A Social History, 1822–1885*. Fayetteville: University of Arkansas Press, 1994.

Harry Reed. *Platform for Change: The Foundations of the Northern Free Black Community, 1775–1865*. East Lansing: Michigan State University Press, 1994.

Judith Kelleher Schafer. *Becoming Free, Remaining Free: Manumission and Enslavement in New Orleans, 1846–1862*. Baton Rouge: Louisiana State University Press, 2003.

Julie Winch. *Philadelphia's Black Elite: Activism, Accommodation, and the Struggle for Autonomy, 1787–1848*. Philadelphia: Temple University Press, 1988.

STATE-LEVEL STUDIES

Barbara Jeanne Fields. *Slavery and Freedom on the Middle Ground: Maryland during the Nineteenth Century*. New Haven, CT: Yale University Press, 1985.

John Hope Franklin. *The Free Negro in North Carolina, 1790–1860*. Chapel Hill: University of North Carolina Press, 1943.

Graham Russell Hodges. *Root and Branch: African Americans in New York and East Jersey, 1613–1863*. Chapel Hill: University of North Carolina Press, 1999.

John H. Russell. *The Free Negro in Virginia, 1619–1865*. 1913. Reprint, New York: Negro Universities Press, 1969.

H. E. Sterkx. *The Free Negro in Antebellum Louisiana*. Rutherford, NJ: Fairleigh Dickinson University Press, 1972.

Marina Wilkramangrake. *A World in Shadow—The Free Black in Antebellum South Carolina*. Columbia: University of South Carolina Press, 1973.

RACE RELATIONS

Francis D. Adams. *Alienable Rights: The Exclusion of African Americans in a White Man's Land, 1619–2000*. New York: HarperCollins, 2003.

Eugene H. Berwanger. *The Frontier against Slavery: Western Anti-Negro Prejudice and the Slavery Expansion Controversy*. Urbana: University of Illinois Press, 1967.

Phyllis F. Field. *The Politics of Race in New York: The Struggle for Black Suffrage in the Civil War Era*. Ithaca, NY: Cornell University Press, 1982.

Noel Ignatiev. *How the Irish Became White*. New York: Routledge, 1995.

David Roediger. *The Wages of Whiteness: Race and the Making of the American Working Class*. New York: Verso, 1991.

Joel Williamson. *New People: Miscegenation and Mulattoes in the United States*. New York: Free Press, 1980.

Carol Wilson. *Freedom at Risk: The Kidnapping of Free Blacks in America, 1780–1865*. Lexington: University Press of Kentucky, 1994.

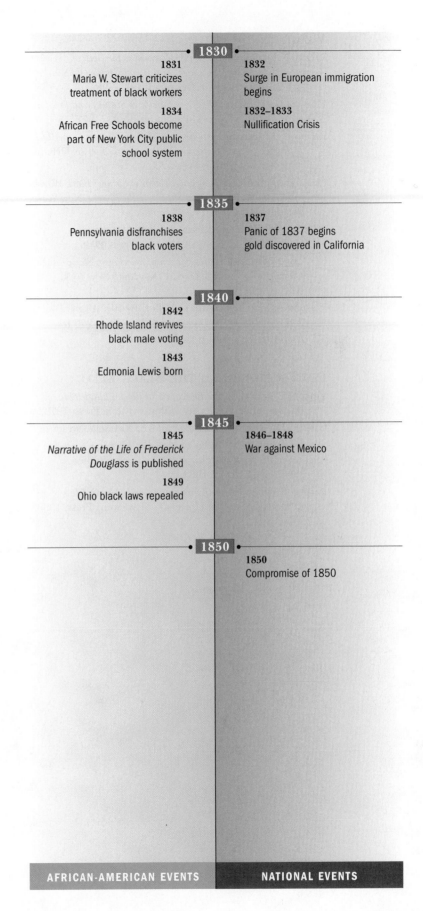

1830

1831
Maria W. Stewart criticizes treatment of black workers

1834
African Free Schools become part of New York City public school system

1832
Surge in European immigration begins

1832–1833
Nullification Crisis

1835

1838
Pennsylvania disfranchises black voters

1837
Panic of 1837 begins
gold discovered in California

1840

1842
Rhode Island revives black male voting

1843
Edmonia Lewis born

1845

1845
Narrative of the Life of Frederick Douglass is published

1849
Ohio black laws repealed

1846–1848
War against Mexico

1850

1850
Compromise of 1850

AFRICAN-AMERICAN EVENTS   NATIONAL EVENTS

WOMEN AND FAMILY

Virginia Meacham Gould, ed. *Chained to the Rock of Adversity: To Be Free, Black, and Female in the Old South.* Athens: University of Georgia Press, 1998.

Herbert G. Gutman. *The Black Family in Slavery and Freedom, 1750–1925.* New York: Pantheon Books, 1977.

Lynn M. Hudson. *The Making of "Mammy Pleasant": A Black Entrepreneur in Nineteenth-Century San Francisco.* Urbana: University of Illinois Press, 2003.

Jacqueline Jones. *Labor of Love, Labor of Sorrow: Black Women, Work and the Family from Slavery to the Present.* New York: Basic Books, 1985.

Wilma King. *Free Black Women during the Slave Era.* Columbia: University of Missouri Press, 2006.

Suzanne Lebsock. *The Free Women of Petersburg: Status and Culture in a Southern Town, 1784–1860.* New York: Norton, 1984.

T. O. Madden Jr., with Ann L. Miller. *We Were Always Free: The Maddens of Culpeper County, Virginia, a 200 Year Family History.* New York: Norton, 1992.

INSTITUTIONS AND THE BLACK ELITE

Vincent P. Franklin. *The Education of Black Philadelphia.* Philadelphia: University of Pennsylvania Press, 1979.

Carlton Mabee. *Black Education in New York State.* Syracuse, NY: Syracuse University Press, 1979.

Eileen Southern. *The Music of Black America.* 2nd ed. New York: Norton, 1983.

Loretta J. Williams. *Black Freemasonry and Middle-Class Realities.* Columbia: University of Missouri Press, 1980.

RETRACING THE ODYSSEY

Boston African-American National Historic Site: Black Heritage Trail and Museum of Afro-American History, Boston, MA. http://www.afroammuseum.org/trail.htm. Visitors may follow the Black Heritage Trail to historic locations located in Boston's antebellum black community on Beacon Hill. Of particular interest are the African Meeting House and the Abiel Smith School.

New Bedford Whaling Museum, New Bedford, MA. http://www.whalingmuseum.org/library/heros/index_h.html. Exhibits include "Heroes in the Ships: African Americans in the Whaling Industry, 1840–1900."

Chattanooga African American Museum, Chattanooga, TN. http://www.caamhistory.org/. A major exhibit focuses on free black businessmen in antebellum Chattanooga.

REVIEW QUESTIONS

1. How was black freedom in the North limited in the antebellum decades?

2. How did northern African Americans deal with these limits?

3. What was the relationship of the African-American elite to urban black communities?

4. How did African-American institutions fare between 1820 and 1861?

5. Compare black life in the North to free black life in the Upper South, Deep South, and California.

myhistorylab Connections

www.myhistorylab.com
Review what you've learned in this chapter and explore the many documents, images, research tools, and activities for this chapter to learn more about African-American history.

✓ Study and Review

READ

Read the Document

- "Reflections, Occasioned by the Late Disturbances in Charleston" (1822)

- Richard Allen, "Address to the Free People of Colour of These United States" (1830)

- Thomas R. Dew's Defense of Slavery (1832)

- Maria Stewart, "The Miseries We Tasted" (1835)

- Senator Sees Slavery as a "Positive Good" (1837)

- Sarah Mapps Douglass, Letter to William Basset (1837)

- North Carolina Codes (1855)

- An African-American Novel Critiques Racism in the North (1859)

- Address to the Free People of Color (1830)

LISTEN

Hear the Audio

Hear the audio files for Chapter 7.

RESEARCH

mysearchlab

Consider these questions in a short research paper.

Compare and contrast the lives of free blacks in the North and the South. What key differences do you note?

EXPLORE

See the Map

- The Slave, Free Black, and White Populations of the United States in 1830

Opposition to Slavery

Why and how did abolitionism begin in America?

How did the revolts of Gabriel, Denmark Vesey, and Nat Turner affect African Americans?

What were the goals of the American Colonization Society?

What role did black women play in the abolition movement?

Why was Walker's *Appeal* important?

▶ **This drawing, known as "Nat Turner Preaches Religion,"** portrays Turner telling "friends and brothers" in August 1831 that God has chosen them to lead a violent "struggle for freedom."

Beloved brethren—here let me tell you, and believe it, that the Lord our God, as true as he sits on his throne in heaven, and as true as our Savior died to redeem the world, will give you a Hannibal [an ancient Carthaginian general], and when the Lord shall have raised him up, and given him to you for your possession, O my suffering brethren! . . . Read the history particularly of Hayti, and see how they were butchered by the whites, and do you take warning. The person whom God Shall give you, give him your support and let him go his length, and behold in him the salvation of your God. God will indeed, deliver you through him from your deplorable and wretched condition under the Christians of America.

David Walker's *Appeal*

◀ **Haitian independence** movement leader Toussant Louverture, who fought successfully against the French and British, provided inspiration for leaders of slave uprisings in America.

Black abolitionist David Walker wrote these words in Boston in 1829. They suggest the sense early nineteenth-century Americans had of the nearness of God and the anguish a free black man felt about his brothers and sisters in bondage.

((•⦁— **Hear** the Audio
Hear the audio files for Chapter 8 at **www.myhistorylab.com**

In his harsh language and demands for action, Walker anticipated the militant black and white abolitionists of the 1830s, 1840s, and 1850s. He bluntly portrayed the oppression African Americans suffered. He urged black men to redeem themselves by defending their loved ones from abuse. If that led to violence and death, he asked, "Had you not rather be killed than be a slave to a tyrant, who takes the life of your mother, wife and dear little children?" Through his provocative language and efforts to have his *Appeal . . . to the Colored Citizens of the World* distributed in the South, Walker became a prophet of violent revolution against slaveholders.

Walker's *Appeal* was not just a reaction to slavery; it was also a response to a conservative brand of antislavery reform. This chapter explores the emergence, during the eighteenth century, of abolitionism in America; its transformation during the early nineteenth century; and the beginning of a more radical antislavery movement by the late 1820s. Slave revolt conspiracies; political, social, and religious turmoil; and wide-ranging reform shaped this process. Black leaders, including Walker, Denmark Vesey, and Nat Turner, were major contributors. So was white abolitionist William Lloyd Garrison.

Abolitionism Begins in America

The antislavery movement in its broadest context reflected economic, intellectual, and moral changes that affected the Atlantic world during the Age of Revolution that began during the 1760s. In the United States, that age forged *two* antislavery movements that survived until the end of the Civil War. Although separate, the two movements influenced each other. The first movement arose in the South among slaves with the help of free African Americans and a few sympathetic white people. As we mentioned in earlier chapters, from the seventeenth century onward enslaved African Americans, individually and in groups, sought their freedom through violent and nonviolent means. Before the revolutionary era, however, they only wanted to free themselves. They did not seek to destroy slavery as a social system.

The second antislavery movement consisted of black and white abolitionists in the North, with outposts in the Upper South. Far more white people were in this movement than in the one southern slaves conducted. In the North, white people controlled the larger antislavery organizations, although African Americans led in direct action against slavery and its influences in the North. In the Upper South, African Americans could not openly establish or participate in antislavery organizations, but they cooperated covertly and informally with white abolitionists.

This second and essentially northern movement began during the 1730s when white Quakers in New Jersey and Pennsylvania realized slaveholding contradicted their belief in spiritual equality. Therefore, they advocated the abolition of slavery—at least among their fellow Quakers—in their home states and in the Chesapeake. As members of a denomination that emphasized nonviolence, Quakers generally expected slavery to be abolished peacefully and gradually.

Quakers remained prominent in the northern antislavery movement for the next 130 years. But the American Revolution, together with the French Revolution that began in 1789 and the Haitian struggle for independence between 1791 and 1804, revitalized the northern and southern antislavery movements and changed their nature. The revolutionary doctrine that all men had a natural right to life, liberty, and property led other northerners besides Quakers and African Americans to endorse the antislavery cause.

In 1775 Philadelphia Quakers organized the first antislavery society in the world. But their organization lapsed during the War for Independence. When they regrouped in 1784 as the Society for the Promotion of the Abolition of Slavery, they attracted non-Quakers. Among the first of these were Benjamin Rush and Benjamin Franklin, both of whom embraced natural rights doctrines. Revolutionary principles also influenced Alexander Hamilton and John Jay, who helped organize New York's first antislavery society. Similarly Prince Hall, the most prominent black abolitionist of his time, based his effort to abolish slavery in Massachusetts on universal rights. He contended that African Americans "have in common with all other men a natural right to our freedom."

Black and white abolitionists were instrumental in abolishing slavery in the North. However, the early northern antislavery movement had several limiting features. First, black and white abolitionists had similar goals but worked in separate organizations. Even white Quaker abolitionists were reluctant to mix socially with African Americans or welcome them to their meetings. Second, except in parts of New England, abolition in the North proceeded *gradually* to protect the economic interests of slaveholders. Third, despite natural rights rhetoric, white abolitionists did not advocate equal rights for black people. In most northern states, laws kept black people from enjoying full freedom after their emancipation. Fourth, early northern abolitionists did little to bring about abolition in the South, where most slaves lived.

All this indicates that neither Quaker piety nor natural rights principles created a truly egalitarian or sectionally aggressive northern abolitionism. Rather, major antislavery efforts carried out by black southerners, widespread religious revivalism, demands for reform, and the growth of northern black institutions established a framework for a more biracial and wide-ranging antislavery movement.

FROM GABRIEL TO DENMARK VESEY

Gabriel's abortive slave revolt conspiracy of 1800 (discussed in Chapter 5) owed as much to revolutionary ideology as did the northern antislavery movement. The arrival of Haitian refugees in Virginia led to slave unrest throughout the 1790s, and Gabriel hoped to attract French revolutionary support. Although he was betrayed and he and 26 of his followers suffered execution, the revolutionary spirit and insurrectionary network he established lived on (see Map 8–1). Virginia authorities had to suppress another slave conspiracy in 1802, and sporadic minor revolts erupted there for years.

Gabriel's conspiracy had two other consequences. The first involved the Quaker-led antislavery societies of the Chesapeake. These organizations had always been small and weak compared with antislavery societies in the North. Unlike their northern counterparts, the Chesapeake societies were more effective in helping free black people illegally held as slaves than in promoting emancipation. The revelation of Gabriel's plot worsened conditions for these organizations. State and local governments suppressed them, or they withered under negative public opinion. The chance that Maryland, Virginia, and North Carolina would follow the northeastern states' example in abolishing slavery gradually and peacefully all but vanished.

The second consequence was that white southerners and many white northerners became convinced that, so long as African Americans lived among them, a race war like the one in Haiti could erupt in the United States. Slaveholders and their defenders argued that this threat did not result from the oppressiveness of

MAP 8–1   SLAVE CONSPIRACIES AND UPRISINGS, 1800–1831
Major slave conspiracies and revolts were rare between 1800 and 1860. This was in part because those that took place frightened masters and led them to adopt policies aimed at preventing recurrences.

⊙ See the Map   *Explore this map at* **www.myhistorylab.com**

slavery. Instead, they claimed, people of African descent were naturally suited for bondage and would be content if a growing class of free black people did not instigate resistance and revolt.

Free African Americans were, slavery's defenders contended, a dangerous, criminal, and potentially revolutionary class that had to be regulated, subdued, and ultimately expelled from the country to prevent catastrophe. No system of emancipation that would increase the number of free black people in the United States could be tolerated. Slaveholders who had never shown a willingness to free their slaves began to claim they would favor emancipation if it were not for fear of enlarging such a dangerous group. As an elderly Thomas Jefferson put it, white southerners had "the wolf by the ear": once they had enslaved black people, it was impossible to free them safely.

Without the restrictions slavery placed on African Americans, southern politicians and journalists argued, they would become economic competitors to white workers, a perpetual criminal class, and a revolutionary threat to white rule.

Events in and about Charleston, South Carolina, in 1822 appeared to confirm the threat. In that year black informants revealed that Denmark Vesey, a free black carpenter, had organized a massive slave revolt conspiracy. Like Gabriel before him, Vesey could read and was well aware of the revolutions that had shaken the Atlantic world. Born most likely on the Danish-ruled Caribbean island of St. Thomas, Vesey—a former sailor—had been to Haiti and hoped for Haitian aid for an antislavery revolution in the South Carolina low country. He understood the significance of the storming of the Bastille (a fortress-prison in Paris) on July 14, 1789, that marked the start of the French Revolution and planned to start his revolution on July 14, 1822. He had read the antislavery speeches of northern members of Congress during the 1820 debates over the admission of Missouri to the Union and may have hoped for northern aid.

However, religion had a more prominent role in Vesey's plot than in Gabriel's. Vesey, a Bible-quoting Methodist who conducted religious classes, resented white authorities' attempts in 1818 to suppress Charleston's African Methodist Episcopal (AME) Church. He believed that passages in the Bible about the enslavement of the Hebrews in Egypt and their deliverance promised freedom for African Americans. But Vesey also relied on aspects of African religion that had survived among low-country slaves to promote his revolutionary efforts. To reach slaves whose Christian convictions blended in with West African spiritualism, he relied on Jack Pritchard—known as Gullah Jack. A "conjure-man" born in East Africa, Pritchard distributed charms and cast spells he claimed would make black revolutionaries invincible.

Vesey and his associates planned to capture arms and ammunition and seize control of Charleston. But Gullah Jack's charms were ineffective against white vigilance and black informers. About a month before the revolt was to begin, the arrest of one of Vesey's lieutenants put authorities on guard. Vesey moved the date of the uprising to June 16. But on June 14, a house servant told his master about the plot, the local government called in the state militia, and arrests followed. Over several weeks, law officers rounded up 131 suspects. The accused received public trials, and juries convicted 76 of them. Thirty-five, including Vesey and Gullah Jack, were hanged. Thirty-seven were banished. Four white men—three of them foreigners—were convicted of inciting slaves to revolt. They received prison sentences and fines.

After the executions, Charleston's city government destroyed what remained of the local AME church, and white churches assumed responsibility for supervising other black congregations. Meanwhile, white South Carolinians sought to make slave patrols more efficient. The state legislature outlawed assemblages of slaves and banned teaching slaves to read. Local authorities jailed black seamen whose ships docked in Charleston until the ships were ready to sail. Assuming that free black and white abolitionists inspired slave unrest, white South Carolinians became more suspicious of local free African Americans and of white Yankees who visited their state.

A Country in Turmoil

During the long period from Gabriel's conspiracy, through Vesey's, to the year Walker wrote his *Appeal* and beyond, the United States was in economic, political, and social turmoil. As we have shown in earlier chapters, the invention of the cotton gin in 1793 led to a vast westward expansion of cotton cultivation. Where cotton went, so did slavery. By the late 1820s, southern slaveholders and their slaves had pushed into what was then the Mexican province of Texas. Meanwhile, the states of the Old Northwest passed from frontier conditions to commercial farming. By 1825 the Erie Canal had linked this region economically to the Northeast. Later, railroads carried the Old Northwest's agricultural products to East Coast cities. An enormous amount of grain and meat also flowed down the Ohio and Mississippi rivers, encouraging the growth of such cities as Pittsburgh, Cincinnati, Louisville, St. Louis, Memphis, and New Orleans. As steamboats became common and networks of macadam turnpikes (paved with crushed stone and tar), canals, and railroads spread, travel time diminished. Americans became more mobile, families scattered, and ties to local communities weakened. For African Americans, subject to the domestic slave trade, mobility came with a high price.

The factory system, which arose in urban areas of the Northeast and spread to parts of the Old Northwest and Upper South, was also disruptive. Cities grew, and increased immigration from Europe meant native black and white people had to compete for employment with foreign-born workers. Farmers became more dependent on urban markets for their crops. The money economy expanded, banks became essential, and private fortunes influenced public policy. Many Americans believed forces beyond their control threatened their way of life and the nation's republican values. They distrusted change and wanted someone to blame for the uncertainties they faced. This outlook encouraged American politics to become paranoid—dominated by fear of hostile conspiracies.

POLITICAL PARANOIA

The charge (discussed in Chapter 7) that John Quincy Adams and Henry Clay had cheated Andrew Jackson out of the presidency in early 1825 reflected this fear of conspiracies. What Jackson's supporters called "the corrupt bargain" and claims that Adams favored a wealthy and intellectual elite at the expense of the common white man led to the organization of the Democratic Party and the election of Jackson to the presidency in 1828. The Democrats claimed to stand for the natural rights and economic well-being of American workers and farmers against what they called the "money power," a conspiratorial alliance of bankers and businessmen.

Yet, from its start, the Democratic Party also represented the interests of the South's slaveholding elite. Democratic politicians, North and South, favored a state rights doctrine that protected slavery from interference by the national government. They sought through legislation, judicial decisions, and diplomacy to make the right to hold human property inviolate. They became the most ardent supporters of expanding slavery into new regions, leading their opponents to claim they were part of a **"slave power"** conspiracy. Most Democratic politicians openly advocated white supremacy. Although their rhetoric demanded equal rights for all and special privileges for none, they were really concerned only with the rights of white men.

The Democratic Party's outlook toward American Indians, women, and African Americans demonstrated this. Democratic politicians led in demanding the removal of Indians to the area west of the Mississippi River, which led to the Cherokee "Trail of Tears" in 1838. Democrats also supported patriarchy, a subservient role for women in family life and the church, and their exclusion from the public sphere. Almost all Democratic leaders believed God and nature had designed African Americans to be slaves. During the 1820s and early 1830s, only a few radicals like Walker saw the hypocrisy of this outlook and contended that real democracy would embrace all men, regardless of race. Reformers did not begin to propose equal rights for women until the late 1830s.

The Trail of Tears, painted in 1942 by Robert Lindneux, dramatizes the westward journey of Cherokees from their homeland in Georgia to what is now Oklahoma. The Democratic Party, which championed the rights of white men, was chiefly responsible for the forced westward relocation of the Cherokees and other southeastern Indian peoples.   Robert Lindneux,

"The Trail of Tears" (the removal of the Cherokee Indians to the West in 1838). Oil on canvas. © The Granger Collection, New York

By the mid-1830s, those Americans who favored a more enlightened political program turned—often reluctantly—to the Whig Party, which opposed Jackson and the Democrats. The Whigs also attracted those who had supported the Anti-Masonic Party during the early 1830s. This small party epitomized political paranoia by contending that the Freemasons conspired to subvert republican government. Politicians such as Henry Clay, Daniel Webster, William H. Seward, and John Quincy Adams, who identified with the Whig Party, emphasized Christian morality and active national government more than the Democrats did. They regarded themselves as conservatives, did not seek to end slavery in the South, and included many wealthy slaveholders within their ranks. But in the North, the party's moral orientation and its opposition to territorial expansion by the United States made it attractive to slavery's opponents.

The Whig Party also served as the channel through which evangelical Christianity influenced politics. In the North, Whig politicians appealed to evangelical voters. Often evangelicals themselves, some Whig politicians and journalists defended the human rights of African Americans and American Indians. They criticized the inhumanity of slaveholders and tried to limit federal support for the "peculiar institution." When and where they could, black men voted for Whig candidates.

THE SECOND GREAT AWAKENING

Under the influence of a wave of religious revivalism, evangelicals carried Christian morality into politics during the 1830s. Religion, of course, had always been important in America. During the 1730s and 1740s, the revival known as the Great Awakening had used emotional preaching and hymn singing to encourage men and women to embrace Jesus and reform their lives. During this period, American churches converted black people, and African Americans in turn helped shape the revival. At the end of the eighteenth century, a new, emotional revivalism began. Known as the **Second Great Awakening,** it lasted through the 1830s. It led laymen to replace established clergy as leaders and seek to impose moral order on a turbulent society.

The Second Great Awakening influenced Richard Allen and Absalom Jones's efforts to establish separate black churches in Philadelphia during the 1790s. It helped shape the character of other black churches that emerged during the 1800s and 1810s. These churches became an essential part of the antislavery movement. However, the Second Great Awakening did not peak until the 1820s. During that decade, Charles G. Finney, a white Presbyterian, and other revivalists helped democratize religion in America. At days-long camp meetings, revivalists preached that all men and women—not just a few—could become faithful Christians and save their souls. Just as Jacksonian democracy revolutionized politics in America, the Second Great Awakening revolutionized the nation's spiritual life and—especially in the Northeast and Old Northwest—led many Americans, black and white, to join reform movements.

THE BENEVOLENT EMPIRE

Evangelicals emphasized "practical Christianity." Those who were truly among the saved, they

This 1844 lithograph by Peter S. Duval, derived from a painting by Alfred Hoffy, portrays Julianne Jane Tillman. Tillman was an AME preacher and one of the few women of her time to be employed in such a capacity.

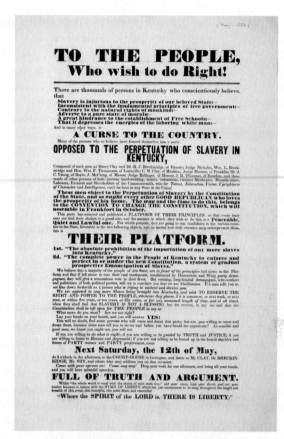

Leaflet appealing to citizens to attend a meeting to hear a platform against slavery, published in Lexington, 1850.

maintained, had actively to oppose sin and save others. Black evangelicals, in particular, called for "a *liberating* faith" applied in ways that would advance material and spiritual well-being. This emphasis on action led during the 1810s and 1820s to what became known as the **Benevolent Empire,** a network of church-related organizations designed to fight sin and rescue souls. The Benevolent Empire launched what is now known as antebellum or Jacksonian reform.

Centered in the Northeast, this social movement flourished through the 1850s. Voluntary associations organized on behalf of a host of causes. Among them were public education, self-improvement, limiting or abolishing alcohol consumption and sales (the temperance movement), prison reform, and aid to the mentally and physically challenged. Other associations distributed Bibles and religious tracts, funded missionary activities, and discouraged prostitution. Still others sought to improve health through diet and medical fads, alleviate shipboard conditions for sailors, and—by the 1840s—gain equal rights for women. The self-improvement, temperance, and missionary associations that free black people—and sometimes slaves—formed in urban areas in conjunction with their churches were part of this movement.

The most important of these reform associations were those that addressed the problem of African-American bondage. Called societies for promoting the abolition of slavery during the eighteenth and early nineteenth centuries, by the 1830s they became known as antislavery societies. Whatever they called themselves, their members were **abolitionists,** people who favored abolishing slavery in their respective states and throughout the country.

COLONIZATION

The most significant antislavery organization of the 1810s and 1820s was the American Colonization Society (ACS). But whether its aim was abolition is debatable. In late 1816 concerned white leaders met in Washington, D.C., to form this organization, formally named the American Society for Colonizing Free People of Colour of the United States. Among its founders were prominent slaveholders, including Bushrod Washington—a nephew of George Washington—and Henry Clay.

The ACS had a twofold program. First, it proposed to abolish slavery gradually in the United States, perhaps giving slaveholders financial compensation for freeing their human property. Second, it proposed to send emancipated slaves and free African Americans to Africa. To achieve this second goal, the ACS—with the support of the U.S. government—established the colony of Liberia on the West African coast. The founders of the ACS claimed that free African Americans had to go to Liberia because masters would never emancipate their slaves if they thought doing so would increase the size of what they regarded as a shiftless and dangerous free black class. Despite this agenda, the ACS became an integral part of the Benevolent Empire and commanded widespread support among many who regarded themselves as friends of humanity. At first black and white abolitionists did not perceive the moral and practical objections to the ACS program.

The ACS always had its greatest strength in the Upper South and enjoyed the support of slaveholders, including—besides Washington and Clay—Francis Scott Key (who wrote the lyrics for "The Spangled Banner"), James Monroe, Andrew Jackson, John Tyler, and John Randolph. But, by the 1820s, it had branches in every northern state. During that decade, such northern white abolitionists as Arthur and Lewis Tappan, Gerrit Smith, and William Lloyd Garrison supported colonization. They emphasized the ACS's abolitionist aspects and hoped free and soon-to-be-emancipated African Americans would be able to choose whether to stay in the United States or go to Liberia. In either case, they assumed black people would become free.

BLACK NATIONALISM AND COLONIZATION

Prominent black abolitionists initially shared this positive assessment of the ACS. They were part of a black nationalist tradition dating back to Prince Hall that, disappointed with repeated rebuffs from white people, endorsed black migration to Africa. During the early 1800s, the most prominent advocate of this point of view was Paul Cuffe of Massachusetts. In 1811, six years before the ACS organized, Cuffe, a Quaker of African and American Indian ancestry, addressed Congress on the subject of African-American Christian colonies in Africa.

The colonization argument that appealed to Cuffe and many other African Americans was that white prejudice would never allow black people to enjoy full citizenship, equal protection under the law, and economic success in the United States. Black people born in America, this argument held, could enjoy equal rights only in the land of their ancestors. The spirit of American evangelicalism also led many African Americans to embrace the prospect of bringing Christianity to African nations. Like white Americans, they considered Africa a pagan, barbaric land that could benefit from

Christianity and republican government. Other black leaders who favored colonization objected to this view of Africa. They considered African cultures superior to those of America and Europe. They were often Africans themselves, the children of African parents, or individuals who had been influenced by Africans.

In 1815 Cuffe, who owned and commanded a ship, took 34 African-American settlers to the British free black colony of Sierra Leone, located just north of what became Liberia. Cuffe's American-Indian wife's reluctance to leave her native land and his death in 1817 prevented him from transporting more settlers to West Africa. Therefore, it was former AME bishop Daniel Coker who in 1820 led the first 86 African-American colonists to Liberia. Pro-ACS sentiment was especially strong among African Americans in Coker's home city of Baltimore and other Chesapeake urban areas. By 1838 approximately 2,500 colonists had made the journey. They lived less than harmoniously with Liberia's 28,000 indigenous inhabitants (see Map 8–2).

In 1847 Liberia became an independent republic. But despite the efforts of such **black nationalist** advocates as Henry Highland Garnet and Alexander Crummell, only about 10,000 African-American immigrants had gone there by 1860. This number amounted to just 3 percent of the increase

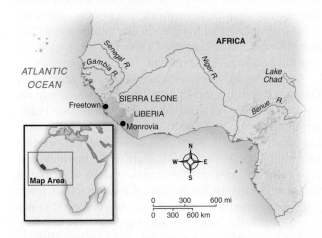

MAP 8–2   THE FOUNDING OF LIBERIA

This map shows the location of Sierra Leone and Liberia in West Africa. British abolitionists established Sierra Leone as a colony for former slaves in 1800. The American Colonization Society established Liberia for the same purpose in 1821.

▶ *Why were Sierra Leone and Liberia established in West Africa?*

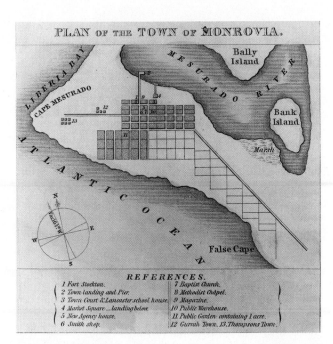

Monrovia, Liberia, c. 1830. This map shows the American Colonization Society's main Liberian settlement as it existed about ten years after its founding.

of the black population in the United States since 1816. Well before 1860, it was clear that African colonization would never fulfill the dreams of its black or white advocates.

Other African Americans regarded Haiti as a potential refuge from the oppression they suffered in the United States. Those whose ancestors had lived in the Caribbean and those who admired Haiti's revolutionary history found it especially attractive. In 1824 about 200 men, women, and children from Philadelphia, New York City, and Baltimore went to Haiti. By the end of the 1820s, between 8,000 and 13,000 African Americans had arrived there. But many of the emigrants found Haitian culture alien. They had difficulty learning French and Creole and distrusted the Roman Catholic Church, to which most Haitians at least nominally belonged. About one-third of the emigrants returned to the United States.

BLACK OPPOSITION TO COLONIZATION

Some African Americans had always opposed overseas colonization, and, as early as 1817, such an influential black leader as James Forten wavered in his support of the ACS. Although in private Forten continued to endorse colonization, he led a meeting that year of 3,000 black Philadelphians who denounced it. By the

mid-1820s, many black abolitionists in cities from Richmond to Boston had criticized colonization in general and the ACS in particular.

Among them was Samuel Cornish, who in New York City in 1827 began publishing *Freedom's Journal*, the first African-American newspaper. Cornish, a young Presbyterian minister, called for independent black action against slavery. The *Journal*—reflecting the values of antebellum reform—also encouraged northern black self-improvement, education, civil rights, and sympathy for slaves. However John Russwurm—the *Journal's* cofounder—was less opposed than Cornish to the ACS. This disagreement contributed to the suspension of the newspaper in 1829. That same year Russwurm, one of the first African Americans to earn a college degree, moved to Liberia. (See *Roots of Culture: Freedom's Journal* on pp. 214–215.)

People like Cornish, however, wanted to improve their condition in the United States. They considered Liberia to be foreign and unhealthy. They had no desire to go to Africa or send other African Americans there. They also feared that ACS proposals for *voluntary* colonization were misleading because nearly every southern state required the expulsion of slaves individually freed by their masters. The Maryland and Virginia legislatures were considering legislation designed to require *all* free black people to leave those states or be enslaved. These efforts had little practical impact, but African Americans feared colonization would be forced on them, much the way state and federal governments forced American Indians from their land.

By the mid-1820s, most black abolitionists had concluded that the ACS was part of a proslavery effort to drive free African Americans from the United States. The ACS, they maintained, was not an abolitionist organization at all but a proslavery scheme to force free black people to choose between reenslavement or banishment. America, they argued, was their native land. They knew nothing of Africa. Efforts to force them to go there were based on a racist assumption that they were not entitled to live in freedom in the land of their birth. "Do they think to drive us from our country and homes, after having enriched it with our blood and tears?" asked David Walker.

Black Abolitionist Women

Black women joined black men in opposing slavery. In considering their role, it is important to understand that the United States in the early nineteenth century had a rigid gender hierarchy. Law and custom

VOICES

WILLIAM WATKINS OPPOSES COLONIZATION

In response to a white clergyman who argued that migration to Africa would help alleviate the plight of African Americans, William Watkins stressed black unity, education, and self-improvement in this country.

The Reverend Mr. Hewitt says] "Let us unite into select societies for the purpose of digesting a plan for raising funds to be appropriated to this grand object" [African colonization]. This we cannot do; we intend to let the burden of this work rest upon the shoulders of those who wish us out of the country. We will, however, compromise the matter with our friend. We are willing and anxious to "unite into select societies for the purpose of digesting a plan": for the improvement of our people in science, morals, domestic economy, &c. We are willing and anxious to form union societies . . . that shall discountenance and destroy, as far as possible, those unhappy schisms which have too long divided us, though we are brethren. We are willing to unite . . . in the formation of temperance societies . . . that will enable us to exhibit to the world an amount of moral power that would give new impetus to our friends and "strike alarm" into the breasts of our enemies, if not wholly disarm them of the weapons they are hurling against us.

▶ *According to Watkins, how will black self-improvement societies help counter colonization?*

▶ *What difficulties does Watkins believe African Americans must overcome to make themselves stronger in the United States?*

Source: "A Colored American [Watkins] to Editors," n.d., in *Genius of Universal Emancipation*, December 18, 1829.

proscribed women from engaging in politics, the professions, and most businesses. Those women deemed respectable by black and white Americans— the women of wealthy families—were expected to devote themselves exclusively to domestic concerns and remain socially aloof. Church and benevolent activities constituted their only opportunities for public action. Even in these arenas, custom relegated them to work in auxiliaries to men's organizations.

This was true of the first *formal* abolitionist groups of black women. Among the leaders were Charlotte Forten, the wife of James Forten, and Maria W. Stewart, the widow of a well-to-do Boston ship outfitter. In 1833 Charlotte and her daughters Sarah, Margaretta, and Harriet joined with other black and white women to found the **Philadelphia Female Anti-Slavery Society.** A year earlier, other black women had established in Salem, Massachusetts, the first women's antislavery society. Women of the black elite also supported the education of black children. They hoped that, as African Americans gained knowledge, white prejudice that supported slavery would diminish.

•••⊣Read the Document
A Black Feminist Speaks Out in 1851

Stewart's brief career as an antislavery orator provoked far more controversy than those of the Fortens or other early black abolitionist women. Influenced by Walker's *Appeal* and encouraged by William Lloyd Garrison, Stewart in 1831 and 1832 became the first American woman publicly to address male audiences. Although she directed some of her remarks to "Afric's daughters" and to "ye fairer sisters," she—as had Walker before her—pointedly called on black men to act against slavery. "It is true," she told a group assembled at the African Masonic Hall in Boston in 1833, "our fathers bled and died in the revolutionary war, and others fought bravely under the command of [General Andrew] Jackson [at New Orleans in 1815], in defense of liberty. But where is the man that has distinguished himself in these modern days by acting wholly in the defense of African rights and liberty?" Such remarks from a woman cut deeply, and Stewart met such hostility from the black community that in September 1833 she retired as a public speaker. Henceforth, she labored in more conventional and respectable female ways for the antislavery cause.

Many African-American women (and white women) did not fit the early nineteenth-century criteria for respectability that applied to the Fortens, Stewart, and others among the African-American elite. Most black women were poor and uneducated. They had to work outside their homes.

(((•⊣Hear the Audio
What If I Am a Woman?

Particularly in the Upper South, these women were *practical* abolitionists.

From the revolutionary era onward, countless anonymous black women, both slave and free, living in such southern border cities as Baltimore, Louisville, and Washington, risked everything to harbor fugitive slaves. Others saved their meager earnings to purchase freedom for themselves and their loved ones. Among them was Alethia Tanner of Washington, who purchased her freedom in 1810 for $1,400 (about 39,200 current dollars). During the 1820s she also purchased the freedom of her sister, her sister's ten children, and her sister's five grandchildren. During the 1830s Tanner purchased the freedom of seven more slaves. Meanwhile, according to an account written in the 1860s, "Mrs. Tanner was alive to every wise scheme for the education and elevation of her race."

The Baltimore Alliance

Among the stronger black abolitionist opponents of the ACS were William Watkins, Jacob Greener, and Hezekiah Grice. All three were associates in Baltimore of Benjamin Lundy, a white Quaker aboli-

tionist who published an antislavery newspaper named the *Genius of Universal Emancipation*. By the mid-1820s, Watkins, a schoolteacher, had emerged, in letters he published in *Freedom's Journal* and in Lundy's paper, as one of the more articulate critics of colonization. Greener, a whitewasher and schoolteacher, helped Lundy publish the *Genius* and promoted its circulation. Grice, who later changed his mind about colonization, became the principal founder of the National Black Convention Movement, which during the 1830s, 1840s, and 1850s served as a forum for black abolitionists.

In 1829 Watkins, Greener, and Grice profoundly influenced William Lloyd Garrison, who later

P R O F I L E : Maria W. Stewart

Maria W. Stewart had a brief but striking career as an abolitionist, feminist, and advocate of racial justice. She was born Maria Miller in Hartford, Connecticut, in 1803 to free parents, and she was orphaned at age five. Raised in the home of a minister, she had little formal education until she began attending "sabbath schools" when she was fifteen. In 1826 she married James W. Stewart, a successful Boston businessman nearly twice her age, in a ceremony conducted by Thomas Paul at his Boston church. When James W. Stewart died in 1829, he left her with limited means.

In 1830, caught up in the Second Great Awakening, Maria W. Stewart determined to dedicate herself to Christian benevolence. When William Lloyd Garrison began publishing the *Liberator* in 1831, she visited him at his office. Later that year, Garrison published her pamphlet *Religion and Pure Principles of Morality, the Sure Foundation on Which We Must Build*, in which she advocated abolition and black autonomy. The following year, Garrison published her second and last pamphlet, which dealt more narrowly with religion.

Meanwhile, Stewart began speaking to black organizations. In early 1832 she addressed Boston's Afric-American Female Intelligence Society. Using prophetic rhetoric, she noted that the world had entered a revolutionary age and called on African-American women to influence their husbands and children on behalf of the cause of black freedom, equality, education, and economic advancement in America. In regard to African colonization, she

said, "before I go, the bayonet shall press me through."

But in February 1833, when she addressed Boston's African Masonic Lodge, Stewart overplayed her role as a prophet. She invoked the glories of ancient Africa and black service in the American Revolution to chastise black men of her time for not being more active on behalf of the liberty of their people. By claiming that black men lacked "ambition and requisite courage," she provoked her audience to respond with hoots, jeers, and a barrage of rotten tomatoes.

Daunted by this stunning rejection, Stewart determined to leave Boston for New York City. In her farewell address of September 1833, which she delivered at a schoolroom in Paul's church, she asserted that her advice had been rejected because she was a woman. Nevertheless, while acknowledging that black men must lead, she called on black women to promote themselves, their families, and their race.

During the rest of her life, Stewart sought to fulfill that role in a less flamboyant manner. In New York she joined the Female Literary Society and became a schoolteacher. She moved to Baltimore in 1852 to start a school for black children. During the Civil War, with the assistance of black seamstress Elizabeth Keckley, she organized a black school in Washington, D.C. Later she worked as a matron at that city's Freedmen's Hospital and organized a Sunday school for poor black children. She died at Freedmen's Hospital in December 1879.

VOICES

A BLACK WOMAN SPEAKS OUT ON THE RIGHT TO EDUCATION

Historians generally believe the antebellum women's rights movement emerged from the antislavery movement during the late 1830s. But as the following letter, published in Freedom's Journal *on August 10, 1827, indicates, some black women advocated equal rights for women much earlier:*

Messrs. Editors,

Will you allow a female to offer a few remarks upon a subject that you must allow to be all-important? I don't know that in any of your papers, you have said sufficient upon the education of females. I hope you are not to be classed with those, who think that our mathematical knowledge should be limited to "fathoming the dish-kettle," and that we have acquired enough of history, if we know that our grandfather's father lived and died. . . . The diffusion of knowledge has destroyed those degraded opinions, and men of the present age, allow, that we have minds that are capable and deserving of culture. There are difficulties . . . in the way of our advancement; but that should only stir us to greater efforts. We possess not the advantages with those of our sex, whose skins are not coloured like our own, but we can improve what little we have, and make our one talent produce two-fold. . . . Ignorant ourselves, how can we be expected to form the minds of our youth, and conduct them in the paths of knowledge? I would address myself to all mothers. . . . It is their bounden duty to store their daughters' minds with useful learning. They should be made to devote their leisure time to reading books, whence they would derive valuable information, which could never be taken from them. . . .

Matilda

▶ *How does Matilda use sarcasm to make her point?*
▶ *What special difficulties did black women like Matilda face in asserting their rights?*

Source: Herbert Aptheker, ed., *A Documentary History of the Negro People in the United States,* 7 vols. (1951; reprint, New York: Citadel, 1990), 1: 89. Reprinted by permission of Bettina Aptheker, Literary Executer, Herbert Aptheker Estate.

William Lloyd Garrison (1805–1879) was the leading American abolitionist during the 1830s. He called for immediate emancipation of American slaves, without compensation to their masters, and led the American Anti-Slavery Society.

well-schooled journalist, had decided before he came to Baltimore that *gradual* abolition was neither practical nor moral. Gradualism was impractical, he said, because it continually put off the date of general emancipation. It was immoral because it encouraged slaveholders to continue sinfully and criminally oppressing African Americans.

Garrison, however, tolerated the ACS until he came under the influence of Watkins, Greener, and Grice. They set him on a course that transformed the abolitionist movement in the United States during the early 1830s. They also initiated a bond between African Americans and Garrison that—although strained at times—shaped the rest of his antislavery career. That bond intensified in 1830 when Garrison served 49 days in Baltimore Jail on charges he had libeled a slave trader. While in jail, Garrison met imprisoned fugitive slaves and denounced *to their faces* masters who came to retrieve them.

In 1831, when he began publishing his abolitionist newspaper, *The Liberator,* in Boston, Garrison led the antislavery movement in a radical direction. It was radical not so much because

Read the Document
Abolitionist Demands Immediate End to Slavery (1831)

became the most influential American antislavery leader. Lundy had convinced Garrison—a young abolitionist and temperance advocate—to leave his native Massachusetts to come to Baltimore as the associate editor of the *Genius.* Garrison, a deeply religious product of the Second Great Awakening and a

Garrison rejected gradual abolition and called for immediate emancipation. He had earlier rejected gradualism and was not the first to endorse **immediatism.** What made his brand of abolitionism revolutionary was the insight he gained from his association with African Americans in Baltimore: that immediate emancipation must be combined with a commitment to racial justice in the United States. Watkins and Greener convinced Garrison that African Americans must have equal rights in America and not be sent to Africa after their emancipation. Immediate emancipation without compensating slaveholders and without expatriating African Americans became the core of Garrison's program for the rest of his long antislavery career.

This is the mashead of William Lloyd Garrison's abolitionist newspaper, the *Liberator*, as it appeared in August 1831. It portrays a slave auction in Washington, D.C., taking place in sight of the U.S. Capitol Building, where the flag of "Liberty" flies.

((•⎯|**Hear** the **Audio**
The Liberator

David Walker and Nat Turner

Two other black abolitionists, David Walker and Nat Turner, helped shape Garrison's brand of abolitionism. They were from the South—Walker from North Carolina and Turner from Virginia—and they were deeply religious. They also advocated employing violent means against slavery and had an impact on both the white South and abolitionists. Otherwise, their circumstances differed, as did the form of their antislavery efforts.

This chapter begins with a quote from Walker's *Appeal . . . to the Colored Citizens of the World,* which he published in 1829. As historian

•◗⎯|**Read** the **Document**
An African American Advocates Radical Action in 1829

Clement Eaton commented in 1936, this *Appeal* was "a dangerous pamphlet in the Old South." In aggressive language, Walker furiously attacked slavery and white racism. He suggested that slaves use violence to secure their liberty. "I do declare," he wrote, "that one good black can put to death six white men."

The *Appeal* shaped the struggle over slavery in three ways. First, although Garrison was committed to peaceful means, Walker's aggressive writing style influenced the tone of Garrison and other advocates of immediate abolition. Second, Walker's effort to instill hope and pride in an oppressed people inspired an increasingly militant black abolitionism. Third, his pamphlet and his ability to have it circulated among free African Americans in the South contributed to white southern fear of encirclement from without and subversion from within. This fear encouraged the

section's leaders to make demands on the North that helped bring on the Civil War.

In this last respect, Nat Turner's contribution was more important than Walker's. Slave conspiracies had not ended with Denmark Vesey's execution in 1822. But in 1831 Turner, a privileged slave from eastern Virginia, became the first African American to initiate a large-scale slave uprising since Charles Deslondes's revolt in Louisiana in 1811. As a result Turner inspired far greater fear among white southerners than Walker had.

During the late 1820s and early 1830s, unrest among slaves in Virginia increased, and Walker's *Appeal* may have contributed to this. Divisions among

1829–1831

THE RADICAL TURN IN THE ABOLITION MOVEMENT

JULY 1829	William Lloyd Garrison joins Benjamin Lundy in Baltimore as associate editor of the *Genius of Universal Emancipation*.
SEPTEMBER 1829	David Walker's *Appeal* is published in Boston and then circulated in the South.
NOVEMBER 1829	William Watkins's anticolonization letters first appear in the *Genius*.
JUNE 1830	Garrison is sentenced to jail in Baltimore for libeling a slave trader.
AUGUST 1830	Walker dies of tuberculosis in Boston.
JANUARY 1831	Garrison begins publication of *The Liberator* in Boston.
AUGUST 1831	Nat Turner's revolt occurs.

white Virginians may have also encouraged slaves to seek advantages for themselves. In anticipation of a state constitutional convention in 1829, white people in western Virginia, where there were few slaveholders, called for emancipation. Poorer white men demanded an end to the property qualifications that denied them the vote. As the convention approached, a "spirit of dissatisfaction and insubordination" became manifest among slaves. Some armed themselves and escaped north. As proslavery Virginians grew fearful, they demanded additional restrictions on the ability of local free black people and northern abolitionists to influence slaves.

Yet no evidence indicates that Turner or any of his associates had read Walker's *Appeal*, had contact with northern abolitionists, or were aware of divisions among white Virginians. Also, although Turner knew about the successful slave revolt in Haiti, he was more a religious visionary than a political revolutionary. Born in 1800, he learned to read as a child. As a young man, he spent much of his time studying and memorizing the Bible. He became a lay preacher and a leader among local slaves. By the late 1820s, he had begun to have visions that convinced him God intended him to lead his people to freedom through violence.

Read the **Document**
The Confessions of Nat Turner (1831)

After considerable planning, Turner began his uprising on the evening of August 21, 1831. His band, which numbered between 60 and 70, killed 57 white men, women, and children—the largest number of white Americans that slave rebels ever killed—before militia put down the revolt the following morning. In November, Turner and 17 others were found guilty of insurrection and treason and were hanged. Meanwhile, panicked white people in nearby parts of Virginia and North Carolina killed more than 100 African Americans whom they—almost always incorrectly—suspected of being in league with the rebels.

The bloodshed in Virginia inspired general revulsion. White southerners—and some northerners—accused Garrison and other abolitionists of inspiring the revolt. In response, northern abolitionists of both races asserted their commitment to a *peaceful* struggle against slavery. Yet black and white abolitionists respected Turner. Black abolitionists accorded him the same heroic stature they gave Toussaint Louverture and Gabriel. White abolitionists compared Turner to George Washington and other leaders of national liberation movements. This tension between lip service to peaceful means and admiration for violence against slavery characterized the antislavery movement for the next 30 years.

Discovery of Nat Turner.

This recently colorized drawing dates to the 1830s. It depicts the capture of Nat Turner. He avoided apprehension for nearly two months following the suppression of his revolt. The artist conveys how Turner maintained his dignity in surrender.

CONCLUSION

This chapter has focused on the two principal antislavery movements in the United States before 1833. One movement existed in the South among slaves. The other centered in the North and the Chesapeake among free African American and white abolitionists. Both movements had roots in the age of revolution and gained vitality from evangelical Christianity. The **Second Great Awakening** and the reforming spirit of the Benevolent Empire shaped the northern antislavery effort. The black church, the Bible, and elements of African religion helped inspire slave revolutionaries.

Gabriel, Denmark Vesey, and Nat Turner had to rely on violence to fight slavery. Northern abolitionists used peaceful means, such as newspapers, books, petitions, and speeches, to spread their message. But the two movements had similarities and influenced each other. David Walker's life in Charleston at the time of Denmark Vesey's conspiracy shaped his beliefs. In turn, his *Appeal* may have influenced slaves. Turner's revolt helped determine the course of northern abolitionism after 1831. During the subsequent decades, the efforts of slaves to resist their masters, to rebel, and to escape influenced radical black and white abolitionists in the North.

The antislavery movement that existed in the North and portions of the Upper South was always biracial. During the 1810s and for much of the 1820s, many black abolitionists embraced a form of nationalism that encouraged them to cooperate with the conservative white people who led the ACS. As the racist and proslavery nature of that organization became clear, northern black and white abolitionists called for immediate, uncompensated general emancipation that would not force former slaves to leave the United States.

Slavery, the legal disabilities imposed on free African Americans, and the widespread religious revivalism of the early nineteenth century created conditions different from those that exist today. But some similarities between then and now are striking. As it was in the 1810s and 1820s, the United States today is in turmoil. Technological innovation and corporate restructuring have contributed to economic fluctuation and a volatile job market that disproportionately affects members of minority groups. As they did in the early nineteenth century, African-American leaders today advocate various strategies to deal with such developments.

Samuel Cornish, William Watkins, and others who opposed the ACS sought through peaceful means to abolish slavery and gain recognition of African Americans as American citizens. David Walker advocated a more forceful strategy to achieve the same ends. Cornish, Watkins, and Walker all cooperated with white abolitionists. Others took a position closer to black nationalism by linking the abolition of slavery to an independent black destiny in Africa. As is true today, African Americans of the early nineteenth century faced difficult choices. Each of the strategies their leaders advocated had virtues, weaknesses, and dangers.

RECOMMENDED READING

Merton L. Dillon. *Slavery Attacked: Southern Slaves and Their Allies, 1619–1865*. Baton Rouge: Louisiana State University Press, 1990. Integrates slave resistance and revolt with the northern abolitionist movement.

Eugene D. Genovese. *From Rebellion to Revolution: Afro-American Slave Revolts in the Making of the Modern World*. Baton Rouge: Louisiana State University Press,

PROFILE : David Walker

David Walker was born free in Wilmington, North Carolina, in 1796 or 1797. Although he learned to read and write, we know nothing of his early life. He may have attended a biracial Methodist church in Wilmington. As a young man, he traveled widely and, according to his *Appeal*, spent time in Charleston, South Carolina, where he attended a religious camp meeting in 1821. This has led historians to conjecture that Walker knew something about Denmark Vesey's conspiracy or, if he was still in Charleston in 1822, that he may even have participated in it.

By 1825 Walker was in Boston dealing in secondhand clothes. He had his own shop, lived in the city's black neighborhood, was married, and had a daughter and a son. At a time when many occupations were closed to African Americans, Walker was doing relatively well. He associated with well-established local black people, including Thomas Paul, an abolitionist minister, and William C. Nell, a foe of Boston's segregated public schools. During the late 1820s, Walker was a circulation agent in Boston for John Russwurm and Samuel Cornish's *Freedom's Journal*.

Walker, who also wrote for the *Journal*, was as conscious of the legal disabilities African Americans faced in Boston as he was of the oppressiveness of slavery. In December 1828 he addressed the Massachusetts General Colored Association on the topic of black cooperation with white abolitionists to improve the conditions of free black people and to liberate the slaves.

Not long after this, Walker became more radical. He wrote his *Appeal* and in September 1829 implemented a clandestine method to circulate it among slaves. He had black and white sailors, to whom he sold used clothes in Boston, take copies of the pamphlet to southern ports and distribute them to African Americans.

When white southerners discovered that slaves had copies of the pamphlet, southern officials demanded that the mayor of Boston stop Walker from publishing. When the mayor refused, rumors circulated that a group of white southerners had offered a reward for Walker, dead or alive. It was not surprising, therefore, that when Walker's daughter and then Walker himself died during the summer of 1830, many assumed they had been poisoned. The most recent biography of Walker, however, indicates that they died of tuberculosis.

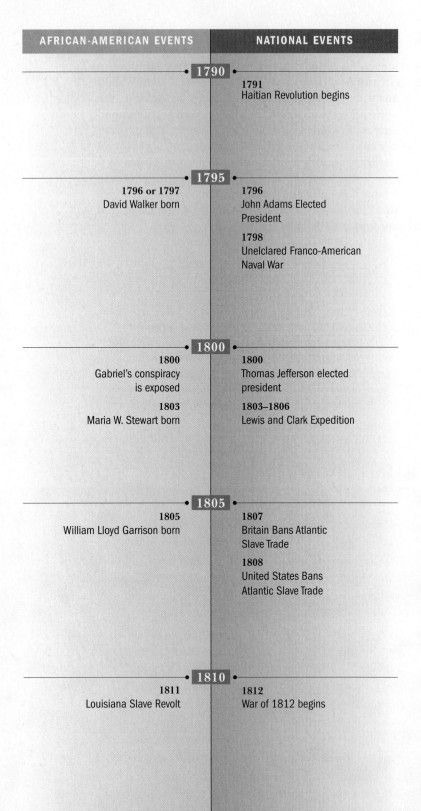

AFRICAN-AMERICAN EVENTS	NATIONAL EVENTS
	1790
	1791 Haitian Revolution begins
	1795
1796 or 1797 David Walker born	1796 John Adams Elected President
	1798 Unelclared Franco-American Naval War
	1800
1800 Gabriel's conspiracy is exposed	1800 Thomas Jefferson elected president
1803 Maria W. Stewart born	1803–1806 Lewis and Clark Expedition
	1805
1805 William Lloyd Garrison born	1807 Britain Bans Atlantic Slave Trade
	1808 United States Bans Atlantic Slave Trade
	1810
1811 Louisiana Slave Revolt	1812 War of 1812 begins

1979. Places the major American slave revolts and conspiracies in an Atlantic context.

Peter P. Hinks. *To Awaken My Afflicted Brethren: David Walker and the Problem of Antebellum Slave Resistance.* University Park: Pennsylvania State University Press, 1997. The most recent biography of Walker, which places him within the black abolitionist movement and attempts to clarify what little we know about his life.

Benjamin Quarles. *Black Abolitionists.* New York: Oxford University Press, 1969. A classic study that emphasizes cooperation between black and white abolitionists.

Harry Reed. *Platform for Change: The Foundations of the Northern Free Black Community, 1775–1865.* East Lansing: Michigan State University Press, 1994. An excellent study of the relationship between free black culture in the North and antislavery action.

P. J. Staudenraus. *The African Colonization Movement, 1816–1865.* New York: Columbia University Press, 1961. Although published in the 1960s, the most recent account of the American Colonization Society.

Shirley J. Yee. *Black Women Abolitionists: A Study in Activism, 1828–1860.* Knoxville: University of Tennessee Press, 1992. Concentrates on the period after 1833, but it is the best place to start reading about black abolitionist women.

ADDITIONAL BIBLIOGRAPHY

THE RELATIONSHIP AMONG EVANGELICALISM, REFORM, AND ABOLITIONISM

Robert H. Abzug. *Cosmos Crumbling: American Reform and the Religious Imagination.* New York: Oxford University Press, 1994.

Gilbert H. Barnes. *The Antislavery Impulse, 1830–1844.* 1933. Reprint, Gloucester, MA: Peter Smith, 1973.

Douglas M. Strong. *Perfectionist Politics: Abolitionism and the Religious Tensions of American Democracy.* Syracuse, NY: Syracuse University Press, 1999.

Ronald G. Walters. *American Reformers, 1815–1860.* Baltimore: Johns Hopkins University Press, 1978.

AMERICAN ABOLITIONISM BEFORE 1831

David Brion Davis. *The Problem of Slavery in the Age of Revolution.* Ithaca, NY: Cornell University Press, 1975.

———. *The Problem of Slavery in Western Culture.* Ithaca, NY: Cornell University Press, 1966.

———. *Slavery and Human Progress.* Ithaca, NY: Cornell University Press, 1987.

Merton L. Dillon. *The Abolitionists: The Growth of a Dissenting Minority.* New York: Norton, 1974.

Richard S. Newman. *The Transformation of American Abolitionism: Fighting Slavery in the Early Republic.* Chapel Hill: University of North Carolina Press, 2002.

SLAVE REVOLTS AND CONSPIRACIES

Herbert Aptheker. *American Negro Slave Revolts.* 1943. New ed., New York: International Publishers, 1974.

Douglas R. Egerton. *Gabriel's Rebellion: The Virginia Slave Conspiracies of 1800 & 1802.* Chapel Hill: University of North Carolina Press, 1993.

———. *He Shall Go Out Free: The Lives of Denmark Vesey.* Madison, WI: Madison House, 1999.

David P. Feggus, ed. *The Impact of the Haitian Revolution on the Atlantic World.* Columbia: University of South Carolina Press, 2001.

Alfred N. Hunt. *Haiti's Influence on Antebellum America: Slumbering Volcano in the Caribbean.* Baton Rouge: Louisiana State University Press, 1988.

John Lofton. *Denmark Vesey's Revolt: The Slave Plot That Lit a Fuse to Fort Sumter.* Kent, OH: Kent State University Press, 1983.

Stephen B. Oates. *The Fires of the Jubilee: Nat Turner's Fierce Rebellion.* New York: Harper & Row, 1975.

T. Stephen Whitman. *Challenging Slavery in the Chesapeake: Black and White Resistance to Human Bondage.* Baltimore: Maryland Historical Society, 2007.

BLACK ABOLITIONISM AND BLACK NATIONALISM

Rodney Carlisle. *The Roots of Black Nationalism.* Port Washington, NY: Kennikat, 1975.

Eddie S. Glaude. *Exodus!: Religion, Race, and Nation in Early Nineteenth-Century Black America.* Chicago: University of Chicago Press, 2000.

Leroy Graham. *Baltimore: Nineteenth-Century Black Capital.* Washington, DC: University Press of America, 1982.

Vincent Harding. *There Is a River: The Black Struggle for Freedom in America.* New York: Harcourt, Brace, Jovanovich, 1981.

Floyd J. Miller. *The Search for Black Nationality: Black Colonization and Emigration, 1787–1863.* Urbana: University of Illinois Press, 1975.

Marilyn Richardson. *Maria W. Stewart: America's First Black Woman Political Writer.* Bloomington: Indiana University Press, 1987.

Sterling Stuckey. *Slave Culture: Nationalist Theory and the Foundations of Black America.* New York: Oxford University Press, 1987.

Lamont D. Thomas. *Rise to Be a People: A Biography of Paul Cuffe.* Urbana: University of Illinois Press, 1986.

Julie Winch. *Philadelphia's Black Elite: Activism, Accommodation, and Struggle for Autonomy, 1787–1840.* Philadelphia: Temple University Press, 1988.

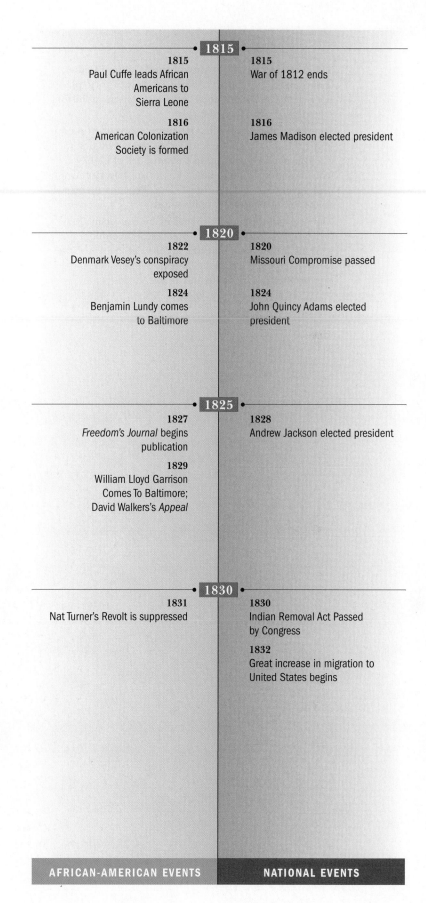

1815

1815
Paul Cuffe leads African Americans to Sierra Leone

1815
War of 1812 ends

1816
American Colonization Society is formed

1816
James Madison elected president

1820

1822
Denmark Vesey's conspiracy exposed

1820
Missouri Compromise passed

1824
Benjamin Lundy comes to Baltimore

1824
John Quincy Adams elected president

1825

1827
Freedom's Journal begins publication

1828
Andrew Jackson elected president

1829
William Lloyd Garrison Comes To Baltimore; David Walkers's *Appeal*

1830

1831
Nat Turner's Revolt is suppressed

1830
Indian Removal Act Passed by Congress

1832
Great increase in migration to United States begins

AFRICAN-AMERICAN EVENTS   **NATIONAL EVENTS**

RETRACING THE ODYSSEY

National Afro-American Museum and Cultural Center, Wilberforce, OH. http://ohsweb.ohiohistory.org/places/sw13/index.shtml. Exhibits on African-American history include the antislavery struggle.

Oberlin College, Oberlin, OH. http://www.oberlin.edu/library/research/aas.html. Oberlin, one of the first racially integrated and coeducational institutions of higher learning in the United States, was an antislavery and underground railroad center. The college maintains a collection of antislavery publications.

The Amistad Research Center, Tulane University, New Orleans, LA. http://www.amistadresearchcenter.org/. This institution maintains the archives of the American Missionary Association, the largest American antislavery organization of the 1840s and 1850s.

REVIEW QUESTIONS

1. What did the program of the ACS mean for African Americans? How did they respond to this program?

2. Analyze the role played in abolitionism (1) by Christianity and (2) by the revolutionary tradition in the Atlantic world. Which was more important in shaping the views of black and white abolitionists?

3. Evaluate the interaction of black and white abolitionists during the early nineteenth century. How did their motives for becoming abolitionists differ?

4. How did Gabriel, Denmark Vesey, and Nat Turner influence the northern abolitionist movement?

5. What risks did Maria W. Stewart take when she called publicly for antislavery action?

PEARSON myhistorylab™ Connections

www.myhistorylab.com
Review what you've learned in this chapter and explore the many documents, images,
research tools, and activities for this chapter to learn more about African-American history.

✓●—[Study and Review

READ
●●●—[Read the Document

- Confession of Solomon (1800)

- An African American
  Advocates Radical Action
  in 1829

- Abolitionist Demands
  Immediate End to Slavery,
  (1831)

- *The Confessions of Nat
  Turner* (1831)

- Angelina E. Grimké, *Appeal
  to the Christian Women of
  the South* (1836)

- Southern Belle Denounces
  Slavery (1838)

- A Black Feminist Speaks
  Out in 1851

LISTEN
((●—[Hear the Audio

Hear the audio files for
Chapter 8.

- *What If I Am a Woman?* Speech
  by Maria W. Stewart; read by
  Ruby Dee

- *The Liberator*

RESEARCH
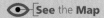

Consider these questions in a
short research paper.

*What forces and events fueled the
antislavery movement?*

*What role did antislavery advocates
see free blacks playing in America
after slavery was abolished?*

EXPLORE
◉—[See the Map

- Slave Conspiracies and
  Uprisings (1800–1831)

FREEDOM'S JOURNAL

Founded in 1827, *Freedom's Journal* was America's first black-owned and operated newspaper. It served as a forum for discussion and debate of the great questions of the day. What was the best way to attack slavery? How could the rights of free African Americans be secured and enlarged? Would whites ever let black people enjoy their full measure of freedom in the United States? As important as these questions were, they were not the only topics readers encountered in the pages of *Freedom's Journal*. The newspaper covered news from around the world, carried birth, marriage, and death announcements, printed biographies of famous African Americans, and ran advertisements for schools, housing, and jobs.

Why did editors think their newspaper was necessary? What did they hope to achieve? What do the pages from the newspaper suggest about the black community and its needs in the late 1820s?

We wish to plead our own cause. Too long have others spoken for us. . . . It is our earnest wish to make our Journal a medium of intercourse between our brethren in the different states of this great confederacy; that through its columns an expression of our sentiments, on many interesting subjects which concern us, may be offered to the publick; that plans which apparently are beneficial may be candidly discussed and properly weighed; if worthy receive our cordial support; if not our marked disapprobation.

Source: Freedom's Journal, Volume 1, Number 1, March 16, 1826

Samuel Cornish was born to free parents in ▶ Sussex County, Delaware. He was formally educated in Philadelphia's Free African School. He was trained for the ministry and served as a missionary to slaves on Maryland's Eastern Shore. A leader in the abolition movement, he cofounded the American Anti-Slavery Society (1835). Cornish is noted for establishing *Freedom's Journal*, the first African-American newspaper in the United States.

John Brown Russwurm (1799–1851) served as the newspaper's editor along with Samuel Cornish. After Cornish resigned in September 1827, Russwurm began to use *Freedom's Journal* to promote colonization. This shift in editorial policy resulted in a significant loss of readership. In 1829 Russwurm emigrated to Liberia, where he became governor of the Maryland colony. He was one of the first African Americans to earn a college degree.

Much of the front page of Volume 1, Number 1, of *Freedom's Journal* was an editorial explaining the purpose and ambitions of the new publication–to advocate for the abolition of slavery, promote racial pride and solidarity, stress the importance of education, and to serve as a vehicle for black protest.

The back page of *Freedom's Journal* carried advertisements of interest to the black community, like these entries from Volume 2, Number 52, March 28, 1829, advertising lodging, shoemaking, and employment.

ROOTS OF CULTURE

9

Let Your Motto Be Resistance

How did the racism and violence of the 1830s and 1840s affect the antislavery movement?

What roles did black institutions and moral suasion play in the antislavery movement?

How did abolitionism become more aggressive during the 1840s and 1850s?

How did the views of Frederick Douglass differ from those of Henry Highland Garnet?

▶ **In this 1867 oil painting by Theo Kaufman,** a group of women and children prepare to ford a river as they escape from slavery. Most escapees were young men, but people of both sexes and all age-groups undertook to reach freedom in the North or Canada. Theodor Kaufmann (1814–1896), "On to Liberty," 1867, Oil on canvas, 36 × 56 in (91.4 × 142.2 cm). The Metropolitan Museum of Art. Gift of Erving and Joyce Wolf, 1982 (1982.443.3) Photograph ©The Metropolitan Museum of Art. /Art Resource, NY

It is in your power to torment the God-cursed slaveholders, that they would be glad to let you go free. . . . But you are a patient people. You act as though you were made for the special use of these devils. You act as though your daughters were born to pamper the lusts of your masters and overseers. And worse than all, you tamely submit, while your lords tear your wives from your embraces, and defile them before your eyes. In the name of God we ask, are you men? . . . Heaven, as with a voice of thunder, calls on you to arise from the dust. Let your motto be RESISTANCE! RESISTANCE! RESISTANCE! No oppressed people have ever secured their Liberty without resistance.

Henry Highland Garnet, "Address to the Slaves of the United States of America"

◀ Entitled "A Bold Stroke for Freedom," this illustration from William Still's *The Underground Railroad* depicts fugitive slaves aiming guns at slave catchers in an attempt to preserve their freedom.

When black abolitionist Henry Highland Garnet spoke these words at the National Convention of Colored Citizens, held in Buffalo, New York, on August 16, 1843, he caused a tremendous stir among those assembled. Garnet had escaped with his family from slavery in Maryland in 1824 when he was a boy. He had received an excellent education

((•─ Hear the Audio
Hear the audio files for Chapter 9 at www.myhistorylab.com

while growing up in New York and became a powerful speaker. But some of the delegates pointed out that he was far away from the slaves he claimed to address. Others believed he had called for a potentially disastrous slave revolt, and, by a narrow margin, the convention refused to endorse his speech.

Yet, in the speech, Garnet rhetorically told slaves, "We do not advise you to attempt a revolution with the sword, because it would be INEXPEDIENT. Your numbers are too small, and moreover the rising spirit of the age, and the spirit of the gospel, are opposed to war and bloodshed." Rather than a slave revolt like Nat Turner's, Garnet advocated a general strike. This, he contended, would put the onus of initiating violence on masters. Nevertheless, Garnet's speech reflected a new militancy among black and white abolitionists that shaped the antislavery movement during the two decades before the Civil War.

This chapter investigates the causes of that militancy and explores the role of African Americans in the antislavery movement from the establishment of the American Anti-Slavery Society in 1833 to the **Compromise of 1850.** Largely in response to changes in American culture, unrest among slaves, and sectional conflict between North and South, the biracial northern antislavery movement during this period became splintered and diverse but more powerful.

A Rising Tide of Racism and Violence

Garnet spoke correctly about the spirit of the gospel but not about the spirit of his time. Militancy among abolitionists reflected increasing American racism and violence from the 1830s through the Civil War. White Americans' embrace of an exuberant nationalism called **Manifest Destiny** contributed to this trend. This doctrine, which defined political and economic progress in racial terms, held that God intended the United States to expand its territory, by war if necessary. Another factor was that American ethnologists—scientists who studied racial diversity—rejected the eighteenth-century idea that the physical and mental characteristics of the world's peoples are the product of environment. Instead, they argued, perceived racial differences were intrinsic and permanent. White people—particularly white Americans—they maintained, were a superior race culturally, physically, economically, politically, and intellectually.

As Manifest Destiny gave divine sanction to imperialism, scientific racism provided white Americans with a justification for the continued enslavement of African Americans and extermination of American Indians. Prejudice against European immigrants to the United States also increased. By the late 1840s, a movement known as *nativism* pitted native-born Protestants against foreign-born Roman Catholics, whom the natives saw as competitors for jobs and as cultural subversives.

A wave of racially motivated violence, committed by the federal and state governments as well as white vigilantes, accompanied these intellectual and demographic developments. Starting in the 1790s, the U.S. Army waged a systematic campaign to remove American Indians from the states and relocate them west of the Mississippi River. This campaign affected several southeastern Indian nations. But it is epitomized by the Trail of Tears, when in 1838 the army forced 16,000 Cherokees from Georgia to what is now Oklahoma. Many Cherokees died along the way. During the same decade, antiblack riots became common in northern cities. Starting in 1829, white mobs attacked abolitionist newspaper presses and wreaked havoc in African-American neighborhoods. Wealthy "gentlemen of property and standing," who believed they defended the social order, led the rioters.

ANTIBLACK AND ANTIABOLITIONIST RIOTS

Antiblack riots coincided with the start of immediate abolitionism during the late 1820s. The riots became more common as abolitionism gained strength during the 1830s and 1840s (see Figure 9–1 and Map 9–1). Although few northern cities escaped attacks on African Americans and their property, riots in Cincinnati, Providence, New York City, and Philadelphia were infamous.

In 1829 a three-day riot instigated by local politicians led many black Cincinnatians to flee to Canada. In 1836 and 1841, mob attacks on the *Philanthropist,* Cincinnati's white-run abolitionist newspaper, expanded into attacks on African-American homes and businesses. During each riot, black residents defended their property with guns. In 1831 white sailors led a mob in Providence that literally tore that city's black neighborhood to pieces. With spectators cheering them on, rioters pulled down the chimneys of black residences and then "with a fire hook and plenty of axes and iron bars" wrecked the buildings and dragged the occupants into the streets. The Rhode Island militia finally stopped the mayhem. In New York City in 1834, a mob destroyed twelve houses owned by black

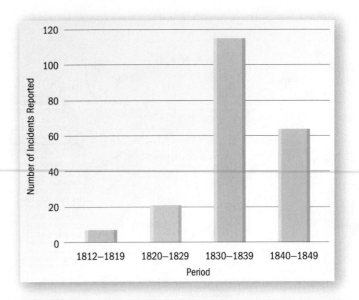

FIGURE 9–1 MOB VIOLENCE IN THE UNITED STATES, 1812–1849
This graph illustrates the rise of mob violence in the North in reaction to abolitionist activity. Attacks on abolitionists peaked during the 1830s and then declined as antislavery sentiment spread in the North.

residents, a black church, a black school, and the home of white abolitionist Lewis Tappan.

No city had more or worse race riots than Philadelphia—the City of Brotherly Love. In 1820, 1829, 1834, 1835, 1838, 1842, and 1849, antiblack rampages broke out. In 1838 a white mob burned Pennsylvania Hall, which abolitionists had just built and dedicated to free discussion. The ugliest riot came in 1842 when Irish immigrants led a mob that assaulted members of a black temperance society, who were commemorating the abolition of slavery in the British colony of Jamaica. When African Americans defended themselves with muskets, the mob looted and burned Philadelphia's principal black neighborhood. Among those who successfully defended their homes was Robert Purvis, the abolitionist son-in-law of James Forten.

TEXAS AND THE WAR AGAINST MEXICO

Not only northern cities experienced violence. Under President James K. Polk, the United States adopted a belligerent foreign policy, culminating in a war against the Republic of Mexico, which lasted from 1846 to 1848. Mexico had gained its independence from Spain in 1822 and in 1829 had abolished slavery within its borders. Meanwhile, slaveholding Americans began settling in the Mexican province of Texas. At the time, the gigantic regions then known as California and

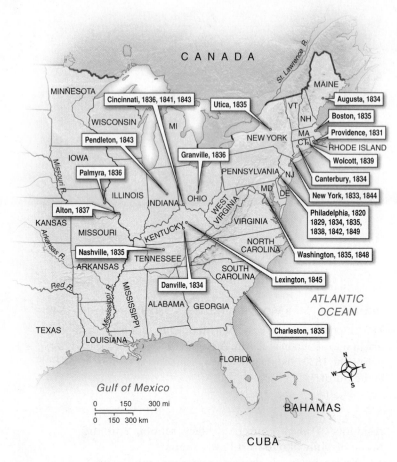

MAP 9–1   ANTIABOLITIONIST AND ANTIBLACK RIOTS DURING THE ANTEBELLUM PERIOD

African Americans faced violent conditions in both the North and South during the antebellum years. Fear among whites of growing free black communities and white antipathy toward spreading abolitionism sparked numerous antiblack and antiabolitionist riots.

▶ *Why did most of these riots occur in the Northeast?*

New Mexico (and now comprising the states of California, Arizona, New Mexico, Utah, and part of Colorado) also belonged to Mexico. In 1836 Texas won independence and, as a slaveholding republic, applied for annexation to the United States as a slave state. Democratic and Whig Party leaders, who realized that adding a large new slave state to the Union would divide the country along North–South lines, rebuffed the application. But the desire for new territory, encouraged by Manifest Destiny and an expanding slave-labor economy, could not be denied. In 1844 Polk, the Democratic presidential candidate, called for the annexation of Texas and Oregon, a huge territory in the Pacific Northwest that the United States and Britain had been jointly administering. After Polk defeated the Whig candidate

Henry Clay, who favored delaying annexation, Congress in early 1845 annexed Texas by joint resolution. This vastly expanded the area within the United States open to slavery.

In early 1846 Polk backed away from a confrontation with Britain over Oregon. A few months later, he provoked the war against Mexico that by 1848 forced that country to recognize American sovereignty over Texas and to cede New Mexico and California (see Map 10–1 on page 245 in Chapter 10). Immediately, the major political question in the United States became, would slavery expand into these southwestern territories? Many northerners suspected slaveholders would create slave states out of the new territories, dominate the federal government, and enact policies detrimental to white workers and farmers.

As these sentiments spread across the North, slaveholders feared they would be excluded from the western lands they had helped wrest from Mexico. The resulting Compromise of 1850 (see Chapter 10) attempted to satisfy both sections. But it subjected African Americans to additional violence because part of the Compromise met slaveholders' demands for a stronger fugitive slave law. This law provided federal aid for masters in recapturing bond people who had escaped to the North. It also encouraged attempts to kidnap free black northerners into slavery.

The Antislavery Movement

The increase in race-related violence caused difficulties for an antislavery movement that was itself not free of racial strife and officially limited to peaceful means. Even though African Americans found loyal white allies within the movement, interracial understanding did not come easily. As white abolitionists assumed they should set policy, their black colleagues became resentful. Meanwhile, abolitionist commitment to nonviolence weakened. It had arisen as a principled rejection of the violence that pervaded America and as a shrewd response to proslavery charges that abolitionists caused unrest among slaves. But rejection of forceful means seemed to limit abolitionist options in a violent environment. By the end of the 1830s, greater autonomy for black abolitionists and peaceful versus violent means became contentious issues within the movement.

THE AMERICAN ANTI-SLAVERY SOCIETY

Before the era of Manifest Destiny, the **American Anti-Slavery Society (AASS)**—the most significant abolitionist organization of the 1830s—emerged from a turning point in the abolitionist cause. This was William Lloyd Garrison's decision in 1831 to create a movement dedicated to immediate, uncompensated emancipation and to equal rights for African Americans in the United States. To reach these goals, abolitionists organized the AASS in December 1833 at Philadelphia's Adelphi Hall.

Read the Document
The American Antislavery Society Declares Its Sentiments (1833)

Well aware of the fears Nat Turner's revolt had raised, those assembled declared, "The society will never, in any way, countenance the oppressed in vindicating their rights by resorting to physical force."

No white American worked harder than Garrison to bridge racial differences. He spoke to black groups, stayed in the homes of African Americans when he traveled, and welcomed them to his home. Black abolitionists responded with affection and loyalty. They provided financial support for his newspaper, *The Liberator;* worked as subscription agents; paid for his speaking tour in England in 1833; and served as his bodyguards. But Garrison, like most other white abolitionists, remained stiff and condescending in conversation with black colleagues, and the black experience in the AASS reflected this.

On one hand, it is remarkable that the AASS allowed black men to participate in its meetings without formal restrictions. At the time, no other American organization did so. On the other hand, that black participation was paltry. Three African Americans—James McCrummell, Robert Purvis, and James G. Barbadoes— helped found the AASS, and McCrummell presided at its first meeting. But, among 60 white people attending that meeting, these three were the only African Americans. Although three white women also participated in the meeting, no black women did. Throughout its history, black people rarely held positions of authority in the AASS.

As state and local auxiliaries of the AASS organized across the North during the early 1830s, these patterns repeated themselves. Black men participated but did not lead, although a few held prominent offices. Among them were Barbadoes and Joshua Easton, who in 1834 joined the board of directors of the Massachusetts Anti-Slavery Society. Also, in 1837

Wealthy black abolitionist Robert Purvis is at the very center of this undated photograph of the Philadelphia Anti-Slavery Society. The famous Quaker abolitionist Lucretia Mott and her husband James Mott are seated to Purvis's left. Equally significant as Purvis's central location in the photograph is that he is the *only* African American pictured.

seven black men, including James Forten, helped organize the Pennsylvania Anti-Slavery Society. Black and white women—with some exceptions—could observe the proceedings of these organizations but not participate in them. It took a three-year struggle between 1837 and 1840 over "the woman question" before an AASS annual meeting elected a woman to a leadership position, and that victory helped split the organization.

BLACK AND WOMEN'S ANTISLAVERY SOCIETIES

In these circumstances, black men, black women, and white women formed auxiliaries to the AASS. Often African Americans belonged to all-black *and* to integrated, predominantly white organizations. Black men's auxiliaries to the AASS formed across the North during the mid-1830s. As mentioned in Chapter 8, the earliest black women's abolitionist organization appeared in Salem, Massachusetts, in 1832, a year before the AASS formed.

The black organizations arose because of racial discord in the predominantly white organizations and because of a black desire for racial solidarity. But, as historian Benjamin Quarles notes, during the 1830s "the founders of Negro societies did not envision their efforts as distinctive or self-contained; rather they viewed their role as that of a true auxiliary— supportive, supplemental, and subsidiary." Despite their differences, black and white abolitionists belonged to a single movement.

The women's organizations exemplified this point. Although their racially integrated societies did not overcome antiblack prejudice, they surpassed men's societies in elevating African Americans to prominent positions. Black abolitionist Susan Paul became a member of the board of the Boston Female Anti-Slavery Society when it organized in 1833. Later that year, Margaretta Forten became recording secretary of the Female Anti-Slavery Society of Philadelphia, founded by white Quaker abolitionist Lucretia Mott. In May 1837 black Quaker Sarah M. Douglass of Philadelphia and Sarah Forten—Margaretta's sister— served as delegates to the First Anti-Slavery Convention of American Women in New York City. At the second convention, Susan Paul became a vice president, and Douglass became treasurer.

Read the **Document**
A Call for Women to Become Abolitionists

All of the women's antislavery societies concentrated on fund-raising. They held bake sales, organized antislavery fairs and bazaars, and sold antislavery memorabilia. The proceeds went to the AASS or to antislavery newspapers. But the women's societies also inspired feminism by creating awareness that women had rights and interests that a male-dominated society had to recognize. By writing essays and poems on political subjects and making public speeches, abolitionist women challenged a culture that relegated *respectable* women to domestic duties. During the 1850s famous African-American speaker Sojourner Truth emphasized that all black women, through their physical labor and the pain they suffered in slavery, had earned equal standing with men and their more favored white sisters.

Hear the **Audio**
*The Rebirth of Sojourner Truth.
Read by Jean Brannon.*

Black men and women also formed auxiliaries during the early 1830s to the Quaker-initiated Free Produce Association, which tried to put economic pressure on slaveholders by boycotting agricultural products produced by slaves. James Cornish led the Colored Free Produce Society of Pennsylvania, which marketed meat, vegetables, cotton, and sugar produced by free labor. With a similar aim, Judith James and Laetitia Rowley organized the Colored Female Free Produce Society of Pennsylvania. Other black affiliates to the Free Produce Association existed in New York and Ohio, and black abolitionist William Whipper operated a free produce store in Philadelphia in 1834. During the 1850s Frances Ellen Watkins Harper, one of the few prominent black female speakers of the time, always included the free produce movement in her abolitionist lectures and wrote newspaper articles on its behalf.

MORAL SUASION

During the 1830s the AASS adopted a reform strategy based on **moral suasion**—what we would today call moral *persuasion*. This was an appeal for Americans to support abolition and racial justice on the basis of their Christian consciences. Slaveholding, the AASS argued, was a sin and a crime that deprived African Americans of the freedom of conscience they needed to save their souls. Simultaneously, slaveholding led masters to damnation through indolence, sexual exploitation of black women, and brutality. Abolitionists also argued that slavery was an inefficient labor system that enriched a few masters while impoverishing black and white southerners and hurting the American economy.

Abolitionists did not just criticize white southerners. They noted that northern industries thrived by manufacturing cloth from cotton produced by slave labor. They pointed out that the U.S. government protected the interests of slaveholders in the District of Columbia, in the territories, in the interstate slave trade, and through the Fugitive Slave Act of 1793. Northerners who profited from slave labor and supported the national government with their votes and taxes bore their share of guilt for slavery and faced divine punishment.

The AASS sought to use these arguments to convince masters to free their slaves and to persuade northerners and nonslaveholding white southerners to put pressure on slaveholders. To reach a southern audience, the AASS in 1835 launched the Great Postal Campaign to send antislavery literature to southern post offices and individual slaveholders. At about the same time, the AASS also organized a petitioning campaign aimed to agitate the slavery issue in Congress. Antislavery women led in circulating and signing the petitions. In 1836 over 30,000 petitions reached Washington.

In the North, AASS agents lectured against slavery and distributed antislavery literature. Often a pair of agents—one black and one white—traveled together.

Ideally, the black agent would be a former slave, so he could testify to the brutality and immorality of slavery from personal experience. During the early 1840s, the AASS paired fugitive slave Frederick Douglass with William A. White, a young white Harvard graduate, in a tour through Ohio and Indiana. In 1843 the Eastern New York Anti-Slavery Society paired white Baptist preacher Abel Brown with "the noble colored man," Lewis Washington. At first all the agents were men. Later, abolitionist organizations also employed women.

The reaction to these efforts in the North and the South was not what the leaders of the AASS anticipated. As the story in the *Voices* box on Frederick Douglass relates, by speaking of racial justice and exemplifying interracial cooperation, abolitionists trod new ground. This created awkward situations that

P R O F I L E : Sojourner Truth

Sojourner Truth does not fit easily into the history of the antislavery movement. She did not identify with a particular group of abolitionists. Instead, as her biographer Nell Irvin Painter points out, Truth served the cause by making herself a symbol of the strength of all black women.

Originally named Isabella, Truth was born a slave—probably in 1797—in a Dutch-speaking area north of New York City. She had several masters, one of whom beat her brutally. Always a hard worker, she grew into a tall, muscular woman. She had a deep voice, and throughout her career enemies charged she was a man—despite her five children.

In 1827 Truth escaped to an antislavery family that purchased her freedom. Two years later, she became a revivalist preacher in New York City. Later she joined a communal religious cult, became an ardent millenarian—predicting that Judgment Day was rapidly approaching—and in 1843 took the name Sojourner Truth. A few years later, while working at a commune in Northampton, Massachusetts, she met abolitionists Frederick Douglass and David Ruggles. This meeting led to her career as a champion of abolition and women's rights.

During the late 1840s and the 1850s, she lectured across the North and as far west as Kansas. Blunt but eloquent, Truth appealed to common sense in arguing

that African Americans and women deserved the same rights as white men because they could work as hard as white men. Truth almost always addressed white audiences and had a strong impression on them. During the Civil War, she volunteered to work among black Union troops, and President Lincoln invited her to the White House in 1864. She continued to advocate black and women's rights until her death in 1883.

As Painter and others note, Truth probably never used the phrase "Ar'n't I a Woman?" for which she is most widely remembered. A white female journalist attributed the phrase to Truth years after the 1851 women's rights meeting in Akron, Ohio, where Truth was supposed to have used it. Contemporary accounts indicate that she did not. Truth did, however, tell those assembled in Akron, "I have as much muscle as any man, and I can do as much work as any man. I have plowed and reaped and husked and chopped and mowed, and can any man do more than that?"

An increase in slave escapes helped inspire the more aggressive abolitionist tactics of the 1840s and 1850s. In this 1845 cover illustration for sheet music composed by white antislavery minstrel Jesse Hutchinson Jr., Frederick Douglass is shown in an idealized rendition of his escape from slavery in Maryland.

are—in retrospect—humorous. But their audiences often reacted violently. Southern postmasters burned antislavery literature, and southern state governments censored the mail. Vigilantes drove off white southerners who openly advocated abolition. Black abolitionists, of course, did not dare denounce slavery while they were in the South.

In 1836 southern representatives and their northern allies in Congress passed the Gag Rule forbidding petitions related to slavery from being introduced in the House of Representatives. In response, the AASS sent 415,000 petitions in 1838, and Congressman (and former president) John Quincy Adams began his struggle against the Gag. Technically not an abolitionist but a defender of the First Amendment right to petition Congress, Adams succeeded in having the Gag repealed in 1844.

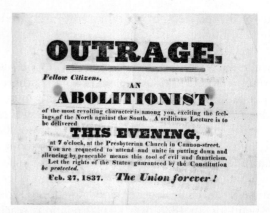

In an effort to stir antiabolitionist feelings, this broadside announces an upcoming abolitionist lecture at a local New York church.

Meanwhile northern mobs continued to assault abolitionist agents, disrupt their meetings, destroy their newspaper presses, and attack black neighborhoods. In 1837 a proslavery mob killed white abolitionist journalist Elijah P. Lovejoy as he defended his printing press in Alton, Illinois. On another occasion, as Douglass, White, and older white abolitionist George Bradburn held an antislavery meeting in the small town of Pendleton, Indiana, an enraged mob attempted to kill Douglass. Some of the rioters shouted, "Kill the nigger, kill the damn nigger." Douglass suffered a broken hand. A rock hit White's head. Finally the two men fled. Years later, Douglass told White, "I shall never forget how like very brothers we were ready to dare, do, and even die for each other. . . . How I looked running you can best describe but how you looked bleeding I shall always remember."

Black Community Institutions

A maturing African-American community undergirded the antislavery movement and helped it survive violent opposition. The free black population of the United States grew from 59,000 in 1790 to 319,000 in 1830 and 434,449 in 1850. Gradual emancipation in the northern states, acts of individual manumission in the Upper South, escapes, and a high birthrate accounted for this sevenfold increase. The concentration of this growing population in such cities as New York, Philadelphia, Baltimore, Boston, and Cincinnati strengthened it. These cities had enough African Americans to support the independent churches, schools, benevolent organizations, and printing presses that self-conscious communities required. These communities became bedrocks of abolitionism.

THE BLACK CONVENTION MOVEMENT

The dozens of local, state, and national black conventions held in the North between 1830 and 1864 manifested the antebellum American reform impulse. Their agenda transcended the antislavery cause. Nevertheless, they provided a forum for prominent black abolitionist men, such as Garnet, Frederick Douglass, and Martin R. Delany. They provided a setting in which abolitionism could grow and adapt to meet the demands of a sectionally polarized and violent time.

Hezekiah Grice, a young black man who had worked with Benjamin Lundy and William Lloyd Garrison in Baltimore during the 1820s (see Chapter 8), organized the first Black National Convention. It met on September 24, 1830, at the Bethel Church in Philadelphia with the venerable churchman Richard Allen presiding. The national convention became an annual event for the next five years, with all but one held in Philadelphia. During the same period, many state and local black conventions met across the North. All the conventions were small and informal—particularly those at the local level—and had no guidelines for choosing delegates. They were nevertheless attractive venues for discussing and publicizing black concerns. They called for the abolition of slavery and improving conditions for northern African Americans. Among other reforms, the conventions advocated integrated public schools and the rights of black men to vote, serve on juries, and testify against white people in court.

The conventions stressed black self-help through temperance, sexual morality, education, and thrift. These causes remained important parts of the black agenda throughout the antebellum years. But by the mid-1830s, the national convention movement faltered as black abolitionists placed their hopes in the AASS.

BLACK CHURCHES IN THE ANTISLAVERY CAUSE

Black churches were even more important than black conventions in the antislavery movement. With few exceptions, leading black abolitionists were ministers. Among them were Garnet, Jehiel C. Beman, Samuel E. Cornish, Theodore S. Wright, Charles B. Ray, James W. C. Pennington, Nathaniel Paul, Alexander Crummell, Daniel A. Payne, and Samuel Ringgold Ward. Some of these men led congregations affiliated with African-American churches, such as the African Baptist Church or the African Methodist Episcopal (AME) Church. Others preached to black congregations affiliated with predominantly white churches. A few black ministers, such as Amos N. Freeman of Brooklyn, New York, served white antislavery congregations. In either case, they used their pulpits to attack slavery, racial discrimination, proslavery white churches, and the American Colonization Society (ACS). Having covered most of these topics in a sermon to a white congregation in 1839, Daniel Payne, who had grown up free in South Carolina, declared, "Awake! AWAKE! to the battle, and hurl the hottest thunders of divine truth at the head of this cruel monster, until he shall fall to rise no more; and the groans of the enslaved are converted into the songs of the free!" Black churches also provided forums for abolitionist speakers, such as Frederick Douglass and Garrison, and meeting places for predominantly white antislavery organizations, which frequently could not meet in white churches.

BLACK NEWSPAPERS

Although less influential than black churches, black antislavery newspapers had an important role in the antislavery movement, particularly by the 1840s. Like their white counterparts, they almost always faced financial difficulties, and few survived for long. This was because *reform*—as opposed to *commercial*—newspapers were a luxury that not many subscribers, black or white, could afford. Black newspapers faced added difficulties finding readers because most African Americans were poor, and many were illiterate. Moreover, white abolitionist newspapers, such as the *Liberator*, served a black clientele. They published speeches by black abolitionists and reported black convention proceedings. Some black abolitionists argued, therefore, that a separate black press was unnecessary. An additional, self-imposed burden was that publishers eager to get their message out almost never required subscribers to pay in advance.

Nevertheless, several influential black abolitionist newspapers existed between the late 1820s and the Civil War. The first black newspaper, *Freedom's Journal*, owned and edited by Samuel Cornish and John B. Russwurm, lasted from 1827 to 1829. It showed that African Americans could produce interesting and competent journalism and attract black and white subscribers. The *Journal* also established a framework for black journalism during the antebellum period by emphasizing opposition to slavery, racial justice, and Christian and democratic values.

The most ubiquitous black journalist of the period was Philip A. Bell. Bell was publisher or copublisher of the *New York Weekly Advocate* in 1837, the **Colored American** from 1837 to 1842, and, during the 1860s, two San Francisco newspapers, the *Pacific Appeal* and the *Elevator*. But black clergyman Charles B. Ray of New York City was the real spirit behind the *Colored American*. Aware of the need for financial success, Ray declared in 1838, "If among the few hundred thousand free colored people in the country—to say

VOICES

Frederick Douglass wrote this passage during the mid-1850s. It is from My Bondage *and* My Freedom, *the second of his three autobiographies. It relates with humor not only the racial barriers that black and white abolitionists had to break but also primitive conditions they took for granted.*

In the summer of 1843, I was traveling and lecturing in company with William A. White, Esq., through the state of Indiana. Antislavery friends were not very abundant in Indiana . . . and beds were not more plentiful than friends. . . . At the close of one of our meetings, we were invited home with a kindly-disposed old farmer, who, in the generous enthusiasm of the moment, seemed to have forgotten that he had but one spare bed, and that his guests were an ill-matched pair. . . . White is remarkably fine looking, and very evidently a born gentleman; the idea of putting us in the same bed was hardly to be tolerated; and yet there we were, and but the one bed for us, and that, by the way, was in the same room occupied by the other members of the family. . . . After witnessing the confusion as long as I liked, I relieved the kindly-disposed family by playfully saying, "Friend White, having got entirely rid of my prejudice against color, I think, as proof of it, I must allow you to sleep with me to-night." White kept up the joke, by seeming to esteem himself the favored party, and thus the difficulty was removed.

▶ *What does this passage reveal about American life during the 1840s?*
▶ *What does Douglass tell us about his personality?*

Source: Michael Meyer, ed., *Frederick Douglass: The Narrative and Selected Writings* (New York: Modern Library, 1984), 170–71.

nothing of the white population from whom it ought to receive a strong support—a living patronage for the paper cannot be obtained, it will be greatly to their reproach."

Other prominent, if short-lived, black newspapers of the 1840s and 1850s included Garnet's *United States Clarion,* published in his home city of Troy, New York; Stephen Myers's *Northern Star and Freeman's Advocate,* published in Albany, New York; Samuel Ringgold Ward's *True American,* of Cortland, New York, which in 1850 became the *Impartial Citizen;* Martin Delany's *Mystery,* published in Pittsburgh during the 1840s; and Thomas Van Rensselaer's *Ram's Horn,* which appeared in New York City during the 1850s.

Frederick Douglass's *North Star* and its successor *Frederick Douglass' Paper* were the most influential black antislavery newspapers of the late 1840s and the 1850s. Heavily subsidized by Gerrit Smith, a wealthy white abolitionist, and attracting more white than black subscribers, Douglass's weeklies gained the support of many black abolitionist organizations. His papers were well edited and attractively printed. They also employed able assistant editors, including Martin R. Delany during the late 1840s, and insightful correspondents, such as William J. Wilson of Brooklyn and James McCune Smith of New York City.

The American and Foreign Anti-Slavery Society and the Liberty Party

In 1840 the AASS splintered. Most of its members left to establish the **American and Foreign Anti-Slavery Society** (AFASS) and the **Liberty Party,** the first antislavery political party. In part the split resulted from long-standing disagreements about the role of women in abolitionism and William Lloyd Garrison's broadening radicalism. By declaring that slavery had irrevocably corrupted the existing American society, by denouncing organized religion, by becoming a feminist, and by embracing a form of Christian anarchy that precluded formal involvement in politics, Garrison seemed to have lost sight of abolitionism's main concern. But the failure of moral suasion to make progress against slavery—particularly in the South—and the question of how abolitionists should respond to slave unrest also helped fracture the AASS.

Garrison and a minority of New England–centered abolitionists who agreed with his radical critique of America retained control of the AASS, which became known as the "Old Organization." By 1842 they had de-emphasized moral suasion and begun calling for dis-union—the separation of the North from the South—as the only means of ending northern support for slavery. The U.S. Constitution, Garrison declared, was a proslavery document that had to be replaced before African Americans could gain freedom.

Those who withdrew from the AASS took a more traditional stand on the role of women, believed the country's churches could be converted to abolitionism, and asserted that the Constitution could be used in behalf of abolitionism. Under the leadership of Lewis Tappan, a wealthy white New York City businessman, some of them formed the church-oriented AFASS. Others created the Liberty Party and nominated James G. Birney, a slaveholder-turned-abolitionist, as their candidate in the 1840 presidential election. Birney received only 7,069 votes out of a total cast of 2,411,187, and William Henry Harrison, the Whig candidate, became president. But the Liberty Party began an increasingly powerful political crusade against slavery.

Black abolitionists joined in the disruption of the Old Organization. Only in New England did most of them remain loyal to the AASS. Among the loyalists were Frederick Douglass, William Wells Brown, Robert Purvis, Charles L. Remond, Susan Paul, and Sarah Douglass. As might be expected, most black clerical abolitionists joined the AFASS. Eight, including Jehiel C. Beman and his son Amos G. Beman, Christopher Rush, Samuel E. Cornish, Theodore S. Wright, Stephen H. Gloucester, Andrew Harris, and Garnet helped create the new organization. After 1840 African Americans were always more prominent as leaders in the AFASS than the AASS.

The Liberty Party also attracted black support, although few black men could vote. Particularly

PROFILE: Henry Highland Garnet

Henry Highland Garnet rivaled Frederick Douglass as a black leader during the antebellum decades. While Douglass emphasized assimilation, Garnet advocated black nationalism. The two men had much in common, however, and by the Civil War, their views were almost indistinguishable.

In 1824, when Garnet was nine, his family fled a Maryland plantation for freedom in the North. His father led the family to New York City, where Garnet enrolled in the Free African School. Influenced by his father's pride in their African heritage, by his vigilance against slave catchers, and by a lameness that led to the amputation of one of his legs in 1840, Garnet brought a profound determination to all he undertook. In 1835 he was among twelve black students admitted to Noyes Academy at Canaan, New Hampshire. When shortly thereafter local farmers reacted by tearing down the school buildings, Garnet defended his black classmates with a shotgun. The following year he enrolled at Oneida Theological Institute near Utica, New York. There, guided by white abolitionist Beriah Green, Garnet prepared for the ministry. In 1842 he became pastor of the black Presbyterian church in Troy, New York.

By that time, he had become an active abolitionist. He worked closely with Gerrit Smith's radical New York wing of the Liberty Party. He also advocated independent antislavery action among African Americans. Referring to white abolitionists, he said, "They are our allies—*Ours* is the battle." But it was within the interracial context of the New York Liberty Party's determination to challenge slavery on its home ground that Garnet delivered his famous "Address to the Slaves" at the 1843 National Convention of Colored Citizens. By demanding that slaves claim their freedom and acknowledging that violence could result, Garnet highlighted his differences with Frederick Douglass and other African Americans who endorsed nonviolence.

Garnet's conviction that African Americans ultimately must free themselves led him to promote migration to Africa. He always regarded the American Colonization Society (ACS) as proslavery and racist. But by 1848 he had come to believe African colonization could be a powerful part of the struggle for emancipation in the United States. Garnet's years abroad during the early 1850s strengthened this outlook. He served as a delegate to the World Peace Conference in Frankfurt, Germany, in 1850; spent 1851 in Great Britain; and was a Presbyterian missionary in Jamaica from 1853 to 1856. Garnet returned to the United States in 1856 and in 1858 organized the African Civilization Society, designed to build an independent Africa through black emigration from America and the cultivation of cotton in Africa.

Few African-American leaders shared Garnet's views, and the Civil War effectively ended his nationalist efforts. Early in the war, he advocated enlisting black troops in the Union armies. In 1863 he became pastor of the 15th Street Presbyterian Church in Washington, D.C., and in 1865 became the first African American to deliver a sermon in Congress. Like Douglass, Garnet was a staunch Republican after the Civil War. In January 1882, he became U.S. ambassador to Liberia and died there a month later.

appealing to black abolitionists was the platform of the radical New York wing of the party led by Gerrit Smith. Philip A. Bell, Charles B. Ray, Samuel E. Cornish, Jermain Wesley Loguen, and Garnet endorsed the New York Liberty Party and influenced its program. Of all the antislavery organizations, the New York party advocated the most aggressive action against slavery in the South and became most directly involved in helping slaves escape.

A More Aggressive Abolitionism

The New York Liberty Party maintained that the U.S. Constitution, interpreted in the light of the Bible and natural law, outlawed slavery throughout the country. While other Liberty abolitionists recognized Congress's power over slavery only in the District of Columbia, the territories, and interstate commerce, the New Yorkers held it could also act against slavery in the states. They contended that neither northern state militias nor the U.S. Army should help suppress slave revolts. Most important, they argued that, since masters had no legal right to own human beings, slaves who escaped and those who aided them acted within the law.

This body of thought, which dated to the late 1830s, reflected northern abolitionist empathy with slaves as they struggled for freedom. At that time, the domestic slave trade in the Border South states of Maryland, Virginia, Kentucky, and Missouri tore black families apart to feed the demand for labor in new cotton-producing areas farther south. As some slaves responded by escaping or staging minor rebellions,

Mutiny, **painted by Hale Woodruff** in 1939, provides a dramatic and stylized portrayal of the successful uprising of African slaves on board the Spanish schooner *Amistad* in 1839.   Savery Library Archives, Talladega College, Talladega, Alabama.

the radical wing of the Liberty Party supported them. It encouraged black and white northerners to go south to help escapees.

THE *AMISTAD* AND THE *CREOLE*

In particular, two maritime slave revolts encouraged northern abolitionist militancy. The first of these revolts, however, did not involve enslaved Americans. In June 1839, fifty-four African captives, under the leadership of Joseph Cinque, seized control of the Spanish schooner *Amistad* (meaning "friendship"), which had been carrying them to slavery in Honduras. After the Africans lost their way in an attempted to return to their homeland, a U.S. warship captured them off the coast of Long Island, New York. Imprisoned in New Haven, Connecticut, the Africans soon gained the assistance of Lewis Tappan and other abolitionists. As a result of that aid and arguments presented by Congressman John Quincy Adams, the Supreme Court in November 1841 freed Cinque and the others.

Later that month, Madison Washington led a revolt aboard the brig *Creole* as it transported 135 American slaves from Richmond to New Orleans. Washington had earlier escaped from Virginia to Canada. When he returned to rescue his wife, he was reenslaved and shipped aboard the *Creole.* At sea, Washington and about a dozen other black men seized control of the vessel and sailed it to the Bahamas, a British colony where slavery had been abolished. There local black fishermen protected the *Creole* by surrounding it with their boats, and most of those on board immediately gained their freedom under British law. A few days later, so did Washington and the other rebels. Although Washington soon vanished from the public eye, the *Creole* revolt made him a hero among abolitionists and a symbol of black bravery.

Cinque and Washington inspired others to risk their lives and freedom to help African Americans escape bondage. The New York Liberty Party reinforced this commitment by declaring their revolts divinely ordained and strictly legal.

THE UNDERGROUND RAILROAD

The famous **underground railroad** must be placed within the context of increasing southern white violence against black families, slave resistance, and aggressive northern abolitionism. Because the underground railroad had to be secret, few details of how it operated are known. Slaves, since colonial times, had escaped from their masters, and free black people and some white people had assisted them. But the organized escape of slaves from the Chesapeake, Kentucky, and Missouri along predetermined routes to Canada became common only after the mid-1830s. A united national underground railroad with a president or unified command never existed. Instead, there were different organizations separated in time and space from one another (see Map 9–2). Even during the 1840s and 1850s, most of the slaves who escaped did so on their own. Sometimes they had to fight pursuing masters.

The best-documented underground railroad organizations centered in Washington, D.C., and Ripley, Ohio. In Washington, Charles T. Torrey, a white Liberty Party abolitionist from Albany, New York, and Thomas Smallwood, a free black resident of Washington, began in 1842 to help slaves escape along a northward route. Between March and November of that year, they sent at least 150 enslaved men, women, and children to Philadelphia. From there, a local black vigilance committee provided the fugitives with transportation to Albany, New York, where a local, predominantly white, vigilance group helped them get to Canada. In southern Ohio and Indiana, some residents, black and white, had since the 1810s helped fugitive slaves as they headed north from Kentucky. The best known of these early underground railroad operatives was John Rankin, a white Presbyterian minister who lit a lantern each night at his Ripley, Ohio, home—located on a hill above the north shore of the Ohio River—to serve as a beacon for escaping slaves. From the late 1840s into the Civil War years, former slave John P. Parker was the most aggressive agent of the Ripley-based underground railroad. With Rankin's support, Parker, who had purchased his freedom in 1845, repeatedly went into Kentucky to lead others north.

The escapees were by no means passive "passengers" in the underground railroad network. They raised money to pay for their transportation, recruited and helped other escapees, and sometimes became underground railroad agents themselves. During the mid-1850s, Arrah Weems of Rockville, Maryland, whose freedom had been recently purchased by black and white abolitionists and whose daughter Ann Maria had been rescued by underground railroad agents, became an agent herself. She brought an enslaved infant from Washington through Philadelphia to Rochester, New York, where she met Frederick Douglass.

This was not an easy journey, and underground railroad work was risky. In 1843 Smallwood had to flee to Canada as Washington police closed in on his home. In 1846 Torrey died of tuberculosis in a Maryland prison while serving a six-year sentence for helping slaves escape. Parker recalled "real warfare" in southern Ohio between underground railroad

MAP 9–2   THE UNDERGROUND RAILROAD

This map illustrates *approximate* routes traveled by escaping slaves through the North to Canada. Although some slaves escaped from the Deep South, most who utilized the underground railroad network came from the border slave states.

▶ *By what means did escaping slaves travel the routes shown on this map?*

⊙ See the Map   Explore this map at www.myhistorylab.com

operators and slaveholders from Kentucky. "I never thought of going uptown without a pistol in my pocket, a knife in my belt, and a blackjack handy," he later recalled.

During the early 1850s, Harriet Tubman, a fugitive slave, became the most active worker on the eastern branch of the underground railroad. Born in 1820 on a Maryland plantation, she suffered years of abuse at the hands of her master. When in 1849 he threatened to sell her and her family south, she escaped to the North. Then she returned about thirteen times to Maryland to help others flee. She had the help of Thomas Garrett, a white Quaker abolitionist who lived in Wilmington, Delaware,

Harriet Tubman, standing at the left, is shown in this undated photograph with a group of people she helped escape from slavery. Because she worked in secret during the 1850s, she was known only to others engaged in the underground railroad, the people she helped, and a few other abolitionists.   Sophia Smith Collection, Smith College

and William Still, the black leader of the Philadelphia Vigilance Association. During the 1850s, Still, who as a child had been a fugitive slave, coordinated the work of many black and white underground agents between Washington and Canada.

TECHNOLOGY AND THE UNDERGROUND RAILROAD

Historian Fergus M. Bordewich notes that before the late 1830s those who helped slaves escape referred to their networks as "lines of posts" or "chains of friends." Only as railroad mileage expanded in the eastern United States did railroad power, speed, and organization serve as a metaphor for escape networks.

But the link between slave escapes and technology was more that a metaphor. Steam engines, whether used to power locomotives or vessels, promoted northward escapes. By the early 1840s, police in Border South cities patrolled steamboat wharves to prevent fugitive slaves from boarding. In 1842 in Washington, D.C., Torrey and Smallwood often helped escapees get

on steamboats. When the men led parties north on foot or by carriage, they headed for Philadelphia, where fugitives boarded northbound trains. As rail lines spread, masters in Maryland and Virginia despaired of recapturing slaves who crossed the Mason-Dixon Line.

Railroads and steamboats were essential in two famous escapes of the late 1840s. In December 1848, Ellen and William Craft (see Chapter 10) used both means of transportation to reach Philadelphia from Macon, Georgia. A few months later, Henry Brown—encased in a shipping box—traveled by train from Richmond to the Potomac River "where the tracks ended," then by steamer to Washington, and once again by train to freedom in Philadelphia. Improving transportation technology posed a threat to slavery.

CANADA WEST

The ultimate destination for many African Americans on the underground railroad was Canada West (present-day Ontario) between Buffalo and Detroit on the northern shore of Lake Erie. Black Americans began to settle in Canada West as early as the 1820s, and, because slavery was illegal in the British Empire after 1833, fugitive slaves were safe there. The stronger fugitive slave law that Congress passed as part of the Compromise of 1850 (see Chapter 10) made Canada an even more important refuge for African Americans. Between 1850 and 1860, the number of black people in Canada West rose from approximately 8,000 to at least 20,000.

There were several communal black settlements in Canada West, including the Refugee Home Society, the Buxton Community at Elgin, and the Dawn Settlement. But most black immigrants lived and worked in Toronto and Chatham. Most of them worked as craftsmen and laborers, although a few became entrepreneurs or professionals.

Mary Ann Shadd Cary was the chief advocate of black migration to Canada West, and she was the only advocate of migration who also supported racial integration. Between 1854 and 1858, she edited the *Provincial Freeman*, an abolitionist paper published in Toronto, and lectured in northern cities promoting emigration to Canada. Cary knew, however, that by

This is the only surviving photograph of Mary Ann Shadd Cary (1823-1893). An advocate, during the 1850s, of black migration to Canada, Cary also promoted racial integration.

the 1850s black people faced the same sort of segregation and discrimination in Canada that existed in the northern United States.

Black Militancy

During the 1840s growing numbers of northern black abolitionists advocated forceful action against slavery. This resolve accompanied a trend toward separate black antislavery action. The black convention movement revived during the 1840s, and there were well-attended meetings in Buffalo in 1843 (where Garnet presented his "Address to the Slaves"); in Troy, New York, in 1844; and in Cleveland in 1848. Meanwhile, more newspapers owned and edited by black abolitionists appeared.

The rise in militancy had several causes. The breakup of the AASS weakened abolitionist loyalty to the national antislavery organizations. All abolitionists, black and white, explored new antislavery tactics. Many black abolitionists came to believe that most white abolitionists enjoyed antislavery debate and theory more than action.

Influenced by the examples of Cinque, Madison Washington, and other rebellious slaves, many black abolitionists during the 1840s and 1850s wanted to do more to encourage slaves to resist and escape. This outlook inspired Garnet, who supported the radical New York wing of the Liberty Party. That organization's willingness to act rather than just talk also attracted other black leaders. However, black abolitionists, like white abolitionists, approached violence and slave rebellion with caution. As late as 1857, Garnet and Frederick Douglass described slave revolt as "inexpedient."

The black abolitionist desire to go beyond rhetoric found its best outlet in the local vigilance organizations. Such associations appeared during the mid-1830s and often had white as well as black members. As the 1840s progressed, African Americans formed more of them and led those that already existed. In this they reacted against a facet of the growing violence in the United States: "slave catchers" use of force to recapture fugitive slaves in northern cities. The most famous of the vigilance associations was the one in Philadelphia led by William Still during the late 1840s and 1850s.

Black militancy also encouraged charges that white abolitionists did not live up to their words in favor of racial justice. Economic slights rankled the most. At the annual meeting of the AFASS in 1852, a black delegate demanded to know why Lewis Tappan did not employ a black clerk in his business. In 1855 Samuel Ringgold Ward denounced Garrison and his associates for failing to have an African American "as clerk in an anti-slavery office, or editor, or lecturer to

VOICES

MARTIN R. DELANY DESCRIBES HIS VISION OF A BLACK NATION

This excerpt comes from the appendix of Martin R. Delany's The Condition, Elevation, Emigration and Destiny of the Colored People of the United States, *Politically Considered, which he published in 1852. It embodies Delany's black nationalist vision.*

Every people should be the originators of their own designs, the projectors of their own schemes, and creators of the events that lead to their destiny—the consummation of their desires.

Situated as we are in the United States, many, and almost insurmountable obstacles present themselves. We are four-and-a-half millions in numbers, free and bond; six hundred thousand free, and three-and-a-half millions bond.

We have native hearts and virtues, just as other nations; which in their pristine purity are noble, potent, and worthy of example. We are a nation within a nation. . . .

But we have been, by our oppressors, despoiled of our purity, and corrupted in our native characteristics, so that we have inherited their vices, and but few of their virtues, leaving us in character, really a broken people.

Being distinguished by complexion, we are still singled out—although having merged in the habits and customs of our oppressors—as a distinct nation of people. . . . The claims of no people, according to established policy and usage, are respected by any nation, until they are presented in a national capacity.

To accomplish so great and desirable an end, there should be held, a great representative gathering of the colored people of the United States; not what is termed a National Convention, representing en masse, such as have been, for the last few years, held at various times and places; but a true representation of the intelligence and wisdom of the colored freemen. . . . A Confidential Council. . . .

By this Council to be appointed, a Board of Commissioners . . . to go on an expedition to the EASTERN COAST OF AFRICA, to make researches for a suitable location on that section of the coast, for the settlement of colored adventurers from the United States, and elsewhere.

The whole continent is rich in minerals, and the most precious metals, as but a superficial notice of the topographical and geological reports from that country, plainly show. . . . The land is ours—there it lies with inexhaustible resources; let us go and possess it. In Eastern Africa must rise up a nation, to whom all the world must pay commercial tribute.

▶ *How does this document express black nationalism?*
▶ *What is Delaney's view of Africa?*

Source: *A Documentary History of the Negro People in the United States,* 5th ed. (New York: Citadel, 1968), Volume 1, pp. 327–28. Reprinted by permission from Bettina Aptheker, Literary Executer, Herbert Aptheker Estate.

---

the same extent . . . as white men of the same calibre." These charges reflected factional struggles between the AASS and the AFASS. But they also represented real grievances among black abolitionists and inconsistencies among their white counterparts.

Frederick Douglass

The career of Frederick Douglass illustrates the impact of the failure of white abolitionists to live up to their egalitarian ideals. Douglass was born a slave in Maryland in 1818. Brilliant, ambitious, and charming, he resisted brutalization, learned to read, and acquired a trade before escaping to New England in 1838. By 1841 he had, with Garrison's encouragement, become an antislavery lecturer, which led to the travels with William White discussed earlier.

But as time passed, Douglass, who had remained loyal to Garrison during the 1840s when most other black abolitionists left the AASS, suspected that his white colleagues wanted him

⊷⊏Read the Document
Frederick Douglass, Independence Day Speech (1852)

By the mid-1840s, Frederick Douglass had emerged as one of the more powerful speakers of his time. He began publishing his influential newspaper, the *North Star,* in 1847. Frederick Douglass (1817?–95). Oil on canvas, ©1844, attr. to E. Hammond. The Granger Collection.

to continue in the role of a fugitive slave even as he was becoming one of the premier American orators. "People won't believe you ever was a slave, Frederick, if you keep on this way," a white colleague advised him.

Finally, Douglass decided he had to free himself from the AASS. In 1847 he asserted his independence by leaving Massachusetts for Rochester, New York, where he began publishing the *North Star*. This decision angered Garrison and his associates but enabled Douglass to chart his course as a black leader. Although Douglass continued to work closely with white abolitionists, especially Gerrit Smith, he could now do it on his own terms and be more active in the black convention movement, which he considered essential to gaining general emancipation and racial justice. In 1851 he completed his break with the AASS by endorsing the constitutional arguments and tactics of the New York Liberty Party as better designed than Garrison's "disunionism" to achieve emancipation.

Revival of Black Nationalism

Douglass always believed that black people were part of a larger American nation and that their best prospects for political and economic success lay in the United States. He was, despite his differences with some white abolitionists, an ardent integrationist. He opposed separate black churches and predicted that African Americans would eventually merge into a greater American identity. Most black abolitionists did not go that far, but they believed racial oppression in all its forms could be defeated in the United States.

During the 1840s and 1850s, however, an influential minority of black leaders disagreed with this point of view. Prominent among them were Garnet and Douglass's sometime colleague on the *North Star*, Martin R. Delany. Although they disagreed over important details, Delany and Garnet both favored African-American migration and nationalism as the best means to realize black aspirations.

Since the postrevolutionary days of Prince Hall and Paul Cuffe, some black leaders had believed African Americans could thrive only as a separate nation. They suggested sites in Africa, Latin America, and the American West as possible places to pursue this goal. But it took the rising tide of racism and violence emphasized in this chapter to induce a respectable minority of black abolitionists to consider migration again. Almost all of them opposed the African migration scheme of the ACS, which they regarded as proslavery and racist. Nevertheless, Garnet conceded in 1849 that he would "rather see a man free in Liberia [the ACS colony], than a slave in the United States."

Douglass and most black abolitionists rejected this outlook, insisting the aim must be freedom in the United States. Nevertheless, emigration plans developed by Garnet and Delany during the 1850s became a significant part of African-American reform culture. Delany, a physician and novelist, was born free in western Virginia in 1812. He grew up in Pennsylvania and by the late 1840s championed black self-reliance. To further this cause, he promoted mass black migration to Latin America or Africa. "We must MAKE an ISSUE, CREATE an EVENT, and ESTABLISH a NATIONAL POSITION for OURSELVES," he declared in 1852.

In contrast, Garnet welcomed white assistance for his plan to foster Christianity and economic development in Africa by encouraging *some*—not all—African Americans to migrate there under the patronage of his African Civilization Society. In 1858 he wrote, "Let those who wished to stay, stay here—and those who had enterprise and wished to go, go and found a nation, if possible, of which the colored Americans could be proud."

Little came of these nationalist visions, largely because of the successes of the antislavery movement. Black and white abolitionists, although not perfect allies, awoke many in the North to the brutalities of

Hear the Audio
If There Is No Struggle, There Is No Progress. *Excerpt from a speech by Frederick Douglass. Read by Ossie Davis.*

1839–1846

THE ANTISLAVERY STRUGGLE INTENSIFIES

JUNE 1839	Joseph Cinque leads a successful revolt of enslaved Africans aboard the Spanish schooner *Amistad*.
APRIL 1840	The Liberty Party nominates James G. Birney for U.S. president.
NOVEMBER 1841	Madison Washington leads a successful revolt of American slaves aboard the *Creole*.
MARCH 1842	Charles T. Torrey and Thomas Smallwood organize an underground railroad network to help slaves escape from Washington, D.C., and its vicinity.
AUGUST 1843	Henry Highland Garnet in Buffalo, New York, delivers his "Address to the Slaves".
DECEMBER 1843	Smallwood flees to Canada to avoid arrest.
JUNE 1844	Torrey is arrested in Baltimore on multiple charges of having helped slaves escape.
MAY 1846	Torrey dies in the Maryland penitentiary.

AFRICAN-AMERICAN EVENTS	NATIONAL EVENTS
• 1830 •	
1831 Publication of *Liberator* begun by William Lloyd Garrison	**1832** Andrew Jackson reelected president
1833 Formation of AASS	**1833** End of Nullification Controversy
• 1835 •	
1835 Abolitionist postal campaign	**1836** Martin Van Buren elected president; Texas independence from Mexico
1839 *Amistad* mutiny	
• 1840 •	
1840 Breakup of AASS	**1840** William H. Harrison elected president
1841 *Creole* revolt	**1844** James K. Polk elected president
1843 Henry Highland Garnet's "Address to the Slaves"	

slavery. They helped convince most white northerners that the slave-labor system and slaveholder control of the national government threatened their economic and political interests. At the same time, abolitionist aid to escaping slaves and their defense of fugitive slaves from recapture pushed southern leaders to adopt policies that led to secession and the Civil War. The northern victory in the war, general emancipation, and constitutional protection for black rights made most African Americans—for a time—optimistic about their future in the United States.

CONCLUSION

This chapter has focused on the radical movement for the immediate abolition of slavery. The movement flourished in the United States from 1831, when William Lloyd Garrison began publishing the *Liberator*, through the Civil War. Garrison hoped slavery could be abolished peacefully. But during the 1840s abolitionists adjusted their antislavery tactics to deal with increasing racism and antiblack violence, both of which were related to the existence of slavery. Slave resistance also inspired a more confrontational brand of abolitionism. Many black abolitionists and their white colleagues concluded that the tactic of moral suasion, typical of abolitionism during the 1830s, could not by itself achieve their goals or prevent violence against free and enslaved black people. Most black abolitionists came to believe they needed a combination of moral suasion, political involvement, and direct action to end slavery and improve the lives of African Americans in the United States. By the late 1840s, a minority of black abolitionists contended they had to establish an independent nation beyond the borders of the United States to promote African-American rights, interests, and identity.

Although much has changed since the abolitionist era, these two perspectives remain characteristic of the African-American community. Most African Americans prefer integration within a larger American nation. But black nationalism still has a powerful appeal. Black people often endorse parts of both views, just as Frederick Douglass embraced some facets of black nationalism and Henry Highland Garnet some integrationism. Reformers also still debate whether peaceful persuasion is more effective than confrontation.

RECOMMENDED READING

Stanley Harrold. *The Abolitionists and the South, 1831–1861*. Lexington: University Press of Kentucky, 1995. Emphasizes the formative impact of slave resistance on northern abolitionism and the aggressiveness of that movement toward the South.

Jane H. Pease and William H. Pease. *They Who Would Be Free: Blacks' Search for Freedom, 1830–1861*. New York: Athenaeum, 1974. Deals with cooperation and conflict between black and white abolitionists. The book emphasizes conflict.

Benjamin Quarles. *Black Abolitionists*. New York: Oxford University Press, 1969. A classic study that emphasizes cooperation between black and white abolitionists.

Harry Reed. *Platforms for Change: The Foundations of the Northern Free Black Community, 1776–1865*. East Lansing: Michigan State University Press, 1994. Places black abolitionism and black nationalism within the context of community development.

Shirley J. Yee. *Black Women Abolitionists: A Study of Activism*. Knoxville: University of Tennessee Press, 1992. Discusses the activities of black women abolitionists in both white and black organizations.

R. J. Young. *Antebellum Black Activists: Race, Gender, Self*. New York: Garland, 1996. A sophisticated study of the motivation of black abolitionists.

ADDITIONAL BIBLIOGRAPHY

GENERAL STUDIES OF THE ANTISLAVERY MOVEMENT

Herbert Aptheker. *Abolitionism: A Revolutionary Movement*. Boston: Twayne, 1989.

Lawrence J. Friedman. *Gregarious Saints: Self and Community in American Abolitionism, 1830–1870*. New York: Cambridge University Press, 1982.

Stanley Harrold. *American Abolitionists*. Harlow, England: Longman, 2001.

———. *The Rise of Aggressive Abolitionism: Addresses to the Slaves*. Lexington: University Press of Kentucky, 2004.

James Brewer Stewart. *Holy Warriors: The Abolitionists and American Slavery*. 2nd ed. New York: Hill and Wang, 1997.

THE BLACK COMMUNITY

John Brown Childs. *The Political Black Minister: A Study in Afro-American Politics and Religion*. Boston: G. K. Hall, 1980.

Leonard P. Curry. *The Free Black in Urban America, 1800–1850: The Shadow of a Dream*. Chicago: University of Chicago Press, 1981.

Martin E. Dann. *The Black Press, 1827–1890*. New York: Capricorn, 1971.

James Oliver Horton and Lois E. Horton. *In Hope of Liberty: Culture, Community, and Protest among Northern Free Blacks, 1700–1860*. New York: Oxford University Press, 1997.

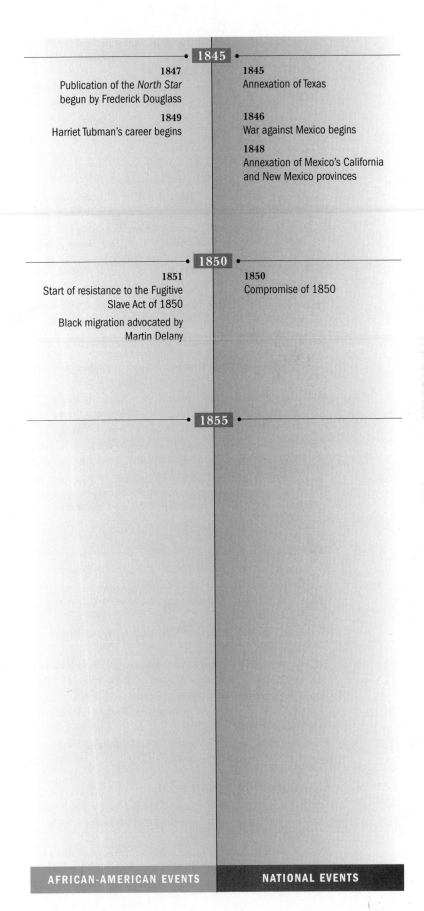

1845

1847
Publication of the *North Star* begun by Frederick Douglass

1849
Harriet Tubman's career begins

1845
Annexation of Texas

1846
War against Mexico begins

1848
Annexation of Mexico's California and New Mexico provinces

1850

1851
Start of resistance to the Fugitive Slave Act of 1850

Black migration advocated by Martin Delany

1850
Compromise of 1850

1855

AFRICAN-AMERICAN EVENTS   **NATIONAL EVENTS**

Patrick Rael. *Black Identity and Black Protest in the Antebellum North.* Chapel Hill: University of North Carolina Press, 2002.

David E. Swift. *Black Prophets of Justice: Activist Clergy before the Civil War.* Baton Rouge: Louisiana State University Press, 1989.

BLACK ABOLITIONISTS

Howard Holman Bell. *A Survey of the Negro Convention Movement, 1830–1861.* New York: Arno, 1969.

———, ed. *Minutes of the Proceedings of the National Negro Conventions, 1830–1864.* New York: Arno, 1969.

R. J. M. Blackett. *Building an Antislavery Wall: Blacks in the Atlantic Abolitionist Movement, 1830–1860.* Baton Rouge: Louisiana State University Press, 1983.

WOMEN

Blanch Glassman-Hersh. *Slavery of Sex: Feminist-Abolitionists in Nineteenth-Century America.* Urbana: University of Illinois Press, 1978.

Darlene Clark Hine, ed. *Black Women in American History: From Colonial Times through the Nineteenth Century.* 4 vols. New York: Carlson, 1990.

Julie Roy Jeffrey. *The Great Silent Army of Abolitionism: Ordinary Women in the Antislavery Movement.* Chapel Hill: University of North Carolina Press, 1998.

Gayle Tate. *Unknown Tongues: Black Women's Political Activism in the Antebellum Era 1830–1860.* East Lansing: Michigan State University Press, 2003.

Jean Fagan Yellin. *Women and Sisters: Antislavery Feminists in American Culture.* New Haven, CT: Yale University Press, 1990.

BIOGRAPHY

Catherine Clinton. *Harriet Tubman: The Road to Freedom.* New York: Little, Brown, 2003.

William S. McFeely. *Frederick Douglass.* New York: Simon & Schuster, 1991.

Nell Irvin Painter. *Sojourner Truth: A Life, a Symbol.* New York: Norton, 1996.

Joel Schor. *Henry Highland Garnet: A Voice of Black Radicalism in the Nineteenth Century.* Westport, CT: Greenwood, 1977.

James Brewer Stewart. *William Lloyd Garrison and the Challenge of Emancipation.* Arlington Heights, IL: Harlan Davidson, 1992.

Victor Ullman. *Martin R. Delany: The Beginnings of Black Nationalism.* Boston: Beacon, 1971.

UNDERGROUND RAILROAD

Fergus M. Bordewich. *Bound for Canaan: The Underground Railroad and the War for the Soul of America.* New York: Amistad, 2005.

Keith P. Griffler. *Front Line of Freedom: African Americans and the Forging of the Underground Railroad in the Ohio Valley.* Lexington: University Press of Kentucky, 2004.

Stanley Harrold. *Subversives: Antislavery Community in Washington, D.C., 1828–1865.* Baton Rouge: Louisiana State University Press, 2003.

William Still. *The Underground Railroad.* 1871. Reprint, Chicago: Johnson Publishing, 1970.

BLACK NATIONALISM

Rodney Carlisle. *The Roots of Black Nationalism.* Port Washington, NY: Kennikat, 1975.

Floyd J. Miller. *The Search for Black Nationality: Black Emigration and Colonization, 1787–1863.* Urbana: University of Illinois Press, 1975.

RETRACING THE ODYSSEY

Frederick Douglass National Historic Site, Washington, D.C. http://www.nps.gov/FRDO/index.htm. This is Douglass's Cedar Hill home, which he purchased in 1878. It contains materials related to his career as an abolitionist and advocate of black rights.

"Free at Last: A History of the Abolition of Slavery in America." A "National Touring Exhibition" sponsored by the Lincoln Home National Historic Site, Springfield, Illinois, that shows how "abolition became a national issue, how the slavery issue drew politicians and moral reformers together, [and] how the efforts of escaped slaves contributed a human face to the horrors of slavery."

National Underground Railroad Freedom Center, Cincinnati. OH. http://www.freedomcenter.org/. Exhibits, programs, and events dealing with "slavery and freedom," with emphasis on the underground railroad.

National Underground Railroad Museum, Maysville, KY. http://www.coax.net/people/lwf/URMUSEUM.HTM. Houses artifacts associated with and provides information on the underground railroad.

REVIEW QUESTIONS

1. What was the historical significance of Henry Highland Garnet's "Address to the Slaves"? How did Garnet's attitude toward slavery differ from that of William Lloyd Garrison?

2. Evaluate Frederick Douglass's career as an abolitionist. How was he consistent? How was he inconsistent?

3. How did black women contribute to the antislavery movement? How did participation in this movement alter their lives?

4. How did the integrationist views of Frederick Douglass compare with the nationalist views of Martin Delany and Henry Highland Garnet?

5. Why did so many black abolitionists leave the AASS in 1840?

PEARSON myhistorylab Connections

www.myhistorylab.com
Review what you've learned in this chapter and explore the many documents, images,
research tools, and activities for this chapter to learn more about African-American history.

✓● Study and Review

READ
●●●—Read the Document

- The American Antislavery Society Declares Its Sentiments (1833)

- A Call for Women to Become Abolitionists

- An Abolitionist Lecturer's Instructions

- Garnet's "Call to Rebellion" (1843)

- Levi Coffin's Underground Railroad Station (1826–1827)

- Frederick Douglass, Independence Day Speech (1852)

LISTEN
((•●—Hear the Audio

Hear the audio files for Chapter 9.

- *If There Is No Struggle, There Is No Progress.* Excerpt from a speech by Frederick Douglass. Read by Ossie Davis.

- *The Rebirth of Sojourner Truth.* Read by Jean Brannon.

RESEARCH
mysearchlab

Consider these questions in a short research paper.

Compare and contrast the attitudes of black and white antislavery activists.

What tensions existed within the antislavery movement?

EXPLORE
Watch the Video

- The Underground Railroad

See the Map

- The Underground Railroad

●●●—Read the Document

- Angelina Grimké

Speaking Out against Slavery

Abolitionist literature was a mainstay of the movement to end slavery. The antislavery press created a wide variety of newspapers, periodicals, publications for children, reports, broadsides, sermons, and other types of printed material to bring their stand against slavery to the public. In addition, many antislavery organizations regularly held public meetings with speeches by prominent leaders of the movement to bring the abolitionist message to people, using music and songs to arouse the crowds. Whites, African Americans, and women were all deeply involved in these determined efforts to abolish slavery.

The title page of *The Penitential Tyrant; or, Slave Trader Reformed* by Thomas Branagan, former slave trader and owner of slaves. Branagan joined the abolitionist movement. His books were a powerful indictment of the institution of slavery.

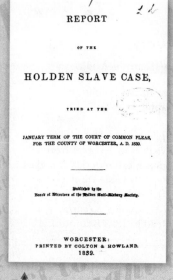

REPORT

OF THE

HOLDEN SLAVE CASE,

TRIED AT THE

JANUARY TERM OF THE COURT OF COMMON PLEAS,
FOR THE COUNTY OF WORCESTER, A.D. 1839.

Published by the
Board of Directors of the Holden Anti-Slavery Society.

WORCESTER:
PRINTED BY COLTON & HOWLAND.
1839.

THE
PENITENTIAL TYRANT;
OR,
Slave Trader Reformed:
A
PATHETIC POEM,
IN FOUR CANTOS.

BY THOMAS BRANAGAN.

THE SECOND EDITION, ENLARGED.

"AM I NOT A MAN, AND A BROTHER!"

New-York:
PRINTED AND SOLD BY SAMUEL WOOD,
NO. 362, PEARL-STREET.
1807.

Antislavery activities included publishing reports on legal cases involving slaves or former slaves.

This illustration shows Wendell Phillips (1811–1884) speaking at a meeting to protest the trial of fugitive slave Thomas Sims in Boston. Sims was eventually returned to slavery in Savannah.

Leaflet appealing to fellow citizens to attend a meeting to hear their platform against slavery, published in Lexington, 1850.

THOMPSON, THE ABOLITIONIST.

That infamous foreign scoundrel THOMPSON, will hold forth *this afternoon*, at the Liberator Office, No. 48, Washington Street. The present is a fair opportunity for the friends of the Union to *snake Thompson out!* It will be a contest between the Abolitionists and the friends of the Union. A purse of **$100** has been raised by a number of patriotic citizens to reward the individual who shall first lay violent hands on Thompson, so that he may be brought to the tar kettle before dark. Friends of the Union, be vigilant!

Boston, Wednesday, 12 o'clock.

◀ This antiabolitionist ad announces an offer of $100 for the capture of an abolitionist.

In an effort to stir ▶ antiabolitionist fervor, this broadside announces an upcoming abolitionist lecture at a local New York church.

OUTRAGE.

Fellow Citizens,

AN
ABOLITIONIST,

of the most revolting character is among you, exciting the feelings of the North against the South. A seditious Lecture is to be delivered

THIS EVENING,

at 7 o'clock, at the Presbyterian Church in Cannon-street. You are requested to attend and unite in putting down and silencing by peaceable means this tool of evil and fanaticism. Let the rights of the States guaranteed by the Constitution be protected.

Feb. 27, 1837. The Union forever!

TO THE PEOPLE, Who wish to do Right!

There are thousands of persons in Kentucky who conscientiously believe that

Slavery is injurious to the prosperity of our beloved State:—
Inconsistent with the fundamental principles of free government:—
Contrary to the natural rights of mankind:—
Adverse to a pure state of morals:—
A great hindrance to the establishment of Free Schools:—
That it depresses the energies of the laboring white man:—
And in many other ways, is

A CURSE TO THE COUNTRY.

Many of the persons who so believe, have formed themselves into a party,

OPPOSED TO THE PERPETUATION OF SLAVERY IN KENTUCKY,

Composed of such men as Henry Clay and Dr. R. J. Breckinridge, of Fayette; Judge Nicholas, Wm. L. Breckinridge and Hon. Wm. P. Thomasson, of Louisville; C. M. Clay, of Madison; Judge Monroe, of Franklin; Dr. J. C. Young, of Boyle; J. McClung, of Mason; Judge Ballinger, of Mercer; J. B. Thornton, of Bourbon, and thousands of other persons of both parties; hard-working, honest, industrious, virtuous Mechanics, Manufacturers, Laborers, Farmers and Slaveholders of the Commonwealth, who for Talent, Education, Virtue, Uprightness of Character and Intelligence, can be best in any State in the Union!

These men object to the Perpetuation of Slavery by the Constitution of the State, and so *ought* every other GOOD REPUBLICAN who loves the prosperity of his home. The *way* and the *time* to do this, belongs to the CONVENTION TO CHANGE THE CONSTITUTION, which will assemble in Frankfort in October.

This party has adopted and published a PLATFORM OF THEIR PRINCIPLES, so that every body may see that their design is a good one, and the manner in which they wish to do this, is a Peaceable, Quiet and Lawful one. For which purpose, they are going to run candidates in the various counties in the State, favorable to the two following objects, and no matter how their enemies may misrepresent them, this is

THEIR PLATFORM.

1st. "The absolute prohibition of the importation of any more slaves into Kentucky."
2d. "The complete power in the People of Kentucky to enforce and perfect in or under the new Constitution, a system of gradual prospective Emancipation of Slaves."

We believe that a majority of the people of this State, are in favor of the principles laid down in this Platform; and that if left alone to vote their real sentiments, uninfluenced by Democratic and Whig party demagogues, they will give a tremendous vote in their favor. But cunning, long-headed demagogues, wire-workers

THE LIBERATOR.

VOL. I.] WILLIAM LLOYD GARRISON AND ISAAC KNAPP, PUBLISHERS. **[NO. 33.**

BOSTON, MASSACHUSETTS.] OUR COUNTRY IS THE WORLD—OUR COUNTRYMEN ARE MANKIND. [SATURDAY, AUGUST 13, 1831.

▲ **The masthead** of William Lloyd Garrison's abolitionist newspaper, *The Liberator*.

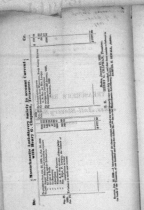

Publications of antislavery ▶ societies included treasurer's reports detailing the financial aspect of abolitionist activities.

THE ANTI-SLAVERY RECORD.

THE RUNAWAY.

The frontispiece of the *Anti-Slavery Record* published in July, 1837 with a woodcut illustration of a runaway slave.

"GET OFF THE TRACK!"

A song for Emancipation. Sung by THE HUTCHINSONS, Respectfully dedicated to NATH'L P. ROGERS,

JESSE HUTCHINSON JUN'.

◀ **Music and songs** were an integral part of abolitionist meetings and publications.

THE NORTH STAR.

▲ **The *North Star*** was one of two abolitionist papers published by Frederick Douglass from 1847–1863 in Rochester, New York.

NATIONAL ANTI-SLAVERY BAZAAR

VOL. I. **NO. II.**

THE OLD CRADLE OF LIBERTY.

GAZETTE.

ANTI-SLAVERY FAIR, TO BE HELD IN **FANEUIL HALL,** AT THE CLOSE OF THE YEAR.

The opening page of ▶ the leaflet *Gazette* features details of a national antislavery bazaar. Organizers describe the need for donations of goods and services to be used in fund-raising at the bazaar.

VISUALIZING THE PAST

"And Black People Were at the Heart of It"

Why was the expansion of slavery such a divisive issue?

What did "free labor" mean to nineteenth-century Americans?

How did African Americans react to the passage of the Fugitive Slave Law of 1850?

Why was the Supreme Court decision in the *Dred Scott* case so controversial?

What was the impact of John Brown's raid on Harpers Ferry?

How did African Americans and white southerners react to the election of Abraham Lincoln in 1860?

▶ **In January 1856,** Margaret Garner, her husband Robert, and their four children escaped from Kentucky to Ohio across the frozen Ohio River. They were pursed to the home of a black man by slave owners as well as deputy marshals. The Garners fiercely resisted. Robert Garner shot and wounded one of the deputies. But when it became clear that they were about to be captured, Margaret killed her daughter rather than have the child returned to slavery.

The Fugitive Slave Bill, (exhibited in its hideous deformity at our previous meeting,) has already in hot haste commenced its bloody crusade o'er the land, and the liability of ourselves and our families becoming its victims at the caprice of Southern men-stealers, imperatively demands an expression, whether we will tamely submit to chains and slavery, or whether we will, at all and every hazard, Live and Die freemen.

Robert C. Nell, "Declaration of Sentiments of the Colored Citizens of Boston on the Fugitive Slave Bill!!!," 1850

◀ **An abolitionist poster** from Massachusetts condemns the Fugitive Slave Law and the politicians who voted for it.

By the end of the 1840s in the United States, no issue was as controversial as slavery. Slavery or, more accurately, its expansion deeply divided the American people and led to the bloodiest war in American history. Try as they might from 1845 to 1860, political leaders could not solve, evade, or escape slavery, nor could they agree on whether to allow it to expand into the nation's western territories.

((•□ **Hear** the **Audio**
Hear the audio files for Chapter 10 at **www.myhistorylab.com**

Caught in this monumental dispute were the South's nearly four million enslaved men, women, and children. Their future, as well as the fate of the country, was at stake. More than 620,000 Americans—northern and southern, black and white—would die before a divided nation would be reunified and slavery would be abolished.

Whether slavery should be permitted in the western territories was not a new issue. As early as 1787, Congress had prohibited slavery in the Northwest Territory, the area north of the Ohio River that became the states of Ohio, Indiana, Illinois, Michigan, and Wisconsin. Then in 1819 a major political controversy erupted when Missouri applied for admission to the Union as a slave state. The Missouri Compromise—which admitted Maine as a free state, Missouri as a slave state, and outlawed slavery north of the 36° 30' line of latitude (see Chapter 5)—settled that controversy, but only postponed for 25 years further conflict over the expansion of slavery.

The country's desire to acquire western lands intensified in the 1830s and 1840s. Most white Americans and many free black Americans assumed that the American people should occupy the entire North American continent from the Atlantic to the Pacific. It was their future, their Manifest Destiny (see Chapter 9). In 1846–1847, U.S. troops fought an 18-month conflict that resulted in the acquisition of more than half of Mexico and was a major step toward the fulfillment of Manifest Destiny.

The Lure of the West

Even before the war with Mexico, hundreds of Americans made the long journey west, drawn by the opportunity to settle the fertile valleys of California and the Oregon Territory, which included what is today the states of Oregon and Washington. African Americans shared these hopes and dreams. In 1844 a black Missouri farmer with the improbable name of George Washington Bush caught "Oregon fever" and set out with his wife, six children, and four other families on the 1,800-mile trek by wagon train to Oregon. Bush settled north of the Columbia River in what later became the Washington Territory because Oregon's territorial constitution forbade black settlement. Although the law was rarely enforced, black residents were legally subject to whipping every six months until they departed. The statute remained Oregon state law until the 1920s.

FREE LABOR VERSUS SLAVE LABOR

Westward expansion revived the issue of slavery's future in the territories. Should slavery be legal or prohibited in western lands? Most white Americans held thoroughly ingrained racist beliefs that people of African descent were not and could never be their intellectual, political, or social equals. Yet those same white Americans disagreed vehemently on where those unfree African Americans should be permitted to work and reside.

Most northern white people adamantly opposed allowing southern slaveholders to take their slaves into the former Mexican territories, and they detested the prospect of slavery spreading westward and limiting their opportunities to settle and farm those lands. Except for the increasing number of militant abolitionists, white northerners detested both slavery as a labor system and the black people who were enslaved.

By the mid-nineteenth century, northern black and white people embraced the system of **free labor**— that is, free men and women who worked for compensation to earn a living and improve their lives. If southern slave owners managed to gain a foothold for their unfree labor on the western plains, in the Rocky Mountains, or on the Pacific coast, then the future for free white laborers would be severely restricted, if not destroyed.

((•— Hear the Audio
Remembering Slavery #1.
Recordings of former slaves talking about slavery.

THE WILMOT PROVISO

In 1846, during the Mexican War, a Democratic congressman from Pennsylvania, David Wilmot, introduced a measure in Congress, the so-called Wilmot Proviso, to prohibit slavery in any lands acquired from Mexico. Wilmot later explained that he wanted neither slavery nor black people to taint territory that should be reserved exclusively for whites: "The negro race already occupy enough of this fair continent. . . . I would preserve for free white labor a fair country . . . where the sons of toil, of my own race and own color, can live without the disgrace which association with negro slavery brings upon free labor."

The **Wilmot Proviso** failed to become law. But white southerners were enraged, and they saw the proviso as a blatant attempt to prevent them from moving west and enjoying the prosperity and way of life that an expanding slave-labor system would create. They considered any attempt to limit the growth of slavery to be the first step toward eliminating it. And the possibility that slavery might be abolished, as remote as that may have seemed in the 1840s, was too awful for them to contemplate.

White southerners had convinced themselves that black people were a childlike and irresponsible race wholly incapable of surviving as a free people if they were emancipated and compelled to compete with white Americans. Most white people believed the black race would decline and disappear if it were freed. Virginia lawyer George Fitzhugh wrote in 1854, "The negro race is inferior to the white race, and living in their midst, they would be far outstripped or outwitted in the chase of free competition. Gradual, but certain, extermination would be their fate." Thus, southern white people considered slavery "a positive good"—in the words of Senator John C. Calhoun of South Carolina—that benefited both races and resulted in a society vastly superior to that of the North.

To prevent slavery's expansion, the Free-Soil Party was formed in 1848. It was composed mainly of white people who vigorously opposed slavery's expansion and the supposed desecration that the presence of black men and women might bring to the new western lands. But some black and white abolitionists also supported the Free-Soilers as a way to oppose slavery. They reasoned that even though many Free-Soil supporters were hostile to black people, the party still represented a serious challenge to slavery and its expansion. Frederick Douglass felt comfortable enough with the Free-Soil Party to attend its convention in 1848. The Free-Soil candidate for president that year was the former Democratic president Martin Van Buren. He came in a distant third behind the Whig victor and hero of the Mexican War, Zachary Taylor, who won, and the Democrat Lewis Cass. Nevertheless, ten Free-Soil congressmen were elected, and the party provided a growing forum to oppose slavery's advance.

AFRICAN AMERICANS AND THE GOLD RUSH

The discovery of gold in California in 1848 sent thousands of Americans hurrying west in 1849. The **Forty-Niners,** as these migrants were called, were almost exclusively male, and most were white Americans. But the desire to get rich had universal appeal, and the gold rush attracted Europeans, Asians (mostly Chinese), and African Americans. By 1850 nearly 900 black men (and fewer than 100 black women) were living in California, including people of African descent from Mexico, Peru, Chile, and Jamaica.

A black sailor known only as Hector deserted a naval vessel, the USS *Southampton,* in 1848 in Monterrey, California, and headed for the gold fields. He returned with $4,000, a large sum at the time. Another African American, Dick, brought $100,000 in gold,

Quartz mining involved heavy and costly machinery that crushed huge quantities of rock and boulders. Only larger corporations—not individual miners—that had the financial resources to buy and install the machinery and to hire the workers to operate it could employ this technology. Moses L. Rodgers was an ex-slave from Missouri who became knowledgeable and successful in quartz mining operations in the late 1860s. He was both an investor and superintendent of several California gold mines, including the Washington Mine, which was producing $500,000 in gold annually by the early 1870s. Most of the laborers under Rodgers's supervision were Chinese immigrants.

CALIFORNIA AND THE COMPROMISE OF 1850

With the gold rush, California's population soared to more than 100,000, and its new residents quickly applied for admission to the Union as a free state. White southerners were aghast at the prospect of California prohibiting slavery, and they refused to consider its admission unless slavery was lawful there. Most northerners would not accept this.

Into this dispute stepped Whig Senator Henry Clay, who 30 years earlier had assisted with the Missouri Compromise. In 1850 the aging Clay put together an elaborate piece of legislation, the **Compromise of 1850,** designed not only to settle the controversy over California but also to resolve the issue of slavery's expansion once and for all. Clay attempted to satisfy both sides. To placate northerners, he proposed admitting California as a free state and eliminating the slave trade (but not slavery) in the District of Columbia. To satisfy white southerners, he offered a stronger fugitive slave law to make it easier for slave owners to apprehend runaway slaves and return them to slavery. New Mexico and Utah would be organized as territories with no mention of slavery (see Map 10–1).

Clay's measures were hammered into a single bill and produced one of the most remarkable debates in the history of the Senate, but it did not pass. Southern opponents like Senator John C. Calhoun of South Carolina could not tolerate the admission of California without slavery. Northern opponents like Senator William Seward of New York could not tolerate a tougher fugitive slave law. President Zachary Taylor shocked his fellow southerners and insisted that California should be admitted as a free state and that Clay's compromise was unnecessary. Taylor promised to veto the compromise if Congress passed it.

Clay's effort had failed—or so it seemed. But in the summer of 1850, Taylor died unexpectedly and was succeeded by Millard Fillmore, who was willing to accept the compromise.

Although white miners often resented the presence of black men during the gold rush, these two black men and two white men are operating a sluice together as they mine for gold in Spanish Flat in northern California in 1852.

a veritable fortune, out of Tuolumne County, only to lose it all gambling in San Francisco.

Most of the Forty-Niners—whatever their race or nationality—were placer miners. Using the most basic technology—little more than a pan, a pick, and a shovel—they sought the chips and flakes of gold deposited in the icy streams that flowed down the western slopes of the Sierra Nevada Mountains. By swishing the water with their pan, they separated the tiny specks and pieces of gold from the sand and gravel. The more enterprising miners built a sluice to wash the rock and gravel more efficiently. Few of these placer miners struck it rich. But many of them made a modest living from the gold they recovered.

The richer veins of the precious metal were deeper underground and required more sophisticated technology and expensive equipment to mine it. Hydraulic mining used high-pressure hoses that sent powerful streams of water into the sides of hills and mountains, scarring the landscape as the sand and soil were ripped away and revealing the rock, stone, and sometimes gold embedded below. A black man known only as Smith worked his mining claim in Amador County with hydraulic equipment. He earned a respectable five to six dollars a day.

Read the **Document**
The Compromise of 1850

MAP 10—1 THE COMPROMISE OF 1850

As a result of the war against Mexico, the United States acquired the regions shown on this map as California, Utah Territory, New Mexico Territory, and the portions of Texas not included in the Province of Texas.

▶ *With the Compromise of 1850, California entered the Union as a free state. In which remaining western lands would slavery be accepted or rejected?*

⊙ See the Map *Explore this map at* **www.myhistorylab.com**

Senator Stephen Douglas, an ambitious Democrat from Illinois, guided Clay's compromise through Congress by breaking it into separate bills. California entered the Union as a free state, and a stronger fugitive slave law entered the federal legal code.

FUGITIVE SLAVE LAWS

Those who may have hoped the compromise would resolve the dispute over slavery forever were mistaken. The **Fugitive Slave Law of 1850** created bitter resentment among black and white abolitionists and made slavery a more emotional and personal issue for many white people who had previously considered slavery a remote southern institution.

Read the **Document**
Fugitive Slave Act

Had runaway slaves not been an increasingly frustrating problem for slave owners—particularly those in the Upper South states of Maryland, Virginia, and Kentucky—the federal fugitive slave law would not have needed to be strengthened in 1850. The U.S. Constitution and the fugitive slave law passed in 1793 would seem to have provided ample authority for slave owners to recover runaway slaves.

The Constitution in Article IV, Section 2, stipulates that "any person held to service or labor in one State" who ran away to another state "shall be delivered up on claim of the party to whom such service or labor may be due." The fugitive slave law of 1793 permitted slave owners to recover slaves who had escaped to other states. The escaped slave had no rights—no right to a trial, no right to testify, and no guarantee of **habeas corpus** (the legal requirement

VOICES

AFRICAN AMERICANS
RESPOND TO THE
FUGITIVE SLAVE LAW

These two passages reflect the outrage the Fugitive Slave Law of 1850 provoked among black Americans. In the first, John Jacobs, a fugitive slave from South Carolina, urges black people to take up arms to oppose the law. In the second, from a speech he delivered a few days after the passage of the law, Martin Delany defies authorities to search his home for runaway slaves.

My colored brethren, if you have not swords, I say to you, sell your garments and buy one. . . . They said that they cannot take us back to the South; but I say, under the present law they can; and now they say unto you; let them take only dead bodies. . . . I would, my friends, advise you to show a front to our tyrants and arm yourselves . . . and I would advise the women to have their knives too.

Source: William F. Cheek, *Black Resistance before the Civil War* (Beverly Hills, CA: Glencoe Press, 1970), 148–49.

Sir, my house is my castle; in that castle are none but my wife and my children, as free as the angels of heaven, and whose liberty is as sacred as the pillars of God. If any man approaches that house in search of a slave—I care not who he may be, whether the constable, or sheriff, magistrate or even judge of the Supreme Court—nay, let it be he who sanctioned this act to become law [President Millard Fillmore] surrounded by his cabinet as his bodyguard, with the Declaration of Independence waving above his head as his banner, and the constitution of this country upon his breast as his shield—if he crosses the threshold of my door, and I do not lay him a lifeless corpse at my feet, I hope the grave may refuse my body a resting place, and righteous Heaven my spirit a home. O, no! He cannot enter that house and we both live.

Source: Victor Ullman, *Martin R. Delany: The Beginnings of Black Nationalism* (Boston: Beacon Press, 1971), 112.

▶ *How and why did these two black men justify the use of violence against those who were enforcing a law passed by Congress?*
▶ *Under what circumstances is it permissible to violate the law or threaten to kill another human being?*

that a person be brought before a court and not imprisoned illegally).

But by the 1830s and 1840s, hundreds if not thousands of slaves had escaped to freedom by way of the underground railroad, and white southerners increasingly found the 1793 law too weak to overcome the resistance of northern communities to the return of escapees. For example, in January 1847 four Kentuckians and a local law officer attempted to capture Adam Crosswhite, his wife, and their four children after the family had escaped from slavery in Kentucky and settled on a farm near Marshall, Michigan. When the would-be abductors arrived, an old black man mounted a horse and galloped through town ringing a bell warning that the Crosswhites were in danger. Having been aroused by this "Black Paul Revere," about one hundred people helped rescue the family and put them on a railroad train to Canada. The local citizens who had aided the Crosswhites were later successfully sued by the slave owner and fined an amount equal to the estimated value of the Crosswhites had the family been sold as slaves.

Northern states had enacted personal liberty laws that made it illegal for state law enforcement officials to help capture runaways. (Michigan passed such a law in 1855 after the Crosswhites escaped to Canada.) Not only did many northerners refuse to cooperate in returning fugitives to slavery under the 1793 law, but they also encouraged and assisted the fleeing slaves. The local black vigilance committees that were created in many northern communities and discussed in Chapter 9—among them the League of Freedom in Boston and the Liberty Association in Chicago—were especially effective in these efforts. These actions infuriated white southerners and prompted their demand for a stricter fugitive slave law.

The Fugitive Slave Law of 1850 was one of the toughest and harshest measures the U.S. Congress ever passed. Anyone apprehended under the law was almost certain to be sent back to slavery. The law required U.S. marshals, their deputies, and even ordinary citizens to help seize suspected runaways. Those who refused to help apprehend fugitives or who helped the runaways could be fined or imprisoned. The law made it nearly impossible for black people to prove they were free. Slave owners and their agents only had to provide legal documentation from their home state or the testimony of white witnesses before a federal commissioner that the captive was a runaway slave. The federal commissioners were paid $10 for captives returned to bondage but only $5 for those declared free. Supporters of the law claimed the extra paperwork involved in returning a fugitive to slavery necessitated the higher fee. Opponents saw it as a bribe to encourage federal authorities to return men and women to bondage. While the law was in effect, 332 captives were returned to the South and slavery, and only 11 were released as free people.

The new fugitive slave law outraged many black and white northerners. An angry Frederick Douglass insisted in October 1850 that "the only way to make the Fugitive Slave Law a dead letter is to make a half dozen or more dead kidnappers." White abolitionist Wendell Phillips exhorted his listeners to disobey the law, declaring that "we must trample this law under our feet."

Fugitive Slaves

The fugitive slave law did more than anger black and white northerners. It exposed them to cruel and heart-wrenching scenes as southern slave owners and slave catchers took advantage of the new law and—with the vigorous assistance of federal authorities—relentlessly pursued runaway slaves. Many white people and virtually all black people felt revulsion over this crackdown on those who had fled from slavery to freedom.

In September 1850 in New York City, federal authorities captured a black porter and returned him to slavery in Baltimore, even though he insisted that because his mother was a free woman he had not been a slave. (In each of the slave states, the law stipulated the status of the mother determined a child's legal status—free or slave.) In Poughkeepsie, New York, slave catchers captured a well-to-do black tailor and returned him to slavery in South Carolina. In Indiana, a black man was apprehended while his wife and children looked on, and he was sent to Kentucky, where his owner claimed he had escaped 19 years earlier.

Not all fugitives were forced back into bondage. A Maryland slave owner attempted to recover a black woman in Philadelphia who, he asserted, had escaped 22 years earlier. Since then, she had given birth to six children, and the slave owner insisted they were also his property. In this instance, the federal commissioner ruled that the woman and her children were free.

Even California was not immune to the furor over fugitive slaves. Although the new state prohibited slavery, several hundred black people were illegally held there as slaves in the 1850s. Nevertheless, some slaves ran away to the far West rather than to the North. Black abolitionist Mary Ellen Pleasant hid fugitive Archy Lee in San Francisco in 1858. Other black Californians provided security for runaways from as far east as Maryland.

Holy Bible
Thou shalt not deliver unto the master his servant which has escaped from his master unto thee. He shall dwell with thee. Even among you in that place which he shall choose in one of thy gates where it liketh him best: Thou shalt not oppress him.
Deut XXIII.15,16

Effects of the Fugitive-Slave-Law.

Declaration of independence
We hold that all men are created equal, that they are endowed by their Creator with certain unalienable rights that among these are life, liberty and the pursuit of happiness.

Leaflets like this reflect the outrage many northerners felt in response to the capture and reenslavement of African Americans that resulted from the passage of a tougher Fugitive Slave Law as part of the Compromise of 1850.

WILLIAM AND ELLEN CRAFT

Black and white abolitionists had organized vigilance committees to resist the fugitive slave law and to prevent—by force if necessary—the return of fugitives to slavery. In October 1850 slave catchers arrived in Boston prepared to capture and return William and Ellen Craft to slavery in Georgia. In 1848 the Crafts had devised an ingenious escape. Ellen's fair complexion enabled her to disguise herself as a sickly young white man who, accompanied by "his" slave, was traveling north for medical treatment. They journeyed to Boston by railroad and ship and thus escaped from slavery—or so they thought.

Slave catchers vowed to return the Crafts to servitude no matter how long it took: "If [we] have to stay here to all eternity, and if there are not enough men in Massachusetts to take them, [we] will bring some from the South." While white abolitionists protected Ellen and black abolitionists hid William, the vigilance committee plastered posters around Boston describing the slave catchers, calling them "man-stealers," and threatening their safety. Within days (which must have seemed slightly less than eternity), the slave catchers left without the Crafts. Soon thereafter, the Crafts sailed to security in England.

PROFILE: Mary Ellen Pleasant

Mary Ellen Pleasant was an influential woman of many accomplishments. But her life is shrouded in mystery and uncertainty. She may have been born in Georgia or Louisiana. She claimed she was born in Philadelphia in 1814 to a free woman of color. Her father may have been Asian, Native American, or even a white planter.

She did live for a time on Nantucket Island off the Massachusetts coast and then in Boston. She was an educated woman. In New England she became acquainted with black and white abolitionists. She married John W. Smith, who was said to have been a Cuban planter. They had a daughter, Elizabeth. Her husband died in 1844. During the gold rush in 1849, she moved to California where she married John Pleasant and became prominent in San Francisco's African-American community. San Francisco had about 500 black residents in the mid-1850s.

The entrepreneurial spirit struck Pleasant who was soon operating three laundries and a boarding house. She also invested in mining stock. She remained committed to abolition and assisted fugitive slaves who fled to the far West. She may have attended the 1855 Colored Convention in San Francisco, and she almost certainly met Mifflin Gibbs, who ran the first black newspaper on the Pacific coast, *The Mirror of the Times*. (See Chapter 13 for a profile on the Gibbs brothers.)

By the late 1850s, Pleasant was in Chatham, Canada West (Ontario), where she collaborated with Martin Delany, Mary Ann Shadd Cary, and other black abolitionists. They had formed the Chatham Vigilance Committee that aided fugitive slaves escaping from the United States. She met John Brown in Chatham and reportedly donated $30,000 to his efforts to organize a slave rebellion.

Pleasant returned to California by the mid-1860s and presided over her daughter's elegant wedding at San Francisco's A.M.E. Zion Church. Ever the entrepreneur, Pleasant operated a fashionable restaurant and a well-appointed boarding house that some people insisted was a brothel patronized by prominent white men.

Through her contacts with powerful politicians and businessmen, she accumulated information—some might call it gossip—about influential white families and the men who governed them. She used her connections to help black Californians find employment. She also worked as a housekeeper for two well-to-do white families, the Woodworths and then the Bells. Believed by some to be a voodoo queen, she was said to have developed peculiar powers over people, especially men.

Pleasant fought racial discrimination and supported legislation to permit black people to testify in California courts. She was loved and respected as well as hated and resented. She twice sued a San Francisco streetcar company that did not allow her to ride in its vehicles. She won $500 in her second suit, but the verdict was overturned on appeal.

She became renowned as "Mammy Pleasant," but she detested the nickname and did not hesitate to tell people so. At age 87 she curtly informed a journalist, "Listen: I don't like to be called Mammy by everybody. Put that down. I'm not Mammy to everybody in California. I got a letter from a minister in Sacramento. It was addressed to Mammy Pleasant. I wrote back to him on his own paper that my name was Mrs. Mary E. Pleasant. . . . If he didn't have better sense he should have had better manners."

Mrs. Mary E. Pleasant died in 1904. Her estate included diamond jewelry, 114 acres in Sonoma County, and a lot on Octavia Street in San Francisco. Even in death she remained a puzzling and curious figure to many people. There was no mystery, however, to her request that her gravestone simply be inscribed: "She was a friend of John Brown."

◄ **Mary Ellen Pleasant** was a fascinating woman who did not disclose much about herself to others. She once said: "Some folks say that words were made to reveal thought. That ain't so. Words were made to conceal thought."

SHADRACH MINKINS

Black and white abolitionists were prepared to use force against the U.S. government and the slave owners and their agents. Sometimes the abolitionists succeeded, sometimes they did not. In early 1851, a few months after the Crafts left Boston, federal marshals apprehended there a black waiter who had escaped from slavery and given himself the name Shadrach Minkins. But a well-organized band of black men led by Lewis Hayden invaded the courthouse and spirited Minkins to safety in Canada on the underground railroad. (Minkins later owned a restaurant in Montreal.) Federal authorities brought charges against four black men and four white men who were then indicted by a grand jury for helping Minkins, but local juries refused to convict them.

THE BATTLE AT CHRISTIANA

In September 1851 a battle erupted in the little town of Christiana, in southern Pennsylvania, when a Maryland slave owner, Edward Gorsuch, arrived to recover two runaway slaves. Accompanied by family members and three deputy U.S. marshals, he confronted a well-armed crowd of at least 25 black men and several white men. Black leader William Parker told Gorsuch to give up any plans to take the runaway slaves. Gorsuch refused, and a battle ensued. Gorsuch was killed, and several black and white men were hurt. The runaway slaves escaped to Canada.

President Fillmore sent U.S. Marines to Pennsylvania, and they helped round up the alleged perpetrators of the violence. Thirty-six black men and five white men were arrested and indicted for treason by a federal grand jury. But after the first trial ended in acquittal, the remaining cases were dropped.

ANTHONY BURNS

Of all the fugitive slave cases, none elicited more support or sorrow than that of Anthony Burns. In 1854 Burns escaped from slavery in Virginia by stowing away on a ship to Boston. After gaining work in a clothing store, he unwisely sent a letter to his brother, who was still a slave. The letter was confiscated, and Burns's former owner set out to capture him. Burns was arrested by a deputy marshal who, recalling Shadrach Minkins's escape, placed him under guard in chains in the federal courthouse. Efforts by black and white abolitionists to break into the courthouse with axes, guns, and a battering ram failed, although a deputy U.S. marshal was killed during the assault.

◆◆◆ **Read the Document**
Letter from Anthony Burns to the Baptist Church (1855)

President Franklin Pierce, a northern Democrat who in 1852 had been elected with southern support, sent U.S. troops to Boston—including marines, cavalry, and artillery—to uphold the law and return Burns to

The "trial" and subsequent return of Anthony Burns to slavery in 1854 resulted in the publication of a popular pamphlet in Boston. Documents like this generated increased support—and funds—for the abolitionist cause.

Virginia. Black minister Leonard A. Grimes and the vigilance committee tried to purchase Burns's freedom, but the U.S. attorney refused. In June 1854, with church bells tolling and buildings draped in black, thousands of Bostonians watched silently—many in tears—as Anthony Burns was marched through the streets to a ship that would take him to Virginia.

The spectacle of a lone black man, escorted by hundreds of armed troops, as he trudged from freedom to slavery moved even those people who had shown no special interest in or sympathy for fugitives or slaves. One staunchly conservative white man remarked, "When it was all over, and I was left alone in my office, I put my face in my hands and I wept. I could do nothing less." William Lloyd Garrison burned a copy of the Constitution on the Fourth of July as thousands looked on with approval.

Yet the government was unrelenting. A federal grand jury indicted seven black men and white men for riot and inciting a riot in their attempt to free Burns. One indictment was set aside on a technicality, and the other charges were then dropped because no Boston jury

PROFILE: Thomas Sims, a Fugitive Slave

By stowing away on a ship in Savannah, Georgia in 1851, Thomas Sims a twenty-three-year-old slave who was a bricklayer, escaped to Boston, where he worked briefly as a waiter. Sims unwisely sent a telegram to his wife who was free and still in Georgia, asking her to send money. The telegram was intercepted, and his owner, James Potter, quickly had agents locate and apprehend the young man. Sims was confined in chains on the third floor of the federal courthouse in Boston. Black leader Lewis Hayden tried to free Sims, but failed. Hayden had difficulty attracting support because many of the men whom he would ordinarily have depended on had fled when authorities began to search for those who had freed fugitive slave Shadrach Minkins a few weeks earlier.

One plan involved piling mattresses under Sims's window and having him jump about 30 feet to freedom. It was abandoned when bars were installed in the window. Neither Sims' lawyers' attempts to win a writ of habeas corpus nor public protests succeeded in gaining his freedom.

On April 11, 1851, a federal commissioner ordered Sims returned to his owner and slavery. At 5 AM on April 12 he was marched in the predawn darkness from the courthouse, "protected" by 200 Boston police and other armed law enforcement personnel, and taken to a ship in the harbor. A desperate plan to free him by twenty armed men aboard another vessel failed because Sims' ship sailed for Savannah before the other ship could get underway.

Opponents of the Fugitive Slave Law and defenders of Sims were stunned and enraged that they, the people of Boston, had been unable to help a man whose sole desire was for freedom. Boston was their cherished home of liberty. It was where a black man, Crispis Attucks, was among those slain in the Boston Massacre in 1770. It was where the Tea Party took place in 1773, it was where Paul Revere set out on his midnight ride in 1775.

Henry Thoreau, the Transcendental writer and author of *Walden*, who preferred calm reflection to angry denunciation, reacted in fury to the forcible return of Thomas Sims. He wrote, "A government which deliberately enacts injustice—& persists in it!—it will become the laughing stock of the world." Later that summer, Sims was sent to Charleston, and then to New Orleans, where he was auctioned off to a brick mason from Vicksburg, Mississippi. Sims spent the next 12 years enslaved as a mason in Mississippi. In 1863, during the Civil War, when Union forces under Gen. Ulysses S. Grant laid siege to Vicksburg, Sims again fled to freedom. This time his wife, child, and four black men joined him in the escape. Sims and his family returned to Boston, where they witnessed the return in 1865 of the all-black 54th Massachusetts Regiment from combat in South Carolina, Georgia, and Florida.

By 1877 Sims was in Washington, D.C. He obtained a job as a messenger in the Department of Justice through the intervention of U. S. Attorney General Charles Devens—the federal marshal who had arrested him in Boston in 1851.

◄ U. S. military forces were sometimes needed to enforce a law that an increasing number of Northerners had come to regard as unjust.

Read the **Document**
Anthony Burns
would convict the accused. Several months later, black Bostonians led by the Rev. Grimes purchased Burns for $1,300. He settled in St. Catherine's, Ontario, in Canada, where he died in 1862.

MARGARET GARNER

If the Burns case was the most moving, then Margaret Garner's was one of the most tragic examples of the lengths to which slaves might go to gain freedom for themselves and their children. In the winter of 1856, Margaret Garner and seven other slaves escaped from Kentucky across the Ohio River to freedom in Cincinnati. But their owner, Archibald Grimes, pursued them. Grimes, accompanied by a U.S. deputy marshal and several other people, attempted to arrest the fugitives at a small house where they had hidden. Refusing to surrender, the slaves were overpowered and subdued.

Before the fugitives were captured, Garner slit the throat of her daughter with a butcher knife rather than see the child returned to slavery. She was disarmed before she could kill her two sons. Ohio authorities charged her with murder, but by that time she had been returned to Kentucky and then sent to Arkansas with her surviving children to be sold. On the trip down the river, her youngest child and 24 other people drowned in a shipwreck, thereby cruelly fulfilling her wish that the child not grow up to be a slave. Margaret Garner was later sold at a slave market in New Orleans. (Her story was the basis of Toni Morrison's novel *Beloved,* which won the 1988 Pulitzer Prize for fiction and was made into a film by Oprah Winfrey in 1998.)

The Rochester Convention, 1853

In 1853, while northern communities grappled with the consequences of the fugitive slave law, African-American leaders gathered for a national convention in Rochester, New York. The **Rochester Convention**

Beginning in 1830 and continuing until the end of the 19th century, black leaders held a series of national conventions. Those that were held prior to the Civil War focused on the abolition of slavery and met in Northern cities such as Philadelphia, Cleveland, and Rochester. Following the war, the gatherings occurred in Washington and Nashville among other places with the emphasis on the rights and opportunities of African Americans.

warned that black Americans were not prepared to submit quietly to a government more concerned about the interests of slave owners than people seeking to free themselves from bondage. The delegates looked past the grim conditions of the times to call for greater unity among black people and to find ways to improve their economic prospects. They asserted their claims to the rights of citizenship and equal protection before the law, and they worried that the wave of European immigrants entering the country would deprive poor black northerners of the menial and unskilled jobs on which they depended. Frederick Douglass spoke of the need for a school to provide training in the skilled trades and manual arts. There was even talk of establishing a Negro museum and library.

Nativism and the Know-Nothings

Not only did many white Americans look with disfavor and often outright disgust at African Americans, but they were also distressed by and opposed to the increasing numbers of white immigrants coming to the United States. Hundreds of thousands of Europeans—mostly Germans and Irish—arrived in the 1840s and 1850s. In one year—1854—430,000 people arrived on American shores.

The mass starvation that accompanied the potato famine of the 1840s in Ireland drove thousands of Irish people to the United States, where they often encountered intense hostility. Native-born, Protestant, white Americans considered the Catholic Irish crude, ignorant drunks. Irish immigrants also competed with Americans for low-paying unskilled jobs. Anti-Catholic propaganda warned that the influence of the Vatican would weaken American institutions. Some even charged there was a Roman Catholic conspiracy to take over the United States. Mobs attacked Catholic churches and convents.

These anti-immigrant, anti-Catholic, anti-alcohol sentiments helped foster in 1854 the rise of a nativist third political party, the American Party—better known as the **"Know-Nothing Party."** (Its members were supposed to reply "I know nothing" if someone asked if they belonged to the party.) The Know-Nothings attracted considerable support. Feeding on resentment and prejudice, the party grew to one million strong. Most Know-Nothings were in New England, and they even for a short time took control of Massachusetts, where many of the Irish had settled. But the party was also strong in Kentucky, Texas, and elsewhere.

Although Know-Nothings opposed immigrants and Catholics, they disagreed among themselves over slavery and its expansion. As a result the party soon split into northern and southern factions and collapsed.

UNCLE TOM'S CABIN

No one contributed more to the growing opposition to slavery among white northerners than Harriet Beecher Stowe. Raised in a religious environment—her father, brothers, and husband were ministers—Stowe developed a hatred of slavery that she converted into a melodramatic but moving novel about slaves and their lives.

Uncle Tom's Cabin, or Life among the Lowly, was first published in installments in the antislavery newspaper *The National Era.* When it appeared as a book in 1852, it sold an astonishing 300,000 copies in a year. In the novel, Stowe depicted slavery's cruelty, inhumanity, and destructive impact on families through characters and a plot that appealed to the sentimentality of nineteenth-century readers. There was Little Eliza, with a babe in arms, barely escaping across the icy Ohio River from a slave owner in hot pursuit. There was Uncle Tom, the noble and devout Christian. Financial necessity forces Tom's decent master to sell the kindly slave to Simon Legree, a vicious brute and a northerner who has embraced slavery. Legree takes perverse delight in beating Tom until the gentle old man dies.

Harriet Beecher Stowe was a prolific writer. She wrote travel accounts, children's books, and ten adult novels. Easily her best-known work was *Uncle Tom's Cabin.* It was first published in serial form in the antislavery weekly newspaper *The National Era* when Stowe was forty years old.

Uncle Tom's Cabin moved northerners to tears and made slavery more emotional to readers who had previously considered it only a distant system of labor that exploited black people. In stage versions of the book that were later produced across the North, Uncle Tom was transformed from a dignified man into a pitiful and fawning figure eager to please white people—hence the emergence of the derogatory term "Uncle Tom."

Uncle Tom's Cabin infuriated white southerners. They condemned it as a grossly false depiction of slavery and their way of life. They pointed out correctly that Stowe had little firsthand knowledge of slavery and had never even visited the Deep South. But she had lived in Cincinnati for 18 years and witnessed with anguish the desperate attempts of slaves to escape across the Ohio River. In response to her southern critics, Stowe wrote *A Key to Uncle Tom's Cabin,* citing the sources for her novel. Many of those sources were southern newspapers.

The Kansas-Nebraska Act

After the Compromise of 1850, the disagreement over slavery's expansion intensified and became violent. In 1854 Senator Stephen Douglas introduced a bill in Congress to organize the Kansas and Nebraska Territories that soon provoked white settlers in Kansas to kill each other over slavery. Douglas's primary concern was to secure the Kansas and Nebraska region for the construction of a transcontinental railroad. Until 1853 it had been part of the Indian Territory that the federal government had promised would not be open to white settlement. To win the support of southern Democrats, who wanted slavery in at least one of the two new territories, Douglas's bill would permit Kansas residents to decide for themselves whether to allow slavery (see Map 10–2).

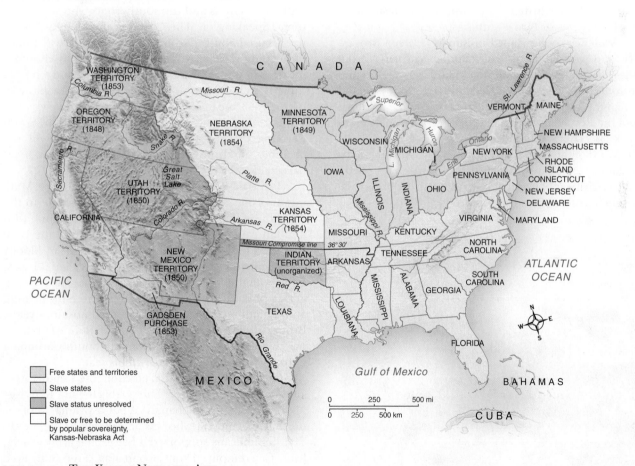

MAP 10–2 THE KANSAS-NEBRASKA ACT

This measure guided through Congress by Democratic Senator Steven A. Douglas opened up the Great Plains to settlement and to railroad development. It also deeply divided the nation by repealing the 1820 Missouri Compromise Line of 36° 30' and permitting—through popular sovereignty—the people in Kansas to determine slavery's fate in that territory. Eastern Kansas became a bloody battleground between proslavery and antislavery forces.

► *Where exactly could slavery conceivably exist where it had previously been prohibited?*

This proposal—known as **"popular sovereignty"**—angered many northerners because it created the possibility that slavery might expand to areas where it had been prohibited. The Missouri Compromise of 1820 banned slavery north of 36° 30' line of latitude. Douglas's **Kansas-Nebraska Act** would repeal that limitation and allow settlers in Kansas, which was north of that line, to vote on slavery there. Thus, if enough proslavery people moved to Kansas and voted for slavery, slaves and their owners would be legally permitted to dwell on land that had been closed to them for more than 30 years.

Douglas managed to muster enough votes in Congress to pass the bill, but its enactment destroyed an already divided Whig Party and drove a wedge between the North and South. The Whig Party disintegrated. Northern Whigs joined supporters of the Free-Soil Party to form the Republican Party, which was organized expressly to oppose the expansion of slavery. Southern Whigs drifted, often without enthusiasm, to the Democrats or Know-Nothings.

Violence soon erupted in Kansas between proslavery and antislavery forces. **"Border ruffians"** from Missouri invaded Kansas to attack antislavery settlers and to vote illegally in Kansas elections. The New England Emigrant Aid Society dispatched people to the territory, and the Rev. Henry Ward Beecher encouraged them to pack "Beecher's Bibles," which were firearms and not the Word of the Lord. By 1856 Kansas had 8,500 settlers, including 245 slaves, and two rival territorial governments. Civil war had erupted—prompting the press to label the territory "Bleeding Kansas."

"Border ruffians" were armed men from Missouri who crossed the border to support proslavery forces in the Kansas territory. They sought the legalization of slavery in Kansas. They—as well as the opponents of slavery—were willing to resort to violence to achieve their aims.

More than 200 people died in the escalating violence. Some 500 border ruffians attacked the antislavery town of Lawrence, damaging businesses and killing one person. Abolitionist John Brown and four of his sons sought revenge by hacking five proslavery men (none of whom actually owned slaves) to death in Pottawattamie. A proslavery firing squad executed nine Free-Soilers. John Brown reappeared in Missouri, killed a slave owner, and freed eleven slaves. Then he fled to plan an even larger and more dramatic attack on slavery.

Preston Brooks Attacks Charles Sumner

The violence in Kansas spread to Congress. In May 1856, Massachusetts Senator Charles Sumner delivered a tirade in the Senate denouncing the proslavery settlers in Kansas and the southerners who supported them. Speaking of "The Crime against Kansas," Sumner accused South Carolina Senator Andrew P. Butler of keeping slavery as his lover. Butler "has chosen a mistress to whom he has made his vows, and who . . . though polluted in the sight of the world, is chaste in his sight—I mean the harlot slavery." Butler was not present for the speech, but his distant cousin, South Carolina Congressman Preston Brooks, was in the chamber, and Brooks did not appreciate Sumner's verbal assault on a member of his family.

Two days later, Brooks exacted his revenge. Waiting until the Senate adjourned, Brooks strode to the desk where Sumner was seated and attacked him with a rattan cane. The blows rained down until the cane shattered and Sumner tumbled to the floor, bloody and semiconscious. Brooks proudly recalled, "I gave him about thirty first rate stripes." Sumner suffered lingering physical and emotional effects from the beating and did not return to the Senate for almost four years. Brooks resigned from the House of Representatives, paid a $300 fine, and went home to South Carolina a hero. He was easily reelected to his seat.

In the 1856 presidential election, the Democrats—although divided over the debacle in Kansas—nominated James Buchanan of Pennsylvania, another northern Democrat who was acceptable to the South. The Republicans supported a handsome army officer, John C. Fremont. Their slogan was "Free Soil, Free Speech, Free Men, and Fremont." But the Republicans were exclusively a northern party, and, with the demise of the Whigs, the South had become largely a one-party region. Almost no white southerners would support the Republicans, a party whose very existence was based on its opposition to slavery's expansion. Buchanan won the presidency with nearly solid southern support and enough northern votes to carry him to victory, but the Republicans gained enough support and confidence to give them hope for the 1860 election. Before then, however, the U.S. Supreme Court intervened in the controversy over slavery.

The *Dred Scott* Decision

Like most slaves, Dred Scott did not know his exact age. But when the Supreme Court accepted his case in 1856, Scott was in his fifties and had been entangled in the judicial system for more than a decade. Scott was born in Virginia, but by the 1830s he belonged to John Emerson, an army doctor in Missouri. Emerson took Scott to military posts in Illinois and to Fort Snelling in what is now Minnesota. While at Fort Snelling, Scott married Harriet, a slave woman, and they had a daughter, Eliza, before Emerson returned with the three of them to St. Louis. In 1846, after Emerson's death and with the support of white friends, Scott and his wife filed separate suits for their freedom. By agreement, her suit was set aside pending the outcome of her husband's litigation. Scott and his lawyers contended that because Scott had been taken to territory where slavery was illegal, he had become a free man.

Read the Document
A Slave Sues for Freedom (1857)

Scott lost his first suit, won his second, but lost again on appeal to the Missouri Supreme Court. His lawyers then appealed to the federal courts where they lost again. The final appeal in ***Dred Scott v. Sanford*** was to the U.S. Supreme Court. Although 79-year-old Chief Justice Roger Taney of Maryland had freed his own slaves, he was an unabashed advocate of the southern way of life. Moreover, Taney, a majority of the other justices, and President Buchanan were convinced that the prestige of the Court would enable it to render a decision about slavery that might be controversial but would still be accepted as the law of the land.

QUESTIONS FOR THE COURT

Taney framed two questions for the Court to decide in the Scott case: Could Scott, a black man, sue in a federal court? And was Scott free because he had been taken to a state and a territory where slavery was prohibited? In response to the first question, the Court, led by Taney, ruled that Scott—and every other black American—could not sue in a federal court because black people were not citizens. Speaking for the majority (two of the nine justices dissented), Taney

The *Dred Scott* case was front-page news on *Frank Leslie's Illustrated Newspaper* in 1857. Harriet and Dred with their two daughters are depicted sympathetically as members of the middle class rather than as abused and mistreated slaves.

emphatically stated that black people had no rights: "They had for more than a century before been regarded as beings of an inferior order; and altogether unfit to associate with the white race, either in social or political relations; and so far inferior that they had no rights which the white man was bound to respect; and that the negro might justly and lawfully be reduced to slavery for his benefit."

Taney was wrong. Although not treated as equals, free black people in many states had enjoyed rights associated with citizenship since the ratification of the Constitution in 1788. Black men had entered into contracts, held title to property, sued in the courts, and voted at one time in five of the original thirteen states.

A majority of the Court also answered no to the second question. Scott was not a free man, although he had lived in places where slavery was illegal. Scott, Taney maintained, again speaking for the Court, was slave property—and the slave owner's property rights took precedence. To the astonishment of those who opposed slavery's expansion, the Court also ruled that Congress could not pass measures—including the Missouri Compromise or the Kansas-Nebraska Act—that might prevent slave owners from taking their property into any territory. To do so, Taney implied, would violate the Fifth Amendment of the Constitution, which protected people from the loss of their life, liberty, or property without due process of law.

Following the decision, a new owner freed Dred and Harriet Scott. They settled in St. Louis, where he worked as a porter at Barnum's Hotel until he died of tuberculosis in 1858.

REACTION TO THE *DRED SCOTT* DECISION

The Court had spoken. Would the nation listen? White southerners were delighted with Taney's decision. Republicans were horrified. But instead of earning the acceptance—let alone the approval—of most Americans, the case further inflamed the controversy over slavery. But if white Americans were divided in their reaction to the *Dred Scott* decision, black Americans were discouraged, disgusted, and defiant. Taney's decision delivered another setback to a people—already held in forced labor—who believed that their toil, sweat, and contributions over the previous 250 years to what had become the United States gave them a legitimate role in American society. Now the Supreme Court said they had no rights. They knew better.

At rallies across the North, black people condemned the decision. Black writer, abolitionist, and women's rights advocate Frances Ellen Watkins Harper heaped scorn on the U.S. government as "the arch traitor to liberty, as shown by the Fugitive Slave Law and the Dred Scott decision."

Black leader H. Ford Douglas (no relation to Frederick Douglass) vented his rage at an American government and a constitution that could produce such a decision:

> To persist in supporting a government which holds and exercises the power . . . to trample a class under foot as an inferior and degraded race is on the part of the colored man at once the height of folly and the depth of pusillanimity. . . . The only duty the colored man owes to a constitution under which he is declared to be an inferior and degraded being . . . is to denounce and repudiate it, and to do what he can by all proper means to bring it into contempt.

Only Frederick Douglass found a glimmer of hope. He believed—and events proved him right—that the decision was so wrong that it would help destroy slavery:

> The Supreme Court . . . [was] not the only power in the world. We, the abolitionists and the colored people, should meet this decision, unlooked for and monstrous as it appears, in a cheerful spirit. The very attempts to blot out forever the hopes of an enslaved people may be one necessary link in the chain of events preparatory to the complete overthrow of the whole slave system.

WHITE NORTHERNERS AND BLACK AMERICANS

Many white northerners were genuinely concerned by the struggles of fugitive slaves, moved by *Uncle Tom's Cabin,* and disturbed by the *Dred Scott* decision. Yet as sensitive and sympathetic as some of them were to the plight of black people, most white Americans—including northerners—remained indifferent to, fearful of, or hostile to people of color. By the 1850s, 200,000 black people lived in the northern states, and many white people there were not pleased with their presence. Many white northerners, especially those living in southern Ohio, Indiana, and Illinois, supported the fugitive slave law and were eager to help return runaway slaves to bondage.

The same white northerners who opposed the expansion of slavery to California or Kansas also opposed the migration of free black people to northern states and communities. In 1851 Indiana and Iowa outlawed the emigration to their territory of black people, slave or free. Illinois did likewise in 1853. White male voters in Michigan in 1850 voted overwhelmingly—32,000 to 12,000—against permitting black men to vote. Only Ohio was an exception. In 1849 it repealed legislation excluding black people from the state.

These restrictive measures were not new. Most northern states had begun to restrict or deny the rights of black Americans in the early 1800s (see Chapter 7). Although only loosely enforced, the laws reflected the prevailing racial sentiments among many white northerners, as did the widespread antiblack rioting of the 1830s and 1840s. During the debate over excluding black people from Indiana, a state senator explained that the Bible revealed God had condemned black people to inferiority. "The same power that has given him a black skin, with less weight or volume of brain, has given us a white skin, with greater volume of brain and intellect; and that we can never live together upon an equality is as certain as that no two antagonistic principles can exist together at the same time."

Foreign observers were struck by northern racism. Alexis de Tocqueville, a French aristocrat, toured America in 1831 and wrote a perceptive analysis of

PROFILE: Martin Delany

"I thank God for making me a man, but Delany thanks Him for making him a black man."
—*Frederick Douglass on Martin Delany*

Martin Delany (1812–1885) was one of the first individuals to insist that African Americans should control their own destiny. In speeches, articles, and books, he evoked pride in his African heritage and stressed black people's need to rely on themselves and not on the white majority.

Delany was a medical doctor, a journalist, an explorer, an anthropologist, an army officer, and a political leader. He was born free in Charlestown, Virginia (now West Virginia), but the family moved to Chambersburg, Pennsylvania, in 1822. In 1831 Martin went to Pittsburgh, where he spent most of the next 25 years. His education was strongly influenced by Lewis Woodson, a young African Methodist Episcopal minister. He also studied medicine as an apprentice under two white physicians.

Delany was active in the Pittsburgh Anti-Slavery Society and helped slaves escape on the underground railroad. In 1843, he married Catherine Richards, the daughter of a well-to-do black butcher, and by 1860, they had seven children, each named for a well-known black figure: Toussaint Louverture, Alexander Dumas, Saint Cyprian, Faustin Soulouque, Charles L. Redmond, and their only daughter, Ethiopia Halle.

In 1843, Delany began publishing *The Mystery*, a four-page weekly newspaper devoted to abolition. It did not thrive, and in 1847 he joined Frederick Douglass briefly as the coeditor of *The North Star* (see Chapter 9). In 1850 Delany was admitted to the Harvard Medical School with two other black students for formal training, but they were forced to leave after one term because of the protests of white students.

In 1852, he wrote and published *The Condition, Elevation, Emigration and Destiny of the Colored People of the United States*—the first major statement of black nationalism. Delany observed, "We are a nation within a nation." He recommended that people of African descent abandon the United States and migrate to Central America, South America, or Hawaii. Delany was the key figure in organizing the National Emigration Convention in Cleveland in 1854.

He and his family left the United States for Canada and lived in Canada West (Ontario), where he organized a meeting of black people and John Brown in 1858. He also wrote a novel, *Blake*, about a West Indian slave who promotes revolution in the United States and Cuba. In 1859–1860, Delany visited Liberia and explored what is today Nigeria.

Once the United States began to enlist black troops in the Civil War, Delany helped recruit black men. His son Toussaint joined the famed 54th Massachusetts Regiment. Delany himself became one of the few black officers. In Charleston, South Carolina, he helped recruit two regiments of former slaves. After the war, he remained in South Carolina, where he entered politics. But he grew disillusioned with the Republicans—both black and white—who dominated southern governments during Reconstruction. He ran for lieutenant governor on a reform party ticket but lost. In 1876, he astounded many black people when he supported white Democrats who favored the restoration of white political control over South Carolina. When Democrats won the election, Governor Wade Hampton rewarded Delany by naming him to a minor political office. In 1878, a group of black South Carolinians and Georgians proposed migrating to Liberia. Delany became their treasurer, but he did not join them. The venture failed.

After he failed to win an appointment to a federal position in Washington, D.C., Delany went to Xenia, Ohio, and Wilberforce University, where his family had lived since the late 1860s. He died there in 1885.

► **Martin R. Delany** played a key role in the emergence of black nationalism in the nineteenth century. He was an abolitionist, a medical doctor, and a journalist. As a major he was the highest-ranking black military officer commissioned during the Civil War.

American society. He considered northerners more antagonistic toward black people than southerners. "The prejudice of race appears to be stronger in the states that have abolished slavery than in those where it still exists; and nowhere is it so intolerant as in those states where servitude has never been known."

The Lincoln-Douglas Debates

In 1858 Senator Stephen Douglas of Illinois, a Democrat, ran for reelection to the Senate against Republican Abraham Lincoln. The main issues in the campaign were slavery and race, which the two candidates addressed in debates around the state. In carefully reasoned speeches and responses, these experienced and articulate lawyers focused almost exclusively on slavery's expansion and its future in the Union. At Freeport, Illinois, Lincoln, a former Whig congressman, attempted to trap Douglas by asking him if slavery could expand now that the *Dred Scott* decision had ruled slaves were property whom their owners could take into any federal territory. In reply, Douglas, who wanted to be president and had no desire to offend northern or southern voters, cleverly defended "popular sovereignty" and the *Dred Scott* decision. He insisted that slave owners could indeed take their slaves where they pleased. But, he contended, if the people of a territory failed to enact slave codes to protect and control slave property, slave owners were not likely to settle there with their slaves.

Abraham Lincoln and Black People

But the **Lincoln-Douglas debates** did not always turn on the fine points of constitutional law or the fate of slavery in the territories. Thanks mainly to Douglas, who accused Lincoln and the Republicans of promoting the interests of black people over those of white people, the debates sometimes degenerated into crude exchanges about which candidate favored white people more and black people less. Douglas proudly advocated white supremacy. "The signers of the Declaration [of Independence] had no reference to the Negro . . . or any other inferior or degraded race when they spoke of the equality of men." He later charged that Lincoln and the Republicans wanted black and white equality. "If you, Black Republicans, think the negro ought to be on social equality with your wives and daughters, . . . you have a perfect right to do so. . . . Those of you who believe the negro is your equal . . . of course will vote for Mr. Lincoln."

Lincoln did not believe in racial equality, and he made that plain. In exasperation, he explained that merely because he opposed slavery did not mean he believed in equality. "I do not understand that because I do not want a negro woman for a slave I must necessarily have her for a wife." He bluntly added,

> I am not, nor ever have been in favor of bringing about in any way the social and political equality of the white and black races—that I am not nor ever have been in favor of making voters or jurors of negroes, nor of qualifying them to hold office, nor to intermarry with white people; and I will say in addition to this that there is a physical difference between the races which I believe will forever forbid the two races living together on terms of social and political equality.

But without repudiating these views, Lincoln later tried to transcend this blatant racism. "Let us discard all this quibbling about this man and the other man— this race and that race and the other race being inferior." Instead, he added, let us "unite as one people throughout this land, until we shall once more stand up declaring that all men are created equal." Lincoln stated unequivocally that race had nothing to do with whether a man had the right to be paid for his labor. He pointed out that the black man, "in the right to eat the bread, without leave of anybody else, which his own hand earns, he is my equal and the equal of Judge Douglas, and the equal of every living man."

Lincoln may have won the debate in the minds of many, but Douglas won the election. (State legislators— not voters—elected U.S. senators until the ratification of the Seventeenth Amendment in 1917.) Lincoln, however, made a name for himself that would work to his political advantage in the near future, and Douglas, despite his best efforts, had thoroughly offended many southerners by suggesting that slave owners would not risk taking their human property to a territory that lacked a slave code. Douglas also antagonized white southerners when he opposed the proslavery Kansas Lecompton constitution that he and many others believed had been fraudulently adopted. In two years, these disagreements over slavery would contribute to a decisive split in the Democratic Party.

John Brown and the Raid on Harpers Ferry

While Lincoln and Douglas were debating, John Brown was plotting. Following his attack on Pottawattamie in Kansas, Brown began to plan the overthrow of slavery in the South itself. In Canada in May 1858, accompanied by eleven white followers, he met 34 black people led by Martin Delany and appealed for their support. Brown was determined to invade the South and end slavery. He hoped to attract legions of slaves as his "army" moved down the Appalachian Mountains into the heart of the plantation system.

PLANNING THE RAID

Only one man at the Canadian gathering agreed to join the raid. Brown returned to the United States and garnered financial support from prosperous white abolitionists. Contributing money rather than risking their lives seemed more realistic to these men, who preferred to keep their identities confidential and thus came to be known as the Secret Six: Gerrit Smith, Thomas Wentworth Higginson, Samuel Gridley Howe, George L. Stearns, Theodore Parker, and Franklin Sanborn.

Brown also asked Frederick Douglass and Harriet Tubman to join him. They declined. By the summer of 1859, at a farm in rural Maryland, Brown had assembled an "army" consisting of 17 white men (including three of his adult sons) and five black men. The black men who enlisted were Osborne Anderson; Sheridan Leary, an escaped slave who had become a saddle and harness maker in Oberlin, Ohio; Leary's nephew John A. Copeland, an Oberlin College student; and two escaped slaves, Shields Green and Dangerfield Newby.

Newby was determined to rescue his pregnant wife Harriet and their six children, who were about to be sold from nearby Warrenton, Virginia, down the river to Louisiana. Harriet sent her husband a letter begging for him. "Oh Dear Dangerfield, com this fall . . . without fail . . . I want to see you so much that is one bright hope I have before me."

THE RAID

Brown's invasion began on Sunday night October 16, 1859, with a raid on Harpers Ferry, Virginia, and the federal arsenal there. Brown hoped to secure weapons and then advance south, but the operation went awry from the start. The dedication and devotion of Brown and his men were not matched by their strategy or his leadership. The first person Brown's band killed was ironically a free black man, Heyward Shepard, who was a baggage handler at the train station. The alarm went out, and opposition gathered.

Although they had lost the initiative, Brown and his men neither advanced nor retreated. Instead they remained in Harpers Ferry while Virginia and Maryland militia converged on them. Fighting began, and two townspeople, the mayor, and eight of Brown's men, including Sheridan Leary, Dangerfield Newby,

and two of Brown's sons, were killed. Newby died carrying his wife's letter. But Brown managed to seize hostages, including Lewis W. Washington, the great grandnephew of George Washington.

By Tuesday morning, Brown, with his hostages and what remained of his "army," were holed up in an engine house. U.S. Marines under the command of Robert E. Lee arrived, surrounded the building, and demanded Brown's surrender. He refused. The marines broke in. Brown was wounded and captured.

About 150 adult slaves lived near Harpers Ferry. Most of them were aware of the raid, and many of them joined the insurrection. Osborne Anderson provided pikes to slaves. Some of them acquired firearms. Several slaves managed to flee to freedom in the North. Perhaps a dozen black men—in addition to those who accompanied Brown—died during and after the raid.

There was no massive slave uprising. Shields Green and John A. Copeland fled but were caught. Osborne Anderson eluded capture and later fought in the Civil War. Virginia tried Brown, Green, and Copeland for treason. They were found guilty and sentenced to hang.

●●●─ **Read** the **Document**
An Abolitionist Is Given the Death Sentence (1859)

But the violence did not end. In the weeks that followed, the barn of every juror who convicted Brown was burned. Many horses and cattle died. They were apparently poisoned.

JOHN BROWN AT HARPER'S FERRY.

John Brown was captured in the Engine House at Harpers Ferry on October 18, 1859. He was quickly tried for treason and convicted. On December 2, 1859, he was hanged. His raid helped catapult the nation toward civil war.

THE REACTION

John Brown's raid had not proceeded as planned. But Brown and his men succeeded in intensifying the deep emotions of those who supported and those who opposed slavery. At first regarded as crazed zealots and insane fanatics, they showed they were willing—even eager—to die for the antislavery cause. The dignity and assurance that Brown, Green, and Copeland displayed as they awaited the gallows impressed many black and white northerners.

Black teacher and abolitionist Frances Ellen Watkins Harper wrote to John Brown's wife two weeks before Brown was executed to express compassion and admiration for both husband and wife:

> Belonging to the race your dear husband reached forth his hand to assist, I need not tell you that my sympathies are with you. I thank you for the brave words you have spoken. A republic that produces such a wife and mother may hope for better days. Our heart may grow more hopeful for humanity when it sees the sublime sacrifice it is about to receive from his hands. Not in vain had your dear husband periled all, if the martyrdom of one hero is worth more than the life of a million cowards.

John A. Copeland wrote his family that he was proud to die:

> I am not terrified by the gallows, which I see staring me in the face, and upon which I am soon to stand and suffer death for doing what George Washington was made a hero for doing. . . . Could I die in a manner and for a cause which would induce true and honest men more to honor me, and the angels more ready to receive me to their happy home of everlasting joy above? . . . I imagine that I hear you, and all of you, mother, father, sisters and brothers, say—"No, there is not a cause for which we, with less sorrow, could see you die."

Brown also eloquently and calmly announced his willingness to die as so many had died before him. "Now, if it is deemed necessary that I should forfeit my life for the furtherance of the ends of justice, and mingle my blood further with the blood of my children and with the blood of millions in this slave country whose rights are disregarded by wicked, cruel, and unjust enactments, I say, let it be done."

For many northerners, the day Brown was executed, December 2, 1859, was a day of mourning. Church bells tolled, and people bowed their heads in prayer. One unnamed black man later solemnly declared, "The memory of John Brown shall be indelibly written upon the tablets of our hearts, and when tyrants cease to oppress the enslaved, we will teach our children to revive his name, and transmit it to the latest posterity, as being the greatest man in the 19th century."

White southerners were traumatized by the raid and outraged that northerners made Brown a hero and a martyr. A wave of hysteria and paranoia swept the South as incredulous white people wondered how northerners could admire a man who sought to kill slave owners and free their slaves.

((•—[Hear the Audio
John Brown: An Address

Brown's raid and the reaction to it further divided a nation already badly split over slavery. Although neither he nor anyone else realized it at the time, Brown and his "army" had propelled the South toward secession from the Union—and thereby moved the nation closer to his goal of destroying slavery.

The Election of Abraham Lincoln

With the country fracturing over slavery, four candidates ran for president in the election of 1860. The Democrats split into a northern faction, which nominated Stephen Douglas, and a southern faction, which nominated John C. Breckenridge of Kentucky. The Constitutional Union Party, a new party formed by former Whigs, nominated John Bell of Tennessee. The breakup of the Democratic Party assured victory for the Republican candidate, Abraham Lincoln (see Map 10–3).

Lincoln's name was not even on the ballot in most southern states because his candidacy was based on the Republican Party's adamant opposition to the expansion of slavery into any western territory. Although Lincoln took pains to reassure white southerners that slavery would continue in states where it already existed, they were not persuaded. A South Carolina newspaper was convinced Lincoln would abolish slavery. "[Lincoln] has openly proclaimed a war of

TABLE 10–1   DEEPENING CRISIS OVER SLAVERY

1846	The Wilmot Proviso
1850	The Compromise of 1850
1854	The Kansas-Nebraska Act
1855–1856	Bleeding Kansas
1857	The *Dred Scott* Decision
1859	John Brown's Raid
1860	Lincoln elected president
1860	South Carolina secedes from the Union
1861	Formation of the Confederacy, Fort Sumter, beginning of the Civil War

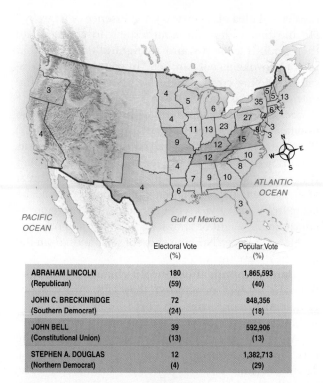

	Electoral Vote (%)	Popular Vote (%)
ABRAHAM LINCOLN (Republican)	180 (59)	1,865,593 (40)
JOHN C. BRECKINRIDGE (Southern Democrat)	72 (24)	848,356 (18)
JOHN BELL (Constitutional Union)	39 (13)	592,906 (13)
STEPHEN A. DOUGLAS (Northern Democrat)	12 (4)	1,382,713 (29)

MAP 10–3 THE ELECTION OF 1860

The results reflect the sectional schism over slavery. Lincoln carried the election, although he won only in northern states. His name did not even appear on the ballot in most southern states.

▶ *How was Lincoln able to win without getting any electoral votes from the South?*

extermination against the leading institutions of the Southern States. He says that there can be no peace so long as slavery has a foot hold in America."

A Georgia newspaper preferred a bloody civil war to a Lincoln presidency. "Let the consequences be what they may—whether the Potomac is crimsoned in human gore, and Pennsylvania Avenue is paved ten fathoms deep with mangled bodies . . . the South will never submit to such humiliation and degradation as the inauguration of Abraham Lincoln."

BLACK PEOPLE RESPOND TO LINCOLN'S ELECTION

Although they were less opposed to Lincoln than white southerners, black northerners and white abolitionists were not eager to see Abraham Lincoln become president. Dismayed by his contradictions and racism—he opposed slavery, but he tolerated it; he was against slavery's expansion, but he condemned black Americans as inferiors—many black people refused to

support him or did so reluctantly. The New York *Anglo-African* opposed both Republicans and Democrats in the 1860 election, telling its readers to depend on each other. "We have no hope from either [of the] political parties. We must rely on ourselves, the righteousness of our cause, and the advance of just sentiments among the great masses of the . . . people."

Abolitionists such as William Lloyd Garrison and Wendell Phillips believed Lincoln was too willing to tolerate slaveholding interests. But Frederick Douglass wrote, "Lincoln's election will indicate growth in the right direction," and his presidency "must and will be hailed as an anti-slavery triumph."

After Lincoln's election, black leaders almost welcomed the secession of southern states. H. Ford Douglas urged the southern states to leave the Union. "Stand not upon the order of your going, but go at once. . . . There is no union of ideas and interests in this country, and there can be no union between freedom and slavery." Frederick Douglass was convinced that there were men prepared to follow in the footsteps of John Brown's "army" to destroy slavery. "I am for dissolution of the Union—decidedly for a dissolution of the Union! . . . In case of such a dissolution, I believe that men could be found . . . who would venture into those states and raise the standard of liberty there."

▶ **Watch the Video**
Dred Scott and the Crises That Led to the Civil War

Disunion

When South Carolina seceded on December 20, 1860, it began a procession of southern states out of the Union. By February 1861 seven states—South Carolina, Mississippi, Alabama, Florida, Louisiana, Georgia, and Texas—had seceded and formed the Confederate States of America in Montgomery, Alabama. Before there could be the kind of undertaking against slavery that Douglass had proposed, Abraham Lincoln tried to persuade the seceding states to reconsider. In his inaugural address of March 4, 1861, Lincoln attempted to calm the fears of white southerners but informed them he would not tolerate their withdrawal from the Union. Lincoln repeated his assurance that he would not tamper with slavery in the states where it was already legal. "I have no purpose, directly or indirectly, to interfere with the institution of slavery in the States where it exists. I believe I have no lawful right to do so, and I have no inclination to do so."

Lincoln added that the "only" dispute between the North and South was over the expansion of slavery. He emphatically warned, however, that he would enforce the Constitution and not permit secession. "Plainly,

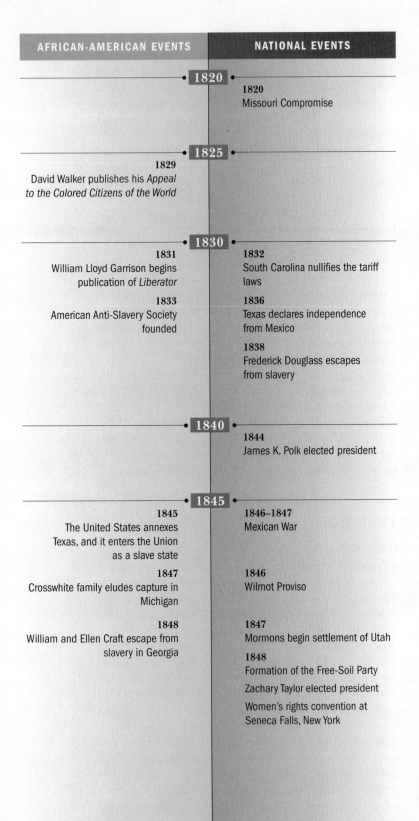

AFRICAN-AMERICAN EVENTS	NATIONAL EVENTS
	1820
	1820 Missouri Compromise
	1825
1829 David Walker publishes his *Appeal to the Colored Citizens of the World*	
	1830
1831 William Lloyd Garrison begins publication of *Liberator*	1832 South Carolina nullifies the tariff laws
1833 American Anti-Slavery Society founded	1836 Texas declares independence from Mexico
	1838 Frederick Douglass escapes from slavery
	1840
	1844 James K. Polk elected president
	1845
1845 The United States annexes Texas, and it enters the Union as a slave state	1846–1847 Mexican War
1847 Crosswhite family eludes capture in Michigan	1846 Wilmot Proviso
1848 William and Ellen Craft escape from slavery in Georgia	1847 Mormons begin settlement of Utah
	1848 Formation of the Free-Soil Party
	Zachary Taylor elected president
	Women's rights convention at Seneca Falls, New York

the central idea of secession is the essence of anarchy." He pleaded with white southerners to contemplate their actions patiently and thoughtfully, actions that might provoke a civil conflict. "In your hands, my dissatisfied fellow-countrymen, and not in mine, is the monumental issue of civil war."

Southern whites did not heed him. Slavery was too essential to give up merely to preserve the Union. Arthur P. Hayne of South Carolina had succinctly summed up its importance in an 1860 letter to President James Buchanan. "Slavery with us is no abstraction—but a great and vital fact. Without it our every comfort would be taken from us. Our wives, our children, made unhappy—education, the light of knowledge—all lost and our people ruined forever. Nothing short of separation from the Union can save us."

Barely a month after Lincoln's inauguration, Confederate leaders demanded that U.S. Army Major Robert Anderson surrender Fort Sumter in the harbor of Charleston, South Carolina. Anderson refused, and on April 12, 1861, Confederate artillery fired on the fort. In the aftermath, Virginia, North Carolina, Tennessee, and Arkansas joined the Confederacy. The Civil War had begun.

CONCLUSION

Virtually every event and episode of major or minor consequence in the United States between 1846 and 1861 involved black people and the expansion of slavery. From the Wilmot Proviso and the Compromise of 1850 to the *Dred Scott* decision and John Brown's raid, white Americans were increasingly perplexed about how the nation could remain half slave and half free. They were unable to resolve the problem of slavery's expansion.

Without the presence of black people in America, neither secession nor civil war would have occurred. Yet the Civil War began because white Americans had developed contradictory visions of the future. White southerners contemplated a future that inextricably linked their security and prosperity to slavery. The South, they believed, could neither advance nor endure without slavery.

Northern white people believed their future rested on the opportunities for white men and their families to flourish as independent, self-sufficient farmers, shopkeepers, and skilled artisans. For their future to prevail, they insisted the new lands in the American West should exclude the slave system that white southerners considered so vital. Neither northern nor southern white people—except for some abolitionists—ever believed people of color should fully participate as free people in American society or in the future of the American nation.

RECOMMENDED READING

Eric Foner. *Free Soil, Free Labor and Free Men: The Ideology of the Republican Party before the Civil War.* New York: Oxford University Press, 1970. An excellent overview of attitudes on free soil, slavery, and race.

Vincent Harding. *There Is a River: The Black Struggle for Freedom in America.* New York: Harcourt, Brace, Jovanovich, 1981. A tribute to and a masterful narrative about the black people who challenged the white majority in nineteenth-century America.

Leon Litwack. *North of Slavery: The Negro in the Free States, 1790–1860.* Chicago: University of Chicago Press, 1961. A story of black northerners and the discrimination they encountered.

James McPherson. *Battle Cry of Freedom: The Civil War Era.* New York: Oxford University Press, 1988. A superb account of the crisis leading up to the Civil War and of the war itself.

David Potter. *The Impending Crisis, 1848–1861.* New York: Harper & Row, 1976. Another fine account of the events leading up to the Civil War.

ADDITIONAL BIBLIOGRAPHY

CALIFORNIA AND THE COMPROMISE OF 1850

Eugene H. Berwanger. *The Frontier against Slavery: Western Anti-Negro Prejudice and the Slave Extension Controversy.* Urbana: University of Illinois Press, 1967.

Holman Hamilton. *Prologue to Conflict: The Crisis and Compromise of 1850.* Lexington: University Press of Kentucky, 1964.

Lynn M. Hudson. *The Making of "Mammy Pleasant," a Black Entrepreneur in Nineteenth-Century San Francisco.* Urbana: University of Illinois Press, 2003.

Rudolph M. Lapp. *Blacks in Gold Rush California.* New Haven, CT: Yale University Press, 1977.

THE FUGITIVE SLAVE LAW AND ITS VICTIMS

Stanley W. Campbell. *The Slave Catchers: Enforcement of the Fugitive Slave Law, 1850–1860.* Chapel Hill: University of North Carolina Press, 1968.

Gary Collison. *Shadrach Minkins.* Cambridge, MA: Harvard University Press, 1998.

Albert J. von Frank. *The Trials of Anthony Burns: Freedom and Slavery in Emerson's Boston.* Cambridge, MA: Harvard University Press, 1998.

Jonathan Katz. *Resistance at Christiana: The Fugitive Slave Rebellion at Christiana, Pennsylvania, September 11, 1851: A Documentary Account.* New York: Crowell, 1974.

Thomas P. Slaughter. *Bloody Dawn: The Christiana Riot and Violence in the Antebellum North.* New York: Oxford University Press, 1991.

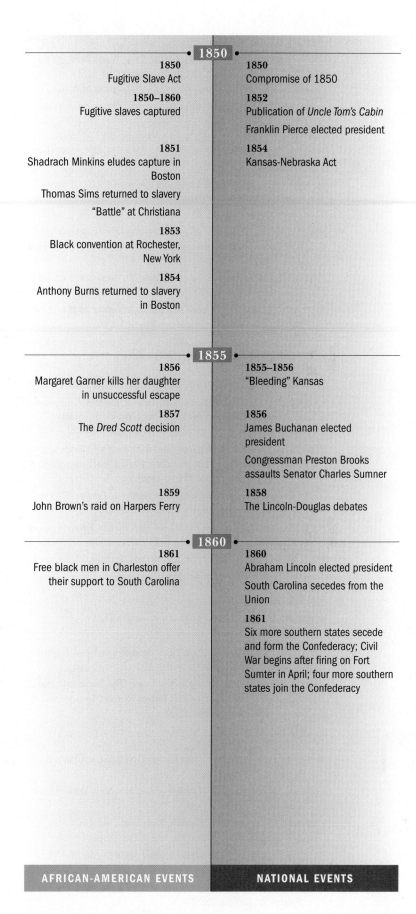

1850

AFRICAN-AMERICAN EVENTS

1850
Fugitive Slave Act

1850–1860
Fugitive slaves captured

1851
Shadrach Minkins eludes capture in Boston

Thomas Sims returned to slavery

"Battle" at Christiana

1853
Black convention at Rochester, New York

1854
Anthony Burns returned to slavery in Boston

1855

1856
Margaret Garner kills her daughter in unsuccessful escape

1857
The *Dred Scott* decision

1859
John Brown's raid on Harpers Ferry

1860

1861
Free black men in Charleston offer their support to South Carolina

NATIONAL EVENTS

1850
Compromise of 1850

1852
Publication of *Uncle Tom's Cabin*

Franklin Pierce elected president

1854
Kansas-Nebraska Act

1855–1856
"Bleeding" Kansas

1856
James Buchanan elected president

Congressman Preston Brooks assaults Senator Charles Sumner

1858
The Lincoln-Douglas debates

1860
Abraham Lincoln elected president

South Carolina secedes from the Union

1861
Six more southern states secede and form the Confederacy; Civil War begins after firing on Fort Sumter in April; four more southern states join the Confederacy

THE 1850s

Walter Ehrlich. *They Have No Rights: Dred Scott's Struggle for Freedom*. Westport, CT: Greenwood Press, 1979.

Don E. Fehrenbacher. *The Dred Scott Case: Its Significance in American Law and Politics*. New York: Oxford University Press, 1978.

William W. Freehling. *The Road to Disunion: Secessionists Triumphant, 1854–1861*. New York: Oxford University Press, 2008.

Henry Lewis Gates Jr. and Donald Yacovone, eds. *Lincoln on Race and Slavery*. Princeton, NJ: Princeton University Press, 2009.

Michael F. Holt. *The Fate of Their Country: Politicians, Slavery Extension, and the Coming of the Civil War*. New York: Hill and Wang, 2005.

Robert W. Johannsen. *Stephen A. Douglas*. New York: Oxford University Press, 1973.

Kenneth M. Stampp. *America in 1857: A Nation on the Brink*. New York: Oxford University Press, 1990.

Eric Walther. *The Shattering of the Union: America in the 1850s*. Wilmington, DE: Scholarly Resources, 2004.

JOHN BROWN AND THE RAID ON HARPERS FERRY

Louis A. DeCaro Jr. *"Fire from the Midst of You": A Religious Life of John Brown*. New York: New York University Press, 2002.

Paul Finkelman. *And His Soul Goes Marching On: Responses to John Brown and the Harpers Ferry Raid*. Charlottesville: University of Virginia Press, 1995.

Truman Nelson. *The Old Man John Brown at Harpers Ferry*. New York: Holt, Rinehart and Winston, 1973.

Stephen Oates. *To Purge This Land with Blood: A Biography of John Brown*. New York: Harper & Row, 1970.

Benjamin Quarles. *Blacks on John Brown*. Urbana: University of Illinois Press, 1972.

SECESSION

William L. Barney. *The Road to Secession*. New York: Praeger, 1972.

Steven A. Channing. *Crisis of Fear: Secession in South Carolina*. New York: Simon & Schuster, 1970.

Kenneth M. Stampp. *And the War Came: The North and the Secession Crisis, 1860–1861*. Baton Rouge: Louisiana State University Press, 1950.

ABRAHAM LINCOLN

Gabor Boritt, ed. *The Lincoln Enigma*. New York: Oxford University Press, 2001.

Orville Vernon Burton. *The Age of Lincoln*. New York: Hill and Wang, 2007.

David Herbert Donald. *Lincoln*. New York: Simon & Schuster, 1995.

Stephen B. Oates. *With Malice toward None: A Life of Abraham Lincoln*. New York: Harper & Row, 1977.

Benjamin Thomas. *Abraham Lincoln: A Biography*. New York: Alfred A. Knopf, 1952.

Ronald C. White Jr. *A. Lincoln: A Life*. New York: Random House, 2009.

NOVELS

Martin R. Delany. *Blake or the Huts of America*. Boston: Beacon Press, 1970.

Harriet Beecher Stowe. *Uncle Tom's Cabin, or Life among the Lowly*. New York: Modern Library, 1985.

RETRACING THE ODYSSEY

Black Heritage Trail, Boston, MA. http://www .afroammuseum.org/trail.htm. This is a 1.6-mile walking tour of fourteen sites. It begins at the Africa Meeting House (built in 1806) and includes the four-story home of black leader Lewis Hayden and his wife Harriet as well as Augustus Saint-Gaudens's powerful 1897 *Memorial to Robert Gould Shaw and the 54th Massachusetts Regiment*.

The Old St. Louis Court House, St. Louis, MO. http:// www.nps.gov/jeff/planyourvisit/och.htm. This restored structure was the scene of two of Dred Scott's trials. It contains some of the legal papers and newspaper articles involving the case.

The First Baptist Church, Chatham, Ontario, Canada. http://www.heritagefdn.on.ca/userfiles/HTML/nts_1_ 10024_1.html. On May 28, 1858, John Brown met with members of Chatham's black community—many of whom had fled to Canada to escape the fugitive slave law. Brown appealed for support to begin an armed uprising of slaves in the South. Fire destroyed the original structure in 1907, and the current church was built in 1908.

Harpers Ferry National Park, WV. http://www.nps.gov/ hafe/index.htm. Picturesquely situated in the Blue Ridge Mountains at the confluence of the Shenandoah and Potomac rivers, this is where John Brown and his "army" in October 1859 attempted to secure weapons to begin a slave rebellion.

REVIEW QUESTIONS

1. How and why did southern and northern white people differ over slavery? On what did white people of both regions agree and disagree about race and slavery?

2. If you were a northern African American in the 1850s, how would you have responded to the policies of the U.S. government?

3. If you were a white southerner in the 1850s, would you have been encouraged or discouraged by U.S. government policies?

4. Why did seven southern states secede from the Union within three months after Abraham Lincoln was elected president in 1860?

5. If you were a black person—either a slave or free—would you have welcomed the secession of the southern states? How might secession affect the future of your people?

myhistorylab Connections

www.myhistorylab.com
Review what you've learned in this chapter and explore the many documents, images,
research tools, and activities for this chapter to learn more about African-American history.

✓● Study and Review

READ

Read the Document

- The Compromise of 1850

- The Lincoln-Douglas Debate (1858)

- Northern State Defies Fugitive Slave Act (1855)

- New England Writer Portrays Slavery (1852)

- Letter from Anthony Burns to the Baptist Church (1855)

- Vilet Lester Letter to Miss Patsey Patterson (1857)

- A Slave Sues for Freedom (1857)

- A Senatorial Candidate Addresses the Question of Slavery (1858)

- An Abolitionist Is Given the Death Sentence (1859)

- Fugitive Slave Act

LISTEN

Hear the Audio

Hear the audio files for Chapter 10.

- *Remembering Slavery #1.* Recordings of former slaves talking about slavery.

- *John Brown: An Address.* Frederich Douglass, pamphlet excerpt.

RESEARCH

mysearchlab

Consider these questions in a short research paper.

Why did the conflict over slavery intensify in the 1840s and 1850s?

What efforts were made to resolve the conflict?

EXPLORE

Watch the Video

- Dred Scott and the Crises That Led to the Civil War

- Trials of Racial Identity in Nineteenth-Century America

- Harriet Beecher Stowe and the Making of *Uncle Tom's Cabin*

See the Map

- The Compromise of 1850

- The Compromise of 1850 and the Kansas-Nebraska Act

- Slave Population Patterns, 1790 and 1860

Read the Document

- Anthony Burns

III THE CIVIL WAR, EMANCIPATION, AND BLACK RECONSTRUCTION:
The Second American Revolution

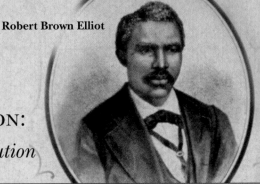

Robert Brown Elliot

RELIGION

1865–1870s Former slaves organize their own religious congregations across the South

1866–1870s Numerous black ministers elected to political office and leadership positions in the South

CULTURE

1865–1870s More than forty black colleges founded in the South

1867 Howard University established

1868 Elizabeth Keckley publishes *Behind the Scenes, or, Thirty Years a Slave and Four Years in the White House*

1869 More than 100,000 students attend Freedmen's Bureau schools in the South

POLITICS & GOVERNMENT

1861 Union Army rejects black volunteers

First Confiscation Act frees slaves who had been used by the Confederate Army

1862 Militia Act authorizes recruitment of black troops for the Union Army

First black troops fight for Union at Island Mountain, MO

1863 Emancipation Proclamation issued

Black troops assault Battery Wagner in Charleston Harbor

1864 Fort Pillow Massacre

1865 Confederate Congress votes to enlist 300,000 black troops

U.S. Congress creates the Freedmen's Bureau

Thirteenth Amendment abolishes slavery

Congress passes a Civil Rights Act

Southern states rejoin the Union and enact black codes

1865–1866 Black conventions held across the South

1867 Reconstruction Acts passed by Congress

1867–1868 Black people participate in southern states' constitutional conventions

1868 Fourteenth Amendment gives black people the rights of citizenship

SOCIETY & ECONOMY

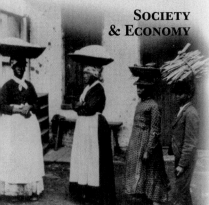

1862 Port Royal Experiment begins in South Carolina

1863 New York City draft riots attack African Americans

1864 Black National Convention meets in Syracuse, NY

1865 Freedmen's Savings Bank and Trust Company established

1866 Ku Klux Klan organized

New Orleans Massacre

White mob lynches twenty-four black men near Pine Bluff, AR

1869 Isaac Myers organizes the Colored National Labor Union

Susie King Taylor

Blanche K. Bruce

P. B. S. Pinchback

1870–1880	1880–1900	NOTEWORTHY INDIVIDUALS

1870 Colored Methodist Episcopal Church established

1870s Black people organize St. Mark's, the first African-American Episcopal congregation in Charleston, SC

1902 Susie K. Taylor publishes her memoir of nursing black troops in the Union Army

1872 Charlotte Ray becomes the first African-American woman lawyer

Alcorn A&M College, the first black state university, founded in Mississippi

1870 Fifteenth Amendment prohibits disfranchisement because of race

Hiram R. Revels, first African-American U.S. senator elected; Joseph Rainey, first African-American congressman elected

1870–1871 Enforcement Acts against Klan terrorism passed by Congress

1877 Reconstruction ends

1883 U.S. Supreme Court strikes down the Civil Rights Act of 1875

1872 Colfax Massacre in Louisiana

1874 Freedmen's Savings Bank closes

1876 Hamburg Massacre in South Carolina

Aaron A. Bradley
(1815–1881)

Elizabeth Keckley
(1818–1907)

Hiram R. Revels
(1822–1901)

Mifflin W. Gibbs
(1823–1915)

Richard H. Cain
(1825–1887)

Jonathan C. Gibbs
(c. 1827–1874)

Isaac Myers
(1835–1901)

William Whipper
(1835–1907)

James T. Rapier
(1837–1883)

Francis L. Cardozo
(1837–1903)

Charlotte Forten
(1837–1914)

P. B. S. Pinchback
(1837–1921)

Robert Smalls
(1839–1915)

Jonathan J. Wright
(1840–1885)

William H. Carney
(1840–c. 1901)

Blanche K. Bruce
(1841–1898)

Robert Brown Elliott
(1842–1884)

Frances Rollin
(1844–1901)

Susie King Taylor
(1848–1912)

Charlotte Ray
(1850–1911)

Katherine Rollin
(1851–1876)

Liberation:
African Americans and the Civil War

When the Civil War began, what was Abraham Lincoln's primary objective?

How did African Americans respond to the outbreak of the Civil War?

How did Lincoln's policies on slavery change as the Civil War continued?

Why did Lincoln issue the Emancipation Proclamation?

How did black and white people react to the Emancipation Proclamation?

How did African Americans affect the outcome of the Civil War?

▶ **The band of** 107th U.S. Colored Infantry at Fort Corcoran in Arlington, Virginia.

If the muse were mine to tempt it
And my feeble voice were strong,
If my tongue were trained to measures,
I would sing a stirring song.
I would sing a song heroic
Of those noble sons of Ham,
Of the gallant colored soldiers
Who fought for Uncle Sam! . . .
Ah, they rallied to the standard
To uphold it by their might;
None were stronger in the labors,
None were braver in the fight.
From the blazing breach of Wagner
To the plains of Olustee,
They were foremost in the fight
Of the battles of the free. . . .
And their deeds shall find a record
In the registry of Fame;
For their blood has cleansed completely
Every blot of Slavery's shame.
So all honor and all glory
To those noble sons of Ham—
The gallant colored soldiers
Who fought for Uncle Sam!

From "The Colored Soldiers," 1895, by
Paul Laurence Dunbar, whose father,
Joshua, served with the all-black 55th
Massachusetts Regiment

◄ **185,000 black men** fought for
the Union during the Civil War.

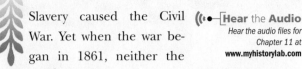

Slavery caused the Civil War. Yet when the war began in 1861, neither the Union nor the Confederacy entered the conflict with any intention or desire to change the status of black Americans. It was supposed to be a white man's war. White southerners would wage war to make the Confederacy a separate and independent nation free to promote slavery. White northerners took up arms to maintain the Union but not to free a single slave. African Americans who wanted to enlist in 1861 were rejected. The Union might be disrupted, but slavery was not going to be disturbed.

Both North and South expected a quick victory. No one anticipated that 48 months of brutal war would rip the nation apart. When the Civil War ended in April 1865, almost 620,000 Americans were dead—including nearly 40,000 black men. The Union was preserved. Four million people had been freed. Nothing in American history compares with it.

Lincoln's Aims

Throughout the war, President Lincoln's unwavering objective was to preserve the Union. Any policies that helped or hindered black people were subordinate to that goal. Following the attack on Fort Sumter in April 1861 and Lincoln's call for state militias to help suppress the rebellion, four more slave states—North Carolina, Virginia, Tennessee, and Arkansas—seceded from the Union and joined the Confederacy. For most of 1861, Lincoln was determined to do nothing that would drive the four remaining slave states—Delaware, Maryland, Kentucky, and Missouri—into the Confederacy. Lincoln feared that if he did or said anything that could be interpreted as interfering with slavery, those four states would leave the Union too.

Meanwhile, Lincoln called for 75,000 men to enlist in the military for 90 days of service to the national government. Many thousands of black and white men, far more than 75,000, responded. White men were accepted. Black men were rejected. Spurned by federal and state authorities, black men remained determined to aid the cause.

Black Men Volunteer and Are Rejected

Black people recognized long before most white northerners that the fate of the Union was inextricably tied to the issue of slavery and the future of slavery was tied to the outcome of the war. "Talk as we may," insisted the *Anglo-African*, a black New York newspaper,

> we are concerned in this fight and our fate hangs upon its issues. The South must be subjugated, or we shall be enslaved. In aiding the Federal government in whatever way we can, we are aiding to secure our own liberty; for this war can end only in the subjugation of the North or the South.

Black men in New York formed their own military companies and began to drill. In Boston, they drew up a resolution modeled on the Declaration of Independence and appealed for permission to go to war:

> Our feelings urge us to say to our countrymen that we are ready to stand by and defend our Government as equals of its white defenders; to do so with "our lives, our fortunes, and our sacred honor," for the sake of freedom, and as good citizens; and we ask you to modify your laws, that we may enlist—that full scope may be given to patriotic feelings burning in the colored man's breast.

Black men in Philadelphia volunteered to infiltrate the South to incite slave revolts but were turned down. In Washington, D.C., Jacob Dodson, a black employee of the Senate, wrote to Secretary of War Simon Cameron shortly after the fall of Fort Sumter volunteering the services of local black men. "I desire to inform you that I know of some 300 reliable colored free citizens of this city who desire to enter the service for the defense of the city." Cameron curtly rejected Dodson, "This Department has no intention at the present to call into the service of the government any colored soldiers."

Union Policies toward Confederate Slaves

Slaves started to liberate themselves as soon as the war began, but Union leaders had no coherent policy for dealing with them. To the disappointment of black northerners and white abolitionists, Union military commanders showed more concern for the interests of Confederate slave owners than for the people in bondage. In May 1861 General George B. McClellan reassured Virginia slave owners, "Not only will we abstain from all interferences with your slaves, but we will, with an iron hand, crush any attempt at insurrection on their part."

General Henry Halleck ordered slaves who escaped in the Ohio valley returned to their owners, and General Winfield Scott, the army's chief of staff, asked that Confederate slave owners be permitted to recover slaves who crossed the Potomac River to what they believed was the freedom of Union lines. In Tennessee in early 1862, General Ulysses S. Grant returned runaway slaves to their owners if the owners supported the Union cause but put them to work on fortifications if their owners favored secession.

"CONTRABAND"

Not all Union commanders were so callous. A month after the war began, three bondmen working on Confederate fortifications in Virginia escaped to the Union's Fortress Monroe on the coast. Their owner, a Confederate colonel, appeared at the fortress the next day under a flag of truce and demanded the return of his slaves under the 1850 Fugitive Slave Act. The incredulous Union commander, General Benjamin Butler, informed him that because Virginia had seceded from the Union, that law was no longer in force. Butler did not free the three slaves, but he

These African-American troops served as teamsters for the Union Army in Virginia. Most northern white people—including political leaders—believed that black men lacked the courage and fortitude for combat. They expected black men would do little more as soldiers than haul freight, erect fortifications, serve guard duty, and prepare food.

did not reenslave them either. He declared them **"contraband"**—enemy property—and put them to work for the Union. Soon, over a thousand slaves fled to Fortress Monroe. The white authorities may have thought of them as contraband, but it is doubtful that while crossing Union lines any slaves declared, "We are contraband." Rather, they were apt to insist, "We are free!"

On August 6, 1861, Congress clarified the status of runaway slaves when it passed the First Confiscation Act. Federal forces could seize any property that belonged to Confederates used in the war effort. Any slaves their masters used to benefit the Confederacy— and only those slaves—would be freed. Almost immediately, Union General John C. Fremont (the 1856 Republican presidential candidate) exceeded the strict limits of the act by freeing all the slaves belonging to Confederates in Missouri. President Lincoln countermanded the order and told Fremont that only slaves actively used to aid the Confederate war effort were to be freed. Lincoln worried that Fremont's decision would drive Missouri or Kentucky into the Confederacy.

Black leaders were—to put it mildly—displeased with Lincoln and with federal policies that both prohibited the enlistment of black troops and ignored the plight of the enslaved. To fight a war against the South without fighting against slavery, the institution on which the South was so dependent, seemed absurd. As Frederick Douglass stated, "To fight against slaveholders, without fighting against slavery, is but a half-hearted business, and paralyzes the hands engaged in it. . . . Fire must be met with water. . . . War for the destruction of liberty must be met with war for the destruction of slavery."

Others were less charitable. Joseph R. Hawley, a white Connecticut Republican, thought Lincoln was foolish to worry about whether the border states might leave the Union: "Permit me to say damn the border states. . . . A thousand Lincolns cannot stop the people from fighting slavery." In the New York *Anglo-African*, a letter writer who identified himself as "Ivanhoe" urged northern black men to decline any request to serve in Union military forces until the slaves were freed and black northerners received treatment equal to that of white people: "And suppose we were invited [to enlist], what duty would we then owe to ourselves and our posterity? . . . Our enslaved brethren must be made freedmen. . . . We of the North must have all of the rights which white men enjoy; until then we are in no condition to fight under the flag [which] gives us no protection."

Lincoln was unmoved. Union military forces occupied an enclave on South Carolina's southern coast and the sea islands in late 1861, and on May 9, 1862, General David Hunter ordered slavery abolished in South Carolina, Georgia, and Florida. Lincoln revoked Hunter's order and reprimanded him. Nevertheless, thousands of slaves along the South Carolina and Georgia coast threw off their shackles and welcomed Union troops as plantation owners fled to the interior.

LINCOLN'S INITIAL POSITION

For more than a year, Lincoln remained reluctant to strike decisively against slavery. He believed the long-term solution to slavery and the race problem in the United States was the compensated emancipation of slaves followed by their colonization outside the country. That is, slave owners would be paid for their slaves. The slaves would be freed but forced to settle in the Caribbean, Latin America, or West Africa.

Read the Document
The Working Men of Manchester, England, Write to President Lincoln on the Question of Slavery (1862)

As a Whig congressman in 1849, Lincoln voted for a bill that would have emancipated slaves and compensated their owners in the District of Columbia if it had passed. In 1861 he tried—but failed—to persuade the Delaware legislature to support compensated emancipation. Then in April 1862, at Lincoln's urging, Republicans in Congress (against almost unanimous Democratic opposition) voted to provide funds to "any state which may adopt gradual abolishment of slavery." Lincoln wanted to eliminate slavery from the border states with the approval of slave owners there and thus diminish the likelihood that those states would join the Confederacy.

But leaders in the border states rejected the proposal. Lincoln brought it up again in July. This time he warned congressmen and senators from the border states that if their states opposed compensated emancipation, they might have to accept uncompensated emancipation. They ignored his advice and denounced compensated emancipation as a "radical change in our social system" and an intrusion by the federal government into a state issue.

To many white Americans, Lincoln's support for compensated emancipation and colonization was a misguided attempt to link the war to the issue of slavery. But to black Americans, abolitionists, and an increasing number of Republicans, Lincoln's refusal to abolish slavery immediately was tragic. Antislavery advocates regarded Lincoln's willingness to purchase the freedom of slaves as an admission that he considered those human beings to be property. They deplored his seeming inability to realize the Union would not win the war unless slaves were liberated.

A Ride for Liberty—The Fugitive Slaves, 1862. On March 23, 1862, artist Eastman Johnson was with General George B. McClellan's Army of the Potomac near Manassas, Virginia. Just before dawn, Johnson witnessed a family of three fleeing slavery, and he was prompted to paint the episode. Oil on board, The Brooklyn Museum, Gift of Miss Gwendolyn O.L. Conkling. Eastman Johnson, A Ride for Liberty–The Fugitive Slaves, 1862, oil on board. The Brooklyn Museum, Gift of Miss Gwendolyn O.L. Conkling.

LINCOLN MOVES TOWARD EMANCIPATION

However, by the summer of 1862, after the border states rejected compensated emancipation, Lincoln concluded that victory and the future of the Union were tied directly to the issue of slavery. Slavery became the instrument Lincoln would use to hasten the end of the war and restore the Union. He told Secretary of the Navy Gideon Welles, "We must free the slaves or be ourselves subdued. The slaves were undeniably an element of strength to those who had their service, and we must decide whether that element should be with us or against us." Emancipation, Lincoln stressed, would "strike at the heart of the rebellion."

In cabinet meetings in July 1862, Lincoln discussed abolishing slavery. Except for Postmaster General Montgomery Blair, cabinet members supported emancipation. Blair feared that eliminating slavery would cost the Republicans control of Congress in the fall elections. Secretary of State William H. Seward supported abolition but advised Lincoln not to issue a proclamation until the Union Army won a major victory. Otherwise, emancipation might look like the desperate gesture of the leader of a losing cause. Lincoln accepted Seward's advice and postponed emancipation.

LINCOLN DELAYS EMANCIPATION

Nevertheless, word circulated that Lincoln intended to abolish slavery. But weeks passed, and slavery did not end. Frustrated abolitionists and Republicans attacked Lincoln. Frederick Douglass was exasperated with a president who had shown inexcusable deference to white southerners who had rebelled against the Union:

> Abraham Lincoln is no more fit for the place he holds than was [previous president] James Buchanan. . . . The country is destined to become sick of both [General George B.] McClellan and Lincoln, and the sooner the better. The one plays lawyer for the benefit of the rebels, and the other handles the army for the benefit of traitors. We should not be surprised if both should be hurled from their places before the rebellion is ended.

In his *Prayer of Twenty Millions*, Horace Greeley, editor of the *New York Tribune*, expressed his disappointment that the president had not moved promptly against slavery, the issue that had led the southern states to leave the Union and go to war: "We ask you to consider that Slavery [is the] inciting cause and sustaining base of treason. . . . We think timid counsels in such a crisis [are] calculated to prove perilous, probably disastrous." Greeley insisted that Lincoln should have long ago warned white southerners that secession would endanger slavery.

On August 22, 1862, Lincoln replied to Greeley and explained his priorities. Placing the preservation of the Union before freedom for the enslaved, Lincoln declared, "My paramount object in this struggle is to save the Union, and is not either to save or destroy slavery. If I could save the Union without freeing any slave I would do it; and if I could save it by freeing all the slaves, I would do it; and if I could do it by freeing some and leaving others alone, I would also do that." He concluded, "I have here stated my purpose according to my view of *official* duty, and I intend no modification of my oft-expressed *personal* wish that all men, everywhere, could be free."

BLACK PEOPLE REJECT COLONIZATION

Lincoln's policy on emancipation had shifted dramatically, but he remained committed to colonization. On August 14, 1862, Lincoln invited black leaders to the White House and appealed for their support for colonization. After condemning slavery as "the greatest wrong inflicted on any people," he explained that white racism made it unwise for black people to remain in the United States. "Your race suffer very greatly, many of them, by living among us, while ours suffer from your presence. There is an unwillingness on the part of our people, harsh as it may be, for you free colored people to remain among us. . . . I do not mean to discuss this, but to propose it as a fact with which we have to deal. I cannot alter it if I would." Lincoln asked the black leaders to begin enlisting volunteers for a colonization project in Central America.

Most black people were unimpressed by Lincoln's words and unmoved by his advice. A black leader from Philadelphia condemned the president. "This is our country as much as it is yours, and we will not leave it." Frederick Douglass accused Lincoln of hypocrisy and claimed that support for colonization would lead white men "to commit all kinds of violence and outrage upon the colored people."

Lincoln would not retreat from his support for colonization. Attempts were already under way to put compensated emancipation and colonization into effect. In April 1862 Congress enacted a bill to pay District of Columbia slave owners up to $300 for each slave they freed and to provide $100,000 to support the voluntary colonization of the freed people in Haiti or Liberia. In 1863 the government tried to settle 453 black American colonists at Ile à Vache, an island near Haiti. The settlers suffered terribly from disease and starvation. This sorry attempt at government-sponsored colonization ended in 1864 when the navy returned 368 survivors to the United States.

The Preliminary Emancipation Proclamation

Finally on September 22, 1862—more than two months after Lincoln first seriously considered freedom for the enslaved—the president issued the Preliminary Emancipation Proclamation. It came five days after General George B. McClellan's Army of the Potomac turned back an invasion of Maryland at Antietam by General Robert E. Lee's Army of Northern Virginia. This bloody but indecisive victory allowed Lincoln to justify emancipation. But this first proclamation freed no people that September—or during the rest of 1862. Instead, it stipulated that anyone in bondage in states or parts of states still in rebellion on January 1, 1863, would be "thenceforward, and forever free." Lincoln's announcement gave the Confederate states one hundred days to return to the Union. If any or all of those states rejoined the Union, the slaves there would remain in bondage. The Union would be preserved, and slavery would be maintained.

What were Lincoln's intentions? It might seem that he expected the Confederate leaders to give his offer serious consideration and perhaps return to the Union and thus was willing to free the slaves only as a last resort. But Lincoln knew there was virtually no chance that white southerners would return to the Union just because he had threatened to free their slaves. Most Confederates expected to win the war, thereby maintaining secession and safeguarding slavery. White southerners ridiculed the preliminary proclamation. Lincoln hoped, however, that the preliminary emancipation proclamation would prepare white northerners to accept freedom for slaves.

During the Civil War, Abraham Lincoln met with a free black family on the lawn of the Executive Mansion. A white woman and Union soldier are observers.

NORTHERN REACTION TO EMANCIPATION

In the Union, the Preliminary Emancipation Proclamation was greeted with little enthusiasm. Most black people and abolitionists, of course, were gratified that Lincoln had finally issued the proclamation. Frederick Douglass was ecstatic. "We shout for joy that we live to record this righteous decree." In *The Liberator*, William Lloyd Garrison wrote that it was "an act of immense historical consequence." But they also worried that—however remote the possibility—some slave states would return to the Union by January 1, denying freedom to those enslaved.

Many white northerners resented emancipation. One New York soldier, more concerned with defeating the South than freeing the slaves, reflected these views: "We must first conquer & then it's time enough to talk about the *dam'd niggers*." A northern newspaper editor vilified Lincoln as a "half-witted usurper" and the Proclamation as "monstrous, impudent, and heinous . . . insulting to God as to man, for it declares those 'equal' whom God created unequal."

Even before the announcement of emancipation, antiblack riots flared in the North. In Cincinnati in the summer of 1862, Irish dockworkers invaded black neighborhoods after black men had replaced the striking wharf hands along the city's riverfront. In Brooklyn, New York, Irish Americans burned a tobacco factory that employed black women and children.

POLITICAL OPPOSITION TO EMANCIPATION

Northern Democrats almost unanimously opposed emancipation. They accused Lincoln and the Republicans of "fanaticism" and regretted that emancipation would liberate "two or three million semi savages" who would "overrun the North" and compete with white working people. The Democratic-controlled lower houses of the legislatures in Indiana and Illinois condemned the Proclamation as "wicked, inhuman, and unholy." Republicans recognized the hostility among many white northerners to black people. Senator Lyman Trumbull of Illinois conceded that "there is a very great aversion in the West—I know it to be so in my state—against having free negroes come among us. Our people want nothing to do with the negro."

And as some Republicans had predicted and feared, the Democrats capitalized on dissatisfaction with the war's progress and with Republican support for emancipation to make gains in the fall elections. New York and New Jersey elected Democratic governors, and Democrats won 34 more seats in the U.S. House of Representatives, although the Republicans retained a majority. Overjoyed Democrats proclaimed,

"Abolition Slaughtered." Republicans took solace that their losses were not greater.

The Emancipation Proclamation

On January 1, 1863, Abraham Lincoln issued the **Emancipation Proclamation.** It was not the first step toward freedom. Since 1861 several thousand slaves had already freed themselves, but it was the first significant effort by Union authorities to assure freedom to nearly four million people of African descent who, with their ancestors, had been enslaved for 250 years in North America. The Civil War was now a war to make people free.

Read the **Document**
The Emancipation Proclamation (1863)

Black communities and many white people across the North celebrated. Church bells pealed. Poems were written, and prayers of thanksgiving were offered. Many considered it the most momentous day in American

The Emancipation Proclamation was essentially a military directive and not a ringing declaration of liberation. Nevertheless, its uninspiring words would free more than three million people from bondage by 1865. Decorative copies such as this circulated for many decades after the Civil War.

1861–1863

THE STEPS TO EMANCIPATION

APRIL 1861	Fort Sumter is attacked; Civil War begins.
MAY 1861	General Butler refuses to return escaped "contrabands" to slavery.
AUGUST 1861	General Fremont orders emancipation of slaves in Missouri; Lincoln countermands him.
AUGUST 1861	First Confiscation Act frees captured slaves used by Confederate Army.
APRIL 1862	Congress provides funds for compensated emancipation; border states spurn the proposal.
MAY 1862	Lincoln revokes General Hunter's order abolishing slavery in South Carolina, Georgia, and Florida.
SUMMER 1862	Lincoln concludes that Union victory requires emancipation.
SEPTEMBER 22, 1862	Lincoln issues Preliminary Emancipation Proclamation after Battle of Antietam.
JANUARY 1, 1863	Emancipation Proclamation takes effect.

history since July 4, 1776. Frederick Douglass had difficulty describing the emotions of people in Boston when word reached the city late on the night of December 31 that Lincoln would issue the Proclamation the next day. "The effect of this announcement was startling beyond description, and the scene was wild and grand. Joy and gladness exhausted all forms of expression, from shouts of praise to sobs and tears. . . . A Negro preacher, a man of wonderful vocal power, expressed the heartfelt emotion of the hour, when he led all voices in the anthem, 'Sound the loud timbrel o'er Egypt's dark sea, Jehovah hath triumphed, his people were free.'" Well into the twentieth century, New Year's Day was commemorated as Emancipation Day, a holiday black Americans zealously observed.

((•—Hear the Audio
Free at Last

LIMITS OF THE PROCLAMATION

Despite this excitement, the language of the Emancipation Proclamation was uninspired and unmoving. It lacked the eloquence of the Declaration of Independence or the address Lincoln would deliver after the Union victory at Gettysburg in July 1863. Lincoln dryly wrote that "as a fit and necessary measure for suppressing said rebellion . . . I do order and declare that all persons held as slaves within said designated States, and parts of States, are, and henceforth shall be free."

Moreover, by limiting emancipation to those states and areas still in rebellion, Lincoln did not include enslaved people in the four border states still in the Union or in areas of Confederate states that Union forces had already occupied. This included forty-eight counties in western Virginia that would soon become the state of West Virginia, parts of Tennessee, and thirteen parishes (counties) in Louisiana, including New Orleans (see Map 11–1). Thus, hundreds of thousands of people would remain in bondage despite the Proclamation. The immediate practical effect of the Proclamation was negligible. Slave owners in the Confederacy did not recognize Lincoln's authority, and they certainly did not free their slaves on January 1 or anytime soon thereafter. Yet the Emancipation Proclamation remains one of the most important documents in American history. It made the Civil War a war to free people as well as to preserve the Union, and it gave the Union cause moral authority. And as many black people had freed themselves before the Proclamation, many more would liberate themselves after.

EFFECTS OF THE PROCLAMATION ON THE SOUTH

The Emancipation Proclamation destroyed any chance that Britain or France would offer diplomatic recognition to the Confederate government. Diplomatic recognition would have meant accepting the Confederacy as a legitimate state equal in international law to the Union, and it would almost surely have led to financial and military assistance for the South. British leaders, who had considered recognizing the Confederacy, now declined to support a "nation" that relied on slavery while its opponent moved to abolish it. In this sense, the Proclamation weakened the Confederacy's ability to prosecute the war.

Even more important, it undermined slavery in the South and contributed directly to the Confederacy's defeat. While the Proclamation may not have freed any of those in bondage on January 1, 1863, word of freedom spread rapidly across the South. Black people—aware a Union victory in the war meant freedom—were far less likely to labor for their owners or for the Confederacy. More slaves ran away, especially as Union troops approached. Slave resistance became more likely, although Lincoln cautioned against insurrection in the Proclamation: "And I hereby enjoin upon the people so declared to be free to abstain from all violence, unless in necessary self-defence." The institution of slavery cracked, crumbled, and collapsed after January 1, 1863.

Without emancipation, the United States would not have survived as a unified nation. Abraham Lincoln, after first failing to make the connection between eliminating slavery and preserving the Union,

MAP 11–1 EFFECTS OF THE EMANCIPATION PROCLAMATION

When Abraham Lincoln issued the Emancipation Proclamation on January 1, 1863, it applied only to slaves in those portions of the Confederacy not under Union authority. No southern slave owners freed their slaves at Lincoln's command. But many black people already had freed themselves as well as family and friends in the aftermath of Lincoln's order. The Emancipation Proclamation was of extreme importance. It helped the Union win the war. It meant that at long last the U.S. government had joined the abolitionist movement.

▶ *Where, according to the map, did slaves reside who were to be freed under the terms of the Proclamation?*

came to understand it fully and grasped what freedom meant to both black and white people. In his annual message to Congress in December 1862, one month before the Proclamation, Lincoln described the importance of emancipation with a passion and with feelings that were absent in the Proclamation itself. "We know how to save the Union. The world knows we do know how to save it. We—even we here—hold the power, and bear the responsibility. In giving freedom to the slave, we assure freedom to the free—honorable alike in what we give, and what we preserve."

Black Men Fight for the Union

The Emancipation Proclamation not only marked the beginning of the end of slavery but also authorized the enlistment of black troops in the Union Army. Just as white leaders in the North came to realize the preservation of the Union necessitated the abolition of slavery, they also began to understand that black men were needed for the military effort if the Union was to triumph in the Civil War.

By early 1863 the war had not gone well for the all-white Union Army. Although Union forces had won victories in Kentucky and Tennessee and had captured New Orleans, the war in the east was a different matter (see Map 11–2). The Union's Army of the Potomac faced a smaller but highly effective Confederate Army—the Army of Northern Virginia—led by General

Robert E. Lee. Confederate troops forced a Union retreat from Richmond during the 1862 Peninsular Campaign. Union forces lost at the first and second battles of Bull Run. Their only victory over Lee at Antietam was followed by a crushing Union loss at Fredericksburg.

Like the decision to free the slaves, the decision to employ black troops proceeded neither smoothly nor logically. The commitment to the Civil War as a white man's war was entrenched, and many white northerners opposed the initial attempts to enlist black troops. As with emancipation, Lincoln moved slowly from outright opposition to cautious acceptance to enthusiastic support for enlisting black men in the Union Army.

Although black men had fought well in the War for Independence and the War of 1812, they were legally prohibited from joining the regular U.S. Army. The Militia Act of 1792 also barred them from the state militias. In 1861 a few black men were able to join Union units and go off to war. H. Ford Douglas, who had a fair complexion, enlisted in the all-white 95th Illinois Infantry, a volunteer regiment.

Read the Document
Letter from H. Ford Douglas to Frederick Douglass's Monthly (1863)

THE FIRST SOUTH CAROLINA VOLUNTEERS

Some Union officers recruited black men long before emancipation was proclaimed and before most white northerners were prepared to accept, much

1861–62

1863

MAP 11–2   THE COURSE OF THE CIVIL WAR

Although the outcome of the Civil War remained in doubt until the autumn of 1864, Union armies, as well as a Union naval blockade, applied increasing pressure on the eleven Confederate states beginning in 1862. Black people freed themselves as Union forces carved out an enclave on the South Carolina coast, captured New Orleans, and pushed through Kentucky and Tennessee into Mississippi and Arkansas. Following the successful Union siege of Vicksburg in 1863, the Confederacy was divided along the Mississippi River. In 1864 General Ulysses S. Grant's Army of the Potomac drove General Robert E. Lee's Army of Northern Virginia into entrenchments around Richmond and Petersburg. General William Tecumseh Sherman marched from Atlanta to Savannah and then into the Carolinas. Several thousand more black people liberated themselves. The war ended in April 1865 with Lee's surrender to Grant at Appomattox Court House and Joseph E. Johnston's capitulation to Sherman near Durham, North Carolina.

▶ *Based on an examination of these maps, what appears to have been the strategy of Union military forces to defeat the Confederacy?*

1864–65

less welcome, black troops. In May 1862 General David Hunter began recruiting former slaves along the South Carolina coast and the sea islands, an area Union forces had captured in late 1861. But some black men did not want to enlist, and Hunter used white troops to force black men to "volunteer" for military service. He managed to organize a 500-man regiment—the **First South Carolina Volunteers.**

The former slaves were outfitted in bright red pants, with blue coats and broad-brimmed hats. Through the summer of 1862, Hunter trained and drilled the regiment while awaiting official authorization and funds to pay them. When Congress balked, Hunter disbanded all but one company of the regiment that August. The troops were dispersed, unpaid and disappointed. The surviving company was sent to

St. Simon's Island off the Georgia coast to protect former slaves.

Although Congress failed to support Hunter, it did pass the Second Confiscation Act and the Militia Act of 1862, which authorized President Lincoln to enlist black men. In Louisiana that fall, two regiments of free black men, the Native Guards, were accepted for federal service, and General Benjamin Butler organized them into the Corps d'Afrique. General Rufus Saxton gained the approval of Secretary of War Edwin Stanton

to revive Hunter's dispersed regiment and to recall the company that had been sent to St. Simon's Island.

As commander, Saxton appointed Thomas Wentworth Higginson. Higginson was an ardent white abolitionist, one of the Secret Six who had provided financial support for John Brown's raid on Harpers Ferry. He was determined not merely to end slavery but to prove that black people were equal to white people, a proposition most white people regarded as preposterous. Disposing of the unit's gaudy red trousers, Higginson set out to

PROFILE: Elizabeth Keckley

Born a slave in 1818, Elizabeth Keckley became a dressmaker for First Lady Mary Todd Lincoln and later wrote one of the first personal accounts of life inside the Lincoln White House. Elizabeth Keckley had experienced the exploitation and degradation common to thousands of slave women. She was born in Dinwiddie Court House, Virginia, and spent her childhood as a slave of the Burwell family. She saw slaves beaten and sold away from their families. She watched as a young boy was sold away from his mother so his owner could buy pigs.

During adolescence, she was loaned to a North Carolina slave owner and beaten and eventually raped. She described what happened: "I was regarded as fair-looking for one of my race, and for four years a white man—I spare the world his name—had base designs upon me. I do not care to dwell upon this subject for it is one that is fraught with pain. Suffice it to say that he persecuted me for four years, and I—I became a mother. The child of which he was the father was the only child I ever brought into the world."

Later one of the Burwell daughters took Keckley and her son George to St. Louis. She already knew how to sew, and she became a proficient seamstress. She also married a slave, James Keckley, but they soon separated. Keckley was able to purchase herself and her son for $1,200. She learned to read and write. In 1860 she moved to Washington, D.C., and attracted a prosperous clientele that included such prominent politicians' wives as Varma Davis, the wife of Mississippi Senator Jefferson Davis, soon to be president of the Confederacy.

After the Lincolns arrived in Washington, Keckley began making dresses for the First Lady and

became Mrs. Lincoln's confidante and traveling companion. She helped convert Mrs. Lincoln, whose family owned slaves in Kentucky, to strong antislavery views. Both women lost sons. Keckley's son George was killed early in the Civil War in Missouri fighting for the Union. Eleven-year-old Willie Lincoln died of a fever in 1862 in the White House. With Mrs. Lincoln's assistance, Keckley founded the Contraband Relief Association to help former slaves in Washington.

In 1868 she published *Behind the Scenes: Or, Thirty Years a Slave and Four Years in the White House.* Although it was a favorable account of life in the Lincoln White House, the book upset the Lincoln family. Keckley denied she had violated Mrs. Lincoln's privacy. "If I have betrayed confidence in anything I have published it has been to place Mrs. Lincoln in better light before the world. My own character as well as the character of Mrs. Lincoln, is at stake, since I have been intimately associated with the lady in the most eventful periods of her life."

Elizabeth Keckley spent the rest of her own life living off the pension from her son's service as a Union soldier. She died in Washington in 1907 at the Home for Destitute Women and Children, which she had helped found years earlier.

 Read the Document

Elizabeth Keckley, *Behind the Scenes: Or, Thirty Years a Slave, and Four Years in the White House, 1868*

Poised with their rifles, these African-American soldiers were members of the Twenty-first U.S. Colored Infantry at the battle of Dutch Gap in Virginia in August 1864.

mold this regiment of mostly former slaves into an effective fighting force. On Emancipation Day, January 1, 1863, near Beaufort, South Carolina, the First South Carolina Volunteer Regiment was inducted into the U.S. Army.

THE SECOND SOUTH CAROLINA VOLUNTEERS

A month later, the Second South Carolina Volunteers began enrolling ex-slaves, many from Georgia and Florida. James Montgomery, another former financial supporter of John Brown, commanded them. Montgomery was determined that the regiment would wipe out all vestiges of slavery, especially the homes, plantations, and personal possessions of families who owned slaves. But like Hunter, Montgomery found that many former slaves were reluctant to volunteer for military service, so he also used force to recruit them. He concluded that black men responded to the call to arms much the way white men did, except black men were less likely to desert once they joined the army:

> Finding it somewhat difficult to induce Negroes to enlist, we resolved to the draft. The negroes reindicate their claim to humanity by shirking the

draft in every possible way; acting exactly like white men under similar circumstances. . . . The only difference that I notice is, the negro, after being drafted does not desert; but once dressed in the uniform with arms in his hands he feels himself a man; and acts like one.

THE 54TH MASSACHUSETTS REGIMENT

While ex-slaves joined the Union ranks in South Carolina, free black men in the North enlisted in what would become the most famous black unit, the **54th Massachusetts Regiment.** In January 1863 Governor John A. Andrew received permission from Secretary of War Stanton to raise a black regiment, but because few black men lived in Massachusetts, Andrew asked prominent black men across the North for help. The **Black Committee**—as it became known—included Frederick Douglass, Martin Delany, Charles Remond, and Henry Highland Garnet.

These black leaders were convinced that by serving in the military, black men would prove they deserved to be treated as equals and had earned the right to be citizens. Frederick Douglass put it succinctly: "Once let the black man get upon his person the brass letters, U.S.; let him get an eagle on his button, and a musket on his shoulder and bullets in his pocket, and there is no power on earth which can deny that he has earned the right to citizenship." Douglass's sons, Charles and Lewis, joined the 54th.

Lincoln, who had opposed emancipation and resisted enlisting black troops, became an enthusiastic supporter of black men in the Union Army. Writing to Andrew Johnson, the Union military governor of Tennessee, Lincoln perhaps overoptimistically predicted that, "the bare sight of fifty thousand armed, and drilled black soldiers on the banks of the Mississippi, would end the rebellion at once. And who doubts that we can present that sight, if we but take hold in earnest."

Governor Andrew selected 25-year-old Robert Gould Shaw to command the 54th Massachusetts Regiment. Shaw was a Harvard graduate from a prominent Massachusetts family, and he had already been wounded at the battle at Antietam. Although not an active abolitionist, he opposed slavery and was determined to prove that black men would fight well. The men the Black Committee recruited came from most of the northern states. Their average age was around 25, and virtually all of them were literate. They were farmers, seamen, butchers, blacksmiths, and teamsters. Only one of them had grown up in a slave state. As the ranks of the 54th filled, the 55th Massachusetts Regiment and the all-black 5th Massachusetts Cavalry Regiment were also formed.

On May 28, 1863, the 54th paraded through Boston to board a ship for the trip to South Carolina and the war. Thousands turned out to see the black men in blue uniforms. As they passed the home of fiery abolitionist William Lloyd Garrison, he stood erect with a bust of John Brown. As they passed the custom-house where Crispus Attucks and four others had been killed in the Boston Massacre in 1770, the regiment sang "John Brown's Body." The departure of the 54th from the city was perhaps the most emotional event Boston had witnessed since Anthony Burns had been forcibly returned to slavery in 1854.

BLACK SOLDIERS CONFRONT DISCRIMINATION

But the enthusiastic departure could not disguise the discrimination and hostility that black troops faced during the war. Many white northerners would accept neither the presence of black troops nor the idea that black men could endure combat. Many white people tolerated black troops only because they preferred that a black man die rather than a white man. A crude bit of verse in an Irish dialect that reflected this racism circulated during the war:

Sambo's Right to be Kilt

Some tell us 'tis a burnin' shame
    To Make the naygers fight;
And that the thrade of bein' kilt
    Belongs but to the white;
But as for me, upon my sowl!
    So liberal are we here,
I'll let Sambo be murthered instead of myself,
    On every day of the Year.

In the same vein, a white Union soldier wrote that a "Negro can fall from a rebel shot as well as me or my friends, and better them than us."

That black troops would serve in separate, all-black units was a matter of course. No one seriously proposed that black men integrate all-white regiments. In 1863 the War Department created the Bureau of Colored Troops, and the Union Army remained segregated throughout the war. The only exceptions were the officers of the black regiments.

Almost all black troops had white officers. Yet many white officers, convinced such service would taint their military record, refused to command black troops. Others believed black men could not be trained for combat. Even those white officers who were willing to command black troops sometimes regarded their men as "niggers" suited only for work or fatigue duty. When the 110th U.S. Colored Infantry joined General William Tecumseh Sherman's army on its march through Georgia and South Carolina in 1864 and 1865, Sherman kept them out of combat. Some were armed with picks and axes. Others served as hospital guards and teamsters.

Black soldiers were paid less than white soldiers. Based on the assumption that black troops would be used almost exclusively for construction, transportation, cooking, and burial details, and not for fighting, the War Department authorized a lower pay scale for them. A white private earned $13 per month, a black private $10 per month. This demoralized black soldiers, particularly after they had shown they were more than capable of fighting.

The 54th Massachusetts Regiment refused to accept their pay until they received equal pay. To take no compensation was an enormous sacrifice for men who had wives, children, and families to support. For some, it was more than a monetary loss. Sergeant William Walker insisted—despite orders—that the men in his company take no pay until they received equal pay. He was charged with mutiny, convicted, and shot. In Texas, a soldier in a black artillery unit from Rhode Island threatened a white officer in the dispute over pay. The white lieutenant shot and killed him, and the regiment's commander declined to press charges.

The pay issue festered for nearly two years. Finally, near the end of the war, Congress enacted a compromise, but many black soldiers remained dissatisfied. The law equalized pay between black and white troops but made it retroactive only to January 1, 1864—except

Read the Document
James Henry Gooding, Letter to President Lincoln (1863)

for black men who had never been slaves. Therefore, the thousands of black men who had been slaves and had joined the military before January 1, 1864, would not be entitled to equal pay for the entire period of their service. The War Department compounded the problem with bureaucratic delays.

BLACK MEN IN COMBAT

Once black men put on the Union uniform, they took part in almost every battle that was fought during the rest of the Civil War. Black troops not only faced an enemy dedicated to the belief that black people belonged in slavery but also confronted white northerners' doubts about their fighting abilities. Yet by war's end, black units had suffered disproportionately more casualties than white units.

In October 1862, the first black unit went into combat in Missouri. James H. Lane, a white Free-Soiler, recruited 500 black men in Kansas. Most were runaway slaves from Missouri and Arkansas. After hasty training, they advanced against a Confederate position at

This young man is Jackson. In the first photo he is shown as a slave who worked as a servant in the Confederate Army. In the second photo he has been freed and has joined the U.S. Colored Troops as a drummer.

Island Mountain. The black troops held off an attack until reinforcements repulsed the Confederates. Soon thereafter, the black unit became the First Kansas Colored Infantry.

On July 17, 1863, at Honey Springs in Indian Territory (now Oklahoma), the Kansas soldiers attacked a Confederate force of white Texans and Cherokee Indians. After a 20-minute battle, the black troops broke through the southern line, won a victory, and captured the flags of a Texas regiment.

In January 1863, Thomas Wentworth Higginson led the First South Carolina Volunteers on raids on the Georgia and Florida coasts. At one point, they were surrounded at night by Confederate cavalry but fought their way out and escaped.

On June 3, 1863, the 54th Massachusetts Regiment arrived in South Carolina and joined the raids in Georgia. Other raids in the Carolina low country devastated rice plantations and liberated hundreds of slaves.

THE ASSAULT ON BATTERY WAGNER

Since 1861 and the Confederate capture of Fort Sumter in Charleston harbor, Union leaders had been determined to retake the fort and occupy nearby Charleston—the heart of secession. In 1863 Union commanders began a land and sea offensive to seize the fort. But **Battery Wagner,** a fortified installation on the northern tip of Morris Island, guarded the entrance to the harbor.

Frustrated in their efforts to enter the harbor, Major General Quincy A. Gilmore and Rear Admiral John Dahlgren decided on a full-scale assault on Wagner. After an unsuccessful attack by white troops, Colonel Shaw volunteered to lead the 54th in a second attack on the battery.

To improve the Union's chances, artillery fired more than 9,000 shells on Wagner on July 18, 1863. Everyone but the fort's Confederate defenders was convinced that no one could survive the bombardment. In fact, it had killed only eight of the 1,620 defenders.

At sunset, 650 men of the first brigade of the 54th prepared to lead more than 5,000 Union troops in storming the battery. The regiment was tired and hungry but eager for the assault. Colonel Shaw told his troops, "Now I want you to prove yourselves men."

At 7:45 P.M., the 54th charged and was met by heavy rifle and artillery fire. Within minutes, the sand was littered with injured and dying men. Sergeant

Major Lewis Douglass (the son of Frederick Douglass) was among those who took part. The 54th reached the walls, only to be thrown back in hand-to-hand combat. Shaw was killed.

Sergeant Major William H. Carney, although wounded four times, saved the regiment's flags. In May 1900, he was awarded the Medal of Honor for his gallantry that night.

Although white troops supported the 54th, the attack could not be sustained, and the battle was over by 1 A.M. But within days, the courage of the 54th was known across the North, putting to rest—for a time—the myth that black men lacked the nerve to fight.

The day after the attack, Shaw and 20 of his men were buried in a trench outside Wagner. Several wounded men had drowned when the tide came in. Altogether 246 black and white men were killed, 890 were wounded, and 391 were taken prisoner. Forty-two percent of the men of the 54th were killed or injured, and 80 men were taken prisoner.

Union forces never took Wagner. The Confederates abandoned Charleston as the war was ending in February 1865. Black Union troops—the 21st U.S. Colored Infantry and the 55th Massachusetts Regiment—occupied the city. Years later Charles Crowley recalled the scene: "Never, while memory holds power to retain anything, shall I forget the thrilling strain of music of the Union, as sung by our sable soldiers when marching up Meeting Street with the battle stained banners flapping in the breeze."

●●◆─ Read the Document
"I Hope to Fall with My Face to the Foe": Lewis Douglass Describes the Battle of Fort Wagner (1863)

OLUSTEE

On February 20, 1864, the 54th fought again and was joined by two black regiments—the First North Carolina and the Eighth U.S. of Pennsylvania—and six white regiments at the battle at Olustee in northern Florida. After almost five hours of combat, Confederate forces forced a Union retreat. The 54th had marched 110 miles in 100 hours before entering the engagement.

THE CRATER

But as impressive as black troops often were in battle, northern commanders sometimes hesitated to commit them to combat. In 1864, after Union troops laid siege to Petersburg, Virginia, white soldiers of the 48th Pennsylvania, who had been coal miners before the

On the evening of July 18, 1863, more than six hundred black men led by their white commander, Colonel Robert Gould Shaw, attacked the heavily fortified Battery Wagner on Morris Island near the southern approach to Charleston harbor. They made a frontal assault through withering fire and managed to breach the battery before Confederate forces threw them back. Shaw was killed, and the 54th suffered heavy losses. It was a defining moment of the Civil War, demonstrating to skeptical white people the valor and determination of black troops.

war, offered to dig a tunnel and set off an explosion under Confederate lines. General Ambrose Burnside assigned black troops to be prepared to lead the attack after the blast.

Four tons of powder were placed in the tunnel, but only hours before the blast was set to go off, Burnside's superior, General George Meade, replaced the black troops with inadequately trained white soldiers commanded by an alcoholic. Meade either lacked confidence in the black unit or was worried he would be blamed for using black men as shields for white soldiers if the attack failed.

On July 30, 1864, at 4:45 A.M., what was perhaps the largest man-made explosion in history up to that time buried a Confederate regiment and an artillery battery and created a crater 170 feet long, 60 feet wide, and 30 feet deep. But the white Union troops rushed down into the crater instead of fanning out around it in pursuit of the stunned enemy. While the Union soldiers marveled at the destruction, the Confederates counterattacked and threw back the Union troops, including the black troops, who were finally brought

After the failed assault on Battery Wagner, Lewis Douglass wrote this letter home to his wife Amelia.

Lewis Douglass
July 20 [1863]

My Dear Amelia:

I have been in two fights, and am unhurt. I am about to go in another I believe tonight. Our men fought well on both occasions. The last one was desperate. We charged that terrible battery on . . . Fort Wagner and were repulsed. . . . I escaped unhurt from amidst that perfect hail of shot and shell. It was terrible. . . . This regiment has established its reputation as a fighting regiment. Not a man flinched, though it was a trying time. Men fell all around me. . . . Our men would close up again, but it was no use. . . . How I got out of that fight alive I cannot tell, but I am here. My dear girl, I hope again to see you. I must bid you farewell should I be killed. Remember if I die, I die in a good cause. I wish we had a hundred thousand colored troops. We would put an end to this war.

Your own loving

Lewis

▶ *How does Douglass describe combat?*
▶ *What motivated him and his fellow troops?*
▶ *Does this account of combat differ in any way from the way a white soldier might describe it?*

Source: Carter G. Woodson, ed., *The Mind of the Negro as Reflected in Letters Written during the Crisis 1800–1860* (Washington, DC: Association for the Study of Negro Life and History, 1926).

Confederate attack. Assistant Secretary of War Charles A. Dana claimed that their valor would change the attitudes of white people toward the use of black troops: "The bravery of the blacks completely revolutionized the sentiment of the army with regard to the employment of negro troops. I heard prominent officers who formerly in private sneered at the idea of negroes fighting express themselves after that as heartily in favor of it."

The southern soldiers who lost at Milliken's Bend, however, felt differently. Enraged by having to fight black troops, they executed several black prisoners and sold others into slavery.

THE ABUSE AND MURDER OF BLACK TROOPS

Confederate leaders and troops refused to recognize black men as legitimate soldiers. Captured black soldiers were abused and even murdered rather than treated as prisoners of war. Confederate Secretary of War James A. Seddon ordered that captured black soldiers be executed: "We ought never to be inconvenienced with such prisoners . . . summary execution must therefore be inflicted on those taken."

Protests erupted across the North after Confederate authorities decided to treat 80 men of the 54th Massachusetts Regiment who had been captured in the attack on Battery Wagner not as prisoners of war but as rebellious slaves. Frederick Douglass refused to recruit any more black men and held Abraham Lincoln personally responsible for tolerating the mistreatment of black prisoners: "How many 54ths must be cut to pieces, its mutilated prisoners killed, and its living sold into slavery, to be tortured to death by inches, before Mr. Lincoln shall say, 'Hold, enough!'"

Lincoln issued General Order 11, threatening to execute southern troops or confine them to hard labor: "For every soldier of the United States killed in violation of the laws of war a rebel soldier shall be executed, and for every one enslaved by the enemy or sold into slavery a rebel soldier shall be placed at hard labor on the public works, and continued at such labor until the other shall be released and receive the treatment due to a prisoner of war."

Lincoln's order did not prevent the Confederates from sending the men of the 54th to trial by the state of South Carolina. The state regarded the black soldiers as either rebellious slaves or free black men inciting rebellion. Four black soldiers went on trial in Charleston police court, but the court declared it lacked jurisdiction. The black prisoners were eventually sent to prisoner-of-war camps.

forward. Some black men were murdered after they surrendered. More than 4,000 Union troops, many of them black, were killed or wounded.

The Confederate Reaction to Black Soldiers

On June 7, 1863, Confederate forces attempting to relieve the Union siege of Vicksburg attacked black Union troops at Milliken's Bend on the Mississippi River. Although armed with outdated muskets and not fully trained, the defenders fought off the

THE FORT PILLOW MASSACRE

The war's worst atrocity against black troops occurred at **Fort Pillow** in Tennessee on April 12, 1864. Confederates under the command of Nathan Bedford Forrest slaughtered 300 black troops and their white commander, William F. Bradford, after many of them had surrendered. (After the Civil War, Forrest gained notoriety as a founder of the Ku Klux Klan. Before the war he had been a slave trader.) The Fort Pillow Massacre became the subject of an intense debate in Lincoln's cabinet. But rather than retaliate indiscriminately—as General Order 11 required—the cabinet decided to punish only those responsible for the killings, if and when they were apprehended. But no one was punished during or after the war. Instead, black troops exacted revenge themselves. In fighting around Petersburg later that year, black soldiers shouting, "Remember Fort Pillow!" reportedly murdered several Confederate prisoners. Captain Charles Francis Adams Jr. reported, "The darkies fought ferociously. . . . If they murdered prisoners, as I hear they did . . . they can hardly be blamed." Confederate troops committed many other racial atrocities during the remainder of the war.

●●●⊏Read the **Document**
Fort Pillow Massacre

On their own, Union commanders in the field also retaliated for the Confederate treatment of captured black troops. When captured black men were virtually enslaved and forced to work at Richmond and Charleston on Confederate fortifications that were under Union attack, Union officers put Confederate prisoners to work on Union installations that were under fire. Aware they were not likely to be treated as well as white soldiers if they were captured, black men often fought desperately.

In April 1864 fifteen hundred Confederate forces under General Nathan Bedford Forrest attacked and captured Fort Pillow, a Union installation on the Mississippi River forty miles north of Memphis, Tennessee, that was defended by 550 black and white troops. After the Union forces surrendered, Confederate troops executed some of the black soldiers. Forrest and his men denied the atrocity, but there is little doubt it occurred.

VOICES

A BLACK NURSE ON THE HORRORS OF WAR AND THE SACRIFICE OF BLACK SOLDIERS

Susie King Taylor was born a slave in Georgia and learned to read and write in Savannah. She escaped to Union forces in 1862 and served as a nurse and laundress with the First South Carolina Volunteers. In these passages, written years later, she recalls her service with the black men who went into combat and pays tribute to them.

It seems strange how our aversion to seeing suffering is overcome in war,—how we are able to see the most sickening sights, such as men with their limbs blown off and mangled by the deadly shells, without a shudder; and instead of turning away, how we hurry to assist in alleviating their pain, bind up their wounds, and press the cool water to their parched lips, with feelings only of sympathy and pity. . . .

I look around now and see the comforts that our younger generation enjoy, and think of the blood that was shed to make these comforts possible for them, and see how little some of them appreciate the old soldiers. My heart burns within me at this want of appreciation. There are only a few of them left now, so let us all, as the ranks close, take a deeper interest in them. Let the younger generation take an interest also, and remember that it was through the efforts of these veterans that we older ones enjoy our liberty today.

▶ How does Taylor describe what men in combat endure?
▶ Who is the object of Taylor's criticism, and why does she offer it?

Source: Susie King Taylor, *Reminiscences of My Life in Camp* (Boston: Taylor, 1902), 31–32, 51–52.

Black Men in the Union Navy

Black men had a tradition of serving at sea and had been in the U.S. Navy almost continuously since its creation in the 1790s. In the early nineteenth century, there were so many black sailors that some white people tried to ban black men from the navy. Nor did black sailors serve in segregated units. Naval crews were integrated.

Nonetheless, black sailors encountered rampant discrimination and exploitation during the Civil War. They were paid less than white sailors. They were assigned the hardest and filthiest tasks, such as loading coal and tending the boilers, on the navy's new steam-powered vessels. Many were stewards who waited on white officers. White officers and sailors often treated black sailors with contempt. On the USS *Constellation* in 1863, white crew members regularly referred to the 33 black sailors as "God-damned nigger," "black dog," and "black bitches" and kicked and swore at them.

But some white men admired the black sailors. One observed, "We never were betrayed when we trusted one of them, they were always our friends and were ready, if necessary, to lay down their lives for us." (He did not say whether white men were willing to lay down their lives for black men.) About 10,000, or 8 percent, of the men who served in the Union Navy during the war were black sailors.

Liberators, Spies, and Guides

Besides serving as soldiers and sailors, black men and women aided themselves and the Union cause as liberators, spies, guides, and messengers. At about 3 A.M. on May 13, 1862, Robert Smalls, a 23-year-old slave, fired the boiler on the *Planter*, a Confederate supply ship moored in Charleston harbor. With the aid of seven black crewmen, Smalls sailed the *Planter* past Confederate fortifications, including Fort Sumter, to the Union fleet outside the harbor and to freedom. Smalls liberated himself and 15 other slaves, including the families of several crewmen and his own wife, daughter, and son.

Smalls managed the daring escape because he knew the South Carolina coast and was familiar with Confederate navigation signals and regulations. He became an overnight hero in the North, a slave who wanted freedom and had possessed the leadership, knowledge, and tenacity to liberate 16 people.

In 1863 Harriet Tubman organized a spy ring in the South Carolina low country, and in cooperation with the all-black Second South Carolina Volunteer Regiment, she helped organize an expedition that destroyed plantations and freed nearly 800 slaves, many of whom joined the Union Army.

In Richmond in 1864, slaves helped more than one hundred escaped Union prisoners of war. Other slaves drew sketches and maps of Confederate fortifications and warned Union forces about troop movements. A black couple near Fredericksburg, Virginia, cleverly transmitted military intelligence to Union general Joseph Hooker. The woman washed laundry for a Confederate officer and hung shirts and blankets in patterns that conveyed information to her husband,

Robert Smalls was born a slave in Beaufort, South Carolina, in 1839. In May 1862 while still a slave and working as a pilot in Charleston on a 150-foot Confederate vessel, the *Planter,* Smalls devised an audacious plan to seize the ship. With the ship's white officers enjoying a night on the town, Smalls sailed the *Planter* with family and friends aboard to the Union Navy outside the harbor. Smalls's exploits created a sensation in the North. He went on to become a successful Republican politician in South Carolina in the decades following the Civil War.

a cook and groom for Union troops, and he relayed the information to Union officers.

Mary Elizabeth Bowser was a former slave who worked as a servant at the Confederate White House in Richmond. She overheard conversations by President Jefferson Davis and his subordinates, and—because she was literate—she covertly examined Confederate correspondence. She relayed the information to Union agents until the Confederates became suspicious. Bowser and slave Jim Pemberton fled after trying to burn down the mansion to distract their pursuers.

In Virginia's Shenandoah Valley, slave John Henry Woodson was a guide for Union General Philip H. Sheridan's cavalry in 1864 and 1865. Woodson was the father of Carter G. Woodson, who would become the "father" of black history in the twentieth century.

Violent Opposition to Black People

No matter how well black men fought, no matter how much individual black women contributed, and no matter how many people—black and white—died "to make men free," many white northerners, both civilian and military, remained bitter and often violently hostile to black people. They used intimidation, threats, and terror to injure and kill people of color.

THE NEW YORK CITY DRAFT RIOT

Irish Catholic Americans, themselves held in contempt by prosperous white Protestants, indulged in an orgy of violence in New York City in July 1863. The New York draft riot arose from racial, religious, and class antagonisms. Democrats, including New York Governor Horatio Seymour, convinced poor, unskilled Irish workers and other white northerners that the war had become a crusade to benefit black people.

The violence began when federal officials prepared to select the first men to be drafted by the Union for military service. An enraged mob of mostly Irish men attacked the draft offices and any black people who were around. Many of the Irish men were angry because black men had replaced striking Irish stevedores on the city's wharves the month before and because rich white northerners could purchase an exemption from the draft.

◆●◆ Read the Document
"If It Were Not for My Trust in Christ I Do Not Know How I Could Have Endured It": Testimony from Victims of New York's Draft Riots (1863)

The riot went on for four days. The police could not control it. Black people were beaten and lynched. The Colored Orphan Asylum was burned to the ground, although the children had already fled. The mob attacked businesses that employed black people. Protestant churches were burned. Rioters set fire to Horace Greeley's *New York Tribune.* The houses of Republicans and abolitionists were destroyed. The violence did not end until the army arrived. Soldiers who had been fighting Confederates at Gettysburg two weeks earlier found themselves firing on New York rioters.

UNION TROOPS AND SLAVES

White Union troops who brutalized southern freedmen sometimes exceeded the savagery of northern civilians. In November 1861 men from the 47th New

York Regiment raped an eight-year-old black girl. Later, in Virginia, a Connecticut soldier told what men in his regiment did to a pair of black women. They took "two niger wenches . . . turned them on their heads, & put tobacco, chips, sticks, lighted cigars & sand into their behinds." On Sherman's march through Georgia in 1864, a drunken Irish soldier from an Ohio regiment shot into a crowd of black children, wounding one youngster. He was tried and convicted but released on a technicality and returned to the army.

However, some Union soldiers wanted to fight for the liberation of black people. One Wisconsin private wrote, "I have no heart in this war if the slaves cannot be free." The desire of slaves for freedom moved many. A Union officer noted that those who believed

PROFILE: Harriet Tubman

Long before her death in 1913, Harriet Tubman had achieved legendary status. Although she never led a slave revolt like Nat Turner or Joseph Cinque, she freed more slaves than any other individual in American history.

Thomas Wentworth Higginson, commander of the First South Carolina Volunteers, called her "the greatest heroine of the age. Her tales of adventure are beyond anything in fiction and her ingenuity and generalship are extraordinary. I have known her for some time—the slaves call her Moses."

Tubman was born in 1821 or 1822 on Maryland's eastern shore, one of eleven slave children of Harriet Greene and Benjamin Ross. While a teenager, she was struck in the head by a rock or chunk of metal hurled by an overseer at a fleeing slave. The incident left her plagued by seizures and with an ugly scar that she sometimes covered with a turban.

In 1849 she married John Tubman, a free black man. Fearing that she would be sold after the death of her owner, she escaped to Pennsylvania, but her husband refused to go with her. He married another woman and died after the Civil War.

Tubman—like Sojourner Truth—never learned to read or write. However, her religious faith sustained her and helped inspire her return to slave states again and again to free people held in bondage. She made at least 15 trips south in ten years as a conductor on the underground railroad.

With the support of William Still and the General Vigilance Committee in Philadelphia and Quaker abolitionist Thomas Garrett in Wilmington, Delaware, she led between 70 and 80 people to freedom on 14 trips to Maryland's Eastern Shore between 1849 and 1860. Among them were her sister, her sister's two children, and her parents. Tubman also helped as many as 200 other people escape slavery. She never lost a passenger.

Aware that she had a reward on her head, Tubman devised detailed plans and elaborate disguises to elude capture. She feigned insanity, pretended to be feeble, forged passes, and acquired real railroad tickets. She also packed a gun, as much to goad any of her charges whose courage might waver as to protect herself.

In 1862, during the Civil War, Tubman journeyed to the South Carolina low country, where Union military forces had established a base. She worked as a nurse, cook, scout, and liberator. She made her way up the Combahee River and helped more than 700 slaves to freedom. She was on Morris Island in 1863 when the 54th Massachusetts Regiment attacked Battery Wagner.

After the war, she married Nelson Davis, a Union veteran who died in 1888. She and her supporters spent years in an effort to gain her federal pension. She finally secured an award of $20 a month that was based on her husband's military service rather than her own contributions to the Union cause.

Tubman was active in the women's rights movement of the late nineteenth century. She attended several women's rights conventions and befriended Susan B. Anthony. She also helped elderly ex-slaves who faced insecurity and uncertainty after emancipation. She bought a home in Auburn, New York, and eventually died there.

Many Americans talk about freedom, but not many have done as much to make it a reality for as many people as did Harriet Tubman.

((•—Hear the Audio

Harriet Tubman; read by Jean Brannon

slaves were satisfied with slavery were wrong. "It is claimed the negroes are so well contented with their slavery; if it ever was so, that day has ceased." Several Union soldiers wept when they witnessed a daughter reunited with her mother ten years after a slave sale had separated them.

Refugees

Throughout the war, black people freed themselves. It was not easy. Confederate authorities did not hesitate to reenslave or even execute black people who sought freedom. Six black people were hanged near Georgetown, South Carolina, in 1862 when they were captured trying to reach Union forces.

As Union armies plunged deep into the Confederacy in 1863 and 1864, thousands of black people liberated themselves and became refugees. When General William Tecumseh Sherman's army of 60,000 troops laid waste to Georgia in 1864, an estimated 10,000 former slaves followed his troops to Savannah, although they lacked adequate food, clothing, and housing. Sherman did not like black people, and his troops tried to discourage the refugees. As one elderly black couple prepared to leave a plantation, Union soldiers as well as their master urged them to remain. They declined: "We must go, freedom is as sweet to us as it is to you."

Black People and the Confederacy

The Confederacy was based on the defense of slavery, and it benefited from the usually coerced but sometimes willing labor of black people. Slaves toiled in southern fields and factories during the Civil War. The greater the burden of work the slaves took on, the more white men there were who could become soldiers. When the war began, southern whites believed their disadvantage in manpower—the twenty-two northern states had 22,339,989 people, and the eleven Confederate states had 9,103,332 (5,449,462 white people, 3,521,110 slaves, and 132,760 free black people)—would be partly offset by the slaves whose presence would free a disproportionately large number of white southerners to go to war. While slaves would tend cotton, corn, and cattle, white southern men would fight.

During the draft riot in New York City in July 1863, black people were attacked, beaten, and killed. A mob lynched this black man near Clarkson Street.

SKILLED AND UNSKILLED SLAVES IN SOUTHERN INDUSTRY

Slave labor helped sustain the Confederate war effort. More than 800 slaves and several hundred free black people, for example, worked at the South's largest industrial complex in Richmond, Virginia. The sprawling Tredegar Iron Works along the James River produced half of the 2,200 cannons that Confederate military forces used. It also furnished locomotives, iron plate, boilers, and nails.

As white men departed for military service, the Tredegar operators relied increasingly on slaves for skilled and unskilled labor. The company typically hired slaves from their owners for one-year terms. By 1864, slaves represented half of the workforce at Tredegar. They toiled in the machine shop, rolling mill, foundry, and as blacksmiths. After a white man quit in a pay dispute, a black engineer operated the Tredegar steam engine. Ed Taylor, who was one of the blacksmiths, performed the highly specialized task of hammering out iron bands that were fixed on artillery pieces to strengthen them. The company paid Taylor's owner the extraordinary sum of $1,000 a year for his technical expertise. Most slaves at Tredegar were hired from their owners at $200 per year. Unfortunately for Tredegar and the Confederacy but fortunately for its slave laborers, many of them escaped as Union military forces closed in on Richmond in 1864. Other black men across the South loaded and unloaded ships, worked on the railroads, and labored in salt mines.

THE IMPRESSMENT OF BLACK PEOPLE

As the war went on, the Confederacy needed more troops and laborers. Slave owners were first asked and then compelled to contribute their slave laborers to the war effort. In July 1861, the Confederate Congress required free black people to register and enroll for military labor. In the summer of 1862 the Virginia legislature authorized the **impressment** of 10,000 slaves between the ages of 18 and 45 for up to 60 days. The owners would receive $16 per month per slave. Despite protests by Tredegar's management, slave laborers were taken from the factory and forced to build fortifications for 60-day terms.

But many slave owners who enjoyed the benefits of forced labor did not want to be forced to turn their slaves over to state authorities. In October 1862, President Davis asked Virginia to draft 4,500 black people to build fortifications around Richmond so that "whites could fight more and dig less."

In South Carolina in 1863, Confederate officials appealed to slave owners for 2,500 slaves to help fortify Charleston. The owners offered fewer than 1,000. During the Union bombardment of Fort Sumter, 500 slaves did the difficult, dirty, and dangerous work of building and rebuilding the fort. Slaves were even forced into combat. Two Virginia slaves who were compelled to load and fire Confederate cannons near Yorktown were shot and killed.

Although many slave owners resisted the impressment of their bondmen, other white southerners who did not own slaves were infuriated when the Confederate conscription law in 1862 exempted men who owned 20 or more slaves from military service. This "20 nigger law" (later reduced to 15) meant that poor white men were drafted while wealthier planters remained home, presumably to supervise and discipline their slaves. One Mississippi soldier deserted the Confederate Army, claiming he "did not propose to fight for the rich men while they were home having a good time." Although the law was widely criticized, planters—always a small percentage of the white southern population—dominated the Confederate government and would not permit the repeal of the exemption.

CONFEDERATES ENSLAVE FREE BLACK PEOPLE

After Lincoln's Emancipation Proclamation, Confederate President Jefferson Davis issued a counterproclamation in February 1863 declaring that free black people would be enslaved, "all free negroes within the limits of the Southern Confederacy shall be placed on the slave status, and be deemed to be chattels . . . forever." This directive was not widely enforced. Davis, however, also ordered Confederate armies that invaded Union states to capture free black people in the North and enslave them: "All negroes who shall be taken in any of the States in which slavery does not now exist, in the progress of our arms, shall be adjudged, immediately after their capture, to occupy slave status."

This was done. Several hundred northern black people were taken south after Confederate forces invaded Pennsylvania in 1863 and fought at Gettysburg. Robert E. Lee's Army of Northern Virginia at Greensburg, Pennsylvania, captured at least 50 black people. A southern victory in the Civil War could have led to the enslavement of more than 132,000 free black residents of the Confederate States.

BLACK CONFEDERATES

Most of the labor black people did for the Confederacy was involuntary, but a few free black men and women offered their services to the southern cause. In Lynchburg, Virginia, in the spring of 1861, 70 free black people volunteered "to act in whatever capacity may be assigned them." In Memphis in the fall, several hundred black residents cheered for Jefferson Davis and sang patriotic songs. These demonstrations of black support were made early in the conflict when the outcome was in doubt and long before the war became a crusade against slavery.

The status of many free black southerners remained precarious. In Virginia in 1861, impressment laws, like those applying to slaves, compelled free black men to work on Confederate defenses around Richmond and Petersburg. Months before the war, South Carolina considered forcing its free black population to choose between enslavement and exile. The legislature rejected the proposal, but it terrified the state's free black people. Many people of color there had been free for generations. Fair in complexion, they had education, skills, homes, and businesses. Some even owned slaves. When the war came, many were willing to demonstrate their devotion to the South in a desperate attempt to gain white acceptance before they lost their freedom and property.

In early 1861, before the formation of the Confederacy but after the secession of South Carolina, 82 free black men in Charleston petitioned Governor Francis W. Pickens "to be assigned any service where we can be useful." To distinguish themselves from slaves and show their solidarity with white southerners, they proclaimed, "We are by birth citizens of South Carolina, in our veins is the blood of the white race in some half, in others much more, our attachments are with you, our hopes of safety and protection is in South Carolina, our allegiance is due alone to her, in her defence we are willing to offer up our lives and all that is dear to us." Pickens rejected the petition, but white South Carolinians were pleased at this show of loyalty.

White southern leaders generally ignored offers of free black support unless it was for menial labor. But when Charleston was under siege between 1863 and 1865, black and white residents were grateful that volunteer fire brigades composed of free black men turned out to fight fires caused by Union artillery.

PERSONAL SERVANTS

Other black men contributed in different ways to the Confederate military effort. Black musicians in Virginia played for Confederate regiments and received the same pay as white musicians. Wealthy white men often took their slaves—personal servants—with them when they went off to war. The servants cooked, cleaned uniforms, cared for weapons, maintained horses, and even provided entertainment. Some were loyal and devoted. They cared for owners who were wounded or fell sick. They accompanied the bodies of dead masters home.

Being the personal servant for a soldier was hard and sometimes dangerous work. Those close to combat could be killed or injured. One white father warned his son not to take Sam, a valuable slave, into battle. "I hear you are likely to have a big battle soon, and I write to tell you not to let Sam go into the fight with you. Keep him in the rear, for that nigger is worth a thousand dollars." The father evidently placed a higher value on the slave than on his son.

BLACK MEN FIGHTING FOR THE SOUTH

Approximately 144,000 black men from the southern states fought with the Union Army. Most had been slaves. Although it was technically not legal until almost the end of the war, a much smaller number of black men also fought for the Confederacy. White New York troops claimed to have encountered about 700 armed black men in late 1861 near Newport News, Virginia. In 1862 a black Confederate sharpshooter positioned himself in a chimney and shot several Union soldiers before he was killed. Fifty black men served as pickets for the Confederates along the Rappahannock River in Virginia in 1863.

John Wilson Buckner, a free black man with a light complexion, enlisted in the First South Carolina Artillery. As a member of the well-regarded free black Ellison family of Stateburg, South Carolina, Buckner was considered an "honorary white man." He fought for the Confederacy in the defense of Charleston at Battery Wagner in July 1863 and was wounded just before the 54th Massachusetts Regiment assaulted the fort.

Some black civilians supported the war effort and stood to profit if the South won. Buckner's uncles grew corn, sweet potatoes, peas, sorghum, and beans on the Ellison family plantation to feed Confederate troops. By hiring out horses, mules, and slaves they owned, the Ellisons had earned nearly $1,000 by 1863. By 1865 they had paid almost $5,000 in taxes to the Confederacy, nearly one-fifth of their total income. They also patriotically invested almost $7,000 in Confederate bonds and notes. Like prosperous white families, the Ellisons lost most of this investment with the defeat of the Confederacy. At war's end, the bonds were as worthless as Confederate cash, and the 80 slaves the Ellisons owned—worth approximately $100,000— were free people (see Chapter 6).

Other black southerners also suffered economically from the Confederate defeat. Richard Mack, a South Carolina slave, went off to war as a personal servant. After his master died, he became an orderly for another Confederate officer. He worked hard and accumulated a large sum in Confederate currency. He later joked, "If we had won, I would be rich."

In Virginia, free black people and slaves also contributed to the Confederate cause. Pompey Scott of Amelia County gave $20 to the war effort. William, a slave who had amassed $150, invested in Confederate State Loan Bonds. Lewis, a Mecklenburg County slave, was not permitted to join a cavalry unit as a bugler, so he donated his bugle and $20 to the Confederacy.

White southerners praised the few black people who actively supported the South. Several states awarded pensions to black men who served in the war and survived. Henry Clay Lightfoot, a slave in Culpeper, Virginia, went to war as a body servant of Captain William Holcomb. After the war, he bought a house, raised a family, and was elected to the Culpeper town council. He collected a pension from Virginia, and when he died in 1931, the United Daughters of the Confederacy draped his coffin in a Confederate flag.

BLACK OPPOSITION TO THE CONFEDERACY

Although many white southerners and some northerners believed most slaves would support their masters, in fact most slaves did not. When a slave named Tom was asked if slaves would fight for their masters, he replied, "I know they say dese tings, but dey lies. Our masters may talk now all dey choose; but one ting's

Black troops were among the first Union military forces to "liberate" the devastated city of Charleston, South Carolina, in the waning weeks of the Civil War. On February 21, 1865, the 55th Massachusetts Regiment occupied Charleston. Black residents—many of them former slaves—eagerly welcomed the soldiers. Defeated and discouraged white residents remained secluded indoors.

sartin,—dey don't dare to try us. Jess put de guns in our hans, and you'll soon see dat we not only knows how to shoot, but who, to shoot. My master wouldn't be wuff much ef I was a soldier."

THE CONFEDERATE DEBATE ON BLACK TROOPS

By late 1863 and 1864, prospects for the Confederacy had become grim. The Union naval blockade had become increasingly effective, and the likelihood of British aid had all but vanished. Confederate armies suffered crushing defeats at Vicksburg and Gettysburg in 1863 and absorbed terrible losses in Tennessee, Georgia, and Virginia in 1864.

As defeat loomed, white southerners began to discuss the possibility of arming black men. Several newspapers advocated it. In September 1863, the Montgomery (Alabama) *Weekly Mail* admitted it would have been preposterous to contemplate the need for black troops

earlier in the war, but it had now become necessary to save the white South:

> We are forced by the necessity of our condition—by the insolence and barbarity of the enemy, by his revengeful and demoniacal spirit—to take a step which is revolting to every sentiment of pride, and to every principle that governed our institutions before the war. But the war has made great changes, and we must meet those changes, for the sake of preserving our very existence. It is a matter of necessity, therefore, that we should use every means within our reach to defeat the enemy. One of these, and the only one which will checkmate him, is the employment of negroes in the military service of the Confederacy.

In early 1864 General Patrick Cleburne recommended enlisting slaves and promising them their freedom if they remained loyal to the Confederacy. Cleburne argued that this policy would gain recognition and aid from Britain and would disrupt Union military efforts to recruit black southerners. Yet the prospect of arming slaves and free black men appalled most white southerners. Jefferson Davis ordered military officers, including Cleburne, to cease discussing it.

Most white southerners were convinced that to arm slaves and put black men in gray uniforms defied the assumptions on which southern society was based. Black people were inferior, and their proper status was to be slaves. The *Richmond Whig* declared in 1864 that "servitude is a divinely appointed condition for the highest good of the slave." It was absurd to contemplate black people as soldiers and as free people. Georgia politician Howell Cobb explained that slaves could not be armed. "If slaves will make good soldiers our whole theory of slavery is wrong."

The Civil War for white southerners was a war to prevent the abolition of slavery. Now white southern voices were proposing abolition to preserve the southern nation. North Carolina Senator Robert M. T. Hunter opposed any attempt to enlist slaves and free them. "If we are right in passing this measure we were wrong in denying to the old government the right to interfere with the institution of slavery and to emancipate slaves. Besides, if we offer slaves their freedom . . . we confess that we were insincere, were hypocritical, in asserting that slavery was the best state for the negroes themselves."

Nevertheless, as the military situation deteriorated, the South moved toward employing black troops. In November 1864, Virginia Governor William Smith enthusiastically supported the idea. "There is not a man that would not cheerfully put the negro in the Army rather than become a slave himself. . . . Standing before God and my country, I do not hesitate to say that I would arm such portion of our able-bodied slaves population as may be necessary." In February 1865, Jefferson Davis and the Confederate cabinet conceded, "We are reduced to choosing whether the negroes shall fight for us or against us."

The opinion of General Robert E. Lee was critical to determining whether the Confederacy would decide to arm black men. No southerner was more revered and respected. Lee had freed nearly 200 slaves in keeping with the instructions of his father-in-law George Washington Parke Custis's will in 1862, which provided that the slaves be emancipated within five years of Custis's death in 1857.

With his army struggling to survive a desperate winter around Petersburg and Richmond, Lee announced in February 1865 that he favored both enrolling and emancipating black troops. "My own opinion is that we should employ them without delay." Their service as slaves would make them capable soldiers. "They possess the physical qualities in an eminent degree. Long habits of obedience and subordination, coupled with

moral influence which in our country the white man possesses over the black, furnish an excellent foundation for that discipline which is the best guarantee of military efficiency."

Less than a month later in March 1865, although many white southerners still opposed it, the Confederate Congress voted to enlist 300,000 black men between the ages of 18 and 45. They would receive the same pay, equipment, and supplies as white soldiers. But those who were slaves would not be freed unless their owner consented and the state where they served agreed to their emancipation.

It was a desperate measure by a nearly defeated government and did not affect the outcome of the conflict. Before the war ended in April, authorities in Virginia managed to recruit some black men and send a few into combat. By the end of March, one company of 35 black men—12 free black men and 23 slaves—was organized. On April 4, 1865, Union troops attacked Confederate supply wagons that the black troops were guarding in Amelia County. Less than a week later, Lee surrendered to Grant at Appomattox Court House, and the Civil War ended.

Watch the Video
The Meaning of the Civil War for Americans

CONCLUSION

The Civil War ended with the decisive defeat of the Confederacy. The Union was preserved. The ordeal of slavery for millions of people of African descent was over. Slavery—having thrived in America for nearly 250 years—was finally abolished by an amendment to the Constitution. Congress passed the Thirteenth Amendment on January 31, 1865. It was ratified by 27 states and declared in effect on December 18, 1865.

Were it not for the presence and labors of more than four million black people, there would have been no Civil War. Had it not been for the presence and contributions of more than 185,000 black soldiers and sailors, the Union would not have won. Almost 40,000 of those black men died in combat and of disease during the war. Twenty-one black men were awarded the Medal of Honor for heroism.

Abraham Lincoln represents the dramatic shift in attitudes and policies toward African Americans during the Civil War. When the war began, Lincoln insisted it was a white man's conflict to suppress rebellious white southerners. Black people, Lincoln remained convinced, would be better off outside the United States. But the war went on, and thousands of white men died. Lincoln issued the Emancipation Proclamation and welcomed the enlistment of black troops. The president came to appreciate the achievements

AFRICAN-AMERICAN EVENTS	NATIONAL EVENTS
	● 1860 ●
	November 1860 Abraham Lincoln elected president
	December 1860 South Carolina secedes from the Union
	● 1861 ●
April–May 1861 Black men volunteer for military service and are rejected	**February 1861** The Confederate States of America is formed
August 1861 First Confiscation Act	**March 1861** Lincoln inaugurated
	April 1861 The firing on Fort Sumter begins the Civil War
	November 1861 Union forces capture the sea islands and coastal areas of South Carolina and Georgia
	● 1862 ●
May 1862 Robert Smalls escapes with the *Planter* and 16 slaves	**September 1862** Battle of Antietam
May–August 1862 The First South Carolina Volunteers, an all-black regiment, forms	
September 1862 Lincoln announces the Preliminary Emancipation Proclamation	
October 1862 Black troops see combat for the first time in Missouri	

and devotion of black troops and condemned the mean-spiritedness of white northerners who opposed the war. Lincoln wrote in 1863, "And then there will be some black men who can remember that, with silent tongue, and clenched teeth, and steady eye, and well-poised bayonet, they have helped mankind on to this great consummation; while, I fear, there will be some white ones, unable to forget that, with malignant heart, and deceitful speech, they have strove to hinder it."

RECOMMENDED READING

Lerone Bennett. *Forced into Glory: Abraham Lincoln's White Dream.* Chicago: Johnson, 2000. Bennett is highly critical of Lincoln in this thought-provoking account.

Dudley Taylor Cornish. *The Sable Arm: Negro Troops in the Union Army, 1861–1865.* New York: Norton, 1956. The best single study of black men in the military during the war.

John Hope Franklin. *The Emancipation Proclamation.* Garden City, NY: Doubleday, 1963. A work written to commemorate the centennial of the Proclamation.

Michael P. Johnson and James L. Roark. *Black Masters: A Free Family of Color in the Old South.* New York: Norton, 1984. A splendid depiction of life among prosperous free black people before and during the Civil War.

Ervin Jordan. *Black Confederates and Afro-Yankees in Civil War Virginia.* Charlottesville: University of Virginia Press, 1995. A rich study of life and society among African Americans in Virginia during the war.

James McPherson. *Battle Cry of Freedom: The Civil War Era.* New York: Oxford University Press, 1988. A superb one-volume account of the Civil War.

George W. Williams. *History of the Negro Troops in the War of the Rebellion.* New York: Harper & Row, 1888. An account of black soldiers in the war by America's first African-American historian.

ADDITIONAL BIBLIOGRAPHY

MILITARY

Joseph T. Glatthaar. *Forged in Battle: The Civil War Alliance of Black Soldiers and White Officers.* New York: Free Press, 1990.

———. *The March to the Sea and Beyond: Sherman's Troops in the Savannah and Carolina Campaign.* New York: New York University Press, 1985.

Herman Hattaway and Archer Jones. *How the North Won: A Military History of the Civil War.* Urbana: University of Illinois Press, 1983.

John Keegan. *The American Civil War: A Military History.* New York: Alfred A. Knopf, 2009.

Geoffrey Ward and Ken Burns. *The Civil War.* New York: Alfred A. Knopf, 1990.

Stephen R. Wise. *Gate of Hell: Campaign for Charleston Harbor, 1863.* Columbia: University of South Carolina Press, 1994.

AFRICAN AMERICANS AND THE WAR

Iver Bernstein. *The New York City Draft Riots: Their Significance for American Society and Politics in the Age of the Civil War.* New York: Oxford University Press, 1991.

Peter Burchard. *One Gallant Rush: Robert Gould Shaw and His Brave Black Regiment.* New York: St. Martin's Press, 1965.

George S. Burkhardt. *Confederate Wrath: No Quarter in the Civil War.* Carbondale: Southern Illinois University Press, 2007.

John Cimpach. *Fort Pillow: A Civil War Massacre and Public Memory.* Baton Rouge: Louisiana State University Press, 2005.

Catherine Clinton. *Harriet Tubman: The Road to Freedom.* Boston: Little, Brown, 2004.

Charles B. Dew. *Ironmaker to the Confederacy: Joseph R. Anderson and the Tredegar Iron Works.* New Haven, CT: Yale University Press, 1966.

Ella Forbes. *African American Women during the Civil War.* New York: Garland, 1998.

Kate Clifford Larson. *Bound for the Promised Land: Harriet Tubman, Portrait of an American Hero.* New York: Ballantine, 2004.

Leon Litwack. *Been in the Storm So Long: The Aftermath of Slavery.* New York: Alfred A. Knopf, 1979.

Edward A. Miller. *Gullah Statesman: Robert Smalls from Slavery to Congress, 1839–1915.* Columbia: University of South Carolina Press, 1995.

Benjamin Quarles. *The Negro in the Civil War.* Boston: Little, Brown, 1953.

Willie Lee Rose. *Rehearsal for Reconstruction: The Port Royal Experiment.* Indianapolis: Bobbs Merrill, 1964.

Milton C. Sernett. *Harriet Tubman: Myth, Memory, and History.* Durham, NC: Duke University Press, 2007.

Richard Slotkin. *No Quarter: The Battle of the Crater, 1864.* New York: Random House, 2009.

Noah A. Trudeau. *Like Men of War: Black Troops in the Civil War, 1862–1865.* Boston: Little, Brown, 1998.

Gregory J. W. Urwin, ed. *Black Flag over Dixie: Racial Atrocities and Reprisals in the Civil War.* Carbondale: Southern Illinois University Press, 2004.

Bell I. Wiley. *Southern Negroes, 1861–1865.* New Haven, CT: Yale University Press, 1938.

DOCUMENTS, LETTERS, AND OTHER SOURCES

Virginia M. Adams, ed. *On the Altar of Freedom: A Black Soldier's Civil War Letters from the Front.* [Corporal James Henry Gooding]. Amherst: University of Massachusetts Press, 1991.

1863

January 1, 1863 Lincoln issues the Emancipation Proclamation

January–March 1863 Troops recruited for the 54th and the 55th Massachusetts Regiments

June 1863 Battle of Milliken's Bend

July 1863 Assault on Battery Wagner; New York City draft riots

March 1863 The U.S. government enacts a Conscription Act

July 1863 Battles of Vicksburg and Gettysburg

1864

February 1864 Battle at Olustee

April 1864 Fort Pillow Massacre

November 1864 Lincoln is reelected

November–December 1864 Sherman's march to the sea

1865

February 1865 Black troops lead the occupation of Charleston

March 1865 Confederate Congress approves the enlistment of black men

December 1865 Thirteenth Amendment ratified

February 1865 Charleston falls

March 1865 Richmond falls

April 1865 Lee surrenders at Appomattox; Lincoln is assassinated

AFRICAN-AMERICAN EVENTS **NATIONAL EVENTS**

Ira Berlin et al., eds. *Freedom: A Documentary History of Emancipation, 1861–1867.* Series 1, Volume I, *The Destruction of Slavery.* New York: Cambridge University Press, 1985.

———. *Freedom: A Documentary History of Emancipation, 1861–1867.* Series 1, Volume III, *The Wartime Genesis of Free Labor: The Lower South.* New York: Cambridge University Press, 1990.

Robert F. Durden. *The Gray and the Black: The Confederate Debate on Emancipation.* Baton Rouge: Louisiana State University Press, 1972.

Michael P. Johnson and James L. Roark, eds. *No Chariot Letdown: Charleston's Free People of Color on the Eve of the Civil War.* Chapel Hill: University of North Carolina Press, 1984.

James McPherson. *The Negro's Civil War: How American Negroes Felt and Acted during the War for the Union.* New York: Pantheon, 1965.

Edwin S. Redkey, ed. *A Grand Army of Black Men: Letters from African American Soldiers in the Union Army, 1861–1865.* New York: Cambridge University Press, 1992.

REMINISCENCES

Thomas Wentworth Higginson. *Army Life in a Black Regiment.* Boston: Beacon Press, 1962.

Elizabeth Keckley. *Behind the Scenes: Or, Thirty Years a Slave and Four Years in the White House.* New York: Oxford University Press, 1968.

Susie King Taylor. *Reminiscences of My Life in Camp.* Boston: Taylor, 1902.

RETRACING THE ODYSSEY

The Penn Center, St. Helena Island, South Carolina. www.penncenter.com. Beginning in 1862, black and white teachers from the North began offering instruction to former slaves on the Carolina coast. Laura Towne and Ellen Murray helped establish Penn school amid the oak trees draped in Spanish moss. The school closed in 1948. During the 1950s and 1960s, civil rights leaders, including Dr. Martin Luther King Jr., gathered at Penn to discuss strategy. Today Penn Center provides programs on health, literacy, landownership, and agriculture. It serves as a cultural and community center, and there is a museum among the historic buildings.

Olustee Battlefield State Historic Site, Olustee, Florida. www.floridastateparks.org/olusteebattlefield.default.cfm. In February 1864 the largest Civil War battle in Florida was fought at Olustee, which is almost fifty miles west of Jacksonville. About one-third of the Union troops were black men. There is a museum with exhibits and artifacts.

Fort Pillow State Park, Tennessee. www.stateparks.com/fort_pillow.html. This was the scene of the April 1864 battle in which Confederate forces attacked the black and white Union defenders of the fort. About 238 black men were killed, some during the battle and others after they surrendered. There is a visitor center, museum, and trail to the fortifications.

The Crater, Petersburg National Battlefield, Virginia. www.nps.gov/pete/index.htm. The longest siege in American military history occurred in and around the town of Petersburg in 1864 and 1865. Union forces attempted to break Confederate lines by setting off an enormous explosion in July 1864. Poor leadership and inept execution turned the Union advantage to disaster for the white and black troops who took part. Portions of the trenches and the crater are still visible.

Harriet Tubman Museum, Auburn, New York. www.nyhistory.com/harriettubman/. In 1896 the famed liberator of slaves bought this property and made it her home. She died here in 1913. The African Methodist Episcopal Zion Church operates the house as a museum. Harriet Tubman is buried nearby at Fort Hill Cemetery.

REVIEW QUESTIONS

1. How did the Union's goals in the Civil War change between 1861 and 1865? What accounts for those changes?

2. How did the Confederate government's policies toward slaves change during the Civil War? When and why did those changes occur?

3. When the Civil War began, why did northern black men volunteer to serve in the Union army if the war had not yet become a war to end slavery?

4. How did Abraham Lincoln's policies and attitudes toward black people change during the Civil War? Does Lincoln deserve credit as "the Great Emancipator"? Why or why not?

5. What did the Emancipation Proclamation seek to achieve? Why was it issued? What did it actually accomplish?

6. What did black men and women contribute to the Union war effort? Was it in their interests to participate in the Civil War? Why or why not?

7. Why did some black people support the Confederacy?

8. Was the result of the Civil War worth the loss of 620,000 lives?

PEARSON myhistorylab Connections

www.myhistorylab.com
Review what you've learned in this chapter and explore the many documents, images,
research tools, and activities for this chapter to learn more about African-American history.

✓● Study and Review

READ

●●● Read the Document

- The Working Men of Manchester, England, Write to President Lincoln on the Question of Slavery (1862)

- President Lincoln Responds to the Working Men of Manchester on the Subject of Slavery in 1863

- The Emancipation Proclamation (1863)

- Abraham Lincoln, The Gettysburg Address (1863)

- Letter from H. Ford Douglas to Frederick Douglass's Monthly (1863)

- "If It Were Not for My Trust in Christ I Do Not Know How I Could Have Endured It": Testimony from Victims of New York's Draft Riots (1863)

- "I Hope to Fall with My Face to the Foe": Lewis Douglass Describes the Battle of Fort Wagner (1863)

- James Henry Gooding, Letter to President Lincoln (1863)

- Elizabeth Keckley, *Behind the Scenes: Or, Thirty Years a Slave, and Four Years in the White House* (1868)

- The Meaning of the Civil War for Americans

LISTEN

((●● Hear the Audio

Hear the audio files for Chapter 11.

- *Harriet Tubman;* read by Jean Brannon

- *When This Cruel War Is Over*

- *Free at Last*

RESEARCH

mysearchlab

Consider this question in a short research paper.

Why were African Americans who wanted to enlist rejected in 1861?

What role did African Americans play in gaining their own freedom, and how did their struggle affect the lives of ordinary people?

EXPLORE

(●) Watch the Video

- What Caused the Civil War?

- *The Meaning of the Civil War for Americans*

(●) See the Map

- Effects of the Emancipation Proclamation

- The Civil War Part I: 1861-1862

- The Civil War Part II: 1863–1865

●●● Read the Document

- Fort Pillow Massacre

- A Nation Divided: The Civil War

12

The Meaning of Freedom:
The Promise of Reconstruction

What did freedom mean to nearly four
million people who had been slaves?

How successful were former slaves
in acquiring land of their own?

What was the Freedmen's Bureau,
and how effective was it?

Why was education so important
to African-Americans?

What was the purpose of the
Fourteenth Amendment?

How did African-American men gain
the right to vote?

▶ **Students assembled in front of James Plantation School** in North
Carolina shortly after the Civil War ended in 1865. Compared to many
such schools, this one was exceptionally well constructed. Notice the
students' clothes and lack of shoes.

Many Thousand Gone

No more auction block for me,
No more, no more,
No more auction block for me,
Many thousand gone.

No more driver's lash for me,
No more, no more,
No more driver's lash for me,
Many thousand gone.

No more peck of salt for me,
No more, no more,
No more peck of salt for me,
Many thousand gone.

No more iron chain for me,
No more, no more.
No more iron chain for me,
Many thousand gone.

An African-American emancipation song

◀ **Many freed blacks** returned to the South looking for family who had been sold away.

Hear the Audio
Hear the audio files for Chapter 12 at www.myhistorylab.com

What did freedom mean to a people who had endured and survived 250 years of enslavement in America? What did the future hold for nearly four million African Americans in 1865? Freedom meant many things to many people. But to most former slaves, it meant that families would stay together. Freedom meant that women would no longer be sexually exploited. Freedom meant learning to read and write. Freedom meant organizing churches. Freedom meant moving around without having to obtain permission. Freedom meant that labor would produce income for the laborer and not the master. Freedom meant working without the whip. Freedom meant land to own, cultivate, and live on. Freedom meant a trial before a jury if charged with a crime. Freedom meant voting. Freedom meant citizenship and having the same rights as white people.

Years after slavery ended, a former Texas slave, Margrett Nillin, was asked if she preferred slavery or freedom. She answered unequivocally, "Well, it's dis way, in slavery I owns nothin' and never owns nothin'. In freedom I's own de home and raise de family. All dat causes me worryment and in slavery I has no worryment, but I takes freedom."

The End of Slavery

With the collapse of slavery, many black people were quick to inform white people that whatever loyalty, devotion, and cooperation they might have shown as slaves had never reflected their inner feelings and attitudes. Near Opelousas, Louisiana, a Union officer asked a young black man why he did not love his master, and the youth responded sharply, "When my master begins to lub me, den it'll be time enough for me to lub him. What I wants is to get away. I want to take me off from dis plantation, where I can be free."

In North Carolina, planter Robert P. Howell was disappointed that a loyal slave named Lovet fled at the first opportunity. "He was about my age and I had always treated him more as a companion than a slave. When I left I put everything in his charge, told him that he was free, but to remain on the place and take care of things. He promised me faithfully that he would, but he was the first one to leave . . . and I did not see him for several years."

Hear the Audio
Remembering Slavery #2

Emancipation was traumatic for many former masters. A Virginia freedman remembered that "Miss Polly died right after the surrender, she was so hurt that all the negroes was going to be free." Another former slave, Robert Falls, recalled that his master assembled the slaves to inform them they were free. "I hates to do it, but I must. You all ain't my niggers no more. You is free. Just as free as I am. Here I have raised you all to work for me, and now you are going to leave me. I am an old man, and I can't get along without you. I don't know what I am going to do." In less than a year, he was dead. Falls attributed his master's death to the end of slavery: "It killed him."

•••▶ Read the Document
Reconstruction: The Struggle to Define the Meaning of Freedom

DIFFERING REACTIONS OF FORMER SLAVES

Other slaves bluntly displayed their reaction to years of bondage. Aunt Delia, a cook with a North Carolina family, revealed that she secretly had been gaining retribution for the indignity of servitude. "How many times I spit in the biscuits and peed in the coffee just to get back at them mean white folks." In Goodman, Mississippi, a slave named Caddy learned she was free and rushed from the field to find her owner. "Caddy threw down that hoe, she marched herself up to the big house, then, she looked around and found the mistress. She went over to the mistress, she flipped up her dress and told the white woman to do something. She said it mean and ugly. This is what she said: 'Kiss my ass!'"

In contrast, some slaves, especially elderly ones, were apprehensive about freedom. On a South Carolina plantation, an older black woman refused to accept emancipation. "I ain' no free nigger! I is got a marster and mistiss! Dee right dar in de great house. Ef you don' b'lieve me, you go dar an' see."

REUNITING BLACK FAMILIES

As slavery ended, the most urgent need for many freed people was finding family members who had been sold away from them. Slavery had not destroyed the black family. Husbands, wives, and children went to great lengths to reassemble their families after the Civil War. For years and even decades after the end of slavery, advertisements in black newspapers appealed for information about missing kinfolk. The *Colored Tennessean* published the following notice on August 5, 1865:

> Saml. Dove wishes to know of the whereabouts of his mother, Areno, his sisters Maria, Neziah and Peggy, and his brother Edmond, who were owned by Geo. Dove of Rockingham County, Shenandoah Valley, Va.

Sold in Richmond, after which Saml. and Edmond were taken to Nashville, Tenn., by Joe Mick; Areno was left at the Eagle Tavern, Richmond. Respectfully yours, Saml. Dove, Utica, New York.

In North Carolina a northern journalist met a middle-aged black man "plodding along, staff in hand, and apparently very footsore and tired." The nearly exhausted freedman explained that he had walked almost 600 miles looking for his wife and children, who had been sold four years earlier.

There were emotional reunions as family members found each other after years of separation. Ben and Betty Dodson had been apart for 20 years when Ben found her in a refugee camp after the war. "Glory! glory! hallelujah," he shouted as he hugged his wife. "Dis is my Betty, shuah. I foun' you at las'. I's hunted and hunted till I track you up here. I's boun' to hunt till I fin' you if you's alive."

Other searches had more heart-wrenching results. Husbands and wives sometimes learned that their spouses had remarried during the separation. Believing his wife had died, the husband of Laura Spicer remarried—only to learn after the war that Laura was still alive. Sadly, he wrote to her but refused to meet: "I would come and see you but I know I could not bear it. I want to see you and I don't want to see you. I love you just as well as I did the last day I saw you, and it will not do for you and I to meet."

Tormented, he wrote again pledging his love: "Laura I do not think that I have change any at all since I saw you last—I thinks of you and my children every day of my life. Laura I do love you the same. My love to you never have failed. Laura, truly, I have got another wife, and I am very sorry that I am. You feels and seems to me as much like my dear loving wife, as you ever did Laura."

One freedman testified to the close ties that bound many slave families when he replied bitterly to the claim that he had had a kind master who had fed him and never used the whip: "Kind! yes, he gib men corn enough, and he gib me pork enough, and he neber gib me one lick wid de whip, but whar's my wife?—whar's my chill'en? Take away de pork, I say; take away de corn, I can work and raise dese for myself, but gib me back de wife of my bosom, and gib me back my poor chill'en as was sold away."

Land

As people embraced freedom and left their masters, they wanted land. Nineteenth-century Americans of virtually every background associated economic security with owning land. Families wanted to work land and prosper

Former slaves assembled in a village near Washington, D.C. Black people welcomed emancipation, but without land, education, or employment, they faced an uncertain future.

and fathers preferred that their wives and daughters not work in the fields as slave women had been forced to do.

THE PORT ROYAL EXPERIMENT

Meanwhile, hundreds of former slaves had been cultivating land for three years. In late 1861 Union military forces carved out an enclave around Beaufort and Port Royal, South Carolina, that remained under federal authority for the rest of the war. White planters fled to the interior, leaving their slaves behind. Under the supervision of U.S. Treasury officials and northern reformers and missionaries who hurried south in 1862, ex-slaves began to work the land in what came to be known as the **"Port Royal Experiment."** When Treasury agents auctioned off portions of the land for nonpayment of taxes, freedmen purchased some of it. But northern businessmen bought most of the real estate and then hired black people to raise cotton.

White owners sometimes returned to their former lands only to find that black families had taken charge. Black farmers told one former owner, "We own this land now, put it out of your head that it will ever be yours again." And on one South Carolina sea island, white men were turned back by armed black men.

as self-sufficient yeomen. Former slaves believed their future as a free people was tied to the possession of land. But just as it had been impossible to abolish slavery without federal intervention, it would not be possible to procure land without the assistance of the U.S. government. At first, federal authorities seemed determined to make land available to freedmen.

SPECIAL FIELD ORDER #15

Shortly after his army arrived in Savannah—after having devastated Georgia—Union General William T. Sherman announced that freedmen would receive land. On January 16, 1865, he issued **Special Field Order #15.** This military directive set aside a 30-mile-wide tract of land along the Atlantic coast from Charleston, South Carolina, 245 miles south to Jacksonville, Florida. White owners had abandoned the land, and Sherman reserved it for black families. The head of each family would receive "possessory title" to 40 acres of land. Sherman also gave the freedmen the use of army mules—hence the slogan, "Forty acres and a mule." (Before the development of motorized equipment, mules, horses, and other draft animals were the key elements of agricultural technology for plowing fields and harvesting many crops.)

Within six months, 40,000 freed people were working 400,000 acres in the South Carolina and Georgia low country and on the sea islands. Former slaves generally avoided the slave crops of cotton and rice and instead planted sweet potatoes and corn. They also worked together as families and kinfolk. They avoided the gang labor associated with slavery. Most husbands

The Freedmen's Bureau

As the war ended in early 1865, Congress created the Bureau of Refugees, Freedmen, and Abandoned Lands—commonly called the **Freedmen's Bureau.** Created as a temporary agency to assist freedmen to make the transition to freedom, the bureau was placed under the control of the U.S. Army, and General Oliver O. Howard was put in command. Howard, a devout Christian who had lost an arm in the war, was eager to aid the freedmen.

The bureau was given enormous responsibilities. It was to help freedmen obtain land, gain an education, negotiate labor contracts with white planters, settle legal and criminal disputes involving black and white people, and provide food, medical care, and transportation for black and white people left destitute by the war. However, Congress never provided sufficient funds or personnel to carry out these tasks.

The Freedmen's Bureau never had more than 900 agents spread across the South from Virginia to Texas. Mississippi, for example, had twelve agents in 1866.

One agent often served a county with a population of 10,000 to 20,000 freedmen. Few of the agents were black because few military officers were black. John Mercer Langston of Virginia was an inspector of schools assigned to the bureau's main office in Washington, D.C.; Major Martin R. Delany worked with freedmen on the South Carolina sea islands.

The need for assistance was desperate as thousands of black and white southerners endured extreme privation in the months after the war ended. The bureau established camps for the homeless, fed the hungry, and cared for orphans and the sick as best it could. By 1866 it had distributed more than thirteen million rations, consisting of flour, corn meal, and sugar. The bureau provided medical care to a half million freedmen and thousands of white people who were suffering from smallpox, yellow fever, cholera, and pneumonia. Many more remained untreated.

In July 1865 the bureau took a first step toward distributing land when General Howard issued Circular 13 ordering agents to "set aside" 40-acre plots for freedmen. But the allocation had hardly begun when the order was revoked, and it was announced that land already distributed under Sherman's Special Field Order #15 was to be returned to its white owners.

The reason for this reversal was that Andrew Johnson, who had become president after Lincoln's assassination in April 1865, began to pardon hundreds and then thousands of former Confederates and restore their lands to them. General Howard had to tell black people that they had to relinquish the land they thought they had acquired. Speaking to some 2,000 freedmen on South Carolina's Edisto Island in October 1865, Howard pleaded with them to "lay aside their bitter feelings, and to become reconciled to their old masters." A black man shouted a response, "Why, General Howard, why do you take away our lands? You take them from us who are true, always true to the Government! You give them to our all-time enemies. This is not right!"

A committee rejected Howard's appeal for reconciliation and forgiveness and an unhappy black man insisted the government provide land:

You ask us to forgive the landowners of our island. You only lost your right arm in war and might forgive them. The man who tied me to a tree and gave me 39 lashes and who stripped and flogged my mother and my sister and who will not let me stay in his

OFFICE OF THE FREEDMEN'S BUREAU, MEMPHIS, TENNESSEE.
[See Page 316.]

Freedmen's Bureau agents often found themselves in the middle of angry disputes over land and labor that erupted between black and white southerners. Too often the Bureau officers sided with the white landowners in these disagreements with former slaves.   *Harper's Weekly*, July 25, 1868

empty hut except I will do his planting and be satisfied with his price and who combines with others to keep away land from me well knowing I would not have anything to do with him if I had land of my own—that man I cannot well forgive.

These appeals moved Howard. He returned to Washington and attempted to persuade Congress to provide land. Congress refused, and President Johnson was determined that white people would get their lands back. It seemed so sensible to most white people. Property that had belonged to white families for generations simply could not be given to freedmen. Freedmen saw it differently. They deserved land that they and their families had worked without compensation for generations. Freedmen believed it was the only way to make freedom meaningful and to gain independence from white people. As it turned out, most freedmen were forced off land they thought should belong to them.

SOUTHERN HOMESTEAD ACT

In early 1866 Congress attempted to provide land for freedmen with the passage of the **Southern Homestead Act.** More than three million acres of public land were

VOICES

A FREEDMEN'S BUREAU COMMISSIONER TELLS FREED PEOPLE WHAT FREEDOM MEANS

In June 1865 Charles Soule, the commissioner of contracts for the Freedmen's Bureau, told freedmen in Orangeburg, South Carolina, what to expect and how to behave in the coming year:

You are now free, but you must know that the only difference you can feel yet, between slavery and freedom, is that neither you nor your children can be bought or sold. You may have a harder time this year than you have ever had before; it will be the price you pay for your freedom. You will have to work hard, and get very little to eat, and very few clothes to wear. If you get through this year alive and well, you should be thankful. . . . You cannot be paid in money, for there is no good money in the District, nothing but Confederate paper. Then, what can you be paid with? Why, with food, with clothes, with the free use of your little houses and plots. You do not own a cent's worth except yourselves.

You do not understand why some of the white people who used to own you do not have to work in the field. It is because they are rich. If every man were poor, and worked in his own field, there would be no big farms, and very little cotton or corn raised to sell; there would be no money, and nothing to buy. Some people must be rich, to pay the others, and they have the right to do no work except to look out after their property.

Remember that all of your working time belongs to the man who hires you: therefore you must not leave work without his leave not even to nurse a child, or to go and visit a wife or husband. When you wish to go off the place, get a pass as you used to, and then you will run no danger of being taken up by our soldiers.

In short, do just about as the good men among you have always done. Remember that even if you are badly off, no one can buy and sell you: remember that if you help yourselves, GOD will help you, and trust hopefully that next year and the year after will bring some new blessing to you.

▶ *According to Soule, what is the difference between slavery and freedom?*
▶ *Does freedom mean that freed people will have economic opportunities equal to those of white people?*
▶ *How should freed people have responded to Soule's advice?*

Source: Ira Berlin et al., "The Terrain of Freedom: The Struggle over the Meaning of Free Labor in the U.S. South," *History Workshop* 22 (Autumn 1986): 108–30.

set aside for black people and white southerners who had remained loyal to the Union. Much of this land, however, consisted of swampy wetlands or unfertile pinewoods unsuitable for farming. More than 4,000 black families—three-quarters of them in Florida—did claim some of this land, but many lacked the financial resources to cultivate it. Eventually timber companies acquired much of it, and the Southern Homestead Act largely failed.

SHARECROPPING

To make matters worse, by 1866 bureau officials tried to force freedmen to sign labor contracts with white landowners—returning black people to white authority. Black men who refused to sign contracts could be arrested. Theoretically, these contracts were legal agreements between two equals: landowner and laborer. But they were seldom freely concluded. Bureau agents usually sided with the landowner and pressured freedmen to accept unequal terms.

Occasionally, the landowner would pay wages to the laborer. But because most landowners lacked cash to pay wages, they agreed to provide the laborer with part of the crop. The laborer, often grudgingly, agreed to work under the supervision of the landowner. The contracts required labor for a full year. The laborer could neither quit nor strike. Landowners demanded that the laborers work the fields in gangs. Freedmen resisted this system. They sometimes insisted on making decisions involving planting, fertilizing, and harvesting as they sought to exercise independence (see Map 12–1).

Thus, it took time for a new form of agricultural labor to develop. But by the 1870s, the system of **sharecropping** dominated most of the South. There were no wages. Freedmen worked land as families—not in gangs—and not under direct white supervision. The landowner provided seed, tools, fertilizer, and work animals (mules, horses, oxen), and the black family received one-third of the crop. There were many variations on these arrangements, and black families were often cheated out of their fair share of the crop. Without land of their own, they remained under white authority well into the twentieth century.

The Black Church

In the years after slavery, the church became the most important institution among African Americans other than the family. It filled deep spiritual needs, offered enriching music, provided charity and compassion to those in need, developed community and political

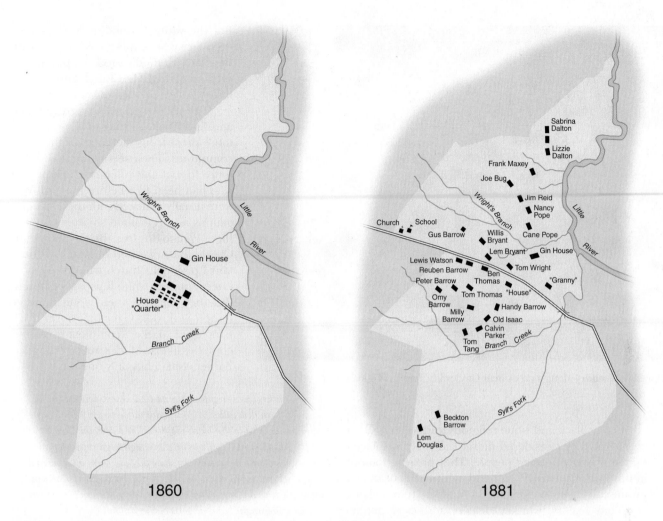

MAP 12–1 THE EFFECT OF SHARECROPPING ON THE SOUTHERN PLANTATION: THE BARROW PLANTATION, OGLETHORPE COUNTY, GEORGIA

With the end of slavery and the advent of sharecropping, black people would no longer agree to work in fields as gangs. They preferred to have each family cultivate separate plots of land, thereby distancing themselves as much as possible from slavery and white supervision.

▶ *Although many freed people worked the same land that they had as slaves, how does this map suggest the changes experienced by black people in family life, religion, education, and their relationships with white people?*

leaders, and was free of white supervision. Before slavery's demise, free black people and slaves often attended white churches where they participated in religious services conducted by white clergymen and where they were treated as second-class Christians.

Once liberated, black men and women organized their own churches with their own ministers. Most black people considered white ministers incapable of delivering a meaningful message. Nancy Williams recalled, "Ole white preachers used to talk wid dey tongues widdout sayin' nothin', but Jesus told us slaves to talk wid our hearts."

Northern white missionaries were sometimes appalled by the unlettered and ungrammatical black preachers who nevertheless communicated effectively and emotionally with their parishioners. A visiting white clergyman was impressed and humbled on hearing a black preacher who lacked education but more than made up for it with his devout faith. "He talked about Christ and his salvation as one who understood what he said. . . . Here was an unlearned man, one who could not read, telling of the love of Christ, of Christian faith and duty in a way which I have not learned."

Freedwomen washing laundry along a creek near Circleville, Texas, c. 1866.

But the white Methodists lost some of their fervor after they failed to persuade the black Methodists to keep political issues out of the CME Church and to dwell instead solely on spiritual concerns.

The Presbyterian, Congregational, and Episcopal churches appealed to the more prosperous members of the black community. Their services tended to be more formal and solemn. Black people who had been free before the Civil War were usually affiliated with these congregations and remained so after the conflict. Well-to-do free black people in Charleston organized St. Mark's Protestant Episcopal Church when they separated from the white Episcopal Church. But they retained their white minister Joseph Seabrook as rector. Poorer black people of darker complexion found churches like St. Mark's unappealing. Ed Barber visited, but only one time:

"When I was trampin' 'round Charleston, dere was a church dere called St. Mark, dat all de society folks of my color went to. No black nigger welcome dere, they told me. Thinkin' as how I was bright 'nough to git in, I up and goes dere one Sunday, Ah, how they did carry on, bow and scrape and ape de white folks. . . . I was uncomfortable all de time though, 'cause they were too "hifalootin" in de ways, in de singin', and all sorts of carryin' ons."

The Roman Catholic Church made modest inroads among black southerners. There were all-black parishes in St. Augustine, Savannah, Charleston, and Louisville after the Civil War. For generations before the conflict, many well-to-do free people of color in New Orleans had been Catholics, and their descendants remained faithful to the church. On Georgia's Skidaway Island, Benedictine monks established a school for black youngsters in 1878 that survived for nearly a decade.

Religious differences notwithstanding, the black churches, their parishioners, and their clergymen would play a vital role in Reconstruction politics. More than one hundred black ministers were elected to political office after the Civil War.

Other black and white religious leaders anguished over what they considered moral laxity and displaced values among the freed people. They preached about honesty, thrift, temperance, and elimination of sexual promiscuity. They demanded an end to "rum-suckers, bar-room loafers, whiskey dealers and card players among the men, and to those women who dressed finely on ill gotten gain."

Church members struggled, scrimped, and saved to buy land and build churches. Most former slaves founded Baptist and Methodist churches. These denominations tended to be more autonomous and less subject to outside control. Their doctrine was usually simple and direct without complex theology. Of the Methodist churches, the African Methodist Episcopal (AME) Church made giant strides in the South after the Civil War.

In Charleston the AME Church was resurrected 40 years after it had been forced to disband during the turmoil over the Denmark Vesey plot in 1822 (see Chapter 8). But by the 1870s, three AME congregations were thriving in Charleston. In Wilmington, North Carolina, the 1,600 members of the Front Street Methodist Church decided to join the AME Church soon after the Civil War ended. They replaced the longtime white minister, the Rev. L. S. Burkhead, with a black man.

White Methodists initially encouraged cooperation with black Methodists and helped establish the Colored (now Christian) Methodist Episcopal (CME) Church.

Education

Freedom and education were inseparable. To remain illiterate after emancipation was to remain enslaved. One ex-slave master bluntly told his former slave,

Charles Whiteside, "Charles, you is a free man they say, but Ah tells you now, you is still a slave and if you lives to be a hundred, you'll STILL be a slave, cause you got no education, and education is what makes a man free!" Almost every freed black person—young or old—desperately wanted to learn. Elderly people were especially eager to read the Bible. During the war and before slavery ended, black people began to establish schools. In 1861 Mary Peake, a free black woman, opened a school in Hampton, Virginia. On South Carolina's sea islands, a black cabinetmaker began teaching openly after having covertly operated a school for years. In 1862 northern missionaries arrived on the sea islands to begin teaching.

●●● Read the Document
Charlotte Forten, Life on the Sea Islands (1864)

Laura Towne and Ellen Murray, two white women, and Charlotte Forten, a black woman, opened Penn school on St. Helena's Island as part of the Port Royal Experiment. They enrolled 138 children and 58 adults. By 1863 there were 1,700 students and 45 teachers at 30 schools in the South Carolina low country.

With the end of the Civil War, northern religious organizations, in cooperation with the Freedmen's Bureau, organized hundreds of schools. Classes were held in stables, homes, former slave cabins, taverns, churches, and even—in Savannah and New Orleans—the old slave markets. Former slaves spent hours in the fields and then trudged to a makeshift school to learn the alphabet and arithmetic. In 1865 black ministers created the Savannah Educational Association, raised $1,000, employed 15 black teachers, and enrolled 600 students.

In 1866 the Freedmen's Bureau set aside $500,000 for education. The Bureau furnished the buildings, while former slaves hired, housed, and fed the teachers.

◉ See the Map
Milestones in Education

By 1869 the Freedmen's Bureau was involved with 3,000 schools and 150,000 students. Even more impressive, by 1870 black people had contributed $1 million to educate their people.

BLACK TEACHERS

Although freedmen appreciated the dedication of the white teachers affiliated with the missionary societies, they usually preferred black teachers. The Rev. Richard H. Cain, an AME minister who came south from Brooklyn, New York, said that black people needed to learn to control their own futures: "We must take into our own hands the education of our race. . . . Honest, dignified whites may teach ever so well, but it has not the effect to exalt the black man's opinion of his own race, because they have always been in the habit of seeing white men in honored positions, and respected."

Black men and women responded to the call to teach. Virginia C. Green, a northern black woman, felt compelled to go to Mississippi: "Though I have never known servitude they are . . . my people. Born as far north as the lakes I have felt no freer because so many were less fortunate. . . . I look forward with impatience to the time when my people shall be strong, blest with education, purified and made prosperous by virtue and industry." Hezekiah Hunter, a black teacher from New York, commented in 1865 on the need for black teachers: "I believe we best can instruct our own people, knowing our own peculiarities—needs—necessities. Further—I believe we that are competent owe it to our people to teach them our speciality." And in Malden, West Virginia, when black residents found that a recently arrived 18-year-old black man could read and write, they hired him to teach.

Charlotte Forten came from a prominent Philadelphia family of color. She joined hundreds of black and white teachers who migrated South during and after the Civil War to instruct the freed people. Some teachers remained for a few months. Others stayed for a lifetime. Charlotte Forten—shown here in an 1866 photograph—taught on the South Carolina sea islands from 1862 to 1864.

In some areas of the South, the sole person available to teach was a poorly educated former slave equipped primarily with a willingness to teach fellow freedmen. One such teacher explained, "I never had the chance of goen to school for I was a slave until freedom. . . . I am the only teacher because we can not doe better now." Many northern teachers, black and white, provided more than the basics of elementary education. Black life and history were occasionally read about and discussed. Abolitionist Lydia Maria Child wrote *The Freedmen's Book*, which offered brief biographies of Benjamin Banneker, Frederick Douglass, and Toussaint Louverture. More often northern teachers, dismayed at the backwardness of the freedmen, struggled to modify behavior and to impart cultural values by teaching piety, thrift, cleanliness, temperance, and timeliness.

Many former slaves came to resent some of these teachers as condescending, self-righteous, and paternalistic. Sometimes the teachers, especially those who were white, became frustrated with recalcitrant students who did not readily absorb middle-class values. Others, however, derived enormous satisfaction from teaching freedmen. A Virginia teacher commented, "I think I shall stay here as long as I live and teach this people. I have no love or taste for any other work, and I am happy only here with them."

BLACK COLLEGES

Northern churches and religious societies established dozens of colleges, universities, academies, and institutes across the South in the late 1860s and the 1870s. Most of these institutions provided elementary and secondary education. Few black students were prepared for actual college or university work. The **American Missionary Association**—an abolitionist and Congregationalist organization—worked with the Freedmen's Bureau to establish Fisk in Tennessee, Hampton in Virginia, Tougaloo in Alabama, and Avery in South Carolina. The primary purpose of these schools was to educate black students to become teachers.

In Missouri, the black enlisted men and white officers of the 62nd and 65th Colored Volunteers raised $6,000 to establish Lincoln Institute in 1866, which would become Lincoln University. The American Baptist Home Mission Society founded Virginia Union, Shaw in North Carolina, Benedict in South Carolina, and Morehouse in Georgia. Northern Methodists helped establish Claflin in South Carolina, Rust in Mississippi, and Bennett in North Carolina. The Episcopalians were responsible for St. Augustine's in North Carolina and St. Paul's in Virginia. These and similar institutions formed the foundation for the historically black colleges and universities.

RESPONSE OF WHITE SOUTHERNERS

White southerners considered black people's efforts to learn absurd. For generations, white Americans had considered people of African descent abjectly inferior. When efforts were made to educate former slaves, white southerners reacted with suspicion, contempt, and hostility. One white woman told a teacher, "I do assure you, you might as well try to teach your horse or mule to read, as to teach these niggers. They can't learn."

Most white people were well aware that black people could learn. Otherwise, the slave codes that prohibited educating slaves would have been unnecessary. After slavery's end, some white people went out of their way to prevent black people from learning. Countless schools were burned, mostly in rural areas. In Canton, Mississippi, black people collected money to open a school—only to have white residents inform them that the school would be burned and the prospective teacher lynched if it opened. The female teacher at a freedmen's school in Donaldsonville, Louisiana, was shot and killed.

Other white southerners grudgingly tolerated black people's desire to acquire an education. One planter

Black and white land-grant colleges stressed training in agriculture and industry. In this late nineteenth-century photograph, Hampton Institute students learn milk production. The men are in military uniforms, which was typical for males at these colleges. Military training was a required part of the curriculum.

conceded in 1870, "Every little negro in the county is now going to school and the public pays for it. This is one hell of [a] fix but we can't help it, and the best policy is to conform as far as possible to circumstances."

Most white people refused to attend school with black people. No integrated schools were established in the immediate aftermath of emancipation. Most black people were more interested in gaining an education than in whether white students attended school with them. When black youngsters tried to attend a white school in Raleigh, North Carolina, the white students stopped going to it. For a brief time in Charleston, black and white children attended the same school, but they were taught in separate classrooms.

Violence

In the days, weeks, and months after the end of the Civil War, an orgy of brutality and violence swept across the South. White southerners—embittered by their defeat and unable to adjust to the end of slave labor and the loss of millions of dollars worth of slave property—lashed out at black people. There were beatings, murders, rapes, and riots, often with little or no provocation.

Black people who demanded respect, wore better clothing, refused to step aside for white people, or asked to be addressed as "mister" or "missus" were attacked. In South Carolina, a white clergyman shot and killed a black man who protested when another black man was removed from a church service. In Texas, one black man was killed for not removing his hat in the presence of a white man and another for refusing to relinquish a bottle of whiskey. A black woman was beaten for "using insolent language," and a black worker in Alabama was killed for speaking sharply to a white overseer. In Virginia, a black veteran was beaten after announcing he had been proud to serve in the Union Army.

In South Carolina, a white man asked a passing black man whom he belonged to. The black man replied that he no longer belonged to anybody, "I am free now." With that, the white man roared, "Sas me? You black devil!" He then slashed the freedman with a knife. The sheriff of DeWitt County, Texas, shot a black man who was whistling "Yankee Doodle." A Freedmen's Bureau agent in North Carolina explained the intense white hostility: "The fact is, it's the first notion with a great many of these people, if a Negro says anything or does anything that they don't like, to take a gun and put a bullet into him, or a charge of shot." In Texas another Freedmen's Bureau officer claimed that white people simply killed black people "for the love of killing."

There was also large-scale violence. In 1865 University of North Carolina students twice attacked peaceful meetings of black people. Near Pine Bluff,

PROFILE: Charlotte E. Ray

Charlotte E. Ray became the first African-American woman to earn a law degree and the first woman admitted to practice law in Washington, D.C. She was born on January 13, 1850, in New York City, one of seven children. Her parents were the Rev. Charles B. Ray and his second wife, Charlotte Augusta Burroughs Ray. They were firm believers in the rights of African Americans and in their potential for success.

Charlotte attended Myrtilla Miner's Institution for the Education of Colored Youth in Washington, D.C., where Myrtilla Miner, a white educator from New York, was determined to demonstrate that black women were as capable of high moral and mental development as white women.

Charlotte completed high school at Miner's in 1869 and taught at the Normal and Preparatory Department of the recently established Howard University. She also enrolled in law classes at Howard and wrote a thesis analyzing corporations. She graduated from the law school in 1872 and a month later was admitted to the bar in Washington. She opened an office and planned to practice real estate law. As a real estate lawyer, she could avoid court appearances and the discrimination that women attorneys encountered. She often used her initials, C. E. Ray, so that her clients would not suffer because their legal counsel could be identified as a woman.

Because of the Panic of 1873 and the ensuing economic depression and the difficulties of being a black woman in a white male profession, Ray gave up the practice of law. She supported women's rights and in 1876 attended the annual meeting of the National American Woman Suffrage Association in New York City. By 1879, she had returned to New York and taught school in Brooklyn. Some time before 1886, she had married, but little is known of her husband. Charlotte Ray died of acute bronchitis on January 11, 1911.

Bearing a remarkable resemblance to a slave auction, this scene in Monticello, Florida, shows a black man auctioned off to the highest bidder shortly after the Civil War. Under the terms of most southern black codes, black people arrested and fined for vagrancy or loitering could be "sold" if they could not pay the fine. Such spectacles infuriated many northerners and led to demands for more rigid Reconstruction policies.

Arkansas, in 1866, a white mob burned a black settlement and lynched 24 men, women, and children. An estimated 2,000 black people were murdered around Shreveport, Louisiana. In Texas, white people killed 1,000 black people between 1865 and 1868.

In May 1866, white residents of Memphis went on a rampage after black veterans forced police to release a black prisoner. The city was already beset with economic difficulties and racial tensions caused in part by an influx of rural refugees. White people, led by Irish policemen, destroyed hundreds of homes, cabins, shacks, churches, and schools in the black section of Memphis. Forty-six black people and two white men died.

On July 30, 1866, in New Orleans, white people—angered that black men were demanding political rights—assaulted black people on the street and in a convention hall. City policemen, who were mostly Confederate veterans, shot down the black delegates as they fled in panic waving white flags in a futile attempt to surrender. Thirty-four black people and three of their white allies died. Federal troops eventually stopped the bloodshed. General Philip H. Sheridan called the riot "an absolute massacre."

Little was done to stem the violence. Most Union troops had been withdrawn from the South and demobilized after the war. The Freedmen's Bureau was usually unwilling and unable to protect the black population. Black people left to defend themselves were usually in no position to retaliate. Instead, they sometimes attempted to bring the perpetrators to justice. In Orangeburg, South Carolina, armed black men brought three white men who had been wreaking violence in the community to the local jail. In Holly Springs, Mississippi, a posse of armed black men apprehended a white man who had murdered a freedwoman.

For black people, the system of justice was thoroughly unjust. Although black people could now testify against white people in court, southern juries remained all white and refused to convict white people charged with harming black people. In Texas during 1865 and 1866, 500 white men were indicted for murdering black people. None were convicted.

The Crusade for Political and Civil Rights

In October 1864 in Syracuse, New York, 145 black leaders gathered in a national convention. Some of the century's most prominent black men and women attended, including Henry Highland Garnet, Frances E. W. Harper, William Wells Brown, Francis L. Cardozo, Richard H. Cain, Jonathan J. Wright, and Jonathan C. Gibbs. They embraced the basic tenets of the American political tradition and proclaimed that they expected to participate fully in it.

●●●━**Read** the **Document**
Integration Quest: Race Relations and Reconstruction

Anticipating a future free of slavery, Frederick Douglass optimistically declared "that we hereby assert our full confidence in the fundamental principles of this government . . . the great heart of this nation will ultimately concede us our just claims, accord us our rights, and grant us our full measure of citizenship under the broad shield of the Constitution."

●●●━**Read** the **Document**
The Civil Rights Act of 1866

Even before the **Syracuse Convention,** northern Republicans met in Union-controlled territory around Beaufort, South Carolina, and nominated the state's delegates to the 1864 Republican national convention.

Among those selected were Robert Smalls and Prince Rivers, former slaves who had exemplary records with the Union Army. The probability of black participation in postwar politics seemed promising.

But northern and southern white leaders who already held power would largely determine whether black Americans would gain political power or acquire the same rights as white people. As the Civil War ended, President Lincoln was more concerned with restoring the seceded states to the Union than in opening political doors for black people. Yet Lincoln suggested that at least some black men deserved the right to vote. On April 11, 1865, he wrote, "I would myself prefer that [the vote] were now conferred on the very intelligent, and on those who serve our cause as soldiers." Three days later he was assassinated.

Presidential Reconstruction under Andrew Johnson

Vice President Andrew Johnson then became president and initially seemed inclined to impose stern policies on the white South while befriending the freedmen.

◄●►Read the Document
President Johnson's Veto of the Civil Rights Act of 1866

He announced that "treason must be made odious, and traitors must be punished and impoverished." In 1864 he had told black people, "I will be your Moses, and lead you through the Red Sea of War and Bondage to a fairer future of Liberty and Peace." Nothing proved to be further from the truth. Andrew Johnson was no friend of black Americans.

Born poor in eastern Tennessee and never part of the southern aristocracy, Johnson opposed secession and was the only senator from the seceded states to remain loyal to the Union. He had nonetheless acquired five slaves and the conviction that black people were so inferior that white men must forever govern them. In 1867 Johnson argued that black people could not exercise political power and that they had "less capacity for government than any other race of people. No independent government of any form has ever been successful in their hands. On the contrary, wherever they have been left to their own devices they have shown a constant tendency to relapse into barbarism."

Johnson quickly lost his enthusiasm for punishing traitors. Indeed, he began to placate white southerners. In May 1865 Johnson granted blanket amnesty and pardons to former Confederates willing to swear allegiance to the United States. The main exceptions were high former Confederate officials and those who owned property valued in excess of $20,000, a large

VOICES

A NORTHERN BLACK WOMAN ON TEACHING FREEDMEN

Blanche Virginia Harris was born in 1842 in Monroe, Michigan. She graduated from Oberlin College in 1860. She became the principal of a black school in Norfolk, Virginia, attended by 230 students. She organized night classes for adults and a sewing society to provide clothing for impoverished students. Later, she taught in Mississippi, North Carolina, and Tennessee. In the following letter she describes her experiences in Mississippi:

23 January 1866
Natchez, Miss.

I have been in this city now nearly five months. . . . The colored teachers three in number, sent out by the [American Missionary] Association to this city, have been brought down here it is true. And then left to the mercy of the colored people or themselves. The distinction between the two classes of teachers (white and colored) is so marked that it is the topic of conversation among the better class of colored people.

My school is very large, some of them pay and some do not. And from the proceeds I pay the board of my sister and myself, and also for the rent of two rooms; rent as well as board is very high so I have to work quite hard to meet my expenses. I also furnish lights, wood and coal. I do not write this as fault-finding, far from it. I shall be thankful if I can in any way help. I sometimes get discouraged. . . .

I have become very much attached to my school; the interest they manifest in their studies pleases me. I will now tell you how I employ my time. From 8 A.M. until 2 P.M. I teach the children. At 3 P.M. I have a class of adults and at night I have night school.

One afternoon we have prayer meeting, another sewing school. And another singing school. I hope my next letter may be more interesting to you.

Very Respectfully,

Blanche Harris

▶ Why was the race of the teacher of such concern?
▶ What did Harris find difficult about teaching, and what did she find rewarding?

Source: Ellen NicKenzie Lawson, ed., *The Three Sarahs: Documents of Antebellum Black College Women* (New York: Edward Mellon Press, 1984).

sum at the time. Yet even these leaders could appeal for individual pardons. And appeal they did. By 1866 Johnson had pardoned more than 7,000 high-ranking former Confederates and wealthier southerners. Moreover, he had restored land to those white people who had lost it to freedmen.

Johnson's actions encouraged those who had supported secession, owned slaves, and opposed the Union. He permitted longtime southern leaders to regain political influence and authority only months after the end of America's bloodiest conflict. As black people and radical Republicans watched in disbelief, Johnson appointed provisional governors in the former Confederate states. Leaders in those states then called constitutional conventions, held elections, and prepared to regain their place in the Union. Johnson merely insisted that each former Confederate state formally accept the **Thirteenth Amendment** (ratified in December 1865, it outlawed slavery) and repudiate Confederate war debts.

The southern constitutional conventions excluded black people in the political system and denied them equal rights. As one Mississippi delegate explained, "'Tis nature's law that the superior race must rule and rule they will."

Black Codes

After the election of state and local officials, white legislators gathered in state capitals across the South to determine the status and future of the freedmen. With little debate, the legislatures drafted the so-called **black codes.** Southern politicians gave no thought to providing black people with the political and legal rights associated with citizenship.

The black codes sought to ensure the availability of a subservient agricultural labor supply controlled by white people. They imposed severe restrictions on freedmen. Freedmen had to sign annual labor contracts with white landowners. South Carolina required black people who wanted to establish a business to purchase licenses costing from $10 to $100. The codes permitted black children ages 2 to 21 to be apprenticed to white people and spelled out their duties and obligations in detail. Corporal punishment was legal. Employers were designated "masters" and employees "servants." The black codes also restricted black people from loitering or vagrancy, using alcohol or firearms, hunting, fishing, and grazing livestock. The codes did guarantee rights that slaves had not possessed. Freedmen could marry legally, engage in contracts, purchase property, sue or be sued, and testify in court. But black people could not vote or

Read the Document
The Mississippi Black Code (1865)

serve on juries. The black codes conceded—barely—freedom to black people.

Black Conventions

Alarmed by these threats to their freedom, black people met in conventions across the South in 1865 and 1866 to protest, appeal for justice, and chart their future. Men who had been free before the war dominated the conventions. Many were ministers, teachers, and artisans. Few had been slaves. Women and children also attended—as spectators, not delegates—but women often offered comments, suggestions, and criticism. These meetings were hardly militant or radical affairs. Delegates respectfully insisted that white people live up to the principles and rights embodied in the Declaration of Independence and the Constitution.

At the AME church in Raleigh, North Carolina, delegates asked for equal rights and the right to vote. At Georgia's convention they protested against white violence and appealed for leaders who would enforce the law without regard to color: "We ask not for a Black Man's Governor, nor a White Man's Governor, but for a People's Governor, who shall impartially protect the rights of all, and faithfully sustain the Union."

Delegates at the Norfolk meeting reminded white Virginians that black people were patriotic: "We are Americans. We know no other country. We love the land of our birth." But they protested that Virginia's black code caused "invidious political or legal distinctions, on account of color merely." They requested the right to vote and added that they might boycott the businesses of "those who deny to us our equal rights."

Two conventions were held in Charleston, South Carolina—one before and one after the black code was enacted. At the first, delegates stressed the "respect and affection" they felt toward white Charlestonians. They even proposed that only literate men be granted the right to vote if it were applied to both races. The second convention denounced the black code and insisted on its repeal.

Read the Document
Address of the Colored State Convention to the People of the State of South Carolina (1865)

Delegates again asked for the rights to vote and testify in court: "These two things we deem necessary to our welfare and elevation." They also appealed for public schools and for "homesteads for ourselves and our children." White authorities ignored the black conventions and their petitions. Instead, they were confident they had relegated the freedmen to a subordinate role.

By late 1865 President Johnson's Reconstruction policies had aroused black people. One black Union veteran summed up the situation: "If you call this

PROFILE: Aaron A. Bradley

At a time when many white people considered it a disgrace that even the most reserved, refined, and well-educated black man might serve in political office, Aaron Bradley's presence in politics was outrageous. White southerners regarded him as a dangerous revolutionary. White Republicans, who normally would have been his allies, considered him belligerent and uncooperative. But most freedmen admired and supported him. Like him or not, he was a major figure in Georgia politics during Reconstruction.

Bradley was born a slave in about 1815 in South Carolina. His father was probably white. He belonged to Francis W. Pickens, who was South Carolina's governor when the state seceded (see Chapter 10). For a time, Bradley worked as a shoemaker in nearby Augusta, Georgia. At about age 20, he escaped and went to Boston, where he studied law and met black and white abolitionists.

In 1865, Bradley moved to Savannah, where he took up the cause of the freedmen and opened a school. He worked closely with the city's black longshoremen and low country and sea island rice field workers.

Bradley demanded that black families keep the land they had occupied under Sherman's Special Field Order #15. He believed that they had to have land to prosper. He criticized the Freedmen's Bureau for attempting to force black people off the land and argued that President Johnson should be impeached for supporting Confederate landowners rather than black and white people who were loyal to the Union.

Bradley also insisted that black people deserved the rights to vote, testify in court, and have jury trials. After he urged black farmers to defend their land by force, federal authorities charged him with advocating insurrection. He was sentenced to a year's confinement but was soon paroled. Almost immediately, another fiery speech got him in trouble again, and he had to leave Georgia.

He returned to Boston and renewed his pleas for land for the freedmen. He wrote the head of the Freedmen's Bureau, "My great object is, to give you Back-bone, and as the Chief Justice of 4 millions of Colored people, and Refugees; You can not, and must not, be a Military Tool, in the hands of Andrew Johnson."

In 1867, Bradley returned to Savannah and attacked the system of sharecropping. He complained that freedmen were compelled to work involuntarily and asked that black men be permitted to arm themselves. He also argued that justice would be fairer if the courts included black men. Although the Freedmen's Bureau considered Bradley a troublemaker, he never backed down.

In 1867, black voters elected Bradley to the state constitutional convention, but he was soon expelled. Then he was elected to the state senate—only to be expelled again along with all the black members of the Georgia legislature.

Meanwhile, Bradley carried on a running battle with Savannah's mayor, a former Confederate colonel affiliated with the Ku Klux Klan. He threatened the "KKK and all Bad Men, . . . if you strike a blow the man or men will be followed, and the house in which he or they shall take shelter, will be burned to the ground."

In 1868, Bradley organized black workers to arm themselves to retain the lands that they believed belonged to them. For a month, black men controlled parts of Chatham County outside Savannah. Eventually, federal authorities jailed one hundred of them. Bradley again fled north.

He returned to Georgia in 1870 and reclaimed his senate seat after Congress forced the legislature to seat its black members. He supported measures to remove Savannah's mayor, reduce taxes on workers, and institute an eight-hour workday.

Democrats regained control of Georgia politics in 1872, and Bradley and the Republicans were swept from power. He ran for Congress in South Carolina in 1874 but lost. He supported black migration to Liberia and Florida, but he moved to St. Louis and died there in 1881.

Aaron Bradley was certainly not a typical Reconstruction leader. He maintained few close ties to black or white politicians. He was constantly embroiled in disputes. He did not cooperate with middle-class black leaders and had no ties with local churches and their clergymen—a rarity among black politicians.

He dressed in expensive and flashy clothes. He could be pompous, abrasive, and intemperate. White people universally detested him. Yet Bradley remained popular among freedmen.

Freedom, what do you call Slavery?" Republicans in Congress also opposed Johnson's policies toward the freedmen and the former Confederate states.

The Radical Republicans

Radical Republicans, as the more militant Republicans were called, were especially disturbed that Johnson seemed to have abandoned the ex-slaves to their former masters. They considered white southerners disloyal and unrepentant, despite their military defeat. Moreover, radical Republicans—unlike moderate Republicans and Democrats—were determined to transform the racial fabric of American society by including black people in the political and economic system.

Among the most influential radical Republicans were Senators Charles Sumner, Benjamin Wade, and Henry Wilson and Congressmen Thaddeus Stevens, George W. Julian, and James M. Ashley. Few white Americans have been as dedicated to the rights of black people as these men. They had fought to abolish slavery. They were reluctant to compromise. They were honest, tough, and articulate but also abrasive, difficult, self-righteous, and vain. Black people appreciated

them. Many white people hated them. One black veteran wrote Charles Sumner in 1869, "Your name shall live in our hearts forever." A white Philadelphia businessman said that Thaddeus Stevens "seems to oppose any measure that will not benefit the nigger."

RADICAL PROPOSALS

To provide freedmen with land, Stevens introduced a bill in Congress in late 1865 to confiscate 400 million acres from the wealthiest 10 percent of southerners and distribute it free to freedmen. The remaining land would be auctioned off in plots no larger than 500 acres. Few legislators supported the proposal. Even those who wanted fundamental change considered confiscation a violation of property rights.

Instead, radical Republicans supported voting rights for black men. They were convinced that black men—to protect themselves and to secure the South for the Republican Party—had to have the right to vote.

Moderate Republicans, however, found the prospect of black voting almost as objectionable as the confiscation of land. They preferred to build the Republican Party in the South by cooperating with President Johnson and attracting loyal white southerners.

The thought of black suffrage appalled northern and southern Democrats. Most white northerners—Republicans and Democrats—favored denying black men the right to vote in their states. After the war, proposals to guarantee the right to vote to black men were defeated in New York, Ohio, Kansas, and the Nebraska Territory. In the District of Columbia, a vote to permit black suffrage lost 6,951 to 35. However, five of the six New England states as well as Iowa, Minnesota, and Wisconsin allowed black men to vote.

As much as they objected to black suffrage, most white northerners objected even more strongly to defiant white southerners. Journalist Charles A. Dana described the attitude of many northerners: "As for negro suffrage, the mass of Union men in the Northwest do not care a great deal. What scares them is the idea that the rebels are all to be let back . . . and made a power in government again, just as though there had been no rebellion."

In December 1865, Congress created the Joint Committee on Reconstruction to determine whether to readmit the

With the adoption of radical Republican policies, most black men eagerly took part in political activities. Political meetings, conventions, speeches, barbecues, and other gatherings also attracted women and children.

southern states to the Union. The committee confirmed reports of widespread mistreatment of black people and white arrogance.

THE FREEDMEN'S BUREAU BILL
AND THE CIVIL RIGHTS BILL

In early 1866 Senator Lyman Trumbull, a moderate Republican from Illinois, introduced two major bills. The first was to provide more financial support for the Freedmen's Bureau and extend its authority to defend the rights of black people.

•••—Read the Document
The Freedmen's Bureau Bill (1865)

The second proposal became the first **Civil Rights Act** in American history. It made any person born in the United States a citizen (except Indians) and entitled them to rights protected by the U.S. government. Black people would possess the same legal rights as white people. The bill was clearly intended to invalidate the black codes.

•••—Read the Document
The Civil Rights Act of 1866

JOHNSON'S VETOES

Both measures passed in Congress with nearly unanimous Republican support. President Johnson vetoed them. He claimed that the bill to continue the Freedmen's Bureau would greatly expand the federal bureaucracy and permit too "vast a number of agents" to exercise arbitrary power over the white population. He insisted that the civil rights bill benefited black people at the expense of white people: "In fact, the distinction of race and color is by the bill made to operate in favor of the colored and against the white race."

The Johnson vetoes stunned Republicans. Although he had not meant to, Johnson drove moderate Republicans into the radical camp and strengthened the Republican Party. The president did not believe Republicans would oppose him to support the freedmen. He was wrong. Congress overrode both vetoes. The Republicans broke with Johnson in 1866, defied him in 1867, and impeached him in 1868 (failing to remove him from office by only one vote in the Senate).

The Fourteenth Amendment

To secure the legal rights of freedmen, Republicans passed the **Fourteenth Amendment.** This amendment fundamentally changed the Constitution by compelling states to accept their residents as citizens and to guarantee that their rights as citizens would be safeguarded.

Its first section guaranteed citizenship to every person born in the United States. This included virtually every black person. It made each person a citizen of the state in which he or she resided. It defined the specific rights of citizens and protected those rights against the authority of state governments. Citizens had the right to due process (usually a trial) before they could lose their life, liberty, or property:

> All persons born or naturalized in the United States, and subject to the jurisdiction thereof, are citizens of the United States and of the State wherein they reside. No State shall make or enforce any law which shall abridge the privileges or immunities of citizens of the United States; nor shall any State deprive any person of life, liberty, or property, without due process of law; nor deny to any person within its jurisdiction the equal protection of the laws.

Eleven years after Chief Justice Roger Taney declared in the *Dred Scott* decision that black people were "a subordinate and inferior class of beings" who had "no rights that white people were bound to respect," the Fourteenth Amendment vested African Americans with the same rights of citizenship other Americans possessed.

The amendment also threatened to deprive states of representation in Congress if they denied black men the vote. The end of slavery had also made obsolete the Three-Fifths Clause in the Constitution, which had counted slaves as only three-fifths (or 60 percent) of a white person in calculating a state's population and in determining the number of representatives each state was entitled to in the House of Representatives. Republicans feared that southern states would count black people in their populations without permitting them to vote, thereby gaining more representatives than those states had before the Civil War. The amendment mandated that if any state—northern or southern—did

1865–1867

FEDERAL RECONSTRUCTION LEGISLATION

1865	Freedmen's Bureau established
1865	Thirteenth Amendment passed and ratified
1866	Freedmen's Bureau Bill and the Civil Rights Act of 1866 passed over Johnson's veto
1866	Fourteenth Amendment passed (ratified 1868)
1867	Reconstruction Acts passed over Johnson's veto

not allow adult male citizens to vote, then the number of representatives it was entitled to in Congress would be reduced in proportion to the number of men denied the right to vote.

Democrats almost unanimously opposed the Fourteenth Amendment. Andrew Johnson denounced it, although he could not prevent its adoption. Except for Tennessee, southern states refused to ratify it. Women's suffragists felt betrayed because the amendment limited suffrage to males. Despite this opposition, the amendment was ratified in 1868.

Radical Reconstruction

By 1867 radical Republicans in Congress had wrested control over **Reconstruction** from Johnson, and they then imposed policies that brought black men into the political system as voters and officeholders. It was a dramatic development, second in importance only to emancipation and the end of slavery.

Republicans swept the 1866 congressional elections despite the belligerent opposition of Johnson and the Democrats. With two-thirds majorities in the House and Senate, Republicans easily overrode presidential vetoes. Two years after the Civil War, Republicans dismantled the state governments established in the South under Johnson's authority. They instituted a new Reconstruction policy.

Republicans passed the first of three **Reconstruction Acts** over Johnson's veto in March 1867. It divided the South into five military districts, each under the command of a general (see Map 12–2). Troops would protect lives and property while new civilian governments were formed. Elected delegates in each state would draft a new constitution and submit it to the voters.

UNIVERSAL MANHOOD SUFFRAGE

The Reconstruction Act stipulated that all adult males in the states of the former Confederacy were eligible to vote, except for those who had actively supported the Confederacy or were convicted felons. Once each state had formed a new government and approved the Fourteenth Amendment, it would be readmitted to the Union with representation in Congress.

The advent of radical Reconstruction was the culmination of the struggle of black people to gain legal and political rights. Since the 1864 black national convention in Syracuse and the meetings and conventions in the South in 1865 and 1866, black leaders had argued that one of the consequences of the Civil War should be the inclusion of black men in the body

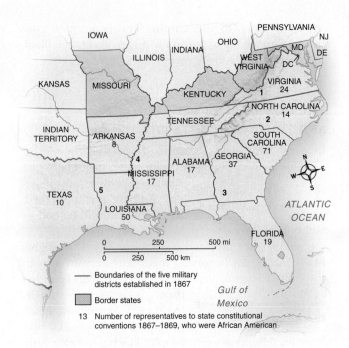

MAP 12–2   CONGRESSIONAL RECONSTRUCTION

Under the terms of the First Reconstruction Act of 1867, the former Confederate states (except Tennessee) were divided into five military districts and placed under the authority of military officers. Commanders in each of the five districts were responsible for supervising the reestablishment of civilian governments in each state.

▶ *In which states were African Americans a majority of delegates to that state's constitutional convention?*

◉ See the Map   Explore this map at www.myhistorylab.com

politic. The achievement of that goal was due to their persistent and persuasive efforts, the determination of radical Republicans, and, ironically, the obstructionism of Andrew Johnson, who had played into their hands.

BLACK POLITICS

Full of energy and enthusiasm, black men and women rushed into the political arena in the spring and summer of 1867. Although women could not vote, they joined men at the meetings, rallies, parades, and picnics that accompanied political organizing in the South. For many former slaves, politics became as important as religious activities. Black people flocked to the Republican Party and the new Union Leagues.

The **Union Leagues** had been established in the North during the Civil War, but they expanded across the South as quasi-political organizations in the late 1860s. The Leagues were social, fraternal, and patriotic groups in which black people often but not always outnumbered white people. League meetings featured ceremonies, rituals, initiation rites, and oaths. They gave people an opportunity to sharpen leadership skills and gain a political education by discussing issues from taxes to schools.

SIT-INS AND STRIKES

Political progress did not induce apathy, satisfaction, or contentment among black people. Gaining citizenship, legal rights, and the vote generated more expectations and demands for advancement. For example, black people insisted on equal access to public transportation. In Charleston, South Carolina, black people were permitted to ride only on the outside running boards of the cars. After a Republican rally there in April 1867, black men staged a "sit-in" on a horse-drawn streetcar before they were arrested. They wanted to sit on the seats inside. Within a month, after military authorities intervened, the streetcar company gave in. Similar protests occurred in Richmond and New Orleans.

Black workers also struck across the South in 1867. Black longshoremen in New Orleans, Mobile, Savannah, Charleston, and Richmond walked off the job. Black laborers were usually paid less than white men for the same work, which led to labor unrest during the 1860s and 1870s. Sometimes the strikers won, sometimes they lost. In 1869 a black Baltimore longshoreman, Isaac Myers, organized the National Colored Labor Union.

The Reaction of White Southerners

White southerners grimly opposed radical Reconstruction. They were outraged that black people could claim the same legal and political rights they themselves possessed. Such a possibility seemed preposterous to people convinced of the absolute inferiority of black people. Benjamin F. Perry, whom Johnson had appointed provisional governor of South Carolina in 1865, captures the depth of this racist conviction: "The African," Perry declared, "has been in all ages, a savage or a slave. God created him inferior to the white man in form, color and intellect, and no legislation or culture can make him his equal. . . . His hair, his form and features will not

compete with the caucasian race, and it is in vain to think of elevating him to the dignity of the white man. God created differences between the two races, and nothing can make him equal."

Some white people, taking solace in their belief in the innate inferiority of black people, concluded they could turn black suffrage to their advantage. White people, they assumed, should easily be able to control and manipulate black voters just as they had controlled black people during slavery. White southerners who believed this, however, would be disappointed, and their disappointment would turn to fury.

CONCLUSION

Why were black southerners able to gain citizenship and access to the political system by 1868? Most white Americans did not suddenly abandon 250 years of deeply ingrained beliefs that people of African descent were their inferiors. The advances that African Americans achieved fit into a series of complex political developments after the Civil War. Black people themselves had fought and died to preserve the Union, and they had earned the grudging respect of many white people and the open admiration of others. Black leaders in meetings and petitions insisted that their rights be recognized.

White northerners—led by the radical Republicans—were convinced that President Johnson was wrong to support policies that permitted white southerners to retain pre–Civil War leaders while the black codes virtually made freedmen slaves again. Republicans were determined that white southerners realize that their defeat had doomed the prewar status quo. Republicans established a Reconstruction program to disfranchise key southern leaders while providing legal rights to freedmen. The right to vote, they reasoned, would enable black people to deal more effectively with white southerners and strengthen the Republican Party in the South.

The result was to make the mid-to late 1860s one of the few high points in African-American history. During this period, not only was slavery abolished, but black southerners were able to organize schools and churches, and black people throughout the South acquired legal and political rights that would have been incomprehensible before the war. Yet black people did not stand on the brink of utopia. Most freedmen still lacked land and had no realistic hope of obtaining much, if any, of it. White violence and cruelty continued almost unabated across much of the South. Still, for millions of African Americans, the future looked more promising than ever before in American history.

AFRICAN-AMERICAN EVENTS	NATIONAL EVENTS
● 1862 ●	
March 1862 The Port Royal Experiment in South Carolina begins	**February 1862** Julia Ward Howe publishes the first version of "Battle Hymn of the Republic" in the *Atlantic Monthly* **July 1862** Morrill Land-Grant College Act signed into law
● 1864 ●	
October 1864 Black national convention in Syracuse, New York	**November 1864** President Lincoln reelected
● 1865 ●	
January 1865 General Sherman's Special Field Order #15 **March 1865** Freedmen's Bureau established **September–November 1865** Black codes enacted	**April 1865** Lincoln is assassinated; Andrew Johnson succeeds to presidency **May 1865** Johnson begins presidential Reconstruction **June–August 1865** Southern state governments reorganized **December 1865** Thirteenth Amendment to the Constitution ratified
● 1866 ●	
February 1866 Southern Homestead Act **March 1866** President Johnson vetoes bill to extend the Freedman's Bureau and the Civil Rights bill **April 1866** Congress overrides Johnson's veto of the Civil Rights bill **May 1866** Memphis riot **July 1866** Congress enacts new Freedmen's Bureau bill over Johnson's veto; New Orleans riot	**November 1866** Republicans gain greater than two-thirds majorities in House and Senate

RECOMMENDED READING

Ira Berlin and Leslie Rowland, eds. *Families and Freedom: A Documentary History of African-American Kinship in the Civil War Era.* New York: Cambridge University Press, 1997. A collection of documents that conveys the aspirations and frustrations of freedmen.

David W. Blight. *Race and Reunion: The Civil War in American Memory.* Cambridge, MA: Harvard University Press, 2001. This outstanding study shows how white Americans "remembered" the Civil War and reconciled their sectional differences by essentially forgetting the role and contributions of African Americans.

W. E. B. Du Bois. *Black Reconstruction in America: An Essay toward a History of the Part Which Black Folk Played in the Attempt to Reconstruct Democracy in America, 1860–1880.* New York: Russell & Russell, 1935. A classic account of Reconstruction challenging the traditional interpretation that it was a tragic era marked by corrupt and inept black rule of the South.

Eric Foner. *Reconstruction: America's Unfinished Revolution, 1863–1877.* New York: Harper & Row, 1988. The best and most comprehensive account of Reconstruction.

Herbert G. Gutman. *The Black Family in Slavery and Freedom, 1750–1925.* New York: Oxford University Press, 1976. An illustration of how African-American family values and kinship ties forged in slavery endured after emancipation.

Steven Hahn. *A Nation under Our Feet: Black Political Struggles in the Rural South from Slavery to the Great Migration.* Cambridge, MA: Harvard University Press, 2003. In a sophisticated analysis, Hahn explores how African Americans conceived of themselves as political people and organized from slavery through Reconstruction and disfranchisement to the 1920s.

Tera W. Hunter. *To Joy My Freedom: Southern Black Women's Lives and Labors after the Civil War.* Cambridge, MA: Harvard University Press, 1997. An examination of the interior lives of black women, their work, social welfare, and leisure.

Gerald D. Jaynes. *Branches without Roots: Genesis of the Black Working Class in the American South, 1862–1882.* New York: Pantheon, 1986. Examines the changes in work patterns and the labor of African Americans after slavery.

Leon F. Litwack. *Been in the Storm So Long: The Aftermath of Slavery.* New York: Alfred A. Knopf, 1979. A rich and detailed account of the transition to freedom largely based on recollections of former slaves.

ADDITIONAL BIBLIOGRAPHY

EDUCATION

James D. Anderson. *The Education of Blacks in the South, 1860–1935.* Chapel Hill: University of North Carolina Press, 1988.

Ronald E. Butchart. *Northern Schools, Southern Blacks, and Reconstruction: Freedmen's Education, 1862–1875.* Westport, CT: Greenwood Press, 1981.

Edmund L. Drago. *Initiative, Paternalism, and Race Relations: Charleston's Avery Normal Institute.* Athens: University of Georgia Press, 1990.

Robert C. Morris. *Reading, 'Riting, and Reconstruction: The Education of the Freedmen in the South, 1861–1890.* Chicago: University of Chicago Press, 1981.

Joe M. Richardson. *Christian Reconstruction: The American Missionary Association and Southern Blacks, 1861–1890.* Athens: University of Georgia Press, 1986.

Brenda Stevenson, ed. *The Journals of Charlotte Forten Grimke.* New York: Oxford University Press, 1988.

Heather Andrea Williams. *Self Taught: African-American Education in Slavery and Freedom.* Chapel Hill: University of North Carolina Press, 2005.

LAND AND LABOR

Paul A. Cimbala and Randall M. Miller, eds. *The Freedmen's Bureau and Reconstruction.* New York: Fordham University Press, 1999.

Barbara J. Fields. *Slavery and Freedom on the Middle Ground: Maryland during the Nineteenth Century.* New Haven, CT: Yale University Press, 1985.

Jacqueline Jones. *Labor of Love, Labor of Sorrow: Black Women, Work and Family, from Slavery to the Present.* New York: Basic Books, 1985.

Edward Magdol. *A Right to the Land: Essays on the Freedmen's Community.* Westport, CT: Greenwood Press, 1977.

Claude F. Oubre. *Forty Acres and a Mule: The Freedmen's Bureau and Black Landownership.* Baton Rouge: Louisiana State University Press, 1978.

Dylan C. Penningroth. *The Claims of Kinfolk: African American Property and Community in the Nineteenth-Century South.* Chapel Hill: University of North Carolina Press, 2003.

Roger L. Ransom and Richard Sutch. *One Kind of Freedom: The Economic Consequences of Emancipation.* New York: Cambridge University Press, 1977.

Elizabeth Regosin. *Freedom's Promise: Slave Families and Citizenship in the Age of Emancipation.* Charlottesville: University of Virginia Press, 2002

Willie Lee Rose. *Rehearsal for Reconstruction: The Port Royal Experiment.* Indianapolis: Bobbs-Merrill, 1964.

Julie Saville. *The Work of Reconstruction: From Slave to Wage Labor in South Carolina, 1860–1870.* New York: Cambridge University Press, 1994.

James D. Schmidt. *Free to Work: Labor, Law, Emancipation, and Reconstruction, 1815–1880.* Athens: University of Georgia Press, 1998.

Leslie A. Schwalm. *A Hard Fight for We: Women's Transition from Slavery to Freedom in South Carolina.* Urbana: University of Illinois Press, 1997.

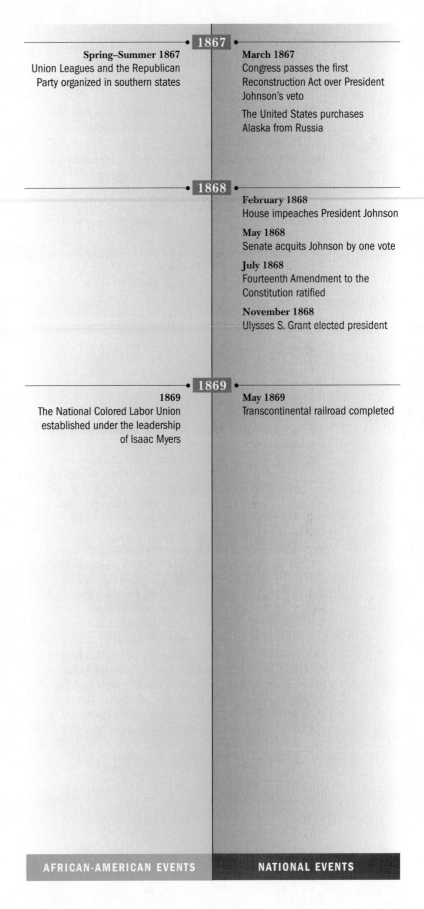

1867

Spring–Summer 1867
Union Leagues and the Republican Party organized in southern states

March 1867
Congress passes the first Reconstruction Act over President Johnson's veto

The United States purchases Alaska from Russia

1868

February 1868
House impeaches President Johnson

May 1868
Senate acquits Johnson by one vote

July 1868
Fourteenth Amendment to the Constitution ratified

November 1868
Ulysses S. Grant elected president

1869

1869
The National Colored Labor Union established under the leadership of Isaac Myers

May 1869
Transcontinental railroad completed

AFRICAN-AMERICAN EVENTS   **NATIONAL EVENTS**

BLACK COMMUNITIES

John W. Blassingame. *Black New Orleans, 1860–1880.* Chicago: University of Chicago Press, 1973.

Cyprian Davis. *The History of Black Catholics in the United States.* New York: Crossroad, 1990.

Robert F. Engs. *Freedom's First Generation: Black Hampton, Virginia, 1861–1890.* Philadelphia: University of Pennsylvania Press, 1979.

William E. Montgomery. *Under Their Own Vine and Fig Tree: The African American Church in the South 1865–1900.* Baton Rouge: Louisiana State University Press, 1993.

Bernard E. Powers Jr. *Black Charlestonians: A Social History, 1822–1885.* Fayetteville: University of Arkansas Press, 1994.

Clarence E. Walker. *A Rock in a Weary Land: The African Methodist Episcopal Church during the Civil War and Reconstruction.* Baton Rouge: Louisiana State University Press, 1982.

James M. Washington. *Frustrated Fellowship: The Black Baptist Quest for Social Power.* Macon, GA: Mercer University Press, 1986.

RETRACING THE ODYSSEY

The Avery Research Center for African-American History and Culture, Charleston, South Carolina. www.avery.cofc.edu. In 1865 the American Missionary Association opened a private school for black youngsters that served the Charleston community until 1954. The renovated structure currently contains an archive, a restored classroom, and exhibits devoted to African-American life in the Carolina low country.

Shaw University and St. Augustine's College, Raleigh, North Carolina. www.shawuniversity.edu. www.st-aug.edu. These are two of the many black colleges established during Reconstruction. The Baptists founded Shaw in 1865, and its impressive Estey Hall has survived almost 130 years. The Episcopal Church and the Freedmen's Bureau collaborated to found St. Augustine's in 1867.

Fisk University, Nashville, Tennessee. www.fisk.edu. The American Missionary Association established Fisk in 1866. Magnificent Jubilee Hall is the nation's oldest building dedicated to the higher education of black students. It was completed in 1876. There is an impressive collection of European and American art on the campus at the Carl Van Vechten Art Gallery.

St. Stephen African Methodist Episcopal Church, Wilmington, North Carolina. Following the Civil War, black members of the Front Street Methodist Church withdrew and founded their own church on Red Cross Street. In 1880 they began construction of the current building. For a time parishioners met in the basement while work continued on the imposing and ornate sanctuary above them.

Gullah/Geechee Cultural Heritage Corridor. www.nps.gov/guge. In 2006 Congress established this 12,000-square-mile corridor that extends along the South Atlantic coast from Wilmington, North Carolina, through South Carolina and Georgia, to Jacksonville, Florida. It was created to recognize the cultural contributions, language, and way of life that has prevailed among people of African descent on the sea islands and the low country since the seventeenth century.

REVIEW QUESTIONS

1. What did freedom mean to ex-slaves? How did their priorities differ from those of African Americans who had been free before the Civil War?

2. What did the former slaves and the former slaveholders want after emancipation? Were these desires realistic? How did former slaves and former slaveholders disagree after the end of slavery?

3. Why did African Americans form separate churches, schools, and social organizations after the Civil War? What role did the black church play in the black community?

4. How effective was the Freedmen's Bureau? How successful was it in assisting ex-slaves to live in freedom?

5. Why did southern states enact black codes?

6. Why did radical Republicans object to President Andrew Johnson's Reconstruction policies? Why did Congress impose its own Reconstruction policies?

7. Why were laws passed to enable black men to vote?

8. Why did black men gain the right to vote but not possession of land?

9. Did congressional Reconstruction secure full equality for African Americans as American citizens?

PEARSON myhistorylab Connections

www.myhistorylab.com

Review what you've learned in this chapter and explore the many documents, images,
research tools, and activities for this chapter to learn more about African-American history.

✓• Study and Review

READ

••• Read the Document

- Charlotte Forten, Life on the Sea Islands (1864)

- "A Jubilee of Freedom": Freed Slaves March in Charleston, South Carolina (1865)

- The Freedmen's Bureau Bill (1865)

- The Mississippi Black Code (1865)

- Address of the Colored State Convention to the People of the State of South Carolina (1865)

- The Civil Rights Act of 1866

- President Johnson's Veto of the Civil Rights Act of 1866

LISTEN

((•• Hear the Audio

Hear the audio files for Chapter 12.

- *Remembering Slavery #2*

RESEARCH

mysearchlab

Consider this question in a short research paper.

Who supported radical Reconstruction? Why?

EXPLORE

Watch the Video

- Trials of Racial Identity in Nineteenth-Century America

See the Map

- Milestones in Education

- Congressional Reconstruction

••• Read the Document

- Reconstruction: The Struggle to Define the Meaning of Freedom

- Integration Quest: Race Relations and the Reconstruction Years

Higher Education for African Americans Begins

Three black colleges were founded before the Civil War. In Pennsylvania, Cheney University opened in 1837, followed by the establishment of Lincoln University in 1854. In 1856, Wilberforce University was founded in Ohio. After the Civil War, northern black and white missionary groups fanned out across the South and—frequently with the assistance of Freedmen's Bureau officials—founded colleges, institutes, and normal schools in the former slave states in the late 1860s and the 1870s. Most of these institutions provided elementary and secondary education. Few black students were prepared for actual college or university work. Even so, black colleges soon offered academic and trade courses and professional and military training. A comprehensive list of current black colleges and universities is included on page U1–U2.

The faculty of Tuskegee Institute poses for ▶ a portrait with Mr. and Mrs. Booker T. Washington and Andrew Carnegie, the industralist (all seated in the front row).

▲ Students perform experiments in the biological laboratory at Agricultural and Mechanical College in Greensboro, North Carolina, which began in 1892 as a land-grant college.

Biological Laboratory

◀ The choir of Fisk University, Nashville, Tennessee, poses in front of the school's organ. Founded in 1866 as a liberal arts college and affiliated with the United Church of Christ, Fisk was also the home of the famed Jubilee singers, who performed in fund-raising concerts in the United States and Europe in the 1870s.

A class learns the craft ▶ of woodworking at Clafin University, Orangeburg, South Carolina, c. 1899. The university was founded in 1869 and affiliated with the United Methodist Church.

This 1850s lithograph offers a view of the buildings that comprised Wilberforce University in Xenia, Ohio, founded as a black college in 1856 by the Methodist Episcopal Church and named after the abolitionist William Wilberforce.

These classes in dressmaking and capillary physics at Hampton Institute (now University) in Virginia illustrate the range of studies available. Hampton was founded as a private university in 1868.

"Tuskegee Normal and Industrial Institute."

The Howard University law graduating class of 1900 poses on the campus in formal attire.

Students gathered on the campus of Berea College, in Berea, Kentucky, which was founded after the Civil War. Established by the Rev. John G. Fee in 1865, the college provided educational opportunities to black and white students, both men and women.

Howard University in Washington, D.C., provided education for African Americans in many professions, including dentistry. Howard first opened its doors in 1867 as a public university.

VISUALIZING THE PAST

The Meaning of Freedom:
The Failure of Reconstruction

What political offices were black men elected to—and not elected to—during Reconstruction?

What issues most concerned black political leaders?

Why were so many white southerners so opposed to black and white Republicans exercising political power?

Why was the Ku Klux Klan founded, and how effective was it?

Why was the Fifteenth Amendment enacted?

How and why did black and white Republicans lose control of every southern state by 1877?

▶ **These are the first African Americans** to serve in the U.S. Congress. Standing, left to right: Robert C. DeLarge, representative, South Carolina; Jefferson Long, representative, Georgia; Seated, left to right: U.S. Senator Hiram R. Revels, Mississippi; Benjamin S. Turner, representative, Alabama; Josiah T. Walls, representative, Florida; Joseph H. Rainey, representative, South Carolina; Robert B. Elliott, representative, South Carolina.

Let us with a fixed, firm, hearty, earnest, and unswerving determination move steadily on and on, fanning the flame of true liberty until the last vestige of oppression shall be destroyed, and when that eventful period shall arrive, when, in the selection of rulers, both State and Federal, we shall know no North, no East, no South, no West, no white nor colored, no Democrat nor Republican, but shall choose men because of their moral and intrinsic value, their honesty and integrity, their love of unmixed liberty, and their ability to perform well the duties to be committed to their charge.

From a speech delivered in 1872, by Jonathan J. Wright, Associate Justice of the South Carolina Supreme Court

▼ **An African-American attorney** confers with white colleagues during a historic session of the Supreme Court in the late 1800s.

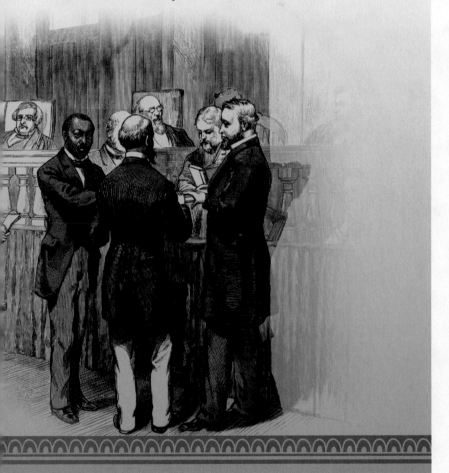

In 1868, for the first time in American history, thousands of black men would elect hundreds of black and white leaders to state and local offices across the South. Would this newly acquired political influence enable freedmen to complete the

Hear the Audio
Hear the audio files for Chapter 13 at
www.myhistorylab.com

transition from slavery to freedom? Would political power propel black people into the mainstream of American society? Equally important, would white southerners and northerners accept black people as fellow citizens?

Events from 1867 to 1877 generated hope that black and white Americans might learn to live together on a compatible and equitable basis. But these developments also raised the possibility that black people's new access to political power would fail to resolve the racial animosity and intolerance that persisted in American life after the Civil War.

Constitutional Conventions

Black men as a group first entered politics as delegates to constitutional conventions in the southern states in 1867 and 1868. Each of the former Confederate states, except Tennessee, which had already been restored to the Union, elected delegates to these conventions. Most southern white men were Democrats. They boycotted these elections to protest Congress's assumption of authority over Reconstruction and the extension of voting privileges to black men. Thus, the delegates to the conventions that met to frame new state constitutions to replace those drawn up in 1865 under President Johnson's authority were mostly Republicans joined by a few conservative southern Democrats. The Republicans represented three constituencies. One consisted of white northern migrants who moved to the South after the war. They were disparagingly called **carpetbaggers** because they were said to have arrived in the South with all their possessions in a single carpetbag. A second group consisted of native white southerners, mostly small farmers in devastated upland regions of the South who hoped for economic relief from Republican governments. Other southern white people denigrated them as **scalawags,** or scoundrels. African Americans made up the third and largest Republican constituency.

Of the 1,000 men elected as delegates to the ten state conventions, 265 were black. Black delegates were a majority only in the South Carolina and Louisiana conventions. In most states, including Alabama, Georgia, Mississippi, Virginia, North Carolina, Arkansas, and

Texas, black men made up 10 to 20 percent of the delegates. At least 107 of the 265 black delegates had been born slaves. About 40 had served in the Union Army. Several were well-educated teachers and ministers. Others were tailors, blacksmiths, barbers, and farmers. Most went on to hold other political offices.

These delegates produced impressive constitutions. Unlike previous state constitutions in the South, the new constitutions ensured that all adult males could vote, and except in Mississippi and Virginia, they did not disfranchise many former Confederates. They conferred broad guarantees of civil rights. In several states they provided the first statewide systems of public education. These constitutions were progressive, not radical. Black and white Republicans hoped to attract support from white southerners for the new state governments these documents created by encouraging state support for private businesses, especially railroad construction.

ELECTIONS

Elections were held in 1868 to ratify the new constitutions and elect officials. The white Democratic response varied. In some states, Democrats boycotted the elections. In others, they participated but voted against ratification, and in still other states they supported ratification and attempted to elect as many Democrats as possible. Congress required only a majority of those voting—not a majority of all registered voters—to ratify the constitutions. In each state a majority of those voting eventually voted to ratify, and in each state, black men were elected to office.

BLACK POLITICAL LEADERS

Over the next decade, 1,465 black men held political office in the South. Although black leaders individually and collectively enjoyed significant political leverage, white Republicans dominated politics during Reconstruction. In general, the number of black officials in a state reflected the size of that state's African-American population. Black people were a substantial majority of the population in just Mississippi and South Carolina, and most of the black officeholders came from those two states and Louisiana, where black people were a slight majority. In most states, such as Arkansas, North Carolina, Tennessee, and Texas, where black people made up between 25 and 40 percent of the population, far fewer black men were elected to office (see Table 13–1).

Initially, black men chose not to run for the most important political offices because they feared their election would further alienate angry white southerners. But as white Republicans swept into office in 1868,

Southern black men cast ballots for the first time in 1867 in the election of delegates to state constitutional conventions. The ballots were provided by the candidates or political parties, not by state or municipal officials. Most nineteenth-century elections were not by secret ballot.

black leaders reversed their strategy, and by 1870 black men had been elected to many key positions. No black man was elected governor, but Lieutenant Governor P. B. S. Pinchback served one month (December 1872 to January 1873) as governor in Louisiana after the white governor was removed from office. Blanche K. Bruce and Hiram Revels represented Mississippi in the U.S. Senate. Beginning with Joseph Rainey in 1870 in South Carolina, fourteen black men served in the U.S. House of Representatives during Reconstruction. Six men served as lieutenant governors. In Mississippi and South Carolina, a majority of the representatives in state houses were black men, and each of these states had two black speakers of the house in the 1870s. Jonathan J. Wright, quoted at the beginning of this chapter, served seven years as a supreme court justice in South Carolina. Four black men served as state superintendents of education, and Francis L. Cardozo served as South Carolina's secretary of state and then treasurer. During Reconstruction, 112 black state senators and 683 black representatives were elected. There were also forty-one black sheriffs, five black mayors, and thirty-one black coroners. Tallahassee, Florida, and Little Rock, Arkansas, had black police chiefs.

TABLE 13–1   African-American Population and Office Holding during Reconstruction in the States Subject to Congressional Reconstruction

	African-American Population in 1870	African Americans as Percentage of Total Population	Number of African-American Officeholders during Reconstruction
South Carolina	415,814	58.9	314
Mississippi	444,201	53.6	226
Louisiana	364,210	50.1	210
North Carolina	391,650	36.5	180
Alabama	475,510	47.6	167
Georgia	545,142	46.0	108
Virginia	512,841	41.8	85
Florida	91,689	48.7	58
Arkansas	122,169	25.2	46
Texas	253,475	30.9	46
Tennessee	322,331	25.6	20

Source: Eric Foner, *Freedom's Lawmakers: A Directory of Black Officeholders during Reconstruction* (New York: Oxford University Press, 1993), xiv; *The Statistics of the Population of the United States, Ninth Census* (1873), xvii.

Hiram R. Revels represented Mississippi in the U.S. Senate from February 1870 until March 1871, completing an unexpired term. He went on to serve as Mississippi's secretary of state. He was born free in Fayetteville, North Carolina, in 1822. He attended Knox College in Illinois before the Civil War. In 1874 he abandoned the Republican Party and became a Democrat. By the 1890s he had acquired a sizable plantation near Natchez.

Many of these men—by background, experience, and education—were well qualified. Others were not. Of the 1,465 black officeholders, at least 378 had been free before the Civil War, 933 were literate, and 195 were illiterate (we lack information about the remaining 337). Sixty-four had attended college or professional school. In fact, fourteen of the leaders had been students at Oberlin College in Ohio, which began admitting both black and female students before the Civil War.

Black farmers and artisans—tailors, carpenters, and barbers—were well represented among those who held political office. There were also 237 ministers and 172 teachers. At least 129 had served in the Union Army, and 46 had worked for the Freedmen's Bureau.

Several black politicians were wealthy, and a few were former slave owners. Antoine Dubuclet, who became Louisiana's treasurer, had owned more than one hundred slaves and land valued at more than $100,000 before the Civil War. Former slave Ferdinand Havis became a member of the Arkansas House of Representatives. He owned a saloon, a whiskey business, and 2,000 acres near Pine Bluff, where he became known as "the Colored Millionaire."

Although black men did not take over any state politically, a few did dominate districts with sizable black populations. Before he was elected to the U.S. Senate, Blanche K. Bruce all but controlled Bolivar County, Mississippi, where he served as sheriff, tax collector, and superintendent of education. Former

Read the Document
Blanche K. Bruce, Speech in the Senate (1876)

slave and Civil War hero Robert Smalls was the political "kingpin" in Beaufort, South Carolina. He served in the South Carolina house and senate and in the U.S. House of Representatives. He was also a member of the South Carolina constitutional conventions in 1868 and 1895.

The Issues

Many but not all black and white Republican leaders favored increasing the authority of state governments to promote the welfare of all the state's citizens. Before the Civil War, most southern states did not provide schools, medical care, assistance for the mentally impaired, or prisons. Such concerns—if attended to at all—were left to local communities or families.

EDUCATION AND SOCIAL WELFARE

Black leaders were eager to increase literacy and promote education among black people. Republicans created statewide systems of public education throughout the South. It was a difficult and expensive task, and the results were only a limited success. Schools had to be built, teachers employed, and textbooks provided. To pay for it, taxes were increased in states still reeling from the war.

In many rural areas, schools were not built. In other places, teachers were not paid. Some people—black and white—opposed compulsory education laws, preferring to let parents determine whether their children should attend school or work to help the family. Some black leaders favored a poll tax on voting to fund the schools. Thus, although Reconstruction leaders established a strong commitment to public education, the results they achieved were uneven.

Furthermore, white parents refused to send their children to integrated schools. Although no laws required segregation, public schools during and after Reconstruction were invariably segregated. Black parents were usually more concerned that their children should have schools to attend than whether the schools were integrated. New Orleans' schools, however, were mixed.

Reconstruction leaders also supported higher education. In 1872 Mississippi legislators took advantage of the 1862 federal Morrill Land-Grant Act, which provided states with funds for agricultural and mechanical colleges, to found the first historically black state university: Alcorn A&M College. Although the university was named after white Republican Governor James L. Alcorn, former U.S. Senator Hiram Revels was its first president. The South Carolina legislature created a similar college and attached it to the Methodist-sponsored Claflin University.

Black leaders in the state legislature compelled the University of South Carolina, which had been all white, to admit black students and hire black faculty. Many of the white students and faculty left. Several black politicians enrolled in the law and medical programs at the university. Richard Greener, a black Harvard graduate, served on the university's faculty and was its librarian.

Despite the costs, Reconstruction leaders also created the first state-supported institutions for the insane, the blind, and the deaf in much of the South. Some southern states during Reconstruction began to offer medical care and public health programs. Orphanages were established. State prisons were built. Black leaders also supported revisions to state criminal codes, the elimination of corporal punishment for many crimes, and a reduction in the number of capital crimes.

CIVIL RIGHTS

Black politicians were often the victims of racial discrimination when they tried to use public transportation and accommodations such as hotels and restaurants. Rather than provide separate arrangements for black customers, white-owned businesses simply excluded black patrons. This was true in the North as well as the South. The Civil War hero Robert Smalls, for example, was ejected from a Philadelphia streetcar in 1864. After protests, the company agreed to accept black riders. In Arkansas, Mifflin Gibbs (see *Profile: The Gibbs Brothers*) and W. Hines Furbish successfully sued a local saloon after they had been denied service. In South Carolina, Jonathan J. Wright won $1,200 in a lawsuit against a railroad after he had purchased a first-class ticket but had been forced to ride in the second-class coach.

Black leaders' determination to open public facilities to all people revealed deep divisions between themselves and white Republicans. In several southern states they introduced bills to prevent proprietors from excluding black people from restaurants, barrooms, hotels, concert halls, and auditoriums, as well as railroad coaches, streetcars, and steamboats. Many white Republicans and virtually every Democrat attacked such proposals as efforts to promote social equality and gain access for black people to places where they were not welcome. White politicians blocked these laws in most states. Only South Carolina—with a black majority in the house and many black senators—enacted such a law, but it was not effectively enforced. In Mississippi, the Republican Governor James L. Alcorn vetoed a bill to outlaw racial discrimination by railroads. In Alabama and North Carolina, civil rights bills were defeated, and Georgia and Arkansas enacted measures that encouraged segregation.

Economic Issues

Black politicians sought to promote economic development in general and for black people in particular. For example, white landowners sometimes fired black agricultural laborers near the end of the growing season and then did not pay them. Some of these landowners were dishonest, but others were in debt and could not pay their workers. To prevent such abuses, black politicians secured laws that required laborers to be paid before the crop was sold or when it was sold. Some black leaders who had been slaves also wanted to regulate wages, but these proposals failed because most Republicans did not believe states had the authority to regulate wages and prices.

PROFILE: The Gibbs Brothers

Among the many black leaders who emerged during Reconstruction were the Gibbs brothers, who had political careers in Arkansas and Florida. Mifflin W. Gibbs and Jonathan C. Gibbs grew up in a well-to-do, free black family in Philadelphia, where their father was a Methodist minister. But their paths diverged, and they spent little time together as adults.

Mifflin was born in 1823 and became a building contractor. By the 1840s, he was an active abolitionist. With the discovery of gold in California in 1849, he went west and eventually established California's first black newspaper, the *Mirror of the Times*. He led a protest in 1851 against a provision in the California constitution that denied black men the right to vote. In 1858 he left California for Canada, again because gold had been discovered. He spent more than ten years in Canada as a businessman involved in real estate and a coal company. In 1866 he was elected to the Victoria City Council in British Columbia. He returned to the United States in 1869. In 1870 he graduated from the law program at Oberlin College.

Mifflin moved to Arkansas in 1871 and was elected municipal judge in Little Rock in 1873. Although defeated for reelection, he remained involved in the Republican Party and was a delegate to every Republican national convention from 1876 to 1904. In 1897, Republican President William McKinley appointed him U.S. consul to Madagascar, a French island colony off the east coast of Africa, where he served until 1901. He died in 1915. A black high school in Little Rock was named in his honor.

Jonathan, born in 1827 or 1828, also joined the abolitionist movement. Rejected by 18 colleges because of his color, he finally graduated from Dartmouth in 1852. He then went to Princeton Theological Seminary and became a Presbyterian minister in Troy, New York.

Jonathan attended the 1864 National Black Convention in Syracuse, New York; taught at a freedmen's school in North Carolina; and then spent two years in Charleston, South Carolina. There he joined those black leaders who favored limiting the right to vote to literate men if that restriction were applied both to black and white people.

In 1867, Jonathan moved to Florida, where he became a key Republican leader and the state's highest-ranking black official. He was elected to the 1868 Florida constitutional convention, and the Republican governor appointed him secretary of state. Although defeated for a seat in Congress in 1868, he remained one of Florida's most visible black leaders and was repeatedly threatened by the Ku Klux Klan. In 1873, another Republican governor appointed him state superintendent of education. Jonathan Gibbs died in 1874, but his son Thomas served in the Florida House of Representatives, where he was instrumental in establishing Florida A&M University.

◄ **Mifflin Gibbs** was probably the only African American in the nineteenth century elected to political office in two nations. He served as a city councilman in Victoria, British Columbia, in Canada in the late 1860s, and he was elected a judge in Little Rock, Arkansas, in 1873.

Legislators also enacted measures that protected the land and property of small farmers against seizure for nonpayment of debts. Black and white farmers who lost land, tools, animals, and other property because they could not pay their debts were unlikely to recover financially. "Stay laws" prohibited, or "stayed," authorities from taking property. Besides protecting poor farmers, Republicans hoped these laws would also end the attachment of white yeomen for the Democratic Party.

Read the Document
James T. Rapier, Testimony before U.S. Senate Regarding the Agricultural Labor Force in the South (1880)

LAND

Black leaders were unable to provide land to landless black and white farmers. Many black and white political leaders believed the state had no right to distribute land. Again, South Carolina was the exception. Its legislature created a state land commission in 1869.

The commission could purchase and distribute land to freedmen. It also gave the freedmen loans on generous terms to pay for the land. Unfortunately, the commission was corrupt and inefficiently managed and had little fertile land to distribute. Yet despite its many difficulties, the commission enabled more than 14,000 black families and a few white families to acquire land in South Carolina. Their descendants still possess some of this land today.

Although some black leaders were reluctant to use the states' power to distribute land, others had no qualms about raising property taxes so high that large landowners would be forced to sell some of their property to pay their taxes. Abraham Galloway of North Carolina explained, "I want to see the man who owns one or two thousand acres of land, taxed a dollar on the acre, and if they can't pay the taxes, sell their property to the highest bidder . . . and then we negroes shall become the land holders."

Read the Document
"When We Worked on Shares, We Couldn't Make Nothing": Henry Blake Talks about Sharecropping after the Civil War

BUSINESS AND INDUSTRY

Black and white leaders had an easier time enacting legislation to support business and industry. Like most Americans after the Civil War, Republicans believed that expanding the railroad network would stimulate employment, improve transportation, and generate prosperity. State governments approved the sale of state-supported bonds to finance railroad construction. In Georgia, Alabama, Texas, and Arkansas, the railroad network did expand. But the bonded debt of these states soared, and taxes increased to pay for it.

Moreover, railroad financing was often corrupt. Most of the illegal money wound up in the pockets of white businessmen and politicians. Black politicians rarely had access to large financial transactions.

So attractive were business profits that some black political leaders formed corporations. They invested modest sums and believed—like so many capitalists—that the rewards outweighed the risks. In Charleston, 28 black leaders (and two white politicians) formed a horse-drawn streetcar line they called the Enterprise Railroad to carry freight between the city wharves and the railroad terminal. Black leaders in South Carolina also created a company to extract the phosphate used for fertilizer from riverbeds and riverbanks in the low country. Neither business lasted long. Black men found it far more difficult than white entrepreneurs to finance their corporations.

Black Politicians: An Evaluation

Southern black political leaders on the state level did create the foundation for public education; for state assistance for the blind, deaf, and insane; and for reforming the criminal justice system. They tried but mostly failed to outlaw racial discrimination in public facilities. They encouraged state support for economic expansion.

But black leaders could not significantly improve the lives of their constituents. Because white Republicans almost always outnumbered them, they could not enact an agenda of their own. Moreover, black leaders often disagreed among themselves about issues and programs. Class and prewar status frequently divided them. Those leaders who had not been slaves and had not been raised in rural isolation were less likely to be concerned with land and agricultural labor. More prosperous black leaders showed more interest in civil rights and encouraging business. Even when they agreed about the need for public education, black leaders often disagreed about how to finance it and whether it should be compulsory.

Republican Factionalism

Disagreements among black leaders paled compared to the conflicts that divided the Republican Party during Reconstruction. Black and white Republicans often disagreed on political issues and strategy, but the lack of party cohesion and discipline was even more harmful. The Republican Party in the South constantly split into factions as groups fought with each other. Most disagreements were over who should run for and hold political office.

Hundreds of would-be Republican leaders—black and white—sought public offices. If they lost the Republican nomination, they often formed a competing slate of candidates. Then Republicans ran against each other and against the Democrats in the general election. It was not a recipe for political success.

These bitter and angry contests were based less on race and issues than on the desperate desire to gain an office that would pay even a modest salary. Most black and white Republicans were not well off. Public office assured them a modicum of economic security.

Ironically, these factional disputes led to a high turnover in political leadership and the loss of that very economic security. It was difficult for black leaders (and white leaders too) to be renominated and re-elected to more than one or two terms. Few officeholders served three or four consecutive terms in the same office during Reconstruction. This made for inexperienced leadership and added to Republican woes.

Opposition

Even if black and Republican leaders had been less prone to fighting among themselves and more effective in adopting a political platform, they might still have failed to sustain themselves for long. Most white southerners led by conservative Democrats remained absolutely opposed to letting black men vote or hold office. As a white Floridian put it, "The damned Republican Party has put niggers to rule us and we will not suffer it." Of course, because black people voted did not mean they ruled during Reconstruction, but many white people failed to grasp that. Instead, for most white southerners, the only acceptable political system was one that excluded black men and the Republican Party.

As far as most white people were concerned, the end of slavery and the enfranchisement of black men did not make black people their equals. They did not accept the Fourteenth Amendment. They attacked Republican governments and their leaders unrelentingly. White southerners blamed the Republicans for an epidemic of waste and corruption in state government. But most of all, they considered it preposterous and outrageous that former slaves could vote and hold office.

James S. Pike spoke for many white people when he ridiculed black leaders in the South Carolina House of Representatives in 1873:

> The body is almost literally a Black Parliament. . . .
> The Speaker is black, the Clerk is black, the door-
> keepers are black, the little pages are black, the
> chairman of the Ways and Means is black, and the
> chaplain is coal-black. At some of the desks sit

colored men whose types it would be hard to find outside of Congo; whose costume, visages, attitudes, and expression only befit the forecastle of a buccaneer. It must be remembered, also, that these men, with not more than a half a dozen exceptions, have been themselves slaves, and that their ancestors were slaves for generations.

Pike's observations circulated widely in both the North and the South.

White southerners were determined to rid themselves of Republicans and the disgrace of having to live with black men who possessed political rights. White southerners would "redeem" their states by restoring white Democrats to power. This meant not just defeating black and white Republicans in elections but removing them from politics entirely. White southerners believed any means—fair or foul—were justified in exorcising this evil.

The Ku Klux Klan

If the presence of black men in politics was illegitimate—in the eyes of white southerners—then it was acceptable to use violence to remove them. This thinking gave rise to militant terrorist organizations, such as the **Ku Klux Klan,** the Knights of the White Camellia, the White Brotherhood, and the White-caps. Threats, intimidation, beatings, rapes, and murder, such groups believed, would restore conservative white Democratic rule and force black people back into subordination.

The Ku Klux Klan was founded in Pulaski, Tennessee, in 1866. It was originally a social club for Confederate veterans who adopted secret oaths and rituals—similar to the Union Leagues but with far more deadly consequences. One of the key figures in the Klan's rapid growth was former Confederate General Nathan Bedford Forrest, who became its leader or grand wizard. The Klan drew its members from all classes of white society, not merely from among the poor. Businessmen, lawyers, physicians, and politicians were active in the Klan, as well as farmers and planters. The Klan and other terrorist organizations functioned mainly where black people were a large minority and where their votes could affect elections. Klansmen virtually took over areas of western Alabama, northern Georgia, and Florida's panhandle. The Klan controlled the up-country of South Carolina and the area around Mecklenburg County, North Carolina. However, in the Carolina and Georgia low

Read the **Document**
Organization and Principles of the Ku Klux Klan (1868)

PROFILE: The Rollin Sisters

Few women, black or white, were as influential in Reconstruction politics as the Rollin sisters of South Carolina. Although they could not vote or hold political office, the five sisters, and especially Frances and Katherine, were closely associated with the black and white Republican leadership in South Carolina. With their education, knowledge, and charm, these black women affected political decisions and policies.

The sisters were born and raised in the elite antebellum free black community in Charleston. Their father, William Rollin, a prosperous lumber dealer, was descended from French Catholic Haitians. He insisted that his daughters obtain a first-rate education. Frances, who was born in 1844, was sent to Philadelphia to take the "ladies course" at the Quaker's Institute for Colored Youth. At least two of the other sisters attended school in Boston. After the war, Frances joined other members of Charleston's prominent people of color and taught at schools sponsored by the American Missionary Association. She also wrote the biography of the black abolitionist leader Martin Delany. This was the first major nonfiction work a black woman published in America, but she felt compelled to conceal her identity under a male name, Frank A. Rollin.

In 1867 and 1868, as black men were entering the political arena, the Rollin sisters also gravitated to politics. Against her father's wishes, Frances married one of South Carolina's most controversial figures, William Whipper, a black attorney from Philadelphia who settled in Beaufort, South Carolina, after the war. (Whipper was the nephew of the antebellum black Pennsylvania businessman, also named William Whipper, profiled in Chapter 7.) He was elected to the state constitutional convention and then to the South Carolina House of Representatives. Whipper was a tough, able, shrewd, and not altogether honest politician. He enjoyed an expensive lifestyle. Most white people detested him.

While the legislature was in session, the Whippers and the Rollin sisters lived in Columbia, the state capital. There, the sisters were extraordinarily popular. They were well educated, intelligent, refined, and sophisticated. One observer described them as "ravishingly beautiful." Katherine Rollin was frequently seen with white State Senator George W. McIntyre.

The Rollin sisters were enthusiastic proponents of women's rights and women's suffrage. They enlisted the wives of prominent black and white Republicans in their cause. Charlotte and Katherine organized a women's rights convention in Columbia in 1870 and formed the South Carolina branch of the American Women's Suffrage Association.

Charlotte Rollin pleaded for the right to vote:

> We ask suffrage not as a favor, not as a privilege, but as a right based on the grounds that we are human beings and as such entitled to human rights. While we concede that woman's ennobling influence should be confined chiefly to the home and society, we claim that public opinion has had a tendency to limit a woman's sphere to too small a circle and until woman has the right of representation this will last, and other rights will be held by insecure tenure.

Their black and white male allies tried to amend South Carolina's constitution to enable women to vote, but the legislature rejected it after a bitter debate.

After the Democrats regained political power in 1877, the Rollin sisters left for the North. Charlotte and Louise settled with their mother in Brooklyn, New York. William and Frances Whipper and their five children moved to Washington, D.C., in 1882, where he practiced law and she was a clerk in the General Land Office. Three of their children survived to adulthood. Their sole son, Leigh Whipper, was a prominent stage and screen actor in the 1940s and 1950s. Sometime in the 1890s, Frances joined her husband in Beaufort. She died there in 1901.

▶ **Frances Rollin Whipper** was an author, teacher, political activist, wife, and mother. With her sisters, she was deeply involved in Reconstruction politics in South Carolina.

country where there were huge black majorities, the Klan rarely, if ever, appeared.

Although the Klan and similar societies were neither well organized nor unified, they did reduce support for the Republican Party and helped eliminate its leaders. Often wearing hoods and masks to hide their faces, white terrorists embarked on a campaign of violence rarely matched and never exceeded in American history.

Read the Document
Hannah Irwin Describes Ku Klux Klan Ride (Late 1860s)

Mobs of marauding terrorists beat and killed hundreds of black people—and many white people. Black churches and schools were burned. Republican leaders were threatened or killed. In South Carolina in 1868, the black chairman of the Republican Party, Benjamin F. Randolph, was murdered as he stepped off a train. Black legislator Lee Nance and white legislator Solomon G. W. Dill were later slain. In 1870 black lawmaker Richard Burke was killed in Sumter County, Alabama, because he was considered too influential among "people of his color."

As his wife looked on, Jack Dupree—a local Republican leader—had his throat cut and was eviscerated in Monroe County, Mississippi. In 1870 North Carolina Senator John W. Stephens, a white Republican, was murdered. After Alabama freedman George Moore voted for the Republicans in 1869, Klansmen beat him, raped a girl who was visiting his wife, and attacked a neighbor. An Irish-American teacher and four black men were lynched in Cross Plains, Alabama, in 1870. The outlaw John Wesley Hardin openly acknowledged he had killed black Texas state policemen.

White men attacked a Republican campaign rally in Eutaw, Alabama, in 1870 and killed four black men and wounded 54 other people. After three black leaders were arrested in 1871 in Meridian, Mississippi, for delivering what many white people considered inflammatory speeches, shooting broke out in the courtroom. The Republican judge and two of the defendants were killed, and in a wave of violence, 30 black people were murdered, including every black leader in the small community. In the same year, a mob of 500 men broke

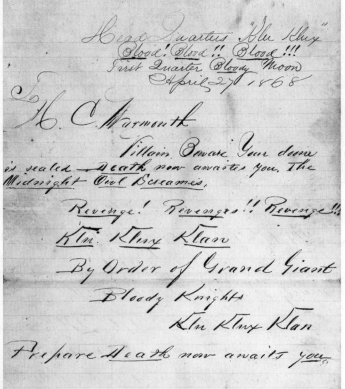

The flowing white robes and cone-shaped headgear associated with the Ku Klux Klan today are mostly a twentieth-century phenomenon. The Klansmen of the Reconstruction era, like these two men in Alabama in 1868, were well armed, disguised, and prepared to intimidate black and white Republicans. The note is a Klan death threat directed at Louisiana's first Republican governor, Henry C. Warmoth.

into the jail in Union County, South Carolina, and lynched eight black prisoners accused of killing a Confederate veteran.

Nowhere was the Klan more active and violent than in York County, South Carolina. Almost the entire adult white male population joined in threatening, attacking, and murdering the black population. Hundreds were beaten and at least eleven killed. Terrified families fled into the woods. Appeals for help were sent to Governor Robert K. Scott (see *Voices: An Appeal for Help Against the Klan*).

But Scott did not send aid. He had already sent the South Carolina militia into areas of Klan activity, and even more violence had resulted. The militia was made up mostly of black men, and white terrorists retaliated by killing militia officers. Scott could not send white men to York County because most of them sympathized with the Klan. Thus, Republican governors like Scott responded ineffectually. Republican-controlled legislatures passed anti-Klan measures that made it illegal to appear in public in disguises and masks, and they strengthened laws against assault, murder, and conspiracy. But enforcement was weak.

A few Republican leaders did deal harshly and effectively with terrorism. Governors in Tennessee, Texas, and Arkansas declared martial law and sent in hundreds of well-armed white and black men to quell the violence. Hundreds of Klansmen were arrested, many fled, and three were executed in Arkansas. But when Governor William W. Holden of North Carolina sent the state militia after the Klan, he provoked an angry reaction. Subsequent Klan violence in ten counties helped Democrats carry the 1870 legislative elections, and the legislature then removed Holden from office.

Outnumbered and outgunned, black people in most areas did not retaliate against the Klan, and the Klan was rarely active where black people were in a majority and prepared to defend themselves. In the cause of white supremacy, the Klan usually attacked those who could not defend themselves.

The West

During the 1830s the U.S. government forced the Five Civilized Tribes—the Cherokee, Chickasaw, Choctaw, Creek, and Seminole—from their southern homelands to Indian Territory in what is now Oklahoma. By 1860 Native Americans there held 7,367 African Americans in slavery. Many of the Indians fought for the Confederacy during the Civil War. Following the war, the former slaves encountered nearly as much violence and hostility from Native Americans as they did

VOICES

AN APPEAL FOR HELP AGAINST THE KLAN

H. K. Roberts, a black lieutenant in the South Carolina militia, described Klan terror in York County in late 1870 to Governor Robert K. Scott. Roberts desperately appealed for aid to protect Republicans and defend the black community.

ANTIOCH P.O.
YORK COUNTY S.C.

Dec. the 6th 1870.

To Your Excelency R. K. Scott

Sir I will tell you that on last friday night the 2nd day of this [month] 8 miles from here thier was one of the worst outrages Commited that is on record in the state from 50 to 75 armed men went to the house of Thomas Blacks a colored man fired shots into the house and cald for him he clibed up in the loft of the house they fired up their and he came down jumped out at a window ran about 30 steps was shot down then they shot him after he fell they then draged him about 10 steps and cut his throat from ear to ear their was about 30 bullet holes in his body some 50 to one hundred shots in the house. . . . [They] abused his wife and enquired for one or two more colored men some of the colored people are leaving and a great many lying out in the woods and they reports comes to me evry day that they Ku Kluxs intend to kill us all out and I heard yesterday that they had 30 stands of arms. . . . I wish you would give me 20 or 25 men or let me enroll that many and I will stop it or catch some of them or send some U S Soldiers on for I tell you their must be something don and that quick to for I do believe that they intend to beat and kill out the Radical party in the upper Counties of the state where the vote is close if we was to have the ellection now the Radicals would turn [out] to vote their ticket I leave the matter with you I hope you will wright back to me by return mail and let me heare what you think you can do for us up here I cant tell whether I can hold my own or not I know some men that stay with us at night for safety but if they come as strong as they were the other night they may kill me and all of my men I remain yours truly as ever

H.K. Roberts, Lieut.
Commanding Post of State Guards Kings Mountain

▶ *Why did Roberts write this letter?*
▶ *Would Roberts have had any reason to exaggerate the violence in York County?*
▶ *According to Roberts, what motivated white men to attack?*

Source: H. K. Roberts to Governor Robert K. Scott, South Carolina Department of Archives and History.

1869–1875

from southern white people. Indians were reluctant to share their land with freedmen, and they vigorously opposed policies that favored black voting rights.

Gradually and despite considerable Indian prejudice, some African Americans managed to acquire tribal land. Also, the Creeks and the Seminoles permitted former slaves to take part in tribal government. Black men served in both houses of the Creek legislature—the House of Warriors and the House of Kings. An African American, Jesse Franklin, served as a justice on the Creek tribal court in 1876. In contrast, the Chickasaw and Choctaw were absolutely opposed to making concessions to freed people. So the U.S. government ordered

This optimistic 1870 illustration exemplifies the hopes and aspirations generated during Reconstruction as black people gained access to the political system. Invoking the legacy of Abraham Lincoln and John Brown, it suggests that African Americans would soon assume their rightful and equitable role in American society.

federal troops onto Chickasaw and Choctaw lands to protect the former slaves.

Elsewhere on the western frontier, black people struggled for legal and political rights and periodically participated in territorial governments. In 1867, 200 black men voted—although white men protested—in the Montana territorial election. In the Colorado Territory, William Jefferson Hardin, a barber, campaigned with other black men for the right to vote, and in 1865 they persuaded 137 African Americans (91 percent of Colorado's black population) to petition the territorial governor to abolish a white-only voting provision. In 1867 black men in Colorado finally gained the right to vote. Hardin later moved to Cheyenne and was elected to the Wyoming territorial legislature in 1879.

The Fifteenth Amendment

The federal government under Republican domination tried to protect black voting rights and defend Republican state governments in the South. In 1869 Congress passed the **Fifteenth Amendment,** which was ratified in 1870. It stipulated that a person could not be deprived of the right to vote because of race: "The right of citizens of the United States to vote shall not be denied or abridged by the United States or by any State on account of race, color, or previous condition of servitude." Black people, abolitionists, and reformers hailed the amendment as the culmination of the crusade to end slavery and give black people the same rights as white people.

Read the Document
Thirteenth, Fourteenth, and Fifteenth Amendments

Northern black men were the amendment's immediate beneficiaries because before its adoption, black men could vote in only eight northern states. Yet to the disappointment of many, the amendment said nothing about women voting and did not outlaw poll taxes, literacy tests, and property qualifications that could disfranchise citizens.

The Enforcement Acts

In direct response to the terrorism in the South, Congress passed the **Enforcement Acts** in 1870 and 1871, and the federal government expanded its authority over the states. The 1870 act outlawed disguises and masks and protected the civil rights of citizens. The 1871 act—known as the Ku Klux Klan Act—made it a federal offense to interfere with a person's right to vote, hold office, serve on a jury, or enjoy equal protection of the law. Those accused of violating the act would be tried in federal court. For extreme violence, the act authorized the president to send in federal troops and suspend the writ of **habeas corpus.** (Habeas corpus is the right to be brought before a judge and not be arrested and jailed without cause.)

Black congressmen, who had long advocated federal action against the Klan, endorsed the Enforcement Acts. Representative Joseph Rainey of South Carolina wanted to suspend the Constitution to protect citizens: "I desire that so broad and liberal a construction be placed on its provisions, as will insure protection to the humblest citizen. Tell me nothing of a constitution which fails to shelter beneath its rightful power the people of a country."

Armed with this new legislation, the Justice Department and Attorney General Amos T. Ackerman moved vigorously against the Klan. Hundreds of Klansmen were arrested—700 in Mississippi alone. Faced with a full-scale rebellion in late 1871 in South Carolina's up-country, President Ulysses S. Grant declared martial law in nine counties, suspended the writ of habeas corpus, and sent in the army. Mass arrests and trials followed, but federal authorities permitted many Klansmen to confess and thereby escape prosecution. The government lacked the human and financial resources to bring hundreds of men to court for lengthy trials. Some white men were tried, mostly before black juries, and were imprisoned or fined. Comparatively few Klansmen, however, were punished severely, especially considering the enormity of their crimes.

The North and Reconstruction

Although the federal government did reduce Klan violence for a time, white southerners remained convinced that white supremacy must be restored and Republican governments overturned. Klan violence did not overthrow any state governments, but it undermined freedmen's confidence in the ability of these governments to protect them. Meanwhile, radical Republicans in Congress grew frustrated that the South and especially black people continued to demand so much of their time and attention year after year. There was less and less sentiment in the North to continue support for the freedmen and involvement in southern affairs.

Many northern Republicans lost interest in civil rights issues and principles and became more concerned with winning elections and the economy. By the mid-1870s, there was more discussion in Congress of patronage, veterans' pensions, railroads, taxes, tariffs, the economy, and monetary policy than about rights for black people or the future of the South.

By the 1870s, the American political system was also awash in corruption, which further detracted from concerns over the South. Although President Grant was a man of integrity, many men in his administration were not. They were implicated in scandals involving the construction of the transcontinental railroad, federal taxes on whiskey, and fraud within the Bureau of Indian Affairs. Nor was the dishonesty limited to Republicans. William Marcy "Boss" Tweed and the Democratic machine that dominated New York City were notoriously corrupt.

Many Republicans began to question the necessity for more moral, military, and political support for African Americans. They were convinced that African Americans had demanded too much for too long from the national government. Former slaves had become citizens and had the right to vote and hold political office. Therefore, they did not need additional help or legislation from the federal government. Equality for black people would come from their labor as free men, which would produce wealth and acceptance by white people. Federal legislation, many northern white people believed, could not create equality.

The *Chicago Tribune*, a Republican newspaper, had wearied of black agitation by 1874: "Is it not time for the colored race to stop playing baby? The whites of America have done nobly in outgrowing old prejudices against them. They cannot hurry this process by law. Let them obtain social equality as every other man, woman, and child in the world obtain it,—by showing themselves in their lives the social equals of those with whom they wish to consort. If they do this, year by year the prejudices will die away."

Other northern white people, swayed by white southerners' views of black people, began to doubt the wisdom of universal manhood suffrage. Many white people who had nominally supported black suffrage began to believe the exaggerated complaints about corruption among black leaders and the unrelenting claims that freedmen were incapable of self-government. Some white northerners began to conclude that Reconstruction had been a mistake.

Economic conditions contributed to changing attitudes. A financial crisis—the Panic of 1873—sent

VOICES

BLACK LEADERS SUPPORT THE PASSAGE OF A CIVIL RIGHTS ACT

Black Congressmen Robert Brown Elliott of South Carolina and James T. Rapier of Alabama spoke passionately in favor of the Sumner civil rights bill in 1874. Both men had been free before the war. Both were also lawyers, and although each accumulated considerable wealth, they died in poverty in the 1880s.

[James T. Rapier]

I must confess it is somewhat embarrassing for a colored man to urge the passage of this bill, because if he exhibit an earnestness in the matter and expresses a desire for its immediate passage, straightaway he is charged with a desire for social equality, as explained by the demagogue and understood by the ignorant white man. But then it is just as embarrassing for him not to do so, for, if he remains silent while the struggle is being carried on around, and for him, he is liable to be charged with a want of interest in a matter that concerns him more than anyone else, which is enough to make his friends desert his cause. So in steering away from Scylla I may run upon Charybdis. But the anomalous, and I may add the supremely ridiculous, position of the Negro at this time, in this country, compel me to say something. Here his condition is without comparison, parallel alone to itself. Just that the law recognizes my right upon this floor as a law-maker, but that there is no law to secure to me any accommodations whatever while traveling here to discharge my duties as a Representative of a large and wealthy constituency. Here I am the peer of the proudest, but on a steamboat or car I am not equal to the most degraded. Is not this most anomalous and ridiculous?

[Robert Brown Elliott]

The results of the war, as seen in Reconstruction, have settled forever the political status of my race. The passage of this bill will determine the civil status, not only of the Negro but of any other class of citizens who may feel themselves discriminated against. It will form the capstone of that temple of liberty begun on this continent under discouraging circumstances, carried on in spite of the sneers of monarchists and the cavils of pretended friends of freedom, until at last it stands in all its beautiful symmetry and proportions, a building the grandest which the world has ever seen, realizing the most sanguine expectations and the highest hopes of those who in the name of equal, impartial and universal liberty, laid the foundation stone.

---

the economy into a long slump. Businesses and financial institutions failed, unemployment soared, and prices fell. In 1874 the Democrats recaptured a majority in the House of Representatives for the first time since 1860 and also took control of several northern states.

The Freedmen's Bank

One of the casualties of the financial crisis was the **Freedmen's Savings Bank,** which failed in 1874. Founded in 1865 when hope flourished, the Freedmen's Savings and Trust Company had been chartered by Congress but was not connected to the Freedmen's Bureau. However, the bank's advertising featured pictures of Abraham Lincoln, and many black people assumed it was a federal agency. Freedmen and black veterans, churches, fraternal organizations, and benevolent societies opened thousands of accounts in the bank. Most of the deposits totaled under $50, and some amounted to only a few cents.

Although the bank had many black employees, its board of directors consisted of white men. They invested the bank's funds in risky ventures, including Washington, D.C., real estate. With the Panic of 1873, the bank lost large sums in unsecured railroad loans. To restore confidence, its directors persuaded Frederick Douglass to serve as president and invest $10,000 of his own money to help shore up the bank. Douglass lost his money, and African Americans across the South lost more than $1 million when the bank closed in June 1874. Eventually about half the depositors received three-fifths of the value of their accounts, but many African Americans believed the U.S. government owed them a debt. Well into the twentieth century, they wrote to Congress and the president in unsuccessful efforts to retrieve their hard-earned money.

▶ *If black men had the right to vote and serve in Congress, why was a civil rights law needed?*

▶ *Who would benefit most from the passage of this bill?*

▶ *What distinction do the congressmen draw between social discrimination and political rights?*

Source: *Congressional Record*, 43rd Congress, 1st sess., 1874, vol. II, pt. 1, 565–67; Peggy Lamson, *The Glorious Failure* (New York: Norton, 1973), 181.

The Civil Rights Act of 1875

Before Reconstruction expired, Congress made one final—some said futile—gesture to protect black people from racial discrimination when it passed the **Civil Rights Act of 1875.** Championed by Senator Charles Sumner of Massachusetts, it was originally intended to open public accommodations—including schools, churches, cemeteries, hotels, and transportation—to all people regardless of race. It passed in the Republican-controlled Senate in 1874. But House Democrats held up passage. It was not enacted until 1875 and then largely as a memorial to Sumner, who had died in 1874. In its final form, the bans on discrimination in churches, cemeteries, and schools were deleted.

The act stipulated "That all persons . . . shall be entitled to the full and equal enjoyment of the accommodations, advantages, facilities, and privileges of inns, public conveyances on land or water, theaters, and other places of public amusement." After its passage, no attempt was made to enforce these provisions, and in 1883 the Supreme Court declared it unconstitutional. Justice Joseph Bradley wrote that the Fourteenth Amendment protected black people from discrimination by states but not by private businesses. Black newspapers likened the decision to the *Dred Scott* case a quarter century earlier.

The End of Reconstruction

Reconstruction ended as it began—in violence and controversy. Democrats demanded **"redemption"**—a word with biblical and spiritual overtones. They wanted southern states restored to conservative, white political control. By 1875 they had regained authority in all the former Confederate states except Mississippi, Florida, Louisiana, and South Carolina (see Map 13–1). Democrats had redeemed Tennessee in 1870 and Georgia in 1871. Democrats had learned two lessons. First, few black men would vote for the Democratic Party—no matter how much white leaders wanted to believe former slaves were easy to manipulate. Second, intimidation and violence would win elections in areas where the number of black and white voters was nearly equal. The federal government had stymied Klan violence in 1871, but by the mid-1870s, the government had become reluctant to send troops to the South to protect black citizens.

◉⃝ Watch the Video
The Promise and Failure of Reconstruction

VIOLENT REDEMPTION

In Alabama in 1874, black and white Republican leaders were murdered, and white mobs destroyed crops and homes. On election day in Eufaula, white men killed

On January 6, 1874, Robert Brown Elliott delivered a ringing speech in the U.S. House of Representatives in support of the Sumner civil rights bill. Elliott was responding in part to words uttered the day before by Virginia Congressman John T. Harris, who claimed that "there is not a gentleman on this floor who can honestly say he really believes that the colored man is created his equal." P.S. Duval and Son, Come and join us brothers; Civil War; Philadelphia, PA; ca. 1863.   P.S. Duval and Son, Come and join us brothers; Civil War; Philadelphia, Pa.; ca. 1863. Chicago Historical Society ICHi-22051.

seven and injured nearly 70 unarmed black voters. Black voters were also driven from the polls in Mobile. Democrats won the election and "redeemed" Alabama.

White violence marred every election in Louisiana from 1868 to 1876. After Republicans and Democrats each claimed victory in the 1872 elections, black people seized the small town of Colfax along the Red River to protect themselves against a Democratic takeover. They held out for three weeks. Then on Easter Sunday in 1873, a well-armed white mob attacked the black defenders. At least 105 were killed in the **Colfax Massacre,** the worst single day of bloodshed during Reconstruction. In 1874 the White League almost redeemed Louisiana in a wave of violence. Black people were murdered, courts were attacked, and white people refused to pay taxes to the Republican state government. Six white and two black Republicans were murdered at Coushatta. In September, President Grant finally sent federal troops to New Orleans after 3,500 White Leaguers nearly wiped out the black militia and the Metropolitan Police. But the stage had been set for the 1876 campaign.

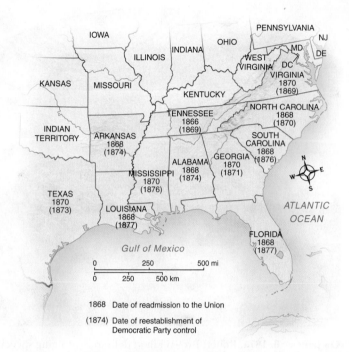

MAP 13–1 DATES OF READMISSION OF SOUTHERN STATES TO THE UNION AND REESTABLISHMENT OF DEMOCRATIC PARTY CONTROL

Once conservative white Democrats regained political control of a state government from black and white Republicans, they considered that state "redeemed." The first states the Democrats "redeemed" were Georgia, Virginia, and North Carolina. Louisiana, Florida, and South Carolina were the last. (Tennessee was not included in the Reconstruction process under the terms of the 1867 Reconstruction Act.)

▶ *In which states did black and white Republicans hold political control for the shortest and longest periods of time?*

 See the Map *Explore this map at* **www.myhistorylab.com**

THE SHOTGUN POLICY

In 1875 white Mississippians, no longer afraid the national government would intervene in force, declared open warfare on the black majority. The masks and hoods of the Klan were discarded. One newspaper proclaimed that Democrats would carry the election, "peaceably if we can, forcibly if we must." Another paper carried a bold banner: "Mississippi is a white man's country, and by the eternal God we'll rule it."

White Mississippi unleashed a campaign of violence known as the **"shotgun policy"** that was extreme even for Reconstruction. Many Republicans fled, and others were murdered. In late 1874 an estimated 300 black people were hunted down outside Vicksburg after black men armed with inferior weapons had lost a "battle" with white men. In 1875, 30 teachers, church leaders, and Republican officials were killed in Clinton. The white sheriff of Yazoo County, who had married a black woman and supported the education of black children, fled the state.

Governor Adelbert Ames appealed for federal help, but President Grant refused: "The whole public are tired out with these annual autumnal outbreaks in the South . . . [and] are ready now to condemn any interference on the part of the Government." The terrorism intensified, and many black voters went into hiding on election day, afraid for their lives and those of their families. Democrats redeemed Mississippi and prided themselves that they—a superior race representing the most civilized of all people—were back in control.

In Florida in 1876, white Republicans noted that support for black people in the South was fading. They nominated an all-white Republican slate and even refused to renominate black Congressman Josiah Walls.

THE HAMBURG MASSACRE

South Carolina Democrats were divided between moderate and extreme factions, but they united to nominate former Confederate general Wade Hampton for governor after the **Hamburg Massacre.** The prelude to this event occurred on July 4, 1876—the nation's centennial—when two white men in a buggy confronted the black militia that was drilling on a town street in Hamburg, a small, mostly black town. Hot words were exchanged, and days later, Democrats demanded the militia be disarmed. White rifle club members from around the state arrived in Hamburg and attacked the armory, where 40 black members of the militia defended themselves. The rifle companies brought up a cannon and reinforcements from Georgia. After the militia ran low on ammunition, white men captured the armory. One white man was killed, 29 black men were taken prisoner, and the other eleven fled. Five of the black men identified as leaders were shot down in cold blood. The rifle companies wrecked the town. Seven white men were indicted for murder. All were acquitted.

The Hamburg Massacre incited South Carolina Democrats to imitate Mississippi's "shotgun policy." It also forced a reluctant President Grant to send federal troops to South Carolina. In the 1876 election campaign, hundreds of white men in red flannel shirts turned out on mules and horses to support Wade Hampton against incumbent Republican governor Daniel Chamberlain and his black and white allies. When Chamberlain and fellow Republicans tried to speak in Edgefield, 600 Red Shirts, many of them armed, ridiculed, threatened, and shouted them down.

Democrats beat and killed black people to prevent them from voting. Democratic leaders instructed their followers to treat black voters with contempt: "In speeches to negroes you must remember that argument has no effect on them. They can only be influenced by their fears, superstition, and cupidity. . . . Treat them so as to show them you are a superior race and that their natural position is that of subordination to the white man."

As the election approached, black people in the up-country of South Carolina knew it would be dangerous if they tried to vote. But in the low country, black people went on the offensive and attacked Democrats. In Charleston, a white man was killed in a racial melee. At a campaign rally at Cainhoy, a few miles outside Charleston, armed black men killed five white men.

A few black men supported Hampton and the Red Shirts. Hampton had a paternalistic view of black people, and, although he considered them inferior, he promised to respect their rights. Martin Delany believed Hampton and the Democrats were more trustworthy than unreliable Republicans; Delany campaigned for Hampton and was later rewarded with an appointment to a minor political post. A few conservative black men during Reconstruction also supported the Democrats and curried their favor and patronage. Most black people despised them. When one black man gave his support to the Democrats, his wife threw him and his clothes out, declaring she would prefer to "beg her bread" than live with a "Democratic nigger."

THE "COMPROMISE" OF 1877

Threats, violence, and bloodshed accompanied the elections of 1876 in the South, but the national results were confusing and contradictory. Samuel Tilden, the Democratic presidential candidate, won the popular vote by more than 250,000 and had a large lead—185 to 167—over Republican Rutherford B. Hayes in the electoral vote. The 20 remaining electoral votes were in dispute. Both Democrats and Republicans claimed to have won in Florida, Louisiana, and South Carolina, the last three southern states that had not been redeemed. (There was also one contested vote from Oregon.) Whoever took the 20 electoral votes of the three contested states (and Oregon) would be the next president (see Map 13–2).

The constitutional crisis over the outcome of the 1876 election was not resolved until shortly before Inauguration Day in March 1877. An informal understanding known as the **Compromise of 1877** ended the dispute. Democrats accepted a Hayes victory, but Hayes

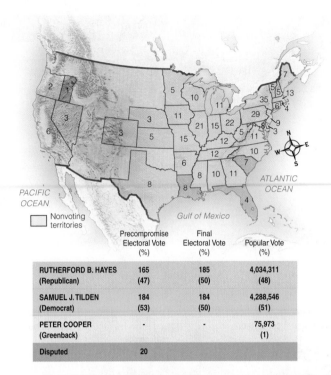

	Precompromise Electoral Vote (%)	Final Electoral Vote (%)	Popular Vote (%)
RUTHERFORD B. HAYES (Republican)	165 (47)	185 (50)	4,034,311 (48)
SAMUEL J. TILDEN (Democrat)	184 (53)	184 (50)	4,288,546 (51)
PETER COOPER (Greenback)	-	-	75,973 (1)
Disputed	20		

MAP 13–2   THE ELECTION OF 1876

Although Democrat Samuel Tilden appeared to have won the election of 1876, Rutherford B. Hayes and the Republicans were able to claim victory after a prolonged political and constitutional controversy involving the disputed Electoral College votes from Louisiana, Florida, and South Carolina (and one from Oregon). In an informal settlement in 1877, Democrats agreed to accept electoral votes for Hayes from those states, and Republicans agreed to permit those states to be "redeemed" by the Democrats. The result was to leave the entire South under the political control of conservative white Democrats. For the first time since 1867, black and white Republicans no longer effectively controlled any former Confederate state.

▶ *What factors explain the loss of political power by southern Republicans?*

let southern Democrats know he would not support Republican governments in Florida, Louisiana, and South Carolina. In 1877 Hayes withdrew the last federal troops from the South, and the Republican administration in those states collapsed. Democrats immediately took control.

Redemption was now complete. White Democrats controlled each of the former Confederate states. Henry Adams, a black leader from Louisiana, explained what had happened: "The whole South—every state in the South had got into the hands of the very men that held us as slaves."

AFRICAN-AMERICAN EVENTS	NATIONAL EVENTS
• **1865** •	
1865	**1865**
The Freedmen's Savings Bank and Trust Company is established	Freedmen's Bureau established
	1866
	President Johnson vetoes Freedmen's Bureau and civil rights bills; Congress overrides both vetoes
	Ku Klux Klan founded in Pulaski, Tennessee
• **1867** •	
1867–1868	**1867**
Ten southern states hold constitutional conventions	Congress takes over Reconstruction and provides for universal manhood suffrage
1867	**1868**
Howard University established in Washington, D.C.	Fourteenth Amendment to the Constitution ratified
	Ulysses S. Grant elected president
1868	
Black political leaders elected to state and local offices across the South	
• **1869** •	
1870	**1869**
Hiram R. Revels elected to the U.S. Senate and Joseph H. Rainey to the U.S. House of Representatives	Knights of Labor founded in Philadelphia
	1870
Congress passes the Enforcement Act	Fifteenth Amendment to the Constitution ratified
	John D. Rockefeller incorporates Standard Oil Co. in Cleveland

CONCLUSION

The glorious hopes that emancipation and the Union victory in the Civil War had aroused among African Americans in 1865 appeared forlorn by 1877. To be sure, black people were no longer slave laborers or property. They lived in tightly knit families that white people no longer controlled. They had established hundreds of schools, churches, and benevolent societies. The Constitution now endowed them with freedom, citizenship, and the right to vote. Some black people had even acquired land.

But no one can characterize Reconstruction as a success. The epidemic of terror and violence made it one of the bloodiest eras in American history. Thousands of black people had been beaten, raped, and murdered since 1865 simply because they had acted as free people. Too many white people were determined that black people could not and would not have the same rights that white people enjoyed. White southerners would not tolerate either the presence of black men in politics or white Republicans who accepted black political involvement. Most white northerners and even radical Republicans grew weary of intervening in southern affairs and became convinced again that black men and women were their inferiors and were not prepared to participate in government. Reconstruction, they concluded, had been a mistake.

Furthermore, black and white Republicans hurt themselves by indulging in fraud and corruption and by engaging in angry and divisive factionalism. But even if Republicans had been honest and united, white southern Democrats would never have accepted black people as worthy to participate in the political system.

Southern Democrats would accept black people in politics only if Democrats could control black voters. But black voters understood this, rejected control by former slave owners, and were loyal to the Republican Party—as flawed as it was.

But as grim a turn as life may have taken for black people by 1877, it would get even worse in the decades that followed.

RECOMMENDED READING

Eric Foner. *Freedom's Lawmakers: A Directory of Black Officeholders during Reconstruction.* New York: Oxford University Press, 1993. Biographical sketches of every known southern black leader during the era.

John Hope Franklin. *Reconstruction after the Civil War.* Chicago: University of Chicago Press, 1961. An excellent summary and interpretation of the postwar years.

William Gillette. *Retreat from Reconstruction, 1869–1879.* Baton Rouge: Louisiana State University Press, 1979. An analysis of how and why the North lost interest in the South.

Thomas Holt. *Black over White: Negro Political Leadership in South Carolina.* Urbana: University of Illinois Press, 1979. A masterful and sophisticated study of black leaders in the state with the most African-American politicians.

Michael L. Perman. *Emancipation and Reconstruction, 1862–1879.* Arlington Heights, IL: Harlan Davidson, 1987. Another excellent survey of the period.

Howard N. Rabinowitz, ed. *Southern Black Leaders of the Reconstruction Era.* Urbana: University of Illinois Press, 1982. A series of biographical essays on black politicians.

Frank A. Rollin. *Life and Public Services of Martin R. Delany.* Boston: Lee and Shepard, 1883. This is the first biography of a black leader by an African American. The author was Frances A. Rollin, but she used a male pseudonym.

ADDITIONAL BIBLIOGRAPHY

RECONSTRUCTION IN SPECIFIC STATES AND TERRITORIES

M. Thomas Bailey. *Reconstruction in Indian Territory: A Story of Avarice, Discrimination, and Opportunism.* Port Washington, NY: Kennikat Press, 1972.

Jane Dailey. *Before Jim Crow: The Politics of Race in Post Emancipation Virginia.* Chapel Hill: University of North Carolina Press, 2000.

Edmund L. Drago. *Black Politicians and Reconstruction in Georgia.* Athens: University of Georgia Press, 1982.

———. *Hurrah for Hampton! Black Red Shirts in South Carolina during Reconstruction.* Fayetteville: University of Arkansas Press, 1998.

Luther P. Jackson. *Negro Officeholders in Virginia, 1865–1895.* Norfolk, VA: Guide Quality Press, 1945.

Peter Kolchin. *First Freedom: The Responses of Alabama's Blacks to Emancipation and Reconstruction.* Westport, CT: Greenwood, 1972.

Merline Pitre. *Through Many Dangers, Toils, and Snares: The Black Leadership of Texas, 1868–1900.* Austin, TX: Eakin Press, 1985.

Joe M. Richardson. *The Negro in the Reconstruction of Florida, 1865–1877.* Tallahassee: Florida State University Press, 1965.

Buford Stacher. *Blacks in Mississippi Politics, 1865–1900.* Washington, DC: University Press of America, 1978.

Ted Tunnell. *Crucible of Reconstruction: War, Radicalism and Race in Louisiana, 1862–1877.* Baton Rouge: Louisiana State University Press, 1984.

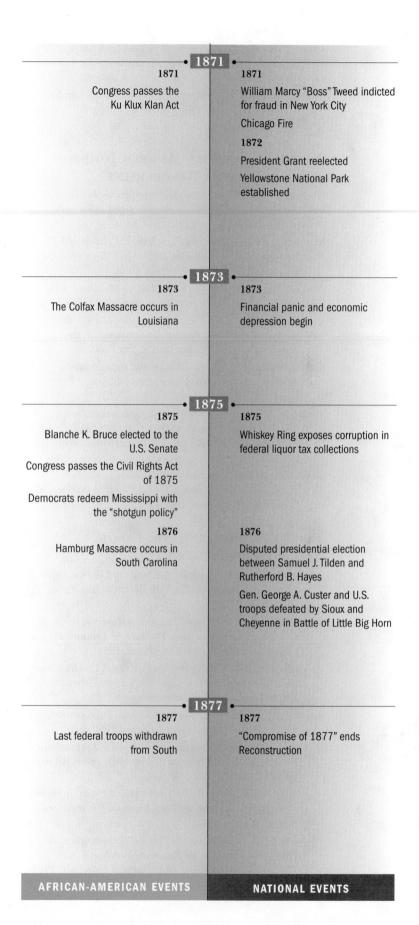

1871

1871
Congress passes the Ku Klux Klan Act

1871
William Marcy "Boss" Tweed indicted for fraud in New York City

Chicago Fire

1872
President Grant reelected

Yellowstone National Park established

1873

1873
The Colfax Massacre occurs in Louisiana

1873
Financial panic and economic depression begin

1875

1875
Blanche K. Bruce elected to the U.S. Senate

Congress passes the Civil Rights Act of 1875

Democrats redeem Mississippi with the "shotgun policy"

1875
Whiskey Ring exposes corruption in federal liquor tax collections

1876
Hamburg Massacre occurs in South Carolina

1876
Disputed presidential election between Samuel J. Tilden and Rutherford B. Hayes

Gen. George A. Custer and U.S. troops defeated by Sioux and Cheyenne in Battle of Little Big Horn

1877

1877
Last federal troops withdrawn from South

1877
"Compromise of 1877" ends Reconstruction

AFRICAN-AMERICAN EVENTS   **NATIONAL EVENTS**

Charles Vincent. *Black Legislators in Louisiana during Reconstruction.* Baton Rouge: Louisiana State University Press, 1976.

Joel Williamson. *After Slavery: The Negro in South Carolina: 1861–1877.* Chapel Hill: University of North Carolina Press, 1965.

NATIONAL POLITICS: ANDREW JOHNSON AND THE RADICAL REPUBLICANS

Michael Les Benedict. *A Compromise of Principle: Congressional Republicans and Reconstruction.* New York: Norton, 1974.

Dan T. Carter. *When the War Was Over: The Failure of Self-Reconstruction in the South, 1865–1867.* Baton Rouge: Louisina State University Press, 1983.

Michael W. Fitzgerald. *The Union League Movement in the Deep South.* Baton Rouge: Louisiana State University Press, 1989.

————. *Splendid Failure: Postwar Reconstruction in the American South.* Chicago: Ivan R. Dee, 2007.

Eric L. McKitrick. *Andrew Johnson and Reconstruction, 1865–1867.* Chicago: University of Chicago Press, 1960.

James M. McPherson. *The Struggle for Equality: Abolitionists and the Negro in the Civil War and Reconstruction.* Princeton, NJ: Princeton University Press, 1964.

Hans L. Trefousse. *The Radical Republicans: Lincoln's Vanguard for Racial Justice.* Baton Rouge: Louisiana State University Press, 1969.

ECONOMIC ISSUES: LAND, LABOR, AND THE FREEDMEN'S BANK

Elizabeth Bethel. *Promiseland: A Century of Life in a Negro Community.* Philadelphia: Temple University Press, 1981.

Carol R. Bleser. *The Promised Land: The History of the South Carolina Land Commission, 1869–1890.* Columbia: University of South Carolina Press, 1969.

Sharon Ann Holt. *Making Freedom Pay: North Carolina Freed People Working for Themselves, 1865–1900.* Athens: University of Georgia Press, 2000.

Lynda J. Morgan. *Emancipation in Virginia's Tobacco Belt.* Athens: University of Georgia Press, 1992.

Donald G. Nieman. *To Set the Law in Motion: The Freedmen's Bureau and Legal Rights for Blacks, 1865–1869.* Millwood, NY: KTO, 1979.

Carl R. Osthaus. *Freedmen, Philanthropy and Fraud: A History of the Freedman's Savings Bank.* Urbana: University of Illinois Press, 1976.

Heather Cox Richardson. *The Death of Reconstruction: Race, Labor, and Politics in the Post–Civil War North, 1865–1901.* Cambridge, MA: Harvard University Press, 2001.

VIOLENCE AND THE KU KLUX KLAN

George C. Rable. *But There Was No Peace: The Role of Violence in the Politics of Reconstruction.* Athens: University of Georgia Press, 1984.

Allen W. Trelease. *White Terror: The Ku Klux Klan Conspiracy and Southern Reconstruction.* New York: Harper & Row, 1973.

Lou Falkner Williams. *The Great South Carolina Ku Klux Klan Trials, 1871–1872.* Athens: University of Georgia Press, 1996.

AUTOBIOGRAPHY AND BIOGRAPHY

Mifflin Wistar Gibbs. *Shadow & Light: An Autobiography.* Lincoln: University of Nebraska Press, 1995.

Peter D. Klingman. *Josiah Walls.* Gainesville: University Press of Florida, 1976.

Peggy Lamson. *The Glorious Failure: Black Congressman Robert Brown Elliott and Reconstruction in South Carolina.* New York: Norton, 1973.

Edward A. Miller. *Gullah Statesman: Robert Smalls: From Slavery to Congress, 1839–1915.* Columbia: University of South Carolina Press, 1995.

Loren Schweninger. *James T. Rapier and Reconstruction.* Chicago: University of Chicago Press, 1978.

Okon E. Uya. *From Slavery to Public Service: Robert Smalls, 1839–1915.* New York: Oxford University Press, 1971.

RETRACING THE ODYSSEY

Howard University, Washington, D.C. www.howard.edu. The Freedmen's Bureau founded this national university in 1867. Also located on the campus is the Moorland-Spingarn Research Center, one of the country's richest archives in African-American history.

Wilberforce University and the National Afro-American Museum and Cultural Center, Wilberforce, Ohio. www.ohsweb.ohiohistory.org/places/sw13/index.shtml; www.wilberforce.edu. Wilberforce University opened in 1856 and was named after English abolitionist William Wilberforce. The African Methodist Episcopal Church took over the school in 1863. It contains exhibits, an art gallery, and a theater, and has a picnic area.

Union Bank Building, Tallahassee, Florida. www.museumoffloridahistory.com/sites/unionbank/ For a time during Reconstruction, a branch of the Freedmen's Savings and Trust Company was located here. The building, constructed in 1840, originally served as a planters' bank. It is currently part of the Museum of Florida History and includes its African-American History teacher in-service program.

The Robert Smalls Home, Beaufort, South Carolina. www.robertsmalls.org The Civil War hero and black political leader bought this house in 1863. He had lived on the premises as a slave, and it remained in his hands until his death in 1915. (The former Smalls house is a privately owned dwelling today.)

REVIEW QUESTIONS

1. What issues most concerned black political leaders during Reconstruction?

2. What did black political leaders accomplish and fail to accomplish during Reconstruction? What contributed to their successes and failures?

3. Were black political leaders unqualified to hold office so soon after the end of slavery?

4. To what extent did African Americans dominate southern politics during Reconstruction? Should we refer to this era as "Black Reconstruction"?

5. Why did the Republican Party fail to maintain control of southern state governments during Reconstruction?

6. What was "redemption"? What happened when redemption occurred? What factors contributed to redemption?

7. How and why did Reconstruction end?

8. How effective was Reconstruction in assisting black people to move from slavery to freedom? How effective was it in restoring the southern states to the Union?

PEARSON myhistorylab Connections

www.myhistorylab.com

Review what you've learned in this chapter and explore the many documents, images, research tools, and activities for this chapter to learn more about African-American history.

✓● Study and Review

READ

● Read the Document

- Diary of Joseph Addison Waddell (1865)

- Organization and Principles of the Ku Klux Klan (1868)

- Hannah Irwin Describes Ku Klux Klan Ride (Late 1860s)

- Blanche K. Bruce, Speech in the Senate (1876)

- Thirteenth, Fourteenth, and Fifteenth Amendments

- The New Slavery in the South—An Autobiography (1904)

- James T. Rapier, Testimony before U.S. Senate Regarding the Agricultural Labor Force in the South (1880)

- "When We Worked on Shares, We Couldn't Make Nothing": Henry Blake Talks about Share-cropping after the Civil War

LISTEN

((● Hear the Audio

Hear the audio files for Chapter 13.

RESEARCH

mysearchlab

Consider this question in a short research paper.

Why did so many whites in the North lose interest in the situation of blacks in the South?

EXPLORE

● Watch the Video

- The Promise and Failure of Reconstruction

● See the Map

- Dates of Readmission of the Southern States to the Union and Reestablishment of Democratic Party Control

● Read the Document

- Did Reconstruction Work for the Freed People?

FRANCES ELLEN WATKINS HARPER, SKETCHES OF SOUTHERN LIFE

Frances Ellen Watkins Harper (1825–1911) was born free in Baltimore, Maryland. Her parents died when she was young, and she was raised by her aunt and uncle. Her uncle, the Rev. William Watkins, had a profound influence on her life. An important member of Baltimore's black community and the founder of a school, Rev. Watkins instilled in Harper a passion for learning, writing, and social activism. Over the course of her life, she would publish poetry, short stories, and a novel. In 1850 Harper moved to Ohio to become the first women to teach at the Union Seminary, a school established by the African Methodist Episcopal Church. She joined the American Anti-Slavery Society in 1853, launching a career as public speaker and political activist. Her activism did not end with the abolition of slavery after the Civil War. She continued to fight for civil rights for women and African Americans as well as for a number of other social causes right up until her death in 1911.

During Reconstruction, she toured the South, meeting newly freed blacks and observing the conditions in which they lived. The poems from her *Sketches of Southern Life* (1872) were inspired by that experience. An elderly ex-slave, Aunt Chole, is the narrator for many of the poems, including the two included below.

What do these two poems say about Reconstruction politics and the importance of literacy to slaves and ex-slaves. How do these poems shed light on these two issues?

Aunt Chloe's Politics

Of course, I don't know very much
   About these politics,
But I think that some who run 'em,
   Do mighty ugly tricks.

I've seen 'em honey-fugle round,
   And talk so awful sweet,
That you'd think them full of kindness,
   As an egg is full of meat.

Now I don't believe in looking
   Honest people in the face,
And saying when you're doing wrong,
   That "I haven't sold my race."

When we want to school our children,
   If the money isn't there,
Whether black or white have took it,
   The loss we all must share.

And this buying up each other
   Is something worse than mean,
Though I thinks a heap of voting,
   I go for voting clean.

Frances Ellen Watkins Harper traveled across the North as an antislavery speaker.

Learning to Read

Very soon the Yankee teachers
  Came down and set up school;
But, oh! how the Rebs did hate it, –
  It was agin' their rule.

Our masters always tried to hide
  Book learning from our eyes;
Knowledge didn't agree with slavery –
  'Twould make us all too wise.

But some of us would try to steal
  A little from the book,
And put the words together,
  And learn by hook or crook.

I remember Uncle Caldwell,
  Who took pot liquor fat
And greased the pages of his book,
  And hid it in his hat.

And had his master ever seen
  The leaves upon his head,
He'd have thought them greasy papers,
  But nothing to be read.

And there was Mr. Turner's Ben,
  Who heard the children spell,
And picked the words right up by heart,
  And learned to read 'em well.

Well, the Northern folks kept sending
  The Yankee teachers down;
And they stood right up and helped us,
  Though Rebs did sneer and frown.

And, I longed to read my Bible,
  For precious words it said;
But when I begun to learn it,
  Folks just shook their heads,

And said there is no use trying,
  Oh! Chloe, you're too late;
But as I was rising sixty,
  I had no time to wait.

So I got a pair of glasses,
  And straight to work I went,
And never stopped till I could read
  The hymns and Testament.

Then I got a little cabin
  A place to call my own –
And I felt as independent
  As the queen upon her throne.

ROOTS OF CULTURE

Appendix

THE DECLARATION OF INDEPENDENCE

When in the course of human events it becomes necessary for one people to dissolve the political bands which have connected them with another and to assume, among the powers of the earth, the separate and equal station to which the laws of nature and of nature's God entitle them, a decent respect to the opinions of mankind requires that they should declare the causes which impel them to the separation.

We hold these truths to be self-evident, that all men are created equal; that they are endowed by their Creator with certain unalienable rights; that among these are life, liberty, and the pursuit of happiness. That, to secure these rights, governments are instituted among men, deriving their just powers from the consent of the governed; that, whenever any form of government becomes destructive of these ends, it is the right of the people to alter or to abolish it, and to institute a new government, laying its foundation on such principles, and organizing its powers in such form, as to them shall seem most likely to effect their safety and happiness. Prudence, indeed, will dictate that governments long established should not be changed for light and transient causes; and, accordingly, all experience hath shown that mankind are more disposed to suffer, while evils are sufferable, than to right themselves by abolishing the forms to which they are accustomed. But when a long train of abuses and usurpations, pursuing invariably the same object, evinces a design to reduce them under absolute despotism, it is their right, it is their duty, to throw off such government and to provide new guards for their future security. Such has been the patient sufferance of these colonies, and such is now the necessity which constrains them to alter their former systems of government. The history of the present King of Great Britain is a history of repeated injuries and usurpations, all having, in direct object, the establishment of an absolute tyranny over these States. To prove this, let facts be submitted to a candid world:

He has refused his assent to laws the most wholesome and necessary for the public good.

He has forbidden his governors to pass laws of immediate and pressing importance, unless suspended in their operation till his assent should be obtained; and, when so suspended, he has utterly neglected to attend to them.

He has refused to pass other laws for the accommodation of large districts of people, unless those people would relinquish the right of representation in the legislature, a right inestimable to them and formidable to tyrants only.

He has called together legislative bodies at places unusual, uncomfortable, and distant from the depository of their public records, for the sole purpose of fatiguing them into compliance with his measures.

He has dissolved representative houses, repeatedly for opposing, with manly firmness, his invasions on the rights of the people.

He has refused, for a long time after such dissolutions, to cause others to be elected; whereby the legislative powers, incapable of annihilation, have returned to the people at large for their exercise; the state remaining, in the meantime, exposed to all the danger of invasion from without and convulsions within.

He has endeavored to prevent the population of these States; for that purpose, obstructing the laws for naturalization of foreigners, refusing to pass others to encourage their migration hither, and raising the conditions of new appropriations of lands.

He has obstructed the administration of justice by refusing his assent to laws for establishing judiciary powers.

He has made judges dependent on his will alone for the tenure of their offices and the amount and payment of their salaries.

He has erected a multitude of new offices and sent hither swarms of officers to harass our people and eat out their substance.

He has kept among us, in time of peace, standing armies, without the consent of our legislatures.

He has affected to render the military independent of, and superior to, the civil power.

He has combined with others to subject us to a jurisdiction foreign to our Constitution and unacknowledged by our laws, giving his assent to their acts of pretended legislation—

For quartering large bodies of armed troops among us;

For protecting them, by mock trial, from punishment for any murders which they should commit on the inhabitants of these States;

For cutting off our trade with all parts of the world;

For imposing taxes on us without our consent;

For depriving us, in many cases, of the benefits of trial by jury;

For transporting us beyond seas to be tried for pretended offences;

For abolishing the free system of English laws in a neighboring province, establishing therein an arbitrary government, and enlarging its boundaries, so as to render it at once an example and fit instrument for introducing the same absolute rule into these colonies;

For taking away our charters, abolishing our most valuable laws, and altering, fundamentally, the powers of our governments.

For suspending our own legislatures and declaring themselves invested with power to legislate for us in all cases whatsoever.

He has abdicated government here by declaring us out of his protection and waging war against us.

He has plundered our seas, ravaged our coasts, burnt our towns, and destroyed the lives of our people.

He is, at this time, transporting large armies of foreign mercenaries to complete the works of death, desolation, and tyranny already begun with circumstances of cruelty and perfidy scarcely paralleled in the most barbarous ages, and totally unworthy the head of a civilized nation.

He has constrained our fellow citizens, taken captive on the high seas, to bear arms against their country, to become the executioners of their friends and brethren, or to fall themselves by their hands.

He has excited domestic insurrections amongst us and has endeavored to bring on the inhabitants of our frontiers, the merciless Indian savages, whose known rule of warfare is an undistinguished destruction of all ages, sexes, and conditions.

In every stage of these oppressions, we have petitioned for redress in the most humble terms; our repeated petitions have been answered only by repeated injury. A prince whose character is thus marked by every act which may define a tyrant is unfit to be the ruler of a free people.

Nor have we been wanting in attention to our British brethren. We have warned them, from time to time, of attempts made by their legislature to extend an unwarrantable jurisdiction over us. We have reminded them of the circumstances of our emigration and settlement here. We have appealed to their native justice and magnanimity, and we have conjured them, by the ties of our common kindred, to disavow these usurpations, which would inevitably interrupt our connections and correspondence. They, too, have been deaf to the voice of justice and consanguinity. We must, therefore, acquiesce in the necessity which denounces our separation, and hold them, as we hold the rest of mankind, enemies in war, in peace, friends.

We, therefore, the representatives of the United States of America, in general Congress assembled, appealing to the Supreme Judge of the world for the rectitude of our intentions, do, in the name and by the authority of the good people of these colonies, solemnly publish and declare, that these united colonies are, and of right ought to be, free and independent states: that they are absolved from all allegiance to the British Crown, and that all political connection between them and the state of Great Britain is, and ought to be, totally dissolved; and that, as free and independent states, they have full power to levy war, conclude peace, contract alliances, establish commerce, and to do all other acts and things which independent states may of right do. And, for the support of this declaration, with a firm reliance on the protection of Divine Providence, we mutually pledge to each other our lives, our fortunes, and our sacred honor.

PROPOSED CLAUSE ON THE SLAVE TRADE OMITTED FROM THE FINAL DRAFT OF THE DECLARATION

He has waged cruel war against human nature itself, violating its most sacred rights of life and liberty in the person of a distant people who never offended him; captivating and carrying them into slavery in another hemisphere, or to incur miserable death in their transportation thither. This piratical warfare, the opprobrium of infidel powers, is the warfare of the Christian king of Great Britain. Determined to keep open a market where men should be bought and sold, he has prostituted his negative for suppressing every legislative attempt to prohibit or restrain this execrable commerce.

THE CONSTITUTION
OF THE
UNITED STATES OF AMERICA

(with clauses pertaining to the status of African Americans highlighted)

We the people of the United States, in order to form a more perfect union, establish justice, insure domestic tranquility, provide for the common defense, promote the general welfare, and secure the blessings of liberty to ourselves and our posterity, do ordain and establish this Constitution for the United States of America.

ARTICLE I

SECTION 1.   All legislative powers herein granted shall be vested in a Congress of the United States, which shall consist of a Senate and House of Representatives.

SECTION 2.   1. The House of Representatives shall be composed of members chosen every second year by the people of the several States, and the electors in each State shall have the qualifications requisite for electors of the most numerous branch of the State legislature.

2. No person shall be a representative who shall not have attained to the age of twenty-five years, and been seven years a citizen of the United States, and who shall not, when elected, be an inhabitant of that State in which he shall be chosen.

3. Representatives and direct taxes[1] shall be apportioned among the several States which may be included within this Union, according to their respective numbers, which shall be determined by adding to the whole number of free persons, including those bound to service for a term of years, and excluding Indians not taxed, three fifths of all other persons.[2]

The actual enumeration shall be made within three years after the first meeting of the Congress of the United States, and within every subsequent term of ten years, in such manner as they shall by law direct. The number of representatives shall not exceed one for every thirty thousand, but each State shall have at least one representative; and until such enumeration shall be made, the State of New Hampshire shall be entitled to choose three, Massachusetts eight, Rhode Island and Providence Plantations one, Connecticut five, New York six, New Jersey four, Pennsylvania eight, Delaware one, Maryland six, Virginia ten, North Carolina five, South Carolina five, and Georgia three.

4. When vacancies happen in the representation from any State, the executive authority thereof shall issue writs of election to fill such vacancies.

5. The House of Representatives shall choose their speaker and other officers; and shall have the sole power of impeachment.

SECTION 3.   1. The Senate of the United States shall be composed of two senators from each State, chosen by the legislature thereof,[3] for six years; and each senator shall have one vote.

2. Immediately after they shall be assembled in consequence of the first election, they shall be divided as equally as may be into three classes. The seats of the senators of the first class shall be vacated at the expiration of the second year, of the second class at the expiration of the fourth year, and of the third class at the expiration of the sixth year, so that one third may be chosen every second year; and if vacancies happen by resignation, or otherwise, during the recess of the legislature of any State, the executive thereof may make temporary appointments until the next meeting of the legislature, which shall then fill such vacancies.[4]

3. No person shall be a senator who shall not have attained to the age of thirty years, and been nine years a citizen of the United States, and who shall not, when elected, be an inhabitant of that State for which he shall be chosen.

---

[1]See the Sixteenth Amendment.
[2]See the Fourteenth Amendment.

[3]See the Seventeenth Amendment.
[4]See the Seventeenth Amendment.

4. The Vice President of the United States shall be President of the Senate, but shall have no vote, unless they be equally divided.

5. The Senate shall choose their other officers, and also a president pro tempore, in the absence of the Vice President, or when he shall exercise the office of the President of the United States.

6. The Senate shall have the sole power to try all impeachments. When sitting for that purpose, they shall be on oath or affirmation. When the president of the United States is tried, the chief justice shall preside: and no person shall be convicted without the concurrence of two thirds of the members present.

7. Judgment in cases of impeachment shall not extend further than to removal from office, and disqualification to hold and enjoy any office of honor, trust or profit under the United States: but the party convicted shall nevertheless be liable and subject to indictment, trial, judgment and punishment, according to law.

SECTION 4.   1. The times, places, and manner of holding elections for senators and representatives, shall be prescribed in each State by the legislature thereof; but the Congress may at any time by law make or alter such regulations, except as to the places of choosing senators.

2. The Congress shall assemble at least once in every year, and such meeting shall be on the first Monday in December, unless they shall by law appoint a different day.

SECTION 5.   1. Each House shall be the judge of the elections, returns and qualifications of its own members, and a majority of each shall constitute a quorum to do business; but a smaller number may adjourn from day to day, and may be authorized to compel the attendance of absent members, in such manner, and under such penalties as each House may provide.

2. Each House may determine the rules of its proceedings, punish its members for disorderly behavior, and, with the concurrence of two thirds, expel a member.

3. Each House shall keep a journal of its proceedings, and from time to time publish the same, excepting such parts as may in their judgment require secrecy; and the yeas and nays of the members of either house on any question shall, at the desire of one fifth of those present, be entered on the journal.

4. Neither House, during the session of Congress, shall, without the consent of the other, adjourn for more than three days, nor to any other place than that in which the two Houses shall be sitting.

SECTION 6.   1. The senators and representatives shall receive a compensation for their services, to be ascertained by law, and paid out of the Treasury of the United States. They shall in all cases, except treason, felony, and breach of the peace, be privileged from arrest during their attendance at the session of their respective Houses, and in going to and returning from the same; and for any speech or debate in either House, they shall not be questioned in any other place.

2. No senator or representative shall, during the time for which he was elected, be appointed to any civil office under the authority of the United States, which shall have been created, or the emoluments whereof shall have been increased, during such time; and no person holding any office under the United States shall be a member of either House during his continuance in office.

SECTION 7.   1. All bills for raising revenue shall originate in the House of Representatives; but the Senate may purpose or concur with amendments as on other bills.

2. Every bill which shall have passed the House of Representatives and the Senate, shall, before it become a law, be presented to the President of the United States; if he approves he shall sign it, but if not he shall return it, with his objections, to that House in which it shall have originated, who shall enter the objections at large on their journal, and proceed to reconsider it. If after such reconsideration two thirds of that House shall agree to pass the bill, it shall be sent, together with the objections, to the other House, by which it shall likewise be reconsidered, and if approved by two thirds of that House, it shall become a law. But in all such cases the votes of both Houses shall be determined by yeas and nays, and the names of the persons voting for and against the bill shall be entered on the journal of each House respectively. If any bill shall not be returned by the President within ten days (Sundays excepted) after it shall have been presented to him, the same shall be a law, in like manner as if he had signed it, unless the Congress by their adjournment prevent its return, in which case it shall not be a law.

3. Every order, resolution, or vote to which the concurrence of the Senate and the House of Representatives may be necessary (except on a question of adjournment) shall be presented to the President of the United States; and before the same shall take effect, shall be approved by him, or being disapproved by him, shall be repassed by two thirds of the Senate and House of Representatives, according to the rules and limitations prescribed in the case of a bill.

SECTION 8.   The Congress shall have the power

1. To lay and collect taxes, duties, imposts, and excises, to pay the debts and provide for the common defense and general welfare of the United States; but all duties, imposts, and excises shall be uniform throughout the United States.

2. To borrow money on the credit of the United States;

3. To regulate commerce with foreign nations, and among the several States, and with the Indian tribes;

4. To establish a uniform rule of naturalization, and uniform laws on the subject of bankruptcies throughout the United States;

5. To coin money, regulate the value thereof, and of foreign coin, and fix the standard of weights and measures;

6. To provide for the punishment of counterfeiting the securities and current coin of the United States;

7. To establish post offices and post roads;

8. To promote the progress of science and useful arts, by securing for limited times to authors and inventors the exclusive right to their respective writings and discoveries;

9. To constitute tribunals inferior to the Supreme Court;

10. To define and punish piracies and felonies committed on the high seas, and offenses against the law of nations;

11. To declare war, grant letters of marque and reprisal, and make rules concerning captures on land and water;

12. To raise and support armies, but no appropriation of money to that use shall be for a longer term than two years;

13. To provide and maintain a navy;

14. To make rules for the government and regulation of the land and naval forces;

15. To provide for calling forth the militia to execute the laws of the Union, suppress insurrections and repel invasions;

16. To provide for organizing, arming, and disciplining the militia, and for governing such part of them as may be employed in the service of the United States, reserving to the States respectively, the appointment of the officers, and the authority of training the militia according to the discipline prescribed by Congress;

17. To exercise exclusive legislation in all cases whatsoever, over such district (not exceeding ten miles square) as may, by cession of particular States, and the acceptance of Congress, become the seat of the government of the United States, and to exercise like authority over all places purchased by the consent of the legislature of the State in which the same shall be, for the erection of forts, magazines, arsenals, dockyards, and other needful buildings; and

18. To make all laws which shall be necessary and proper for carrying into execution the foregoing powers, and all other powers vested by this Constitution in the government of the United States, or any department or officer thereof.

SECTION 9.   1. The migration or importation of such persons as any of the States now existing shall think proper to admit, shall not be prohibited by the Congress prior to the year one thousand eight hundred and eight, but a tax or duty may be imposed on such importation, not exceeding ten dollars for each person.

2. The privilege of the writ of habeas corpus shall not be suspended, unless when in cases of rebellion or invasion the public safety may require it.

3. No bill of attainder or ex post facto law shall be passed.

4. No capitation, or other direct, tax shall be laid, unless in proportion to the census or enumeration herein-before directed to be taken.[5]

5. No tax or duty shall be laid on articles exported from any State.

6. No preference shall be given by any regulation of commerce or revenue to the ports of one State over those of another: nor shall vessels bound to, or from, one State be obliged to enter, clear, or pay duties in another.

7. No money shall be drawn from the treasury, but in consequence of appropriations made by law; and a regular statement and account of the receipts and expenditures of all public money shall be published from time to time.

8. No title of nobility shall be granted by the United States: and no person holding any office of profit or trust under them, shall, without the consent of the Congress, accept of any present, emolument, office, or title, of any kind whatever, from any king, prince, or foreign State.

SECTION 10.   1. No State shall enter into any treaty, alliance, or confederation; grant letters of marque and reprisal; coin money; emit bills of credit; make any thing but gold and silver coin a tender in payment of debts; pass any bill of attainder, ex post facto law, or law impairing the obligation of contracts, or grant any title of nobility.

2. No State shall, without the consent of the Congress, lay any imposts or duties on imports or exports, except what may be absolutely necessary for executing its inspection laws: and the net produce of all duties and imposts laid by any State on imports or exports, shall be for the use of the treasury of the United States; and all such laws shall be subject to the revision and control of the Congress.

3. No State shall, without the consent of the Congress, lay any duty of tonnage, keep troops, or ships of

---

[5]See the Sixteenth Amendment.

war in time of peace, enter into any agreement or compact with another State, or with a foreign power, or engage in war, unless actually invaded, or in such imminent danger as will not admit of delay.

ARTICLE II

SECTION 1.   1. The executive power shall be vested in a President of the United States of America. He shall hold his office during the term of four years, and, together with the Vice President, chosen for the same term, be elected, as follows:

2. Each State shall appoint, in such manner as the legislature thereof may direct, a number of electors, equal to the whole number of senators and representatives to which the State may be entitled in the Congress: but no senator or representative, or person holding any office of trust or profit under the United States, shall be appointed an elector.

The electors shall meet in their respective States, and vote by ballot for two persons, of whom one at least shall not be an inhabitant of the same State with themselves. And they shall make a list of all the persons voted for, and of the number of votes for each; which list they shall sign and certify, and transmit sealed to the seat of the government of the United States, directed to the president of the Senate. The president of the Senate shall, in the presence of the Senate and House of Representatives, open all the certificates, and the votes shall then be counted. The person having the greatest number of votes shall be the President, if such number be a majority of the whole number of electors appointed; and if there be more than one who have such majority, and have an equal number of votes, then the House of Representatives shall immediately choose by ballot one of them for President; and if no person have a majority, then from the five highest on the list the said House shall in like manner choose the President. But in choosing the President, the votes shall be taken by States, the representation from each State having one vote; a quorum for this purpose shall consist of a member or members from two thirds of the States, and a majority of all the States shall be necessary to a choice. In every case after the choice of the President, the person having the greatest number of votes of the electors shall be the Vice President. But if there should remain two or more who have equal votes, the Senate shall choose from them by ballot the Vice President.[6]

3. The Congress may determine the time of choosing the electors, and the day on which they shall give their votes; which day shall be the same throughout the United States.

4. No person except a natural born citizen, or a citizen of the United States, at the time of the adoption of this Constitution, shall be eligible to the office of President; neither shall any person be eligible to the office who shall not have attained to the age of thirty-five years, and been fourteen years a resident within the United States.

5. In case of the removal of the President from office, or of his death, resignation, or inability to discharge the powers and duties of the said office, the same shall devolve on the Vice President, and the Congress may by law provide for the case of removal, death, resignation or inability, both of the President and Vice President, declaring what officer shall then act as President, and such officer shall act accordingly until the disability be removed, or a President shall be elected.

6. The President shall, at stated times, receive for his services a compensation which shall neither be increased nor diminished during the period for which he shall have been elected, and he shall not receive within that period any other emolument from the United States, or any of them.

7. Before he enter on the execution of his office, he shall take the following oath or affirmation:—"I do solemnly swear (or affirm) that I will faithfully execute the office of president of the United States, and will to the best of my ability, preserve, protect and defend the Constitution of the United States."

SECTION 2.   1. The President shall be commander in chief of the army and navy of the United States, and of the militia of the several States, when called into the actual service of the United States; he may require the opinion in writing, of the principal officer in each of the executive departments, upon any subject relating to the duties of their respective offices, and he shall have power to grant reprieves and pardons for offenses against the United States, except in cases of impeachment.

2. He shall have power, by and with the advice and consent of the Senate, to make treaties, provided two thirds of the senators present concur; and he shall nominate, and by and with the advice and consent of the Senate, shall appoint ambassadors, other public ministers and consuls, judges of the Supreme Court, and all other officers of the United States, whose appointments are not herein otherwise provided for, and which shall be established by law; but the Congress may by law vest the appointment of such inferior officers, as they think proper, in the President alone, in the courts of laws, or in the heads of departments.

3. The President shall have power to fill up all vacancies that may happen during the recess of the Senate, by

[6]See the Twelfth Amendment.

granting commissions which shall expire at the end of their next session.

SECTION 3.   He shall from time to time give to the Congress information of the state of the Union, and recommend to their consideration such measures as he shall judge necessary and expedient; he may, on extraordinary occasions, convene both houses, or either of them, and in case of disagreement between them with respect to the time of adjournment, he may adjourn them to such time as he shall think proper; he shall receive ambassadors and other public ministers; he shall take care that the laws be faithfully executed, and shall commission all the officers of the United States.

SECTION 4.   The President, Vice President, and all civil officers of the United States, shall be removed from office on impeachment for, and conviction of, treason, bribery, or other high crimes and misdemeanors.

ARTICLE III

SECTION 1.   The judicial power of the United States shall be vested in one Supreme Court, and in such inferior courts as the Congress may from time to time ordain and establish. The judges, both of the Supreme and inferior courts, shall hold their offices during good behavior, and shall, at stated times, receive for their services, a compensation, which shall not be diminished during their continuance in office.

SECTION 2.   1. The judicial power shall extend to all cases, in law and equity, arising under this Constitution, the laws of the United States, and treaties made, or which shall be made, under their authority;—to all cases of admiralty and maritime jurisdiction;—to controversies to which the United States shall be a party;[7]—to controversies between two or more States;—between a State and citizens of another State;—between citizens of different States;—between citizens of the same State claiming lands under grants of different States, and between a State, or the citizens thereof, and foreign States, citizens or subjects.

2. In all cases affecting ambassadors, other public ministers and consuls, and those in which a State shall be party, the Supreme Court shall have original jurisdiction. In all the other cases before mentioned, the Supreme Court shall have appellate jurisdiction, both as to law and fact, with such exceptions, and under such regulations as the Congress shall make.

3. The trial of all crimes, except in cases of impeachment, shall be by jury; and such trial shall be held in the State where the said crimes shall have been committed; but when not committed within any State, the trial shall be such place or places as the Congress may by law have directed.

SECTION 3.   (1) Treason against the United States shall consist only in levying war against them, or in adhering to their enemies, giving them aid and comfort. No person shall be convicted of treason unless on the testimony of two witnesses to the same overt act, or on confession in open court.

2. The Congress shall have power to declare the punishment of treason, but no attainder of treason shall work corruption of blood, or forfeiture except during the life of the person attained.

ARTICLE IV

SECTION 1.   Full faith and credit shall be given in each State to the public acts, records, and judicial proceedings of every other State. And the Congress may by general laws prescribe the manner in which such acts, records and proceedings shall be proved, and the effect thereof.

SECTION 2.   1. The citizens of each State shall be entitled to all privileges and immunities of citizens in the several States.[8]

2. A person charged in any State with treason, felony, or other crime, who shall flee from justice, and be found in another State, shall on demand of the executive authority of the State from which he fled, be delivered up to be removed to the State having jurisdiction of the crime.

3. No person held to service or labor in one State under the laws thereof, escaping into another, shall, in consequence of any law or regulation therein, be discharged from such service or labor, but shall be delivered up on claim of the party to whom such service or labor may be due.[9]

SECTION 3.   1. New States may be admitted by the Congress into this Union; but no new State shall be formed or erected within the jurisdiction of any other State, nor any State be formed by the junction of two or more States, or parts of States, without the consent of the legislatures of the States concerned as well as of the Congress.

2. The Congress shall have power to dispose of and make all needful rules and regulations respecting the territory or other property belonging to the United States; and nothing in this Constitution shall be so construed as to prejudice any claims of the United States, or of any particular State.

---

[7]See the Eleventh Amendment.

[8]See the Fourteenth Amendment, Sec. 1.

[9]See the Thirteenth Amendment.

SECTION 4.   The United States shall guarantee to every State in this Union a republican form of government, and shall protect each of them against invasion; and on application of the legislature, or of the executive (when the legislature cannot be convened) against domestic violence.

ARTICLE V

The Congress, whenever two thirds of both Houses shall deem it necessary, shall propose amendments to this Constitution, or, on the application of the legislatures of two thirds of the several States, shall call a convention for proposing amendments, which in either case shall be valid to all intents and purposes, as part of this Constitution, when ratified by the legislatures of three fourths of the several States, or by conventions in three fourths thereof, as the one or the other mode of ratification may be proposed by the Congress; Provided that no amendment which may be made prior to the year one thousand eight hundred and eight shall in any manner affect the first and fourth clauses in the ninth section of the first article; and that no State, without its consent, shall be deprived of its equal suffrage in the Senate.

ARTICLE VI

1. All debts contracted and engagements entered into, before the adoption of this Constitution, shall be as valid against the United States under this Constitution, as under the Confederation.[10]

2. This Constitution, and the laws of the United States which shall be made in pursuance thereof; and all treaties made, or which shall be made, under the authority of the United States, shall be the supreme law of the land; and the judges in every State shall be bound thereby, any thing in the Constitution or laws of any State to the contrary notwithstanding.

3. The senators and representatives before mentioned, and the members of the several State legislatures, and all executive and judicial officers, both of the United States and of the several States, shall be bound by oath or affirmation to support this Constitution; but no religious test shall ever be required as a qualification to any office or public trust under the United States.

ARTICLE VII

The ratification of the conventions of nine States shall be sufficient for the establishment of this Constitution between the States so ratifying the same.

---

[10]See the Fourteenth Amendment, Sec. 4.

Done in Convention by the unanimous consent of the States present the seventeenth day of September in the year of our Lord one thousand seven hundred and eighty-seven, and of the independence of the United States of America the twelfth. In witness whereof we have hereunto subscribed our names.

Articles in addition to, and amendment of, the Constitution of the United States of America, proposed by Congress, and ratified by the legislatures of the several States, pursuant to the fifth article of the original Constitution.

AMENDMENT I [FIRST TEN AMENDMENTS RATIFIED DECEMBER 15, 1791]

Congress shall make no law respecting an establishment of religion, or prohibiting the free exercise thereof; or abridging the freedom of speech, or of the press; or the right of the people peaceably to assemble, and to petition the government for a redress of grievances.

AMENDMENT II

A well regulated militia, being necessary to the security of a free State, the right of the people to keep and bear arms, shall not be infringed.

AMENDMENT III

No soldier shall, in time of peace be quartered in any house, without the consent of the owner, nor in time of war, but in a manner to be prescribed by law.

AMENDMENT IV

The right of the people to be secure in their persons, houses, papers, and effects, against unreasonable searches and seizures, shall not be violated, and no warrants shall issue, but upon probable cause, supported by oath or affirmation, and particularly describing the place to be searched, and the persons or things to be seized.

AMENDMENT V

No person shall be held to answer for a capital or otherwise infamous crime, unless on a presentment or indictment of a grand jury, except in cases arising in the land or naval forces, or in the militia, when in actual service in time of war or public danger; nor shall any person be subject for the same offense to be twice put in jeopardy of life or limb; nor shall be compelled in any criminal case to be a witness against himself, nor be deprived of life, liberty, or property, without due process of law; nor shall private property be taken for public use, without just compensation.

AMENDMENT VI

In all criminal prosecutions, the accused shall enjoy the right to a speedy and public trial, by an impartial jury of the State and district wherein the crime shall have been committed, which district shall have been previously ascertained by law, and to be informed of the nature and cause of the accusation; to be confronted with the witnesses against him; to have compulsory process for obtaining witnesses in his favor, and to have the assistance of counsel for his defense.

AMENDMENT VII

In suits at common law, where the value in controversy shall exceed twenty dollars, the right of trial by jury shall be preserved, and no fact tried by a jury shall be otherwise reexamined in any court of the United States, than according to the rules of the common law.

AMENDMENT VIII

Excessive bail shall not be required, nor excessive fines imposed, nor cruel and unusual punishments inflicted.

AMENDMENT IX

The enumeration in the Constitution of certain rights shall not be construed to deny or disparage others retained by the people.

AMENDMENT X

The powers not delegated to the United States by the Constitution, nor prohibited by it to the States, are reserved to the States respectively, or to the people.

AMENDMENT XI [JANUARY 8, 1798]

The judicial power of the United States shall not be construed to extend to any suit in law or equity, commenced or prosecuted against one of the United States by citizens of another State, or by citizens or subjects of any foreign State.

AMENDMENT XII [SEPTEMBER 25, 1804]

The electors shall meet in their respective States, and vote by ballot for President and Vice President, one of whom, at least, shall not be an inhabitant of the same State with themselves; they shall name in their ballots the person voted for as President, and in distinct ballots, the person voted for as Vice President, and they shall make distinct lists of all persons voted for as President and of all persons voted for as Vice President, and of the number of votes for each, which lists they shall sign and certify, and transmit sealed to the seat of the government of the United States, directed to the President of the Senate;—The President of the Senate shall, in the presence of the Senate and House of Representatives, open all the certificates and the votes shall then be counted;—The person having the greatest number of votes for President, shall be the President, if such number be a majority of the whole number of electors appointed; and if no person have such majority, then from the persons having the highest numbers not exceeding three on the list of those voted for as President, the House of Representatives shall choose immediately, by ballot, the President. But in choosing the President, the votes shall be taken by States, the representation from each State having one vote; a quorum for this purpose shall consist of a member or members from two thirds of the States, and a majority of all the States shall be necessary to a choice. And if the House of Representatives shall not choose a President whenever the right of choice shall devolve upon them, before the fourth day of March next following, then the Vice President shall act as President, as in the case of the death or other constitutional disability of the President. The person having the greatest number of votes as Vice President shall be the Vice President, if such number be a majority of the whole number of electors appointed, and if no person have a majority, then from the two highest numbers on the list, the Senate shall choose the Vice President; a quorum for the purpose shall consist of two thirds of the whole number of Senators, and a majority of the whole number shall be necessary to a choice. But no person constitutionally ineligible to the office of President shall be eligible to that of Vice President of the United States.

AMENDMENT XIII [DECEMBER 18, 1865]

SECTION 1.   Neither slavery nor involuntary servitude, except as punishment for crime whereof the party shall have been duly convicted, shall exist within the United States, or any place subject to their jurisdiction.

SECTION 2.   Congress shall have power to enforce this article by appropriate legislation.

AMENDMENT XIV [JULY 28, 1868]

SECTION 1.   All persons born or naturalized in the United States, and subject to the jurisdiction thereof, are citizens of the United States and of the State wherein they reside. No State shall make or enforce any law which shall abridge the privileges or immunities of citizens of the United States; nor shall any State deprive any person of life, liberty, or property, without due process of law; nor deny to any person within its jurisdiction the equal protection of the laws.

SECTION 2.   Representatives shall be apportioned among the several States according to their respective numbers, counting the whole number of persons in each State, excluding Indians not taxed. But when the right to vote at any election for the choice of electors for President and Vice President of the United States, representatives in Congress, the executive and judicial officers of a State, or the members of the legislature thereof, is denied to any of the male inhabitants of such State, being twenty-one years of age, and citizens of the United States, or in any way abridged, except for participating in rebellion, or other crime, the basis of representation there shall be reduced in the proportion which the number of such male citizens shall bear to the whole number of male citizens twenty-one years of age in such State.

Section 3.   No person shall be a senator or representative in Congress, or elector of President and Vice President, or hold any office, civil or military, under the United States, or under any State, who having previously taken an oath, as a member of Congress, or as an officer of the United States, or as a member of any State legislature, or as an executive or judicial officer of any State, to support the Constitution of the United States, shall have engaged in insurrection or rebellion against the same, or given aid or comfort to the enemies thereof. But Congress may by a vote of two thirds of each House, remove such disability.

Section 4.   The validity of the public debt of the United States, authorized by law, including debts incurred for payment of pensions and bounties for services in suppressing insurrection or rebellion; shall not be questioned. But neither the United States nor any State shall assume or pay any debt or obligation incurred in aid of insurrection or rebellion against the United States, or any claim for the loss or emancipation of any slave; but all such debts, obligations, and claims shall be held illegal and void.

Section 5.   The Congress shall have the power to enforce, by appropriate legislation, the provisions of this article.

Amendment XV [March 30, 1870]

Section 1.   The right of citizens of the United States to vote shall not be denied or abridged by the United States or by any State on account of race, color, or previous condition of servitude.

Section 2.   The Congress shall have power to enforce this article by appropriate legislation.

Amendment XVI [February 25, 1913]

The Congress shall have power to lay and collect taxes on incomes, from whatever source derived, without apportionment among the several States, and without regard to any census or enumeration.

Amendment XVII [May 31, 1913]

The Senate of the United States shall be composed of two senators from each State, elected by the people thereof, for six years; and each senator shall have one vote. The electors in each State shall have the qualifications requisite for electors of the most numerous branch of the State legislature.

When vacancies happen in the representation of any State in the Senate, the executive authority of such State shall issue writs of election to fill such vacancies: Provided, That the legislature of any State may empower the executive thereof to make temporary appointments until the people fill the vacancies by election as the legislature may direct.

This amendment shall not be so construed as to affect the election or term of any senator chosen before it becomes valid as part of the Constitution.

Amendment XVIII[11] [January 29, 1919]

After one year from the ratification of this article, the manufacture, sale, or transportation of intoxicating liquors within, the importation thereof into, or the exportation thereof from the United States and all territory subject to the jurisdiction thereof for beverage purposes is thereby prohibited.

The Congress and the several States shall have concurrent power to enforce this article by appropriate legislation.

This article shall be inoperative unless it shall have been ratified as an amendment to the Constitution by the legislatures of the several States, as provided in the Constitution, within seven years from the date of the submission hereof to the States by Congress.

Amendment XIX [August 26, 1920]

The right of citizens of the United States to vote shall not be denied or abridged by the United States or by any State on account of sex.

Congress shall have the power to enforce this article by appropriate legislation.

Amendment XX [January 23, 1933]

Section 1.   The terms of the President and Vice President shall end at noon on the 20th day of January and the terms of Senators and Representatives at noon on the 3d day of January, of the years in which such terms would have ended if this article had not been ratified; and the terms of their successors shall then begin.

Section 2.   The Congress shall assemble at least once in every year, and such meeting shall begin at noon on the 3d day of January, unless they shall by law appoint a different day.

Section 3.   If, at the time fixed for the beginning of the term of president, the President-elect shall have died, the Vice President-elect shall become President. If a President shall not have been chosen before the time fixed for the beginning of his term, or if the President-elect shall have failed to qualify,

---

[11]Repealed by the Twenty-first Amendment.

then the Vice President-elect shall act as president until a President shall have qualified; and the Congress may by law provide for the case wherein neither a President-elect nor a Vice President-elect shall have qualified, declaring who shall then act as President, or the manner in which one who is to act shall be selected, and such person shall act accordingly until a President or Vice President shall have qualified.

SECTION 4.   The Congress may by law provide for the case of the death of any of the persons from whom, the House of Representatives may choose a President whenever the right of choice shall have devolved upon them, and for the case of the death of any of the persons from whom the Senate may choose a Vice President whenever the right of choice shall have devolved upon them.

SECTION 5.   Sections 1 and 2 shall take effect on the 15th day of October following the ratification of this article.

SECTION 6.   This article shall be inoperative unless it shall have been ratified as an amendment to the Constitution by the legislatures of three-fourths of the several States within seven years from the date of its submission.

AMENDMENT XXI [DECEMBER 5, 1933]

SECTION 1.   The Eighteenth Article of amendment to the Constitution of the United States is hereby repealed.

SECTION 2.   The transportation or importation into any State, Territory, or possession of the United States for delivery or use therein of intoxicating liquors in violation of the laws thereof, is hereby prohibited.

SECTION 3.   This article shall be inoperative unless it shall have been ratified as an amendment to the Constitution by conventions in the several States, as provided in the Consitution, within seven years from the date of the submission thereof to the States by the Congress.

AMENDMENT XXII [MARCH 1, 1951]

No person shall be elected to the office of the President more than twice, and no person who has held the office of President, or acted as President, for more than two years of a term to which some other person was elected President shall be elected to the office of the President more than once.

But this article shall not apply to any person holding the office of President when this article was proposed by the Congress, and shall not prevent any person who may be holding the office of President, or acting as President, during the term within which this article becomes operative from holding the office of President or acting as President during the remainder of such term.

This article shall be inoperative unless it shall have been ratified as an amendment to the Constitution by the legislatures of three-fourths of the several States within seven years from the date of its submission to the States by the Congress.

AMENDMENT XXIII [MARCH 29, 1961]

SECTION 1.   The District constituting the seat of Government of the United States shall appoint in such manner as the Congress may direct:

A number of electors of President and Vice President equal to the whole number of Senators and Representatives in Congress to which the District would be entitled if it were a State, but in no event more than the least populous State; they shall be in addition to those appointed by the States, but they shall be considered, for the purposes of the election of President and Vice President, to be electors appointed by a State; and they shall meet in the District and perform such duties as provided by the twelfth article of amendment.

SECTION 2.   The Congress shall have power to enforce this article by appropriate legislation.

AMENDMENT XXIV [JANUARY 23, 1964]

SECTION 1.   The right of citizens of the United States to vote in any primary or other election for President or Vice President, for electors for President or Vice President, or for Senator or Representative in Congress, shall not be denied or abridged by the United States or any State by reason of failure to pay any poll tax or other tax.

SECTION 2.   The Congress shall have power to enforce this article by appropriate legislation.

AMENDMENT XXV [FEBRUARY 10, 1967]

SECTION 1.   In case of the removal of the President from office or of his death or resignation, the Vice President shall become President.

SECTION 2.   Whenever there is a vacancy in the office of the Vice President, the President shall nominate a Vice President who shall take office upon confirmation by a majority of both Houses of Congress.

SECTION 3.   Whenever the President transmits to the President pro tempore of the Senate and the Speaker of the House of Representatives his written declaration that he is unable to discharge the powers and duties of his office, and until he transmits to them a written declaration to the contrary, such powers and duties shall be discharged by the Vice President as Acting President.

SECTION 4.   Whenever the Vice President and a majority of either the principal officers of the executive departments or of such other body as Congress may by law provide, transmit to the President pro tempore of the Senate and the Speaker of the House of Representatives their written declaration that the President is unable to discharge the powers and duties of his office, the Vice President shall immediately assume the powers and duties of the office as Acting President.

Thereafter, when the President transmits to the President pro tempore of the Senate and the Speaker of the House of Representatives his written declaration that no inability exists, he shall resume the powers and duties of his office unless the Vice President and a majority of either the principal officers of the executive departments or of such other body as Congress may by law provide, transmit within four days to the President pro tempore of the Senate and the Speaker of the House of Representatives their written declaration that the President is unable to discharge the powers and duties of his office. Thereupon Congress shall decide the issue, assembling within forty-eight hours for that purpose if not in session. If the Congress, within twenty-one days after receipt of the latter written declaration, or, if Congress is not in session, within twenty-one days after Congress is required to assemble, determines by two-thirds vote of both houses that the President is unable to discharge the powers and duties of his office, the Vice President shall continue to discharge the same as Acting President; otherwise, the President shall resume the powers and duties of his office.

AMENDMENT XXVI [JUNE 30, 1971]

SECTION 1.   The right of citizens of the United States who are eighteen years of age or older to vote shall not be denied or abridged by the United States or by any State on account of age.

SECTION 2.   The Congress shall have power to enforce this article by appropriate legislation.

AMENDMENT XXVII[12] [MAY 7, 1992]

No law, varying the compensation for services of the Senators and Representatives, shall take effect until an election of Representatives shall have intervened.

---

[12]James Madison proposed this amendment in 1789 together with the ten amendments that were adopted as the Bill of Rights, but it failed to win ratification at the time. Congress, however, had set no deadline for its ratification, and over the years—particularly in the 1980s and 1990s—many states voted to add it to the Constitution. With the ratification of Michigan in 1992 it passed the threshold of of the states required for adoption, but because the process took more than 200 years, its validity remains in doubt.

THE EMANCIPATION PROCLAMATION

BY THE PRESIDENT OF THE UNITED STATES OF AMERICA:

Whereas, on the twenty-second day of September, in the year of our Lord one thousand eight hundred and sixty-two, a proclamation was issued by the President of the United States, containing, among other things, the following, to wit:

That on the first day of January, in the year of our Lord one thousand eight hundred and sixty-three, all persons held as slaves within any State or designated part of a State, the people whereof shall then be in rebellion against the United States, shall be then, thenceforward, and forever free; and the Executive Government of the United States, including the military and naval authority thereof, will recognize and maintain the freedom of such persons, and will do no act or acts to repress such persons, or any of them, in any efforts they may make for their actual freedom.

That the Executive will, on the first day of January aforesaid, by proclamation, designate the States and parts of States, if any, in which the people thereof, respectively, shall then be in rebellion against the United States; and the fact that any State, or the people thereof, shall on that day be, in good faith, represented in the Congress of the United States by members chosen thereto at elections wherein a majority of the qualified voters of such State shall have participated, shall, in the absence of strong countervailing testimony, be deemed conclusive evidence that such State, and the people thereof, are not then in rebellion against the United States.

Now, therefore I, Abraham Lincoln, President of the United States, by virtue of the power in me vested as Commander-in-Chief, of the Army and Navy of the United States in time of actual armed rebellion against the authority and government of the United States, and as a fit and necessary war measure for suppressing said rebellion, do, on this first day of January, in the year of our Lord one thousand eight hundred and sixty-three, and in accordance with my purpose so to do publicly proclaimed for the full period of one hundred days, from the day first above mentioned, order and designate as the States and parts of States wherein the people thereof respectively, are this day in rebellion against the United States, the following, to wit:

Arkansas, Texas, Louisiana, (except the Parishes of St. Bernard, Plaquemines, Jefferson, St. John, St. Charles, St. James Ascension, Assumption, Terrebonne, Lafourche, St. Mary, St. Martin, and Orleans, including the City of New Orleans), Mississippi, Alabama, Florida, Georgia, South Carolina, North Carolina, and Virginia, (except the forty-eight counties designated as West Virginia, and also the counties of Berkley, Accomac, Northampton, Elizabeth City, York, Princess Ann, and Norfolk, including the cities of Norfolk and Portsmouth), and which excepted parts, are for the present, left precisely as if this proclamation were not issued.

And by virtue of the power, and for the purpose aforesaid, I do order and declare that all persons held as slaves within said designated States, and parts of States, are, and henceforward shall be free; and that the Executive government of the United States, including the military and naval authorities thereof, will recognize and maintain the freedom of said persons.

And I hereby enjoin upon the people so declared to be free to abstain from all violence, unless in necessary self-defense; and I recommend to them that, in all cases when allowed, they labor faithfully for reasonable wages.

And I further declare and make known, that such persons of suitable condition, will be received into the armed service of the United States to garrison forts, positions, stations, and other places, and to man vessels of all sorts in said service.

And upon this act, sincerely believed to be an act of justice, warranted by the Constitution, upon military necessity, I invoke the considerate judgment of mankind, and the gracious favor of Almighty God.

In witness whereof, I have hereunto set my hand and caused the seal of the United States to be affixed. Done at the City of Washington, this first day of January, in the year of our Lord one thousand eight hundred and sixty-three, and of the Independence of the United States of America the eighty-seventh.

By the President: Abraham Lincoln
William H. Seward, Secretary of State

KEY PROVISIONS OF
THE CIVIL RIGHTS ACT OF 1964

AN ACT

To enforce the constitutional right to vote, to confer jurisdiction upon the district courts of the United States to provide injunctive relief against discrimination in public accommodations, to authorize the Attorney General to institute suits to protect constitutional rights in public facilities and public education, to extend the Commission on Civil Rights, to prevent discrimination in federally assisted programs, to estab-lish a Commission on Equal Employment Opportunity, and for other purposes.

Be it enacted by the Senate and House of Representatives of the United States of America in Congress assembled, that this Act may be cited as the "Civil Rights Act of 1964."

TITLE I—VOTING RIGHTS

SECTION 101 . . . (2) No person acting under color of law shall—

(A) In determining whether any individual is qualified under State law or laws to vote in any Federal election, apply any standard, practice, or procedure different from the standards, practices, or procedures applied under such law or laws to other individuals within the same county, parish, or similar political subdivision who have been found by State officials to be qualified to vote;

(B) deny the right of any individual to vote in any Federal election because of an error or omission on any record or paper relating to any application, registration, or other act requisite to voting, if such error or omission is not material in determining whether such individual is qualified under State law to vote in such election;

(C) employ any literacy test as a qualification for voting in any Federal election unless (i) such test is administered to each individual and is conducted wholly in writing, and (ii) a certified copy of the test and of the answers given by the individual is furnished to him within twenty-five days of the submission of his request made within the period of time during which records and papers are required to be retained and preserved pursuant to title III of the Civil Rights Act of 1960 (42 U.S.C. 1974–74e; 74 Stat. 88): Provided, however, That the Attorney General may enter into agreements with appropriate State or local authorities that preparation, conduct, and maintenance of such tests in accordance with the provisions of applicable State or local law, including such special provisions as are necessary in the preparation, conduct, and maintenance of such tests for persons who are blind or otherwise physically handicapped, meet the purposes of this subparagraph and constitute compliance therewith.

TITLE II—INJUNCTIVE RELIEF AGAINST DISCRIMINATION IN PLACES OF PUBLIC ACCOMMODATION

SECTION 201.   (a) All persons shall be entitled to the full and equal enjoyment of the goods, services, facilities, and privileges, advantages and accommodations of any place of public accommodation, as defined in this section, without discrimination or segregation on the ground of race, color, religion, or national origin.

(b) Each of the following establishments which serves the public is a place of public accommodation within the meaning of this title if its operations affect commerce, or if discrimination or segregation by it is supported by State action:

(1) any inn, hotel, motel, or other establishment which provides lodging to transient guests, other than an establishment located within a building which contains not more than five rooms for rent or hire and which is actually occupied by the proprietor of such establishment as his residence;

(2) any restaurant, cafeteria, lunchroom, lunch counter, soda fountain, or other facility principally engaged in selling food for consumption on the premises, including, but not limited to, any such facility located on the premises of any retail establishment; or any gasoline station;

(3) any motion picture house, theater, concert hall, sports arena, stadium or other place of exhibition or entertainment;

(4) any establishment (A)(i) which is physically located within the premises of any establishment otherwise covered by this subsection, or (ii) within the premises of which is physically located any such

covered establishment, and (B) which holds itself out as serving patrons of such covered establishment. . . .

(d) Discrimination or segregation by an establishment is supported by State action within the meaning of this title if such discrimination or segregation

(1) is carried on under color of any law, statute, ordinance, or regulation; or

(2) is carried on under color of any custom or usage required or enforced by officials of the State or political subdivision thereof; or

(3) is required by action of the State or political sub-division thereof. . . .

SECTION 202. All persons shall be entitled to be free, at any establishment or place, from discrimination or segregation of any kind on the ground of race, color, religion, or national origin, if such discrimination or segregation is or purports to be required by any law, statute, ordinance, regulation, rule, or order of a State or any agency or political subdivision thereof.

SECTION 203. No person shall (a) withhold, deny, or attempt to withhold or deny, or deprive or attempt to deprive, any person of any right or privilege secured by section 201 or 202, or (b) intimidate, threaten, or coerce, or attempt to intimidate, threaten, or coerce any person with the purpose of interfering with any right or privilege secured by section 201 or 202, or (c) punish or attempt to punish any person for exercising or attempting to exercise any right or privilege secured by section 201 or 202.

SECTION 204. (a) Whenever any person has engaged or there are reasonable grounds to believe that any person is about to engage in any act or practice prohibited by section 203, a civil action for preventive relief, including an application for a permanent or temporary injunction, restraining order, or other order, may be instituted by the person aggrieved and, upon timely application, the court may, in its discretion, permit the Attorney General to intervene in such civil action if he certifies that the case is of general public importance. Upon application by the complainant and in such circumstances as the court may deem just, the court may appoint an attorney for such complainant and may authorize the commencement of the civil action without the payment of fees, costs, or security. . . .

SECTION 206. (a) Whenever the Attorney General has reasonable cause to believe that any person or group of persons is engaged in a pattern or practice of resistance to the full enjoyment of any of the rights secured by this title, and that the pattern or practice is of such a nature and is intended to deny the full exercise of the rights herein described, the Attorney General may bring a civil action in the appropriate district court of the United States by filing with it a complaint

(1) signed by him (or in his absence the Acting Attorney General),

(2) setting forth facts pertaining to such pattern or practice, and

(3) requesting such preventive relief, including an application for a permanent or temporary injunction, restraining order or other order against the person or persons responsible for such pattern or practice, as he deems necessary to insure the full enjoyment of the rights herein described . . . .

TITLE III—DESEGREGATION OF PUBLIC FACILITIES

SECTION 301. (a) Whenever the Attorney General receives a complaint in writing signed by an individual to the effect that he is being deprived of or threatened with the loss of his right to the equal protection of the laws, on account of his race, color, religion, or national origin, by being denied equal utilization of any public facility which is owned, operated, or managed by or on behalf of any State or subdivision thereof, other than a public school or public college as defined in section 401 of title IV hereof, and the Attorney General believes the complaint is meritorious and certifies that the signer or signers of such complaint are unable, in his judgment, to initiate and maintain appropriate legal proceedings for relief and that the institution of an action will materially further the orderly progress of desegregation in public facili-ties, the Attorney General is authorized to institute for or in the name of the United States a civil action in any appropriate district court of the United States against such parties and for such relief as may be appropriate. And such court shall have and shall exercise jurisdiction of proceedings instituted pursuant to this section. The Attorney General may implead as defendants such additional parties as are or become necessary to the grant of effective relief hereunder. . . .

TITLE IV—DESEGREGATION OF PUBLIC EDUCATION

SECTION 401. As used in this title—. . . .

"Desegregation" means the assignment of students to public schools and within such schools without regard to their race, color, religion, or national origin, but "desegregation" shall not mean the assignment of students to public schools in order to overcome racial imbalance . . . .

Survey and Report of Educational Opportunities

SECTION 402. The Commissioner shall conduct a survey and make a report to the President and the Congress, within two years of the enactment of this title, concerning the lack of availability of equal educational opportunities for individuals by reason of race, color, religion, or national origin in public educational institutions at all levels in the United States, its territories and possessions, and the District of Columbia. . . .

TITLE V—COMMISSION ON CIVIL RIGHTS . . .
Duties of the Commission

SECTION 104.   (a) The Commission shall—

(1) investigate allegations in writing under oath or affirmation that certain citizens of the United States are being deprived of their right to vote and have that vote counted by reason of their color, race, religion, or national origin; which writing, under oath or affirmation, shall set forth the facts upon which such belief or beliefs are based;

(2) study and collect information concerning legal developments constituting a denial of equal protection of the laws under the Constitution because of race, color, religion or national origin or in the administration of justice;

(3) appraise the laws and policies of the Federal Government with respect to denials of equal protection of the laws under the Constitution because of race, color, religion or national origin or in the administration of justice;

(4) serve as a national clearinghouse for information in respect to denials of equal protection of the laws because of race, color, religion or national origin, including but not limited to the fields of voting, education, housing, employment, the use of public facilities, and transportation, or in the administration of justice;

(5) investigate allegations, made in writing and under oath or affirmation, that citizens of the United States are unlawfully being accorded or denied the right to vote, or to have their votes properly counted, in any election of presidential electors, Members of the United States Senate, or of the House of Representatives, as a result of any patterns or practice of fraud or discrimination in the conduct of such election; . . .

TITLE VI—NONDISCRIMINATION IN FEDERALLY ASSISTED PROGRAMS

SECTION 601.   No person in the United States shall, on the ground of race, color, or national origin, be excluded from participation in, be denied the benefits of, or be subjected to discrimination under any program or activity receiving Federal financial assistance.

SECTION 602. Each Federal department and agency which is empowered to extend Federal financial assistance to any program or activity, by way of grant, loan, or contract other than a contract of insurance or guaranty, is authorized and directed to effectuate the provisions of section 601 with respect to such program or activity by issuing rules, regulations, or orders of general applicability which shall be consistent with achievement of the objectives of the statute authorizing the financial assistance in connection with which the action is taken. No such rule, regulation, or order shall become effective unless and until approved by the President. Compliance with any requirement adopted pursuant to this section may be effected

(1) by the termination of or refusal to grant or to continue assistance under such program or activity to any recipient as to whom there has been an express finding on the record, after opportunity for hearing, of a failure to comply with such requirement, but such termination or refusal shall be limited to the particular political entity, or part thereof, or other recipient as to whom such a finding has been made and, shall be limited in its effect to the particular program, or part thereof, in which such non-compliance has been so found, or

(2) by any other means authorized by law:

Provided, however, that no such action shall be taken until the department or agency concerned has advised the appropriate person or persons of the failure to comply with the requirement and has determined that compliance cannot be secured by voluntary means. In the case of any action terminating, or refusing to grant or continue, assistance because of failure to comply with a requirement imposed pursuant to this section, the head of the federal department or agency shall file with the committees of the House and Senate having legislative jurisdiction over the program or activity involved a full written report of the circumstances and the grounds for such action. No such action shall become effective until thirty days have elapsed after the filing of such report. . . .

TITLE VII—EQUAL EMPLOYMENT OPPORTUNITY . . .
Discrimination Because of Race, Color, Religion, Sex, or National Origin

SECTION 703.   (a) it shall be an unlawful employment practice for an employer—

(1) to fail or refuse to hire or to discharge any individual, or otherwise to discriminate against any individual with respect to his compensation, terms, conditions, or privileges of employment, because of such individual's race, color, religion, sex, or national origin; or

(2) to limit, segregate, or classify his employees in any way which would deprive or tend to deprive any individual of employment opportunities or otherwise adversely affect his status as an employee, because of such individual's race, color, religion, sex, or national origin.

(b) it shall be an unlawful employment practice for an employment agency to fail or refuse to refer for employment, or otherwise to discriminate against, any individual because of his race, color, religion, sex, or national origin, or to classify or refer for employment any individual on the basis of his race, color, religion, sex, or national origin.

(c) it shall be an unlawful employment practice for a labor organization—

(1) to exclude or to expel from its membership, or otherwise to discriminate against, any individual because of his race, color, religion, sex, or national origin;

(2) to limit, segregate, or classify its membership, or to classify or fail or refuse to refer for employment any individual, in any way which would deprive or tend to deprive any individual of employment opportunities, or would limit such employment opportunities or otherwise adversely affect his status as an employee or as an applicant for employment, because of such individual's race, color, religion, sex, or national origin; or

(3) to cause or attempt to cause an employer to discriminate against an individual in violation of this section.

(d) It shall be an unlawful employment practice for any employer, labor organization, or joint labor-management committee controlling apprenticeship or other training or retraining, including on-the-job training programs to discriminate against any individual because of his race, color, religion, sex, or national origin in admission to, or employment in, any program established to provide apprenticeship or other training. . . .

Other Unlawful Employment Practices

SECTION 704.   (a) It shall be an unlawful employment practice for an employer to discriminate against any of his employees or applicants for employment, for an employment agency to discriminate against any individual, or for a labor organization to discriminate against any member thereof or applicant for membership, because he has opposed any practice made an unlawful employment practice by this title, or because he has made a charge, testified, assisted, or participated in any manner in an investigation, proceeding, or hearing under this title.

(b) It shall be an unlawful employment practice for an employer, labor organization, or employment agency to print or publish or cause to be printed or published any notice or advertisement relating to employment by such an employer or membership in or any classification or referral for employment by such a labor organization, or relating to any classification or referral for employment by such an employment agency, indicating any preference, limitation, specification, or discrimination, based on race, color, religion, sex, or national origin, except that such a notice or advertisement may indicate a preference, limitation, specification, or discrimination based on religion, sex, or national origin when religion, sex, or national origin is a bona fide occupational qualification for employment.

Equal Employment Opportunity Commission

SECTION 705.   (a) There is hereby created a Commission to be known as the Equal Employment Opportunity Commission, which shall be composed of five members, not more than three of whom shall be members of the same political party, who shall be appointed by the President by and with the advice and consent of the Senate. One of the original members shall be appointed for a term of one year, one for a term of two years, one for a term of three years, one for a term of four years, and one for a term of five years, beginning from the date of enactment of this title, but their successors shall be appointed for terms of five years each, except that any individual chosen to fill a vacancy shall be appointed only for the unexpired term of the member whom he shall succeed. The President shall designate one member to serve as Chairman of the Commission, and one member to serve as Vice Chairman. The Chairman shall be responsible on behalf of the Commission for the administrative operations of the Commission, and shall appoint, in accordance with the civil service laws, such officers, agents, attorneys, and employees as it deems necessary to assist it in the performance of its functions and to fix their compensation in accordance with Classification Act of 1949, as amended. . . .

TITLE VIII—REGISTRATION AND VOTING STATISTICS

SECTION 801. The Secretary of Commerce shall promptly conduct a survey to compile registration and voting statistics in such geographic areas as may be recommended by the Commission on Civil Rights.

Such a survey and compilation shall, to the extent recommended by the Commission on Civil Rights, only include a count of persons of voting age by race, color, and national origin, and determination of the extent to which such persons are registered to vote, and have voted in any statewide primary or general election in which the Members of the United States House of Representatives are nominated or elected, since January 1, 1960. Such information shall also be collected and compiled in connection with the Nineteenth Decennial Census, and at such other times as the Congress may prescribe. The provisions of section 9 and chapter 7 of title 13, United States Code, shall apply to any survey, collection, or compilation of registration and voting statistics carried out under this title: Provided, however, that no person shall be compelled to disclose his race, color, national origin, or questioned about his political party affiliation, how he voted, or the reasons therefore, nor shall any penalty be imposed for his failure or refusal to make such disclosure. Every person interrogated orally, by written survey or questionnaire or by any other means with respect to such information shall be fully advised with respect to his right to fail or refuse to furnish such information.

Lyndon B. Johnson July 2, 1964

KEY PROVISIONS OF
THE VOTING RIGHTS ACT OF 1965

AN ACT

To enforce the fifteenth amendment to the Constitution of the United States, and for other purposes.

Be it enacted by the Senate and House of Representatives of the United States of America in Congress assembled, That this Act shall be known as the "Voting Rights Act of 1965."

SECTION 2.   No voting qualification or prerequisite to voting, or standard, practice, or procedure shall be imposed or applied by any State or political subdivision to deny or abridge the right of any citizen of the United States to vote on account of race or color.

SECTION 3.   (a) Whenever the Attorney General institutes a proceeding under any statute to enforce the guarantees of the fifteenth amendment in any State or political subdivision the court shall authorize the appointment of Federal examiners by the United States Civil Service Commission in accordance with section 6 to serve for such period of time and for such political sub-divisions as the court shall determine is appropriate to enforce the guarantees of the fifteenth amendment

(1) as part of any interlocutory order if the court determines that the appointment of such examiners is necessary to enforce such guarantees or (2) as part of any final judgment if the court finds that violations of the fifteenth amendment justifying equitable relief have occurred in such State or subdivision: Provided, That the court need not authorize the appointment of examiners if any incidents of denial or abridgment of the right to vote on account of race or color (1) have been few in number and have been promptly and effectively corrected by State or local action, (2) the continuing effect of such incidents has been eliminated, and (3) there is no reasonable probability of their recurrence in the future.

(b) If in a proceeding instituted by the Attorney General under any statute to enforce the guarantees of the fifteenth amendment in any State or political subdivision the court finds that a test or device has been used for the purpose or with the effect of denying or abridging the right of any citizen of the United States to vote on account of race or color, it shall suspend the use of tests and devices in such State or political subdivisions as the court shall determine is appropriate and for such period as it deems necessary. . . .

SECTION 4.   (a) To assure that the right of citizens of the United States to vote is not denied or abridged on account of race or color, no citizen shall be denied the right to vote in any Federal, State, or local election because of his failure to comply with any test or device in any State with respect to which the determinations have been made under subsection (b). . . .

(b) The provisions of subsection (a) shall apply in any State or in any political subdivision of a state which (1) the Attorney General determines maintained on November 1, 1964, any test or device, and with respect to which (2) the Director of the Census determines that less than 50 per centum of the persons of voting age residing therein were registered on November 1, 1964, or that less than 50 per centum of such persons voted in the presidential election of November 1964. . . .

(c) The phrase "test or device" shall mean any requirement that a person as a prerequisite for voting or registration of voting (1) demonstrate the ability to read, write, understand, or interpret any matter, (2) demonstrate any educational achievement or his knowledge of any particular subject, (3) possess good moral character, or (4) prove his qualifications by the voucher of registered voters or members of any other class. . . .

SECTION 6.   Whenever (a) a court has authorized the appointment of examiners pursuant to the provisions of section 3 (a), or (b) unless a declaratory judgment has been rendered under section 4 (a), the Attorney General certifies with respect to any political subdivision named in, or included within the scope of, determinations made under section 4 (b) that (1) he has received complaints in writing from twenty or more residents of such political subdivision alleging that they have been denied the right to vote under color of law on account of race or color, and that he believes such complaints to be meritorious, or (2) that in his judgment (considering, among other factors, whether the ratio of nonwhite persons to white persons registered to vote within such subdivision appears to him to be reasonably attributable to violations of the fifteenth amendment or whether substantial evidence exists that bona fide efforts are being made within such subdivision to comply with the fifteenth amendment), the appointment of examiners is otherwise necessary to enforce the guarantees of the fifteenth amendment, the Civil Service Commission shall appoint as many examiners for such subdivision as it may deem appropriate to prepare and maintain lists of persons eligible to vote in Federal, State, and local elections. . . . Examiners and hearing officers shall have the power to administer oaths. . . .

Lyndon B. Johnson August 6, 1965

EXECUTIVE ORDER 13050
PRESIDENT'S ADVISORY BOARD ON RACE

By the authority vested in me as President by the Constitution and the laws of the United States of America, including the Federal Advisory Committee Act, as amended (5 U.S.C. App.), and in order to establish a President's Advisory Board on Race, it is hereby ordered as follows:

SECTION 1.   Establishment. (a) There is established the President's Advisory Board on Race. The Advisory Board shall comprise 7 members from outside the Federal Government to be appointed by the President. Members shall each have substantial experience and expertise in the areas to be considered by the Advisory Board. Members shall be representative of the diverse perspectives in the areas to be considered by the Advisory Board.

(b) The President shall designate a Chairperson from among the members of the Advisory Board.

SEC. 2.   Functions. (a) The Advisory Board shall advise the President on matters involving race and racial reconciliation, including ways in which the President can:

(1) Promote a constructive national dialogue to confront and work through challenging issues that surround race;

(2) Increase the Nation's understanding of our recent history of race relations and the course our Nation is charting on issues of race relations and racial diversity;

(3) Bridge racial divides by encouraging leaders in communities throughout the Nation to develop and implement innovative approaches to calming racial tensions;

(4) Identify, develop, and implement solutions to problems in areas in which race has a substantial impact, such as education, economic opportunity, housing, health care, and the administration of justice.

(b) The Advisory Board also shall advise on such other matters as from time to time the President may refer to the Board.

(c) In carrying out its functions, the Advisory Board shall coordinate with the staff of the President's Initiative on Race.

SEC. 3.   Administration. (a) To the extent permitted by law and subject to the availability of appropriations, the Department of Justice shall provide the financial and administrative support for the Advisory Board.

(b) The heads of executive agencies shall, to the extent permitted by law, provide to the Advisory Board such information as it may require for the purpose of carrying out its functions.

(c) The Chairperson may, from time to time, invite experts to submit information to the Advisory Board and may form subcommittees or working groups within the Advisory Board to review specific matters.

(d) Members of the Advisory Board shall serve without compensation but shall be allowed travel expenses, including per diem in lieu of subsistence, as authorized by law for persons serving intermittently in the Government service (5 U.S.C. 5701–5707).

SEC. 4.   General. (a) Notwithstanding any other Executive order, the functions of the President under the Federal Advisory Committee Act, as amended, except that of reporting to the Congress, that are applicable to the Advisory Board shall be performed by the Attorney General, or his or her designee, in accordance with guidelines that have been issued by the Administrator of General Services.

(b) The Advisory Board shall terminate on September 30, 1998 unless extended by the President prior to such date.

William J. Clinton June 13, 1997

Glossary of Key Terms and Concepts

54th Massachusetts Regiment: This all-black volunteer infantry regiment was recruited in the Northern states for service with Union military forces in the Civil War. It was made up almost entirely of black men who had been free. It was commanded by white officers.

Abolitionists: Those who sought to end slavery within their colony, state, nation, or religious denomination. By the 1830s the term best applied to those who advocated immediate rather than gradual emancipation.

Acculturation: Change in individuals who are introduced to a new culture.

Affirmative action: Civil rights policy or program that seeks to redress the effects of past discrimination due to race or gender by giving preference to women and minorities in education and employment.

African Methodist Episcopal (AME) Church: Founded in Philadelphia in 1816, it was the first and became the largest independent black church.

Afrocentricists: Scholars who view history from an African perspective.

Afrocentricity: A philosophy of culture that celebrates Africa's role in history and stresses the enduring African roots and identity of black America.

Age of Revolution: A period in Atlantic history that began with the American Revolution in 1776 and ended with the defeat of Napoleonic France in 1815.

Agricultural Adjustment Act (AAA): A federal program that provided subsidies to farmers to grow less to help stabilize prices.

American and Foreign Anti-Slavery Society (AFASS, 1840–1855): An organization of church-oriented abolitionists.

American Anti-Slavery Society (AASS, 1833–1870): The umbrella organization for immediate abolitionists during the 1830s and the main Garrisonian organization after 1840.

American Colonization Society (ACS, 1816–1912): An organization founded in Washington, D.C., by prominent slaveholders. It claimed to encourage the ultimate abolition of slavery by sending free African Americans to its West African colony of Liberia.

American Convention for Promoting the Abolition of Slavery and Improving the Condition of the African Race (1794–1838): A loose coalition of state and local societies, dominated by the Pennsylvania Abolition Society, dedicated to gradual abolition.

American Missionary Association: This religious organization sent teachers and clergymen throughout the South following the Civil War to tend to the spiritual and educational needs of former slaves. It was instrumental in establishing dozens of schools, including Fisk, Hampton, and Avery.

Amistad: A Spanish schooner on which West African Joseph Cinque led a successful slave revolt in 1839.

Animism: The belief that inanimate objects have spiritual attributes.

Antimiscegenation laws: In 1967 in Loving v. Virginia the U.S. Supreme Court declared that all laws making it a crime for black and white citizens to marry were unconstitutional. This decision struck down the last of the measures that southerners had passed to keep the races separate and unequal in the Jim Crow era.

Asiento: The monopoly over the slave trade from Africa to Spain's American colonies.

Assimilation: The process by which people of different backgrounds become similar to each other in culture and language.

Barbados: An island nation in the Lesser Antilles, located to the southeast of Puerto Rico.

Battery Wagner: This defensive fortification guarded Fort Sumter near the entrance to Charleston Harbor in South Carolina. It was the scene in July 1863 of a major Union assault by the 54th Massachusetts Regiment, a black unit. The assault failed, but the bravery and valor of the black troops earned them fame and glory.

Benevolent Empire: A network of church-related voluntary associations designed to fight sin and save souls. It emerged during the 1810s in relationship to the Second Great Awakening.

Berbers: A people native to North Africa and the Sahara Desert.

Black arts movement: Artistic movement that seeks to promote black art by black artists for black people.

Black Cabinet: Informal group of highly placed African-American advisors to President Franklin D. Roosevelt.

Black codes: Laws that were passed in each of the former Confederate states following the Civil War that applied only to black people. While conceding such rights as the right to marry, to contract a debt, or to own property, the codes severely restricted the rights and opportunities of former slaves in terms of labor and mobility.

Black Committee: An organization of prominent black men in the North who assisted in recruiting African Americans to fight for the Union in the Civil War.

Black English (or African-American Vernacular English): A variety of American English that is influenced by West African grammar, vocabulary, and pronunciation.

Black laws: Laws passed in states of the Old Northwest during the early nineteenth century banning or restricting black settlement and limiting the rights of black residents.

Black Manifesto: In 1969 James Forman demanded, in a position paper, that white religious denominations and churches that had benefited from racial slavery and exploitation pay $500 million dollars in reparations to black Americans.

Black nationalism: A belief held by some African Americans that they must seek their racial destiny by establishing separate institutions and, perhaps, migrating as a group to a location (often Africa) outside the United States.

Black Panther Party: Black militant organization set up in 1966 by Huey P. Newton and Bobby Seale.

Black Power: A nationalist ideology popularized by Stokely Carmichael that advocated black control of community resources and social institutions and the election of political representatives who would speak to the needs and interests of black people.

Black studies: Scholarly study of the history and experiences of persons of African descent.

Border ruffians: Pro-slavery advocates and vigilantes from Missouri who crossed the border into Kansas in 1855–1857 to support slavery in Kansas by threatening and attacking antislavery settlers.

Brooks-Sumner Affair: South Carolina congressman Preston Brooks attacked and severely beat Massachusetts senator Charles Sumner on the floor of the U.S. Senate after Sumner had denounced the proslavery position of Brooks's uncle, South Carolina senator Andrew Butler.

Brotherhood of Sleeping Car Porters (BSCP): Black men and women who worked on Pullman passenger coaches on the nation's railroads organized this labor union in 1925 with A. Philip Randolph as its leader. It struggled until the passage in 1935 of the National Labor Relations Act, after which it became one of the powerful unions within the American Federation of Labor (AFL). In 1978 it was absorbed into the Brotherhood of Railway and Airline Clerks.

Brown v. Board of Education of Topeka: Decision by the Supreme Court in 1954 that overturned the "separate but equal" doctrine.

Brownsville Affair: In 1906, a shooting in Brownsville, Texas, was blamed on black soldiers from the 25th Infantry Regiment. President Theodore Roosevelt summarily dismissed 167 black men from the U.S. Army. Later investigations exonerated the men.

Buffalo soldiers: Four regiments of black soldiers that served with the U.S. Army on the western frontier from the 1870s to the 1890s. The Plains Indians called them the buffalo soldiers.

Call-and-response: An African-American singing style rooted in Africa. A solo call tells a story to which a group responds, often with repeated lyrics.

Carpetbagger: The derogatory term used during Reconstruction to describe Northerners who came South following the Civil War to take advantage of political and economic opportunities. They were labeled "carpetbaggers" because they ostensibly carried all of their possessions in a solitary carpetbag.

Cash crop: A crop grown for sale rather than subsistence.

Chattel slavery: A form of slavery in which the enslaved are treated legally as property.

Chicago Renaissance: Flourishing of the arts that made Chicago the center of black culture in the 1940s.

Church of England: A Protestant church established in the sixteenth century as the English national or Anglican church with the English monarch as its head. After the American Revolution, its American branch became the Episcopal Church.

Civil Rights Act, 1866: This act nullified the black codes and made African Americans citizens with the basic rights of life, liberty, and due process. It was passed over President Andrew Johnson's veto. Its main features were subsequently embedded in the Fourteenth Amendment to the Constitution.

Civil Rights Act of 1875: This federal legislation outlawed racial discrimination in public accommodations such as hotels and restaurants, and in transportation, including railroad coaches and steamboats. The Supreme Court invalidated it in 1883.

Civil Rights Act of 1964: Federal law banning discrimination in places of public accommodation.

Civil Rights Act of 1968: Federal law banning discrimination in housing.

Coffle: A file of slaves chained together that was typical of the domestic slave trade.

Colfax Massacre: At least 105 African Americans were murdered on Easter Sunday in 1873 in Colfax, Louisiana, in the single worst episode of violence during Reconstruction.

Colored American **(New York, 1837–1842):** The leading African-American newspaper of its time.

Colored Farmers' Alliance: A large organization of black southern farmers in the 1880s and 1890s that had as many as one million members who agitated for improved conditions and income for black landowners, renters, and sharecroppers.

Committee for Industrial Organization (CIO): Labor organization that was committed to inter-racial and multiethnic organizing.

Communist Party: Political party formed to promote communism.

Community Action Programs (CAPS): Anti-poverty programs involving "maximum feasible participation" by the poor themselves.

Compromise of 1850: An attempt by the U.S. Congress to settle divisive issues between the North and South, including slavery expansion, apprehension in the North of fugitive slaves, and slavery in the District of Columbia.

Compromise of 1877: This informal arrangement between national Democrats and Republicans settled the disputed presidential election of 1876 by permitting Republican Rutherford B. Hayes to become president while allowing Democrats to complete redemption by taking political control of Louisiana, Florida, and South Carolina.

Congress of Racial Equality: Protest group committed to nonviolent direct action.

Continental Army: The army created by the Continental Congress in June 1775 to fight British troops. George Washington was its commander in chief.

Continental Congress: A representative assembly that first met in October 1775 and served as the de facto central government of the United States during the Revolutionary War.

Contraband: Slaves who escaped to the Union or were captured by Union troops early in the Civil War were considered enemy property or contraband.

Convict lease system: Southern states and communities leased prisoners to privately operated mines, railroads, and timber companies. These businesses forced the prisoners, who were usually black men, to work in brutal, unhealthy, and dangerous conditions. Many convicts died of abuse and disease.

Cotton gin: A simple machine invented by Eli Whitney in 1793 to separate cotton seeds from cotton fiber. It greatly speeded this task and encouraged the westward expansion of cotton-growing in the United States.

Creole: An American brig on which Madison Washington led a successful slave revolt in 1841.

Creoles: Persons of African or European parentage born in the Americas.

Deindustrialization: Beginning in the late 1960s major manufacturing companies and industries moved the production of their goods and products off shore and relocated to countries with lower wage standards and little protection against labor exploitation. While companies maximized profits, the closing of plants and loss of jobs at home had a devastating impact on black workers whose high unemployment rates continued to soar into the new millennium.

Disfranchisement: White southern Democrats devised a variety of techniques in the late nineteenth and early twentieth centuries to prevent black people from voting. Those techniques included literacy tests, poll taxes, and the grandfather clause as well as intimidation and violence.

Divination: A form of magic aimed at telling the future by interpreting a variety of signs.

Domestic slave trade: A trade dating from the first decade of the nineteenth century in American-born slaves purchased primarily in the border South and sent overland or by sea to the cotton-growing regions of the Old Southwest.

Double V campaign: Slogan during World War II that stood for victory over fascism abroad and over racism at home for blacks.

Dred Scott v. Sanford: The 1857 U.S. Supreme Court case that ruled against Missouri slave Dred Scott by declaring that black people were not citizens, that they possessed no constitutional rights, and were considered to be property.

Economic Opportunity Act of 1964: Federal law creating the Office of Economic Opportunity and a number of programs aimed at poor communities.

Emancipation Proclamation: President Abraham Lincoln issued the Preliminary Emancipation Proclamation on September 22, 1862. It declared that slaves in states or portions of states still in rebellion 100 days later would be freed. On January 1, 1863, the Emancipation Proclamation freed slaves in areas of the Confederate states not under Union control.

Enforcement Acts: Also known as the Force Acts, these measures were passed by Congress in the early 1870s to undermine the Ku Klux Klan and other terrorist organizations by authorizing the president to use military force and to suspend the writ of habeas corpus.

Executive Order #8802: Order issued by President Franklin D. Roosevelt in 1941 banning discrimination in employment in defense industries and the federal government.

Executive Order #9346: Order establishing a new Committee on Fair Employment Practices, with greater resources, and direct oversight by the Executive Office of the President.

Executive Order #9981: Order issued by President Harry Truman in 1948 desegregating the armed forces.

Exodusters: Black migrants who left the South during and after Reconstruction and settled in Kansas, often in all-black towns.

Factory: A headquarters for a European company that traded for slaves or engaged in other commercial enterprises on the West African coast.

Fair Employment Practices Committee (FEPC): A committee created by Franklin Roosevelt to investigate complaints of discrimination.

Fair Play Committee: Organization formed to promote black actors in the movie industry and improve the image of blacks in film.

Family Assistance Plan (FAP): Plan giving financial assistance to families with no wage earner.

Federal Arts Project: New Deal agency formed to promote the creation of public art.

Federal Elections bill, 1890: A measure, also known as the Force bill, to protect the voting rights of black men in the South by providing federal supervision of elections. It passed in the House of Representatives but failed in the Senate.

Fetish: A natural object or an artifact believed to have magical power. A charm.

Fifteenth Amendment, 1870: This constitutional amendment stipulated that the right to vote could not be denied on account of race, color, or because a person had been a slave.

First South Carolina Volunteers: This black military unit consisted of former slaves recruited in the South Carolina and Georgia low country in 1862 and 1863 for service with Union military forces in the Civil War.

Fort Pillow: This fort on the east bank of the Mississippi River north of Memphis, Tennessee, was the scene of a massacre of black Union troops as well as some white soldiers and officers by Confederate cavalry in April 1864.

Forty-Niners: The men and women who rushed to California in 1849 after gold had been discovered there.

Fourteenth Amendment, 1868: This amendment ratified during Reconstruction made any person born in the United States a citizen of the United States and of the state in which they lived. It guaranteed citizens the rights of life, liberty, and due process—usually a trial or judicial proceeding—as well as equal protection of the law. It also contained a provision reducing a state's representation in Congress if that state denied the right to vote to any adult males.

Free labor: Mid-nineteenth-century Americans who were free and worked for income or compensation to advance themselves, as opposed to slave labor, which was work done with no financial compensation by people who were not free.

Free papers: Proof of freedom that free black people had to carry at all times in the southern states prior to emancipation. The papers, issued by state governments, identified an individual by name, age, sex, color, height, and so forth.

Free-Soil Party (1848–1853): An almost entirely northern political coalition opposed to the expansion of slavery into western territories. It included former supporters of the Whig, Democratic, and Liberty parties.

Freedmen's Bureau: Congress established the Bureau of Refugees, Freedmen, and Abandoned Lands in February 1865 to assist black and white Southerners left destitute by the Civil War.

Freedmen's Savings Bank: A private financial institution chartered by Congress in 1865. Many black people and organizations deposited funds in the bank, which went bankrupt in 1874.

Freedom Rides: Effort in 1961 to desegregate interstate bus and rail travel.

Freedom suits: Legal cases in which slaves sued their master or master's heirs for freedom.

French and Indian War: A war between Great Britain and its American Indian allies and France and its American Indian allies, fought between 1754 and 1763 for control of the eastern portion of North America.

Fugitive Slave Act of 1793: An act of Congress permitting masters to recapture escaped slaves who had reached the free states and, with the authorization of local courts, return with the slave or slaves to their home state.

Fugitive Slave Law, 1850: Part of the Compromise of 1850. It required law enforcement officials as well as civilians to assist in capturing runaway slaves.

Fur trade: A North American colonial industry involving American Indians trapping fur-bearing animals (chiefly beavers) and exchanging their pelts for European products.

Gang system: A mode of organizing labor that had West African antecedents. In this system American slaves worked in groups under the direction of a slave driver.

Gansta rap: A genre of rap music characterized by violent and sexist lyrics.

Gary Convention: Meeting of black leaders and organizations in Gary, Indiana to develop an agenda for black empowerment.

Grandfather clause: A method southern states used to disfranchise black men. It stipulated that only men whose grandfathers were eligible to vote were themselves eligible to vote. The U.S. Supreme Court invalidated the grandfather clause in 1915.

Great Dismal Swamp: A heavily forested area on the Virginia–North Carolina border that served as a refuge for fugitive slaves during the eighteenth and nineteenth centuries.

Griot: A West African self-employed poet and oral historian.

Guinea Coast: The southward-facing coast of West Africa, from which many of the people caught up in the Atlantic slave trade departed for the Americas.

Habeas corpus: A court order that a person arrested or detained by law enforcement officers must be brought to court and charged with a crime and not held indefinitely.

Hamburg Massacre: White Democrats attacked black Republicans in July 1876 in the village of Hamburg, South Carolina. Five black men were murdered as the Democrats began a violent effort to redeem the state.

Harlem Renaissance: As New York City became a destination for black migrants before, during, and after World War I, most of them settled in Harlem—a large neighborhood in the northern portion of Manhattan Island—which by the 1920s became a center of African-American cultural activities including literature, art, and music.

Harpers Ferry: *See* John Brown's raid.

Hierarchical: Refers to a social system based on class rank.

Hieroglyphics: A writing system based on pictures or symbols.

Hip-Hop: The backup music for rap. It is also the term for the youth culture that developed with the rise of rap music.

Hired their own time: Refers to a practice in which a master allowed slaves to work for wages paid by someone other than the master himself.

House of Burgesses: A representative body established at Jamestown, Virginia, in 1619.

House Un-American Activities Committee (HUAC): Congressional committee formed to investigate the activities of communists and "communist sympathizers" in America.

Humanism: The belief that human achievement and interests are more important than theological issues.

Hunting and gathering societies: Small societies dependent on hunting animals and collecting wild plants rather than on agriculture.

Immediatism: Refers to an antislavery movement that began in the US during the late 1820s, which demanded that slavery be abolished immediately rather than gradually.

Import duties: Taxes on goods brought into a country or colony.

Impressment: During the Civil War, Southern states and the Confederate government required slave owners to provide slaves to work on such public projects as fortifications, roads, and wharves. The owners (not the slaves) were usually compensated for the work.

Incest taboos: Customary rules against sexual relations and marriage within family and kinship groups.

Indentured servant: A person who sold his or her freedom to a master for a term of years.

Indigo: A bluish-violet dye produced from the indigo plant.

Industrial Revolution: An economic change that began in England during the early eighteenth century and spread to Continental Europe and the United States. Industry rather than agriculture became the dominant form of enterprise.

Jim Crow: Jump Jim Crow was a nineteenth-century dance ridiculing black people that was transformed by the twentieth century into a term meaning racial discrimination and segregation.

John Brown's raid: Brown's raid on Harpers Ferry, Virginia, in October 1859 failed to lead to a major slave insurrection, but it inflamed the controversy over slavery in the North and South.

Joint-stock companies: Primitive corporations that carried out British and Dutch colonization in the Americas during the seventeenth century.

Kansas-Nebraska Act, 1854: Legislation introduced by Democratic Senator Stephen Douglas to organize the Kansas and Nebraska territories. It provided for "popular sovereignty," whereby settlers would decide whether slavery would be legal or illegal.

"Know-Nothing Party": The nickname applied to members of the American Party, which opposed immigration in the 1850s.

Ku Klux Klan: A secret society founded by former Confederates in Pulaski, Tennessee, in 1866. It transformed itself into a terrorist organization during Reconstruction to drive black and white Republicans from political power in southern states. It disappeared by the late nineteenth century but was revived near Atlanta, Georgia, in 1915, as a powerful, white, Anglo-Saxon, Protestant political force in many states outside the South. It was revived again in the 1950s to oppose the civil rights movement.

Liberty Party (1840–1848): The first antislavery political party. Most of its supporters joined the Free-Soil Party in 1848, although its radical New York wing maintained a Liberty organization into the 1850s.

Lien: Black and white farmers purchased goods on credit from local merchants. The merchant demanded collateral in the form of a lien on the crop, typically cotton. If the farmer failed to repay the loan, the merchant had the legal right to seize the crop.

Lincoln-Douglas debates: Abraham Lincoln and Stephen Douglas debated seven times in the 1858 U.S. Senate race in Illinois. They spent most of their time arguing over slavery, its expansion, the *Dred Scott* decision, and the character of African Americans. Douglas won the election.

Lineage: A type of clan, typical of West Africa, in which members claim descent from a single ancestor.

Lowndes County Freedom Organization (LCFO): Political organization founded in 1965 by Stokely Carmichael.

Loyalists: Those Americans who, during the Revolutionary War, wished to remain within the British Empire.

Lynching: Killing by a mob without the benefit of a trial or conviction.

Manifest Destiny: A doctrine, prevalent during the nineteenth century, holding that God intended the United States to expand territorially over all of North America and the Caribbean islands, or over the entire Western Hemisphere.

Manumission: The act of freeing a slave by the slave's master.

March on Washington Movement (MOWM): Movement created by A. Philip Randolph to pressure the federal government to end discrimination in the defense industry and government.

Market revolution: The process between 1800 and 1860 by which an American economy based on subsistence farming, production by skilled artisans, and local markets changed into an economy marked by commercial farming, factory production, and national markets.

Martinique: An island in the eastern Caribbean Sea that was a French sugar-producing colony from the seventeenth into the nineteenth centuries.

Master class: Slaveholders.

Matrilineal: Descent traced through the female line.

Middle Passage: The voyage of slave ships (slavers) across the Atlantic Ocean from Africa to the Americas.

Mississippi Freedom Democratic Party: Inter-racial group set up to challenge Mississippi's all-white delegation to the Democratic National Convention in 1964.

Missouri Compromise, 1820: A congressional attempt to settle the issue of slavery expansion in the United States by permitting Missouri to enter the Union as a slave state, admitting Maine as a free state, and banning slavery in the rest of the Louisiana Purchase north of the 36° 30' line of latitude.

Montgomery Bus Boycott: Refusal from 1955 to 1957 of African Americans in Montgomery, Alabama to ride the city's buses until the bus lines were desegregated.

Moral suasion: A tactic endorsed by the American Anti-Slavery Society during the 1830s. It appealed to slaveholders and others to support immediate emancipation on the basis of Christian principles.

Moynihan Report: Report attributing many of the problems of poor black communities to the breakdown of the "lower-class" black family.

Nation of Islam: Religious movement that combines Islam with black nationalism.

National Industrial Recovery Act (NIRA): Federal law intended to promote the revival of manufacturing by allowing for cooperation among industries.

National Negro Congress (NCC): Organization founded in 1926 to unite African-American protest groups.

Negro National League: A professional baseball league for black players and teams organized in 1912.

New Deal: Set of policies proposed by the Roosevelt administration in response to the Great Depression.

New York City draft riot: In early July 1863 in opposition to the forthcoming military draft, rioting erupted in New York City. Many of the victims were black men, women, and children.

North Atlantic Treaty Organization: Military alliance formed to counter the threat posed by the Soviet Union and its allies.

North Star: A weekly newspaper published and edited by Frederick Douglass from 1847 to 1851. *Fredrick Douglass's Paper* (1851–1860) succeeded it.

Northwest Ordinance, 1787: Based on earlier legislation drafted by Thomas Jefferson, it organized the Northwest Territory, providing for orderly land sales, public education, government, the creation of five to seven states out of the territory, and the prohibition of slavery within the territory.

Nuclear family: A family unit consisting solely of one set of parents and their children.

Nullification Crisis (1832–1833): Arose when the South Carolina legislature declared the United States tariff "null and void" within the state's borders. President Andrew Jackson denounced the action as treasonous and threatened to use military force to uphold national supremacy.

Orangeburg Massacre: In February 1968 three students were killed and 28 were injured on the campus of South Carolina State College when Highway Patrolmen opened fire. Students had been protesting the persistence of segregation in the community.

Pan-Africanism: A movement of people of African descent from sub-Saharan Africa in the early twentieth century that emphasized their identity, shared experiences, and the need to liberate Africa from its European colonizers.

Patriarchal: A society ruled by a senior man.

Patrilineal: Descent through the male line.

Patriots: Those Americans who, during the Revolutionary War, favored independence.

Peace Mission Movement: Religious movement led by Father Major Jealous Divine.

Pennsylvania Society for Promoting the Abolition of Slavery (Pennsylvania Abolition Society: 1787–present): An antislavery organization centered in Philadelphia and based on an earlier Quaker society. Exclusively white, it promoted gradual abolition, black self-improvement, freedom suits, and protection of African Americans against kidnapping.

Peonage: The system that forbade southern farmers, usually sharecroppers and renters, who accumulated debts to leave the land until the debt was repaid—often an impossible task. The U.S. Supreme Court outlawed peonage, but many landowners and merchants still forced farmers to remain on the land.

Philadelphia Female Anti-Slavery Society (1833–1870): A biracial abolitionist organization aligned with the American Anti-Slavery Society. White Quaker women dominated the society, but it included a significant number of black women.

Pidgin: A simplified mixture of two or more languages used to communicate between people who speak different languages.

Plessy v. Ferguson: In 1896 in an 8-to-1 decision, the U.S. Supreme Court ruled that segregation did not violate the equal protection clause of the Fourteenth Amendment. The "separate but equal" doctrine remained the supreme law of the land until the 1954 *Brown vs. Board of Education* decision overturned *Plessy.*

Polygynous family: A family unit consisting of a man, his wives, and their children.

Polytheism: The worship of many gods.

Poor People's Campaign: Project supported by Martin Luther King involving the march of tens of thousands of poor people on Washington.

Popular sovereignty: The residents of a territory (such as Kansas) would vote to legalize or prohibit slavery in that territory.

Populist Party: Also known as the Peoples' Party, the Populists supported inflation, the free and unlimited coinage of silver and gold, government ownership of railroads, telephone, and telegraph companies, and an eight-hour workday. They won state and congressional elections but lost the presidential contests in 1892 and 1896.

Port Royal Experiment: An effort by Northern white missionaries, educators, and businessmen in the Sea Islands near Beaufort, South Carolina, to transform former slaves into educated, reliable, and industrious wage earners. Most of the freedmen did not acquire the land they worked.

Prince Hall Masons: A black Masonic order formed in 1791 in Boston under the leadership of Prince Hall. He became its first grand master and promoted its expansion to other cities.

Project 100,000: Military project with the goal of reducing the number of African Americans rejected by the military.

Race films: Movies made for African-American audiences in the 1930s and 1940s.

Radical Republicans: Members of the Republican Party during Reconstruction who vigorously supported the rights of African Americans to vote, hold political office, and to have the same legal and economic opportunities as white people.

Rain forest: A dense growth of tall trees characteristic of hot, wet regions.

Rainbow Coalition: Political coalition of African Americans, workers, liberals, feminists, gay people, environmentalists, and others formed by Jesse Jackson in the 1980s.

Reconstruction: The twelve years (1865–1877) following the Civil War, during which the former Confederate states were restored to the Union and former slaves became citizens and gained the right to vote and hold political office. It was also a time of violence and terrorism as many southern white people resisted the change in the status of African Americans.

Reconstruction Acts, 1867: Led by Radical Republicans, Congress divided the South into five military districts. Each former Confederate state (except Tennessee) was to frame a new state constitution and establish a new state government. The first Reconstruction Act provided for universal manhood suffrage, which granted the right to vote to all adult males, including black men.

Red Scare: The widespread fear among any Americans in the years immediately after World War I from about 1918 to about 1924 that Russia's 1917 Bolshevik Revolution might result in communists attempting to take over the U.S. government.

Redemption: The term used for the process, often violent, by which white conservative Democrats regained political control of a southern state from black and white Republicans during Reconstruction.

Renaissance: A humanist and artistic movement that began in Italy during the late fourteenth century and spread across Europe.

Rochester Convention, 1853: African-American leaders assembled in Rochester, New York, to discuss slavery, abolition, the recently passed Fugitive Slave Law, and their prospects for life in America.

Savannah: A flat, nearly treeless grassland typical of large portions of West Africa.

Scalawag: The derogatory term used during Reconstruction to identify a native white southerner who supported black and white Republicans. They were considered traitors to their people and the Democratic Party.

Scottsboro Boys: Nine young African-American men unjustly accused of raping two white women in Alabama in 1931. The Supreme Court overturned their convictions in 1937.

Seasoning: The process by which newly arrived Africans were broken in to slavery in the Americas.

Second Great Awakening (1790s–1830s): A widespread religious revival, centered in the North and upper South, that encouraged reform movements.

Secret societies: Social organizations that have secret ceremonies that only their members know about and can participate in.

Secularism: The belief that the present public welfare should predominate over religion in civil affairs.

Segregation: The separation of people based on their race in the use of such public facilities as hotels, restaurants, restrooms, drinking fountains, parks, and auditoriums. In many instances segregation meant the exclusion of black people.

Semitic: Refers to people who speak languages, such as Arabic and Hebrew, native to southwest Asia.

Sharecropping: The system following the Civil War in which former slaves worked land owned by white people and "paid" for the use of the land and for tools, seeds, fertilizer, and mules by sharing the crop—usually cotton—with the owner.

Shotgun policy: In Mississippi in 1875 white men resorted to violence and intimidation against black and white Republicans to regain political control of the state for conservative Democrats.

Slave codes: Colonial and state laws that defined the status of slaves and the prerogatives of masters.

Slave power: A term used to indicate the political control exercised by slaveholders over the U.S. government before the Civil War.

Slaver: A ship used to transport slaves from Africa to the Americas.

Sons of Liberty: A secret American organization formed in the Northeast during the summer of 1765 and committed to forcible opposition to the Stamp Act.

Southern Christian Leadership Conference (SCLC): Organization spearheaded by Martin Luther King, Jr. to provide an institutional base for the Civil Rights Movement.

Southern Homestead Act, 1866: Congress passed this measure that set aside over 3 million acres of land for former slaves and loyal white Southerners to farm following the Civil War. Most of the land was not fertile or suitable for agriculture, and the act largely failed.

Southern Regional Council (SRC): Organization that conducted research and focused attention on social, political, and educational inequality in the South.

Spanish Armada: A fleet that unsuccessfully attempted to carry out an invasion of England in1588.

Special Field Order #15: General William Tecumseh Sherman issued this military directive in January 1865. It set aside lands along the coast from Charleston, South Carolina, to Jacksonville, Florida, for former slaves. President Andrew Johnson revoked the order six months later.

Spirit possession: A belief rooted in West African religions that spirits may possess human souls.

Student Non-Violent Coordinating Committee (SNCC): Civil rights organization founded by black college students in 1960 at the initiative of Ella Baker.

Syracuse Convention, 1864: A meeting of black leaders in Syracuse, New York, to discuss the future of African Americans following the abolition of slavery. They insisted that black people had earned and deserved the same political and legal rights as white Americans.

Talented Tenth: Term coined by W. E. B. Du Bois for the educated black elite of the late nineteenth and early twentieth centuries. The upper 10 percent was supposed to assume responsibility for the leadership and advancement of the remaining 90 percent of African Americans.

Ten-Point Program: The Black Panther Party under the leadership of Huey Newton and Bobby Seale devised a ten point platform to help black people achieve liberation including demands for exemption from military service, freedom for all political prisoners, and an end to police brutality. It also asserted black people's rights to decent housing, jobs, and an empowering education.

Term slavery: A type of slavery prevalent in the Chesapeake from the late 1700s to the Civil War in which slaves were able to purchase their freedom from their masters by earning money over a number of years.

Terra-cotta: a hard, waterproof, ceramic clay.

Terrell law: The Terrell law was a Texas law banning African-American participation in the Democratic primary.

The Great Society: Programs created in response to the problems of poor Americans championed by President Johnson.

Thirteenth Amendment, 1865: This amendment to the U.S. Constitution outlawed slavery and involuntary servitude.

Three-Fifths Clause: A clause in the U.S. Constitution providing that a slave be counted as three-fifths of a free person in determining a state's representation in Congress and the electoral college and three-fifths of a free person in regard to per capita taxes levied by Congress on the states.

Tuskegee Airmen: All-black combat air unit during World War II.

Tuskegee Machine: As the president of Tuskegee Institute, Booker T. Washington developed an extensive network of contacts that gave him extraordinary influence with white political leaders and philanthropists as well as with black businesspeople, journalists, and college presidents.

Tuskegee Study: A medical study by the U.S. Public Health Service of the effects of syphilis on 622 black men. The study ran from 1932 to the 1970s, and the men were given only placebos and no treatment for the disease.

Uncle Tom's Cabin: This antislavery novel by Harriet Beecher Stowe was a best seller in the 1850s and it helped inflame the controversy over slavery.

Underground Railroad: Refers to several loosely organized, semisecret biracial networks that helped slaves escape from the border South to the North and Canada. The earliest networks appeared during the first decade of the nineteenth century; others operated into the Civil War years.

Union League: A social and fraternal organization that stirred political interest and support among black and white Republicans in the South during Reconstruction.

Universal Negro Improvement Association (UNIA): Established in 1914 in Jamaica by Marcus Garvey, it fostered racial pride, African heritage, Christian faith, and economic uplift.

Voting Rights Act of 1965: Federal law banning the methods that had systematically excluded African Americans from registering or voting in southern elections.

Wilmot Proviso: A measure introduced in Congress in 1845 to prohibit slavery in any lands acquired from Mexico. It did not pass.

Presidents and Vice Presidents of the United States*

PRESIDENT	VICE PRESIDENT
1. George Washington (1789)	John Adams (1789)
2. John Adams (1797)	Thomas Jefferson (1797)
3. Thomas Jefferson (1801)	Aaron Burr (1801) George Clinton (1805)
4. James Madison (1809)	George Clinton (1809) Elbridge Gerry (1813)
5. James Monroe (1817)	Daniel D. Tompkins (1817)
6. John Quincy Adams (1825)	John C. Calhoun (1825)
7. Andrew Jackson (1829)	John C. Calhoun (1829) Martin Van Buren (1833)
8. Martin Van Buren (1837)	Richard M. Johnson (1837)
9. William H. Harrison (1841)	John Tyler (1841)
10. John Tyler (1841)	
11. James K. Polk (1845)	George M. Dallas (1845)
12. Zachary Taylor (1849)	Millard Fillmore (1849)
13. Millard Fillmore (1850)	
14. Franklin Pierce (1853)	William R. King (1853)
15. James Buchanan (1857)	John C. Breckinridge (1857)
16. Abraham Lincoln (1861)	Hannibal Hamlin (1861) Andrew Johnson (1865)
17. Andrew Johnson (1865)	
18. Ulysses S. Grant (1869)	Schuyler Colfax (1869) Henry Wilson (1873)
19. Rutherford B. Hayes (1877)	William A. Wheeler (1877)
20. James A. Garfield (1881)	Chester A. Arthur (1881)
21. Chester A. Arthur (1881)	
22. Grover Cleveland (1885)	Thomas A. Hendricks (1885)
23. Benjamin Harrison (1889)	Levi P. Morton (1889)

PRESIDENT	VICE PRESIDENT
24. Grover Cleveland (1893)	Adlai E. Stevenson (1893)
25. William McKinley (1897)	Garret A. Hobart (1897) Theodore Roosevelt (1901)
26. Theodore Roosevelt (1901)	Charles Fairbanks (1905)
27. William H. Taft (1909)	James S. Sherman (1909)
28. Woodrow Wilson (1913)	Thomas R. Marshall (1913)
29. Warren G. Harding (1921)	Calvin Coolidge (1921)
30. Calvin Coolidge (1923)	Charles G. Dawes (1925)
31. Herbert C. Hoover (1929)	Charles Curtis (1929)
32. Franklin D. Roosevelt (1933)	John Nance Garner (1933) Henry A. Wallace (1941) Harry S. Truman (1945)
33. Harry S Truman (1945)	Alben W. Barkley (1949)
34. Dwight D. Eisenhower (1953)	Richard M. Nixon (1953)
35. John F. Kennedy (1961)	Lyndon B. Johnson (1961)
36. Lyndon B. Johnson (1963)	Hubert H. Humphrey (1965)
37. Richard M. Nixon (1969)	Spiro T. Agnew (1969) Gerald R. Ford (1973)
38. Gerald R. Ford (1974)	Nelson A. Rockefeller (1974)
39. James E. Carter Jr. (1977)	Walter F. Mondale (1977)
40. Ronald W. Reagan (1981)	George H. Bush (1981)
41. George H. Bush (1989)	James D. Quayle III (1989)
42. William J. Clinton (1993)	Albert Gore (1993)
43. George W. Bush (2001)	Richard B. Cheney (2001)
44. Barack H. Obama (2009)	Joseph R. Biden (2009)

* Year of inauguration

Historically Black Four-Year Colleges and Universities

INSTITUTION AND LOCATION	YEAR FOUNDED	LAND-GRANT, PUBLIC, PRIVATE, OR CHURCH-AFFILIATED DENOMINATION
Alabama A&M University, Normal, Alabama	1875	Land-grant
Alabama State University, Montgomery, Alabama	1867	Public
Albany State University, Albany, Georgia	1903	Public
Alcorn State University, Lorman, Mississippi	1871	Land-grant
Allen University, Columbia, South Carolina	1870	AME
Arkansas Baptist College, Little Rock, Arkansas	1884	Baptist
Barber-Scotia College, Concord, North Carolina	1904	Presbyterian
Benedict College, Columbia, South Carolina	1870	Baptist
Bennett College, Greensboro, North Carolina	1873	United Methodist
Bethune-Cookman College, Daytona Beach, Florida	1904	United Methodist
Bluefield State College, Bluefield, West Virginia	1895	Public
Bowie State University, Bowie, Maryland	1865	Public
Central State University, Wilberforce, Ohio	1887	Public
Cheyney University, Cheyney, Pennsylvania	1837	Public
Claflin College, Orangeburg, South Carolina	1869	United Methodist
Clark Atlanta University, Atlanta, Georgia	1988	United Methodist
Concordia College, Selma, Alabama	1922	Lutheran
Coppin State University, Baltimore, Maryland	1900	Public
Delaware State University, Dover, Delaware	1891	Land-grant
Dillard University, New Orleans, Louisiana	1930	Congregational/United Methodist
Edward Waters College, Jacksonville, Florida	1866	AME
Elizabeth City State University, Elizabeth City, North Carolina	1891	Public
Fayetteville State University, Fayetteville, North Carolina	1867	Public
Fisk University, Nashville, Tennessee	1866	United Church of Christ
Florida A&M University, Tallahassee, Florida	1887	Land-grant
Florida Memorial College, Miami, Florida	1879	Baptist
Fort Valley State College, Fort Valley, Georgia	1895	Land-grant
Grambling State University, Grambling, Louisiana	1901	Public
Hampton University, Hampton, Virginia	1868	Private
Harris-Stowe State College, St. Louis, Missouri	1857	Public
Howard University, Washington, DC	1867	Public
Huston-Tillotson University, Austin, Texas	1952	United Church of Christ/United Methodist
Jackson State University, Jackson, Mississippi	1877	Public
Jarvis Christian College, Hawkins, Texas	1913	Disciple of Christ Christian Church
Johnson C. Smith University, Charlotte, North Carolina	1867	Presbyterian
Kentucky State University, Frankfort, Kentucky	1886	Land-grant
Knoxville College, Knoxville, Tennessee	1875	Presbyterian
Lane College, Jackson, Tennessee	1882	Christian Methodist Episcopal
Langston University, Langston, Oklahoma	1897	Land-grant
LeMoyne-Owen College, Memphis, Tennessee	1870	United Church of Christ
Lincoln University, Jefferson City, Missouri	1866	Land-grant

INSTITUTION AND LOCATION	YEAR FOUNDED	LAND-GRANT, PUBLIC, PRIVATE, OR CHURCH-AFFILIATED DENOMINATION
Lincoln University, Lincoln, Pennsylvania	1854	Public
Livingstone College, Salisbury, North Carolina	1879	AME
Miles College, Birmingham, Alabama	1908	Christian Methodist Episcopal
Mississippi Valley State University, Itta Bena, Mississippi	1946	Public
Morehouse College, Atlanta, Georgia	1867	Baptist
Morgan State University, Baltimore, Maryland	1867	Public
Morris Brown College, Atlanta, Georgia	1881	AME
Morris College, Sumter, South Carolina	1908	Baptist
Norfolk State University, Norfolk, Virginia	1935	Public
North Carolina A&T State University, Greensboro, North Carolina	1892	Land-grant
North Carolina Central University, Durham, North Carolina	1909	Public
Oakwood College, Huntsville, Alabama	1896	Seventh Day Adventist
Paine College, Augusta, Georgia	1882	United Methodist
Paul Quinn College, Dallas, Texas	1872	AME
Philander Smith College, Little Rock, Arkansas	1877	United Methodist
Prairie View A&M University, Prairie View, Texas	1878	Land-grant
Rust College, Holly Springs, Mississippi	1866	United Methodist
Saint Augustine's College, Raleigh, North Carolina	1867	Episcopal
Saint Paul's College, Lawrenceville, Virginia	1888	Episcopal
Savannah State College, Savannah, Georgia	1890	Public
Selma University, Selma, Alabama	1878	Baptist
Shaw University, Raleigh, North Carolina	1865	Baptist
Sojourner-Douglass College, Baltimore, Maryland	1980	Private
South Carolina State University, Orangeburg, South Carolina	1896	Land-grant
Southern University and A&M College, Baton Rouge, Louisiana	1880	Land-grant
Southern University at New Orleans, New Orleans, Louisiana	1956	Public
Southwestern Christian College, Terrell, Texas	1949	Church of Christ
Spelman College, Atlanta, Georgia	1876	Presbyterian
Stillman College, Tuscaloosa, Alabama	1876	Presbyterian
Talladega College, Talladega, Alabama	1867	United Church of Christ
Tennessee State University, Nashville, Tennessee	1912	Land-grant
Texas College, Tyler, Texas	1894	Christian Methodist Episcopal
Texas Southern University, Houston, Texas	1947	Public
Tougaloo College, Tougaloo, Mississippi	1869	United Church of Christ/United Missionary Society
Tuskegee University, Tuskegee, Alabama	1881	Land-grant
University of Arkansas at Pine Bluff, Pine Bluff, Arkansas	1873	Land-grant
University of the District of Columbia, Washington, DC	1977	Public
University of Maryland Eastern Shore, Princess Anne, Maryland	1886	Land-grant
University of the Virgin Islands, St. Thomas, United States Virgin Islands	1962	Public
Virginia State University, Petersburg, Virginia	1882	Land-grant
Virginia Union University, Richmond, Virginia	1865	Baptist
Voorhees College, Denmark, South Carolina	1897	Episcopal
West Virginia State College, Institute, West Virginia	1891	Public
Wilberforce University, Wilberforce, Ohio	1856	AME
Wiley College, Marshall, Texas	1873	United Methodist
Winston-Salem State University, Winston-Salem, North Carolina	1892	Public
Xavier University of New Orleans, New Orleans, Louisiana	1925	Roman Catholic

Photo and Text Credits

PART TIMELINE I: *Images that appear on page 2:* Tina Chambers © Dorling Kindersley, Courtesy of the National Maritime Museum, London; The Library Company of Philadelphia; Library of Congress; Anne S.K. Brown Military Collection, John Hay Library, Brown University; Courtesy of the Library of Congress; Courtesy of the Library of Congress; Geoff Dann/Wisdom Omoda Omodamwe - modelmaker © Dorling Kindersley; Library of Congress; Courtesy of the Library of Congress. *Images that appear on page 3:* Library of Congress; Courtesy of the Library of Congress; The Historical Society of Pennsylvania; William Ranney, "The Battle of Cowpens." Oil on canvas. Photo by Sam Holland. Courtesy South Carolina State House.

CHAPTER 1: *Photos:* British Museum, London/Bridgeman Art Library, London/Superstock, 4; Library of Congress, 6; © (Photographer)/CORBIS All Rights Reserved, 8; Peter Hayman © The British Museum, 9; Dr. Timothy Kendall, 11; Werner Forman/Art Resource, N.Y., 12; The Granger Collection, 15; Michael Holford, 17; Roderick J. McIntosh, Rice University, 17; Yoruba Offering Bowl from Ekiti Efon-Alaye, (BON46967) Bonhams, London, UK/Bridgeman Art Library, London/New York, 18; Courtesy of the Library of Congress, 21; Christie's Images Ltd., 2005/The Bridgeman Art Library International Ltd, 23; Mike Row © The British Museum, 24.

ROOTS OF CULTURE: *Images that appear on page 28:* National Archives of South Africa; National Archives of South Africa; Courtesy of the Library of Congress. *Images that appear on page 29:* Courtesy of the Library of Congress; Courtesy of the Library of Congress.

CHAPTER 2: *Photos:* Library of Congress, 30; Copyright © North Wind Picture Archives/ North Wind Picture Archives—All rights reserved, 32; Werner Forman/Art Resource, N.Y., 33; Albrecht Duerer (1471–1528), "Portrait of the Moorish Woman Katharina." Drawing. Uffizi Florence, Italy. Photograph © Foto Marburg/Art Resource, NY, 34; The Granger Collection, New York, 37; Culver Pictures, Inc., 39; Courtesy of the Library of Congress, 40; EX 17082 Portrait of a Negro Man, Olaudah Equiano, 1780s, (previously attributed to Joshua Reynolds) by English School (18th century) Royal Albert Memorial Museum, Exeter, Devon, UK/Bridgeman Art Library, 42; Copyright The British Museum, 43; The New York Public Library/Art Resource, NY, 47; Courtesy of the Library of Congress, 49; The Granger Collection, 50; The Granger Collection, New York, 51. © Dorling Kindersley, Courtesy of the Wilberforce House Museum, Hull, 56; Library of Congress, 56; Courtesy of the Library of Congress, 56; Eugene Gordon, 56; Hulton Archive/Getty Images, 56; US Dept of the Interior Museum, 57; US Dept of the Interior Museum, 57; Art Resource/Schomburg Center for Research in Black Culture, 57; Public Domain, 57; Wilberforce House © Hull Museums, 57; Courtesy of the Library of Congress, 57. *Text:* Derek Walcott, Omeros. Reprinted with permission, 32.

VISUALIZING THE PAST: *Images that appear on page 56:* © Dorling Kindersley, Courtesy of the Wilberforce House Museum, Hull; Library of Congress; Courtesy of the Library of Congress; Eugene Gordon; Hulton Archive/Getty Images. *Images that appear on page 57:* US Dept of the Interior Museum; US Dept of the Interior Museum; Art Resource/Schomburg Center for Research in Black Culture; Public Domain; Wilberforce House © Hull Museums; Courtesy of the Library of Congress.

CHAPTER 3: *Photos:* Courtesy of the Library of Congress, 58; Courtesy of the Library of Congress, 60; From the collections of the South Carolina Historical Society, 62; North Wind Picture Archives, 71; Abby Aldrich Rockefeller Folk Art Museum, Colonial Williamsburg Foundation, VA, 72; CORBIS- NY, 74; John F. Watson, "Annals of Philadelphia," being a collection of memoirs, anecdotes, & incidents of Philadelphia. The London Coffee House. The Library Company of Philadelphia, 77; Arizona State Library, Archives and Public Records, Archives Division, Phoenix, #99-9996, 78; CORBIS- NY, 79.

CHAPTER 4: *Photos:* William Ranney, "The Battle of Cowpens." Oil on canvas. Photo by Sam Holland. Courtesy South Carolina State House, 86; Library of Congress, 88; CORBIS- NY, 91; Courtesy of the Library of Congress, 93; Courtesy of the Library of CongressCollections of The Virgina State Historical Society, Richmond, VA/Bridgeman Art Library, NY, 93; Library of Congress, 95; The Maryland Historical Society, Baltimore, Maryland, 97; University of Virginia Library, Special Collections Dept, 99; The Granger Collection, 100; Valley Forge National Historical Park, 101; Courtesy, American Antiquarian Society, 102.

CHAPTER 5: *Photos:* Dennis MacDonald/PhotoEdit Inc., 110; Courtesy of the Library of Congress, 112; The Library Company of Philadelphia, 113; Courtesy of the Massachusetts Historical Society, Boston, 116; 2001-196-1 Krimmel, John Lewis Pepper Pot, A Scene in the Philadelphia Market Philadelphia Museum of Art: Gift of Mr. & Mrs. Edward B. Leisenring, Jr. in honor of the 125th Anniversary of the Museum, 2001. Sumpter Priddy III, Inc, 118; Courtesy of the Library of Congress, 120; Schomburg Center for Research in Black Culture, The New York Public Library, 123; Delaware Art Museum, 124; The Library Company of Philadelphia, 125; The New York Public Library, 125; The Historical Society of Pennsylvania, 128; Library of Congress, 130; © Curt Teich Postcard Archives, Lake County Discovery Museum, 132.

PART TIMELINE II: *Images that appear on page 138:* © Wilberforce House Museum, Hull City Council, UK; Photographer/Hulton Archive/Getty Images; Courtesy of the Library of Congress; Courtesy of the Library of Congress; Courtesy of the Library of Congress; Courtesy of the Library of Congress; Courtesy of the Library of Congress; Library of Congress; Library of Congress. *Images that appear on page 139:* Courtesy of the Library of Congress; Courtesy of the Library of Congress; Courtesy of the Library of Congress; Courtesy of the Library of Congress.

CHAPTER 6: *Photos:* North Wind Picture Archives, 140; Library of Congress, 142;The New York Public Library/Art Resource, NY, 143; The Granger Collection, New York, 148; Neg.# ICHi-00013/Chicago History Museum, 149; Louisiana State Museum, 151; National Archives and Records Administration, 152; South Carolina Department of Parks, Recreation, and Tourism, 154; Courtesy of the Library of Congress, 155; Abby Aldrich Rockefeller Folk Art Museum, Williamsburg, VA, 157; Library of Congress, 158; John Antrobus, "Negro Burial." Oil painting. The Historic New Orleans Collection. #1960.46, 160.

CHAPTER 7: *Photos:* Courtesy of the Library of Congress, 166; Manigault Family Papers, Southern Historical Collection, Wilson Library, The University of North Carolina at Chapel Hill, 168; Three Sisters of the Copeland Family, 1854; William Matthew Prior, American (1806–1873). Oil on canvas; $26\frac{7}{8} \times 36\frac{1}{2}$ in. (68.3 × 92.7 cm). Bequest of Martha C. Karolik for the M. and M. Karolik Collection of American Paintings, 1815–1865, 48.467. Courtesy, Museum of Fine Arts, Boston. Reproduced with permission. © 2004 Museum of Fine Arts, Boston. All Rights Reserved, 173; The Granger Collection, 175; The Granger Collection, New York, 177; Courtesy of the Library of Congress, 179; The Boston Athenaeum, 179; Courtesy of the Library of Congress, 180; Courtesy of the Library of Congress, 181; Fenimore Art Museum,

Index

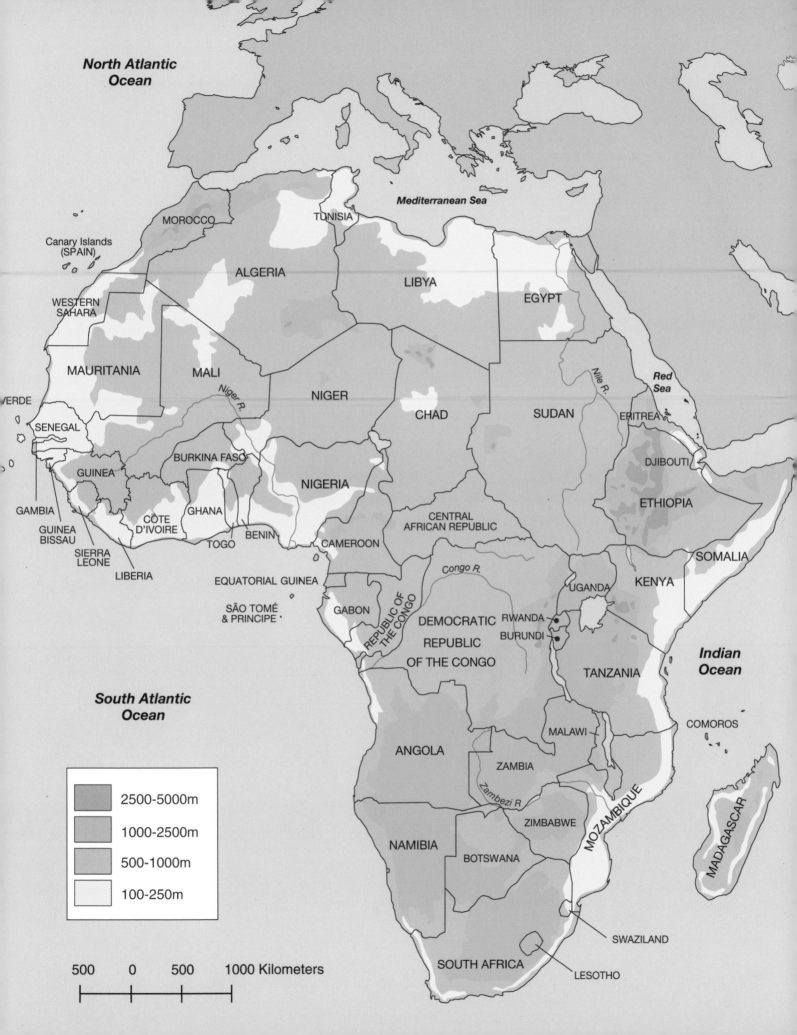

North Atlantic Ocean

Mediterranean Sea

MOROCCO

TUNISIA

Canary Islands (SPAIN)

WESTERN SAHARA

ALGERIA

LIBYA

EGYPT

Red Sea

MAURITANIA

MALI

NIGER

CHAD

SUDAN

ERITREA

Niger R.

Nile R.

VERDE

SENEGAL

BURKINA FASO

DJIBOUTI

GUINEA

NIGERIA

ETHIOPIA

GAMBIA

GHANA

CENTRAL AFRICAN REPUBLIC

SOMALIA

GUINEA BISSAU

CÔTE D'IVOIRE

TOGO

BENIN

CAMEROON

SIERRA LEONE

LIBERIA

EQUATORIAL GUINEA

Congo R.

UGANDA

KENYA

SÃO TOMÉ & PRINCIPE

GABON

REPUBLIC OF THE CONGO

DEMOCRATIC

RWANDA

REPUBLIC

BURUNDI

Indian Ocean

South Atlantic Ocean

OF THE CONGO

TANZANIA

MALAWI

COMOROS

ANGOLA

ZAMBIA

Zambezi R.

ZIMBABWE

MOZAMBIQUE

MADAGASCAR

NAMIBIA

BOTSWANA

	2500–5000m
	1000–2500m
	500–1000m
	100–250m

SWAZILAND

SOUTH AFRICA

LESOTHO

500   0   500   1000 Kilometers